THE SELECTED CORRESPONDENCE OF
MICHAEL FARADAY

VOLUME 2
1849–1866

To the Managers of the Royal Institution.

Royal Institution
11 Octᵇʳ 1861.

Gentlemen,

It is with the deepest feeling that I address you.

I entered the Royal Institution in March 1813, nearly forty-nine years ago; and, with the exception of a comparatively ■■ that period during which I was absent on the continent with Sir Humphry Davy, have been with you ever since.

During that time I have been most happy in your kindness, and in the fostering care which the Royal Institution has bestowed upon me. I am very thankful to you, and your predecessors, for the unswerving encouragement and support which you have given me during that period. My life has been a happy one and all I desired. During its progress I have tried to make a fitting return for it to the Royal Institution and through it to Science.

But the progress of years (now amounting in number to three score and ten) having brought forth, first, the period of development; and then that of maturity; have ultimately produced for me that of gentle decay. This has taken place in such a manner as to render the evening of life a blessing; — for whilst increasing physical weakness occurs, a full share of health free from pain is granted with it; and whilst memory and certain other faculties of the mind diminish, my good spirits and cheerfulness do not diminish with them.

First page of Faraday's letter offering to resign from The Royal Institution

Frontispiece

THE SELECTED
CORRESPONDENCE OF
MICHAEL FARADAY

VOLUME 2   1849-1866

Edited on behalf of the Royal Institution
of Great Britain by

L. PEARCE WILLIAMS

with the assistance of
Rosemary FitzGerald & Oliver Stallybrass

CAMBRIDGE
AT THE UNIVERSITY PRESS
1971

Published by the Syndics of the Cambridge University Press
Bentley House, 200 Euston Road, London N.W.1
American Branch: 32 East 57th Street, New York, N.Y.10022

Library of Congress Catalogue Card Number: 77–138377

ISBN: 0 521 07913 6

Printed in Great Britain
at the University Printing House, Cambridge
(Brooke Crutchley, University Printer)

CONTENTS

VOLUME 2

v

LIST OF ABBREVIATIONS FOR JOURNALS, PUBLISHED WORKS AND MANUSCRIPTS

ABLP	*Annuaire* du Bureau des Longitudes, Paris
AC	*Annales de Chimie et de Physique*
AE	*Archives d'Electricité*
AJS	*American Journal of Science*
AKAWB	*Abhandlungen* der Königlichen Akademie der Wissenschaften zu Berlin
AOP	*Annals of Philosophy*
AP	*Annalen der Physik*
ASPN	*Archives des Sciences Physiques et Naturelles*; Supplément à la *Bibliothéque Universelle et Revue Suisse*
BAAS	British Association for the Advancement of Science
BAASR	British Association for the Advancement of Science; *Reports*
BASB	*Bulletin* de l'Académie Royale des Sciences, des Lettres, et Belles-Lettres de Bruxelles
BF	*Biblioteca Fisica*
B.J.	Henry Bence Jones, *The Life and Letters of Faraday*, 2 vols., London, 1870
BSd'E	*Bulletin* de la Société d'Encouragement pour l'Industrie Nationale
BU	Bibliothèque Universelle des Sciences, Belles-Lettres et Arts, faisant suite à la Bibliothèque Britannique rédigée à Genève
CDMJ	*The Cambridge and Dublin Mathematical Journal*
CGA	L. de Launay, editor, *Correspondance du Grand Ampère*, 3 vols., Paris, 1936–43
CR	*Comptes Rendus Hebdomadaires des Séances* de l'Académie des Sciences, Paris
DJMCS	*Dublin Journal of Medical and Chemical Science*
EJS	*The Edinburgh Journal of Science*
ENPJ	*The Edinburgh New Philosophical Journal*
EPJ	*The Edinburgh Philosophical Journal*
ERCP	M. Faraday, *Experimental Researches in Chemistry and Physics*, London, 1859
ERE	M. Faraday, *Experimental Researches in Electricity*, 3 vols., London, 1839–55
IEE	Institution of Electrical Engineers
JGC	*Journal de Génie Civil*

JP	*Journal de Physique, de Chimie, et d'Histoire Naturelle*
JRAS	*Journal* of the Royal Agricultural Society of England
JRI	*Journal* of the Royal Institution of Great Britain
LG	*The Literary Gazette*
LPW	L. Pearce Williams, *Michael Faraday, A Biography*, London and New York, 1965
MAS	*Mémoires* de l'Académie des Sciences, Paris
MASB	*Mémoires* de l'Académie Royale des Sciences, des Lettres et Belles-Lettres de Bruxelles
MASN	*Memorie* della Reale Accademia delle Scienze, Napoli
MAWB	*Mémoires*; Akademie der Wissenschaften, Berlin
MCASB	*Mémoires Couronnés* publiés par l'Académie Royale des Sciences, des Lettres et Belles-Lettres de Bruxelles
MNASL	*Monthly Notices* of the Astronomical Society of London
MNGB	Mittheilungen der Naturforschenden Gesellschaft in Bern
MSA	*Mémoires de Physique et de Chimie* de la Société d'Arcueil
MSIM	*Memorie di Matematica e di Fisica* della Società Italiana delle Scienze residente in Modena
MSSN	*Mémoires* de la Société Royale des Sciences, Lettres et Arts de Nancy
NASN	*Nuovi Annali delle Scienze Naturali*
NBSP	*Nouveau Bulletin des Sciences* de la Société Philomatique de Paris
NJ	*Nicholson's Journal of Natural Philosophy, Chemistry and the Arts*
NM	*Nautical Magazine*
NRRS	*Notes and Records* of the Royal Society of London
PM	*The Philosophical Magazine.* After 1832, *The London and Edinburgh Philosophical Magazine and Journal of Science.* After 1840, *The London, Edinburgh and Dublin Philosophical Magazine and Journal of Science*
PRI	*Proceedings* of the Royal Institution of Great Britain
PRS	*Proceedings* of the Royal Society of London
PT	*Philosophical Transactions* of the Royal Society of London
PVSP	*Extraits des Procès-verbaux* de la Société Philomatique de Paris
QCM	Quételet, *Correspondance Mathématique et Physique*
QJS	*The Journal of Science and the Arts* edited at the Royal Institution of Great Britain (known as the *Quarterly Journal of Science*)
QR	*The Quarterly Review*
RI	The Royal Institution of Great Britain
RS	The Royal Society of London

RSAE	*Recueil des Travaux* de la Société Libre d'Agriculture, des Sciences, des Arts et des Belles-Lettres du Département de l'Eure
RSCSP	*Catalogue of Scientific Papers* compiled and published by the Royal Society of London, 19 vols., London, 1867–1925
TCPS	*Transactions* of the Cambridge Philosophical Society
TLCS	*Transactions* of the London Chemical Society
TLES	*Transactions* of the London Electrical Society
TRSE	*Transactions* of the Royal Society of Edinburgh
TSM	Richard Taylor, *Scientific Memoirs*, selected from the Transactions of Foreign Academies of Science and Learned Societies and from Foreign Journals, 5 vols., London, 1837–52
VEKNIW	Verhandelingen der Eerste Klasse van het Koninklijk Nederlandsche Instituut van Wetenschappen, Letterkunde, en Schoone Kunsten te Amsterdam

THE
CORRESPONDENCE

385 M. FARADAY to R. OWEN,[1] 14 January 1849

[*British Museum, Add. mss. 39954, f. 138, previously unpublished*]

Royal Institution
14 Jany 1849

MY DEAR OWEN

I have had your letter and am very sorry for the cause; and far more for the Dean of Westminsters[2] sake than our own. I had before to give an Eveng for him on account of illness and from what I knew then from Mr. Buckland should never have thought of asking him for one. But when he advertised in the newspapers that he would give a lecture on Artesian wells in this house, I felt that not to accept it would be to insult him; & told Barlow so. Barlow is out about the matter. Our only plea for the change must be the indisposition of the Dean for otherwise certain wrong interpretations which the Dean himself hinted at to me & which he seemed to fear; are sure to be made by some who think his views not quite correct

What would have happened if we had gone on with another offer which he voluntarily made of giving *Six* lectures here for some Charity!!!

Ever yours
M. FARADAY

[1] Richard Owen (1804–92), comparative anatomist and (later) opponent of Darwin.
[2] William Buckland.

386 J. PLÜCKER to M. FARADAY, 7 February 1849

[*I.E.E., previously unpublished*]

Bonn
7 Febr. 1849

DEAR SIR!

I thank you very much for your kind letter of the 14^Th of Dec.[1] by which you give me a short notice of your newest discoveries. You may think that I was axious [*sic*] to repeat them instantly, but being a poor german professor, obliged to give 3 lectures a day & charged too with different functions at the University, I found time to work only a few days ago. As my results are in some respect different from yours, I take liberty to comunicate [*sic*] the following ones.

1. I first tried antimony and was extremely surprised to find that its magne-crystallic axis (perpendicular to the chief cleavage planes) points not axially but *equatorially*. It has been confirmed by all different modes of suspension. I could not attribute the different effects to the state of impurity of my specimen of Antimony, nevertheless I tried pure antimony taken from the laboratory of Professor Bischof:[2] but allways the same result.

2. Secondly I tried very fine and pure bismuth, and was satisfied to find its magnecrystallic power *very strong*, the magnecrystallic axis pointing axially quite so as you describe it. Then I experimented with the less perfect cleavage planes and I found that there is another corresponding magnecrystallic axis, that axis belonging to the chief cleavage planes being more affected by the

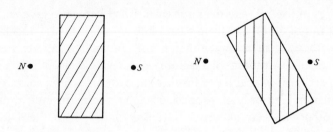

magnet than the other ones. The following experiment may prove it. A plate of bismuth bounded by chief cleavage planes, showed in these planes several parallel lines, indicating a second less perfect cleavage. If suspended horizontally in the level of the poles (the principal magnecrystallic axis being vertically and the two poles as near as possible) it pointed like a comon [*sic*] diamagnetic body, but lifted up one centimeter or nearly so, it turned instantly taking such a position, that the parallel lines mentioned above pointed equatorially and continued to do so even at a height of 10–15 centimeter [*sic*] above the level of the poles. It proves that there is another magnecrystallic axis contained in a plane perpendicular to these lines and perpendicular itself to the less perfect cleavage planes.

If you think my observations wrong, I'll send you in a letter some of the pieces of antimony and bismuth used in my experiments.

My head turns round by the multitude of new facts. I am about to get new ones.

I hope you will realize Your imagination to see Germany, and then I hope too your first stay will be at Bonn. In this case I shall be happy to give you any information you like, and if you should desire to work then I'll be your assistant (My Electromagnet will become more powerfull than it is now, I think it proper to put on it 100 pounds more of copper wire). You have many things better in England than we have in Germany, but our climate, mainly in the spring, is better than yours, and I am certain, that even a short stay in our country wou[ld] [ms. torn and missing] do good to your health. No doubt our political s[tate] [ms. torn and missing] is a disturbed one, but travelling or residing in our country you will scarcely perceive it; none of the English families, living here, left Bonn for that reason.

I did not yet see any of my papers in the English dress, though Mr Francis promised me some copies of them. I join to this letter a copy of my last papers. and will be very glad to see yours about the magnecrystallic axes.

I am Sir
very truly yours
PLÜCKER

P S. Excuse Sir my bad English.

[1] See letter 383.
[2] Carl Gustav Christoph Bischof (1792–1870), Professor of Chemistry and Technology at the University of Bonn.

387 J. PLATEAU to M. FARADAY, 25 March 1849
[*Faraday's 'Diary', 5, 196*]

Gand,
25 Mars 1849

MON CHER MONSIEUR FARADAY,

Permettez-moi de vous offrir un exemplaire du mémoire que je viens de publier.[1] Ce travail constitue la suite de celui que j'ai eu l'honneur de vous envoyer il y a quelques années, et au sujet duquel vous avez bien voulu m'écrire une lettre flatteuse que je conserve comme un témoignage de vos bons sentiments pour moi. Dans ce premier mémoire, je n'ai guère eu recours qu'à l'expérience; aussi renferme-t-il plus d'une chose hasardée, et même de petites erreurs théoriques. Dans le mémoire actuel, au contraire, la theorie et l'expérience; marchent de front, et se prêtent un mutuel appui. Vous y verrez se produire sur une grande échelle, des phénomènes de l'ordre de ceux auxquels on a donné l'épithète de *Capillaires* à cause de leur exiguité; vous y trouverez en même temps une suite de confirmations inattendues de l'admirable théorie sur laquelle repose l'explication des phénomènes capillaires; enfin, vous arriverez à une application qui consiste dans la theorie complète d'un phénomène dont l'étude expérimentale a formé la matière de l'un des plus beaux mémoires de Savart.[2]

J'ai reçu l'exemplaire que vous avez bien voulu m'envoyer de votre mémoire sur les nouveaux phénomènes dont vous avez enrichi la science; je vous en remercie, et je saisis cette occasion un peu tardive de vous exprimer toute mon admiration pour ces brillantes découvertes. On pouvait penser que c'était assez pour votre gloire d'avoir ajouté à vos travaux antérieurs la découverte de l'induction électro-dynamique avec toutes ses conséquences si extraordinaires; eh bien non! voilà que vous constatez d'une manière inespérée l'influence des courants électriques sur la lumière, puis l'universalité de l'action du magnétisme. En vérité, créer une nouvelle branche de la physique, ce n'est qu'un jeu pour vous.

A propos de magnétisme, causons un peu, si vous le voulez bien. Vos belles expériences sur les gaz vous ont conduit à établir l'état magnétique ou dia-magnétique d'un gaz donné, par rapport à un autre gaz donné; mais, ainsi que vous l'avez fait remarquer, elles ne permettent pas de constater si tel gaz est, par lui-même, magnétique ou dia-magnétique. Or, il m'a semblé qu'il serait possible d'arriver à cette connaissance absolue, et cela au moyen d'un procédé que je vais avoir l'honneur de vous soumettre.

Supposons l'électro-aimant renfermé dans une cage transparente remplie d'un gaz donne. Si ce gaz est magnétique, ses molécules, seront attirées par les pôles de l'électro-aimant, et elles seront, au contraire, repoussées si le gaz est dia-magnétique. Or, dans le premier cas, l'attraction des pôles aura nécessairement pour effet d'augmenter la densité du gaz autour de ces mêmes pôles, et, dans le second cas, la repulsion devra, au contraire, diminuer cette densité. Si donc le gaz est magnétique, la densité de la couche qui environne les pôles ira en croissant rapidement depuis une petite distance de la surface du métal jusqu'à cette même surface, et, si le gaz est dia-magnétique, ce sera un décroissement rapide de densité qui aura lieu. Par conséquent, lorsqu'un rayon lumineux traversera très obliquement la couche dont il s'agit, il sera quelque peu dévié dans un sens ou dans l'autre, suivant que la couche sera condensée ou dilatée.

Cela étant, et l'électro-aimant étant supposé vertical, placez verticalement derrière lui, à la distance d'une dixaine de pieds, par exemple, une feuille de papier blanc sur laquelle vous aurez marqué un point noir, et faites en sorte que ce point soit à la hauteur des pôles; puis, avant de faire agir le courant, placez-vous du cote opposé, à une distance au moins aussi grande de l'électro-aimant, et de manière que la droite qui va du point noir à votre oeil rase la surface supérieure de l'un des pôles; enfin, faites agir le courant. Alors, si le gaz est magnétique, le point noir devra paraître s'élever un peu au-dessus de la surface du pôle, et, si le gaz est dia-magnétique, le point devra disparaître derrière ce même pôle.

Il est inutile de vous faire remarquer que, dans cette expérience, l'oeil devra être bien immobile, et que, par conséquent, il faudra regarder à travers un petit trou percé dans une plaque portée par un support fixe. Il me semble, en outre, que les pôles ne devront pas être munis des armatures coniques dont vous vous êtes servi pour vos expériences: car les pointes de ces armatures étant tres voisines, le magnétisme de chacun des pôles doit être en partie dissimulé par celui de l'autre; je crois que les pôles devraient être terminés par des surfaces horizontales très legèrement convexes. Le plus ou moins d'effet dépendra surtout de la force de l'électro-aimant; mais je pense qu'on pourrait augmenter ce même effet, en plaçant les deux pôles suivant la ligne qui va du point noir à l'oeil: car alors le rayon, après avoir traversé la couche qui environne l'un des pôles, traverserait ensuite celle qui environne l'autre, et sa déviation serait doublée. Peut-être aussi serait-il bon de remplacer le point noir par une ligne noire horizontale et suffisamment longue: cette ligne devrait paraître brisée. Si l'action était trop faible, vous pourriez regarder à travers une lunette munie d'un fil horizontal. Enfin, il est possible que l'action de la pile échauffe notablement les fils de l'électro-aimant, d'où résulterait un courant d'air ascendant et dilaté, qui pourrait devenir une cause de déviation du rayon lumineux; dans ce cas, il faudrait garantir les pôles de ce courant d'air chaud, au moyen d'écrans convenables.

Je vous expose ces idées telles qu'elles me sont venues à l'esprit, et vous en ferez l'usage qu'il vous plaira; seulement, si vous les mettez en pratique, j'attends de votre conte que vous me fassiez part des résultats positifs ou négatifs auxquels vous serez arrivé.

Puis-je espérer que vous aurez l'obligeance de faire remettre les exemplaires ci-joints à Sir J. Herschel et à Messieurs Wheatstone et Grove dont j'ignore les adresses, ainsi qu'à Société Royale?

Tout à vous

J. PLATEAU

professeur à l'Université place du Casino 18

P.S. Je m'aperçois qu'au commencement de ma lettre, en parlant de mon premier mémoire sur les masses liquides, je semble faire le procès aux méthodes expérimentales. Telle n'a pas été mon intention; j'ai trop souvent moi-même employé ces méthodes pour ne pas en reconnaître toute l'importance; j'ai voulu dire uniquement, que comme le sujet de ce premier mémoire pouvait être abordé à la fois par la théorie et par l'expérience, j'ai eu tort, dans ce cas, de m'en tenir à l'expérience seule.

¹ See Letter 384, fn. 1.
² F. Savart, 'Mémoire sur la constitution des veines liquides lancées par des orifices circulaires en mince paroi', *AC*, 2 s., 53 (1833), 337.

---

388 J. PLÜCKER to M. FARADAY, 30 April 1849
[*I.E.E., previously unpublished*]

Bonn
30ᵗʰ of April 1849

Sir: I received your kind letter, by which you announced to me your last paper; I am very anxious to get it and will read it, with the greatest attention.

The new facts I alluded to in my last letter are the following ones. Since my first experiments I was convinced, that there ought to be an influence of Magnetism on crystallisation and I expected, that any salt crystallising *slowly* between the poles of a strong Magnet, would have its optical axes perpendicular to the line joining the two poles. Having tried in vain to prove it experimentally I did not speak about it. But when I repeated your last experiments with bismuth, I thought this metal excedingly [*sic*] proper to be subjected to the former experiments, and this time I had a full success. Melted bismuth, crystallising slowly between the poles of a strong Magnet gets such a crystalline structure that the chief cleavage plan [*sic*] becomes perpendicular to the line joining the two poles.[1] I prove the same, even without cleaving the crystallized bismuth, by the following experiment. A piece of bismuth, crystallised between the two poles, takes, whatever may be its shape, when suspended in such a way, that it may turn freely around a vertical axis allways and exactly (according to the magnecrystallic action) the same position it had during the crystallisation.

This result proves strikingly that the force acting on the magnecrystallic axis (and also I think on the optic axes) is a *molecular* one. That has been allways my opinion.

All my experiments confirm that this force produces, as you call it an effect of position only and not an effect of place When I say „repulsion of the optical axes" as I may say „attraction of the magnecrystallic one" I meaned [*sic*] only to explain the facts, without anticipating any conception about the nature of the acting forces.

About the 20th of March I gave my paper to Poggendorff; as soon as I get a copy of it, I'll send it to you by post.

Since I have been at Paris. Tired by lectures & a „changement d'air" was necessary for my health – Being restored by travelling, I'll find time to go on in my researches, even, I may say, in spite of the government, which does not at all favour them.

Yours very sincerely
PLÜCKER

[1] See [9646]. Also *LPW*, 433.

389 J. PLÜCKER to M. FARADAY, 20 May 1849
[*I.E.E.*, *P.M.*, *n.s.*, *34 (1849), 450*]

Bonn,
the 20th of May 1849

[in Faraday's hand?]

On the Magnetic relations of the Positive & Negative of the axes of crystals by Professor Plücker of Bonn in a letter to, & communicated [?] by Dr Faraday.

Allow me, Sir, to communicate to you several new facts, which, I hope, will spread some light over the action of the Magnet upon the optic and magnecrystallic axes.

I. The first and general law, I deduced from my last experiments is the following one

„There will be *either repulsion or attraction* of the optic axes by the poles
of a Magnet, according to the crystalline structure of the crystal. If the

crystal is a *negative* one, there will be *repulsion,* if it is a *positive* one there will be *attraction*"

The crystals most fitted to give the evidence of this law are *diopside* (a positive crystal) *cyanite, topaƶe* (both negatives) and other ones, crystallising in a similar way. In these crystals the line (*A*) bisecting the acute angles, made by the two optic axes, is neither perpendicular nor parallel to the axis (*B*) of the prism. Such a crystal, suspended horizontally like a prism of turmaline, staurotite or „cyanure rouge de fer & potasse" in my former experiments, will point neither axially nor equatorially, but will take allways a fixed intermediate direction. This direction will continually change if the prisme [*sic*] will be turned round its own axis *B*. It may be proved by a simple geometrical construction, which shows, that during one revolution of the prism round its axis (*B*), this axis without passing out of two fixed limits *C* & *D*, will go through all intermediate positions. The directions *C* & *D*, where the crystal returns, make *either* whith [*sic*] the line joining the two poles, *or* with the line perpendicular to it, on both sides of these lines, angles equal to the angle included by *A* and *B*: the first being the case, if the crystal is a *positive* one, the last if a *negative* one. There it follows that if the crystal by any kind of horizontal suspension may point to the poles of the Magnet, it is a *positive* one; if it may point equatorially it is a *negative* one. This last reasoning conducted me at first to the law mentioned above.

The magnecrystallic axis, I think, is, optically speaking, the line bisecting the (acute) angles made by the two optic axes, or in the case of one single axis, this axis itself. The crystals of bismuth and arsenic are positive crystals, Antimony, according to my experiments, is a negative one. All are uniaxal [*sic*].

II The cyanite is by far the most interesting crystal, I examined till now. If suspended horizontally it points very nicely, *only by the magnetic power of the Earth,* to the north. It is a true compass needle, and more than that, you may comand over its declination. If for instance, you suspend it in such a way that the line bisecting the two optic axes of the crystal, be in the vertical plane passing through the axis *B* of the prism, the crystal will point exactly as a compass needle does. By turning the crystal round the line *B* you may make it point exactly to the north of the Earth &c The crystal does non [*sic*] point according to the Magnetisme [*sic*] of its substance, *but only by following the magnetic action upon its optical axes.* This is in full concordance to the different law of diminution by distance of the pure magnetic and the optomagnetic action. If you approach to the north end of the suspended crystal the south pole of a permanent magnetic bar, strong enough to overpowering [*sic*] the magnetism of the Earth, the axis *B* of the prism will make with the axis of the bar (this bar having any direction whatever in the horizontal plane) an angle exactly *the same* it made before with the meridian plane: the crystal being directed either more towards the East or more towards the West.

The crystal showed, resembling for that also to a magnetic needle, strong polarity: the same end being allways directed to the north. I dare say, if it may be a *polarity of the optomagnetic power*. Two questions too may easily be answered. 1° Is the north pole indicated by the form of crystallisation 2° did the crystal get, when formed, its polarity by the magnetism of the Earth. Between the poles of the strong Electromagnet the permanent polarity disappeared as long as the Magnetism was excited.

I am obliged by the new facts, mentioned above, to take up my former memoir,[1] I must reproduce it under a quite new shape. I'll examine again the rock crystal, which being acted upon weakly by a magnet induced me to deny in that memoir, what I ascertain now and what I thought most probably, as soon as I got the first notice of your recent researches. (That you will find in the Memoir given to Mr Poggendorff 2 or 3 month [*sic*] ago.) Perhaps the exceptional molecular condition of rock crystal, as indicated by the passage of light trough [*sic*] it, will produce a particular magnetic action.

I should be very obliged to you, if you would give notice of the contents of my present letter to Mr. de la Rive, when he calls on you, as he intended to do. I showed him several of my experiments when he passed through Bonn the 12th of Mai [*sic*]. The following day I got the different results, mentioned above.

My best whishes [*sic*] for your health!

Very truly yours
PLÜCKER

[1] See his 'Ueber das Verhältniss zwischen Magnetismus und Diamagnetismus', *AP*, 148 (1847), 343.

390   J. B. DUMAS to M. FARADAY, 23 May 1849
[*I.E.E., previously unpublished*]

[Marked 'Rec'd, 23 May 1849']

MON CHER CONFRERE ET AMI

Cette lettre vous sera remise par M. D'Eichtal[1] l'un des plus honorables et des plus distingués parmi les Membres de la chambre des députés de l'ancien tems. Il veut bien se charger de vous remettre en même occasion, des échantillons qui vous intéresseront je l'espère. Le premier consiste en une reproduction obtenue sur un enduit d'amidon, au moyen de l'Iode. Le procédé de M. Niepce[2] vous est bien connu, mais personne n'est en état de le pratiquer aussi habilement que lui et son oeuvre peut vous le prouver. La gravure très imparfaite qui se trouve reportée sur la glace amidonnée y a produit une image plus agréable à l'oeil qu'elle ne l'étoit elle même. Vous remarquerez que j'ai fait encadrer la gravure dans un Cadre fait avec du bois injecté par le procédé de M. Boucherie.[3] il y en a divers échantillons.

Vous trouverez en second lieu, une série d'épreuves obtenues soit sur pierre, soit sur acier ou cuivre, pour des gravures en relief, tirées avec de l'encre ordinaire. C'est un problème très heureusement résolu par nos artistes et très proprement fournit des papiers qui résistent aux tentatives de faux, soit pour les effets de commerce, soit pour les actes publics. examinez ces papiers avec une bonne loupe et vous serez frappé de la pureté des lignes et de la perfection du tirage, qui est plus facile avec l'encre aqueuse qu'avec l'encre grasse d'Imprimerie. C'est une nouvelle ressource pour l'Industrie et pour les arts.

M. D'Eichtal vous entretiendra lui même d'un objet nouveau plein d'intérêt. Il s'agit de l'oxide de zinc et de fer [illeg. derivée [reading doubtful]] qu'il substitue aux matières à base de plomb employées en peinture. J'ai employé ses couleurs pour des Laboratoires et des amphithéatres avec le plus complet succès. Nous avons à paris déjà une grande experience de ce procédé qui me semble destiné à jouer un rôle trés considérable dans le monde industriel. Je suis persuadé que vous en aurez à Londres le parti le plus avantageux, tant à cause de l'Innocuité des produits que de leur résistance a l'action du gaz hydrogène sulfuré.

Enfin, M. D'Eichtal vous dira quelques mots d'une découverte faite dans mon laboratoire par un de mes éleves qui avoit bien voulu m'accompagner à Londres et qui a eu l'honneur de vous voir, M. Melsens.[4] Il s'agit d'un procédé merveilleux qui permet d'extraire de la canne à sucre, *tout le sucre* qu'elle contient. L'expérience avoit si bien réussi avec les Betteraves que j'ai voulu la vérifier sur la canne. J'ai fait venir une Centaine de livres de canne à sucre fraiches d'Andalousie et elles ont été traitées sous mes yeux avec le résultat le plus satisfaisant et le plus décisif.

M. Melsens vouloit que je vous fisse connaitre Son procédé, je m'y suis refusé. Je sais par ma propre expérience combien un secret embarasse son dépositaire. Si, cependant, vous permettiez qu'on vous le fit savoir et si vôtre gouvernement y mettait le moindre intérêt, vous consentiez à examiner la question, sans lui donner vôtre opinion, Je Vous transmettrais tout ce que Je sais à ce sujet.

M. Melsens lui même iroit au besoin repéter sous vos yeux toutes ses expériences. Ce seroit un immense service rendu à M. Melsens, qui en est bien digne par son dévouement à la Science et à qui Je porte un intérêt de père.

Je suis très à court de nouvelles purement Scientifiques. Vous savez déjà par nos comptes rendus que M. Boutigny a trouvé le moyen de plonger la main dans la fonte en fusion, sans le moindre accident.[5] L'Epreuve du feu est expliquée désormais. Il étoit bien du à la France, *ou l'on joue avec le feu*, tous les jours, de voir cette découverte faite par un des Savans qu'elle compte dans son Sein. La recette de M. Boutigny pourra être utile à nos hommes politiques.

Je me recommande à toute votre amitié. Vous verrez que le Dept. du Nord vient de m'envoyer à l'assemblée législative, plaignez moi et soyez bien assuré que s'il avoit été possible de refuser ce dangereux honneur, je me serois empressé de la faire, pour me consacrer tout entier à mes travaux. heureusement, qu'il reste encore au monde un coin paisible où la philosophie conserve un asile. Vous étiez digne plus que personne qu'il vous fut réservé, Jouissez de vôtre bonheur et qu'il vous soit longtems conservé.

Mille amitiés
DUMAS

Mad.ᵉ Dumas se rappele au bon souvenir de Madame Faraday à qui Je vous prie de présenter mes respectueux hommages.

¹ Adolphe Séligman d'Eichtal (1805–?), deputy from Le Mans (Dept. of La Sarthe) from 1846 to 1848.
² Abel Niepce de Saint-Victor (1805–70), inventor of the process of photography on glass.
³ Auguste Boucherie (1801–71), Bordeaux physician and discoverer of a process of preserving wood by injecting copper sulfate into it.
⁴ Louis Henri Fréderic Melsens (1814–86), later Professor at the School of Veterinary Medicine in Brussels.
⁵ P. H. Boutigny, 'Quelques faits relatifs à l'état sphéroïdal des corps. Epreuve du feu. Homme incombustible, etc.' *CR*, 28 (1849), 593.

391 M. FARADAY to J. PLÜCKER, 23 May 1849
[*Nat. Res. Counc. Canada, previously unpublished*]

R.I.,
23 May, 1849

MY DEAR PLÜCKER

Not 10 minutes ago I received your letter of the 20th. instant[1] & write at once to congratulate you on the beautiful facts you describe. How wonderfully this branch of Science is progressing! – I saw De la Rive two days ago & he gave me the pieces of bismuth from you about which I say nothing because I have not experimented with them & I conclude you have not yet received my paper. I shall see de la Rive in a day or two & will show him yours.

I am not quite sure what you would like but I think (if I can get the letter back from De la Rive in time) I shall send it to Mr Taylor to print in the next Number of the Phil Mag

In haste but
Most truly Yours
M. FARADAY

¹ See Letter 389.

392 M. FARADAY to J. PLÜCKER, 31 May 1849
[*Nat. Res. Counc. Canada, previously unpublished*]

31 May 1849

MY DEAR PLÜCKER

The inclosed will appear in the Phil Magazine tomorrow morning.[1] – I have altered a word or two here & there – I hope that what I have done meets your approbation & is agreeable to you. I could not resist my desire to make it known.

Ever Truly Yours
M. FARADAY

[1] See Letter 389.

393 J. PLÜCKER to M. FARADAY, 2 June 1849
[*I.E.E., previously unpublished*]

Bonn
2th [*sic*] of June 1849

Sir, I thank you very much for the unexpected kindness, with which you received my last comunication. A letter not being a memoir, I am very satisfied you sent mine to be printed by Mr. Taylor. My bad English, I know very well, is to be changed before going to press; therefore I am much obliged to you, for having altered some expressions. There is only one word, introduced by you, which I do not understand. You say „It is a true compass-needle and more than that, *you may obtain its declination*"[1] My meaning was „you may dispose on the direction, it shall take" or „you may give to it any declination you like, from about 25° to the East to 65° to the West".

I'll go again to work as soon as I get crystals, I am expecting from Berlin. Since my last letter I tried only a few crystals, ascertaining all the general law. I found that angite is acted upon by the magnetic power of the Earth, quite in the same way as cyanite.

I examined also rock crystal. If you suspend a prism of it horizontally it will, according to the *smaler* or *greater* distance from the poles, point either *equatorially* by the diamagnetism of its substance or *axially; its optic axis being attracted.* Why did I not try that before? To excuse my stupidity I might write a long psychological memoir.

I did not yet receive your paper.

Most sincerely
Yours
PLÜCKER

[1] Compare with Letter 389 as written by Plücker.

[Arch. de l'Acad. des Sciences, Paris, Dossier Faraday, previously unpublished]

Royal Institution,
5 June 1849

MY VERY DEAR FRIEND

I expect to see M. de la Rive in half an hour who afterwards will leave London for Paris and I rejoice in the opportunity (though a hasty one) of acknowledging both your letters & the presents you sent me by M. Eichtal [*sic*].[1] I grieved very much for a long time thinking of the unapt and adverse circumstances under which you must as a man of peace order & science have felt yourself oppressed and I thought I knew how far the fine natural tone of your mind would make these things distasteful to you. But now I hope things are better not externally merely but as respects the feelings of mens minds and to hear that *you* are nominated a deputy and intend to act in that position makes me think that matters must be righting fast.

Mr. Niepce's result which you sent me is beautiful and has excited the admiration of many. It keeps very well for the present but I conclude will not be permanent. The frame also of dyed wood is very beautiful. Surely that must be a valuable result.

M. D'Eichtal is busy in some communications which if I understand him rightly may concern both you and me about Sugar. From all he says I shall be most happy to be joined in the matter i. e. provided it is necessary here for I am never willing to be the depository of a *secret* unless there be a necessity. However as he understands the matter thoroughly and will take the trouble of guarding it aright I will leave it all to him to explain. All I can say is that I feel it a great pleasure & a great honor to be joined with you in any thing – or in the smallest matter.

I am greatly behind in Scientific reading & hardly know what is doing – and my encouragement to read is sadly diminished by the daily consciousness that I cannot keep what I read. Still as I know you feel an interest in me let me say that I am pretty well and cheerful & happy in mind.

My wife desires her kindest remembrances to you and Madame Dumas. We often speak of the kindness we received together & wonder you could so consent to loan your time and powers idling with us. and now my dear friend with the most earnest wishes for your health & happiness and that of those around you who make your happiness, Believe me to be

Ever
Most truly Yours
M. FARADAY

[1] See Letter 390.

395 M. FARADAY to L. THOMPSON, 9 June 1849

[*Burndy Library, Norwalk, Conn., Michael Faraday Collection 79, previously un-published*]

Rl Institution
9 June 1849

MY DEAR SIR

Olifiant [reading doubtful] gas requires a pressure of 42 1/2 atmospheres to liquefy it at 30° F. I have not succeeded in liquefying coal gas or light hydrocarbon but it requires a much higher pressure than that. – Again – Babbage I think bored a hole in a very compact limestone rock, poured in acid & closed it up hoping to confine the gas & blow up the rock but the gas gradually found its way through the body of the rock

Ever Truly Yours
M. FARADAY

[1] Probably Lewis Thompson, chemist. See *RSCSP*.

396 M. FARADAY to B. HAWES,[1] 13 June 1849[2]

[*Duke University Library, previously unpublished*]

R.I.,
June 13, 1849

MY DEAR SIR,

I received your letter of the 9th instant and I have also received a letter from the discoverer of the process of extracting sugar, and another from M. Dumas stating to me the results which he witnessed.[3] I am willing to answer your enquiry as far as lies in my power: provided I can guard myself from the possible charge, hereafter, of having given a hasty and ill-considered opinion. Let me remind you, therefore, that circumstances connected with the season and the time of the year forbid that I should have the opportunity at present of seeing the operation of extraction performed: and that I can only know the process by description; can only judge of it by a consideration of the principles of chemical action which it involves, and can only be aware of the effects by the testimony of M. Dumas and the discoverer.

Having, then, considered the communications carefully, I see nothing to make me doubt that the facts are as stated: – namely that a very large proportion, approaching toward the whole, of the sugar in the sugar cane may be extracted from it in the form of unchanged white crystalline sugar: and at an expence not greater and probably very much less than that of the present process.

I am My dear Sir
Ever Most Truly Yours
M. FARADAY

[1] Sir Benjamin Hawes (1797–1862), soap manufacturer, M.P. for Kinsale and under-secretary for war.
[2] This letter has not been checked against the original.
[3] See Letter 390.

[I.E.E., previously unpublished]

Genève
le 14 juin 1849

MON CHER MONSIEUR,

Me voici à Genève depuis deux jours; je ne suis resté à Paris que trois à quatre jours.[1] J'ai trouvé nos amis si préoccupé de la politique & du choléra que j'ai cru qu'il n'y avait grand chose à espérer d'eux au point de vue de la Science. Arago avec qui j'ai passé une heure, ne m'en a presque pas parlé. Regnault a été cependant plus scientifique; mais il est découragé & peu entrain de continuer ses travaux. Le jeune Becquerel[2] (le père etait absent) m'a entretenu de ses dernières expériences qui me paraissent assez curieuses mais qui ont encore besoin de vérification.

J'ai été bien heureux de me retrouver chez moi au milieu de tous les miens que j'ai trouvés en très bonne santé; ma femme a été très sensible à votre bon souvenir & à celui de Made Faraday & elle me charge bien de la rappeler [illeg.] à votre bonne amitié. Je n'ai point vu Mr. Dumas; c'est à Made. Dumas que j'ai remis votre lettre; elle avait l'air bien & elle m'a beaucoup demandé de vos nouvelles & de celles de Made. Faraday.

J'ai vu à Paris de tristes effets du choléra; des quartiers dans lesquels une charette receuillait les morts; & cependant il régnait au milieu de ce fléau envoyé par la Providence une apparence d'indifférence qui faisait mal. On dansait & on chantait à l'un des bouts de Paris pendant qu'on mourrait à l'autre. Ce peuple est courageux, mais il n'est pas *sérieux*.

Le but de ma lettre n'est pas de vous parler uniquement de mon voyage & de mon arrivée. J'en ai un autre plus important, c'est de vous demander d'avoir la bonté de m'écrire le plus tot que vous pourrez, *un seul mot* pour me dire si vous avez effectivement fait mon expérience, comment elle a réussi & les particularités qu'elle vous a presentées. Vous m'obligerez infiniment en me faisant cette communication; j'espère que vous ne me trouverez pas trop indiscret. Si en même temps vous avez quelque nouvelle scientifique à m'apprendre, vous savez le plaisir que vous me ferez en me la donnant. – Peut-être avez-vous à l'occasion de l'expérience dont je vous ai parlé, fait quelques observations qui m'auraient échappé. –

Mille remerciements des jolis moments que j'ai passés avec vous à Londres, mes compliments bien respectueux à Made Faraday

Votre tout dévoué & affectionné
AUGUSTE DE LA RIVE

[1] See Letter 394.
[2] Alexandre Edmond Becquerel (1820–91), physicist. Son of Antoine César Becquerel and father of Henri Becquerel, the discoverer of radioactivity.

398 M. FARADAY to J. B. DUMAS, 18 June 1849

[*Arch. de l'Acad. des Sciences, Paris, Dossier Faraday, previously unpublished*]

Royal Institution
18 June 1849

MY DEAR FRIEND,

My first thought in writing or thinking of you is are you happy – for so much turns up near & about you that seems to me incompatible with your habit of mind & occupation that I mourn a little at times. What comes to pass due from the hand of God, as the serious illness of your Son, we must indeed strive to receive with patience but that which is evolved through the tumults & passions of man. does not bring with it that chastening & in some degree alleviating thought. I rejoice however to hear that your Son is better and that in respect of him you and Madame Dumas are relieved from all present anxiety. I think I remember him well as he went with us through the Jardin des Plantes –

In reference to M. Melsens matter[1] I have written to our Colonial Secretary Mr Hawes and could not say other than what you have said. but M. D'Eichthal will inform you of that matter. Surely it must become very important & I hope will in one way or another produce its fitting return to M Melsens.

I think I wrote a short time ago by De la Rive and fear that you or still more Madame Dumas will have reason to be weary of my letters but I trust in the kindness of both for forgiveness. Ever my dear friend, Yours most faithfully.

M. FARADAY

[1] See Letter 390.

399 W. THOMSON to M. FARADAY, 19 June 1849

[*Silvanus P. Thompson, 'The Life of William Thomson Baron Kelvin of Largs', London, 1910, Vol. 1, 214*]

32 Duke Street,
St. James',
Saturday, June 19

MY DEAR SIR,

After our conversation to-day I have been thinking again on the subject of a bar of diamagnetic non-crystalline substance, in a field of magnetic force which is naturally uniform, and I believe I can now show you that your views lead to the conclusion I had arrived at otherwise, that such a bar, capable of turning round an axis, would be set stably with its length along the lines of force. As I may not have another opportunity of seeing you again before you leave town, I hope you will excuse my continuing our conversation by writing a few lines on the subject.

Let the diagram represent a field of force naturally uniform, but influenced by the presence of a ball of diamagnetic substance. It is clear that in the localities A and B the lines of force will be less densely arranged, and in the localities D and C they will be more densely arranged than in the undisturbed field. Hence

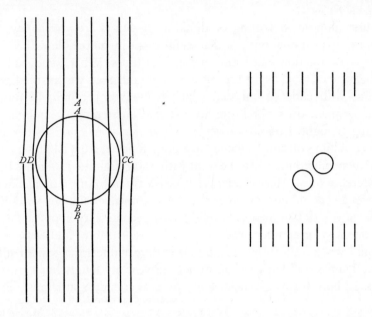

a second ball placed at A or at B would meet and disturb fewer lines than if the first ball were removed; but a second ball placed at D or C would meet and disturb more lines of force than if the first ball were removed. It follows that two equal balls of diamagnetic substance would produce more disturbance on the lines of force of the field if the line joining their centres is perpendicular to the lines of force than if it is parallel to them. But the disturbance produced by a diamagnetic substance is an effect of worse "conducting power," and the less of such an effect the better. Hence two balls of diamagnetic substance, fixed to one another by an unmagnetic framework, would, if placed obliquely and allowed to turn freely round an axis, set with the line joining their centres *along* the lines of force.

The same argument, for a contrary reason, shows that two balls of soft iron similarly arranged would set with the line joining their centres also *along* the lines of force. For this position more disturbance is produced on the lines of force than in any other, but now the *more* disturbance (being of better "conduction") the better. Hence the conclusion. Of course similar conclusions follow for bars, or elongated masses, of the substances.

I can never, however, make any assertion regarding the tendency of a diamagnetic bar in a uniform field without repeating that I believe no experiments can make it sensible. I doubt even whether the corresponding tendency in the case of a neutral bar in as strong a solution of sulphate of iron as could be got could be rendered sensible by actual experiments, as excessively slight deviations from uniformity in the field would entirely mask the results of this tendency, even if by themselves they might produce appreciable effects. – I remain, my dear sir, yours very truly,

WILLIAM THOMSON.

400 W. DE LA RUE[1] to M. FARADAY, 6 July 1849

[*I.E.E., previously unpublished*]

No. 7 St. Mary's Road
Canonbay
July 6th 1849

MY DEAR SIR

This is a begging letter – if not convenient to you to comply with my request lay it on one side and do not trouble yourself any more about it – I apply to you on behalf of a worthy man judging by his works and acts – a Mr. Nobert[2] of Greifswald in Pomerania – a maker of microscopes and other philosophical instruments – He says "I have already asked so much & yet, cannot refrain from enquiring whether you could procure from Mr. Faraday a piece of his heavy glass".

The applicant has accomplished, at my suggestion, some dividing on glass of such extreme fineness that it is a question whether the physical properties of light do not prevent our resolving it – the divisions being about the one hundred & ten thousandths of an inch apart from centre to centre and therefore, less than a wave-length of even the violet ray –

I have but just received the specimen and have not yet examined it but it will I have little doubt serve to elucidate some of the properties of light – it is a mechanical wonder at any rate and reflects the highest credit on the patience and skill of Mr. Nobert. This is the man who wishes for a bit of your glass. I do not think that it will be lost on him if you have it to spare – but I am quite aware that these applications have been repeatedly made since you terminated your experiments and shall therefore not be at all surprised to learn that this comes too late.

Yours Very truly
WARREN DE LA RUE

[1] Warren de la Rue (1815–89), astronomer who pioneered in the application of photography to astronomy.
[2] Friedrich Adolph Nobert (1806–81), maker of the first diffraction gratings.

401 M. FARADAY to A. DE LA RIVE, 9 July 1849

[Bibliothèque publique et universitaire de Genève, ms. 2316, f. 65–6, previously unpublished]

Royal Institution
9 July 1849

MY DEAR DE LA RIVE

Though I have delayed writing this letter until the last minute still I have nothing satisfactory to tell you for as yet I have not made your experiment. I gave orders to Newman at once for an apparatus but illness rendered me unable to follow him up or even to go on regularly with my lectures and when at last he produced an apparatus it would not do. I have waited 'till today for a perfect one but have not yet received it & as we leave London directly for 6 or 7 weeks in the North I must defer the result until I come back. I have no doubt of a repetition in every point of the results you have obtained. and I hope you will before then have given them to the world.

My thoughts are sluggish & heavy or I would say fifty things to you for though I have little to *tell* there is much I could *ask* of you. But head ach [*sic*] & weariness make me quiet I am afraid that the condition of Italy sadly affects her scientific men. for I had a letter from Majocchi[1] the other day seeming to say that he was driven [reading doubtful] from Turin & knew not what to do. For me, who never meddle with politics and who think very little of them as one of the games of life, it seems sad that Scientific men should be so disturbed by them. and so the progress of pure [two words illeg] philosophy be much & so often disturbed by the passions of men.

Ever my dear De la Rive
Yours Most Truly
M. FARADAY

[1] Giovanni Alessandro Majocchi (?–1854), physicist.

402 M. FARADAY to B. C. BRODIE,[1] 16 July 1849

[R.I., previously unpublished]

Filey
Yorkshire
16 July 1849

MY DEAR SIR

I do not at all share in your feeling as regards the Managers & their judgment If their Professor of Chemistry[2] neither asks for nor suggests any change either in the general system or the assistants it is hardly possible that they can imagine or have any reason for making a change without also having a strong judgment *against him*; and that I suppose they have not. Whatever prosperity the Institution *now has* has been acquired during his Professorship and he would have a right to say so supposing that any difference of opinion or discussion arose. I conclude that such thoughts as these must be on the mind of several of the Managers & I do not wonder at it, and though I may wish very earnestly to infuse young blood & new Science into the chemical part of the establishment; I cannot overrule what others may think the common sense view of the case. To those who see the surface or even who may see some depth beneath the surface, it may appear quite unnecessary to make a change whilst the men who have thus far brought the Institution on its way are in their places: and who shall say they are wrong.

As regards the proposed lectures you write that your first impulse was to throw them entirely up, and I would say now *do not give them* unless you in your mind leave the Institution authorities as free to close them at the end of the season as you feel yourself to be either now or at any other time. There are probably *three* views of these lectures: – your own which is to make them strict logical expositions of chemical science & by that useful & very important: – then mine which is that though strict logical accurate & excellent, they are of little practical or influential character except in association with a practical school; *which you admit cannot exist in the Institution* – & thirdly the possible view of the Managers who have I think wished only for such simple elementary developments of chemical principles as should, like Mr Brandes former lectures, give a correct but popular idea of chemistry to their members who not being students are amateurs only & hardly that.

Remember also as respects your judgment of the Managers that your letter was a private letter to me & that though I read it to the Managers they have it not in their possession and could not even lay it before their Professor of Chemistry if they desired You can of course easily make it a letter to them by referring to it & expressing your wish; if you saw any end to be gained by that: but of that I must leave you to be the judge.

Ever Very Truly Yours
M. F A R A D A Y.

[1] Benjamin Collins Brodie (1817–80), later Waynflete Professor of Chemistry at Oxford.
[2] William Thomas Brande was Professor of Chemistry at the Royal Institution at this time. Faraday was Fullerian Professor of Chemistry, a quite different chair.

403 W. T H O M S O N to M. F A R A D A Y, 24 July 1849
[Silvanus P. Thompson, 'The Life of William Thomson Baron Kelvin of Largs', London, 1910, Vol. 1, 216]

9 Barton Street,
Westminster,
July 24, 1849.

My dear Sir – In the conversation which we had about the beginning of this month I mentioned several objects of experimental research which occurred to me as of much importance with reference to a theory of Diamagnetic, and, still more, of Magnecrystallic [*sic*], action. I now take the liberty of addressing to you a few memoranda on the subject.

1. If a ball, cut out of a crystal of bismuth, be placed so as to be repelled by a magnet, will the repulsion not be stronger when the magnecrystallic axis is held perpendicular to the lines of force than when it is held in the direction of these lines. (Reference to §2552 of your Researches).

2. It would be a valuable acquisition to our experimental elements if a ball cut from a crystal of bismuth were suspended in the manner described by you in §2551, and experiments were made by varying the length of the lever, and altering the general disposition so as to perceive cases in w^h the tendency to move, due to the repulsive action, might be exactly balanced by a tendency to move in the contrary direction arising from the magnecrystallic action. A sketch, with dimensions, of the arrangements in any such case of equilibrium would be most valuable.

3. In such a case as the preceding, if the strength of the magnet (a pure electro-magnet without soft iron would be the most satisfactory kind for such an experiment) be increased or diminished, will the equilibrium remain undisturbed?

4. Is the repulsion on a non-crystalline or crystalline diamagnetic ball or the attraction on a ferro-magnetic ball exactly proportional to the square of the strength of the magnet? Thus in any case of pure repulsion, or of pure attraction, if the strength of the magnet be doubled, would the force be quadrupled; if the strength of the magnet be increased threefold would the force be increased ninefold? In this investigation, as in the preceding, a pure electro-magnet would be the best, since in such a magnet the strength may be altered in any ratio, which ratio may be measured with much precision by a torsion galvanometer, while the character and form of the lines of force remains absolutely invariable.

5. How are crystals of magnetic iron ore related to other crystals in their magnetic properties? Are they intrinsically polar, or are they merely axial? For example, if, supposing that to be possible, a crystal of magnetic iron ore have its polarity reversed, will it remain permanently magnetized in this reverse way? or, if a crystal of magnetic iron be demagnetized, will it remain non-magnetic? Will it not, in virtue of an intrinsic tendency to magnetization, gradually become magnetized in its original way?

I have a small ball of loadstone from the island of Elba which I have employed in place of a needle in a torsion galvanometer, and which appears to be susceptible of inductive action like soft iron (returning apparently to its primitive magnetic state when the inducing magnet is removed), and to be susceptible of this action to a greater degree when its axis is along the lines of inducing force than when it is perpendicular to them. My means of experimenting are, however, so very limited that I cannot be confident with reference to any such conclusions.

My intended departure for Norway, of w^h I spoke to you, has been necessarily delayed for a fortnight by important and unexpected business. I hope to-morrow, however, to be on my way to Copenhagen by steamer.

I hope you are at present enjoying a pleasant and refreshing tour, as I heard to-day at the Royal Institution that you are travelling.

Believe me, my dear Sir, yours very truly,

WILLIAM THOMSON.

404 J. PLÜCKER to M. FARADAY, 10 August 1849
[*I.E.E., previously unpublished*]

Bonn,
Aug. 10th, 1849

DEAR SIR!

I feel myself very much obliged to you for having proposed me a member of the Royal Institution, and find no words to express my thanks in a proper way; but believe me Sir the kindness you showed to me on several occassions [*sic*] gave to me the greatest satisfaction I ever felt in my scientific career.

Permitt [*sic*] me to offer to you a „Resumé" of all my researches on Magnetism til July 1849. Since my last letter I had scarcely any time to continue them. I found only crystals of Oxide of Tin showing a *very* strong magnetic polarity in the direction of their single axis; they were directed very well by the Earth. Then I examined most attentively the sulfate of iron. The line attracted by the poles of the Magnet is not perpendicular to the cleavage planes but makes with them an angle of 75°. According to that you will observe that a piece of such a crystal, bounded by cleavage planes, points differently, when turned round its magnecrystallic axis, this axis being allways horizontal. The difference is measured by an angle of 15° on both sides. The line attracted by the poles is one of the midle [*sic*] lines between the optic axes (which include an angle of 90°), the other one being not at all affected by the Magnet. In this (exceptional) case the resulting effect cant be deduced from the attraction of both the optic axes. Therefore I inquired, if the action may directly depend on the distribution of the Ether within the crystals, all the lines of less elasticity being attracted, the lines of greater elasticity repelled by the poles. But this law does not hold. Therefore new investigations only may give the true and complete law of nature.

I cut out of a very nice crystal of sulfate of iron a cube, two surfaces of which were perpendicular to the middle line attracted by the poles. By a sensible balance I found *no* difference in the magnetic attraction whatever a surface might be put on the approached poles of the Magnet. This result, fully according to your experiments, appears to me very strange: the directing [reading doubtful] power of the midle [*sic*] line being in this case so very strong.

These last days I tried again to prove that there is a diamagnetic polarity. The mutual action between magnetised iron being many thousand times stronger than that of magnetised iron on diamagnetic bismuth, you may never expect to see any mutual action between two pieces of diamagnetised bismuth. Such an action must be many – many *million* times weaker. But if you give to a piece of bismuth being acted upon by a magnet and suspended within a copper wire, by means of a current sent trough [*sic*] this wire alternately in opposite direction [*sic*], a new diamagnetic polarity, the repulsion may be altered in the ratio of the intensity of the diamagnetic polarity, given to the bismuth by the Magnet, to to [*sic*] the intensity of that polarity, altered by the current. In this way I succeded [*sic*] to show by means of the balance that a cylindre [*sic*] of bismuth obtained by the wire a magnetic polarity opposite to that which a magnetic body would obtain under the same conditions. But the action is very weak and I must before I may pronounce on this important point, repeat the same experiment in a varied way.

Being elected by the University of Bonn a deputy to the deliberations on the Universities's [*sic*] reform, which will take place at Berlin by ordre [*sic*] of the Prussian government in the month of September, I am not able to accept the kind invitation from Birmingham. But I hope tis not the last time I crossed the Channel.

I had the pleasure to see Prof. Wheatstone here at Bonn, and was excedingly [*sic*] glad to learn from him, you were now of very good health.

Most truly
Yours
PLÜCKER

405 M. FARADAY to C. R. WELD, 21 August 1849
[*R.S., previously unpublished*]

Royal Institution,
21 Aug, 1849

MY DEAR SIR

I returned to town only a few days ago & now send you back Mr. Wards[1] paper with the following remarks.

The paper does not carry conviction to my mind and as yet I retain my own view of *revulsion* &c.

The point whether a substance like *lead* or *zinc*, can, in a *perfectly free state* & free from any ordinary magnetic substance assume either the magnetic or the diamagnetic condition according to the degree of magnetic force to which it is subjected – though assumed in the paper is not I think yet settled by the experiments in the paper: and would require far more care about [*sic*] even than appears from the paper to have been taken Yet upon that point depends all the rest – its Sluggishness & contrary revulsions &c. – I do not say it may not be so but as yet I have seen no results either in my own experiments or those of others that prove it to be so. Plucker himself I believe doubts whether a *perfectly pure substance* can become both Magnetic & diamagnetic.

The hypothesis at the end is all dependant on this questionable point.

At pp. 32–33 of the MS. the writer appears quite unaware of my suppositions in N°s 2429. 2430. 2431. of my old Exp. Researches or of the Experiments & investigations made by Weber, Plücker, Reiss[2] [*sic*] in support of that view.

Still I have no right to decide on a case of difference of conclusions where I am one of the parties concerned & I am anxious never to stand in the way of the publication of opinions which are contrary to my own – & therefore must leave it to others to judge whether the communication is proper for insertion in the Phil Transactions.

Ever My dear Sir
Very Truly Yours
M. FARADAY

[1] William Sykes Ward, 'On some phenomena and motions of metals under the influence of magnetic force', *PRS*, 5 (1849), 853.
[2] Peter Theophil Riess (1805–83). For his many papers on electricity, magnetism and diamagnetism, see *RSCSP*.

406 M. FARADAY to W. WHEWELL, 29 October 1849
[*Trinity College Library, Trinity College, Cambridge, previously unpublished*]

Royal Institution,
29 Oct. 1849

MY DEAR SIR,

Mr. Barlow asks me to support his application to you for a Friday Evg in the coming season.[1] I would most willingly do so for our sakes and my own gratification but considering to whom I write I feel I ought not to say more than if such a thing comes within the scope of your convenience & willingness it will be the source of very high delight and of something more to me.

Ever My dear Sir,
Your Oblgd Servt,
M. FARADAY

[1] See Letter 407.

407   W. WHEWELL to M. FARADAY, 31 October 1849
[*Trinity College Library, Trinity College, Cambridge, previously unpublished*]

Trin. Lodge,
Cambridge,
Oct. 31. 1849

MY DEAR DR. FARADAY

I had not answered Mr. Barlow's application sooner because I was not certain that I could comply with it to any good purpose. Your joining in it adds much to my wish to assent, but still I do not see the possibility of doing so. I could have wished to say something about the constitution of matter, but I dare not do so till I see my way better, or at least till I can bring out the difficulties more clearly. Your paper about axiality is highly important in its bearing upon this point, but I cannot yet bring it into any definite relation with other things. I am at present in far too puzzled a condition to pretend to teach any one. If my ideas should grow any clearer I may perhaps [try to express] [reading doubtful] them if you are willing to hear them; but I fear that will not be this year.

Always my dear Dr Faraday
Yours most truly
W. WHEWELL

408   E. DU BOIS-REYMOND[1] to M. FARADAY,
15 November 1849
[*R.I., previously unpublished*]

Berlin
21. Carlstr.
November 15, 1849

SIR,

According to your own statement, natural philosophy is indebted for the most important steps it has made at your hands to the strong conviction you always felt, that the various forms of force have one common origin, any form of force admitting of being converted into another under appropriate circumstances. Nor have you, on several occasions, refrained from extending this view even to the mysterious agent of the nerves, and, in your paper on the Gymnotus,[2] you have suggested some experiments for the purpose of discovering some new relation between nervous power and electricity.

I therefore venture to hope you will look with some interest on the results of an experimental inquiry, in which I have been engaged for these last eight years. This inquiry has led me to the most striking facts bearing upon the long-suspected identity of the nervous and muscular power and the electro-chemical form of force. The greater part of my investigations are detailed at length in the two accompanying volumes,[3] which I beg you to accept as a proof of my deepest veneration.

I am very sorry to find, from your "Experimental Researches" you do not read German. Unfortunately, the subject I have treated is such a complicated one, and the various series of experiments are so extensive, that the shortest extract, to be intelligible at all, would far exceed the limits of a letter and probably of your patience also. You will, however, perhaps be kind enough to prevail upon some friend of yours to bring you and the scientific public of England acquainted with some parts, if not the whole, of my work; and, at least, you will see by a mere inspection of the plates, that it is not without having previously laid a new and somewhat large experimental groundwork, that I am so bold as, once more and that so positively, to bring forward theoretical views like those of old Priestley and Galvani.

The second copy you would greatly oblige me by presenting, as a token of respect, to the Royal Society.

I am, Sir, yours most respectfully

DR. E. DU BOIS-REYMOND

[1] E. du Bois-Reymond (1818–96), Professor of Physiology at the University of Berlin.
[2] M. Faraday, 'Notice of the character and direction of the electric force of the Gymnotus', *PT* (1839), 1.
[3] E. du Bois-Reymond, *Untersuchungen über thierische Elektricität*, 2 vols., Berlin, 1848–9.

409   T. GRAHAM to M. FARADAY, 3 December 1849
[I.E.E., previously unpublished]

4 London Square
December 3, 1849.

DEAR FARADAY

Your understanding of the passage in my paper[1] to which you refer in your note of Dec. 1 is perfectly right. As also is the illustration you give afterwards speaking of *weight* instead of volume. The numbers, however, which you give in illustration of the last, 2172 of time & 5292 of time are, I find, from a table of results (page 384) which illustrate a *divergence* from the law, owing to the capillary being too short to give resistance enough. The one number should be double of the other, according to the law.

Air or coal gas of 4 atmos. density should pass through a long tube, such as Perkins 1 inch drawn-iron tubes, with 4 times the velocity of the same gas of 1 atmos. density, for equal volumes; & consequently with 16 times the velocity for equal "weights", the propulsive force being the same in both experiments. Hence a great facility in conveying coal gas in a *dense* state, by these pipes for long distances – such as many miles.

In the table head of page 385, would you be so good as to alter with your

pen the first row of figures under 1 atmosphere from 1095 . 1096 .
1095.5 . 1095.5
                                        into

1105 . 1107 . 1106 . 1106.

Your calling my attention to the point has led me to discover that I had
calculated the last column of that table from a set of observations on air of
1 atmos. made last, & which I have omitted to give in the paper, & not from
those observations for 1 atmos which are actually given.

It has been probably this which put you out. With the change, the numerical
relations of the calculated times appear at once – 553 being 1/2 of 1106, &c.

Very faithfully yours
THO. GRAHAM

¹ See Thomas Graham, 'On the motion of gases', *PT* (1849), 349.

410   J. PLÜCKER to M. FARADAY, 8 December 1849
[*I.E.E., previously unpublished*]

Bonn
8th of December 1849.

DEAR SIR!

A few days ago I received your long expected paper.¹ Belonging to sulfate
of iron I found my observations mentioned in the latin Memoir² in complete
accordance with yours. Your arsenic is diamagnetic, mine magnetic; nevertheless in both cases the axis is attracted by the poles. Respecting Iodi, [reading
doubtful] many our [*sic*] observations dont agree. I examined a great number
of crystals and allways the optic axis, which is perpendicular to the cleavage
plane, was repulsed like in calcareous Spar. A piece of crystallised Antimony I
brought from Paris (containing there is no doubt a small quantity of iron),
showed very complicated phenomena. There was diamagnetic magnetic and
crystallamagnetic action: all these three actions varying differently with
distance.

Being returned from Berlin, – where I lost a good time in fruitless deliberations on University reform – I took up again my magnetic researches. During
the last two years I have been much tantalized, not being able to imagine any
force whatever producing the paradox phenomena presented by crystals. Now
I may reduce all to the comon law of magnetic attraction and repulsion and
confirm my theoretical views as well by calculous [*sic*] as by direct experiment.
I gave an incomplete notice of it to Mr Poggendorff and I am now writing a
more elaborate Memoir.³ I dare not believe you will adopt my views, but
nevertheless let me beg to give in a few words an idea of it.

I got by experiment new proofs of diamagnetic polarity, induced by electric currents: Ampère would say there are in diamagnetic bodies induced currents going round the molecules in a direction opposite to that in magnetic bodies. (There is some analogy in this explication with that given by Fresnel of the phenomena of light passing along the axis trough [*sic*] rock crystal and in any direction whatever trough the well known fluids, there being circular rotations of the ether in opposite directions.) That is also I think the first explication you gave of diamagnetic action, which I adopted myself since I found, that there were no necessity to adopt for the diamagnetic and magnetic force a different law of diminution by distance, and since I thought it without doubt that Bismuth gets polarity by becoming diamagnetic. Join to this hypothesis the new one, that in magnetic crystals the polarity of the molecules be induced in different directions with a different facility, energy or stability; that the same take place belonging to the diamagnetic polarity in diamagnetic crystals – and you may explain all phenomena. The meaning of the new hypothesis will be completely understood, when for instance I say that a cylindrical bar of soft iron gets its polarity more easily along the axis of the bar, and with more stability and power, than in any other direction; quite the contrary takes place, when the bar will be reduced to a plate.

By putting thin iron bars into a piece of wood or copper, you may, by choosing properly their directions, imitate all experiments with magnetic crystals.

Allow me to explain a single case, for instance that of a prism of turmaline [*sic*]. By considerations taken from the elasticity of the ether, in accordance with its conducting power for Electricity, you may deduce, that the magnetic polarity of such a bar is most easily and strongly excited perpendicularly to its axis. Suppose it be so.

Now take a bar *C* of any indifferent substance, suspended horizontally between the two poles, to which ends a small iron bar *AB* is attached. Such a bar will point equatorially with great energy: *the iron going away from the poles.* In that way you may, in the case of turmaline reproduce the magnecrystallic action by small iron bars, perpendicular to its axis. You may too reproduce the magnetic action of its mass by a small iron wire passing through it in the direction of its greatest dimension i.e. its axis. Thus you will have two groups of forces, acting one oppositely to the other. You may take only two forces, one driving *A* towards to the nearer pole [*sic*], the other one driving away from

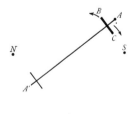

it the bar *BC*. By giving to the two bars *BC* and *AA'* a convenient relative thickness, you will, for a given distance of the poles, have a state of equilibrium; and the poles being far enough, the equilibrium will subsist in every position of the system of the two bars. Then you may mathematically prove that the system will point either *axially* or *equatorially* if you go either *farther* or *nearer* with the poles. &c. &c. An iron helix will point equatorially &c &c.

Tis a consequence of my theoretical views, confirmed by experiment, that the attraction of a given crystal by the poles of the Magnet be only dependant of its exterior form, but independant of the direction of its optical or crystallographical axis with regard to the poles of the Magnet.

Some weeks ago, in repeating Boutigny's experiments,[4] I put my hand into melted iron at 1500 C, without feeling within any heat whatever. Tis curious.

My best thanks for your paper. At the same time I got Mr. Grove's.[5] When I write again I will have repeated his interesting experiments as well as Zantedchi's [*sic*] very strange ones.[6] Unhappily for myself nearly all my time is absorbed by public lectures at the University.

Very truly
Yours
PLÜCKER

[1] M. Faraday, 'On the crystalline polarity of bismuth and other bodies, and on its relation to the magnetic and electric form of force (continued). IV. Crystalline condition of various bodies, V. Nature of the magnecrystallic force, and general observations', *PT* (1849), 1.

[2] *Sacram memoriam regis serenissimi divi Friderici Guilelmi III . . . natali eius die III mensis Augusti . . . ab Litterarum Universitate Fridericia Guilelmia Rhenana . . . celebrandam indicit I. Plücker . . . Praemissa enumeratione novorum phaenomenorum recentissime a se in doctrina de magnetismo inventorum*, Bonn, 1849.

[3] J. Plücker, 'Ueber die magnetischen Beziehungen der positiven und negativen optischen Axes der Crystalle', *AP*, 153 (1849), 447. This small paper (2 pp.) must be the 'incomplete notice'. The elaborate memoir is his 'Ueber die Theorie des Diamagnetismus, die Erklärung des Uebergangs magnetischen Verhaltens in diamagnetisches und mathematische Begründung der bei Krystallen beobachteten Erscheinungen', *AP*, 162 (1852), 1.

[4] See Letter 390.

[5] Probably W. R. Grove, 'On the effect of surrounding media on voltaic ignition', *PT* (1849), 49.

[6] Francesco Zantedeschi (1797–1873), Professor of Physics at the University of Padua. I am unable to identify the paper.

[*Nat. Res. Counc. Canada, previously unpublished*]

Royal Institution
11 Dec\ 1849

MY DEAR PLÜCKER

I received your last letter a day or two ago. and I think I have one before that to acknowledge dated August. I am very thankful to you for them & they are always a great pleasure. Your last views are very interesting but my head aches too much just now for me to say I have considered them and indeed they are fitted to remain in the mind for meditation again & again until by the growing up of facts they are developed confirmed & extended as the future progression of discovery may be. One part of your letter I do not quite understand where you say that it is a consequence of your theoretical views confirmed by experiments. that the attraction of a given crystal by the poles of a magnet be *only* dependant of its exterior form but *independant* of the direction of its optical or crystallographical axes with regard to the poles of the magnet For my own part I believe at present that the subjections of any crystal to the magnetic force depends upon its internal structure – or rather *on the forces* which give it its particular structure and that in any such crystal that line which coincides with the Magnetic axis may conveniently be called the Magnecrystallic axis. I do not suppose it necessary that the Magnecrystallic axis should coincide either with the Crystallographical axis or with the Optic axis. but I conclude that a very definite relations of these axis will in every case be found. and that though they be convenient forms of expression in reference to three sets of phenomena. that the ruling power is *one* and that when we properly understand it we shall see that *one law* will include all these phenomena. and so all the forms of expression as *axes* etc. by which we for the time represent theirs.

I have been at work endeavoring to establish *experimentally* any character of polarity in bismuth etc. when in the magnetic field. I am sorry to say that I can get no stronger facts than those in my original paper and no stronger persuasion than that that I gave in Par 2429, 2430. Weber did me the honor to work upon this thought. I believe I have obtained the effects he obtained in a far higher degree up to deflexions of 40°. 50°. or 60°, but if they are the same they are not effects of polarity. I am just writing the paper.[1]

I shall see Mr. Grove in an hour or too and shall tell him you have his paper.

Ever Yours Very Truly
M. FARADAY

[1] M. Faraday, 'On the polar or other condition of diamagnetic bodies', *PT* (1850), 171. See also *LPW*, 431.

[*I.E.E., previously unpublished*]

Gand,
14 décembre 1849.

MON CHER MONSIEUR FARADAY.

J'ai reçu votre excellente lettre, et vous pouvez vous figurer tout le plaisir qu'elle m'a fait éprouver. De pareils témoignages d'approbation de la part d'un homme tel que vous sont l'une des plus douces compensations que je puisse recevoir aux peines et aux fatigues que m'a causées mon travail; ils sont, en outre, un bien vif stimulant pour m'engager à poursuivre activement mes recherches. Une chose cependant m'a beaucoup contrarié: C'est la nullité absolu d'effet dans l'expérience relative à la couche gazeuse en contact avec les poles d'un aimant.[1] Mais vous ne me dites point si vous avez opéré sur un gaz unique, sur l'oxygène pur, par exemple, or, si votre électro-aimant était simplement plongé dans l'air, il serait possible que les pouvoirs magnétiques des deux gaz dont l'air se compose fussent de nature contraire, et qu'ainsi leurs effets se détruisissent mutuellement, du moins en très-grande partie. Si votre expérience a été faite avec un gaz unique, je ne conçois rien à l'absence totale d'effet, et ce résultat négatif me semble inexplicable: Car vos autres expériences montrent que l'action exercée par les aimants sur les gaz n'est pas si petite, et qu'elle se manifeste à des distances très-sensibles; Comment se ferait il donc que ces attractions ou répulsions si notables ne produisissent, dans la couche gazeuse environnante, aucune condensation ou expansion appréciable?

J'ai maintenant à vous demander un léger service: j'ai adressé à M⁻ Taylor, l'éditeur du philosophical magazine, un exemplaire de mon mémoire; je lui ai écrit, en même temps, que j'espérais qu'il accorderait à cette *deuxième série*[2] les honneurs de la traduction et de l'insertion dans les *Scientific Memoirs*, comme il les avait accordés à la *première*; j'ai ajouté qu'il pouvait, à ce sujet, vous demander votre avis. Lorsque j'ai écrit cela à Mr Taylor, je ne connaissais pas encore votre opinion sur mon travail; maintenant que vous m'avez exprimé un jugement si favorable, j'espère que vous voudrez bien appuyer ma demande auprès de Mr Taylor, et, s'il y accède, l'engager à m'envoyer un exemplaire de la traduction.

La prière que je viens de vous adresser est peut être indiscrète; mais les sentiments d'affection que vous voulez bien me témoigner, me donnent l'espoir que vous ne le considererez pas comme telle

Agréez, Mon cher Monsieur Faraday, l'assurance de mes sentiments de respectueuse amitié.

Jʰ PLATEAU

Professeur à l'Université, place du Casino, 18

[1] See Letter 387.
[2] See Letter 384, fn. 1.

413 M. FARADAY to B. C. BRODIE, 17 December 1849
[*B.J. 2, 251*¹]

Royal Institution,
December 17, 1849.

My dear Brodie, I owe you many and sincere thanks for your kind note. As to your letter to the Secretary, which was of course read to the Managers, it contained so absolute a negative on your part to their request to give another course of lectures at the Institution, that everybody felt there was no more to say upon the matter. The Secretary might, and very probably by this time has, acknowledged the receipt of it.

And now, my dear Sir, though it was this affair that chiefly made you and me known to each other, and though it has ended otherwise than I hoped, still I shall not, as regards ourselves, let matters return to their former state.

I hope much from you, and shall, as long as I remain in life, look with expectation, and, I trust, rejoicing, to your course. If any word from me is of the least value as a word of encouragement and exhortation, I say *proceed, advance.*

Here things have reverted very much to their former state, I rather think perhaps fitly. The time was probably too soon for any change. But when such an one as myself gets out of the way, then new conditions, new men, new views, and new opportunities may allow of the development of other lines of active operation than those heretofore in service; and then perhaps will be the time for change.

Ever, my dear Sir, Very truly yours,

M. FARADAY.

¹ See Letter 402.

414 H. C. OERSTED to M. FARADAY, 27 December 1849¹
[*Det kongelige Bibliotek, Copenhagen, previously unpublished*]

Copenhagen
the 27 Decr. 1849.

MY DEAR SIR,

Permit me to recall myself in your remembrance in introducing to the honour of your acquaintance the bearer of this letter Mr Colding,² Inspector of the Waterworks of Copenhagen, & at the same time a successful and mathematical investigator of several philosophical questions. He is a former pupil of our Danish polytechnical school & since many years well known to me as a man of the most respectable character. He visits England particularly in the view to be acquainted with the great improvements which are made in your Country in regard to the Waterworks: sewers and gas-pipes, but he will as much as his limited time permits him take an interest in all other scientific objects. I beg that you will be so kind as to favour him with your good counsels & to recommend him to such gentlemen who can facilitate his pursuits.

I shall avail myself of this opportunity to give you a short notice of my continued diamagnetical researches which still I have now been obliged to interrupt through the now ending year.

In the meetings of the Royal Society of Copenhagen the 5th and 19 January this year I have communicated some researches upon diamagnetism.[3] Most of them are already contained in a printed French notice[4] of which I sent a copy to you in the Octr 1848. but since the publication of this notice I have been able to shew some of the phenomena in a clearer light & to state some others more correctly. I find that the positions taken by the suspended diamagnetical needles are determined by the borders of the magnetical body. In order to give a clearer view of the phenomena, I shall first suppose that one of the poles of the electromagnet bears a rectangular parallelopipedic [sic] polar piece of soft iron, & that two of its sides are horizontal the four others perpendicular. If an attractive diamagnetical needle (for instance brass) is suspended vis-à-vis one of the perpendicular sides, the action of the magnetism will make it point at this surface; but if the needle is suspended above one of the superior borders or below one of the inferior borders the magnetism will make it parallel to the border. A repulsive diamagnetic body takes in all cases the opposite positions & is thus parallel to the perpendicular side vis-à-vis of which it is suspended, but perpendicular to it & to one of the borders when it is placed above a superior or below an inferior border.

The same principle holds good in regard to all other forms of the poles of the magnet, when each of the electro-magnetical poles is provided with its polar pieces they will act together after the same principles but of course with much more effect.

My new & often repeated experiments have given me a more correct view of the distribution of magnetism in the diamagnetic body.

The diagrams here joined will illustrate this distribution. [A] *N.* and *S.* represent the ends of two parallel (epipedic) polar pieces of an electromagnet, *ns. ns.* The transversal section of an attractive dia-magnetical needle which suspended above the polar pieces will take a position parallel to the two neighbouring borders. In this case the distribution of the magnetism in the needle is such as the small letters *s* and *n* indicate but if the diamagnetic needle in [sic] the contrary is a repulsive one, it takes the position perpendicular to the two neighbouring borders.

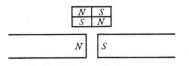

572

The distribution of its magnetism is likewise here indicated by the small letters n and s. –

When an attractive diamagnetic needle of inferior power is suspended in a powerfully attractive fluid & exposed to the action of the electromagnet, it will obtain the same magnetical distribution as a repulsive diamagnet, which is quite in conformity with your discoveries. In order to discover the distribution of magnetism in the diamagnetical needle I make use of very thin iron wires

bent in different manners mostly as ⌐ or ⌐ . –

You have in earlier years had the kindness to send me your series of researches, of which I possess the first 17. Though I have the whole series in the Transactions, I should be glad to be in possession of the continuation of these immortal papers, I consider already those which I have as one of the most distinguished ornaments of my library.

I am dear Sir with sincere admiration
most faithfully Yours
H. C. ØRSTED

[1] The letter as printed in M. C. Harding, *Correspondance de H. C. Ørsted avec divers savants*, 2 vols., Copenhagen, 1920, 2, 325, is incomplete, lacking the first paragraph.
[2] Ludwig August Colding (1815–88), engineer. Colding was one of the contributors to the discovery of the Principle of the Conservation of Energy.
[3] See Oversigt over det kgl. danske Videnskabernes Selskabs Forhandlinger og dets Medlemmers Arbeider i Aaret 1849, 2.
[4] *AC*, 3 s., 24 (1848), 424.

415 M. FARADAY to J. B. DUMAS, 28 December 1849
[*Bibliothèque Nationale, N.A.Fr., 2480, f. 229, previously unpublished*]

Royal Institution,
28 Decr 1849

MY DEAR FRIEND

I feel as if I were writing a last letter to you; for I can hardly think your duty & high occupation, apart as it is from every link that can recall or relate to a remembrance of me, can ever leave you a moment for imagination to travel hitherward: but, whatever our different destinies in, and paths through, life; that you may be prosperous in your proceedings & happy in your heart and home is the earnest hope & wish of one who will never forget you. It was a great grief to me to miss the meeting with your Son. They told me at the Hotel he would leave England in the evening & I found afterwards he was a day or two longer in London. I think I must have made some mistake between him & the son whom I met with at the Jardin des Plants; however, I trust he will be as kind as his father, and excuse any written mistakes in my note to him

Though I was very glad to see your hand writing, yet I must confess, that, in the matter of M. Milne Edwards, I felt somewhat humbled in the thought that he would not come to me without a letter: – does he think that I have forgotten the Evening when he & I passed over from your house to his? he was too kind, for me to lose the remembrance of it. If you see him again tell him I am almost inclined to reproach him.

But I must consider your time and thoughts. I do not know where I ought to direct this letter, but, for the old associations sake, shall send it to the Institute: and as I have a paper in hand, when it is printed I shall still send you a copy, and so on indeed till I hear I ought not. With our kindest remembrances to Madame Dumas and to both your Sons – I remain Ever My dear friend

Yours

M. FARADAY.

416 J. PLÜCKER to M. FARADAY, 4 January 1850
[*I.E.E., previously unpublished*]

Bonn,
the 4th of January, 1850

DEAR SIR!

My best thanks for your kind letter of the 11th of December[1] last since – I think so at least – I got a satisfactory explication of all the questioned phenomena, discovered by you and by myself. This explication is founded on the principles exposed in my last letter. The indications already given by me, are written down under the preoccupation of my mind, that there ought to be in crystals, brought between the two poles, a *conflict* of an attractif and a repulsif power, as it is the case with charcoal. But we dont want such a coexistence of two opposite actions. In magnetic crystals tis *allways* a comon magnetic attraction, producing the known effects; in diamagnetic crystals tis *allways* a diamagnetic repulsion. The *freely* suspended magnetic crystal will allways go to the pole, the diamagnetic away from it: but, when the crystal *is obliged to turn round a vertical line*, the forces producing the rotatory motion of the crystal, deduced by mechanic law from the original ones, will, by different distance from the pole, act in an *opposite* way.

I adopt the views you explained 2439, 2440. There is no difference at all between Magnetism and Diamagnetism, only the kind of inducing them is the opposite one in both cases. In diamagnetic bodies the „coercitif force„ is greater than in magnetic ones. From that I deduced by new experiments, the known observations made by charcoal. Belonging to crystals the only hypothesis I adopt is, that such a crystal take *magnetic* polarity *with different facility in different directions* if it is a *magnetic* crystal, and *diamagnetic* polarity if it is a

574

diamagnetic one. The molecules of positif crystals, when magnetic or diamagnetic by induction, will have the line joining their poles (completely or at
least by preference) directed parallel to the axis; in negatif crystals this line is
perpendicular to the optic axis. The turmaline for instance may
be represented by lines of molecules, parallel to its axis, having
their poles perpendicular to these lines, and may be imitated by
a row (a line) of small pieces of iron wire, arranged in this

way ⊥ . If such a line is brought, like the crystal between the

two poles, you will find by a comon calculus, *that the molecules
are, according to their distance from the centrum, either repelled or
attracted by the poles*. Instead of the analytical results I have joined to my letter
a figure, representing them. The two curves are the geometrical locus for the
neutral points, where is respecting to each of both poles neither attraction
nor repulsion. The kind of action on the molecules of the line *AB* is indicated
by arrows. From this figure you may deduce the phenomena exhibited by
turmaline.

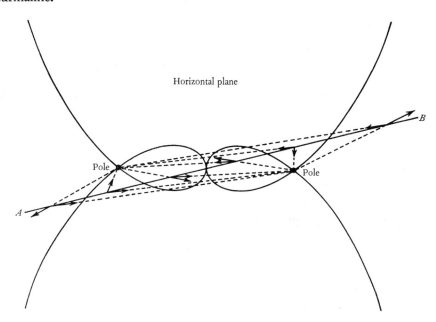

The figure remains the same when there is a diamagnetic repulsion of the
crystallic molecules: the terms attraction and repulsion are only to be com-
mutated.

Every magnetic molecule, having two poles, is attracted by the pole of the
Electro-magnet but the calculus proves that, the distance of the two poles of

the molecule being *exceedingly small* with relation to the distance from the pole of the Magnet, this attraction is to be neglected with relation (par rapport) to the power which gives to the molecule a rotatory motion, whatever may be the direction of this motion. Tis a case quite analogous to that of a compass needle, acted upon by the Earth.

That is the explication you asked from me in your last letter. Hence it follows, according to my experiments made by the balance, that even when the attraction of the mass of a crystal be not absolutely independent of the position of its axes, the difference *of action* cant [*sic*] produce the questioned effect.

But I fear, Sir, you will not return to your own first conception, which includes diamagnetic polarity, and therefore you will be against my theoretical views. Nevertheless you will think it right from my part, to defend them as long as I am not convinced of the contrary. Therefore let me conclude by in[di] [ms. torn] cating a very easy experiment, which, according to me proves, against Weber's theory, that the questioned diamagnetic polarity may be a *permanent* one, like in steel, even, for a short time, strong enough to be demonstrated by experiment.

Let a bar of bismuth be suspended in the common way between the two poles and by the torsion of the silk thread put against a piece of glass or copper (*a*). It will be, with greater force, retained in the same position, when repelled by the magnet, but, if you change by means of a gynotrope, the polarity of the magnet, the bar, in the first moment, will be decidedly *attracted* by the poles.

Bonn the 4ᵗʰ of January

Yours very truly
PLÜCKER

¹ See Letter 411.

417   W. V. HARCOURT to M. FARADAY, 7 January 1850¹
    [*I.E.E., previously unpublished*]

Residence
York
Jan. 7.

DEAR FARADAY

I cannot refrain from sending you my congratulations at this commencement of a new year on the great discovery you have made in placing so universal & important an element as oxygen side by side with iron in the "*Paramagnetics*".

May I enquire whether you obtain a neutral point at which there is neither Dia- nor Para-magnetism by mixing oxygen & nitrogen in a certain proportion, and whereabouts that proportion is? also whether any of the chemical compounds of these gases exhibit such *neutrality*, or whether the most oxygenous are themselves in any degree *para* magnetic at common temperatures? I am curious also to know whether Chlorine Bromine or Iodine, have, or approach to, this property and whether their admixtures or combinations with oxygen counteract its *para*magnetism in the same degree with other substances? I would not ask these questions if I supposed it would give you any trouble to answer: but they are points which I dare say you have ascertained.

Believe me
Y^{rs} sincerely
WM. VERNON HARCOURT

[1] Faraday discovered the paramagnetism of oxygen late in 1849, thus permitting the dating of this letter in 1850.

418   M. FARADAY to J. PLÜCKER, 8 January 1850
[*Nat. Res. Counc. Canada, previously unpublished*]

Royal Institution
8 January 1850

MY DEAR PLÜCKER

I mean to write you a short letter at once though I only received yours[1] yesterday and have not much to say But I want to establish on your mind very clearly that you must not think I deny all that I do not admit. On the contrary I think there are many things which may be true and which I shall receive as such hereafter though I do not as yet receive them but that is not because there is any proof to the contrary but that the proof in the affirmative is not yet sufficient for me. It is so as regards the diamagnetic polarity of bismuth phosphorous etc. my view is just the same as it was when I wrote paragraphs 2429–2430. I think that may be the true view but I do not think that such a state is as yet proved.

Now I rejoice to see all your active reasonings experiments and consideration and am sure that your exertions are & will be successful in clearing up the present mystery of the subject. I am not quite sure I understand all the meaning of your last letter but that is because of my own ignorance You also do me the honor to refer to paragraphs 2439. 2440. and I am not quite sure whether you mean them or the paragraphs 2429. 2430. and that makes a little confusion in my mind. Besides which, my memory is so bad that I cannot recall the purport of the enquiry I may have made of you in my last letter & so am not sure of the bearings of the answer you have sent me. How continually I grieve that I cannot read German for if I could I suppose I could follow you in Poggendorf very quickly. But I have no right to complain for Providence has been very kind to me.

I finished a paper at the close of the last year and sent it on the first of

January to the Royal Society. It was devoted to a rigid examination of the assumed polarity of bismuth phosphorous etc.[2] I think my apparatus must at the last have been very much like Webers but I really regret to say that my conclusions were against the polarity. I obtained effects with bismuth of the kind Weber describes but I obtained far greater effects of the same kind with Gold silver copper tin & lead. On examining them I found they were all effects of the currents induced in the mass of metal employed as a whole and not of any polarity. When I divided the metal so as to interfere with these currents as by making up a cylinder from wires then the action was entirely stopped. whereas when I divided it so as to have the currents uninterfered with as by making the cylinder of discs of metal then the action was good as ever. The *reverse* of this was the case when polarity was concerned as in iron. for then division into wires did not interfere with the final effect but division into discs did.

I have also tested the question of polarity or of induced currents in the mass by reference to the *time* during which the moving metal was in motion i.e. to the velocity of the motion, and which in the form of apparatus is in striking contrast, as presented by the two views. Velocity does nothing in the case of polarity as with iron but the result depends entirely upon the whole amount of journey or motion; in the case of the induced currents it does every thing.

I have also constructed a commutator which because of the existence of a difference in the plane [reading doubtful] of maximum action of polarities & plane [reading doubtful] of maximum action of induced currents can separate or oppose or combine the results of these two kinds of action in any degree. All these means & investigations shew that as yet the effects obtained with bismuth have been the result of induced currents in the mass & not of any polarity, and that if there be such a polarity we have no proofs of it as yet beyond the first simple fact of a repulsion from the poles of the magnet. I have endeavored in every way to repeat Reich's experiment as described by Weber & can not obtain the result.

All this does not make me deny the polarity. but only the sufficiency of the proofs thus far advanced. My opinion is exactly the same as when I wrote 2429. 2430. You will find in my paper when it appears what I think the explication of your experiment with bismuth. it is simply a case of revulsion $\left(\begin{array}{c} 2310.\ 2315 \\ 2338. \end{array}\right)$.

due to currents in the mass: this revulsion I have of late raised to a very high degree by division into discs & destroyed altogether even in Gold silver & copper by division into wires. Yet if the effects were due to polarity the reverse of these results ought to take place

Ever My dear Plucker
Most Truly Yours
M. FARADAY

[1] See Letter 416.
[2] See Letter 410, fn. 1

419   M. FARADAY to E. DU BOIS-REYMOND, 15 January 1850

[Darmstaedter Collection, Westdeutsche Bibliothek, Marburg, B.J. 2, 272]

Royal Institution
15 Jany 1850

Dear Sir I this day received your kind present of books (your great work) and also the letter.[1] I regret that I have no better thanks to offer you than those of a man who cannot estimate the work properly. I look with regret at the pages which are to me a sealed book and but that increasing infirmities too often warn me off I would even now attack the language of science & knowledge, for such the German language is.

M. Magnus[2] whom I rejoice to call a friend told me of your great experiment in which from the muscular excitement of the living human being you obtained a current of Electricity. I endeavoured a few months ago to procure the result, but did not succeed no doubt being unacquainted with all the precautions needful, & the exact manner of proceeding, I was at fault – and now I am so engaged by the duties of my station & the Season that I have no time for anything else. During the season I trust to pick up the information that will give me success the next time that I try.

The second copy of your work is already on the road to the Royal Society and I shall do all I can to direct the attention of the men of Science & others to the copy you have sent me by placing it before them on the tables of this Institution

I am Sir Your Very obliged & grateful Servt,

M. FARADAY.

[1] See Letter 408.
[2] Heinrich Gustav Magnus (1802–70), Professor of Physics at the University of Berlin.

420   M. FARADAY to A. QUÉTELET, 25 February 1850

[Académie Royale des Sciences de Belgique, Quételet papers; J. Pelseneer, 'Notes on some unpublished letters from Faraday to Quételet', 'Annals of Science', 1 (1936), 448]

Royal Institution
25 Feby 1850

MY DEAR FRIEND

I must write you a letter that I may say in it how great pleasure I have had in reading and studying the third part of your Essays on the climate of Belgium;[1] *i. e.* your results in atmospheric electricity. They are, I think, very admirable; and I admire the truly philosophic spirit in which you have been content to give them, without any addition of imagination or hypothesis. They are FACTS and ought not too hastily to be confounded with opinion; for the facts are for all time, whilst opinion may change as a cloud in the air. I think, you know, that I cannot adopt Peltiers views of the relation of the Earth & space;[2] and I was encouraged, therefore, to hold more confidently to my own conclusions in that respect, when I saw how carefully you abstained from any phrase that might commit you to the expression of such an opinion. I took the liberty of giving our Members here an account of your results,[3] and they appeared to be most highly interested in them. In doing so I pointed out your philosophic caution, and expressed my opinion that such was the true method by which advances in science in this very difficult part could be really made.

I have just receiv^d from you a few leaves in which I find a letter to you from young M. Peltier. It is quite natural that he should hold to his fathers views, but he must remove the fundamental objection before he can make any impression, at least on my mind. That objection is, that it is absolutely impossible to charge any body with one electricity independent of direct relationship with the other electricity. Or in other words that it is absolutely impossible that the earth as a whole, or any other single body, as a globe, should have negative electricity appearing on its surface or be *driven into its interior* merely by variation in the electric intensity of the whole surrounding space. If an insulated ball of metal or earth be suspended within a much larger sphere of metal, or wire gauze or any thing else (to represent the space action), which can be charged simultaneously in all parts, no amount of charge which can be given to the sphere representing space, can induce any charge on the ball; nor would the discharge of that space electricity induce any charge on the ball: – and further; that representation of space could not exert any inducing action inwards; – nor could it receive charge, unless it could induce equivalently to something external & outside of itself; – and even in so doing would shew no sign of action inwards.

I have carefully considered all the reasonings and views which Peltier has put forth that seem to bear upon or touch this point; but with the best judgment I could exercise have come to the conclusion that none of them do really touch it.

> Ever My dear Sir
> Your Very obliged & faithful
> M. FARADAY

[1] A. Quételet, *Sur le climat de la Belgique*, 2 vols., Brussels, 1845–53. The essays were taken from the *Annales de l'observatoire royale de Bruxelles*, 10 vols., Brussels, 1834–53.
[2] See Letter 306.
[3] Lecture 'On the electricity of the air' given at the Royal Institution, 1 February 1850. Faraday's ms. notes for it are at the Royal Institution.

421   M. Faraday to H. C. Oersted, 15 March 1850

[*M. C. Harding, 'Correspondance de H.C. Ørsted avec divers savants', 2 vols., Copenhagen, 1920, Vol. 2, 327*]

Royal Institution,
London,
15 March, 1850.

My dear Sir

I received your very kind letter[1] 2 or 3 weeks ago and was very greatly gratified that you should remember me. Since then I have waited in hopes I should see Mr. Colding your friend. But as I have heard nothing of him . . . . . I thought I would not longer delay writing a word or two in acknowledgement of yours. This is a time of the year in which formal matters occupy me so much that (together with a system soon wearied) they prevent me from working to any good purpose so that I have little or nothing to say. I have it is true sent a paper to the Royal Society[2] two or three months ago which was read lately, and in it I describe my failure to produce the results of Weber, Reich, & some others or (of such as were produced) my reference of them to other principles of action than those they had adopted. This branche [*sic*] of science is at present in a very active & promising state. Many men (and amongst them yourself) are working at it, and it is not wonderful that views differ at first. Time will gradually sift & shape them & I believe that we have little idea at present of the importance they may have 10 or 20 years hence.

As soon as my paper is printed I shall send it to you and I hope with copies of those you have not received. I thought I had sent you all in order, for it was to me a delight to think I might do so. I do not know what can have come in the way of them. But if I have copies left you shall have them with the next paper.

I am constrained to make this letter a short one as much through the poverty of matter as the want of time. Hoping it will find you in excellent health I am My dear Sir

Your very obliged & faithful servant –
M. Faraday

[1] See Letter 414.
[2] See Letter 410, fn. 1.

422   W. de la Rue to M. Faraday, 23 March 1850

[*I.E.E., previously unpublished*]

1101 Bunhill Row [London]
March 23rd 1850

My dear Sir

I enclose a printed table of Nobert's lines arranged in series.[1] The single band on your slide is the $\frac{1}{24}$th of a Parisian inch divided in[to] 500 lines.

On the envelope enclosing your note for him you have directed for Paris, but M. Nobert is a german residing at Griefswald [*sic*] in Pomerania; would it be troubling you too much, as you have been kind enough to acknowledge his little present, to write another envelope directed as above; as you have left the present one unsealed I will transfer the enclosure?

I was not aware last Friday week that my name had been proposed for the Royal Society and that you had been good enough to sign the nomination paper, otherwise I would have taken that opportunity of thanking you; I beg that you will now accept my best thanks for your great kindness; I will endeavour by my work to prove myself worthy of it [word illeg. but probably crossed out anyway] when my leisure permits me to devote myself to pure science.

I remain
Yours Very truly
WARREN DE LA RUE

[1] See Letter 400.

423   G. WILSON[1] to M. FARADAY, 29 March 1850
[*I.E.E., previously unpublished*]

24 Brown Square
Edin*b*
March 29, 1850

SIR

I trust you will forgive the liberty I take in addressing you, although personally unknown to you. Mr George Buchanan[2] kindly offered me an introduction two years ago, but I have always felt so reluctant to occupy your valuable time that I have never availed myself of his kindness. The visit, however, of my friend Dr Stenhouse to London induces me to trouble you with the copy of a paper,[3] with a view to ask your answer to this question "Is it possible to render a gas absolutely anhydrous?" I do not use the word *absolutely* in an unqualified sense as excluding the possibility of moisture being present through the practical difficulties attending the realisation of the drying process; but as referring to the sufficiency of the process could it be realised in practice. In other words are our present methods of drying gases, theoretically perfect, & fitted to secure the deprivation of moisture, or are they essentially imperfect and from their nature certain to leave a certain amount of water in every gas?

My object in asking the question, is to request your advice as to the best method of drying gases, with a view to its application to researches resembling those recorded in the accompanying paper. If you would kindly glance at your leisure at Section V. page 489, entitled "*On the methods applicable to the drying of gases*" you would see in the compass of some two pages, the difficulty which has arrested my researches, and which your great experience in the liquefaction of gases, probably enables you to remove.

I know too well your many occupations to wonder if it is out of your power, to write a reply. But, perhaps, you will find time to send a verbal message through Dr Stenhouse, if unable to write. I have enclosed two other papers and remain

Your Obedt Servant

GEORGE WILSON

1 George Wilson (1818–59), chemist, Regius keeper of the Industrial Museum of Edinburgh.
2 George Buchanan (1790–1852), engineer.
3 George Wilson, 'On the Action of the Dry Gases on Organic Colouring Matters, and its relation to the Theory of Bleaching', *TRSE*, 16 (1849), 475.

424   C. DICKENS to M. FARADAY, 28 May 1850

[*W. L. Randell, 'Michael Faraday', London, 1924, 127*]

Devonshire Terrace

Twenty-eight May, 1850

Dear Sir, – I take the liberty of addressing you as if I knew you personally; trusting that I may venture to assume that you will excuse that freedom.

It has occurred to me that it would be extremely beneficial to a large class of the public to have some account of your late lectures on the breakfast-table, and of those you addressed, last year, to children. I should be exceedingly glad to have some papers in reference to them, published in my new enterprise *Household Words*. May I ask you whether it would be agreeable, to you, and, if so, whether you would favour me with the loan of your notes of those lectures for perusal?

I am sensible that you may have reasons of your own, for reserving the subject to yourself. In that case, I beg to assure you that I would on no account approach it.

With great respect and esteem, I am Dear Sir   Your faithful Servant,

CHARLES DICKENS.

425   C. DICKENS to M. FARADAY, 31 May 1850

[*I.E.E., W. L. Randell, 'Michael Faraday', London, 1924, 129*]

Devonshire Terrace,

Thirty-First May, 1850

MY DEAR SIR,

I really cannot tell you how very sensible I am of your great kindness or what an honour I feel it to be to have interested you in my books.

I think I may be able to do something with the candle; but I would not touch it, or have it touched, unless it can be relighted with something of the beautiful simplicity and clearness of which I see the traces in your notes.[1]

Since you are so generous as to offer me the notes of your lectures on the breakfast table, I will borrow them when you have done with them, if it be only for my own interest and gratification. I deeply regret now, not having heard the lectures to children as it would have been a perfect delight to me to have described them, however generally.

I should take it as a great favour if you could allow me (in the event of my being unfortunately unable to come myself) to introduce my sub-editor to your next lecture; for a subsequent comparison of his recollection of it, with your notes, might enlighten us very much.

Pray let me add, as one who has long respected you, and strongly felt the obligations society owes to you, that the day on which I took the liberty of writing to you will always be a memorable day in my calendar, if I date from it – as I now hope I shall – the beginning of a personal knowledge of you.

My dear Sir,
Yours faithfully and obliged
CHARLES DICKENS.

[1] For what Dickens did with Faraday's lectures on the chemical history of a candle, see *Household Words, A Weekly Journal*, 1 (1850), 439.

426 J. PLATEAU to M. FARADAY, 8 July 1850
[I.E.E., previously unpublished]

Gand
8 Juillet 1850

MON CHER MONSIEUR FARADAY.

Recevez d'abord mes bien vifs remerciements pour le morceau de verre pesant dont vous avez eu la bonté de me faire cadeau: je le conserve comme un précieux souvenir de vos bons sentiments pour moi.

Maintenant, je viens vous importuner, et c'est avec grand regret que je m'y décide; mais voici ce qui est arrivé. Au commencement du mois de Janvier, Monsieur Wheatstone m'a écrit que mon Mémoire (*Recherches expérimentales et théoriques sur les figures d'équilibre d'une masse liquide sans pesanteur, deuxième série*) allait être reproduit dans les *Scientific Memoirs* de Mr Taylor, et paraîtrait probablement le mois suivant, c'est à dire en février; Mr Wheatstone ajoutait qu'il se chargeait [reading doubtful] lui même de la traduction, ainsi que de la correction des épreuves. Après avoir attendu plus de quatre mois sans recevoir aucune nouvelle de cette traduction, j'ai écrit à Mr Wheatstone, pour le remercier d'abord de la peine qu'il voulait bien se donner, et pour le prier de me faire savoir à quel point en était l'affaire; mais je n'ai reçu aucune réponse, quoiqu'il y ait près de deux mois de cela. Mr Wheatstone est il absent, ou bien ma lettre ne lui est elle point parvenue? Dans cette incertitude, j'ai pris le parti de recourir à votre extrême obligeance, et je sais que ce ne sera pas inutilement: car vous, si grand comme physicien, vous êtes encore l'un des hommes les meilleurs. Voici donc ce que j'attends de votre bonté: si Mr Wheatstone est à Londres, veuillez l'engager à me répondre de suite; s'il est absent, j'espère que vous voudrez bien vous informer si la traduction de mon Mémoire a parue ou va paraître, ou s'il n'en est rien, et me le faire savoir par un mot de réponse. Le Mémoire dont il s'agit m'a coûté extrêmement de temps et de travail, et j'y attache une très grande importance. Je dois donc faire tout ce qui dépend de moi pour répandre parmi les savants la connaissance des résultats qu'il renferme, et je tiens beaucoup à sa reproduction dans les *Scientific Memoirs*

J'attends votre lettre avec impatience, et je vous prie de me croire, avec tous les sentiments d'une respectueuse amitié,

Votre entièrement dévoué

J^h PLATEAU

place du Casino, 22, à Gand

427 M. FARADAY to B. VINCENT,[1] 25 July 1850
[*R.I., previously unpublished*]

Upper Norwood,
25 July, 1850.

MY DEAR FRIEND

A few words together even on paper (if it cannot be by mouth) are pleasant though I do not find myself good for either just now. Because of much pain in my jaw & the known bad state of my teeth, which I had only hoped to keep through the lectures, I went on Monday morning to the dentist. He pulled out five teeth & a fang He had much trouble & I much pain in the removal of a deep stump and I think from the feeling then & now he must have broken away part of the jaw bone to get at it, for it is very sore & the head is rather unsteady. On the whole the operation was well & cleverly carried on by the dentist, the fault was in the teeth Just let me say in addition about myself that the cold shiverings which came on on Saturday night are gone & I believe my tendency to chill is very much less

I should like to know how you are & the family but I am at the wrong end of the post for that – Mr Barnard was here yesterday – Mrs Hillhouse left this place yesterday and I hope she reached home in safety Mr Hillhouse[2] was with her so that all that could be done in the way of assistance would be done.

On Saturday morning *and Sabbath day* I trust to see you. I am afraid I shall be of no use to others on the Sabbath for my voice is a queer one having lost some of the alphabetical sounds for the present, it is not wonderful that both the dental & labial modifications should be touched: but I hope Mr. H. Deacon is in good ease.

I am My dear friend,
Yours Very affectionately,
M. FARADAY.

1 Benjamin Vincent (1818–99), Assistant Secretary and Keeper of the Library of the Royal Institution. Vincent, like Faraday, was a Sandemanian.
2 All members of the Sandemanian congregation.

428 M. FARADAY to W. WHEWELL, 1 August 1850
[Trinity College Library, Trinity College, Cambridge, previously unpublished]

Royal Institution
1 Aug 1850

MY DEAR SIR

I want a distinctive word. It may only be for a time for I am quite in uncertainty as to how finally the subject of Magnetism may settle down But taking the word *Magnetic* to represent the *general action* of the forces so called, and having already employed the word diamagnetic to represent that part of the general action which is manifest in bismuth, Phospherous, &c. I want a word to represent the other and more known [reading doubtful] part of the action manifested in Iron, Nickel, Cobalt, &c. The distinction is very important to me just now & I can hardly write my notes without it. Assuming the Earth as a Planet or a whole to represent one of these actions I have written Terro magnetic or Terra-magnetic & so made the following distinctions in my notes.

$$\text{Magnetic} \begin{cases} \text{Terromagnetic} \\ \text{Diamagnetic} \end{cases}$$

I feel that *Terro* & *Dia* are not in fair relation. Can you give me a better word, or considering the transitory state of Magnetic language is Terro magnetic or something like it admissible into printed papers for the present?

At present my head is full of visions: whether they will disappear as experiment wakens me up or open out into clear distinct views of the truth of nature is more than I dare say. But my hopes are strong.

Ever My dear Sir,
Very Truly Yours,
M. FARADAY

429 W. WHEWELL to M. FARADAY, 12 August 1850

[*Trinity College Library, Trinity College, Cambridge, I. Todhunter, 'William Whewell', 2 vols., London, 1876, Vol. 2, 363*]

Kreuznach,
Rhenish Prussia,
[postmarked 12 8 1850]

MY DEAR SIR

I am always glad to hear of your wanting new words, because the want shows that you are pursuing new thoughts, and your new thoughts are worth something: but I always feel also how difficult it is for one who has not pursued the train of thought to suggest the right word. There are so many relations involved in a new discovery and the word ought not glaringly to violate any of them. The purists would certainly object to the opposition or coordination of terro-magnetic and diamagnetic, not only on account of the want of symmetry in the relation of *terro* and *dia*, but also because the one is Latin and the other Greek. But these objections, being merely relative to the form of the words would not be fatal, especially if the new word were considered as temporary only to be superseded by a better when the relation of the phenomena are more clearly seen. But a more serious objection to *terromagnetic* seems to me to be that diamagnetic bodies have also a relation to the earth as well as the other class; namely a tendency to place their length transverse to the lines of terrestrial magnetic force. Hence it would appear that the two classes of magnetic bodies are those which place their length *parallel* or *according to* the terrestrial magnetic lines, and those which place their length *transverse* to such lines. Keeping the preposition *dia* for the latter then the preposition *para* or *ana* might be used for the former; perhaps *para* would be best as the word *parallel*, in which it is involved, would be a mechanical memory for it. Thus we should have this distinction

magnetic { Paramagnetic: Iron, Nickel, Cobalt &c
{ Diamagnetic: Bismuth, Phosphor &c.

If you like *anamagnetic* better than *paramagnetic*, as meaning magnetic *according to our standard*, terrestrial magnetism, I see no objection. I had at one time thought of *orthomagnetic* and *diamagnetic*, directly magnetic and diametrally magnetic, but here the symmetry is not so complete as with two prepositions.

In considering whether I quite understand the present state of the subject, I have asked myself what would be the effect of a planet made up of bits of bismuth, phosphor &c, of which the general mass had their lengths parallel to a certain axis of the planet. I suppose all *paramagnetic* bodies would arrange themselves transverse to its meridian, and all diamagnetic bodies in its meridian. Am I right?

I rejoice to hear that you have new views of discovery opening to you. I always rejoice to hail the light of such when they dawn upon you.

I have been at the meeting of Swiss naturalists at Aarau where I met Schön-bein who talked much of you, and told me you were going to explain his views of ozone.

I shall be in London in a few days and shall perhaps try to see you when I am there. Letters sent to Cambridge always find me.

Believe me, my dear Sir, yours most truly,

W. WHEWELL

430   M. FARADAY to A. F. SVANBERG,[1] 16 August 1850
[*Kungl. Vetenskapsakademiens Bibliotek, Stockholm, previously unpublished*]

Royal Institution,
16 Aug 1850

MY DEAR SIR,

I cannot resist my desire to write at once & to thank you for the great pleasure your letter (received yesterday) gave me first as coming from you whom my bad memory well retained in mind, and next for the delight which the facts therein described occasioned.[2] They came with the force of truth and are very beautiful & consistent.

How wonderful it is to me the simplicity of nature when we rightly interpret her laws and how different the convictions which they produce on the mind in comparison with the uncertain conclusions which hypothesis or even theory present.

I am not sorry that you find some things unexpected or curious or a little anomalous, for they serve to shew that there are more treasures to be obtained & I see from your letter that you both know how to work for them & will work. The earnest ardent experimentalist is ever rewarded for his labour.

I have got some fancies in my head but they will require a good deal of development & elaboration before I dare venture to trust them forth. Nevertheless I am in hopes they will be fruitful in due time if health be spared me. But the head becomes giddy

Ever my dear Sir,
Your Oblgd & faithful Servt
M. FARADAY

[1] Adolph Ferdinand Svanberg (1806–57), Professor of Physics and Mechanics at Uppsala University.
[2] I have been unable to find this letter. It may have dealt with some of the ideas presented in a letter written to V. Regnault at the same time. See 'Expériences sur le pouvoir thermo-électrique du bismuth et de l'antimoine cristallisés' (Extrait d'une Note de M. Svanberg communiquée par M. Regnault), Séance du Lundi 19 Août 1850, *CR*, 31 (1850), 250.

[Trinity College Library, Trinity College, Cambridge, previously unpublished]

Upper Norwood,
22 Aug, 1850

MY DEAR SIR,

I am living and working at Norwood, and so lost the great pleasure of seeing you & what would have been more of hearing you. One can consider many things in talking which writing is very unfit for. I received with thankfulness your kind letter and have since then in my notes & W. P.[1] used the word *Paramagnetic* which will serve my purpose well if after a little further explanation you think it is is [*sic*] (as I imagine) right. I conclude that a long piece of *soft iron* unable to *retain* magnetism would in a field of equal magnetic force stand in the direction of the lines of force, still the power which can make it do so must be exceedingly small in effect, for I imagine it would require an extremely delicate apparatus to shew the pointing of a bar of such iron under the Earths force which we may take as presenting a field of equal force. The diamagnetic power of bismuth or phosphorous is exceedingly small as compared to the corresponding magnetic power of iron & there is no chance that a bar of either would stand transverse to the Earths lines of force. I have found lately that such a bar does stand transverse in a field of equal force made by two walls of iron 5 inches by 3 inches and 3/4 of an inch apart. But then a piece of Iron[2] (or a piece of phosphorous) destroys such a field as one of equal force for it generates contingent poles in the parts of the iron wall opposed to its ends & the phosphorous as I believe produces a reverse effect equivalent to a destruction of the power there. Hence both the case of the iron & the phosphorous fall as respects by far the greater part of their effect & perhaps the whole as to position into the law I gave originally – that Magnetic (paramagnetic) bodies pass or tend to pass from weaker to stronger places of magnetic action and diamagnetic bodies from stronger to weaker.

I have been driven to assume for a time especially in relation to the gases a sort of conducting power for magnetism. Mere space is Zero. One substance being made to occupy a given portion of space will cause more lines of force to pass through that space than before and another substance will cause less to pass. The former I now call Paramagnetic & the latter are the diamagnetic. The former need not of necessity assume a polarity of particles such as iron has when magnetic and the latter do not assume any such polarity either direct or reverse. I do not say More to you just now because my own thoughts are only in the act of formation but this I may say that the atmosphere has an extraordinary magnetic constitution & I hope & expect to find in it the cause of the *annual & diurnal variations*, but *keep this to yourself* until I have time to see what harvest will spring from my growing ideas.

I am My dear Sir
Most Truly Yours,
M. FARADAY

[1] Written Papers.
[2] The ms. had '...a piece of Iron or a piece of phosphorus...' with the last five words crossed out.

[*R.I., previously unpublished*]

Lancaster
Sept. 2, 1850

DEAR DR FARADAY

Since I wrote to you I have read your "Twenty Third Series" as well as the letter which you sent me: and the result is that I have some doubts whether the suggestions which I sent you respecting names are sound. I had entertained a view which your paper is employed in refuting, that the magnetism of bismuth &c on the one hand and of iron &c on the other is of a coördinate kind, and that therefore it was desirable to designate the two by two coördinate words, such as paramagnetic and diamagnetic. But as I now understand your view is that bismuth &c have no real polarity but only a seeming polarity arising from each particle having a tendency to go from strong to weak magnetic spaces; while iron &c have a polarity, or at least hard iron is capable of a polarity which may be defined directly and finally as a tendency to arrange its polar axes parallel to the magnetic lines of the earth. This want of exact symmetry in the two kinds of magnetism, and the seeming connection of one with the *earth's* magnetism make me hesitate about the term *paramagnetic*, and reconsider whether your term *terromagnetic*, or the corresponding Greek compound, *geomagnetic*, might not be better. But all things considered, I am still disposed to recommend the use of the term *paramagnetic*, advising only that the term should be explained at the outset (if I am right in my view) as implying that iron &c have a (seeming) polarity which places them *parallel* to the magnetic lines of the earth. Perhaps it is still conceivable that there may be planets so constituted that diamagnetic bodies shall arrange themselves parallel to *their* lines of force; but whether or not, the reference to the earth may I think be *understood* in your sense, as safely as *expressed*.

I am much interested in the hints you give me about the magnetic constitution of the atmosphere and its results. I am exceedingly struck by the uniformity of the modes of experimenting explained in your 23^d Series, but I think you might have given a Diagram to make the construction of the apparatus more evident. For instance, in 2643 what is the position of the brass rod and the core with reference to the wooden lever? I suppose at right angles, and in the plane of the motion; but I think you have not said so.

I am travelling in the lake country but am always accessible at Cambridge. I was there the other day and perceived your card, so if I have missed seeing you there also, which I am sorry for

Believe me always
Yours most truly
W. WHEWELL

433 M. FARADAY to W. WHEWELL, 6 September 1850
[*Trinity College Library, Trinity College, Cambridge*]

R Institution,
6 Septr 1850

MY DEAR SIR

I ought to have sent you the enclosed before. Another friend found the difficulty you refer to & this word cut was the consequence.

I was only waiting to send with it something better. Many thanks for your last letter. I will use Para*magnetic* and restrain its intention as you suggest. The atmospheric magnetism works out beautifully, but my head aches with thinking of it & I am now so giddy I must lay the matter down for a few days.

Ever Truly Yours
M. FARADAY

434 E. SABINE to M. FARADAY, 11 September 1850
[*I.E.E., previously unpublished*]

Geneva.
Sept. 11th. 1850.

DEAR FARADAY.

Capt. Younghusband[1] has informed me of the communications which you have lately had with him; I rejoice greatly that any of your investigations should lead you to desire a knowledge of the facts which we have been engaged in obtaining, or give you a prospect of being able to throw light on their causes. I need not add how delighted [we] [ms. torn] shall be to arrange the facts in such ways as shall be either most clear to your apprehension, or illustrative of your opinions. Younghusband tells me you are pleased with the plate in the Hobarton Volume,[2] shewing the diurnal movements of the magnetic direction & force in each month of the year in that quarter of the Globe. I have a precisely similar *drawing* (not yet lithographed) of the diurnal variation in direction & force in the diferent [*sic*] [reading doubtful] months at Toronto, as nearly as maybe in the same Lat^d. as Hobarton, but in the other hemisphere. It is in a drawer in my cottage, and I will have it copied for you, if you wish it, immediately I return, which will be early next month. It [is to] [ms. torn] be lithographed in the 2^d. Vol. of the Toronto Ch^m. [reading doubtful], of which the printing is now commencing; but you can make any use of it, or indeed of any thing else of mine, that may suit you. I am now engaged on a plate, for which I have the materials with me, which will exhibit the actual curve made by the one extremity of a freely suspended needle in its mean diurnal motion in every month of the year at the 4 observatories of Toronto, Hobarton, St. Helena & the Cape of Good Hope. I mention this because I think it is exactly the plate that will suit you, and I will endeavour to have it ready for you towards the end of October, if you wish it. It will differ from plates such as the one you have seen for Hobarton, inasmuch as it will shew the actual movement which the end of the needle would itself describe or a plane [reading doubtful] [illeg.] perpendicular to the axis of the needle. The plate that you have seen exhibits the movements in *Declination & Inclination*. If the 2 kinds of plates belonged to a station on the *magnetic Equator*, they would be identical; but every where else they differ; the movement in declination requiring to be multiplied by the cosine of the Inclination when the experimentation is to be of the *space* travelled over by the needle.

We are on our way home via Paris, but if you have occasion to write, send your letter to Capt. Younghusband who will forward it.

Always [reading doubtful] truly yours
EDWARD SABINE

[1] Charles Wright Younghusband (1821–99), Royal Artillery. Faraday was working at this time on terrestrial magnetism and was interested in Sabine's investigations. Younghusband was associated with Sabine in this work. See *LPW*, 399.
[2] *Hobart Town* [*sic*], *Observations made at the Magnetical and Meteorological Observatory*, printed under the superintendence of E. Sabine, 1850.

435 J. PLÜCKER to M. FARADAY, 10 October 1850
[*I.E.E.*, *previously unpublished*]

Bonn
10th of October 1850.

DEAR SIR!

Doctor Brandeis[1] of our University, who particularly applies himself to organic Chemistry is going to visit London, invited by the Prussian Ambassador, Chevalier Bunsen.[2] He wished for this letter, which would give to him the opportunity to see you.

Since I received your last kind letter I continued my experimental researches about the magnetic axes of cristals. I hope allways to reach finally the true & general law of nature, but my researches, presenting continually new difficulties are not yet finished. I sent a first paper, six weeks ago, to Poggendorff, and will be able in a few days, I hope, to present to you a copy of it.[3] Then I'll give to you a short account of the results it contains.

I had preferred by far to publish all my results at once, but I was obliged to go on by the papers of Knoblauch[4] & Tyndall[5] and by the fact, that two of my papers of a former date and written in french, have by the fault of the Editor, not yet been printed.

With my best wishes for your health

Yours
very truly
PLÜCKER

[1] Probably Dieterich Brandis [*sic*] (1824–?). See Letter 440. I have been unable to discover anything further about him.
[2] Christian Karl Josias Freiherr von Bunsen (1791–1860), Minister Plenipotentiary and Envoy Extraordinary of His Majesty, Frederic William IV at the Court of St. James.
[3] J. Plücker, 'Ueber das magnetische Verhalten der Gase', *AOP*, 159 (1851), 87.
[4] Karl Herrmann Knoblauch (1820–95), Extraordinary Professor of Physics at the University of Marburg.
[5] John Tyndall (1820–93), student at Marburg from which he received the Ph.D. in 1850. Later, Professor of Natural Philosophy at the Royal Institution.

See John Tyndall and H. Knoblauch, 'Ueber das Verhalten krystallisirter Körper zwischen den Polen eines Magnetes', *AP*, 155 (1850), 233; 157 (1850), 481.

436 M. FARADAY to W. WHEWELL, 10 October 1850
[*Trinity College Library, Trinity College, Cambridge, previously unpublished*]

Folkestone,
10 Octr 1850

MY DEAR SIR

I snatch a few moments to send you some account of the points I referred to in my last. I will not occupy your time by leading you through the successive investigations which are described in two or three papers now sent into the R. S. but go at once to the chief results. Oxygen is a magnetic body in its gaseous state & rather strongly so. The kind of proof is this. *N*. & *S*. are the poles of an electro-

magnet and *c c* a piece of soft iron connecting them but turned away in the middle The consequence is that I have a strong field of action all round the attenuated part equal in force & condition. If I take two equal diamagnetic bodies as for instance 2 glass cylinders & suspend these about 1 1/2 or 2 inches apart on a cross bar fixed to the end of a horizontal line supported by a fibre of cocoon silk & then adjust this so that the cylinders hang on opposite sides of the keeper described & then put on the magnetic power – immediately the whole arrangement takes up a position in which the glass cylinders are equidistant from the core. If for one of the glass cylinders I substitute a cylinder of bismuth or phosphorous or a tube of water the two stand at different distances & by putting on a force of torsion (by a wire not a cocoon thread) I can measure the relative diamagnetic force of the bodies. I have a

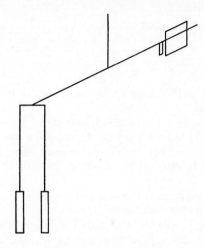

differential balance with the capability of measuring very accurately & yet of removing or at least balancing & estimating interfering circumstances.

Now I have the power of examining *gases* at *different pressure* and *different temperature*, a power which I have long been searching after. First I prepare flint glass bulbs & obtain them so as to be nearly equal in diamagnetic force Then I fill them with gases & seal them up hermetically & I do this when the gas has been by the air pump reduced to half an atmosphere or a third or as nearly as may be to a vacuum, for I reason that if a body (gaseous) were diamagnetic it ought to become less diamagnetic by rarefaction or if magnetic less magnetic by rarefaction.

When two bulbs with Oxygen and Nitrogen were put up the oxygen went close up to the angle & the nitrogen was carried out. With oxygen at 1 atmosphere & 1/2 atmosphere – the 1 atmosphere went up to the core the other out. A bulb with 1/2 atmosphere Ox against another of 1 atmosphere went out but against another of 1/3 of an atmosphere it went inwards. In fine the denser the oxygen the more magnetic it was and when I put a bubble containing 1/3 of a cubic inch of oxygen against an equal bubble containing only an oxygen vacuum, it went inwards with such power as to require force equal to 0.1 of a grain to carry it back to equidistance. With Nitrogen no such thing happens, expansion causes no difference, and three bulbs being Nitrogen 1 atmosphere – Nitrogen Vacuum & Oxygen Vacuum – When compared against each other are alike. Nitrogen is neither Magnetic nor diamagnetic but stands at Zero.

Oxygen is magnetic & in proportion to its quantity: Another experiment will give you a notion of the degree. I took crystals of proto sulphate of iron which is a pretty magnetic salt & dissolved it in water & diluted it until it was bulk for bulk equal to oxygen on the differential balance it then contained sulphate of iron equal to 17 1/2 times the weight of the oxygen which was opposed to it.

Now for another point in the Magnetism of Oxygen. Like iron it loses its magnetism or magnetic condition by heat & is at common temperatures in the condition of iron about to alter. You have a paper of mine about the diamagnetic condition of flame air & gases in which I shew that air heated by a platina helix is rendered more diamagnetic &c. &c. Well all the effect there is due to the oxygen by very careful experiments I find that Oxygen rapidly loses its magnetic character by heat whilst Nitrogen Carbonic acid, &c. are unchanged.

All these properties of oxygen keeps in the atmosphere & I formerly shewed that by cooling the air it was made either more magnetic or less diamagnetic as the case might be. Now I know where the Zero is & that it is the oxygen of the air that was altering in its magnetic relation Again I must refer you to the papers which are long but I trust not too long, for the steps of the reasoning by which I found upon this property of oxygen a branch of physics which I have called atmospheric Magnetism. I think I see the cause in the heating power of the Sun in the atmosphere for all the *periodic solar variations* of the needle both annual & diurnal & as far as I have gone the results of observations tally with the theory – besides these variations there are many others due to atmospheric changes & I am in hopes we shall be able to refer so many to this cause as to give us a far clearer view of the power as it exists in the Earth as its origin. than we have hitherto had & so help us to discriminate that which belongs essentially to its source

The postman is at the door & I must stop

Ever Your Oblgd,
M. FARADAY

437 H. W. ACLAND[1] to M. FARADAY, 17 October 1850

[*I.E.E., previously unpublished*]

Oxford,
Oct. 17, 1850

MY DEAR SIR,

I scarce know whether, (if you remember my existence here,) that remembrance will justify me in troubling you; the more as I expect you will consider my Question an idle one.

My chief avocation is that of a humble Physician but I am dragged out of the routine of the medical life (if indeed the observation of Human disease allows routine at all) by my Physiological lectures.

And these two twin avocations often lead me of course to reflect on the causes & influences which produce the varied effects seen in our frames. In short one's mind cannot be kept off the consideration of how very little we really know of the relation between the greater Cosmical arrangements, and organic life. I really cannot, (for instance) speak precisely of the amount of humidity which is good for my Consumptive Patient. The Dewpoint, & the Temperature varies perpetually, so does he. He alters in weight & chemical composition before & after every meal, and at every hour – so does the atmosphere in its water, its Electrical state &c.

Now, I have I fear neither knowledge, skill, or leisure to clear up any of what we do not know, or to understand & master half of what is known, and mainly thro' your means; but I have a great fancy for seeing in my minutes of leisure (if I can) something of the workings of the great Atmospheric sea. I live in the middle of the town – and I should like to know what goes on where I & other people live – I have a little garden – as big as a room with every aspect. I can therefore have and have Barometer, Thermometer, and Hygrometer. But I am utterly in the dark about the Magnetic, & Electrical states – This is what I wanted to ask you very kindly to tell me. Is there any means of watching any thing of these, without very costly instruments, and a special observatory? And much time & labour?

I must own that I am not 'au courant' with all that is known of the relation of the great imponderable agents and our nervous system, & therefore all our faculties of body & mind – but most certainly more has to be understood about this, and one's mind reels in the contemplation of even what we perceive of the at once greatness, & simplicity of this connexion which probably exists between our mind & the material universe thro' the subtle powers which surround the Earth.

I fear you will think me very impertinent, or very stupid – or both – But I must plead my distance from London as the excuse for my backwardness.

If you are kind enough to answer my question will you tell me what instruments I could easily manage for observing the Magnetic, & Electric variations – & where I can get them – or whether this is so delicate a matter that it is useless to meddle with it, except by reading results. And is there any way that one can note or measure one's own condition in these respects? I suspect that sleep has something to do with the Electro-magnetic condition of the body: only, I beseech you not to think me a Mesmerist in "disguise", but only, yr. faithful servt.

H. W. ACLAND

[1] Henry Wentworth Acland (1815–1900), became Regius Professor of Medicine at Oxford in 1858.

438 H. W. ACLAND to M. FARADAY, 22 October 1850
[*I.E.E., previously unpublished*]

Oxford,
Oct. 22, 1850

MY DEAR PROFESSOR FARADAY,

I am greatly obliged to you for your kind answer to my vague Question. I feared you would say that nothing is to be done in this matter without great labour & costly instruments. I have learned accidentally that I did not know that there is a large & valuable work of M. Dubois Raymont [*sic*] on the Electric currents of Animals.[1] I must try to become acquainted with this.

Your account of the discovery of the magnetic properties of oxygen is deeply interesting, and I will not say throws light upon the electrical properties of animal life, but adds a marvelous & mysterious character to them. The oxygen which we supposed to play an ordinary chemical part, in the changes of textures, and primarily thro' the blood, is then also the great feeder of the nervous system, mediately thro' the blood. At least so it seems to shadow itself forth if it itself bears high magnetic properties with it into the system. However I am out of my depth – But I am very grateful to you for your kind forbearance.

I am My dear Professor Faraday yr. faithful
& obliged servant
HUGH W. ACLAND

[1] See Letter 408, fn. 3.

439 M. FARADAY to J. TYNDALL, 19 November 1850
[*B.J. 2, 275*]

Royal Institution,
November 19, 1850.

DEAR SIR,

I do not know whether this letter will find you at Marburg, but, though at the risk of missing you, I cannot refrain from thanking you for your kindness in sending me the rhomboid of calcareous spar. I am not at present able to pursue that subject, for I am deeply engaged in terrestrial magnetism; but I hope some day to take up the point respecting the magnetic condition of associated particles. In the meantime, I rejoice at every addition to the facts and to the reasoning connected with the subject. It is wonderful how much good results from different persons working at the same matter. Each one gives views and ideas new to the rest. When science is a republic, then it gains; and though I am no republican in other matters, I am in that.

With many thanks for your kindness, I am, Sir, your very obedient servant,

M. FARADAY.

[*Nat. Res. Counc. Canada, previously unpublished*]

Royal Institution
23 Nov[r] 1850

MY DEAR FRIEND

I feel as if I ought to have written to you before but I have been so engaged in researches about Terrestrial Magnetism that I have lost my remembrances of other things & am only slowly coming back to them. I had your kind letter by D[r] Brandis but saw very little of him far less than I desired and I hope you will say so to him. I believe I was in the country the chief part of his time in London but my chief difficulty in the way of intercourse with foreigners and even with society in general is my failing memory. I often intend to do things & then entirely forget their performance until too late.

You still work as I know & cannot work without making discoveries. One of my sorrows is that they are to me concealed as it were in the German language Still by degrees I get hold of the matter. I hope one day to return to the subject of magnetic & diamagnetic bodies and their *inchangeability* or their *convertibility*. I cannot conceive the latter in my mind & think that if it be so there must be some far higher point of philosophy hanging thereby

Ever My dear Sir
Yours Very faithfully
M. FARADAY

[*J. Pelseneer, 'Notes on some unpublished letters from Faraday to Quételet', 'Annals of Science', 1 (1936), 449*]

Royal Institution
23 November

MY DEAR SIR

I ought long ago to have returned you my heartiest thanks for your very great kindness in sending the Portrait I so much desired for my book.[1] It forms a great addition to the pleasure I take in looking into the volume. The only excuse I have is that I have been deeply occupied and I hope that the subject of my thoughts will be acceptable to you. I am vain enough to think that I have found the true physical cause for the periodical & many of the irregular variations of the magnetic needle and perhaps even in part for the magnetic storms. You remember that three years ago I made known the magnetic characters of oxygen in a letter in the Philosophical magazine devoted to the diamagnetic condition of flame & gases[2] and spoke generally of its effect in the atmosphere. Since then I have continually thought & worked on the subject & of late have devised experimental means of ascertaining the effects of rarefaction and of temperature separately in relation to the different gases.[3] I find that all the effects of these two modes of change are exerted on the oxygen & none on the nitrogen. That if oxygen is rarefied by the air pump it loses in magnetic power in proportion, that if it is heated it loses in proportion, but that in regard to the nitrogen neither rarefaction nor change of temperature produces any effect – Then by a chain of reasoning which is given in the three papers that I have sent in to the Royal Society supported by facts drawn from other bodies than oxygen & nitrogen I deduce the effect which the daily changes of temperature ought to produce upon the direction of the lines of force of the earth & as far as I have been able to compare the conclusions with the results obtained at Hobarton, Toronto, Washington, Lake Alhabasen, Fort Simpson, Greenwich, St Petersburgh, Cape of Good Hope, St Helena and Singapore the one accords with the other. You will hear more about them soon.

You desire me to send you a copy of the last portrait that was taken of myself and I shall do so on the first occasion that I can find conveyance perhaps by the Royal Society when the papers are printed. Believe it to represent one who has the highest feelings for your character as a Gentleman a Philosopher and a kind friend

Ever My dear Sir
Most Truly Yours
M. FARADAY.

[1] See *B.J.* 2, 268.
[2] M. Faraday, 'On the diamagnetic Conditions of Flame and Gases', *PM*, 3 s., 31 (1847), 401.
[3] See Letter 436.

---

442 F.C.O. VON FEILITZSCH to M. FARADAY, 3 December 1850[1]
[*I.E.E.*, *previously unpublished*]

Greifswald in Prussia,
3 Dec. 1850

HONOURABLE SIR!

If the exhibition of a new theory conditionates likewise a progress in science, because the apparitions alredy known are comprised under one point of sight engaging to new essays to prove or to disprove them – then I dare hope to have made by my efforts one though but little an advance in that branch, that you Sir the great discoverer of diamagnetism have opened. I dared not so assure you of my unbounded esteem, to express you of what a veneration I am penetrated by following your disinterested indeavours in that science that I love over all, and of which I have made the task of my life, – before I could not put to your feets a little work so unimportant it might be. I wish so vehemently to give you a mark of my deference, that I can not wait longer, to manifest the awe with which I look up to you, might you pardon to such feelings and kindly excuse, that I take now the liberty, to dedicate you this little work. –

I could not be entierly satisfied by that theoretical contemplation of the nature of the diamagnetism, that you and after you Messrs. Reich, Poggendorff, Weber & Plücker have settled. This theory asked the hypothesis: that in every molecule of a magnetical substance by exterial induction the magnetism is *in such manner* distributed, that to the inducing Southpole is turned a Northpole, and to the inducing Northpole a Southpole; but that in diamagnetical substances the distribution takes in such a manner place that in every molekule to the inducing Southpole a Southpole and to the inducing Northpole a Northpole is turned too. Or what is the same thing, that the currents of the theory of Ampère in the magnetical substances are in a contrary direction *moved as* in the diamagnetical substances – I tried rather to explicate myself the apparitions by an hypothesis that Mr. van Rees had explained; consequently I suppose, that in magnetical as in diamagnetical substances the polarity of the molekules have the same direction so that all the Northpoles are turned to the Southpole, and all the Southpoles to the Northpole of the inducing Magnet, only whith that difference, that in a bar of *magnetical* substance the *intensity* of the distribution of the molekules *increases* from the ends to the midst, while it *decreases* in a bar of diamagnetical substance from the ends to the midst. The currents of Ampère in magnetical substances would be consequently more *feebly directed* in *every particles that is situated next one of* the centres of the excitation, as in one more distant, but in diamagnetical substances *they would be more strongly directed.*

These suppositions are permitted, if we attribute to the two groups of substances a diverse resistance against the magnetical excitation (a different Coërcitiv-power). The particles of a magnetical body have a very little Coërcitiv-power, thus the distribution of magnetism must take place in such a manner, that the magnetism dispensed by the primitive excitation in every particle acts distributing on his part on the others, and particulary on the neighbouring particles. Because the molekules are situated very near one to the other, it is to be thought that this part of magnetism is stronger, than that of the primitive excitation. – But in the diamagnetical bodies the Coërcitiv-power is so important, that this portion of magnetism, that takes place by the excitation of the molekules one to the other, is more feeble, than that which is produced by the primitive excitation. A bar of magnetical or diamagnetical substance can we excite in two manners, either from the ends to the midst, or from the midst to the ends ――――

―――― A. The excitation from the ends to the midst is done usually thereby, that a bar is suspended between two magnetpoles.

1.′ Is the Coercitiv-power so important that the effect of the molekules to each other can be neglected, then every particle that is nearer to the magnetpole will be more strongly excited than *that next* neighbouring and more distant particle.

If we such observe two neighbouring particles near the exterial Southpole then will the more near exert a Southpole with the intensity s, the more distant will turn to a Northpole with the intensity n', but in such a manner that $n' < s$. But outwardly these two excited magnetisms with the difference of their power $s - n'$, but this is in our case *southpolar*, consequently of the same kind, as the exciting Southpole. The contrary will take place near the North-pole, so that *the disengaged magnetism, extended over the bar, grows southpolar on that half which is turned to the Southpole, but northpolar on the other half, that is turned to the Northpole.* A substance, where this takes place is *diamagnetical*, it puts itself equatorial.

2. Is the bar of a magnetical substance therefore so qualified, that the separating action of the molekules on each other must be taken in consideration than can it grow so strong, that the molekules in the midst of the substance are more strongly magnetical, than towards the ends. If we observe once more two such particles near the exterial Southpole, of [illeg.] intensity [illeg.] so will the next avert a Southpole of the intensity s, from this exterial Southpole, but the more distant turn towards it a Northpole of the intensity n_1'; but in such a manner, that $n_1' > s_1$ [illeg.] outwardly works both with the intensity $n_1' - s_1$, but this is northpolar, therefore of a contrary nature, as the exciting South-pole. The contrary shall take place near the Northpole, so that *the disengaged magnetism, extended over the bar, grows northpolar on the half that is turned towards the Southpole, but southpolar on that half, that is turned towards the Northpole.* A substance where this takes place is *magnetical*, it puts itself *axial*.

3 Besides of this observed disengaged magnetism must be yet considered that magnetism that grows disengaged on the final surface of the bar and that can not be conpensated by the neighbouring particles. This is always of a contrary nature than the exciting neighbouring pole. For magnetical bodies [word illeg.] it supports the effect of the disengaged magnetism extended over the bar; in diamagnetical bodies acts it in the contrary, and it is to be thought, that even it is preponderating. Perhaps might this be cause of the feeble magnetism, that you were finding in the Platin, Paladium and Osmium. –

B An excitation from the midst to the ends takes place if we do lay a bar in an electrical spiral. But in this case all the substances must gain an equal polarity as the iron.

To prove that, I pushed a thick bar of Bismouth in a very strongly acting spiral, which were excited by 4 cells of Mr. Grove every one of twelve [illeg.] [square] inch of platin plate. I set this spiral on a side near a little declinations-needle suspended on a silk-thread, and I compensated its effect by a magnet of steel, that I dislocated as long on the other side of the needle, as it was returned to its first place. And I withdrew[2] the bismuth bar out of the spiral, than the needle declined in favour of the compensating magnet, but if I pushed it again in the spiral, then the needle declined in favour of the spiral. Unlucky the poor fortune of the physical establishment of our university did not allow, to prove also other substances, than the bismouth, but I schall supply this defect as soon as it is to be done; but you will allow me the consequence: that the diamagnetismus and the magnetismus are only modifications of the same power, that are produced partly by the different Coercitiv power of the substances, partly by the different manner of excitation.

In applying the former in the theory of Ampère I startled, because it has teached hitherto only: Currents, that are parallel and directed in the same way, attracts themselves, but if they are parallel but not directed in the same manner they are repulsive; therefore that a current, moving in the sense of a hand of a watch, in a spiral produces a Southpole on the entrance point in the spiral, but a Northpole on the egression point. But one has only constructed spirals, where the currents in every winding schows an equal intensity.*

But I tried, to construct spirals in such a manner as these which I have adjointed. One of them is in such a way constructed that on two copper wires are solderd to each of them 15 thin threads spined over with silk. With all this 15 threads is the first winding layed [reading doubtful] backwards over the copperwire; the second winding is only winded with 14 threads, during that the fifteenth moves itself along the axis etc. Consequently has every of the 15 windings a thread less, and the ends of all the other threads have the direction of the axis. Are soldered in the midst the latter ends of the 2. 15 threads and are the two thick threads without touching themselves, in each a manner bowed, that they can be suspended in the little cups of the apparatus of Ampère, than a current, passing by the spiral, will divide itself in such a manner, that it is the most strong on the exterior ends of the spiral, but decreases more and more to the midst. If the winding of the spiral took place in the direction of the hand of a watch, then must the end of it, where the current enters, grow a Southpole: but a Northpole, kept parallel of the spiral, will it repulse. Only the final winding will be attracted and it representing this disengaged magnetism of the final surface. The second spiral is winded like this, only with that difference, that the strongest windings are laying in the midst and the feeblest near the ends. This spiral will be attracted of the Northpole of a magnet over the half in which the current moved at first, but the other half will be repulsed by it. Of the third spiral at last has all the windings the same strength, over all the extension, it is indifferent against a magnetpole, that is not too near, and only their last ends are attracted or repulsed.

Therefore it is permitted to enlarge the theory of Ampère in this manner If an electrical current passes through a spiral in the direction of a hand of a watch, and a., if the current is more feeble in every winding that is nearer to the midst of the spiral, then that half is *attracted* by a Southpole, in which enters the current excepted the first winding,

b., but if the current is more strong in every winding that is nearer to the midst of the spiral, then that half is *repulsed* by a Southpole, in which enters the current including the first winding

The contrary will be adopted for that half in which deserts the current and likewise for the Northpole of the magnet opposed.

In consequence of this extension of the theory of Ampère, it is easy to transfer them in the opinions above produced. In the molecules of magnetical and diamagnetical bodies are to find electrical currents: By the magnetism they will be in such a way directed, that they put themselves parallel of the exterial acting currents. In the diamagnetical bodies is opposed a very great resistance to the direction of these currents of molekules, therefore will their intensity decrease from the centre of the excitation; these bodies will comply with the opinion that is given in *a.*, they will be repulsed. But in magnetical bodies acts the currents of the molekules, that are diverted by exterial influence, on their part also directing on the neighbouring currents of molekule, and in such a manner that these currents are the most energical directed in the midst of the bar, but are more feebly directed near the ends. These bodies comply with the opinion given in *b.*, they will by attracted and put themselves axial.

But I fear to tire you, would I transfer the opinions that I have explained on the different apparitions, that followed to the your discovery of the diamagnetism. The apparitions of the minglings of magnetical and diamagnetical substances; the predominating attraction or repulsion of the axis of the crystals; the apparitions of the magne-crystallic axis; the currents of induction that gives a bar of Bismuth exhibited by Mr Weber: – all this apparitions follows by themselves by plain adaptions. –

– I ask your pardon, Sir, that I have dared to write you in your own language, that I know so very imperfectly: but I hope I have not to much deformed the sense of what I would express.

I have the honour to be Sir, your most humble servant

DR. VON FEILITZSCH
Professor of the university of Greifswald

[1] See *PM*, 4 s., 1 (1851), 46, for this letter as edited by Faraday. What is given here is the letter as written by von Feilitzsch.
[2] From here to the asterisk was missing in the microfilm against which the transcript was checked.

[*I.E.E., previously unpublished*]

St Mary's Lodge
York
Dec. 5 1850

MY DEAR FARADAY.

Many thanks for your kind explanations of the meaning which ought to be attached to your lines of magnetic force, which I quite comprehend and (I think) see the bearings of.

Believing from the interest you appeared to take in the question of Aurora – that you may be induced to try to bring that *recusant* within the pale of your magnetism, I will venture to send you my little Hypothesis derived from my many nights of gazing, & not a few of needle scrutinizing.

In my little page[2] only the peculiar Aurora of 1847 is described, but to comprehend my view fully it is necessary to take two cases.

1. The *Auroral Arch, really weak,* viz. a narrow white 'ring of light' stretched across the dipping needle like the ordinary conjunctive wire. This moves from NNW to SSE, at a pretty regular rate. I esteem it to be a simple Electrical Current.

2. *The Beam,* which if commonly seen at a great distance & seen edgeways, appears like a brush or pencil of light, *parallel* to the Dipping Needle, of the plane or nearly so. But I apprehend this appearance is not to be trusted altogether – I suppose that the *beam* when it is viewed from beneath has a different aspect, & such a structure as to justify me in regarding it as an Electrical Magnet. When the sky is so favorably covered by Aurora as in 1847 & 1834, the great area of light is found to be subject to intermittence, as

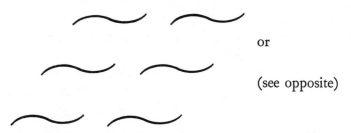

or

(see opposite)

This is as the swift flashing, or curtain waving.

This is the wonderful 'Pulsation' (so called by Airy & Buff independently)[3] and I conceive that the Electric discharges thus subject to fits of alternate brightness & darkness, in a line ↓ parallel to dipping needle may have the effect of interrupted spirals – or continuous spirals, & affect the Needle – though when looked at edgeways they seem (at 70 miles distance) to be like travelling pencils of light.

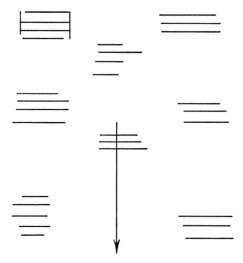

They certainly lie parallel to the dipping needle, & some (or probably all) affect the Compass; this could hardly be if they were simple brushes of light – for in that case they have no business to look to the same Star as the Dipping Needle & the Compass ought not to *see* them. The simple *Arch* or ring of Auroral Light is rather uncommon.

See what a penalty you pay for being famous!

I have just refixed my old Suspension Magnet, in hopes to get some further evidence of the influence of Aurora on it this winter.

My Sister joins in kind Comps to Mrs Faraday with your faithful friend

JOHN PHILLIPS

[1] John Phillips (1800–74), Professor of Geology in King's College, London.
[2] I am unable to identify this reference.
[3] G. B. Airy, 'Account of an Aurora Borealis seen at Cambridge on the 13th of March', *PM*, 3 s., 22 (1833), 315. Airy does not use the term 'pulsation' but describes the phenomenon.

I am unable to discover where Buff discusses the aurora.

444 J. PHILLIPS to M. FARADAY, 14 December 1850

[*I.E.E., previously unpublished*]

14 Dec. 1850
York

MY DEAR FARADAY

It is indeed too true that the *exact* relation of the effect of an Auroral Arch or beam to its position, is not to be stated, except with extreme reserve. The Phenomena are normally of too exciting a kind, & come on us when we are too

5-2

unprepared, to allow of all being done which should be done. In 1833 it was almost a *novelty* to assure the Meteorologist that the needle was powerfully affected at all. Few persons have a needle fit for the purpose of observing *horizontal* deviation, still fewer a *Dipping* needle worthy of the name: & of these almost o has the needle or needles mounted & conveniently placed for use.

In 1839 I changed house, & now it is 1850 – In these 11 years I have never had time & power to mount either of my needles. *Thank God!* both are now mounted, in my study & *so good*, that I intend to devote some time to them, & to make such regular Observations as to give me well their normal state (or rather the *Mean* state) & be prepared against all Auroras – If we have any good arches or Beams I hope to see them with my needles

In turning over old papers I find a duplicate of some notes of the great aurora of 12 Oct 1833. Pray accept it – as being pretty full of Magnetical notes – The *displacements* of the needle are always rather sudden, by little starts.

Ever Yours truly
JOHN PHILLIPS

445 J. S. HENSLOW[1] to M. FARADAY, 27 December 1850
[*I.E.E., previously unpublished*]

Hitcham Hadleigh
Suffolk
27 Dec 1850

MY DEAR SIR,

Tho' it is a shame to apply to one so occupied as yourself, I know there is nothing like appealing to the highest authority – We have determined on forming a collection of objects for the Ipswich Museum which may serve as *types* of the principal groups under the 3 Kingdoms of nature – & to keep such collections well labelled & illustrated by models & drawings apart from the ever shifting series of specimens arranged in the cases of a continually increasing collection – At the head of the Mineral Kingdom I wish to illustrate the Elementary substances by exhibiting as many of them as possible contenting ourselves with the names of those which cannot be exhibited – My idea is to give the S. G. & Chemical Equivalent where known, & to place the specimens under glasses – Circular disks of the metals, one half polished & the other not, with an exhibition of their *fracture* seem to me the best way of showing these Though I cannot ask you to assist further than by offering any suggestion that may occur, perhaps you can inform me where I am likely to pick up examples of the more uncommon substances properly put up (as Iodine, Bromine &c) or of such metals as may require rather severer treatment to reduce them into the required shape than I am able to bestow on them – As I am asking on account

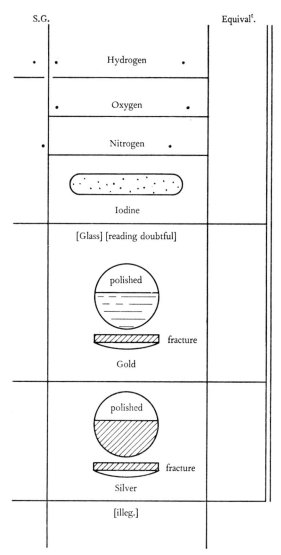

	S.G.		Equival.^t

Hydrogen

Oxygen

Nitrogen

Iodine

[Glass] [reading doubtful]

polished

fracture

Gold

polished

fracture

Silver

[illeg.]

of the public, I feel less scrupulous than if it were on my own account alone, though I shall not be less obliged – Some such arrangement as this is what I am thinking of – a small watch glass over the metals – Where can I find the best arrangement? Will that in Gregory do?

Believe me
very truly yrs
J. S. HENSLOW

[1] John Stevens Henslow (1796–1861), botanist and Charles Darwin's teacher and friend at Cambridge. Henslow was one of the founders of the Ipswich Museum in 1848.

Royal Institution,
December 30, 1850

MY DEAR SIR,

It is with great pleasure that I receive a letter from you, for much as I have thought of your name and the high scientific labours connected with it, I do not remember that I have seen your handwriting before. I shall treasure the letter in a certain volume of portraits and letters that I keep devoted to the personal remembrance of the eminent men who adorn science whom I have more or less the honour and delight of being acquainted with.

In reference to the queries in your letter, I suppose the following will be sufficient answer.

I developed and *published* the nature and principles of the action of magnetic and diamagnetic media upon substances *in* them, more or less magnetic or diamagnetic than themselves, in the year 1845, or just *five* years ago. The paper was read at the Royal Society, January 8, 1846, and is contained in the "Philosophical Transactions" for 1846, p. 50, &c. If you refer to the numbered paragraphs 2357, 2363, 2367, 2400k, 2406, 2414, 2423, 2438, you will see at once how far I had gone at that date. The papers were republished in Poggendorf's "Annalen," and I believe in the Geneva, the Italian, and German journals in one form or another.

In reference to the magnetism of oxygen, *three* years ago, i.e. in 1847, I showed its high magnetic character in relation to nitrogen and all other gases, and that air owed its place amongst them to the oxygen it contained. I even endeavoured to analyse the air, separating its oxygen and nitrogen by magnetic force, for I thought such a result possible. All this you will find in a paper published in the "Philosophical Magazine," for 1847, vol. xxxi. page 401, &c. This paper was also published at full length in Poggendorff's "Annalen," 1848, vol. lxxiii. page 256, &c. I shall send you a copy of it immediately by M. Bailliere, who has undertaken to forward it to you. I have marked it in ink to direct your attention. In it also you will find the effect of *heat on oxygen and air*; the experiments were all devised and made upon the principles before developed, concerning the mutual relation of substances and the media surrounding them.

This year I have been busy extending the above researches, and have sent in several papers to the Royal Society, and have also given a Bakerian lecture in which they were briefly summed up.[1] I fortunately have a copy in slips of the Royal Society's abstract of these papers, and therefore will send it with the paper from the "Philosophical Magazine." I suppose it will appear in the outcoming number of the "Philosophical Magazine." The papers themselves are now in the hands of the printer of the "Transactions."

I was not aware, until lately, of that paper of M. Edmond Becquerel, to which you first refer. My health and occupation often prevent me from reading up to the present state of science. Immediately that I knew of it, I added a note (by permission) to my last paper, series xxvi., in which I referred to it, and quoted at length what it said in reference to atmospheric magnetism, calling attention also to my own results as to oxygen three years ago, and those respecting media five years ago. I have no copy of this note, or I would send it to you. It was manifest to me that M. Edmond Becquerel had never heard of my results, and though that makes no excuse to myself, I hope it will be to him a palliation that I had not before heard of his. The second one I had not heard of until I received your letter the day before yesterday.

I was exceedingly struck with the beauty of M. E. Becquerel's experiments, and though the differential balance I have described in my last paper will, I expect, give me far more delicate indications, when the perfect one, which is in hand, is completed, still I cannot express too freely my praise of the apparatus and results which the first paper describes and which is probably surpassed by those in the second.

I know the severe choice of your Academy of Sciences, and I also know that France has ever been productive of men who deserve to stand as candidates, whenever a vacancy occurs in any branch of knowledge; and though, as you perceive, I do not know all that M. E. Becquerel has done, I know enough to convince me that he deserves the honour of standing in that body and to create in me strong hopes that he will obtain his place there.

Ever, my dear M. Becquerel, your faithful admirer,

M. FARADAY.

¹ *ERE*, 24th–27th Series.
The references Faraday gives in this letter are sufficient to locate the items he mentioned. It did not, therefore, seem necessary to duplicate them.

447 J. S. HENSLOW to M. FARADAY, 5 January 1851
[*I.E.E., previously unpublished*]

Hitcham Hadleigh
Suffolk
5 Jany 1851

MY DEAR SIR,

I shall be most careful in unpacking the box – I know of old what a disagreeable inmate is Bromine. I had some in a glass stoppered bottle which gradually evaporated & attacked several minerals in the same drawer – I do not mention it that you should think of repeating the preparations of this & Chlorine – but the thought strikes me a *globe*, rather than a tube, would be the best way of securing mass enough to see the colour of the gases – I have had some correspondence with an assayer, & have asked his advice about the mode of securing the metal disks. My idea is to procure a number of square blocks of wood, all of the same size, & coat them with some (?) varnish, which may serve as a cement to the disks, the glass covers, & keep out the air. This would admit of ready re-arrangement in an additional covering of a glass case large enough to contain the whole series – Perhaps one of the simplest arrangements

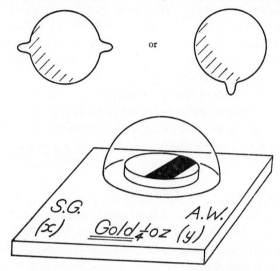

would be to take either the S. G's, or the Atomic Weights, leaving such as are not known at the bottom of the series – According to intrinsic values I have suggested disks of 4 sizes suitable to 1. oz – 1/2 oz – 1/4 oz – 1/8 oz – I never saw Silicium, & do not know whether it can be thus exhibited – As for carbon, I suppose a very *small* diamond would be the best specimen – with a sample of charcoal? or plumbago? – or these latter are hardly pure enough – I see the Assayer has some of the Earths also – & it will be as well to have a selection of such as are common, as an introduction to the geological series –

Believe me
Very sincerely Yrs
J. S. HENSLOW

448 M. FARADAY to M. A. BECQUEREL, 17 January 1851
[*B.J.* 2, *292*]

Royal Institution,
January 17, 1851.

MY DEAR M. BECQUEREL,
   I received your letter of the 14th instant yesterday, and hasten to reply to it, as you desire; first, however, thanking you for your kind expressions, which will be a strong stimulus to me, coming as they do from a master in science. I

would not have you for a moment think that I put my paper of three years ago and that of M. E. Becquerel's of last year on the same footing, except in this, that we each discovered for ourselves at those periods the high magnetic relation of oxygen to the other gases. M. E. Becquerel has made excellent measurements, which I had not, and his paper is, in my opinion, a most important contribution to science.

I am not quite sure whether you are aware that in my paper of 1847 the comparison of one gas with another is always at the *same* temperature, i.e. at common temperatures, and it was a very striking fact to me to find that oxygen was magnetic in relation to hydrogen to such an extent as to be equal in attractive force to its force of gravity, for the oxygen was suspended in the hydrogen by magnetic force alone, "Phil. Mag." xxxi. pp. 415, 416. I do not think that much turns upon the circumstance of calling oxygen magnetic or diamagnetic in 1847, when the object was to show how far oxygen was apart from the other gases in the magnetic direction, these terms being employed in relation to other bodies, and with an acknowledgment that the place of zero was not determined. If I understand rightly, M. Edmond Becquerel still calls bismuth and phosphorus magnetic, whilst I call them diamagnetic. He considers space as magnetic: I consider it as zero. If a body should be found as eminently diamagnetic in my view as iron is magnetic, still I conclude M. Edmond Becquerel would consider it magnetic. He has not yet adopted the view of any zero or natural standard point. But this does not prevent us from fully understanding each other, and the facts upon which the distinction of oxygen from nitrogen and other gases are founded, remain the same, and are just as well made known by the one form of expression as the other. It was, therefore, to me a great delight, when I first saw his paper in last November, to have my old results confirmed and so beautifully enlarged in the case of oxygen and nitrogen by the researches of M. E. Becquerel, and beyond all to see the beautiful system of measurement applied to them which is described in his published paper.

Pray present my kindest remembrances and wishes to him, and believe me to be, with the highest respect, my dear M. Becquerel, your faithful, obliged servant,

M. FARADAY.

449 M. FARADAY to T. BELL,[1] 3 February 1851
[*R.S., previously unpublished*]

Royal Institution,
3 Feby. 1851

MY DEAR SIR

As far as I have have [*sic*] any power of judgment I find reason to commend Col! Sabines paper[2] as a most important contribution to Magnetic science. It resolves a multitude of apparently wild extravagance of action into an important degree of order and develops a new law of periodicity amongst terrestrial effects which can be explained only after it is (as in this paper) made known. I cannot doubt that Terrestrial magnetism is rapidly advancing when such a paper as Sabine's comes forth and not only explains but provokes others also to give explanations

Ever Truly Yours
M. FARADAY

[1] Thomas Bell (1792–1880), Junior Secretary of the Royal Society 1848–53, Professor of Zoology at King's College, London.
[2] Edward Sabine, 'On periodical laws discoverable in the mean effects of the larger magnetic disturbances', *PT* (1851), 123.

450 M. FARADAY to A. DE LA RIVE, 4 February 1851
[*Bibliothèque publique et universitaire de Genève, ms. 2316, f. 67–8, B.J. 2, 257*]

Royal Institution
4 February 1851

MY DEAR DE LA RIVE,

My wife & I were exceedingly sorry to hear of your sad loss:[1] it brought vividly to our remembrance the time when we were at your house; and you, & others with you, made us so welcome. What can we say to these changes but that they shew by comparison the Vanity of all things under the Sun. I am very glad that you have spirits to return to work again; for that is a healthy & proper employment of the mind under such circumstances.

With respect to my views & experiments I do not think that anything shorter than the papers (& they will run to above 100 pages in the Transactions) will give you possession of the subject; because a great deal depends upon the comparison of observations in different parts of the world with the facts obtained by experiment and with the deductions drawn from them: but I will try to give you an idea of the root of the matter. You are aware that I use the phrase *line of magnetic force* to represent the presence of magnetic force & the direction (of polarity) in which it is exerted; and, by the idea which it conveys one obtains very well, and I believe without error, a notion of the distribution of the forces about a bar magnet or between near flat poles presenting a field of equal force; or in any other case. Now if circumstances be arranged so as to present a field of equal force, which is easily done as I have shewn by the Electro-magnet, then if a sphere of iron or nickel be placed in the field it immediately disturbs the direction of the lines of force for they are concentrated within the sphere. They are, however, not merely concentrated but *contorted*; for the sum of forces in any one section across the field is always equal to the sum of forces in any other section; and therefore their condensation in the iron or nickel cannot occur without this contortion. Moreover the contortion is easily shewn by using a small needle, ($\frac{1}{10}$ of an inch long) to examine the field: for, as before the introduction of the sphere of Iron or nickel, it would always take up a position parallel to itself: afterwards it varies in position in different places near the sphere. – That being understood let us then suppose the sphere to be raised in temperature; at a certain temperature it begins to lose its power of affecting the lines of magnetic force, and ends by retaining scarcely any; so that as regards the little needle mentioned above, it now stands every where parallel to itself within the field of force. This change occurs with iron at a very high temperature & is passed through within the compass, apparently, of a small number of degrees: With Nickel it occurs at much lower temperatures being effected by the heat of boiling oil.

Now take another step. Oxygen as I shewed above three years ago. in the Philosophical Magazine for 1847, vol. 31, pp. 410, 415, 416, is magnetic in relation to Nitrogen and other gases. E. Bequerel, [sic] without knowing of my results, has confirmed & extended them in his paper of last year, and given certain excellent measures. In my paper of 1847 I shewed, also, that oxygen (like iron & nickel) lost its magnetic power & its ability of being attracted by the magnet when heated p. 417; and I further shewed that the temperatures at which this took place was within the range of common temperature; for the oxygen in the air i.e the air altogether increased in magnetic power when cooled to 0°F. page 406.

Now I must refer you to the papers themselves for the (to me) strange results of the incompressibility (magnetically speaking) of oxygen and the inexpansibility of nitrogen & other gases: for the description of a differential balance by which I can compare gas with gas: or the same gas at different degrees of rarefaction: – for the determination of the true zero or point between Magnetic & diamagnetic bodies: – and for certain views of magnetic conduction & polarity. You will there find described certain very delicate experiments upon diamagnetic and very weak magnetic bodies concerning their action on each other in a magnetic field of equal force: the magnetic bodies repel each other and the diamagnetic bodies repel each other; but a magnetic & a diamagnetic body *attract* each other: and these results combined with the qualities of oxygen as just described convince me that it is able to deflect the lines of magnetic force passing through it just as iron or nickel is; but to an infinitely smaller amount; and that its power of deflecting the lines varies with its temperature & degree of rarefaction.

Then comes in the consideration of the atmosphere and the manner in which it rises & falls in temperature by the presence & absence of the Sun. The place of the great warm region nearly in his neighbourhood; – of the two colder regions which grow up & diminish in the northern & southern hemispheres as the sun travels between the tropics; – the effect of the extra warmth of the Northern hemisphere over the Southern; – the effect of accumulation from the action of preceding months; – the effect of dip & mean declination at each particular station; – the effects that follow from the noncoincidence of magnetic and astronomical conditions of polarity, meridians and so forth; – the results of the distribution of land & water for any given place; – all these and many other things I must refer you for, to the papers. I could not do them justice in any account that a letter could contain, and should run the risk of leading you into error regarding them. But I may say that, deducing from the experiments & the theory what are the deviations of the magnetic needle at any given station, which may be expected as the mean result of the heating & cooling of the atmosphere for a given Season & hour, I find such a general accordance with the results of observations, especially in the direction & generally in the amount for different seasons of the *declination* variation, as to give me the strongest hopes that I have assigned the true physical cause of those variations and shewn the modus operandi of their production.

And now, my dear De la Rive I must leave you and run to other matters. As soon as I can send you a copy of the papers I will do so and can only say I hope that they will meet with your approbation. With the kindest remembranches to your Son Believe me to be My dear friend

Ever Truly Yours,

M. FARADAY

1 De la Rive's wife had just died.

451   W. SCORESBY[1] to M. FARADAY, 6 March 1851
[*I.E.E.*, *previously unpublished*]

Torquay,
6th March 1851.

DEAR DR. FARADAY,

Whilst *you* are working so sucessfully on great laws & phenomena, I am, as time admits, doing a little, or rather trying to do something, though in the matter to which I refer in this note, the results are merely negative.

I have been trying the effect of the magnetic condition, in iron, as also of a galvanic current, with a view to the inquiry, whether any alterations in *dimensions* are thereby occasioned? My experiments, within the limits of observation in my apparatus, indicate no sensible effect, except what belongs to temperature. The value of my scale, however, observed by reflection in a mirror, is not well determined on account of the different points of contact & leverage – the lengths not being easily determinable. I wish therefore, to verify my present impression, as to the value by the interposition of a disc or slip of metal of *known* thickness. I thought that you, perhaps, might be able to advise me how I could procure such a disc or plate? The mint has a fine rolling apparatus, which I believe has values attached & [illeg.], you possibly, might have some little bit of sheet metal of known dimensions: What I require is a disc or blank or slip of small size – that of a shilling is large enough, and of a thickness of 1/50th or any where from 1/50th to 1/100th of an inch. This I could interpose between two of my bars which would verify or correct my present estimations.

The apparatus which I constructed myself here, works so beautifully, that *a degree of temperature produces near 1/4 inch movement in the reflected scale* – consequently the *quarter of a degree of temperature,* or the alteration in length due to that small quantity, is easily determinable.

Thinking the experiments might not be altogether uninteresting, though negative as to results, I am preparing a paper for the Royal Soc. thereon.[2]

I am, my dear Dr. Faraday,
Yours very faithfully,
WILLIAM SCORESBY.

[1] William Scoresby (1789–1857), naval captain, chaplain and amateur scientist especially interested in magnetism.
[2] The paper was never printed.

452   A. QUÉTELET to M. FARADAY, 20 March 1851
[*I.E.E., previously unpublished*]

Bruxelles
le 20 mars 1851

MON CHER AMI,

J'ai reçu par Mm. Schlagintweit[1] le beau présent que vous m'avez fait: rien ne pouvait m'être plus agréable que de recevoir Votre portrait avec une inscription de Votre main qui témoigne de l'Amitié dont Vous Voulez bien m'honorer. Je veux désormais avoir toujours ce portrait sous mes yeux; il se trouve dans le lieu le plus apparent de mon cabinet de travail, dont il fait le principal ornement.

Je Vous félicite sur les résultats remarquables que Vous avez obtenus au sujet des propriétés magnétiques du gaz oxygène. Notre Academie a qui j'ai cru pouvoir communiquer ce que Vous m'en avez dit dans votre dernière lettre, en a pris connaissance avec un Vif intéret. j'aurais du vous exprimer mes remerciments [*sic*] depuis longtemps; mais je voulais, en vous écrivant, Vous transmettre la suite de mes travaux sur l'électricité de l'air, travaux auxquels Vous avez bien Voulu prêter quelqu'attention. je trouve enfin, aujourd'hui, un moment pour satisfaire à ce desir.

Mon principal but en vous fesant [*sic*] cette communication est de vous prier d'examiner si vos découvertes récentes sur l'oxygène peuvent aussi rendre compte des Variations périodiques de l'électricité. Je ne doute aucunement que cet important sujet n'ait déjà fixé Votre attention. Mon premier travail sur l'électricité contenait les résultats de quatre années et demie d'observations; je puis y joindre aujourd'hui, une des deux années 1849 et 1850, et du commencement de 1851: peut être ne les verrez vous pas sans interêt.[2] Ils confirment en général les principaux faits déduits de mes observations antérieures; et cependant l'année 1849 a présenté une anomalie trés sensible pendant les sept premiers mois: l'électricité a été notablement inférieure à ce qu'elle est dans son état ordinaire: vous pourrez en juger par le TABLEAU cijoint qui, outre les Valeurs moyennes et extremes de chaque mois *observés directement*, contient aussi les moyennes mensuelles, en ramenant à une même échelle les déterminations de chaque jour.

on y retrouve aussi la même loi de continuité; les mêmes différences entre l'hiver et l'été, pour autant, bien entendu, que le permettent les années considérées individuellement.

Rien n'est plus propre à faire apprécier la lacune qui existe encore dans nos connaissances relativement à l'électricité de l'air, que le doute qui entoure les anomalies que j'ai observées pendant la première partie de l'année 1849. Il m'a été impossible de trouver des observations qui pussent servir de contrôle aux miennes. Aucun observatoire, du moins à ma connaissance, ne publie jusqu'à ce jour des observations quotidiennes régulières sur l'électricité atmosphérique: c'est là une lacune trés facheuse, comme on ne tardera pas à le reconnaître.

Quand une année est remarquable par une température anormale, par des pluies excessives ou des sècheresses, tous les méteorologistes s'accordent pour constater ces irrégularités dans le [illeg.] où elles se sont manifestées: malheureusement il n'en est pas de même ici. J'ai consulté des recueils d'observations des plus estimés et je n'y ai trouvé aucun renseignement qui peut me satisfaire.

Il en résulte qu'on peut me demander si l'affaiblissement dans l'état électrique de l'air était un fait bien réel, ou s'il n'était qu'apparent; s'il n'était point du, par exemple, à un dérangement de mon instrument? et en supposant cet affaiblissement d'électricité bien constaté, était il purement local? toutes ces questions peuvent prendre d'autant plus d'importance que l'anomalie signalée coincidait à peu près avec le retour du fléau qui a si cruellement éprouvé nos populations. ces difficultés m'ont porté à rechercher s'il n'y aurait pas moyen de rendre *un électromètre comparable à lui même à différentes époques*.

J'avais montré déjà, dans mon premier travail, qu'il est facile de comparer entre eux deux électromètres de Peltier, et de construire des tables d'équivalents pour leurs indications mais, quand une comparaison a été faite, et que l'instrument comparé a été transporté dans un autre pays; ou même, sans qu'il y ait eu transport, après qu'il s'est écoulé un certain temps, il importe de s'assurer que les indications n'ont pas Varié, qu'elles ont bien conservé leurs Valeurs absolues.

Cette Vérification peut se faire d'une manière très facile. il suffit en effet de s'assurer que l'aiguille a conservé toute sa mobilité et que sa force directrice est restée la même. or, cette force directrice, ici, est donnée par la petite aiguille

Degrés d'électricité aux différents mois (observatoire royal de Bruxelles)

Moyenne des degrés observés à l'électromètre

	1844	45	46	47	48	49	50	51	1844-50
Janvier	...	50	50	63	50	39	49	52	50
Février	...	55	45	45	44	36	38	52	44
Mars	...	44	26	47	36	27	36	31(1)	35
Avril	...	27	23	30	27	20	19	...	24
Mai	...	26	19	21	18	16	22	...	20
Juin	...	18	18	18	18	13	14	...	17
Juillet	...	21	14	18	22	14	12	...	17
Août	28	27	22	6	24	21	19	...	21
Septembre	29	29	23	17	24	24	28	...	25
Octobre	31	42	26	30	32	31	36	...	33
Novembre	33	44	41	35	36	45	34	...	38
Décembre	46	53	57	48	45	38	50	...	48
Année	...	36	30	31	31	27	30	...	31

(1) jusqu'au 20 mars [Quételet's note]

Maxima

	1844	45	46	47	48	49	50	51	1844-50
Janvier		65	71	77	76	65	74	75	71
Février		70	60	73	62	62	55	74	64
Mars		64	56	62	47	55	66	...	58
Avril		48	40	48	51	35	65	...	48
Mai		41	33	41	40	25	75	...	42
Juin		48	30	24	36	39	22	...	35
Juillet		43	32	31	44	24	25	...	33
Août	36	45	37	23	38	34	44	...	37
Septembre		42	29	30	22	44	50	...	40
Octobre	48	67	55	48	54	57	67	...	56
Novembre	51	60	65	53	57	77	64	...	61
Décembre	67	73	74	66	65	74	71	...	70
[Année]		55	49	49	50	49	56	...	51

Moyenne des nombres proportionnels

	1844	45	46	47	48	49	50	51	1844-50
Janvier	...	471	562	957	487	219	507	462	534
Février	...	548	256	413	295	163	180	532	309
Mars	...	262	95	282	164	90	194	125	173
Avril	...	93	94	221	155	132	70	...	128
Mai	...	163	49	67	59	32	220	...	98
Juin	...	51	39	47	48	27	24	...	39
Juillet	...	58	33	43	61	25	21	...	40
Août	90	89	57	11	64	92	55	...	65
Septembre	91	95	62	39	63	69	96	...	74
Octobre	110	299	98	107	120	122	172	...	147
Novembre	127	334	274	160	152	364	155	...	224
Décembre	340	742	799	356	281	304	451	...	468
Année	...	267	202	225	162	137	179	...	192
(1) jusqu'au 20 mars	...	49	44	46	39	36	41	...	43

Minima

	1844	45	46	47	48	49	50	51	1844-50
Janvier		32	8	38	19	0	0	12	16
Février		28	0	23	11	17	0	31	13
Mars		25	0	21	19	0	13	...	13
Avril		10	0	0	8	0	3	...	4
Mai		0	0	0	0	0	0	...	0
Juin		0	3	0	0	0	0	...	0
Juillet		3	0	4	0	0	0	...	1
Août	4	2	9	0	12	0	0	...	4
Septembre		15	8	0	0	13	11	...	8
Octobre	6	0	0	12	22	16	0	...	8
Novembre	13	24	18	4	9	11	11	...	14
Décembre	21	30	24	27	7	5	20	...	19
[Année]		15	6	11	9	5	5	...	8

aimantée attachée à l'aiguille indicatrice de l'électromètre. il suffira alors de soumettre la petite aiguille aimantée aux procédés ordinaires qui servent à constater son énergie magnétique; c'est à dire de la faire osciller librement dans un plan horizontal et de constater si son état magnétique est resté le même. On doit tenir compte, bien entendu, des corrections ordinaires employées en pareil cas pour la température, la torsion des fils, la variation de l'intensité horizontale du magnétisme terrestre, &c.

On conçoit que, par des procédés analogues, on peut faire dépendre aussi la détermination de la force électrique absolue de la terre, de celle de son magné-tisme absolu: problème important, mais dont je n'ai point à m'occuper pour le moment. Il me suffit d'avoir établi qu'on peut par un procédé fort simple reconnaître qu'un électromètre de Peltier est resté comparable à lui même. Bien que la chose soit très simple en soi, je m'étonne que cette précaution n'ait pas été indiquée encore. Si l'idée m'était Venue de Vérifier ainsi l'aiguille directrice de mon électromètre, en 1849, et aux époques qui ont precédé et suivi, je n'aurais pas à rechercher aujourd'hui, si mon instrument a pu subir un dérangement temporaire, ni à m'occuper d'observations étrangères qui puissent contrôler les miennes.

Si vous pensez que ces remarques si simples puissent être de quelqu'utilité, ou qu'elles puissent porter d'autres physiciens à entreprendre des séries d'observations électriques si nécessaires à la Science, je vous prie de faire de cette lettre tel usage que vous jugerez convenable. Je me soumets entièrement à vous, comme au juge le plus compétent en ces matières.

Je vous prie de vouloir bien présenter mes hommages à Madame Faraday, et de recevoir, mon cher et illustre confrère, mes compliments les plus respectueux,

Votre ami
QUÉTELET

Je ne vous parle pas de la mort d'Oersted:[3] cette nouvelle m'est d'autant plus penible que ce grand physicien m'honorait de son amitié. Oersted et Schumacher[4] à des termes si rapprochés!

[1] There are three Schlagintweit's (brothers) listed in Poggendorff. The eldest, Hermann Rudolph Alfred (1826–82), was 25 years old in 1851; his brothers were 22 and 18, respectively. This leads me to choose him as the one referred to by Quételet. His main works were on trips he took to England, Scotland, India, and Asia.
[2] A. Quételet, 'Sur l'électricité de l'air pendant ces derniers années, et sur les moyens d'obtenir des observations comparables', *BASB*, 18 (1851), 269.
[3] Hans Christian Oersted died 9 March 1851.
[4] Heinrich Christian Schumacher (1780–1850), Ordinary Professor of Astronomy at the University of Copenhagen.

[*Hollandse Maatschappij der Wetenschappen, previously unpublished*]

Royal Institution
22. March 1851

SIR

I have been greatly honored by the receipt of Your letter; and though proud of such a mark of confidence fear that I shall hardly prove deserving of it. If I understand rightly you desire me to say what great experiment or research there is, which, being important to science, is in the matter of expence beyond the reach of an individual, and deserves the assistance of the Royal Society of Sciences. For my own part I am so happily situated in this Institution, that I am sure if I could say that I needed even a very large sum up to £1000 or even £2000 to decide a great enquiry; I could raise it amongst our members, for my personal use, in a week. I therefore have every want satisfied; and am not able to mention a subject from amongst those which form the object of my own especial studies.

But there is a research which I will venture to suggest to your consideration for its importance which is to a large extent proved; — because of the character of the philosopher who has already entered into it; — and because of the circumstances which, as I have reason to suppose, have in part caused its cessation: — I refer to that on *Respiration* by Regnault[2] — which he has carried so far already; and the first fruits of which he has published

I cannot doubt that your meeting of 1852 will be important for Science, not merely as respects your own country but as regard [*sic*] the world. Such determinations for the advancement of knowledge do good every where not only by the direct fruits but by the example. I doubt not the meeting will be a happy one for the Society as a body & for its members individually: and in that happiness though at a distance I shall feel that I have the honor to share

I am Sir
With every respect
Your Most Obliged & Humble Servnt
M. FARADAY

[1] Jacques Gisbert Samuel van Breda (1788–1867), Secretary of the Dutch Academy of Science.
[2] Victor Regnault, the French chemist.

454 M. FARADAY to SIR J. F. W. HERSCHEL, 8 April 1851

[*R.S., previously unpublished*]

Royal Institution,
8 April 1851

MY DEAR SIR JOHN

I have no doubt you are aware of the lines on glass produced by M. Nobert[1] – I have received from him some rulings & a paper which he wishes me to present to the Royal Society & I propose doing so by next Thursday[2] but I thought you would like in the mean time to see an attempt to measure the length & velocity of the undulations of a ray of light by the direct application of a scale to them.

Ever Yours Truly,
M. FARADAY.

[1] See Letter 400.
[2] See *PRS*, 6 (1850–4), 43.

455 M. F. MAURY[1] to M. FARADAY, 16 April 1851

[*I.E.E., previously unpublished*]

National Observatory,
Washington W.6
April 16$\frac{\text{th}}{}$ 1851

MY DEAR SIR,

I have rec^{d}. your letter of the 24th. Ult^{o} with the Copy of the "Experimental researches in Electricity 24$\frac{\text{th}}{}$ 25$\frac{\text{th}}{}$ 26th & 27$\frac{\text{th}}{}$ Series" which you had the kindness to send, and for which I thank you most heartily.

I need not say how eagerly these several papers were devoured; I have studied them with profit and pleasure; and admired, step by step as I went along, the true spirit of philosophical research that pervades them.

To me, some of your results look very much like a clew which you have placed in the hands of physicists to guide them through dark and doubtful places of research.

It may lead through many tortuous windings before it brings us to the end, but we look to you still further; You must not tire.

Will you not therefore embrace in your researches the electric or magnetic properties of Sea water at various temperatures? for it appears to me that our philosophy is as much at fault in accounting for the velocity of the Gulf Stream, as it is for the cause of magnetism.

The Mississippi river, where its fall has been computed at 2$\frac{1}{2}$ inches to the mile, is said to have an hourly velocity of 1$\frac{1}{2}$ miles. *But*, the Gulf Stream, running on a *water level*, maintains a velocity of 4, and reaches occasionally a velocity of 5 miles, an hour.

I am prepared to show that the Trade Winds have very little to do with giving direction and force to the currents of the sea, and there is room for the conjecture that the submarine currents are as regular if not as active as those at the surface.

What is the cause of this great velocity of the Gulf stream on a *water* level? Not gravitation certainly

The difference of Specific gravity between the hot waters of the Gulf Stream and the cold waters of the poles would cause *motion*; but unless some other agent were concerned, not with such velocity as that of the Gulf Stream; nor can it be comprehended how, without the help of some other agent, the waters of the Gulf Stream should collect themselves together, and flow to the North in a body, as they do.

That the waters of the Gulf stream do not readily mingle with those of the ocean about them, we know; and if you will do me the favor to look at pp 15–20 "Investigations of the Winds and Currents of the Sea"[2] several copies of which I have caused to be placed at your disposal, you will find some striking evidence of this fact.

Why is this? the very waters through which the Gulf Stream is flowing, are themselves bound down to the Trade Wind regions, to supply the air with vapor, to have their temperature raised, to enter the Gulf, to perform their circuit, and to issue thence as Gulf Stream water, invested with antagonistic principles – so to speak – Whence is this antagonism derived? meaning by Antagonism, in this place, simply the indisposition of the two waters – those flowing from the Gulf and those through which they flow, to commingle.

The reluctance of the waters of any two streams when they meet, to mingle is often manifested, and perhaps the display of this propensity by those of the Gulf Stream may not be considered remarkable, except as to distance and extent.

If you will look at the shape of the Gulf Stream you will be struck with its cuniform proportions; From the Straits of Bemini to the Grand Banks it is like a wedge, with its apex cleaving the Straits

What has this form and the pressure of the cold and therefore heavier waters which make the bed and banks of the Gulf Stream, to do with its velocity? *S*triking analogies might be pointed out in this connexion.

You will observe too, that according to the Storm tracks which meteorologists assign to the West India Hurricanes, those storms manifest by their course, a tendency towards the waters of the Gulf Stream, conforming with it in their general direction

Can therefore the waters of this Stream, and the air above them, be more or less paramagnetic or diamagnetic, than the sea waters generally?

Why may not the oxygen of the water be paramagnetic, as well as the oxygen of the air? or are the gasses and salts of sea water capable of any magnetic influences? If the oxygen of the water be magnetic will not that of its vapor be magnetic also? If an affirmative reply be given to these interrogations, would it not be suggestive of the agency through which, or by which, the Gulf Stream rules the course of the Storm, and preserves its own peculiarities?

You will, I hope, understand me in making the above remarks, and in propounding the above interrogatories.

I make the remarks with the hope of interesting you, and of engaging your thoughts upon these captivating subjects; and I ask the questions, in the true spirit of philosophical inquiry, so well described in your 2702 et seq, as moving you to your beautiful train of researches.

Will you not therefore – or is it your intention to do so, or would it be useless – to extend your "Researches in Electricity" to the sea, its gases, & its salts, and its vapors, and determine as to the degree and nature of "Aqueous Magnetism" if there be such a thing.

Reading your remarks as to the great "Magnetic lense" [*sic*] which follows the sun through the atmosphere and studying the diagrams of magnetic declination at Toronto & St. Petersburg[3] I was led to ask myself the question, What have the Gulf Stream and the mantle of warmth which it spreads over the extra tropical North and places between St. Petersburg and Toronto to do with the time and period of the great "sun swing" of the needle at the two places. One place has a great extent of land surface to the East – the other to the West and the two are separated by the warm waters of the Gulf Stream.

I hope you will pardon me for trying so earnestly to tempt you out to sea. I am there, and often find myself bewildered, and shall be most happy to come within your hail, and get fresh points of departure from you now and then

Respectfully &c
M. F. MAURY

The charts &c referred to by Lieut Maury, will be forwarded to you in a package to John W. Parker, Bookseller, if possible by next London Packet [word illeg.] of 24 inst – or 1st [word illeg.]

Very truly yours
GEO MANNING[4]

New York April 23/51

[1] Matthew Fontaine Maury (1806–73), U.S. Naval officer and pioneer oceanographer.
[2] *Lieut. Maury's investigations of the winds and currents of the sea*, Washington, D.C., 1851.
[3] See Series 26, *ERE*.
[4] George Manning, Lieutenant (1824), R.N. Ret.

[*R.I., Tyndall's Journal,*[1] *previously unpublished*]

Hastings
April 19, 1851.

DEAR SIR,

Whilst here resting for a while I take the opportunity of thanking you for your letter of February 4 and also for the copy of the paper in the "philosophical Magazine" which I have received.[2] I had read the paper before, and was very glad to have the development of your researches more at large than in your letter. Such papers as yours make me feel more than ever the loss of memory I have sustained, for there is no reading them, or at least retaining the argument, under such a deficiency.

Mathematical formulae more than anything require quickness and surety ... in receiving and retaining the true value of the symbols used and when one has to look back at every moment to the beginning of a paper, to see what H or α or β mean, there is no making way. Still though I cannot hold the whole train of reasoning in my mind at once I am fully able to appreciate the value of the results you arrive at, and it appears to me they are exceedingly well established and of very great consequence. These elementary laws of action are of so much consequence in the development of the nature of a force which, like magnetism, is as yet new to us.

My views with regard to the cause of the annual, diurnal, and some other variations are not yet published though printed. The next part of the "Philosophical Transactions" will contain them. I am very sorry I am not able to send you a copy from those allowed to me, but I have had so many applications from those who had some degree of right that they are all gone. I only hope that when you see the "Transactions" you may find reason to think favourably of my hypotheses. Time does not lessen my confidence in the view I have taken but I trust when relieved from my present duties, and somewhat stronger in health to add experimental results regarding oxygen so that the mathematicians may be able to take it up.

As you say in the close of your letter I have far more confidence in the one man who works mentally and bodily at a matter than in the six who merely talk about it – and I therefore hope and am fully pursuaded that you are working.

Nature is our kindest friend and best critic (exciter?) in experimental science, if we only allow her intimations to fall unbiassed on our minds. Nothing is so good as an experiment which, whilst it sets an error right, gives (as a reward for our humility in being reproved) an absolute advancement in knowledge.

I am, my dear Sir,
your very obliged and faithful Servant
M. FARADAY

[1] Copied in by John Tyndall.
[2] J. Tyndall, 'On the Laws of Magnetism', *PM*, 4 s., 1 (1851), 266.

457 M. FARADAY to A. QUÉTELET, 19 April 1851

[*J. Pelseneer, 'Notes on some unpublished letters from Faraday to Quételet', 'Annals of Science', 1 (1936), 451*]

Royal Institution
19 April 1854[1]

MY DEAR QUETELET

Directly that I received your letter I translated it and sent it to the Philosophical Magazine where I have no doubt you have seen its insertion and I trust it will induce some to join with you in the observation of atmospheric electricity. Your observations regarding the first part of the year 1849 are most interesting and I have full confidence in them so that though it may in some degree (& a large one) be unfortunate that there are not other observations made elsewhere to compare with yours still it is of the utmost consequence that yours have been made & I hope they will awake the sleepy observers.

You flatter me by the manner in which you receive my portrait. I do not think much of my own face but I have very great pleasure in looking upon yours and it brings by association all your kind feelings towards me back to my mind and very pleasant they are.

I have sent you a long paper or rather several papers a little while ago[2] certain were on atmospheric magnetism I have no fear as to the experimental part & I entertain hopes that the hypothetical part may find favour before your philosophic mind. My hopes in it are not as yet any less than at any former time – but I shall leave the paper to tell its own story.

I am not quite right in health and though I have from habit dated from the Royal Institution am really at Hastings on the Seashore waiting on rest & fresh air

Ever My dear M. Quetelet
Your faithful Servant
M. FARADAY

[1] See Letter 452. The date is clearly 1851.
[2] Series 26 and 27, *ERE*.

458 W. SNOW HARRIS to M. FARADAY, 25 April 1851

[*I.E.E., previously unpublished*]

Plymouth,
25 April 1851

MY DEAR FARADAY

I am in possession of your late researches in Elect[y]. printed in the First Part of the Philosophical Transactions for this present year, with which I am greatly charmed and instructed, and for which I feel deeply indebted to you When I look at what you have done in Science, and your still brilliant progress, I am inclined to say of you, as the Marquis de L'Hospital said of Newton "Does

Faraday eat drink and sleep like other men"? Your new discovery of Atmospheric Magnetism has opened a vast field of further research and impressed upon every new fact in this department of Science a peculiar Interest.

Having lately been myself engaged in the further prosecution of inquiries concerning the nature, laws, and mode of action of this species of force, and having arrived at several conclusions, apparently novel and important I have assembled them under the form of a Communication to the Royal Society. my first impulse however was to send the Paper to you, with a view of your looking it over, and presenting it, should you have thought it worthy of that honor – that would have been the course which my great admiration of your Labours and I will add my sincere personal regard toward you, would have led me, to adopt – but I considered, that I ought not to trouble you on such an occasion seeing how much you are hourly occupied in matters of such vast importance to the interests of Science. Thinking however, that the experimental part of my paper, may possibly be interesting to you, seeing that it is involved in those very researches in which you are engaged, and that it embraces new phenomena on Magnetism requisite to be considered & accounted for in any further view, we may be led to take of this mysterious power, I have determined on forwarding for your information a rough copy of my paper,[1] with the few following notices, so that you may have no trouble about it, and refer to the facts in it in such way as may suit your convenience. – I trust you will not think me intrusive in having ventured on this step – for after all I am not sure whether what I have done may be esteemed of sufficient importance to merit your consideration or not

The First pages consist of Introductory remarks and a reference to Instruments principally those you saw at the Geological Museum – but with improvements – This is followed by a particular view of the nature and mode of Operation of Magnetic Force, which is considered to arise out of what I have called waves of Induction or Magnetic reverberations set up between the surfaces of the opposed bodies, this may after all come to your Theory of Polarized particles – however if you think it worth while you may see what is said see 4 and 5. –

The laws of these inductive forces, as given in sec. 11 – may perhaps be found very well worth consideration – more especially when taken in connection with sec[ns] 23. 24 &c in which various laws of reciprocal force are fully elucidated – and all the several results of experiments by Hauksbee, Brook Taylor, Muschenbrek [*sic*] and others quite reconciled with the primary or more elementary laws of Magnetic force. I think this is so far interesting inasmuch as it helps to throw light on the nature of Magnetism – more especially in any reference of this peculiar Physical Force, to a general or universal principle as you seem disposed to do. So far as I see – we have in the phenomenon of a Magnet attracting Iron or that of two Magnetic poles attracting each other, the end only of a chain in our grasp, the other end of which is out of sight – Taking the reciprocal force near the magnet, it is certainly in no inverse ratio greater than that of the simple distance – as we recede from this into Space – the force becomes as the 3/2 power of the distance inversely then as the squares next the $\frac{5}{2}$ power then as the cubes of the distances inversely as stated by Newton and to what other inverse powers of the distances the force may extend as the action fades away in distance, it is almost impossible to say, without instruments of extreme sensibility such as we can not at present Boast of it is not possible to further investigate this point – You will see what I have said about this at Sec. 28 – Observe I do not say that you obtain the above laws in every instance successively with the same Magnet so much depends on the stability of the Inductive force. But I have no doubt whatever, not the slightest, of the facts, or that the experiments can in any way, either mathematical or Physical, be called in question –

In Sec 14 and following I think you will find a new class of Phenomena, unless I am unacquainted with all you & others have effected – e.g. you will find a curious and interesting example of *a diminished Magnetic Intensity by an increase of* SURFACE, being in magnetism, precisely the same experiment and class of fact, which Franklins [*sic*] Expe^t. of the can and Chain is in Electricity, or of any analogous experiment in which by extending the Surface the Electro-meter falls see Fig 7 sec (15). – You will further see (16) that a hollow tempered steel Cylinder becomes equally if not more powerfully magnetic than a similar solid-tempered steel Cylinder of the same diameter – shewing that it is the *Surface* and not the *mass* which is concerned – That a soft Iron Cylinder made to fit, and passed into a tempered hollow magnetic Cylinder operates as a sort of discharging rod, and permanently discharges as it were the opposite polarities, leaving a residuum as in the Leyden Jar &c &c. There are a class of facts here which perhaps may be interesting to you We have not I think as yet done enough in the way of investigating *internal* magnetism, as in your Electrical cage, you suspended and lived in.

– Sec. 34 – which treats of magnetic *quantity*, and the *law* of *measurement* is necessarily in association with some of your views sec. 2870. – I have not the slightest doubt but the law and condition of charge, is identical with Electricity *the force of attraction is as the square of* THE QUANTITY Sec. 35 contains my apology for terms, and refers to an Experiment Fig 8. with which I have been much satisfied & pleased from the great, I may say the *extreme precision* of its results–I do not think that such a combined action for the measurement of Volta magnetic force has been as yet effected. It served me in magnetism as the Unit Jar did in Electricity–and we have now I think a means at command for deter-mining how much more magnetism we have in the pole of any one magnet, or in any other point, than in the pole of any other magnet – the Exp^t in detail is given (36) the Law for quantity is in (34) afterward proved to be true.–

In sec. (42) is the problem of the magnetic development in different points of a Magnetic Bar, which has not always been accurately and definitely stated Finally – I have thought it worth while to refer in the end of this Paper to the peculiar parallism [*sic*] in the phenomena of the *Electrical Jar* and the *Magnetic Bar*, and to what Newton and others of the more remote periods of the R.S. have advanced on this subject, and which instead of being open to the severe animadversions and unmerited criticisms of many current mathematicians, are I firmly believe perfectly true in all their details and results, and quite consistent with demonstrable laws of magnetic force – you will see my views on this subject (45).

I do not see how it is possible to consider Magnetism as a central force or *emanation from a magnet* spreading out into space and getting weaker in Proportion to the amount of space spread over – all our experience is to my humble apprehension against such a deduction – and [reading doubtful] the action must be after all referred to an action between terminating planes; much after the fashion you have described in 1299.. 1302. 1301. 1163 &c – and in various other parts of your researches. Two terminating planes or surfaces with *something going on* or *established* between them is the immediate feature to me of both Electrical and magnetic force thus

In the attraction of a magnetic Pole *n* and a similar  mass of Iron *m*, end on, as it were, as in the above Diagram I do not at all believe, that the forces uniting in the other parts & about the center of the Bar *m* enter into the surface action at the pole – and for the reasons

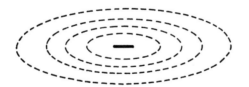

I have given (7) (18) (44) &c. It is not therefore as stated by Robison[2] a sort of balance of Electrical attractions & repulsions we have to consider, as referred to all the points of the mass of the opposed bodies in such a case; but an *exclusive* action between surfaces. – The *something which goes on between* the surfaces you call polarization of particles – So far as I see the general principle is true, but I think we shall have to refer this polarization to some medium different from that of air for I have no doubt whatever but that the force between a plane magnetic pole and an Iron Plate which goes on in vacuo in no sense differs in its nature from the force between a plane polar electrified surface and a neutral conducting plate. – I am quite sure that both these actions are identical all that the air does in Elec.y of high Intensity may be to arrest the passage of the Electy, thus [reading doubtful] in magnetism is not wanted –

627

Robison seems to think (Mech. Phil. vol iv p. 273) that the law of attraction as observed between magnets or between magnets & Iron, must be different from the REAL law of magnetic action – because he says the magnetism is always increasing or decreasing with the distance – but the ground I take in my paper is, that it is *really* this *increasing* or *decreasing* magnetism as depending on induction which *constitutes magnetic action* – it is in fact the combined effect of induction between the opposite poles at different distances which gives the law of the force; this IS the *real* magnetic action – there is *no other* – It appears to me that there has been a great bias with many profound mathematicians in favor of a certain law of magnetic force, which they think must be the same as the law of Gravity, and if we do not find it so by Exp^t. the Experiments are false, we *ought to find it so* – The more modern & French Theorys of Electricity & Magnetism depend much on the truth of this position all their fine mathematical superstructures are built on it – and I really do think in many instances, that if it were a point at issue between Poissons Mathematics and the course of Nature, very many would give it in favor of Poisson It is quite curious to see how severely every Experimental result is handled which does not coincide with the law of the inverse duplicate ratio of the distance. Robison cuts down at one sweep all the valuable exp^{ts} of Hauksbee,[3] Brook Taylor[4] Whiston,[5] Muschenbroek[6] & others, in as many words says they are worthless – that Electrical attractions & repulsions are not the most proper phenomena for declaring the precise law of variation yet was it from *those same attractions and repulsions* that both *Coulomb and Lambert*[7] deduced their law of magnetic force – Lambert especially resorted to the method of Hauksbee & Brook Taylor, certainly in a more refined way – now *their experimental enquiries* are quoted with confidence; and in no way objected to, in fact they were considered to have arrived at the *true law of the Force*: then again Newton having observed that magnetic attraction decreases in a certain case in the Inverse triplicate ratio of the distance – we are told in as many words by Biot,[8] that Newton was ignorant of the whole matter, and had not accurate Ideas of magnetic Phenomena, and so in a variety of other instances. In fact without in any way entering as you have done into a severe and close investigation of nature by Experiment many profound Mathematical men have been content to adopt a certain set of principles, derived it seems to me, not always from very unexceptionable experiments – and they seem determined to bend every thing to those principles. For my self I have no belief in Electrical & Magnetic fluids in their hypothetical density & distribution, in virtue of the assumed law of their constitution &c there is something to come yet far beyond all this – however we are still in the dark about it. – I have read over your attempt to establish a relation between Gravity & Electricity – I have not myself much hope of success by any direct experiment. – The results of the two forces being so very different – I can conceive no identity in these forces except through a sort of Aethereal medium in which all matter may be conceived to float and different relations or affections of which to the particles of common matter is in one case Gravity in another Electricity: but it is in vain for me to speculate on such things at this moment – You are the only Philosopher on Earth likely to throw light on the question.

I had always great misgivings relative to the changes which might ensue in vibrating a magnetic needle in air, and I pointed out some of these changes in my paper in the Edinb. Phil. Transactions for 1834 vol xiii. "On the Investigations of Magnetic Intensity &c" – and I felt quite assured at that time, that Christies Expts. relative to the Influence of Light Phil. Trans. 1825 were disturbed by taking the oscillations in air – all of which I have enlarged on at the close of that Paper see 33. – and I think you may find some Experiments there immediately coinciding with and bearing on what you say 2871 and the direct connection of the two is really very striking see also sec 34 and 35 of my paper above quoted. – Your observations on Atmospheric Magnetism confirm my view of the propriety of observing Intensity oscillations in vacuo – which I have always done as in the long series of Exp^{ts} in the Phil Trans for 1831 p 69.

I take it for granted, that by this time I have tired you out, but I find the subject so very interesting that I could continue to write about it to almost any extent, especially to you. I will however now bid you adieu & will subscribe myself your very faithful & affect. friend

W. SNOW HARRIS

1 See W. Snow Harris, 'On induced and other Magnetic forces', *PRS*, 6 (1850–4), 87.
2 John Robison, *A System of Mechanical Philosophy*, 4 vols., Edinburgh (1822), 4, 272.
3 Francis Hawksbee (?–1713), Curator of Experiments for the Royal Society in the early years of the eighteenth century.
4 Brook Taylor (1685–1731), mathematician and, with Hauksbee, an early investigator of the law of magnetic action.
5 William Whiston (1667–1752), Lucasion Professor of Mathematics at Cambridge from 1702 to 1710.
6 Pieter van Musschenbroek (1692–1761), Professor of Mathematics at the University of Leyden and natural philosopher.
7 Johann Heinrich Lambert (1728–77), 'Analyse de quelques expériences sur l'aimant', *MAWB*, 1766.
8 J. B. Biot, 'Notice historique sur la vie et les ouvrages de Newton', in Michaud, *Biographie Universelle*, 30, Paris, n.d., 366.

459 M. FARADAY to J. HENRY, 28 April 1851

[*Smithsonian Institution, previously unpublished*]

Royal Institution,
April 28, 1851

MY DEAR HENRY

The instant that I received your letter I applied to an Architect whom we employ Mr. Vulliamy,[1] to make me the necessary drawings of our Lecture room. I have only just received them. I do not know what has occasioned the delay but I could not help it. Why did you not come over yourself & see the room[2] & hear in it; & if needful speak in it (we should have been very glad to listen to you) so that you might have been well able to judge of your own knowledge how far it was worthy to suggest any thing or serve for imitation in your own great room? We should have been very glad to see you for we have not forgotten the pleasure we received at Your last visit.

Besides the Exhibition is coming on & though I am very little moved or excited by such things yet it would have been pleasant to see you here for any reason and as it is we do expect a number of very good things from your Country which we reckon also as half ours

I wonder whether I shall ever see America – I think not – the progress of years tells & their effect on me is to blot out many a fancy which in former days I thought might perhaps work up into realities – and so we fade away. Well I have had & have a very happy life at home nothing should make me regret that I cannot leave it & indeed when the time for decision comes – home always has the advantage Mrs. Faraday wishes to be kindly remembered to you We look at your face painted in light by Mayall & I dare say it like He & nature together have made you look very comfortable & I suspect that we have both altered much since last we saw each other My wife mourns with half mimic half serious countenance over my changes & chiefly that a curly head of hair has become a mere unruly grisly mop. I think that is on the whole the worst part of the change that 60 years nearly have made

and now having scratched this letter I merely wait for the Architects charge which is —— and shall then send it & the drawing off.

> Ever My dear Henry,
> Most truly Yours
> M. FARADAY

2 May. I have just obtnd the bill 5. 16. 6 which I have enclosed

> Yours Ever MF.

[1] Lewis Vulliamy (1791–1871), architect.
[2] The Lecture Theatre at the Royal Institution. See Letter 462.

460 A. DE LA RIVE to M. FARADAY, 27 May 1851
[*I.E.E., previously unpublished*]

> Vichy (Dept. de l'Allier)
> le 27 mai 1851.

MON CHER MONSIEUR,

Je ne veux pas tarder plus long-temps à venir vous remercier de votre bonne & aimable lettre que vous m'avez écrite il y a quelques mois.[1] Je suis, comme vous le verrez par la date de cette lettre à Vichy où m'ont envoyé les Médecins à la suite d'une indisposition assez grave que j'ai eue ce printemps. Je me trouve bien de cette cure & je crois qu'elle me guérira. Mais qu'est-ce que la guérison du corps quand le coeur est malade? Sous ce dernier rapport je ne vais guére mieux & il n'y a guère de chance que mon état s'améliore; je ne le voudrais même pas; car, chose singulière, dans la triste situation où je suis, on déteste sa souffrance & pourtant on ne voudrait pas ne pas l'avoir. Il n'y a, je le sais, qu'un seul remède à ce genre de douleurs morales; je le cherche autant que je puis, mais je suis homme & très homme, parconséquent [*sic*] faible & très faible & parconséquent [*sic*] j'ai des moments de désolation où il me semble que je n'ai plus la foi & que Dieu m'abandonne. Je suis sur [*sic*] que vous me comprenez & que vous me plaignez; je voudrais bien être soutenu d'en Haut comme vous l'êtes.

Je vois beaucoup Arago qui est aussi ici pour sa santé; il est arrivé bien malade, mais il semble qu'il est déjà un peu mieux. Vous savez combien sa conversation est intéressante; c'est incroyable combien il sait de choses & comme il les sait bien; aussi sa conversation est pour moi d'un immense intérêt. Nous parlons souvent de vous, car il est aussi l'un de vos grands admirateurs. Nous attendons avec une grande impatience votre mémoire sur les variations diurnes du magnétisme terrestre. Ce sujet nous intéresse d'autant plus que nous nous en sommes tous les deux beaucoup occupés. Je vous avertis que, jusqu'à ce que je connaisse votre théorie, je tiens assez à celle que j'ai donnée de ces phénomènes & que je n'entrevois pas encore trop bien comment vous pouvez rendre compte des anomalies du phénomène (*Cap de Bonne Espérance*) & de la différence qui existe entre l'hémisphère Sud & l'hémisphère Nord quant au tour dans lequel a lieu la variation diurne. Mais tout cela sera probablement éclairci quand on aura lu votre mémoire.

Je suis bien sûr que vous avez quelque chose de nouveau sur le métier; car vous êtes infatigable. Vous savez l'intérêt que je mets à vos recherches, aussi j'ose vous prier de m'écrire quelques lignes quand vous avez quelque chose de nouveau. L'intérêt de la Science est le seul parmi les intérêts humains avec celui de ma famille que j'essaie de conserver encore; & rien ne peut m'y aider davantage que quelques communications de votre part.

J'ai eu bien de la peine à me remettre à mon ouvrage;[2] c'est pour moi un travail plein de souvenirs doux & amers en même temps. Enfin j'ai pris courage & j'avance; mais, j'ai de temps à autre des moments de découragement qui m'ôtent toute possibilité de m'en occuper; alors je suis obligé momentanément de faire autre chose. Cette inconstance jointe à la maladie que j'ai eue ce printemps vous expliquera tous les retards qu'éprouve la publication de cet ouvrage qui aurait dû paraitre, il y a plus d'un an.

J'espère que votre santé est passablement bonne dans ce moment & qu'elle ne souffre pas de vos travaux multipliés. J'espère également que Madame Faraday est bien; veuillez avoir la bonté de me rappeler à son bon souvenir.

Pardonnez moi cette mauvaise lettre; j'ai obéi en vous écrivant au désir que j'avais de me rapprocher de vous par la pensée pendant quelques moments. Croyez moi, mon cher Monsieur, votre bien dévoué & affectionné

A. DE LA RIVE

Si vous avez le temps de m'écrire quelques lignes, je dois vous prévenir que je serai à *Vichy* jusqu'au 8 juin seulement & que de là je retournerai à *Genève* d'où je ne bougerai plus.

¹ See Letter 450.
² A. de la Rive, *Traité d'électricité théorique et appliquée*, 3 vols., Paris, 1854–8.

461   M. FARADAY to C. BABBAGE, 3 June 1851
[*British Museum, Add. mss. 37194, f. 541, previously unpublished*]

Royal Institution
3 June 1851

MY DEAR BABBAGE
I have received & heartily thank you for your book.¹ I have begun to read it – I dare say if I had seen it before it was in print I should have been amongst those who would have tried to persuade you from publishing it The fact is I grieve that your powerful mind ever had cause to turn itself in such a direction and away as it were from its high vocation & fitting occupation Still I know that we cannot avoid the checks & jars of a naughty world and that at times we are driven from our most direct courses by very unworthy objects under our feet

Ever My dear Babbage
Very Truly Yours
M. FARADAY.

¹ C. Babbage, *The Exposition of 1851; or, Views of the Industry, the Science and the Government of England*, London, 1851.

462   J. HENRY to M. FARADAY, 4 June 1851
[*I.E.E., previously unpublished*]

Smithsonian Institution
June 4ᵗʰ 1851

MY DEAR DR. F.
I owe you many thanks for your prompt attention to my inquiries relative to the lecture room of the Royal Institution¹ and also for your very interesting letter of the 28ᵗʰ of april. It was received in Washington while I was absent on a visit to Cincinnati to attend an extra meeting of the American Association for

the advance of science. This was my first visit to the great basin of the Mississippi and I have returned with ideas much expanded of the fertility, resources, and extent of this country. The site of Cincinnati was about fifty years ago a wilderness and it is now occupied by a city which contains 120.000 inhabitants. The houses are built of brick and free stone and the whole country around has the appearance of a long settled place We, (Mr. A. Bache and myself) returned by the way of Niagara Falls, a distance, from Cincinnati, of upwards of 1100 miles, which can now be travelled in three days by rail road and steam boat. Steam as a locomotive power is of great importance in every part of the world, but is no where of as much value as in this country. A friend of mine, one of the Judges of the supreme court of the U.S. has just returned to Washington after deciding 200 law cases and traveling 9000 miles since the 1st of March. I have also been much impressed with the effects produced by the telegraph; lines of which are now forming a net work over the whole inhabited part of the United States. In my late tour I could every where immediately communicate with Washington. On one occasion I held a conversation with a gentleman at a distance of 600 miles; the answers were immediately returned. In dry winter weather I am informed that communications can be sent immediately from Philadelphia to Louisville through 1200 miles of wire This is effected by calling into action a series of batteries distributed along the line.

It would give me much pleasure to see Mrs. F. and yourself in this country and though in comparison with england we could show you nothing of much interest in the way of art, I think you would be gratified with the objects of nature. In our boasted improvements you might possibly be disappointed. An englishman and an american look on these things from different points of view & arrive at very different conclusions. The european finds cities here which in comparison with those he is familiar with in the old world often appear in no respect remarkable while the american after a few years absence returns to a place which he left a wilderness finds it the site of a large and prosperous city. The one compares this country with the conditions of Europe as they now are, the other this country with itself at different times and is astonished at the change.

I am pleased to learn that I still hold a place in the memory of Mrs. F. and yourself The presentation of the daguerrotypes was a proposition of Mayoll [reading doubtful] himself which I did not know he had carried into execution. I had some thoughts of going to London this summer but felt myself too poor to bear the expense of the voyage besides this I would not care to be there during the excitement of the great exhibition and indeed I would by far prefer seeing one of your recent experiments on Diamagnetism than all the contents of the crystal palace.

I send you a copy of an engraving of the smithsonian building and also of a portrait of Smithson[2] with whom I believe you were acquainted. I regret to say that the building, though picturesque, is not well adapted to the uses of the

Institution. This architecture of the 12th century is not well adapted to the wants of the 19th. I consider the crystal palace the true architectural exponent of the feelings and wants of the present day.

Please give the accompanying draft to Mr Vulliamy and ask him to send me a receipt for the amount which may serve as my [word illeg.]. Please also to request the secretary of the Royal Institution to address any communications intended for me to Washington instead of Princeton my former residence.

> With my best wishes for your
> continued health and prosperity
> I remain very truly
> your friend & servant
> JOSEPH HENRY

1 See Letter 459.
2 James Lewis Smithson (1765–1829), chemist, who left the U.S. Government the money with which the Smithsonian Institution was created.

463 M. FARADAY to A. DE LA RIVE, 5 June 1851

[*Bibliothèque publique et universitaire de Genève, ms. 2316, f. 71–2, previously unpublished*]

Royal Institution
5 June 1851

MY DEAR DE LA RIVE

Your last letter[1] has affected me deeply and has renewed my sorrow on your account. I knew of your sad loss and had heard also of your personal illness & its very serious character: but I knew also that you had that within that might sustain you under such deep trials – Do not be discouraged – remember – wait patiently. Surely the human being must suffer when the dearest ties are rent but in the midst of the deepest affliction there is yet present consolation for the humble minded which (through the power that is over us) may grow up and give peace & quietness & rest. Your letter draws me out to say so much for I feel as if I could speak to you on account of something more than mere philosophy or reason. They give but a very uncertain consolation in such troubles as yours. and indeed nothing is more unsatisfactory to me than to see a mere rational philosopher's mind fighting against the afflictions that belong to our present state & nature – as on the contrary nothing is more striking than to see such afflictions met by the weakest with resignation & hope. Forgive me if my words seem to you weak and unfit for the occasion. I speak to you as I have felt and as I still hope to feel to the end. and your affectionate letter has drawn me forth

I have nothing to say to you about Philosophy. For the duties of the season & the exhibition Jury work occupy all my poor ability which through a failing memory becomes less & less. As to my last papers I hope you will find them at home & there you will see how I consider the Cape of Good Hope & other cases.

I intended to have written to you at Vichy but I think that now I had better send to Geneva. Indeed I ought to apologize for this letter both for its bad writing & its unconnected matter but if I wait to write a better it may turn out worse. for I have let my thoughts run on though unconnectedly and as to my hand writing. I find the muscles will not obey my will as they used to do and that I cannot write as well as I would The machine is becoming rusty. Let it. there is a time for all things – and there is a time without end coming

Ever My dear De la Rive
Your affectionate friend
M. FARADAY

¹ See Letter 460.

464   G. WILSON to M. FARADAY, 12 June 1851
[*I.E.E., previously unpublished*]

24 Brown Square
Edinburgh
June 12th 1851

DEAR SIR

Observing from the Athenaeum that you are about to Lecture on Ozone,¹ I take the liberty of addressing a few lines to you on the subject, though afraid that they may not reach you in time.

Schönbein has suggested that Ozone may be the cause of Influenza, & Mr Robert Hunt has drawn attention to the probable increased presence of the substance in question in the atmosphere at the period when the last Epidemic of Cholera was passing away.² What I wish to suggest in the way of a query is that if Ozone can produce influenza it should be possible to induce that artificially by causing Ozonised Air to be breathed, as Berzelius produced in himself severe bronchitis, by inspiring air containing Seleniuretted Hydrogen, which Dr Prout thought *might be* the cause of Influenza. Experiments, however, on the Subject seem scarcely needed, since for more than a Century Electricians have undesignedly developed around their persons large quantities of Ozone, and have been exposed for hours together to Air, much more highly charged with Ozone, than upon any hypothesis the atmosphere can ever be. I should like to put this question to you, in case you think it worth while answering publicly. Has it happened in your own very extensive experience of the action of the largest Friction Hydro-Electric- & Galvanic Machines, & batteries to observe in yourself or your assistants *or audience*, any development of a disease resembling influenza? Surely within a Century we should have heard of a *Morbus Electricus*, if Electricians had been sufferers from the action of Ozone?

Conclusions have been drawn as to the relative quantity of Ozone in the air, from the development of a blue colour of varying intensity in Starch-paste mixed with Iodide of Potassium, but according to M. Chatin's communication made to the Academy of Sciences at Paris (Séance du 5 Mai 1851 L'Institut pour 7 Mai 1851. p 148), the atmosphere always contains free Iodine, so that experiments thought to prove the presence of Ozone in the Air are exposed to a serious fallacy. In the case also of Iodide of Potassium *used alone*, I venture to suggest that the same Agency, Electricity of High Tension which developes Ozone in the Air, also developes at least when undergoing discharge, Nitric Acid, which by liberating Iodine from Iodide of Potassium may give a deceptive appearance as to the presence of free Ozone. I do not wish to call in question the presence of Ozone in the atmosphere, but merely to refer to the doubtful character of some of the supposed proofs of its presence, and to suggest the improbability on the ground of the impunity with which Electricians breathe Ozone, (if I am right in believing in this impunity) of the Ozone-theory of Influenza.

I trust you will excuse this intrusion. Your Courtesy on former occasions induces me to send this hasty scrawl to catch the post.

I Remain
Yours very truly
GEORGE WILSON M.D

1 Faraday delivered a lecture at the Royal Institution 'On Schönbein's Ozone' on 13 June 1851.
2 I have been unable to discover the sources of either of these statements.

465 H. FOX TALBOT to M. FARADAY, 15 June 1851
[*Ms. collection of Dr E. T. Conybeare, OBE, No. 137, Catalogue of Historical Manuscripts Commission, previously unpublished*]

Lacock Abbey,
Chippenham
June 15/51

DEAR SIR

The important experiment tried yesterday at the Royal Inst^n. succeeded perfectly. A printed paper was fastened to a disk, which was then made to revolve as rapidly as possible. The battery was discharged, and on opening ye Camera it was found to have received an impression. The image of the printed letter was just as sharp as if the disk had been motionless. I am not aware of this experiment having ever been made before – I should be happy to repeat it in the presence of some of our Scientific friends, but I wish first to obtain effects on a greater scale of development and therefore I should be very glad if you would devise means of augmenting the brilliancy of the flash. Two methods occur to me which I submit for your judgment. (1) Professor Hare of America says that if a flat coil of copper ribbons is placed in the circuit the spark from a Leyden jar is greatly increased in brilliancy. Supposing this to be equally true of a battery, would it not be desirable to adopt it?

(2) If the battery discharge were taken thro' a tube lined spirally with pieces of tinfoil (one of which is at the R. Inst[n].) would not the total effect of these numerous sparks light up the room more than the single discharge does?

If a truly instantaneous photographic representation of an object has never been obtained before (as I imagine that it has not) I am glad that it should have been first accomplished at the Royal Inst[n]. –

Believe me
Dear Sir
Ever truly yours
H. F. TALBOT

466 · J.PLÜCKER to M. FARADAY, 18 June 1851
[*I.E.E.*, *previously unpublished*]

Bonn,
18th of June 1851

DEAR SIR!

A longe [*sic*] [reading doubtful] time ago I got your last kind letter. Soon after receiving it I sent you „sous bande" the two first papers on the magnetic axes of cristals (a third and last one is not yet finished). I paid them at the post office, but four months after I got [reading doubtful] them back, with the words "Rowland [reading doubtful] refused". Newspapers are sent to England in the same way for a trifle of money. When there is a mistake, I would be angry if by my fault. You will get the papers now by a gentlemen [*sic*] returning to London. With pleasure I had brought them myself, in this time of the Exhibitions fever and the meetings of the British Association; but I cannot leave Bonn befor August.

I have joined to the papers a new metal, named Donarium (Do) discovered by professor Bergeman[1] of Bonn, thinking it may interest yourself and perhaps also the chemical section of the Association. M. H Rose[2] confirmed prof. Bergeman's results. Fearing the reduced metal might be altered by crossing the Channel, he (*B*) prefers to present the hydrat of the oxyd (. . .+Aq.) You may reduce it easily, better by potassium or natrium than by hydrogenium. I give allso a specimen of the mineral (Orangit), which is very rare, containing the new metal. –

Last sumer unhappily I did not succede [*sic*] in repeating E Becquerels

7-2

experiments with oxigenium absorbed by charcoal.[3] At the same time I convinced myself that the results of my former experiments which induced me to admit the dilatation of air in the neighbourhood of of [sic] a magnetic pole, were illusorious. It may be proved mathematically, that there can be in such cases no sensible effect at all. In that desolate state of my head, regarding the magnetisme [sic] of the gases, I received with great satisfaction the first notice of your recent experiments with oxigenium. I instantly undertook a long series of experiments, making use of a very fine balance of glass, indicating with full certainty $\frac{1}{10000}$ of a gramme. In that way I may determine the magnetic power nearly with the same accuracy, then the weight of a body. I concluded first from my experiments that the specific magnetism of a body is a quantity as constant as the specific heat &c. &c. The specific magnetism of oxigenium is exactly proportional to its density; it is not changed in a sensible way, when this gase [sic] is mixed with hydrogenium nitrogenium, carbonic oxyd, chlore &c &c. The specific magnetism of pure iron being 1000000, that of oxigenium is very near 3500. Hydrogenium, Chlore, Cyanic acid, carbonic oxyd, carbonic acid, (protoxide d'azote) &c &c were not affected, the first one showing only a trace of diamagnetic action, but certainly not amounting to $\frac{1}{200}$ of that on oxigenium.

Two months ago I sent two elaborate papers to Poggendorff but till now I got no copies of them. Two weeks ago I sent a new paper, schowing [sic] by experiment the coercitiv force of the gases, similar to that of steel.[4]

By far the most curious and allways unexpected results presented Nitrogenium in its different combinations with oxigenium. I undertook about it a laborious series of experiments not yet quite finished. But I hope to overpower these days the last difficulty by condensing ... (acide hyponitrique) in its purity. I expect the condensed gase will be strongly magnetic, as it is in its aëriform state. Then I shall be able to answer in a most accurate way one important question, by comparing the specific magnetism of the same substance in the two different states.

Within the narrow limits of a letter it seems to me rather impossible to give a true account of my researches. I'll spare some of the results already obtained to a next comunication.

I hope your health be quite good now; with great satisfaction at least I may conclude it from what you worked in science. Tis only the impulse given by you, from which originates my recent researches.

With all my heart, Sir I am
Yours very truly
PLÜCKER

[1] Carl Wilhelm Bergemann (1804–84), Professor of Chemistry at the University of Bonn. See his 'Beiträge zur Kenntniss eines neuen metallischen Körpers', *AP*, 158 (1851), 561.
[2] Heinrich Rose (1795–1864), Professor of Chemistry at the University of Berlin.
[3] See E. Becquerel, 'De l'action du magnétisme sur tous les corps', *AC*, 3 s., 28 (1850), 283.
[4] For these papers, see *RSCSP*.

[*I.E.E., previously unpublished*]

Nancy,
le [ ] July 1851.

Monsieur et illustre promoteur de la Science magneti que &c.

Je profite avec bien de l'empressemant [*sic*] du voyage de L'un de mes compatriotes qui va visiter lexposition Europeenne pour me rapeller a votre bienveillant Souvenir et vous remercier de votre bonne reception l an dernier. j'étais alors plein de vigueur quoique fort agé mais les fatigues de mon voyage qui ont éccedé [*sic*] mes forces m'ont donné une gastralgie des plus pénibles [reading doubtful] et des plus menacantes. toutes fois je ne me repentirai jamais d'avoir visité un eminant [*sic*] physicien, d'avoir vu l une des plus belles ville du monde et d'avoir eu des relations avec des personnes dun peuple qui brille aux premiers rangs – par son industrie, *son bon sens son attachemant* [*sic*] *a Ses* loix et Son respect pour l autorité de Son gouvernemant [*sic*]. je Suis parti de ce pays avec le desir de le voire [*sic*] de nouveau et plus en detail mais ma Santé Sy oppose encore plus que mes 82 ans et c'est un grand Sujet de regret.

j ai lu dans les ouvrages periodiques quelques notices Sur vos ingenieux travaux relatifs au magnétisme des gaz mais ils me Sont insuffisants je serais bien reconnaissant Si vous pouviez me donner le memoire qui les contient – ou quelque [illeg.] quelquanalyse bien faite. le jeune becquerel[2] fils de mon ami a ausi [*sic*] travaillé Sur ce Sujet mais que dire du vide ou [*sic*] il fait jouer à lether le meme role quaux gaz. lEther est une hipothese commode mais. . . .

j ai lhonneur de vous faire hommage de quelques petits travaux extraits des memoires de l'academie de Nancy ou [*sic*] j'habite.[3] veuillez aggréer avec indulgence et les communiquer a Mrs vos confreres aux quels je les adresse *parmi ces memoires il en est un Sur le quel je desire extremement fixer de nouveau votre attention.* cest celui ou [*sic*] jai etabli l'universalité du magnetisme[4] depuis vigoureusement prouvé par vos decouvertes mon but principal est de vous demander *franchemant* [*sic*] votre opinion Sur la pretention que j'éléve d'avoir le premier depuis votre illustre compatriote Gilbert qui en avait deja donné quelqu'idee; d'avoir, deja, contre lopinion de Coulomb alors generallemant [*sic*] adoptée proclamé au nom de tous les physiciens qui m'ont fourni les preuves l'universalite de la force, ou puissance &c magnetique. *votre opinion Sera pour moi d'un grand poid veuilleʒ ne pas me refuser cette grace.* Si vous avez la bonté de menvoyer quelques uns de vos memoire en original ou en extrait vous pouvez me les adresser par l'intermédiaire de la maison de librairie J. B. Balliere regent Street et a paris rue de lEcole de médecine

agreéz [*sic*] Monsieur les humbles temoignages de la plus haute consideration de Votre Serviteur

Mr Haldat

¹ Charles Nicolas Haldat (1770–1852), Secretary of the Academy of Sciences, Letters and Arts of Nancy.
² Edmond Becquerel.
³ For these papers, see *RSCSP*.
⁴ Probably C. N. Haldat, 'Recherches sur l'universalité de la force magnétique', *MSSN*, 1845–55.

468 M. FARADAY to J. HENRY, 23 July 1851
[*Smithsonian Institution, previously unpublished*]

Royal Institution
London
23 July 1851.

MY DEAR DR. HENRY

I received your last letter and herewith enclose Mr. Vulliamy's receipt¹ I thought I had sent it in the former letter but found out my mistake

Your account of the country you have been through excites me far more than Palaces or Exhibitions. The beauties of nature are what I most enjoy. Scenery, and above [all] the effects of light & shadow – Morning & Evening & Midday or a storm or a cloudy sky My predeliction is for out of door beauties & just now I and my wife have run away from London to the seaside to get quiet & rest. My head even now aches & I feel very weary

When I left London I had not received the Engraving of the Smithsonian Building but I dare say I shall find it upon my return I thank you very heartily for it. I did not know Mr Smithson though I think I used to hear his name I was then of no consequence My wife send[s] [*sic*] her kindest remembrances with mine.

Ever my dear friend
Yours very Truly
M. FARADAY

¹ See Letter 462.

469 M. FARADAY to B. VINCENT, 27 July 1851
[*R.I., previously unpublished*]

Tynemouth
27 July, 1851.

MY DEAR FRIEND

I purposed writing to you about this time but did not expect to do so under such circumstances. It is the Sabbath day & yet I am confined to this place and unable to meet with the very few brethren who are at Newcastle – My system had sunk too low and last week it settled into an attack of sore throat so that I speak with labour can hardly swallow even the Saliva because of the pain &

have at last called in the Dr. We are glad of it for he has put us on the right track (and we were not quite right in that which we had been pursuing) and I hope in a day or two to get out of the house again Mrs. Geo Buchanan came to us here & last Sabbath day we had the very unexpected pleasure of her husbands company on his way home. She has been very poorly and so little benefitted by Tynemouth that on Thursday she went away to Newcastle or rather to Rye Hill – We had a letter from her this morning in which she says she is better. She tells us of the death of Mrs. Macnaughton the wife of a brother at Edinburgh – and also the death of Mr Pratts grandson Thomson very suddenly.

Mr. Paradise seems very fairly well We had an outing one day, (last Tuesday) he, D. Reid & I, and enjoyed it very much together though I rather think I was not in a state to be braced up but rather knocked down by it. Mr. & Mrs. Deacon have arrived but I have not yet been able to see them, perhaps in two or three days I may get into Newcastle.[1]

We do not think of coming home until about Wednesday week – if all goes on well Now on looking at my list of remembrance dates yesterday I found that would be after your holiday had begun. I do not expect that will be any inconvenience to you since the arrangements are all made not to interfere one with another and Anderson is fully instructed & trusted by me in his duties, but if there is anything I have not perceived or that you wish attended to write me a line In any case I should be very glad to see a word from you – I feel very weary as to letter writing myself but I am glad when others write to me My wife sends her love to you and yours with mine.

Ever My dear friend,
Yours affectionately
M. FARADAY

[1] All the above-named people were Sandemanian friends of Faraday's whom I am unable to identify further.

470 M. FARADAY to J. TYNDALL, 1 August 1851
[*R.I., Tyndall's Journal,*[1] *previously unpublished*]

Tynemouth
1st Aug. 1851

MY DEAR SIR,

Your letter finds me here ill of a quinsey but now recovering and though I cannot write much I determined to answer you at once. In the first place many thanks for the specimens which I shall find presently at home. I was very sorry not to see you make your experiments but hope to realise the [blank in ms.] results which interest me extremely. I want to have a very clear view of them.

But now for the Toronto matter. In such a case private relationships have much to do in deciding the matter, but if you are comparatively free from such considerations and have simply to balance your present power of doing good with that you might have at Toronto then I think I should (in your place) choose the latter. I do not know much of the university but I trust it is a place where a man of science and a true philosopher is required and where in return such a man would be nourished and cherished in proportion to his desire to advance natural knowledge. I cannot doubt indeed that the university would desire the advancement of its pupils and also of knowledge itself so I think that you would be exceedingly fit for the position and I hope the position fit for you. If I had any power of choosing or recommending I would aid your introduction both because I know what you have already done for science and I heard how you could state your facts and treat your audience.

Now I do not, for I cannot profer you a certificate because I have in every case refused for many years past to give on the application of Candidates: neither indeed have you asked me for one. Nevertheless I wish to say that when I am asked about a candidate by those who have the choice or appointment I never refuse to answer and indeed if my opinion could be useful and there was a need of it you might use this letter as a private letter shewing it or any part of it to any whom it might concern.

And now you must excuse me from writing more, for my muscles are stiff and weak and my head giddy.

Ever my dear Dr. Tyndall
Yours most truly
M. FARADAY

¹ Transcribed by John Tyndall into his journal.

471 M. FARADAY to [no addressee, but one of the secretaries of the Royal Society], 19 August 1851
[R.S., previously unpublished]

Royal Institution,
19 Aug 1851.

I consider Harris' paper¹ as an important experimental paper and one which should be printed in the Transactions not only because of the character of the author & the right he has to speak as a philosophical authority – but for its own manifest merit – It contains the proofs of what I believe to be facts in magnetism and which as they may not be set aside must be admitted & finally explained in any view of the nature of magnetic force which can hope to keep its place in the future progression of science

M.F.

¹ The paper was not published in the *PT*. See *PRS*, 6 (1850–4), 87 for an account of it.

472   G. B. AIRY to M. FARADAY, 2 September 1851
[*Royal Observatory, Herstmonceux, Misc. Corres., 1851, Sect. 50*]

Royal Observatory
Greenwich (copy)
1851 Sept. 2

MY DEAR SIR

Dr. Tyndall writes to me in reference to his candidature for a Toronto professorship.[1] I had just read his last paper in the Phil. Mag.[2] & thought it good. But he refers me distinctly to you – and thus I am as it were compelled to trouble you with the question whether *you* do not think him a good man? Yours very truly,

G. B. AIRY

[1] See *B.J.* 2, 296.
[2] J. Tyndall, 'On the polarity of bismuth, including an examination of the magnetic field', *PM*, 4 s., 2 (1851), 334.

473   M. FARADAY to G. B. AIRY, 5 September 1851
[*Royal Observatory, Herstmonceux, Misc. Corres., 1851, Sect. 50*]

Royal Institution
5 Septr 1851

MY DEAR SIR

I think so well of Dr Tyndalls papers[1] that I should be very glad to hear he had the Toronto Professorship because I think it would give him the power of working & that he would work to the honor of the University.

He spoke so well & clearly at Ipswich in explaining his results that I think he would make a very good Lecturer With kindest remembrances to Mrs. & Miss Airy

I am as Ever
Yours Most Truly
M. FARADAY

[1] It should be noted that Dr Tyndall's papers were generally hostile to Faraday's views on diamagnetic action.

474   M. FARADAY to J. E. PORTLOCK,[1] 1 December 1851
[*B.J. 2, 239*]

December 1, 1851

MY DEAR PORTLOCK,

...As one of the Senate of the University of London, and appointed with others especially to consider the best method of examination, I have had to think very deeply on the subject, and have had my attention drawn to the practical working of different methods at our English and other Universities; and know there are great difficulties in them all. Our conclusion is that examination by papers is the best, accompanied by *viva voce* when the written answers require it. Such examinations require that the students should be collected together, each with his paper, pens, and ink; that each should have the paper of questions (before unknown) delivered to him; that they should be allowed three, or any sufficient number of hours to answer them, and that they should be carefully watched by the examiner or some other officer, so as to prevent their having any communication with each other, or going out of the room for that time. After which, their written answers have to be taken and examined carefully by the examiner and decided upon according to their respective merits. We think that no numerical value can be attached to the questions, because everything depends on how they are answered; and that is the reason why I am not able to send you such a list at the present time.

My verbal examinations at the Academy go for very little, and were instituted by me mainly to keep the students' attention to the lecture for the time, under the pressure of a thought that inquiry would come at the end. My instructions always have been to look to the note-books for the result; and so the verbal examinations are only used at last as confirmations or corrections of the conclusions drawn from the notes.

I should like to have had a serious talk with you on this matter, but my time is so engaged that I cannot come to you at Woolwich for the next two or three weeks, so I will just jot down a remark or two. In the first place, the cadets have only the lectures, and no practical instruction in chemistry, and yet chemistry is eminently a practical science. Lectures alone cannot be expected to give more than a general idea of this most extensive branch of science, and it would be too much to expect that young men who at the utmost hear only fifty lectures on chemistry, should be able to answer with much effect in writing, to questions set down on paper, when we know by experience that daily work for eight hours in *practical laboratories* for *three months* does not go very far to confer such ability.

Again: the audience in the lecture-room at the Academy always, with me, consists of four classes, i.e. persons who have entered at such different periods as to be in four different stages of progress. It would, I think, be unfair to examine all these as if upon the same level; they constitute four different classes, and we found it in our inquiries most essential to avoid mixing up a junior and a senior class one with the other. Even though it were supposed that you admitted only those who were going out to examination, and such others from the rest as chose to volunteer, yet as respects them it has to be considered that I may not go on from the beginning to the end of their fifty lectures increasing the importance and weight of the matter brought before them, for I have to divide the fifty into two courses, each to be begun and finished in the year, and

I ever have to keep my language and statements so simple as to be fit for mere beginners and not for advanced pupils.

I have often considered whether some better method of giving instruction in chemistry to the cadets could not be devised, but have understood that it was subordinate to other more important studies, and that the time required by a practical school, which is considerable, could not be spared. Perhaps, however, you may have some view in this direction, and I hasten to state to you what I could more earnestly and better state by word of mouth, that you must not think me the least in the way. I should be very happy, by consultation, in the first instance, to help you in such a matter, though I could not undertake any part in it. I am getting older, and find the Woolwich duty, taking in as it does large parts of two days, as much as I can manage with satisfaction to myself; so that I could not even add on to it such an examination by written papers as I have talked about: but I should rejoice to know that the whole matter was in more practical and better hands.

Ever, my dear Portlock, yours very truly,

M. FARADAY.

I refused to be an examiner in our University.

M.F.

¹ Joseph Ellison Portlock (1794–1864), Major General RE, at this time, inspector of studies at the Royal Military Academy, Woolwich.

475   M. FARADAY to E. MAGRATH, 6 December 1851
[*R.I., previously unpublished*]

Royal Institution
6 Dec͏ʳ 1851

MY DEAR MAGRATH
The progress of Old time bringing with him in my case and in all others the usual effects tends with me to the dimunition of income and therefore necessarily the dimunition of pleasures depending upon it. One of the first of these which I am constrained to give up is my Membership at the Athenaeum. Will you therefore have the goodness to communicate to the Committee my resignation.

Ever My dear Magrath
Very Truly Yours
M. FARADAY

476 M. FARADAY to E. MAGRATH, 8 December 1851
[*R.I., previously unpublished*]

8 Dec.ʳ 1851

MY DEAR MAGRATH

I send you another note I do not wish the Club to think that I withdraw from any pique or coolness and therefore prefer assigning a reason which I have made as general as possible. You need not be sorry for the reason of my withdrawal there are plenty of means left for all that is needful.

Ever Truly Yours
M. FARADAY

477 W. DE LA RUE to M. FARADAY, 16 December 1851
[*I.E.E., previously unpublished*]

7 St. Mary's Road
Canonbay
December 16th 1851

MY DEAR SIR

In reference to our conversation, I must inform you that immediately after leaving you I took home the iron core which has been prepared now about a twelvemonth or perhaps more and placed it on the stage of my microscope, and was glad to find that it would answer well. Being desirous, however, that no slight defect should cause the waste of your time, I determined on making the core part of the instrument, so as to ensure steadiness and to avoid its sliding about in screwing up the ends. A little consideration enabled me to decide on the plan, which I drew out before I went to bed and the next morning I placed the drawing in the hands of Mr. Ross who pledged himself not to divulge what was in preparation or to allow the core to be seen by his workman or any other person. Tonight at $9\frac{1}{2}$ o'clock I received back the instrument.

As I conceive it to be very important to get the points as nearly in the same plane as possible with the object to be operated upon so as to enable us to bring them very close and [word illeg.] the lines I intend taking my instrument to Bunhill Row so as to turn up the moveable end high enough in order that the thinnest film of mica may be used instead of glass on some occasion; and also to see if our workmen can make make [*sic*] *microscopic points* as at present they look like clumsy fractures of stout wire. Thirdly to see that there is conducting communication from end to end, that is that the wire has not been injured.

I am having constructed 6 holders of glasses so that an experiment may be prepared whilst another is observed; at present I have only one but I have descried that its thickness might be guaged in order that the top surface of the plate in all should be the same height from the stage.

646

As there is a nichols prism *P* which fits under the stage experiments on polarized light or the changed properties of crystals with respect to it may be observed with facility.

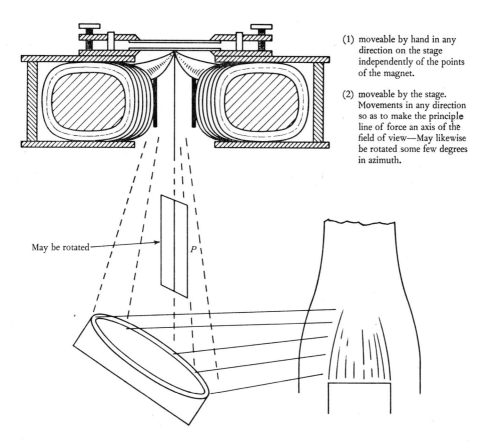

(1) moveable by hand in any direction on the stage independently of the points of the magnet.

(2) moveable by the stage. Movements in any direction so as to make the principle line of force an axis of the field of view—May likewise be rotated some few degrees in azimuth.

May be rotated

If there is any other preparation which you would like to have made I will get it done. A contrivance might easily be made by means of a slip of silver to heat the glass plates if you think this provision desirable.

I remain Yours Very truly
WARREN DE LA RUE

478 G. B. AIRY to M. FARADAY, 29 December 1851 [copy]

[*Royal Observatory, Herstmonceux, Sci. Soc., 1851–2, Sect. 2, previously unpublished*]

Clayford near Ipswich,
1851 Dec 29

MY DEAR SIR

Thank you for your magnetic remembrance, which has followed me hither.[1]
I wish I could instantly convey your kind wishes to Mrs. Airy: she is I trust
safe either on the sea or in Madeira, for which place she has embarked with our
eldest daughter, whose health has given us much uneasiness.

About the Eclipse. First, pray let me yet believe for some time that I am
under no engagement of any kind ∵ [punctuation doubtful] I have been sitting,
this morning, three hours by the fire without doing or thinking of anything,
and begin to understand in what happiness consists. In the next place, the
Eclipse wil be a very meagre subject: ten minutes would suffice for it: but I will
in some more active state turn it over and report to you.

I am, my dear Sir,
Yours very truly
G. B. AIRY

[1] Faraday sent pictures (formed by iron filings and fixed with shellac) of the lines of magnetic
force under different magnetic circumstances to his friends. This is probably to what Airy
refers.

479 M. FARADAY to T. BELL, 13 January 1852

[*R.S., previously unpublished*]

Royal Institution,
Jany. 13 1852

MY DEAR BELL

I do not see that I need alter my report. Lloyd[1] I perceive gives up practically,
i.e. as respects real magnets, both the idea of resultant poles and also the law of
the inverse square of the distance, and if it all were like him, then indeed Harris'[2]
paper would be superfluous, except as a proof that experiment & theory
agreed. But there are many who are of opinion that the law of the inverse
square of the distance is the true law of magnetic action Tyndall & others for
instance who have been working and publishing very lately. Now Harris
probably feels that that is no law which does not apply to the near intervals,
which are perhaps the most important intervals in determining the true nature
of magnetic action and that one might as well say that the revolution of a
parabola produces a cone neglecting the consideration of all the parts about the
focus which are the best fitted to make manifest the truth. As long, therefore, as
the law of the inverse square of the distance is assented to in a superficial manner

he may feel bound to offer experimental proof to the contrary. In these remarks I am not putting myself either in the place of Harris or Lloyd and I think if I were Harris I should like to know of Lloyd's letter and reconsider what modification such admission as it contains might require but whether that is proper or not I cannot say. I perceive that the hope I have expressed in the first of the two papers of mine that you now have,[3] that the apparently contrary results of Harris and others will be reconciled & coalesce is near upon being fulfilled

Ever My dear Bell
Truly Yours
M. FARADAY

[1] Humphrey Lloyd (1800–81), Fellow of Trinity College, Dublin. Faraday would appear to be alluding here to a letter, rather than to a formal paper. See below.
[2] See Letter 458.
[3] See Series 29, *ERE*.

480 J. PLATEAU to M. FARADAY, 16 January 1852
[*I.E.E.*, *previously unpublished*]

Gand,
16 Janvier 1852

MON CHER MONSIEUR FARADAY.

J'ai l'honneur de vous adresser, par la poste, un exemplaire de la première livraison d'un petit traité de physique[1] à l'usage des gens du monde, auquel je travaille depuis une couple d'années. Si vous daignez jeter les yeux sur l'avant-propos, vous comprendrez que ce petit ouvrage qui, au premier abord, peut paraître aisé à composer, a dû cependant m'offrir des difficultés considérables; on m'en a chargé à peu près malgré moi, et c'est lui qui, depuis deux ans, m'a empêché de publier la suite de mes recherches sur les figures d'équilibre liquides. Je n'ai pu mettre de suscription sur la couverture de l'exemplaire que vous recevrez, parce que la poste ne le permet pas.

Permettez-moi maintenant de vous demander un petit service. Je ne le fais qu'avec grand regrêt, parceque je vous ai déjà importuné pour la même chose; mais vous me pardonnerez, j'espère, en réfléchissant que mon infirmité rend pour moi les voyages impossibles, et que, ne pouvant ainsi aller moi-même à Londres m'occuper de mes affaires, je suis contraint de recourir à l'obligeance des personnes qui veulent bien m'honorer de leur amitié; vous, qui êtes si bienveillant pour moi, je suis certain que vous ne rejetterez pas ma requête. Voici ce dont il s'agit: il y a plus de six mois que la traduction anglaise de mon mémoire sur les figures d'équilibre liquides, traduction destinée à paraître dans les Scientific Memoirs de Mr Taylor, est imprimée, je n'ai aucune nouvelle de sa publication, et je désirerais vivement savoir si je dois renoncer à l'espoir de cette publication; n'est-ce point trop abuser de vos bontés pour moi que de vous prier de vouloir bien prendre des informations à cet égard, et me les transmettre?[2]

J'ai encore une petite demande à vous faire. Mr Wheatstone a eu l'obligeance d'envoyer, il y a environ sept mois, au Journal des Sciences d'Edimbourg, une analyse de mon mémoire rédigée par moi.[3] Si vous recevez ce journal, puis-je espérer que vous voudrez bien vous assurer si l'analyse en question y a été insérée?

Je le répète, Monsieur, c'est avec grand regrêt que je viens vous prier de perdre ainsi pour moi une partie d'un temps aussi précieux que le Vôtre, et je vous supplie de nouveau de me pardonner mon importunité.

J'ai reçu les exemplaires de vos dernières séries que vous m'avez fait l'honneur de m'envoyer. J'ai admiré vos belles expériences sur de légères boules de verre pleines d'oxigène ou d'un autre gaz à différentes densités et soumises à l'action d'un électro-aimant; j'ai admiré aussi, en particulier, les moyens ingénieux que vous avez employés, indépendamment de celui dont il a déjà été question entre nous, pour montrer que les gaz n'éprouvent ni condensation ni dilatation dans le voisinage des pôles, et je suis encore à me demander comment cela est possible.

Agréez, Monsieur, l'assurance de tous mes sentiments de respectueuse affection.

J^h PLATEAU

P.S. J'ai envoyé également à Mr Wheatstone un exemplaire de mon petit ouvrage; veuillez avoir la bonté de lui dire, à la première occasion, pourquoi je n'ai pas mis de suscription sur la couverture.

[1] J. Plateau, *Physique*, Brussels, n.d.
[2] *TSM*, 5 (1852), 584.
[3] See *PM*, 4 s., 1 (1851), 531. This is the only publication in an English journal by Plateau I can discover for 1851 or 1852. The PM's full title, it should be remembered, was *The London, Edinburgh, and Dublin Philosophical Magazine and Journal of Science*, hence, perhaps, the source of Plateau's citation. The *EJS* had ceased publication years before.

481 W. WHEWELL to M. FARADAY, 7 February 1852
[*R.I., previously unpublished*]

Trin. Lodge,
Cambridge
Feb. 7, 1852

MY DEAR SIR

I am much obliged to you for the specimens of magnetic curves which I received two days ago.[1] I have been thinking what word will best answer your purpose, but it is difficult to decide such a question without knowing the kind of connection in which it is to be used. *Spheroid* would describe the surface which you wish to express but is not mechanical enough. You might perhaps get on in English by calling it the *spindle shaped* surface or *fusiform* surface, but a new word would be better. I should recommend you to call it the *sphondyloid* surface, and then, the *sphondyloid* simply, making it a substantive. *Sphondylos* in Greek is a pulley or socket which turns on an axis, a spindle, a vertebra, and the like, and is already familiar in anatomy and botany. Used as a substantive *spondyloid* will group well enough with *solenoid* which has been adopted by English writers.

It is rash to suggest anything to you in the way of manipulation; but would not some magnetic curves come out more neatly if instead of filings you were to use fine wire cut into minute lengths.

I am glad you are going on with your magnetic speculations and am always

Yours Truly

W. WHEWELL

¹ Faraday sent out his 'magnetic curves' to a number of friends. See Letter 478.

482   M. FARADAY to W. WHEWELL, 9 February 1852

[*Trinity College Library, Trinity College, Cambridge, previously unpublished*]

Royal Institution,

Feb. 9, 1852

MY DEAR SIR,

I hasten to thank you for your kind suggestions. The term Sphondyloid will I suppose answer my purpose. I may want it for I just enclose a figure to make sure that I have not deceived. Supposing *c.c.* a magnet as marked on the back of the paper. Then various lines of force are shown at the axis AB and the lines $DD. E. F.$ Now I have occasion to consider the solid which would be generated by the revolution of the area between F and C round the axis AB, or that produced by the like revolution of the area enclosed by E and C or by D and C, or even that enclosed between the lines of force D and E and such like. But in saying this I do not wish to give you the trouble of answering this letter. If you should however, desire to do so tell me at the same time what the fair English meaning of the *Solenoid* is meant to be.

Ever Your Very Obliged

M. FARADAY

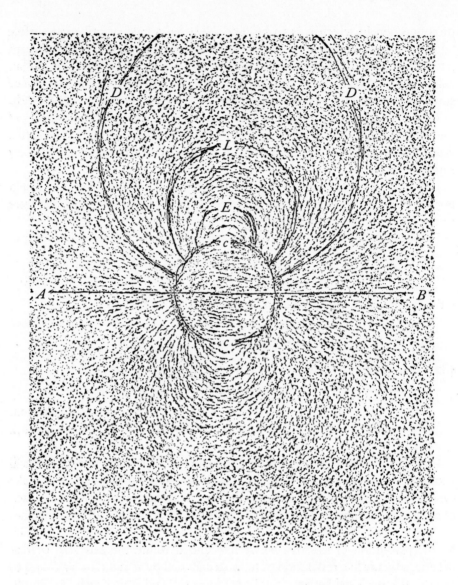

483   W. WHEWELL to M. FARADAY, 10 February 1852
[*R.I., previously unpublished*]

Trin. Lodge,
Cambridge
Feb. 10, 1852

MY DEAR SIR

I think *sphondyloid* will answer your purpose. I have just stumbled on a paper in Jeremy Taylor[1] which will show you that the term sphondyl is not new in English. It is at the beginning of the Dedication to the Cases of Conscience.[2]

"The circles of Divine Providence turn themselves upon the affairs of the world so that every *spondyl* of the wheels may mark out those virtues which we are then to exercise." *Spondyl* is the Ionic, *sphondyl* the Attic form. Perhaps you may think it wise to introduce the word in some such way as this – The sphondyloid body contained between the two surfaces of revolution E and F, which for the sake of brevity I shall call simply *the sphondyloid*".

Solen in Greek means a pipe or gutter. I think Ampere and his followers use it for a figure generated by a ring formed curve sliding along any other line and so with the termination *oid* it may mean any pipelike surface

Believe me yours very truly

W. WHEWELL

[1] Jeremy Taylor (1613–67), Bishop of Down and Connor and of Dromore.
[2] Jeremy Taylor, *Ductor Dubitantium or the Rule of Conscience in all her generall measures; serving as a great instrument for the determination of Cases of Conscience*, 2 vols., London, 1660.

484   M. FARADAY to W. WHEWELL, 11 February 1852

[*Trinity College Library, Trinity College, Cambridge, previously unpublished*]

R Institution,
11 Feb.ʸ 1852.

MY DEAR SIR

Many thanks for your last letter which is curiously to the point in respect of Jeremy Taylor.

I enclose a notice of certain views –

Ever Truly Yours,
M. FARADAY

485   G. G. LEWIS[1] to M. FARADAY, 9 March 1852

[*R.S., previously unpublished*]

Royal Military Academy,
Woolwich;
March 9th 1852

DEAR SIR

Having submitted to His Lordship the Master General Your communication of the 9*th* Ultimo, expressing a wish to retire from the Office of Chemical Lecturer to the Royal Military Academy as soon as Convenience would permit, – I have the honor to state that a person Competent to fill the situation of Chemical Lecturer to this Institution having been found in the person of Mr. Abel[2] – the Master General has been pleased to accept your resignation and to appoint Mr. Abel Your Successor –

I beg to subjoin an Extract from the Official Letter of the Master General's

Secretary expressive of His Lordships high sense of the advantage the Ordinance Service & Gentlemen Cadets of the Royal Military Academy have gained from your instruction for so many Years. –

I have the honor to be
Dear Sir
Your most obt. Servant
Lt Governor [reading doubtful] G. G. LEWIS, *Major General*

Extract
Officer of Ordinance
8*th* March 1852

SIR

"The Master General cannot allow Mr. Faraday to withdraw from the Ordinance Service, without expressing his high sense of the advantage which it has derived from the Professor's instruction. The Lectures of so distinguished a Chemist cannot fail to have encouraged amongst the Cadets a taste for a science intimately Connected with professional objects, and to have laid the foundation of practical attainments which must be eminently useful in their future career."

I have the honor to be
Sir
Your obedient Servant
Signed/EDWARD ELLIOT

M. General Lewis C.B.

Pro: Secty

[1] Griffith George Lewis (1784–1859), Governor of the Royal Military Academy at Woolwich, 1851–6.
[2] Frederick Augustus Abel (1827–1902) served as Lecturer on chemistry until 1854.

486 M. FARADAY to T. BELL, 10 April 1852
[*R.S., previously unpublished*]

Royal Institution,
10 April 1852

MY DEAR BELL

Having carefully read Mr. Grove's paper[1] I arrive at the conclusion that it is correct in the experiments and sound in the deductions and touching as it does upon the unity of electrical phenomena, whether in the static or dynamic form, is of great value in the development of that part of science. My voice therefore is for the paper. Personally I hail it as a great aid in the expansion of that subject which I love.

Ever Very Truly Yours
M. FARADAY

[1] William Robert Grove, 'On the electro-chemical polarity of gases, including the striae in electrical discharges', *PT* (1852), 87.

487 M. FARADAY to T. ANDREWS, 20 April 1852

[Science Museum, S. Kensington, previously unpublished]

Royal Institution
20 April 1852

MY DEAR ANDREWS

Receive my sincere thanks for your kind letter and for the paper & for all your good will & favours to me: tell Mrs. Andrews I hope to thank her personally & trust when the time comes she will put up with me & not be dissappointed.

As to your proposed experiments, it will be of extreme interest to me to know how electrified bodies behave in a perfect vacuum. Perhaps you know that Masson[2] not long since concluded that Electric currents or discharges *cannot exist* in an absolute vacuum As an introduction to his memoires[3] of which there are four or five I may refer you to the Annales de Chimie 1851. Vol xxxi. p. 125. At pp. 149. 150 you will see some of his conclusions

I have sent my papers to Williams & Magrath [reading doubtful].

Ever Truly Yours
M. FARADAY

[1] Probably T. Andrews, 'On a method of obtaining a perfect vacuum in the receiver of an air pump', *PM*, 4 s., 3 (1852), 104.

[2] Antoine Philibert Masson (1806–60), Professor of Chemistry at Caen.

[3] For Masson's papers on this subject, see *RSCSP*.

488 M. FARADAY to CONSTANCE REID,[1] 19 May 1852

[Vassar College, Department of Physics, previously unpublished]

Royal Institution
19 May 1852

MY DEAR CONSTANCE

First a kiss – s – s – s – ss. Next thank you for Your good letter – very well written and very pleasant – and now thanks for the letter you are going to write to me in which you must tell me how Papa & Mamma do – and what you are about – I went this morning to see a fish like a great eel take his breakfast – This morning he had three frogs for breakfast – yesterday he eat [*sic*] 9 fish in the course of the day each as large as a sprat and the day before *14*. When the fish are put into the water he electrifies and kills them & then swallows them up. – and if a man happens to have his hands in the water at the same time the fish that is the eel, electrifies the man too. The eel is now above 12 years old and is heavier I think than you are

Yesterday I saw the Royal children the Prince of Wales & the duke of York. Such nice children they would make famous playmates for you but I do not

655

know whether Princes do play much I do not think they can be so happy in their play as you are.

As to the magnet when you & I meet we will have a long talk about it and make some *experiments* –

and so with my love to Papa & Mamma and curious Constance with a kiss for each I am

Your loving old Uncle
M. FARADAY

¹ Faraday's niece.

489 G. B. AIRY to M. FARADAY, 7 June 1852
[*I.E.E., previously unpublished*]

Royal Observatory
Greenwich
1852 June 7

MY DEAR SIR

At the late meeting of the Board of Visitors, there was a wish expressed by almost every member of the Board that I should confer with you respecting the reduction of our Magnetic Observations. The object – at least the ultimate object – of the reductions being understood to be, the reference of the phaeno-mena to their physical causes.

I do therefore by this writing take the first step in the conference, and I earnestly hope that you will respond to it.

Assuming that you will do so, I now proceed to consult you on the best method of proceeding. And I will beg leave to commence with the following statement.

We have, as you probably know, very full and accurate records (such as I firmly believe to be unequalled in the world) of the constant changes of magnetic elements, formed by our photographic apparatus. Without examina-tion of these, I do not think that any body can form an accurate notion of the phaenomena that stand to be explained. There are, as is commonly believed, the regular phaenomena of

Annual variation
Diurnal variation

but there are also the anomalous phaenomena of

Fret
Irregularity
Storms

which are so much greater in magnitude than the others, that I have no con-fidence (and in this I was supported by several members of the Board) in deductions applying to the socalled [*sic*] regular phaenomena until the irregular ones are cleared out of the way.

Now would you like to look over a volume or two (say a years [*sic*] collection) of our Photographs, and form a general notion of the things? On receiving your assent, I will send you the bound collections. And then, in due time, would you make an appointment for me to wait on you and talk over the matter? – Or do you see any better course?

I am, my dear Sir,
Yours very truly
G. B. AIRY

---

490 W. WHEWELL to M. FARADAY, 8 June 1852

[*Trinity College Library, Trinity College, Cambridge, previously unpublished*]

June 8, 1852

MY DEAR DR. FARADAY,

You find such admirable fields of research for yourself, and work them so well that it is not a light matter to offer to you any suggestion in that way; but what you have already done with regard to the local peculiarities of the declination needle in your most important paper on that subject,[1] points out you as the person most fit to undertake the remainder of the problem. We want some explanation or at least some beginning of explanation of the *magnetic storms* which agitate the needle from time to time, and of which the mean results affect the daily and monthly changes of declination. The Astronomer Royal has a large mass of accumulated photographic observations of the daily changes of the needle, and among them, of course are included the records of various kinds of such storms; from a mere magnetic *fact* which takes place in some degree to a state of frantic oscillating leaps which occur at other times. He will, I know, be very glad if you will look at them and suggest any probable or even possible connexion of these with other physical phenomena.

I saw your "sphondyloid" paper in the Phil. Mag.[2] and I saw that I had led you into saying a sphondyloid *body* instead of *solid*; which would have been [more proper] as it is a new geometrical solid, not a mechanical body which you speak of.

I leave England today; but I shall be glad to hear from you at Kreuznach, Rhine-Prussia; and am always

Yours very truly
W. WHEWELL

[1] See Series 27, *ERE*.
[2] M. Faraday, 'On the Physical Character of the Lines of Magnetic Force', *PM*, 4 s., 3 (1852), 401.

[*Trinity College Library, Trinity College, Cambridge, previously unpublished*]

Royal Institution,
10 June 1852

MY DEAR WHEWELL

I received your pleasant letter which I take as a great compliment; or rather (for I do not care for compliments) as a great encouragement. Now I do not know that I have the ability to enter upon the irregular variations of the Earths magnetism, but I have the wish; and shall some day be encouraged to do so, but not immediately, for the following reasons. The *seat* of the terrestrial magnetic force is (for us at present) in the earth: and *within* the earth there may be causes of variation, not in the distribution of the power only, but also in its amount; the latter varying not simply for the whole mass but probably in different parts at different times. Such variations (*within the earth*) are I suspect the chief, perhaps the only, cause of magnetic storms, frets, etc. etc.; and as yet we have scarcely any other hold than that of the imagination upon them. On the other hand considering the seat of the force to be *in the earth*, the force itself extends externally around the planet & its *distribution* is, as I believe, affected by the medium which is there present, and which, under the influence of the sun, is the chief cause of the daily and of some other regular variations. Now I think I have a hold, by experiment, on this cause of variation; & I further think that if I succeed in making that clear, I shall do far more good to the whole cause & aid more rapidly in the elucidation of the other set of variations, than by going to them at once. For this reason I mean to devote all my thoughts & means to a determination of the rate of variations of the paramagnetic force of oxygen from summer heat or higher, down to $0°$ or if possible $20°$, $30°$ or $40°$ below $0°$. If by such experiments my expectations are confirmed, and we should be able to know surely what is the amount of atmospheric variation; then, subtracting this from the whole amount of effect, how much better we should be able to comprehend the proportion & also the nature of the effect due to internal causes of variation? – and we might then hope that not one or two minds only, but many would start on the search after the cause of the irregular phenomena with far greater advantage, because from a far more assured position than at present. Whatever hopes we have of solving the riddle of terrestrial magnetism must depend upon our successive elimination of the causes of variation; and any one which presents itself in a tangible shape should be pursued as far as possible and estimated in value so that it may be taken from the rest, that they may be studied in a simple form. If we could begin with a magnetic storm the process would be the same as regards the residual phenomena: – but we have as yet little or no hold (on) the storms, & I think we have a grasp on the annual & daily variation.

When we really come to magnetic storms I think we shall want needles far lighter than such as are now used for the observations. Needles for such a use ought to be without weight, so as to have neither inertia or momentum. How can a bar of some pounds weight tell us the frequency or the extent of rapid variations, or give us anything more than a slurring [reading doubtful] mean? Yet it may be that these vibrations in their full development are essential to the explication of the mystery. But we shall see by degrees what is wanted & I dare say at last obtain it

Ever My dear Sir
Yours Most Truly
M. FARADAY

492   M. FARADAY to G. B. AIRY, 10 June 1852

[*Royal Observatory, Herstmonceux, Mag., Corr. & Misc., 1849–61, Sect. 11, previously unpublished*]

Royal Institution
10 June 1852

MY DEAR SIR

Your letter stirs up a great many thoughts in my mind which I have been obliged to leave at rest for a time, simply because experimental work is slow work, & strength & health are limited. My next occupation must be the determination, if possible, of the amount of change in the paramagnetic force of oxygen (or air) by depression of temperature to $0°$, and if possible to $-40°$. or $-50°$; and at different degrees of pressure or condensation. These data are essentially necessary for the development of the effects which occur under the head of atmospheric magnetism; and which as I believe include a large part if not the whole of the daily variation & much of the annual variation. In the mean time it is a great thing that other persons should be moved to collate and analyse the results of observation; & separate as much as possible the compound result which appears in the continuous stream of a continued set of perfect observations, into such subordinate parts as the periodical variations and the irregular or anomalous phenomena: – for until the great result is in some measure analysed & referred to the various parts that make it, there can be but little hopes of clearing up the scheme of these most complicated phenomena. Therefore I think that such analyses as Sabines of the larger variations will be very useful in due time. – M. Laurent[1] has already been moved to search, & has, he says, found a recurring cycle of ten years

To me, the phenomena of fret, storms &c have far greater attraction than the periodical variations already referred to: but we have now some hold of the latter and little or none of the former. They, i.e. the former appear to me as probably due chiefly to actions within the magnet i.e the earth; and may have little or no relation to the action of the surrounding medium – If it be so, to determine the condition of a magnet (as the earth) producing variations of such large extent, with such rapidity, and so general in their influence, is a problem of such difficulty that we can only hope for its solution by degrees. and knowing so little of the interior of the earth as we do, at first seems almost *hopeless*. Nevertheless to know, as I now do, that a perfectly invariable magnet, as regards the amount of force, may have the external *disposition* of its power varied to a very large extent, either suddenly or slowly, without the least change in the *sum* of power externally, is one point of rest and one ground of hope for the mind. Another is the power which, I hope, the mathematician has of pointing out what sources of change or irregularity are external to the magnet (or earth) and what internal. I think I have heard that Gauss has done something of this kind. If we could separate the variations due to external causes from those caused by internal action, it would certainly clear up the subject in some degree. – Hence it is that I must, (being already in the path,) work out the effect of temperature on air as far as I can, before I attempt to meddle with the causes of action within the earth; and, indeed, if I succeed in this first object there are then others waiting for me, which seem to present better handles for experiment than the internal state of the earth.

But I hope in a week or two to have another paper for you, and then if you like I will come some day to the Observatory. It would be a great treat to me, and a source of great instruction, to have a talk with you over some of the records of irregularity, storms &c and over the instruments

I am My dear Sir
Most Truly Yours
M. FARADAY

[1] Pierre Alphonse Laurent (1813–54), of the French Corps of Engineers.

493   W. WHEWELL to M. FARADAY, 20 June 1852

[*Trinity College Library, Trinity College, Cambridge, previously unpublished*]

Trin. Lodge,
Cambridge
June 20, 1852

MY DEAR DR FARADAY,

As I expected, a single line from you has turned my darkness into day. I ought never to have been *so* dark; and I believe I had formerly understood you better; but I have not attended to such subjects for a long time; and turning to them again for a few hours [reading doubtful], I found myself in a puzzle of which you had the result, and which is now quite dissipated. I think, at the same time, that it may be useful to others of your readers that you should draw some figures in which you delineate the currents inside the magnets; for readers are much led by the eye. To explain my getting into such perplexity, I may say that I have been generally in the habit of thinking of your curves as identical with the old magnetic curves, which only give the active part of the curves. Also, when I gave you the word *sphondyl* I thought rather of a solid generated by the revolution of this figure than this.

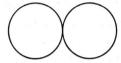

though the word may describe either. The sphondyl is in fact an [illeg.] described by the revolution of a closed curve round an axis.

You will find a calculation of the properties of the magnetic curve, besides the places you have mentioned, in Leslie's [reading doubtful] Geometrical Analysis (1821) but undoubtedly I have seen it in much older works

With regard to Newton's views of lines of force, I have given some account of them, as well as of other ways of expressing gravity, in the Philosophy of the Inductive Sciences. B. III. Ch. IX, Sect. 7.

I know that you try carefully to keep yourself free from all assumptions as to the mode and machinery of the actions which you investigate: but I think the incautious followers of the same line of speculation may run into something very like Descartes' system of *vortices*. I do not at all mean that because it is a system of vortices it must be wrong; but if it be that it must be an assumption which [reading doubtful] requires a good deal of proof.

> Believe me dear Dr Faraday
> Yours very truly
> W. WHEWELL

494 R. WOLF[1] to M. FARADAY, 2 August 1852
[*I.E.E., previously unpublished*]

> Bern
> 2/8 1852

HOCHGEEHRTER HERR.

Ich habe soeben eine Entdeckung gemacht und veröffentlicht (Mittheilungen der Naturforschenden Gesellschaft in Bern Nr⁰. 245–247),[2] die für Sie so viel Interesse haben dürfte, um mich zu entschuldigen, weñ ich mir erlaube Sie in einigen Worten damit bekañt zu machen.

Ein vergleichendes Studium der von Herrn Hofrath Schwabe[3] beobachteten jährlichen Anzahl von Fleckengruppen der Soñe, und der von Herrn Professor Lamont[4] mitgetheilten Jahresmittel für die Declinationsvariationen der Magnetnadel (oder auch der mittlern täglichen Bewegung der Horizontalintensität) hat mich nämlich zu folgendem Gesetze geführt: *Die Anzahl der Fleckengruppen und die mittlere Variation sind nicht nur derselben Periode von circa 10 1/3 Jahren unterworfen, sondern diese Perioden correspondieren bei beiden bis ins kleinste Detail; in demselben Jahre, wo die Anzahl der Fleckengruppen ihr Maximum oder Minimum erreicht, hat dasselbe auch für die mittlere Variation statt.* Es geht wohl mit Evidenz daraus hervor, daß die Soñenflecken und die Declinationsvariationen sich auf dieselbe Endursache zurückführen lassen müssen, und es eröffnet sich ein weites Feld der Speculation. Möchte es Ihnen gefallen an der Hand dieses Gesetzes neue Felder der Wissenschaft zu erleuchten, so würde sich seiner kleinen Mitwirkung herzlich freuen

Dero hochachtungsvollst Ergebensten

RUDOLF WOLF
Director der Sternwarte

[1] Rudolf Wolf (1816–93), Instructor in Mathematics and Physics in the College (Realschule) of Bern.
[2] See the number of short papers on sunspots given in *RSCSP*.
[3] Samuel Heinrich Schwabe (1789–1875), Hofrath and Apothecary in Dessau. For his yearly observations of sun spots see *AN* from 1840 on.
[4] Johann Lamont (1805–79), Professor of Astronomy at the University of Munich. See *RSCSP* for his papers on terrestrial magnetism.

494 a R. WOLF to M. FARADAY, 2 August 1852[1]
[*I.E.E., previously unpublished*]

Bern
2/8 1852

HIGHLY HONORED SIR

I have just made a discovery & explained it (communications of the natural philosophical society in Bern Nos. 245–247) which will have so much interest for you as to excuse me if I permit myself to make it known to you in a few words.

A comparative study of the yearly number of the groups of spots in the sun observed by Herr Hofrath Schwabe [(illeg. 3 words)] and of the communicated yearly mean of the variations of declination of the magnet needle by Professor Lamont (or also of the mean daily movement of the horizontal intensity) has led me to the following view: *The number of the groups of spots & the mean variation are not only subject to the same period of about 10 1/3 years but these periods will correspond in both to the smallest detail in the same year when the number of the groups of spots reaches its maximum or minimum Has*[2] – *the same also for the mean variation.* It agrees with the evidence therefore that the sun spots & the variations of declination must allow themselves to be referred to the same – cause & a wide field for speculation opens itself. If you were pleased, on the suggestion of this view, to enlighten new fields of science Of his small share in the work would heartily rejoice.

Devoted
RUDOLF WOLF
Director of the Observatory

[1] This is the English translation which was made for Faraday. It is rather poor.
[2] The translator here is following Wolf literally. The 'Has' is Wolf's 'hat' and it makes no sense in English.

495 M. FARADAY to C. M. SYKES, 6 August 1852
[*R.I., previously unpublished*]

Royal Institution
6 Aug 1852

MY DEAR SIR,

Yesterday a friend & a friend of Liebigs told me that Liebig having the desire of sending his son (who has now completed his medical education) to India had been advised to apply to you as able to assist him being both a man of Science & having the power to direct an appointment his way I was asked to speak to you but said I could scarcely make so free: that if such a thing were fit in itself, I was sure you would do what you could for Liebigs sake that if not duty would come first. As far as a love for science might lead you I thought that Liebig's name ought to have more weight with you than mine.

At first I thought I would say nothing to you about it, but on consideration concluded that I would let you know. To oblige Liebig would be to oblige myself – but other considerations must come before – Do not trouble yourself to answer this note.

Ever Yours,
M. FARADAY

[1] C. M. Sykes, Colonel, Indian Army. See Letter 474.

496 M. FARADAY to T. ANDREWS, 14 August 1852
[*Science Museum, S. Kensington, previously unpublished*]

Royal Institution
14 August 1852

MY DEAR ANDREWS

I look rather anxiously at my remembrancer as the time passes on & the 1st Septr draws nigh. and the sanguine hopes I entertained in the distance fade much as the period approaches when I thought of enjoying myself with you & Mrs Andrews.[1] There is no chance of my dear wife being with you for her inability to walk much increases and without the power of moving about rather freely there could be no ability to use the privileges of the meeting. A walk even of a few hundred yards makes her require a little rest. Our medical friends think it is rheumatism, but Sir B Brodie & some others think it rather a deficiency of energy in the nerves of the limbs She is very thankful for your kind invitation but dares not accept it For myself my obstruction is just the old one and as I had to run away from Oxford after three days so I fear it would be at Belfast I find in myself an illustration of one of the chapters of Dr Hollands late volume on physiological subjects namely that on the *time* essentially required in mental operations[2] That time is now with me considerable in proportion to what it was naturally & the consequence is that I can only hold my way in a quiet progression of things When I am involved in rapid changes of thoughts or persons then I have to use extra exertion mentally & then confusion & giddiness comes on. All this I forget when I have been in the country for a few weeks doing nothing, & then I think myself as able as ever to race with others. But having come home and gone to work upon oxygen & a magnetic torsion balance for a little while I find the old warning coming on & I have to suspend my occupation. Formerly I thought that to enter into such a thing as the Association meeting would be rest in comparison but found that it was equivalent to work & that under pressure, and so may not look to my visit to Belfast in that point of view.

However I mean to do the best I can between this and the end of the Month, and have not yet given up hopes of seeing you. Do not suppose however that the association would be so chief a reason for my coming as the earnest desire to thank you for your kindness by enjoying it; and when [reading doubtful] I think of giving up Belfast my regret is to lose the pleasure of seeing you & Mrs. Andrews at home. Remember that if I come any closet or corner will do for me to sleep in. I will write again in the course of 12 or 14 days.

Ever My dear Andrews
Affectionately Yours
M. FARADAY

[1] The *BAAS* met in Belfast in 1852.
[2] See Letter 534.

497 M. FARADAY to T. ANDREWS, 30 August 1852

[*Science Museum, S. Kensington, previously unpublished*]

Royal Institution
30 August 1852

MY DEAR ANDREWS

When I received your last letter & the instructions from the Secretaries as to the Routes, I made up my mind to leave London on the Sabbath Eve^g &, passing by Dublin, to be with you on the Monday evening, for the rest of the time. But since that [*sic*] I have been so weak & depressed as to rejoice that I was not with you in that state, as I should have been a mere burden; & shackle on your kind exertions to others: – indeed home & even the bed room were the only fit places. I do not know whether it was the season or not – I cannot tell – it was one of the old time depressions I am better now but not in a fit state for the excitement of the meeting. – I may go on improving & if I feel able enough mean to fulfil the intentions: – still I hardly expect it; – I could not come as I am; and I do not know which way matters will go this week. I shall be sorry, & much disappointed, to be away; but I ought not to complain, and when I do so, & murmering [*sic*] thoughts arise, it seems to me that I am very ungrateful to a kind providence.

Wishing you a happy and prosperous meeting in every case and with most earnest thanks to Mrs. Andrews & yourself for your great kindness I am

My dear Andrews
Yours gratefully
M. FARADAY

498   M. FARADAY to the Secretary, Trinity House, 27 September 1852

[*Lightning Rod Conference, Report, London, 1882, Appendix l, General Correspondence, 187*]

Royal Institution,
27th September, 1852.

MY DEAR SIR,

I fortunately reached the Nash Low Lighthouse last Thursday, before any repairs were made of the injury caused by the discharge of lightning there, and found everything as it had been left: the repairs were to be commenced on the morrow.

The night of Monday, 30th August, was exceedingly stormy, with thunder and lightning; the discharge upon the lighthouse was at six o'clock in the morning of the 31st, just after the keeper had gone to bed. At the same time, or at least in the same storm, the flagstaff between the upper and lower lights was struck, and some corn stacks were struck and fired in the neighbourhood. It is manifest that the discharge upon the tower was exceedingly powerful, but the lightning conductor has done duty well – has, I have no doubt, saved the building; and the injury is comparatively slight, and is referable almost entirely to circumstances which are guarded against in the report made by myself and Mr. Walker[1] 22nd September, 1843.

The conductor is made fast to the metal of the lantern, descends on the inside of the tower to the level of the ground, and passes through the wall and under the flag pavement which surrounds the tower. It is undisturbed everywhere, but there are signs of oxidation on the metal and the wall at a place where two lengths of copper are rivetted together, which show how great an amount of electricity it has carried.

A water-butt stands in the gallery outside the lantern. A small copper pipe, 1 inch in diameter, brings the water from the roof of the lantern into this butt; it does not reach it, but terminates 10 or 12 inches above it. A similar copper pipe conducts the surplus water from the butt to the ground, but it is not connected metallically with the other pipe, or with the metal of the conductor, or the lantern. Hence a part of the lightning which has fallen upon the lantern has passed as a flash, or, as we express it, by disruptive discharge from the outside of the lantern to this tub of water, throwing off a portion of the cement at the place, and has used this pipe as a lightning conductor in the rest of its course to the ground. The pipe has holes made in it in three places, but these are at the three joints, where, it being in different lengths, it is put together with tow and white lead, and where of course the metallic contact is again absent; and thus the injury there (which is very small) is accounted for. The pipe ends below at the level of the ground in a small drain, and at this end a disruptive discharge has (naturally) occurred, which has blown up a little of the cement that covered the place. Some earth is thrown up at the outer edge of the pavement round the tower over the small drain, which tends to show how intense the discharge must have been over the whole of the place.

Inside of the lantern there are traces of the lightning, occurring at places where pieces of metal came near together but did not touch, thus at the platform where a covering copper plate came near to the top of the stair railing, but the effects are very slight. All the lamps, ventilating tubes &c., remained perfectly undisturbed, and there was no trace of injury or effect where the conductor and the lantern were united.

Inside of the tower and the rooms through which the conductor passes there were and are no signs of anything (except at the rivetting above mentioned) until we reach the kitchen or living-room which is on a level with the ground, and here the chair was broken and the carpets and oil-cloth fired and torn. To understand this, it must be known that the separation between this room and the oil-cellar beneath is made by masonry consisting of large stones, the vertical joints of which are leaded throughout, so that the lead appears as a network upon the surface, both of the kitchen floor above, and the roof of the oil cellar beneath, varying in thickness in different places up to $\frac{1}{3}$ or more of an inch, as in a piece that was thrown out. The nearest part of this lead to the conductor is about 9 inches or a little more distant, and it was here that the skirting was thrown off, and the chair broken; here also that the fender was upset and the little cupboard against the skirting emptied of its articles. If this lead had been connected metallically with the conductor, these effects would not have happened.

666

The electricity which in its tendency to pass to the earth took this course, naturally appeared in the oil-cellar beneath, and though the greater portion of it was dissipated through the building itself, yet a part appeared in its effects to have been directed by the oil cans, for though they were not at all injured or disturbed, the wash or colour in the wall above four or five of them was disturbed, showing that slight disruptive connections or sparks had occurred there.

At the time of the shock, rain was descending in floods, and the side of the tower and the pavement was covered with a coat of water, This being a good conductor of electricity has shown its effects in connection with the intense force of the discharge. A part of the electricity leaving the conductor at the edge of the pavement and the tower, broke up the cement there, in its way to the water on the surface, which for the time acted to it as the sheet of copper – which I conclude is at the end of the conductor – does, *i.e.*, as a final discharge to the earth. Also on different parts of the external surface of the tower near the ground, portions of cement, the size of half a hand, have been thrown off by the disruptive discharges from the body of the tower to this coat of water: all testifying to the intensity of the shock.

I should state that the keeper says he was thrown out of bed by the shock. However, no trace of lightning appears in the bedroom, still there are evidences that powerful discharges passing at a distance, and on the other side of thick walls may affect bodies and living systems, especially by spasmodic action, and something of the kind may have occurred here. It may be as well for me to state that the upper floors are *leaded* together like that of the kitchen. The reason why they did not produce like effect is evident in that they from their position could not serve as conductors to the earth as the lower course could.

The keeper said he had told the coppersmith to make the necessary repairs in the pipe, and I instructed him to connect the waste pipe and the upper pipe by a flat strap of copper plate. I would recommend that the lead of the lower floor be connected metallically with the conductor to a plate of copper in the earth. I could not see the end of the present conductor, not being able by any tools at the lighthouse to raise the stonework, but I left instructions with the keeper to have it done, and report to me the state of matters.

I am, &c.,

M. FARADAY

[1] James Walker (1781–1862), one of the founders of the Institution of Civil Engineers and designer of the Bishop Rock Lighthouse (1847) which was destroyed in February 1848.

[*I.E.E., previously unpublished*]

Giessen,
6 Oct. 1852

MY DEAR FARADAY

Perhaps you know already that my son has been fortunate enough to obtain the appointment as Assistant Surgeon in the Indian Army, which I had endeavoured to gain for him. Colonel Sykes wrote me that he would appoint him if he passes the necessary examinations.

To you chiefly my dear faraday I am no doubt indebted for the fulfillment of this favourite wish of mine and I find it difficult to say how sensible I am of the proof you have thus given me of your friendship by using your interest in behalf of my son on this occasion. Never will I forget this service.

Hoping that you will continue in your kindness towards my son I remain with all my heart

Yours very sincerely
JUSTUS LIEBIG

500 M. FARADAY to A. DE LA RIVE, 16 October 1852
[*Bibliothèque publique et universitaire de Genève, ms. 2316, f. 73–4, previously unpublished*[1]]

Royal Institution
16 Octr 1852

MY DEAR DE LA RIVE

From day to day and week to week I put off writing to you, just because I do not feel spirit enough; not that I am dull or low in mind, but I am as it were becoming torpid: – a very natural consequence of that kind of mental fogginess which is the inevitable consequence of a gradually failing memory. I often wonder to think of the different courses (naturally) of different individuals, and how they are brought on their way to the end of this life. Some with minds that grow brighter & brighter but their physical powers fail; as in our friend Arago, of whom I have heard very lately by a nephew who saw him on the same day *in bed* & at *the Academy*: such is his indomitable spirit – Others fail in mind first, whilst the body remains strong. Others again fail in both together; and others fail partially in some faculty or portion of the mental powers, of the importance of which they were hardly conscious until it failed them. One may, in one's course through life, distinguish numerous cases of these and other natures; and it is very interesting to observe the influence of the respective circumstances upon the characters of the parties and in what way these circumstances bear upon their happiness. It may seem very trite to say that *content* appears to me to be the great compensation for these various cases of natural change; and yet it is forced upon me, as a piece of knowledge that I have ever to call afresh to mind. both by my own spontaneous & unconsidered desires and by what I see in others. No remaining gifts though of the highest kind; no grateful remembrance of those which we have had, suffice to make us willingly content under the sense of the removal of the least of those which we have been conscious of. – I wonder why I write all this to you: Believe me it is only because some expressions of yours at different times make me esteem you as a thoughtful man & a true friend: – I often have to call such things to remembrance in the course of my own self examination and I think they make me happier. Do not for a moment suppose that I am unhappy. I am occasionally dull in spirits but not unhappy. there is a hope which is an abundantly sufficient remedy for that. and as that hope does not depend on ourselves. I am bold enough to rejoice in that I may have it.

I do not talk to you about philosophy for I forget it all too fast to make it easy to talk about. When I have a thought worth sending you it is in the shape of a paper before it is worth speaking of; and after that it is astonishing how fast I forget it again; so that I have to read up again & again my own recent communications and may well fear that as regards others. I do not do them justice. However I try to avoid such subjects as other philosophers are working at; and for that reason have nothing important in hand just now. I have been working hard but nothing of value has come of it.

Let me rejoice with you in the Marriage of Your daughter. I trust it *will be* as I have no doubt it *has been* a source of great happiness to you. Your Son too whenever I see him makes me think of the joy he will be to you. May you long be blessed in your children and in all the things which make a man truly happy; even in this life. Ever My dear friend – Yours Affectionately   M. FARADAY

---

[1] See *B.J.* 2, 314. *B.J.* has omitted one phrase; otherwise the letter is complete.

501 R. WOLF to M. FARADAY, 4 November 1852[1]
   [*I.E.E., previously unpublished*]

Berne,
4/11 1852

MONSIEUR.

Je ne saurais Vous remercier d'une manière plus convenable de Votre lettre bienveillante du 27 Août passé,[2] qu'en Vous indiquant les progrès que je viens de faire dans l'étude des relations entre les tâches solaires et la terre. Je terminerai sous peu un mémoire, qui les développera en détail, et je prendrai la liberté de Vous en présenter un exemplaire; mais en attendant je Vous en doñe[3] [*sic*] le résumé suivant. Mon mémoire se divisera en six parties:

Dans le premier chapitre je démontrerai, appuyé sur 16 époques différentes, établies pour le Minimum et le Maximum des taches solaires, que la durée moyenne d'une période des taches solaires doit être fixée à $11,111 \pm 0,038$ années de sorte que 9 périodes équivalent justement à un siècle.

Dans le second chapitre j'établirai que dans chaque siècle les añées

$$0,00 \quad 11,11 \quad 22,22 \quad 33,33 \quad 44,44 \quad 55,56 \quad 66,67 \quad 77,78 \quad 88,89$$

correspondent à des Minimums des taches solaires. L'intervalle entre le Minimum et le Maximum suivant est variable; la moyenne en est de 5 années.

Le troisième chapitre contiendra l'énumération de toutes les observations des taches solaires depuis Fabricius et Scheiner jusqu'à Schwabe, continuellement mise en parallèle avec ma période. L'accord est surprenant.

Le quatrième chapitre établira des analogies remarquables entre les taches solaires et les étoiles variables, par lesquelles on peut présumer une liaison intime entre ces phénomènes singuliers.

Dans le cinquième chapitre je démontrerai que ma période de $11,111$ añées coincide encore plus exactement avec les variations en déclinaison magnétique que la période de 10 1/3 añées établie par Mr Lamont.[4] Les variations magnétiques suivent même les taches solaires non seulement dans leurs changemens réguliers, mais aussi dans toutes les petites irrégularités, – et je pense que cette dernière remarque suffira pour avoir prouvé définitivement cette relation importante.

Le sixième chapitre traitera d'une comparaison entre la période solaire et les indications météorologiques contenues dans une chronique Zuricoise sur les añées 1000–1800. Il en résulte (conformément aux idées de William Herschel)[5] que les années où les taches sont plus nombreuses sont aussi en général plus sèches et plus fertiles que les autres, – ces dernières au contraire plus humides et plus orageuses. Les aurores boréales et les tremblements de terre indiqués dans cette chronique, s'accumulent d'une manière frappante sur les années de taches.

Si ces petites découvertes Vous semblent avoir assez d'importance pour en faire le sujet d'une communication à la Société royale ou à la Société astronomique et surtout à Mr Herschel, je Vous prie d'en disposer, – Vous m'obligeriez infiniment par une telle communication.

Agréez, Monsieur, l'assurance de la plus haute considération de Votre très dévoué serviteur

RODOLPHE WOLF
Directeur de l'Observatoire de Berne

[1] See Letter 494.
[2] I have been unable to locate this letter.
[3] Wolf follows the same practice with double n's as Plücker does with double m's.
[4] See Letter 494.
[5] See William Herschel, 'Observations tending to investigate the Nature of the Sun, in order to find the Causes or Symptoms of its variable Emission of Light and Heat; with Remarks on the Use that may possibly be drawn from Solar Observations', *PT* (1801), 265.

502   M. FARADAY to SIR J. F. W. HERSCHEL, 8 November 1852

[*R.S., previously unpublished*]

Royal Institution,
8 Nov.ʳ 1852

MY DEAR HERSCHELL [*sic*]

I send you a letter I have received from M Wolf as he especially desires. After you have seen it I will send it if you approve according to his wish to the Royal Society or to the Astronomical if you think it better.

Ever faithfully Yours
M. FARADAY

[Note by Herschel] Period of solar spots 9 Periods in 100 y or 11 y 11 Min[inum] to Min[inum]
    The commencement 1800, &c. of each century is a *minimum*

503   SIR J. F. W. HERSCHEL to M. FARADAY, 10 November 1852

[*I.E.E., previously unpublished*]

Harley Street
Nov. 10 1852

MY DEAR FARADAY

Wolf's letter excited great expectations.[1] A law of perioding [*sic*] in the recurrence of the Solar Spots seems to be established by Schwabe's observations referred to by Sabine in his recent paper on Magnetic disturbances,[2] and the period (of somewhere about 10 or 11 years if I remember right) agrees with Wolff [*sic*]. – Sabine has in that paper (whether originally or not I know not) distinctly connected the two Phaenomena – extraordinary Magnetic disturbances and few Solar Spots. Their identity of period. – If all this be not premature we stand on the verge of a vast cosmical discovery such as nothing hitherto imagined can compare with. Compare what I have said about the exciting cause of the Solar light – referring it to Cosmical electric currents traversing space and finding in the upper regions of the Suns [*sic*] atmosphere matter in a fit state of tenuity to be *auroralized* by them (Astron. Note on Aur. 400)[3]

(Query the red Clouds seen in Solar Eclipses – are they not reposing auroral masses)

As Sabines paper was read to the R.S.[4] and the subject is one of quite as much physical as purely astronomical Interest I should think the R S would be the fit point of delivery of M. Wolfe's [sic] ideas – only in what form I know not – perhaps in some conversational form – or in that of a statement from the chair (but ? as this would be a precedent).

However I would not pre[reading doubtful]clude the Astronomical Society from inquiring and discussing it and I don't see why it might not keep on from one to the other in the way of scientific news or gossip.

Yours very sincerely
J. F. W. HERSCHEL

P S. What treatise on Chemistry (not organic) should I put into my Son's library as a text book in furnishing him with matter for meditation in India?

[1] See Letter 502.
[2] Edward Sabine, 'On periodical laws discoverable in the mean effects of the larger magnetic disturbances', *PT* (1852), 103.
[3] Sir John F. Herschel, *Outlines of Astronomy*, London, 1849, 400.
[4] *PRS*, 6 (1850–4), 174.

504   E. SABINE to M. FARADAY, 11 November 1852
[*I.E.E., previously unpublished*]

Woolwich,
Nov. 11, '52

DEAR FARADAY

I return Mr Wolf's *german* letter with thanks[1] – The first letter shall be given to Mr Christie for communication. Humboldt wrote me some time since an account of Mr. Wolfe's [sic] discovery of the connexion between the Magnetic variations & the solar spots, & remarked that I had preceded him in publication by between 4 & 5 months: and I have reason to believe that he will notice my priority in his forthcoming vol. of Cosmos, which I am glad of, as the thing itself has excited but little interest in this country, & foreign countries are not always ready to do justice to a man of a country which is comparatively regardless, of a matter in which they take a far greater interest. I believe that I have a claim to be considered as the first announcer of the probable existence of a *secular magnetic period in the Sun*.

Mr. Wolf has been forestalled by Lamont in the period of the variations of the magnetic declination. By myself in the period of the variations of the magnetic dip & total force, & in the period of the supposed irregular disturbances or storms – and in the coincidence of these periods with that of the solar spots. There remains to him of original suggestion therefore the examination of the earlier solar spot observations from the time of [illeg.], & their connection with the recent far more ample research of Schwabe to a supposed correction of the *period* from 10.33 to 11.11 years – the suggestion of a connexion between the *solar spots & variable stars*, which would be indeed surprising, as one cannot well see how the solar spots are to affect beyond the solar system, & it would seem to make the solar magnetic period only one phenomenon of a general cosmical magnetic period. The proof of the years of maximum solar spots being years of dryness & fertility would seem to be very difficult to establish if the proof is to extend, as it ought to do, *over the surface of the Globe generally*. I should doubt greatly whether this will prove more than a mere speculation.

The connexion between the appearance of Aurora & the magnetic storms has long since been established – the greater frequency of the storms carries with it therefore the greater frequency of Aurora –

Robinson at Belfast[2] suggested that the variable light of the stars might be analogous to the solar spots, as indicative of a magnetic period, but not the *same* period for *sun & stars*

Sincerely yours
EDWARD SABINE

[1] See Letter 494.
[2] Probably Thomas Romney Robinson (1792–1882) of the Armagh Observatory. I am unable to locate Sabine's reference.

505 M. FARADAY to SIR J. F. W. HERSCHEL,
  12 November 1852[1]
  [*R.S., previously unpublished*]

Royal Institution,
12 Nov. 1852

MY DEAR HERSCHEL

I have not read up the different elementary Treatises on Chemistry and should rather ask advice than give it but I will mention three, Fowne's,[2] Graham's[3] and Brande's.[4] The first is the smallest but excellent. The third is the largest.

Ever truly yours
M. FARADAY

I have sent Wolf's letter to Sabine for I thought he was far the best judge as to fitness.

M.F.

The original given by J.F.W. H. to Is. H. [?]

[1] From a copy written in Herschel's hand.
[2] George Fownes, *A Manual of Elementary Chemistry, Theoretical and Practical*, London, 1844.
[3] Thomas Graham, *Elements of Chemistry*, London, 1842.
[4] William Thomas Brande, *A Manual of Chemistry*, London, 1819.

506 M. FARADAY to T. T. W. WATSON,[1] 20 December 1852

[*Burndy Library, Norwalk, Conn., Michael Faraday Collection 83, previously unpublished*]

Royal Institution
20 Decr 1852

SIR

On Saturday I was at the Trinity House & consulted with the Secretary who agreed with my general statement of what I had said to you & Mr. Presler.[2] It will therefore be expedient first to have a day of 8 hours at the Trinity house placing the Electric light in the Dioptric light room in the corner by the steps so as to have it as far from the French light as possible but with the sight clear from one to the other between the Iron pillars.

If the days trial is encouraging then a daily trial for a fortnight excepting Sunday of at least 8 hours each day will be required – also at the Trinity House. Upon the result of these trials further steps can be taken

Now the single days trial might be this week excepting Saturday – but the successive trials could not well come on until the week beginning 10th January because of the possible absence of some who would have to regard the light from day to day. I leave it with you therefore to decide whether the single trial shall take place this week or at that time – & would be glad if you would let me know at once on what you decide and when the day is to be Above all I most earnestly beg of you to produce no imperfectly prepared apparatus or any thing that requires excuse. If the apparatus is not yet complete keep it back until it is. The Trinity House has not time to Witness incomplete trials and it would only do harm to call their attention to any thing avowedly imperfect

I think I have said nothing here to which you did not freely assent If you make a trial this week let me know the day as soon as possible

I am Sir
Your Obdt Servt
M. FARADAY

[1] Possibly Sir Thomas Watson, Bart. (1792–1882).
[2] Presler contrived an electric light for lighthouses.

Geneve
le 24 x^bre 1852

MONSIEUR & TRÈS CHER AMI,

Je n'ai pas répondu plus tôt à votre bonne & amicale lettre[1] parce que j'aurais voulu avoir quelque chose d'intéressant à vous dire. Je suis peiné de ce que votre tête est fatiguée; cela vous est déjà arrivé quelquefois à la suite de vos travaux si nombreux & si persévérants; mais vous vous rappellez qu'il suffit d'un peu de repos pour vous remettre en très bon état. Vous avez ce qui contribue le plus à la sérénité de l'âme & au calme de l'esprit, une foi pleine & entière aux [word illeg.] de notre Divin Maitre & une conscience pure & tranquille qui remplit votre coeur des espérances magnifiques que nous donne le Evangile. [*sic*] Vous avez en outre l'avantage d'avoir toujours mené une vie douce & bien réglée exempte d'ambition & parconséquent de toutes les agitations & de tous les mécomptes qu'elle entraine après elle. La gloire est venue vous chercher malgré vous; vous avez su, sans la mépriser, la réduire à sa juste valeur. Vous avez su vous concilier partout à la fois la haute estime & l'affection de ceux qui vous connaissent. Enfin vous n'avez été frappé jusqu'ici, grâce à la bonté de Dieu, d'aucun de ces malheurs domestiques qui brisent une vie. C'est donc sans crainte comme sans amertume que vous devez sentir approcher la vieillesse, en ayant le sentiment bien doux que les merveilles que vous avez su lire dans le livre de la nature doivent contribuer pour leur bonne part à en faire encore plus admirer & adorer le Suprême Auteur.

Voilà, très cher ami, l'impression que votre belle vie m'a toujours fait éprouver. Et quand je la compare à nos vies agitées & si mal remplies, à tout cet ensemble de mécomptes & de douleurs dont la mienne en particulier a été obscurcie, je vous estime bien heureux surtout parceque vous êtes digne de votre bonheur. Tout cela m'amène à penser au malheur de ceux qui n'ont pas cette foi religieuse que vous avez à un si haut degré, & en particulier à la pauvre Lady Lovelace; avez-vous su quelque chose sur ses derniers moments & sur ses dispositions morales & religieuses à cette heure suprême?

Mon fils qui vous remettra cette lettre est dans ce moment à Londres avec sa jeune femme; ils ont été voir leur excellente grand-mère Madame Marcet qui semble être mieux maintenant qu'elle ne l'a été depuis long-temps.

Mon premier volume sur l'Electricité doit avoir paru dans ce moment; le second avance & ne tardera pas à suivre son ainé. Si vous le lisez (je vous en enverrai un exemplaire aussitôt qu'il aura paru), faites moi la grande amitié de me présenter toutes vos observations, afin que j'en fasse encore profit pour l'édition française. – Je suis bien sur que malgré ce que vous me dites, vous saurez encore trouver quelque belle mine à exploiter dans ce riche domaine que vous cultivez avec tant d'ardeur & de succès. N'oubliez pas de m'en faire part, car vous savez tout l'intéret que je mets à ce qui vient de vous parceque c'est de vous avant tout & ensuite parceque c'est toujours original & remarquable.

Merci de toutes vos précédentes communications. Votre affectionné & bien dévoué

A. DE LA RIVE

1 See Letter 500.

508   E. SABINE to M. FARADAY, 4 January 1853
[*I.E.E., previously unpublished*]

11 Old Burleigh S.
January 4, 1853

DEAR FARADAY

I have just read Mr. Wolf's little pamphlet[1] on the period of the sun's spots –

Having some time since noticed to you that I felt some degree of disapointment in contrasting the interest with which the announcement which I made last March to the R.S.[2] of the connexion between the period of the sun's spots & that of the magnetic variations had been received on the Continents of Europe & America as compared with this country – a remark which perhaps you thought might stand in need of some justification, – Mr. Wolf's pamphlet furnishes me I think with a very fine illustration of it, which I notice at once to yourself because you are concerned, & to mark more particularly that what I regret is rather the *general indifference of Englishmen to the scientific discoverys* [*sic*] *of their own countrymen*, than *individual* indifference; for from no Englishman should I look for more consideration & regard than from you. – But now to my point – In page 16 Mr. Wolf quotes in two notes, long extracts from letters from Humboldt & yourself, Humboldt's dated Sept. 10, yours Augt. 27; both acknowledging letters from him announcing the coincidence of the 2 periods, the magnetic variations & the solar spots. – Humboldt does me the justice to inform Mr. Wolf of my previous announcement of the same first & refers to date & place of publication. You writing from England take no notice whatsoever of the previous publication of the very same coincidence which had been communicated to you some months before by a friend & countryman of your own! –

The fact is a remarkable one; and will no doubt be adverted to by Mr Wolf in the reply which he will probably make to the remarks which I must make on the injustice which overlooking Mr. de Humboldts letter he has done to me in placing the date of my publication in *September* instead of March or May (at which latter date the printed copies were in general circulation), and thus countermanding his own claim to a nearly simultaneous publication in the Comptes Rendus for September 13.

Sincerely yours
EDWARD SABINE

[1] R. Wolf, 'Neue Untersuchungen über die Sonnenfleckenperiode und ihre Bedeutung', Bern, 1852.
[2] See Letter 479, fn. 4.

509   G. G. STOKES[1] to M. FARADAY, 7 January 1853
[*I.E.E., previously unpublished*]

Pembroke College,
Cambridge
Jan 7th 1853

MY DEAR SIR,

I found your letter on my return to Cambridge this evening. As you seem to be disengaged in the early part of next week, I propose to go to Town on Monday, so as to be ready to try experiments on Monday evening. Please to leave word with the Porter, or with your assistant, what hour you would like to begin. It is a matter of perfect indifference to me.

By way of fixing on something, I would propose on Monday evening to try the effects of different flames, especially sulphur burning in oxygen, the effect of which, from your account, must be very powerful. I should be glad also to try the experiment you mentioned respecting the light given by the explosion of oxygen and hydrogen in a glass vessel, and some others which that suggested to me.

The glass vessel which I ordered is destined to hold a very weak solution of chromate or bichromate of potash. I am not sure which will answer best, but I am inclined to think the chromate. It is no consequence whether the salt be or be not chemically pure.

I should be glad to have some Canton's phosphorus. I have got some here, but as I made it myself merely in my fire I am afraid it may not be good.

If there be an Argand lamp at the R.I.I. should be glad to repeat the experiment of Draper's[2] which I have referred to at p. 547 of my paper[3] l.10 from the bottom. According to Becquerel,[4] the rays of low refrangibility cause Canton's phosphorus *if previously excited by rays of high refrangibility* to give out more quickly than it otherwise would the light which it is capable of giving out. It strikes me as possible that the phosphorus with which Draper worked when he obtained this result may have been previously excited.

I dare say the experiments I have mentioned, and some things I should like to show you, (such as the absorption-bands of permanganate of potash mentioned in Note D of my paper) will afford work enough for one evening without the electrifying machine.

Art. 224 of my paper will explain what I wanted with a revolving mirror. The experiment could be performed in any place where there are these two things, a revolving mirror apparatus, and an electrifying machine If Prof.

Wheatstone will kindly lend his apparatus, or else undertake the experiment himself, it might be performed at his house [reading doubtful] or at King's College as might be convenient.

Yours very truly

G. G. STOKES

[1] George Gabriel Stokes (1819–1903), Lucasian Professor of Mathematics at Cambridge.
[2] John William Draper, 'Account of a remarkable difference between the Rays of Incandescent Lime and those emitted by an Electric Spark', *PM*, 3 s., 27 (1845), 435.
[3] G. G. Stokes, 'On the change of refrangibility of Light', *PT* (1852), 463.
[4] E. Becquerel, 'Note sur la phosphorescence produite par insolation', *CR*, 25 (1847), 632.

510   E. SABINE to M. FARADAY, 8 January 1853

[*I.E.E., previously unpublished*]

11 Old Burleigh S,
January 8, '53

DEAR FARADAY

I think that the facts point to a more distinct recognition of distinct causes than appears in your note: that we must separate the effects which are occasioned by the earths revolution in its orbit, from those which are occasioned by its revolution on its axis: the one producing a variation in the magnetic direction which is properly called "annual" because its period is a *year*, and the other "diurnal" because its period is a *day*. Now with respect to the first, or annual variation, & confining ourselves to *our* element, viz the Declination: and (the better to fix our ideas) to *one* hour, viz 8 am, (as that is one of the hours followed out in the dates which I sent to you). Now, as far as we have yet experience, if a declination be observed at the same hour of 8 am in *any part of the world*, i. e. in *any* meridian, or in *any part of any meridian*, whether north or south of the Equator, or on the Equator, the declination so observed will shew an annual variation, the *direction and amount of which will be every where the same*: i. e. at the northern solstice the needle will be at its eastern extreme, at the southern solstice at its western extreme, and it will pass through its mean position at the two equinoxes: in the one case when proceeding from east to west, & in the other when returning from west to east. The direction of the motion is every where the same, i.e. of the north end of the needle from east to west from June 21 to December 21, and from west to East from December 21 to June 21, without reference to whether the one end of the needle be directed upwards (by reason of the Dip) or the other end of the needle be directed upwards, or whether the needle be horizontal: – and the amount is also every where the same, or very nearly so, viz five minutes of Arc.

Now, having found & measured this annual variation, we can eliminate it; and when it is eliminated, the needle will have its mean place for 8 am all the

678

year round, *so far as the annual variation is concerned.* Now let the same thing be done for each of the 24 hours separately, (assuming that you have hourly observations to deal with), and let it be done for three places, one in Northern Latitude, a second in Southern Latitude, and a third on the Equator; (the annual variation so eliminated will have been the same amount, & have had the same direction at each of the three locations as already stated) – Now then the comparison of the direction of the needle at the different *hours* of the day will give us the *diurnal* variation, and, as the result of the diurnal variation, we find that at 8 am the north end of the needle is considerably to the *East* of its mean position in the 24 hours at the station in *North* Latitude, – considerably to the *West* of its mean position at the station in South Latitude; whilst at the Equator the diurnal variation is null; the needle at 8 am pointing the same as it does on the mean of the 24 hours. The *character* of the diurnal variation at 8 am then is that the north end of the needle is affected in opposite senses in opposite hemispheres, passing thro' a Zero on the Equator – and that its amount varies from 0 at the Equator to several minutes in the high Latitudes being continually variable according to some law into which we need not now enter – whereas the Character of the *annual* variation is that the same end of the needle is affected in the same sense, and to the same amount, equally whether the locality be in the North or South hemisphere or on the Equator.

There is another feature in the Annual Variation which is a very remarkable one, which is shown I think well by the Plate I sent you. I have said that the annual variation passes thro' its mean position at the Equinoxes; it not only does so on the very day of the Equinox, but in one week after the Equinox is passed, it has *reached* IN AMOUNT *the full extent (or very nearly so indeed) of* the half amplitude of the whole movement; in the same way that a week before the Equinox the position of the needle depending on the annual variation & almost if not quite as distant from the mean position in the other direction. This phenomena is most markedly the same at St Helena & the Cape of Good Hope – whilst at St Helena the dip is 21° & at the Cape 54′; the Lat of the one 17′, & of the other 34.5°.

You can lay bye this note till you have more time to look into the subject, and then I shall be very glad to receive your remarks.

Very truly yours
EDWARD SABINE

Royal Institution,
24th January, 1853.

MY DEAR SIR,

In reference to the remarkable stroke of lightning which occurred at the Eddystone Lighthouse, at midday on 11th January of this year, and made itself manifest by a partial flash discharge in the living rooms, I have to call your attention to the drawing herewith returned and to the circumstances which appear (from it) to have accompanied and conduced to the discharge.

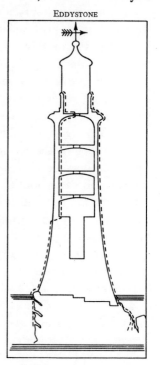

EDDYSTONE

In the body of the stone work above the store-room exist eight rings of metal; each going round the building, and each being four inches square of solid iron and lead. Also, latterly the bed-room and sitting-room have been lined with a framework of iron bars, situated vertically, and pinned by long bolts into the stonework.

The part of the tower above the floor of the living-room is, therefore, filled with a metallic system, which, with the metal lantern, gives a very marked character to the upper half of the structure.

The recent metallic arrangements (but not the rings) are connected with the lightning rod; and the copper part of this rod, beginning at the floor of the living-room, then proceeds downwards by the course which can be followed in the drawing, and terminates on the outside of the rock between high and low water marks.

Considering all these circumstances, I was led to conclude that the conductor was in a very imperfect condition at the time of low water; and I had little doubt that I should find that the discharge had taken place when it was in this state, and very probably with a spring tide.

The day of the stroke was the 11th January – a new moon occurred on the 9th, so that it was at a time of spring tide.

The occurrence took place at midday; and, according to the tide tables, that was close upon the time of low water at Devonport. The end of the conductor would then be 6 feet from the water, if the latter were quiescent, and I cannot doubt that this circumstance gave rise to that diverted discharge which became so manifest to the keepers. Mr. Burges,[1] with whom I have conversed about the matter, thinks it probable that, through the violence of the waves, the conductor does not now descend so much as is represented in the drawing.

I think it essential that the lower end of the conductor be made more perfect in its action; and I should prefer this being done on the *outside* of the tower and rock, if the rod can be rendered permanent in such a situation.

If it be impossible to prolong and fix the lower end of the conductor where it now is, so that it shall have large contact with the sea at low water, then I would suggest, whether or no, on the more sloping part of the rock, about midway between high and low water, three or four holes could not be sunk to the depth of 3 feet, and about 3 or 4 feet apart, and that copper rods being placed in these, they should be connected together, and the lightning rod continued to them.

If this *cannot* be done, then it might be right to consider the propriety of the making a hole through the centre of the building and rock, about 2 or more inches in diameter, and 30 feet deep, and continuing the conductor to the bottom.

A conversation with Mr. Burges regarding the present state of the Bishop's Rock Lighthouse, now in course of construction, induces me also to suggest the propriety of making provision for the lightning conductor as the work proceeds.

It would be easy now to fix terminal rods of copper, and to combine them upwards with the work. Considering the isolated and peculiarly exposed condition of a lighthouse on this site, I would propose that there be *two* conducting rods from the lantern, down the outside on opposite sides of the tower, each terminating below in two or three prolongations, entering as proposed into the rock, or into fissures below low water mark, so as to be well and permanently fixed.

I am, &c.
(Signed) M. FARADAY

[1] Possibly William Burges, civil engineer.

512 C. WHEATSTONE to M. FARADAY, 26 January 1853

[*I.E.E., previously unpublished*]

Lower Mall
Hammersmith
Jany 26th 1853

MY DEAR FARADAY

If you will send to King's College Dr Miller[1] will let you have the original revolving mirror with the whirling table to which it is fitted;[2] I have spoken to him about it. I have at home a small revolving mirror (1/2 of an inch square)

681

with a watch movement making 200 revolutions per second with a tolerably accurate means of measuring the angular elongation of a spark, which I have used to measure the duration of sparks in electro-magnetic coils; Mr Stokes can also have this if it will be of any service to him.

Yours very truly
C. Wheatstone

[1] William Allen Miller (1817–70), Professor of Chemistry, King's College, London.
[2] See Letter 509.

513 M. Faraday to W. Whewell, 29 January 1853
[Trinity College Library, Trinity College, Cambridge, previously unpublished]

Royal Institution,
29 Jany 1853

My dear Sir

You frighten me; for if I have not conveyed to you a clear idea of my meaning by my papers, how can I expect I have succeeded in relation to others. And then how *obscure and confused* my three last papers must have seemed. As you have thought it worth while to look at them once I hope you will again: – for a great deal must have appeared to you to be utter nonsense, which I trust will now have a new meaning & some value in your eyes. My idea of lines of force as closed curves passing through the magnet is, that they pass from *end to end*, or in a direction coinciding therewith: every line of force, wherever it may

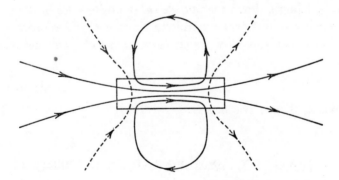

issue from the regular magnet, is *within* it at the magnetic equator; and passes through its *section* at that place. The black lines represent my curves *not* the red lines: the latter could not form continuous lines of force because their polarities would be opposed at the poles of the magnet. I recognize *no poles or centres of action* in that respect. It is curious that I do not find in all my figures one in which the lines of force are marked within the magnet. Of course all those given by filings could give only the direction of the external parts of the lines. But in

(3116) I speak of the full action of the moving internal radius wire alone (b.d. fig 6. par3095. 3098) and in 3117. say that the curve portions of the lines are continuations of the outer portions *absolutely unchanged in their nature*: which would not be true of the red lines on the previous page, where the polarity is suddenly inverted. In (3120) I compare the magnet to an Electromagnetic helix in regard to the direction of the lines; a comparison further illustrated by figs. 5 and 20 of the plate. In 3276 of the paper on the physical lines of force I compare it to a Voltaic battery immersed in a decomposable or conducting fluid; & to a Gymnotus surrounded by water; and I am in hopes the Paragraphs 3277. 3278. 3283. 3287. 3288. 3295. will have a new interest to you, now that you will have caught my idea. 3271. 3265. etc. 3231. also: in fact I think you will be induced to read the papers again.

Dr. Rogets determination of the forms of the lines of magnetic force, is given in the Journal of the Royal Institution 1831, vol I, page 311: and *his* further account of them in the Treatise on Magnetism published in the Library of Useful Knowledge Natural Philosophy vol. II, page 19 of the particular treatise. Wheatstone promised to shew me a folio volume containing demonstrations & forms by a German author but has never kept his word.

In a few days I hope to send you Newtons testimony in favour of physical lines of force as regards Gravity. If that idea is necessary to gravitation, how much more so it must be in relation to the dual powers of Magnetism and Electricity which act in curve lines, and which in the case of a magnet act at all times and when only a single system is concerned.

> Ever My dear Sir,
> Truly Yours,
> M. FARADAY

[1] I have been unable to discover the letter from Whewell to Faraday to which this is a response.

514 J. PLÜCKER to M. FARADAY, 9 February 1853
[*I.E.E., previously unpublished*]

> Bonn,
> 9th February 1853.

DEAR SIR!

After a longer silence, allow me at first to thank you for your last paper, I received two months ago. From your admirable activity in science I may conclude, that your health be improved, and I am happy to do so.

I take liberty to send you my last mémoir on the way of library, two former ones will have reached you, six months ago, on the same way. The indications you gave of the contents of your lecture at the Royal Institution on magnetic lines of force,[1] engaged myself to send a paper of mine, unfinished as it was, to Poggendorff. When I was last time at London, I intended to explain to you what it contains, but I desisted to do so in that troublesome period, not thinking then I might need you in these researches.

I part from the law of the action of an element of the current on a magnetic pole, as given by Biot,[2] immediately after Oerstedt's [sic] discovery. From that law I deduce the law of the induction of a current by a revolving pole, admitting the Newtonian principle, of the equality of action and reaction, as existing between both classes of phenomena. A pole turning round a conducting wire is acting on this wire as an electromotrice force, I deduce the laws of its action, both experimentally and mathematically. In the case of a revolving magnet bar (if you take the case of the Earth) I conclude that there is a tension of negative Electricity in the equatorial zone and a tension of positive one in the arctic regions [etc etc etc] [reading doubtful].

Mr Geissler,[3] our clever artist, constructed a year ago, for the use of a wine-maker's, an apparatus, indicating the quantity of alcool, by the tension of the vapours of the mixture mixed with a certain quantity of air, all at the temperature of 100 C. This apparatus improved on my advice by excluding all air, is that which Dr Waller[4] bought from Mr Geissler and for which he took a „brevet" for England. Dr Hofmann,[5] as it is written to Mr. G., intends to present it at the R. Institution. This apparatus startled me by the *regularity* of its indications, non [sic] only on mixtures containing alcool but also in many other cases, namely in the case of solutions. I left to Mr Geisser [sic] the care to work out (exploiter) his technical apparatus, reserving to myself, after that was done, to take use of the principle, well known before, but not at all sufficiently appreciated, for scientific researches on the affinity of vapours, on Dalton's law, modified for the case of mixed vapours &c &c. After Dr Waller's departure I look up the question and I intend now to send to Poggendorff the first part of the results I obtained, assisted by Mr Geissler.[6] For this purpose new apparatus were constructed, the „Vaporimeter" not being able for scientific researches.

I beg you Sir to present my respects to Mad. Faraday.   Yours very truly
PLÜCKER

[1] *ERE*, 3, 402.
[2] See Letter 416.
[3] Heinrich Geissler (1814–79), inventor of Geissler tubes.
[4] Augustus Waller (1816–70), later Professor of Physiology at University of Birmingham. In 1851, Waller did 'Graduate' work at Bonn.
[5] August Wilhelm Hofmann (1818–92), at this time Professor of Chemistry at the Royal College of Chemistry in London.
[6] This paper does not seem to have been published.

[*I.E.E., previously unpublished*]

Pembroke College,
Cambridge
Feb 14th 1853

MY DEAR SIR,

You will receive I hope some time tomorrow a tin can containing some diagrams. I enclose you the key. Will you have the goodness to order them to be laid flat? I do not think that I shall use more than the 4 outside ones; I merely send the rest for fear I should wish for them and regret having left them behind. They are what I need at Belfast, and they have got a good deal dirtied and rubbed. Will you have the goodness to look at the four outside ones, to see if you think they are decent to produce before a London audience? If not, perhaps there would be time to have them copied or retouched.

I intend to go to the Royal Institution on Thursday evening. I should be glad to have some oxygen ready, as I wish to try some more experiments with the sulphur light. I think it would be possible, and interesting, to show the audience some chemical reactions observed by means of the effects produced by the media on the invisible rays. For this purpose I should wish to have a little of a solution of quinine, (not a quinine salt) in alcohol.

I have found an easy way of purifying the horse-chestnut solution. I mean to bring some of the purified solution with me but in case of any accident please tell Anderson to make a decoction of a good part or the whole of the bark which is left, to the fluid decanted or filtered, & add a little carbonate of ammonia, and then leave it in a shallow open vessel, so as to be exposed to the air. It requires a day or two's exposure. It will be time enough when I come to go on with the process.

I should be very sorry that you should forego any engagement on my account. Anderson can attend me. Indeed you have always got *one* engagement, namely to go on with your most important investigations.

I should like a little hydrogen as well as oxygen, to try the effect of the lime light once more with absorbing media.

I am dear Sir
Yours very truly
G. G. STOKES

Two sliding tables of deal to be made according to this pattern.

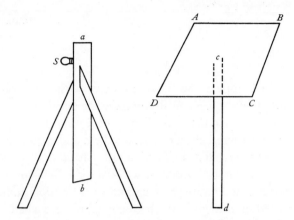

ab is a vertical hollow square tube of board resting firmly on three legs nailed to it (only two are represented in the figure). The base *b* not to reach quite to the floor on which the whole stands. The top *a* may stand 2 ft. 9 in. from the floor. *S* is a coarse wooden screw for clamping, *ABCD* is a square table 1 ft. 4 in. square, fixed to a thick square rod *cd*, which is attached at the centre, and stands perpendicular to its plane. The rod is of the same size as the interior of the tube *ab*, so as to slide within it, and to be clamped by means of the screw *S* to any height that may be desired. The length *cd* is not quite 2 ft. 9 in, so that when *S* is not screwed home *d* does not quite touch the ground.

The bases of the legs ought to form pretty nearly an equilateral triangle with the base *b* of the tube nearly over its centre.

516   W. Stevenson[1] to M. Faraday, 1 March 1853

[*P.M., 4 s., 5 (1853), 465*]

Dunse (N. Britain),
March 1, 1853

Dear Sir, – In the report in the Athenæum of your lecture at the Royal Institution on the 21st of January,[2] I observe that you refer to the highly interesting observations of Schwabe, Sabine, Wolf,[3] Gautier,[4] &c., from which it would appear that a connection exists between the solar spots and the variations of the terrestrial magnetic forces. Since a connection has been demonstrated to exist between the latter and auroral phenomena, I was induced to look over my notes relating to the auroræ observed at this place, with a view to ascertain whether these also exhibited maxima and minima, and if so, whether the periods of such agreed with those of the solar spots and of the magnetic variations. The subjoined table shows the distribution of the auroræ seen here in the years 1838 to 1847 inclusive: –

	Jan.	Feb.	Mar.	Apr.	May	June	July	Aug.	Sept.	Oct.	Nov.	Dec.	Sum.
1838	5	3	4	3	...	...	...	2	4	1	2	3	27
1839	9	1	2	4	1	...	...	...	11	7	2	1	38
1840	5	5	2	4	...	...	...	3	7	6	6	5	43
1841	6	3	4	4	2	...	...	3	3	3	7	7	42
1842	2	2	...	...	...	...	1	...	3	...	1	...	9
1843	2	1	1	1	...	...	...	2	...	3	...	...	10
1844	1	...	2	...	...	...	...	...	1	3	4	2	13
1845	1	2	...	1	...	...	...	1	2	1	1	1	10
1846	...	1	...	...	...	...	1	2	7	4	1	...	16
1847	2	2	3	1	...	...	...	1	5	6	6	4	30
	33	20	18	18	3	...	2	14	43	34	30	23	238

These figures speak for themselves. I may remark that the returns for 1842 are incomplete, as I was absent from home during March and April of that year. In 1848 I was also absent for some months, but from the number of auroræ which I have noted during that year, I am satisfied that a maximum then occurred, both as regards the number and the intensity of auroral displays. This present winter has been very barren in auroral phenomena.

Of crimson auroræ I find I have noted two in 1837, one in 1839, one in 1846, three in 1847, and no less than six in 1848.

A discussion of the auroræ seen in North America and the North of Europe during a series of years would be interesting with reference to the points in question.

Apologizing for troubling you,

I am, dear Sir,
With the greatest respect, yours faithfully,
WM. STEVENSON.

[1] William Stevenson (1805–73), Minister of South Leith near Edinburgh.
[2] 'Observations on the magnetic force', reported on in *The Athenaeum*, 19 February 1853, 230.
[3] See Letters 494, 501 and 504.
[4] Alfred Gautier (1793–1881), 'Recherches relatives à l'influence que le nombre et la permanence des taches observées sur le disque du Soleil peuvent exercer sur les températures terrestres', *AC*, 3 s., 12 (1844), 57.

[Ms. Collection of Dr E. T. Conybeare, OBE, No. 139, Catalogue of Historical Manuscripts Commission, previously unpublished]

Dunse, (N.B.)
5 March 1853

DEAR SIR,

I have no objection to your bringing the substance of my communication under the notice of the Royal Institution. – On the contrary I feel very much gratified that you consider it of so much interest. –

I have for many years paid a good deal of attention to the phenomena of the Aurora & have often sent notice of the more remarkable displays to various public journals. – Some of these have probably come under your notice. – Mr. Glaisher[1] & I have had a good deal of correspondence regarding the connection of the Auroral displays seen here, with the disturbances of the magnetic instruments at Greenwich. –

In 1840, I communicated to Sir D. Brewster some observations on the connection of *cirri* with Auroral phenomena. – These were laid by him before the Phil. Society of St. Andrews & I have often since then sent similar communications to that body. As many of my observations bear upon the subject of atmospheric magnetism, and, on that account, would probably be of some interest to you, – I shall have much pleasure in looking over my notes when I have a little leisure & extracting such obs^{ns} as are likely to be of interest. –

I may state that the communication referred to above as made in 1840, related chiefly to the tendency of cirri to effect a linear arrangement in the direction of the Magnetic meridian. – For two or three years previous to 1840 I had been particularly struck by this tendency, which was all the more remarkable since the direction of the motion of these clouds was generally at *right angles* to that of the Mag. meridian. – Exceptions, due principally to cyclonic movements of the atmosphere, were of pretty frequent occurrance, [*sic*] but from what I observed I was satisfied that the normal or undisturbed position of the long parallel lines of cirrus & cirrostratus clouds coincided with that of the Mag. meridian. – For some years I supposed that I had been the first to detect this magnetic tendency of these clouds. – I was however surprised & gratified (tho' it took from me all title in the eyes of the world to claim originality of discovery,) to find in the "Cosmos", that its illustrious Author had remarked in South America, (under circumstances certainly much more favorable than are presented in our climate) the same tendency of cirri to an arrangement in "meridional bands". –

I have at this moment an impression that for two or three years somewhere between 1840 & 1848, fine, regular displays of cirri were much rarer than for a year or two prior to 1840; but I must look into this matter. –

> I Remain
> Dear Sir
> With the Greatest Respect
> Ever Faithfully Yours
> WM. STEVENSON

[1] James Glaisher was an Assistant at the Greenwich Observatory.

518 M. FARADAY to E. W. BRAYLEY, 10 March 1853
[*Lady Yolande Eddis*,[1] *previously unpublished*]

> Royal Institution.
> 10 Mar. 1853

MY DEAR SIR,

I owe you many thanks for your kindness in sending me the extract from O'Shaughnessy's report.[2] By degrees the evidence of facts accumulates and I hope we shall before very long be able to form a much better notion of the Electro magnetic or Magneto electric state of our earth than we have at present.

Your kindness in sending me the extract reminds me of a little chat we had once about my title "On the *Magnetization of light*". When you told me (what I knew) of the objections of others I held my own and said I was looking a little beyond their views – and I added to the title *a note*. If you happen to look at Walker's translation of De la Rive [*sic*] recent work on Electricity[3] p. 522 at the bottom – p. 523 and page 524 bottom where De la Rive is speaking his own mind on the facts, you will see that I have reason to be satisfied.

My lectures after Easter will be very common place and old in matter for I have had no health or strength to construct or devise new matter but such as they may be I send you on order.

> Ever Truly Yours,
> M. FARADAY

[Brayley's remarks on next page]

"De la R's expression, p. 524, at the last par. "the Phen." to "action...."" "on the *manner*" to "the ether" is exactly equivalent to those in yr. note."[4]

"It appears to me, however, that the *resultant* of all yr. researches in E. is the establishment or at the least the indivisible indication of the existence of the ether."

[1] Lady Yolande Eddis, of Longcroft, Aldeburgh, Suffolk.
[2] Probably Sir William Brooke O'Shaughnessy. I am unable to identify the report.
[3] A. de la Rive, *A Treatise on Electricity in Theory and Practice*, London, 1853. Only the first volume had appeared when Faraday wrote.

4 The passage reads:

'To sum up: in the ideas at present received on the constitution of matter, we think that the phenomena discovered by Faraday ought to be attributed to an action of magnets and electric currents, exercised neither on the particles alone, nor on the ether alone, but on the manner of the existence of the particles in respect to the ether.'

519   M. FARADAY to the Editor of 'The Times', 28 June 1853
['*The Times*', *30 June 1853, 8*]

Royal Institution,
June 28, 1853.

SIR, – I have recently been engaged in the investigation of table-turning. I should be sorry that you should suppose I thought this necessary on my own account, for my conclusion respecting its nature was soon arrived at, and is not changed; but I have been so often misquoted, and applications to me for an opinion are so numerous, that I hoped, if I enabled myself by experiment to give a strong one, you would consent to convey it to all persons interested in the matter. The effect produced by table-turners has been referred to electricity, to magnetism, to attraction, to some unknown or hitherto unrecognized physical power able to affect inanimate bodies – to the revolution of the earth, and even to diabolical or supernatural agency. The natural philosopher can investigate all these supposed causes but the last; that must, to him, be too much connected with credulity or superstition to require any attention on his part. The investigation would be too long in description to obtain a place in your columns. I therefore purpose asking admission for that into the 'Athenæum' of next Saturday, and propose here to give the general result. Believing that the first cause assigned – namely, *a quasi* involuntary muscular action (for the effect is with many subject to the wish or will) – was the true cause; the first point was to prevent the mind of the turner having an undue influence over the effects produced in relation to the nature of the substances employed. A bundle of plates, consisting of sand-paper, millboard, glue, glass, plastic clay, tinfoil, cardboard, gutta-percha, vulcanized caoutchouc, wood, and resinous cement, was therefore made up and tied together, and being placed on a table, under the hand of a turner, did not prevent the transmission of the power; the table turned or moved exactly as if the bundle had been away, to the full satisfaction of all present. The experiment was repeated, with various substances and persons, and at various times, with constant *success*; and henceforth no objection could be taken to the use of these substances in the construction of apparatus. The next point was to determine the place and source of motion, *i. e.* whether the table moved the hand, or the hand moved the table; and for this purpose indicators were constructed. One of these consisted of a light lever, having its fulcrum on the table, its short arm attached to a pin fixed on a cardboard, which could slip on the surface of the table, and its long arm projecting as an index of motion. It is evident that if the experimenter willed the table to move towards the left, and it did so move before the hands, placed at the time on the cardboard, then the index would move to the left also, the fulcrum going with the table. If the hands involuntarily moved towards the left without the table, the index would go towards the right; and, if neither table nor hands moved, the index would itself remain immoveable. The result was, that when the parties saw the index it remained very steady; when it was hidden from them, or they looked away from it, it wavered about, though they believed that they always pressed directly downwards; and, when the table did not move, there was still a resultant of hand force in the direction in which it was wished the table should move, which, however, was exercised quite unwittingly by the party operating. This resultant it is which, in the course of the waiting time, while the fingers and hands become stiff, numb, and insensible by continued pressure, grows up to an amount sufficient to move the table *or* the substances pressed upon. But the most valuable effect of this test-apparatus (which was afterwards made more perfect and independent of the table) is the corrective power it possesses over the mind of the table-turner. As soon as the index is placed before the most earnest, and they perceive – as in my presence they have always done – that it tells truly whether they are pressing downwards only or obliquely, then all effects of table-turning cease, even though the parties persevere, earnestly desiring motion, till they become weary and worn out. No prompting or checking of the hands is needed – the power is gone; and this only because the parties are made conscious of what they are really doing mechanically, and so are unable unwittingly to deceive themselves. I know that some may say that it is the cardboard next the fingers which moves first, and that it both drags the table, and also the table-turner with it. All I have to reply is, that the cardboard may in practice be reduced to a thin sheet of paper weighing only a few grains, or to a piece of goldbeaters' skin, or even the end of the lever, and (in principle) to the very cuticle of the finger itself. Then the results that follow are too absurd to be admitted: the table becomes an incumbrance, and a person holding out the fingers in the air, either naked or tipped with goldbeaters' skin or cardboard, ought to be drawn about the room, &c.; but I refrain from considering imaginary yet consequent results which have nothing philosophical or real in them. I have been happy thus far in meeting with the most honourable and candid though most sanguine persons, and I believe the mental check which I propose will be available in the hands of all who desire truly to investigate the philosophy of the subject, and, being content to resign expectation, wish only to be led by the facts and the truth of nature. As I am unable, even at present, to answer all the letters that come to me regarding this matter, perhaps you will allow me to prevent any increase by saying that my apparatus may be seen at the shop of the philosophical instrument maker – Newman,

122 Regent-street. Permit me to say, before concluding, that I have been greatly startled by the revelation which this purely physical subject has made of the condition of the public mind. No doubt there are many persons who have formed a right judgment or used a cautious reserve, for I know several such, and public communications have shown it to be so; but their number is almost as nothing to the great body who have believed and borne testimony, as I think, in the cause of error. I do not here refer to the distinction of those who agree with me and those who differ. By the great body, I mean such as reject all consideration of the equality of cause and effect, who refer the results to electricity and magnetism, yet know nothing of the laws of these forces, – or to attraction, yet show no phenomena of pure attractive power, – or to the rotation of the earth, as if the earth revolved round the leg of a table, – or to some unrecognized physical force, without inquiring whether the known forces are not sufficient, – or who even refer them to diabolical or supernatural agency, rather than suspend their judgment, or acknowledge to themselves that they are not learned enough in these matters to decide on the nature of the action. I think the system of education that could leave the mental condition of the public body in the state in which this subject has found it, must have been greatly deficient in some very important principle.

I am, Sir, your very obedient Servant,
M. FARADAY.

520 M. FARADAY to G. TOMLIN,[1] 23 July 1853
[*Burndy Library, Norwalk, Conn., previously unpublished*]

R Institution
23 July 1853

SIR

I cannot give you the opinion you ask for – I can only say that I should not publish such a paper in *my own name* – My reasons are that being an experimentalist I do not think theory alone of much force in Magnetism; since many theories as to the natural mode of action, are apparently equally probable. When we have devised new experimental proofs, so as to separate these theories from each other, then we shall be better able to judge which is the nearest to the truth of nature. Hence for my own part I refrain from forming ny conclusion as to the real nature of magnetic action & am content for the resent in trying to find out the *laws* which govern this extraordinary exertion of force.

I am Sir
Your Obt Servt
M. FARADAY

[1] Possibly Frederick Guest Tomlins (1804–67), manager of the Athenaeum Institution for Literary and Scientific Men, editor and publisher. Faraday's advice appears to have been taken for there is no paper on magnetic theory by anyone named either Tomlin or Tomlins.

[*R.I., previously unpublished*]

Royal Institution,
1 August 1853

MY DEAR BARLOW

I only learned on Friday last that you had left a post office reference to Geneva or I should have written to you before I am so accustomed to communicate with you that even when there is no other occasion than kind feeling I do not like to give it up. In real truth the kind feeling is after all the most important of any. I am hoping to hear from you some day soon and to hear also that you are better I should like you to be so well as to be unconscious of it. Tell me soon how you both are and that you are enjoying the scenery & the circumstances: give us a delightful account but let it be a true one. We most sincerely hope & wish that both these points may coincide in one. We have had a fortnights trip into N Wales with constant wet weather – so after living in the hotels for a while we came back not having seen much of the country, but we are pretty well Nothing to brag about: nothing to complain of.

To day Mr. Vincent begins his holiday and the work folk go into the Library *etc*. He wished me to offer his respects & to say that there was nothing particular to mention. Anderson also begins his holiday today – the Porters have had theirs. I wished Anderson to take his whilst I was here: he is very well & I expect will enjoy himself – i. e. if the rainy weather ceases. We have had thus far a very rainy season & it still continues.

The works in the corner of the Hall are now in progress; but here again the rain teazes us sadly & much retards their progress but I think they will be a great comfort when they are finished Mr Wright[1] of the Clarendon was somewhat frightened when he saw them & called whilst I was away. He saw Mr. Vincent & sent his surveyor I suppose he had forgotten that he was upon our wall & not we upon theirs.

As to our painters it is a sad thing that drunkenness should take them away one after another. I have taken the man who succeeded Mr Newsham for the present jobs of the season. He is I understand quite sober, he knows the house and he works for Mr. Ellis & others gaining their approbation. We shall see how things turn out

I am glad to tell you that Percy[2] will lecture here next season. He has chosen the Metals for his course and I have no doubt that he will make it very interesting to our audience. In the point of character (which you know is often apart from the attraction) they are sure to do us good. The Museum of Economic Geology *etc* is no longer the Museum having changed its name into some other long phrase as Metropolitan School of *etc etc* but I hear that it may perhaps change its name again as the point does not appear decided. I fancy the College of Chemistry is by this time identified with it but as you know I am an exceedingly bad Newsmonger & shall make all sorts of mistakes

You would laugh when you heard of our Cab revolution – only think of a strike for three days. It must have been a petty annoyance spread over a very large extent of population & I have no doubt produced extreme irritation with a great number of persons which yet was often extremely ludicrous. We expect much good will result from it in relation to cab conduct

Whether this will find you at Geneva or whether it will have to follow you elsewhere I do not know. If you see De la Rive give my kindest remembrances to him & also to Marcet if in your company We want to know something of you & Mrs. Barlow, for nothing had come to our ears or eyes in any way until I heard on Friday last that you were at Geneva & at the same time through two or three reporters, that Miss Grant[3] had heard of you – the report being pretty good – I hope it is so in truth. My wife & I often think of where you will be & what you may be doing and we hope that Mrs. Barlow will think this part of the letter is as much to her as to you and that it is the bearer of many kindly remembrances founded upon a long continued course of affectionate intercommunication. Ever My dear Barlow

Yours most truly
M. FARADAY.

[1] The Clarendon would appear to be a hotel next to the Royal Institution and Mr. Wright, whom I am unable to identify further, was probably its manager or owner.

[2] John Percy. See Letter 287.

[3] Probably the daughter of Robert Edmund Grant, Fullerian Professor of Anatomy and Physiology at the Royal Institution.

522 M. FARADAY to DR HENRY,[1] 9 August 1853

[*R.I., previously unpublished*]

R Institution
9 August 1853

MY DEAR SIR

I have not the slightest objection[2] only as the letter was written carelessly & in a hurry it may convey my ideas very imperfectly I cannot find a spare copy of my Speculation (printed in Phil Mag for first six months of 1844) or I would send it If you are led to look at it then for "*mere* philosopher" near the top of the second page read "*wise* philospher"[3]

I am My dear Sir
Most truly Yours
M. FARADAY

[1] Possibly Michael Henry (1830–75), then an assistant editor of the *Mechanics Magazine*. See fn. 2.

[2] The first sentence would indicate that Dr. Henry had asked Faraday's leave to do something with a letter from Faraday. Michael Henry is the only Henry I can locate who was associated with a journal, hence my use of him as the recipient of this letter. There is, however, no letter from Faraday published in the *Mechanics Magazine* for 1853 or 1854.

[3] The correction is made in the paper reprinted in *ERE*, 2, 284. This should be noted, for it shows that the collected papers are not printed *exactly* as they first appeared.

523 M. FARADAY to G. B. AIRY, 19 October 1853

[*Royal Observatory, Herstmonceux, Astrology-Optics, 1853 and 1854, Sect. 12, previously unpublished*]

R Institution
19 Octr. 1853

MY DEAR SIR

From what you said about the notes last Saturday night I send you mine to look at if you like. Because of my very bad memory I am obliged to make them long. I must ask you to return them but make any abstract or copy that you like. I have even sent the notes I made the week before at the Wharf on the same subject.

In regard to your note I send back the diagram with the wires marked a and b.[1] Then for simplicitys sake let us suppose that the action [*sic*] are perfect & permanent i.e that the whole of a shall in each case be equally electrified – the insulation being *perfect*. Then no induction would take place in any of the cases if the wires b were also perfectly insulated. It is only when being uninsulated they can assume the contrary state that the induction occurs. (I neglect that which theoretically would ocur [*sic*] across the *thickness* of the wire for it is as nothing)

But if b was in each case uninsulated or touching the ground then induction would occur but the amount of induction would be twice as much on it in the cases 3 & 4 as in those 1. & 2. the battery being of the same power –

I hope I have caught your meaning & that any case which may occur to your mind will be included in the explanation I have endeavoured to give.

Ever Truly Yours
M. FARADAY

[1] No diagram accompanies this letter.

524   G. B. Airy to M. Faraday, 25 October 1853

[*I.E.E., previously unpublished*]

Royal Observatory
Greenwich
1853 October 25

My dear Sir

You know that in all matters magnetical, meteorological, and chemical, I consider myself and Co. here as mere machines, fit to act up to other people's ideas, but having no ideas of our own.

In this consideration I take leave to ask you —

What is the value of Schönbein's Ozonometer?

Is it worth while for us to observe with it here?

If you say that it is, I shall put it in hand for daily observation and registry.

I am, my dear Sir,

Yours very truly
G. B. Airy

525   M. Faraday to G. B. Airy, 27 October 1853

[*Royal Observatory, Herstmonceux, Astrology-Optics, 1853 and 1854, Sect. 12, previously unpublished*]

Royal Institution,
27 Octr. 1853

My dear Sir

I am very glad you are about to observe for ozone. — I think it may, and probably will, become a matter of great importance in relation to the atmosphere & its natural actions. Schonbein's Ozonometer is the best thing we have at present; but the subject is very likely to open out.

Referring to your previous note; May I say that perhaps your mind has been for a moment embrarrassed [*sic*] by thoughts, mingling the conditions of dynamic & static induction; which differ very greatly from each other. In our recent observations together, though the source of Electricity was the Voltaic pile, still the induction we looked after was pure *static* induction; with the one exception of the phenomenon which you noticed, namely the *advance* of the needle on breaking battery contact.

I have thought much on Induction and series xi. xii & xiii of my Exp Researches (which I think you have) are on the subject. — I will not ask you to go through them but perhaps paragraphs 1175–8 and 1295–306 might suggest a chancy [reading doubtful] thought to you in relation to the wire results. You will see at Par 1333 that I have *in principle* anticipated the effect as *to time.* of conduction by the wire consequent upon induction exerted by neighbouring matter. I had quite forgotten the anticipation.

The case of dynamic induction you will find in Paragraphs 1048 &c.

Ever My dear Sir
Yours
M. FARADAY

526 J. LATIMER CLARK[1] to M. FARADAY, 31 October 1853
[*I.E.E., previously unpublished*]

The Electric Telegraph Company,
Engineer's Office,
448 West Strand,
London,
31 Oct[r] 1853

DEAR SIR,

I return you the notes you were so kind as to lend me, with many thanks for their perusal. I have taken the liberty to enclose a list of corrections on some points on which you were not rightly informed, and a diagram of the sending apparatus used in some of the Experiments.

I find we get a return charge quite sensible to the tongue from a coil of 100 yards of gutta percha wire covered with lead – I even reduced the Experiment so far as to receive a perceptible charge from 10 feet of percha wire in a tumbler of Acidulated Water, and lastly from a Leyden Jar – I have no doubt a Leyden battery would give a very perceptible charge –

I am determined to get evidences (if possible) of the disturbance of one wire by another, we ought to see it when circuit [*sic*] is *broken* despite of imperfect insulation. I am making some careful experiments to demonstrate this last link of identity between Galvanic & frictional Electricity of which I will send you a full account & you can then if you wish see them repeated – If you would like a coil or two of wire to Experiment upon either lead covered or plain I have no doubt our people will be glad to send them to you – We are always anxious to further the objects of science in any way – I am anxious to try some delicate Electrometer Experiments about which I shall perhaps have an opportunity of speaking to you –

I remain
Yours very faithfully
LAT. CLARK

[1] Josiah Latimer Clark (1822–98), Chief Engineer of the Electric Telegraph Company.

527 D. BREWSTER to M. FARADAY, 24 November 1853
[*I.E.E., previously unpublished*]

> St. Leonard's College,
> St. Andrew's,
> Novr. 24*th* 1853

MY DEAR MR. FARADAY,

I was much obliged to you for your kind attention to my request respecting the subscription for the statue to M. Arago; and I was gratified to find that we had thought of the same sum.

I have examined the interesting specimen of *Tourmaline* which you requested Dr. Herapath[1] to send me. I have sent him my Report by the same Post which carries this; it expressed my wish that he would shew it to you. It is *certainly* all *Tourmaline*, without Quartz or Feldspar.

> I am,
> My Dear Mr. Faraday,
> Ever most Truly yrs
> D. BREWSTER

P.S. Will you kindly answer the following Queries.

1. What crystals change colour by simply pricking them, and where has any notice of them been published? I think *Iodide of Mercury* is one, & I think Mr. Talbot has somewhere described the experiment.

2. A Lady in whom I am interested has a Red mark of some extent on her cheek. Would it be safe to apply white lead, or zinc paint to hide it? Or do you [know] of any process for this purpose?

[1] William Bird Herapath (1820–68), discoverer and manufacturer of artificial tourmalines.

---

528 M. MELLONI to M. FARADAY, 12 December 1853
[*I.E.E., previously unpublished*]

> Moretti di Portini près Naples
> ce 12 Decembre 1853.

MON ILLUSTRE AMI!

J'ai consigné, il y a quelques jours, au Consul piémontais de Naples un exemplaire de mon second mémoire sur le magnétisme des roches[1] avec prière de vous le faire parvenir le plutôt possible. Cependant comme je sais, par expérience, la lenteur de ces sortes de transmissions, je crois convenable de vous écrire directement par la poste afin de vous informer d'avance des principaux resultats contenus dans ce travail . . . . Je ne sais si je me trompe, mais il me semble que quelques uns d'entre eux ne sont pas tout-à-fait indignes de fixer l'attention de la Societé Royale.

Ma position dans ce pays est toujours la même . . . . je ne conserve plus que ma place d'académicien et les restes d'un patrimoine sérieusement compromis par la passion fatale qui m'a poussé dans le tourbillon scientifique . . . . . Encore dois-je la possibilité de continuer, tant bien que mal, ma vie d'étudiant à la protection des Ambassadeurs prussiens ou pour mieux dire à l'influence de l'illustre savant,² que vous avez déjà déviné, [*sic*] sur le Roi de Prusse leur seigneur et maître! D'autre part Arago de glorieuse mémoire ne pouvant plus agir comme autrefois en ma faveur auprès des puissances politiques à l'ordre du jour a néanmoins continué à me prodiguer les trésors de sa plus vive amitié jusqu'aux derniers moments de sa précieuse existence . . . . . Et vous même, cher et illustre confrère, ne m'avez-vous pas comblé de bontés toutes les fois qu'il vous a été possible de le faire? . . N'ai-je pas encore entre mes mains cette lettre si affectueuse que vous voulûtes bien m'écrire pour me consoler de mes dernières mésaventures?. Ces marques d'estime et d'interêt de la part d'hommes tels que Humboldt, Arago et Faraday sont pour moi le plus haut dégre [*sic*] de bonheur auquel puissent atteindre les veritables *amoureux de la science* et tant qu'elles se maintiendront actives et florissantes à mon égard, les vicissitudes malheureuses de la vie ne parviendront jamais à abattre le courage de

votre très dévoué et très reconn^t Servit. et ami
MACÉDOINE MELLONI

¹ Macédoine Melloni, 'Richerche intorno al magnetismo delle Rocce; 2ᵈ Sopra la calamitazione delle lave in virtu del calore, e gli effetti dovuti alla forza coercitiva di qualunque roccia magnetica', *MASN*, 1 (1852–4), 121.
² Alexander von Humboldt.

529   M. FARADAY to HOPE SHAW, 19 December 1853
[*Sidney M. Edelstein, Dexter Chem. Corp., N.Y.C., previously unpublished*]

Royal Institution
19 Decr. 1853

SIR

I deeply regret that I cannot accede to your request: but the progress of time & the state of my head are entirely against it. I have under medical advice been obliged to restrain my exertions for years past to the Royal Institution where I have been for 40 years. I have there lessened my lecturing duty from year to year and though now announced to deliver six at Christmas – it was up to Yesterday doubtful (& is so still) whether I shall be able because of an attack in the throat to which I am liable accompanied for the first time with extreme deafness.

I am sorry to give you such an answer but it has been accepted as sufficient for several years past by my nearest & highest friends – and it is known that I speak no where out of the Royal Institution: not even at our meetings of the British Association

I have the honor to be
Sir
Your Obt humble Servt
M. FARADAY

530   W. DE LA RUE to M. FARADAY, 22 December 1853
[*I.E.E., previously unpublished*]

7 St. Mary's Road,
Canonbay,
December 22nd 1853

DEAR MR. FARADAY

Permit me to say that I am much flattered that so much of your attention has been bestowed on my drawing of Saturn as to have called forth the conjectures respecting the relative positions of that planet's rings which you are so good as to communicate to me.

The engraving represents the shadow of the planet on the rings correctly for a given epoch, but in other respects except for the position of the two satellites, it must be regarded as a summary of many observations: for the moments of fine or even fair definition on the most favorable night are of too short duration to admit of a complete drawing being made, and I found it generally better to confine my attention to the recording of some one phenomenon only.

The inference I drew from the configuration of the shadow of the planet on the rings, coincides with your own, namely, that the middle ring is in a plane less elevated than the outer ring: – the outline, moreover, of the nebulous ring shows that *it* is more elevated than the two others, and on several occasions of fine definition I have had a distinct impression of its overlaying the middle ring as I have depicted it.

I have repeatedly remarked that the outer and middle rings and the division between them were of different breadth at opposite ends of the same diameter, showing that their centres of gravity as well as their centres of rotation must be eccentric. This joined to their planes not being coincident must produce a complexity in their mutual perturbations and their action on the planet very interesting to the Saturnian mathematicians.

With respect to the probable section of the rings I would remark that on Oct. 15th of this year I observed this appearance

700

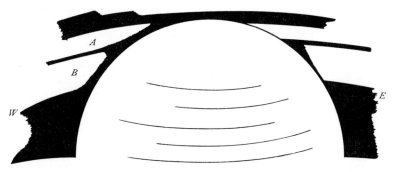

the shadow .. the ring *B* being convex toward the planet – indicating *its*

section to be thus ⬭ ; there was a faint penumbra visible

beyond the dark shadow which was not itself so dark as the division between *A* & *B*. The night was as fine as any I have observed on. The shadow on the ring *B* was just visible on the Eastern side of the ball – but not on the ring *A* on that side.

One subject of interest with respect to Saturn is that the distance of the inner edge of the ring *B* from the planet's centre is less than the drawings of the older observers would appear to indicate was the case in their day, and hence M. Otto Struve[1] who has studied the subject suggests that the ring may be gradually (or rather I should say rapidly) collapsing. He consequently felt desirous to have Huyghens' object glass mounted in order to ascertain if the appearance was due to the telescope and in accordance with his request the Royal Society have as you know determined on so doing. My own belief is that the older astronomers did not clearly observe the darker portions of the ring *B* and hence that its edge appeared to them more distant from the planet than it really was.

I enclose a few diagrams which I employed myself and furnished to other observers, and which, being drawn out in accordance with the data given in the Nautical Almanac, so far as it goes, will show by comparison with my drawing how much I have had to change the relative diameters of the rings to agree with my impressions, which I would remark are in the main confirmed by M. Otto Struve's micrometric measurements.[2]

I must apologize for the length of this note which I fear will have tired your patience.

Very truly Yours

WARREN DE LA RUE

---

[1] Otto Wilhelm Struve (1819–1905), Russian astronomer at Pulkowa. See his 'On the dimensions of the rings of Saturn', *MNASL*, 13 (1852–3), 22.
[2] These diagrams have been lost.

[*I.E.E., previously unpublished*]

Paris
57 rue Cuvier. au jardin des plantes
30 decembre 1853

Monsieur et illustre physicien

il y a bien longtemps que je voulais vous envoyer quelques épreuves de spectres solaires faites sur la préparation chimique que j'ai obtenu il y a plusieures années, (ann. de physique et de chimie 3eme serie tome 25 – page 447.) afin que vous puissiez juger de quelle manière les différentes couleurs de la lumière peuvent se reproduire sur une substance chimiquement impressionnable, et même se conserver pourvu que les impressions soient conservées à l'abri de la lumière du jour.

je n'ai malheureusement que quelques épreuves assez médiocres, et qui sont même en partie décomposées, par suite des expériences que j'ai faites avec elles; cependant j'ai voulu profiter du départ de monsieur Odling[1] pour londres pour vous les envoyer, car cela me procure l'honneur d'entrer en correspondance avec un des plus illustres physiciens de l'europe. comme actuellement je me remets a travailler de nouveau cette question, je vous enverrai cet été de nouvelles épreuves, car elles sont beaucoup plus belles au moment où on les forme, que lorsqu'on les a faites depuis un certain temps; en effet, chaque fois qu'on les observe à la lumière, les teintes s'altèrent un peu.

je vous enverrai également, lorsque la saison permettra de faire les experiences, des images faites à la chambre obscure et colorées d'elles mêmes, afin de vous montrer que l'on peut peindre avec la lumière, ainsi que je l'ai fait voir il y a bientot six ans. il me restait bien quelques peintures que j'aurais pu vous expédier, mais bien plus alterées que les images des spectres que je vous adresse, et c'est pour ce motif que j'ai mieux aimé attendre une nouvelle occasion.

je regarde donc le problème de *la possibilité de peindre avec la lumière*, comme scientifiquement résolu. je ne dis pas pratiquement, car les images sont assez longues à obtenir, et une fois obtenues, elles ne sont fixes qu'autant qu'on les conserve à l'obscurité. la substance chimiquement sensible, qui a reçu des teintes diverses, n'a pas perdu toute impressionnabilité pour cela, et change encore quand on l'expose à l'action d'une lumière quelconque. je n'ai pas encore pu fixer les teintes de façon a ce qu'elles ne changent plus même a la lumière; je ne sais si cela est possible mais je cherche toujours a résoudre la question.

pour voir les images que je vous adresse il est nécessaire de les regarder dans une piéce bien eclairée, mais de ne les considérer que peu de temps, et de les enfermer bien vite dans une boite pour les laisser à l'obscurité jusqu'à ce que on veuille les voir de nouveau. on peut les regarder aussi à la lampe. à chaque fois qu'on les observe, elles s'altèrent de plus en plus; car telles qu'elles sont, elles sont déjà bien alterées et bien moins belles que lorsque je les ai faites il y a 5 ans.

je termine cette lettre, Monsieur, en me felicitant que ce petit envoi m'ait donné l'occasion d'avoir l'honneur de vous écrire, et de vous prier d'agréer l'assurance de la plus haute consideration d'un de vos admirateurs

EDMOND BECQUEREL

Mon père me prie Monsieur de vouloir bien le rappeler a votre bon souvenir.

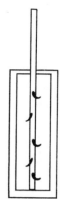

cylindre interieur
5 centi de diametre
13 cent haut

400^{gr} sulfate plomb pulvérisé et 125 à 135 centi cubes d'eau salée saturée (à 25° Marconit [reading doubtful])

Couche de plâtre de $\frac{1}{2}$$^{centi.}$ = tout autour.

---

un couple avec un cylindre en zinc, et de l'eau salée interieur [*sic*] au 1/4 de saturation, a une force electromatrice qu'est mortu [reading doubtful] de celle d'un couple à sulfate de cuivre.

Sa resistance a la conductibilité equivaut à 400 metres de fil de cuivre pur de 1 milli' de diamètre.

---

[1] William Odling (1829–1921), English chemist.

E. BECQUEREL

532   A. DE LA RIVE to M. FARADAY, 6 January 1854
[*I.E.E., previously unpublished*]

Geneve
le 6 janvier 1854

MONSIEUR & TRÈS CHER AMI,

Je ne puis vous dire combien j'ai été sensible à votre bon souvenir. Votre lettre[1] m'a profondément touché. Il est si rare de voir des hommes de Science comme vous, mettre audessus de tout, les sentiments élevés de l'âme & les espérances éternelles, que rien ne peut faire autant de bien à un coeur affligé comme le mien, que des paroles comme celles que vous voulez bien m'adresser. Voilà bientôt quatre années que ma vie a été brisée & mon isolement m'est toujours plus pénible, non pas que je ne sois entouré d'enfants grands & petits aussi aimables que possible; mais il me manque cette compagne confidente de toutes mes impressions, de mes soucis comme de mes jouissances, que rien ne peut remplacer sur cette terre. Il faut donc aller en avant avec des espérances d'un autre ordre; chaque année est un pas de plus vers ce moment où mes espérances, s'il plait à Dieu, seront realisées; mais en attendant on a souvent des moments de découragement & de tristesse qui font trouver la vie bien longue & bien dure. Cependant la Providence me traite encore avec bien de la bonté. Ma fille qui est mariée à un jeune homme excellent plein de piété, est entrée dans une famille pieuse & respectable à tous égards (la famille *Tronchin*).[2] Elle a un petit garçon de neuf mois très prospère & très gentil. Mon fils a épousé sa cousine, la petite fille de Madame Marcet, et il va bientôt être père. J'ai encore deux charmantes filles bien jeunes, l'une de 16 l'autre de 9 ans. Enfin mon fils cadet qui va bientôt avoir vingt ans, est entré l'année dernière comme élève à l'Ecole Polytechnique, après des examens assez brillants. Voilà mon histoire; je vous la fais sans craindre de vous ennuyer, parceque votre amitié pour moi, héritage précieux de mon excellent père, fait que je suis sûr que vous voudrez bien y mettre quelque intéret.

J'aimerais bien vous voir & m'entretenir avec vous; mais je n'ai plus le courage d'aller en Angleterre; les bon amis que j'y ai perdus & surtout le souvenir de ma chère femme avec qui je devais y aller il y a quatre ans, me rendent ce voyage trop mélancolique pour que j'ose encore y penser. Mais vous qui n'avez pas les mêmes impressions, pourquoi ne viendriez-vous pas cet été passer quelques semaines chez moi à la campagne avec Madame Faraday? J'ai un appartement à vous offrir, ma nièce & belle-fille qui a eu le plaisir de vous voir à Londres, vous recevrait de son mieux. Vous meneriez une vie calme & tranquille comme cela convient à des hommes de notre âge & sérieux; vous vous feriez du bien dans notre bon air de la Suisse, & vous en feriez beaucoup à votre ami. Je n'ai aucun projet d'absence du 1er Mai au 1er Novembre 1854; ainsi vous pouvez choisir l'époque qui vous conviendrait le mieux dans cet intervalle de six mois. – Faites cela; le voyage est très rapide & très facile maintenant; je suis sur que Made Faraday s'en trouverait bien aussi.

Je vous remercie des détails intéressants que vous m'avez donnés dans votre lettre sur les expériences faites avec les fils télégraphiques. Ne croyez-vous pas que le retard observé dans la transmission de l'électricité quand le fil plonge dans l'eau vient précisément de ce qu'il joue le role d'une bouteille de Leyde qui exige un certain temps pour se charger; cela n'en est pas moins très curieux.

J'ai donné l'ordre qu'on vous envoyât mon premier volume sur l'Electricité qui vient de paraitre en français. Je suis bien avancé dans le second, & j'attends une occasion pour en envoyer le manuscrit en Angleterre. – Pour en revenir aux succès, vous trouverez dans le volume *français* beaucoup de choses nouvelles & en particulier à la fin (§6 du chap. VIème de la 3ème partie), une théorie nouvelle du magnétisme & du diamagnétisme que je crois assez satisfaisante; je n'entre pas dans plus de détails puisque vous pensez lire le morceau, si cela vous intére[sse].

Oserais-je vous adresser deux questions auxquelles vous pouvez seul me répondre:

1°) Avez-vous jamais réussi dans vos expériences à produire des courants d'induction dans d'autres liquides que le mercure – ou des métaux fondus, par exemple dans les solutions acides ou salines?

2°) Croyez-vous que les liquides puissent conduire une partie quelconque de l'électricité qu'ils transmettent, sans éprouver de décomposition & avez-vous, depuis que vous avez traité ce sujet, été apellé à l'examiner de nouveau & à arrêter vos idées sur ce point important? Je suis, je l'avoue, très perplexe à cet égard, & je serais plutôt disposé maintenant à admettre que dans quelques cas l'électricité peut traverser en partie les liquides électrolytiques sans les décomposer. Cependant je reconnais que c'est un point très difficile à constater à cause des effets secondaires qui jouent toujours un grand rôle dans ces phénomènes. Je mettrais un grand intéret à savoir où vous en êtes à cet égard.

J'espère que vous avez reçu dans le temps ma petite notice sur Arago[3] que je vous ai envoyée par Marcet; je l'ai faite en quelques heures & elle s'est bien ressentie de la précipitation que j'ai été, malgré moi, obligé d'apporter à cet hommage que je tenais à rendre promptement à la mémoire de notre ami.

Veuillez avoir la bonté de me rappeler au bon souvenir de Madame Faraday sur laquelle je compte pour vous engager à nous faire une visite l'été prochain, & agréez, très cher maitre & ami, l'assurance des sentiments de respect & d'affection que je vous porte [reading doubtful]

Votre dévoué

A. DE LA RIVE

[1] This letter does not appear to have survived. Faraday's last letter to de la Rive is number 500 to which de la Rive replied in number 507.
[2] The Tronchin family was of the Genevan aristocracy.
[3] A. de la Rive, *François Arago*, Geneva, 1853.

533 M. FARADAY to J. P. GASSIOT, 17 January 1854
[*R.I., previously unpublished*]

17 Jany 1854

[No salutation]

Three long bands of fine oiled silk crape (each being effectively a plate of fine dry oil – umpervious [*sic*] & insulating.) respectively 108 inches long and $6\frac{1}{2}$ inches wide

Two similar bands of tin foil each 106 or 107 inches long and only 6 inches wide

These made into a common band of Silk————————————
                    foil ————————————
                    silk ————————————
                    foil ————————————
                    silk ————————————
so that the oiled silk shall overlap the edges of the tin foil

The compound band is then bent backwards and forwards thus so as to

 make a packet 6½ inches wide & 18 inches long which lies in the bottom of the box and yet is equivalent to 702 square inches of doubly coated surface or a square of 25 inches in the side – the induction being through a thickness no more than that of *one oiled silk*. Then by proper easy fittings one end of one of these plates is connected with the primary current wire on one side of the *breaker* & the other plate with the same current wire at the other side of the breaker – hence the good effect.

Ever dear Gassiot
Truly yours
M. FARADAY

534   M. FARADAY to J. PLÜCKER, 27 January 1854

[*Nat. Res. Counc. Canada, previously unpublished*]

Royal Institution
27 January 1854

MY DEAR PLÜCKER

I am very tired – rather poorly – and want something to cheer me – so I have resolved to write to you. – For it seems to me very long since I have seen your handwriting and the last time we met was for a very short time – It begins to come back upon me that I saw you on your way to Hull[1] & that you shewed me some beautiful tables & curves of the progression of magnetic and diamagnetic force and I am most desirous of seeing them in an English dress that I may slowly & deliberately embue my mind with them. – I hope you reached home safely I could not be with you at Hull. Every year I feel less able to encounter the quick hurry and excitement of vigorous & active spirits. One of our philosophic physicians Sir Henry Holland[2] has in one of his medical essays dealt with the question of *time* in regard to the operation of thought He shews that the time often becomes sensible: – and in advancing years especially – often increases to a very considerable amount. I feel persuaded by my own experience and by many observations of others that he is right: – for with me the time necessary to apprehend an idea is very sensible and when it becomes necessary to take up many dissimilar ideas in *quick* succession then the necessity of a certain amount of time makes the operation a real labour. Such is the case at meetings like those of the B. association at Hull and I cannot bear them.

I have not been working much lately only a little upon metal wires covered with Gutta Percha – When these are immersed in water they form remarkable Leyden arrangements Only think of a cylinder of Gutta Percha coated inside with copper & outside with Water and though the wire be but 1/4 of an inch thick still 100 meters [reading doubtful] give an inside coating of about 8270 square feet and an outside coating of 33000 square feet. I have worked with 1500 miles of such wire at once and the results are exceedingly curious & interesting. The report of the experiments is now in the Printers hand and though I have not separate copies to send yet I trust you will soon get it in the proceedings of the Friday Evenings[3]

With kindest remembrances of the mutual pleasures we have had together

I am
My dear Plücker
Ever Truly Yours
M. FARADAY

[1] The British Association for the Advancement of Science met in Hull in 1853.
[2] Sir Henry Holland (1788–1873), *Medical Notes and Reflections*, London, 1839. See Chapter 29, 'On Time as an Element in Mental Functions'.
[3] M. Faraday, 'On electric induction: Associated cases of current and static effects', *PRI*, I (1851–4), 345.

535   M. FARADAY to A. DE LA RIVE, 28 January 1854

[*Bibliothèque publique et universitaire de Genève, ms. 2316, f. 78–9, B.J. 2, 322*]

Royal Institution
28 January 1854

MY DEAR & KIND FRIEND

It seems a very long time since I wrote to or heard from you, but I have no doubt it has been my own fault. I often verify to myself the truth of an old school copy. "Procrastination is the thief of time"; and when I purpose to write it seems to me as if my thoughts now were hardly worth utterance to the men of persisting intellect & strength. But there are ties besides those of mere science and worldly relationship and I venture to think I have some such with you. These I can not easily relinquish for they grow dearer as other more temporal things dissolve away and though one cannot talk so often or so glibly about them because of their far more serious character still from time to time we may touch these cords and I shall think it a happiness whilst they respond and vibrate between us. Such ties exist but in few directions but they are worth all the rest.

I had a word from Schonbein a little while ago and he called you to mind by speaking of his daughter who was I think then with you: and it called up afresh the thoughts of the place when very many years ago. I first saw it and your father 1814 or 5 but the remembrances of that time are very shadowy with me Then came up the picture of the time when I and my wife were there with you and your happy family and a strong thought of the kindness I have had from your house through two generations and now comes the contemplation of these generations passing away Surely though we have both had trials & deep ones yet we have also had great mercies & goodness shewn us; above all the *great hope*. May the year that we have entered be full of peace to you, – and sweet pleasure among your children

I have lately had a subject brought before me, in electricity, full of interest. My account of it is in the printers hands & when I receive it I will send you a copy by post Briefly it is this. Copper telegraph wires are here covered perfectly with Gutta Percha so that hundreds of miles may be immersed in water and yet a very small discharge *through* the gutta percha occur [*sic*] when a very intense voltaic battery (300 or 400 pr of plates) is connected with it – 100 miles of such wire in water with the two exposed extremities insulated can be charged by one pole of a Voltaic battery and after separation from the battery for 5 or 10 minutes will give a shock or a current to the body or a galvanometer – or fire gunpowder or effect other electric actions either static or dynamic. The 100 miles is in fact an immense Leyden jar & because the copper is 1/16 of an inch in diameter and the gutta percha 1/10 of an inch thick or 4/16 of an inch extreme diameter, the surface of the copper or inner lining of the jar is equal to 8270 square feet. & the outer coating or water surface equal to 33000 square feet. – But besides this fact of a charge given, kept, and then employed, such a wire in water has its power of conveying electricity wonderfully affected – not its final power for that is the same for that is the same [*sic*] for an equal length of the wire in air or in water but its power in respect of brief currents or waves of electric force even to the extent of making the time occupied in the transmission vary as 100 to 1. or more. In a few days you shall have the account. – I do not know whether I have told you yet of the pleasure I have had in your Vol. I. but I long for Vol. II Many thanks for all your kindness in it & on every occasion

Ever My dear De la Rive
Yours
M. FARADAY

536 M. FARADAY to P. A. FAVRE,[1] 1 February 1854
[*Mrs. Dannie N. Heineman, previously unpublished*]

London
Royal Institution
1 February 1854

MY DEAR SIR

I hope you will excuse my letter though written in English: – for I cannot resist the pleasure of saying how much I have enjoyed both your letter and your Thesis:[2] both of which, if I may make free to say so, bear the impress of the sound philosopher and the hard working careful experimentalist. Both have been very interesting to me and the latter especially and the more so because it not only traces the heat function of the forces of matter round the circuit in a most definite and decided manner but because it justifies the ideas one entertains more or less that all the functions of these forces are mutually related or convertible. It is very delightful when such researches as yours appear for they enable the philosopher to take a firm stand where before all was hesitation doubt and suspicion. I may illustrate that point by referring to the question whether it is the mere oxidation of the zinc or the sum of all the actions up to its combination with the acid which produces the final amount of current power and I think you have very happily settled the question by testing it through the *heat* concerned.

I am My dear Sir
With great regard your
Very faithful Servant
M. FARADAY

[1] Pierre Antoine Favre (1813–80), Director (Chef des travaux) of the Laboratory of Analytical Chemistry of the *Ecole centrale des arts et manufactures* of Paris.

[2] Probably P. A. Favre, 'Notes sur les effets calorifiques développés dans le circuit voltaïque, dans leurs rapports avec l'action chimique qui donne naissance au courant', *CR*, 36 (1853), 342. There is no 'Thesis' as such listed in the catalogue of the *Bibliothèque nationale*.

537   J. PLÜCKER to M. FARADAY, 8 February 1854
[*I.E.E., previously unpublished*]

Bonn
8[Th] of February 1854.

MY DEAR SIR!

I have been very much enjoiced [reading doubtful] to receive your last kind letter; I'll bring against forward [*sic*] my bad English for answering it.

Three weeks ago I gave two copies of a rather extensive paper to my bookseller, one of them addressed to you, the other one to Prof. Wheatstone. Unhappily just the day before a parcel had departed for London. The next departure will take place, I hope, very soon. To this paper on magnetic and diamagnetic induction[1] the table with the curves, you speak of in your last letter, is annexed. The general conclusions are enumerated p. 51–56. The fundametel [*sic*] fact, represented by the curves, is deduced from observations carefully made by the large Electromagnet and a delicate balance. Take as unity of the magnetic attraction that corresponding to the unity of intensity of the current; then you may find experimentally the attraction (y). corresponding to any given intensity &c. In this way you will get for different substances very different curves, but following all the same general law. (First set of curves). To the intensity of the current I substituted that of the acting power of the Magnetic pole (second set) and finally to the attraction, wich [*sic*] undergo the different substances, the intensity of the magnetism induced by the pole in these substances (third set of curves).

I operated only on gaz oxigene, melted phosphorus and different powders. The conclusions I anticipated with regard to bars of soft iron and steel (acier trempé) have been since plainly confirmed by experiment. Iron is nearly double as strong magnetic then [reading doubtful] steel but the magnetism of steel increases more rapidly then [*sic*] that of soft iron does. I am engaged in a new series of experimental researches, wich will, I hope, confirm all my theoretical views.

Going on at the same time in my experimental Essays relatif [*sic*] to magnetisme [*sic*] and electromagnetism, I have just finished for the „Annalen" the first part of a paper on *mixed vapours*.[2]

I hapily [*sic*] returned home last September. Since that time I worked as much as I could, not so much as I would. I have every day two or three public lectures to give; after having given them I feel myself rather tired. That is very hard work, allso, [*sic*] as soon as the lectures are closed, I want to make up my mind and therefore I run during one month or two through the world. Being returned home I feel myself restored.

Pray, sir, present my compliments to Mad. Faraday With my best wishes for your health very truly

Yours
PLÜCKER

[1] J. Plücker, 'Ueber das Gesetz der Induction bei paramagnetischen und diamagnetischen Substanzen', *AP*, 167 (1854), 1.
[2] J. Plücker, 'Untersuchungen über Dampfe und Dampfgemenge', *AP*, 168 (1854), 193.

538   J. D. HOOKER[1] to M. FARADAY, 8 February 1854

[*Ms. Collection of Dr E. T. Conybeare, OBE, No. 74, Catalogue of Historical Manuscripts Commission, previously unpublished*]

Kew
Feby 8th/54

MY DEAR SIR

I have to thank you for the very kind letter which you have written me, in your own name & that of the Managers of the R.ˡ Institution. I assure you that I not only feel most deeply the warm interest expressed in myself, but the flattering opinion formed of my capabilities. It is with sincere regret that I definitely decline the proposals made in your letter, & not without the most earnest consideration of the whole matter. My reasons are very numerous, & I feel that several of them are conclusive in themselves. In the first-place I have always felt very strongly (& often expressed myself so) that when officers in a public service undertake scientific duties that should engross their whole attention, & receive salaries for the same, it becomes their duty to *devote* themselves to the accomplishment of their tasks. I have been twice abroad, on Government employ, & have collected materials on both, that are not half worked out; that will not be for years to come, & for the prosecution of which, I have received many years' salary & continue to receive it.

On my return from the Antarctic Voyage, the Treasury voted me £1000 to be spent in illustrating a Flora of the Southern ocean, & the Admiralty have kept me in the full pay list (of Asst. surgeons) for my own salary; – that work is not completed nor can it be for 2 years to come.[2] The materials of all succeeding voyages have been sent to me for the purpose of incorporation, & my pay was increased by the Admiralty two years ago mainly on this account. The Tasmanian Flora is to form one part, & the colonists of that Island only last week, sent me the announcement that they had voted me £350 in the Legislative Council, which they beg of my acceptance, in the hope that I will allow no consideration to interfere with the speedy performance of the work, which has been announced for now *9 years*. This little matter alone, for which I was wholly unprepared (for I do not know a single member of the council & never had any communication with them) renders it my first duty to go on with that work.

My Indian collections stand next in order, these alone cannot be arranged & distributed (as I have engaged that they shall be) within three years more, & until they are gone over & catalogued I can make no satisfactory progress in the development of those laws that have governed the distribution of the Plants of the Asiatic continent upon whose investigation I have long been engaged, nor can I proceed with the "Flora Indica', upon which Dr. Thomson & I are at work, & which our fellow-Botanists consider the most important that can be undertaken.[3]

There are personal considerations, at present pressing upon me, but there are others in prospect. Had I any time at my disposal, it should be given to my Father,[4] who has neither the leisure nor the means to devote the necessary attention to his Library & Herbarium. This latter is the finest in Europe, it is maintained at considerable private cost, much more for my use than his own, it is absolutely essential to my daily work that it should be kept in scientific order, but owing to its rapid increase & the want of the means of providing a scientific curator, it is rapidly deteriorating in some respects. Added to this my father's public duties are increasing with his years, & being allowed no assistant of any kind, it becomes the more incumbent upon me to allow of no consideration interfering with my duty to him. At present the whole charge of Library, Herbarium, & Scientific correspondence devolve entirely upon himself in a private capacity though all maintained as essential to his public position; the correspondence for the Museum, Garden & arboretum besides the superintendence of the whole, equally devolves upon himself, & except myself he has no assistant in any one capacity. With his advancing age these duties will very shortly become ostensibly too onerous for one man, they are so already in reality; & this constitutes the third reason I have for declining the invitation from the Royal Institution, (& your most kind offer of an application to Lord John Russell[5]) – that there is no possible prospect of my being able to continue my duties at the R.[l]. Institution, were I to commence them. It has been for some time the unanimous opinion of my (Botanical) friends that I should be attached to the Garden, applications to that effect have indeed been laid before the Government, now two years ago, when Lord John Russell gave me the temporary salary of £400, for 3 years in lieu, as the means of enabling me to publish my Indian materials, & keeping me at Kew till circumstances should favor my permanent attachment to the Gardens. Had I the materials for lecturing prepared, the case would be somewhat altered, but having performed the duties of the Botanical Professor in Edinburgh University, I know from experience that lectures in this department of science beyond all others, require copious illustrations by diagrams. I had then 400 diagrams (of my Father's) which have since been parted with, together with my lectures, so that I should have to start afresh, with the certain prospect of not being able to continue long at my post. My distance from Town (where I have no other business) is another objection, for though we have a rail-road, I cannot make the journey without losing 3 hours in the transit.

I fear I have trespassed upon your patience with these details, but I most truly feel the responsibility of declining an invitation couched in such terms as that you forward, & backed by considerations involving the progress of Botanical Science (however little I should prove capable of forwarding it by the means at my disposal.)

I need hardly say that the position of Lecturer at the Royal Institution, is one of which I should be very proud, & should (as is very possible) the government desire me to lecture at Kew, in connection with any position they may appoint me to, I would feel it a privilege to be allowed to offer my services, for an occasional lecture, to the Managers of the Institution. As it is, the opinion of all my friends so entirely coincides with my own, as to the inexpediency of my undertaking any such duty, that I must definitely decline.

Believe me Ever
most respectfully y'rs
Jos. D. HOOKER

[1] Joseph Dalton Hooker (1817–1911), botanist.
[2] J. D. Hooker, *The Botany of the Antarctic Voyage of H.M. Discovery – Ships Erebus and Terror in . . . 1839–1843, under the command of Sir J. C. Ross.* 1. *Flora Antarctica, 2 pt.* – II. *Flora Nova Zelandicae. 2 pt.* – III. *Flora Tasmaniae,* London, 1844–60.

³ J. D. Hooker and Thomas Thomson, *Flora Indica, being a systematic account of the plants of British India*, Vol. 1 (all published), London, 1855.
⁴ Sir William Jackson Hooker (1785–1865), formerly Regius Professor of Botany at Glasgow University and Director of the Royal Botanical Gardens at Kew.
⁵ Lord John Russell (1792–1878), at this point leader of the House of Commons and member of the Cabinet without office.

539   G. B. Airy to M. Faraday, 17 February 1854

[Royal Observatory, Herstmonceux, Astrology-Optics, 1853 and 1854, Sect. 14, previously unpublished]

Greenwich
1854 Feb 17 (copy)

My dear Sir

From time to time I look at your lecture of January 20 and reflect thereon.¹

Page 3 at the bottom, you refer very pointedly to the great extent of *surface* of the copper wire as producing the striking results, and you do not refer to any other character of the metal. But do you not suppose that the *longitudinal* extension had much to do with it: and in plain words that it depends on the wire's being long and thin? Do you suppose that a set of copper sheets amounting in the aggregate to 8300 square feet would produce the same effect? As the world is full of sheets of copper, I should think that this experiment might be tried without great expense, if desirable.

In your lecture you have not adverted to the peculiar character which the galvanic pulse seemed to have acquired at the third galvanometer, nearly a double or treble throb lasting in the whole a full second of time. When I was making longitude-signals with Edinburgh we [illeg.] something of the same kind, so that we were induced by what we then saw to extend our interval of certain signals from 2^s to 3^s in order to avoid confusion. There is always a difficulty in ascertaining the place of force at intervals shorter than or comparable with the time of natural vibration of the needle. Can you devise anything which will exhibit it for shorter intervals? I conjecture it as quite possible that there is a [illeg.] affection of the same kind at Galvanometer No. 2.

I am, my dear Sir,
Yours very truly
G. B. Airy

¹ See Letter 534, fn. 3.

713

[*Royal Observatory, Herstmonceux, Astrology-Optics, 1853 and 1854, Sect. 14, previously unpublished*]

Royal Institution
18 Feby 1854

My dear Sir

With respect to all the phenomena described *up to A* page 4 of the accompanying report,[1] length goes for *nothing*, except as affording surface, and therefore needed no other notice at bottom of page 3. Plates of copper & water would do just as well in association with Gutta Percha; but one would have to adjust the amount of surfaces: thus, with the wire one surface of the Gutta percha is 8300 square feet & the other 33000 square feet: if arrayed as plates one must take the mean of these numbers or 20650 as the square feet of Gutta percha in plates $\frac{1}{10}$ of an inch thick, which has to be coated on one side with copper sheathing & on the other with water. – So a hundred sheets of such gutta percha each 14 feet by 15 feet or thereabouts, arranged in any of the many ways by which their surfaces could be coated with metal & water, so as to form a Leyden arrangement, would answer the same purpose as the 100 miles of wire.

In the phenomena described *after* A. length goes for much, and is referred to pp 6. 8 10 &c as you will see by the marginal ink numbers 1. 2. 3. 4: – and if you wish to see the reasoning more developed I must refer you back to the Philosophical Transactions for 1838 and especially to paragraphs 1328, *1330*, *1331*, 1334, of the Experimental Research there printed.

In the latter results, described after A, where induction effects are combined with that effect due to *length* of wire which may be indifferently considered as either conduction or retardation, the induction effect is distributed along the wire; not being equal in every part as in the previous experiment, but diminishing in amount from the battery to the earth end; but all such variations are evident at a glance & I need say no more about them

As to the double or treble throbs. preparations for their observation with a view to the determination of their character would require great care. I saw nothing which struck my mind as indicating any thing which was not referable to momentum of the needles, disturbance of their polarity, – trembling contact, & other circumstances; all of which would have to be sought for & then cleared away, before I should be able to draw any conclusion in favour of a resolution of one pulse of power into several, by simple length of wire. The expansion of the time. i.e. the production of a slow action in the distance by a quick action at the battery end was clear enough, and is referred to page 9 fig 5; briefly it is true, but I thought the point too evident to need many words

Ever My dear Sir
Very Truly Yours
M. Faraday

¹ I am unable to identify this report with certainty. It is possible that it is the report of the lecture delivered on 20 January 1854, 'On electric induction: – Associated cases of current and static effect', *PRI*, 1 (1851–4), 345. See Letter 534.

541   M. FARADAY to G. B. AIRY, 20 February 1854
[*Royal Observatory, Herstmonceux, Astrology-Optics, 1853 and 1854, Sect. 14, previously unpublished*]

Royal Institution,
20 Feby, 1854

MY DEAR SIR

It has occurred to me that perhaps the fact (described in p 2 of the Evening notice)¹ that many successive shocks could be obtained from one charge of the wire by quick tapping touches, has directed your mind to the condition of length; for there is an effect of length of wire in that case, though almost insensible, as the results with 100 miles of wire in air described at p. 3, shew. The effect is of this kind. With a given wire, length opposes resistance to conduction: – so when the static electricity, employed in sustaining the induction in the wire, is discharged by touching one end, the resistance of the length of wire has to be overcome and so *time* is required. If the wire is touched for discharge at both ends at once, which was the case in several of our experiments at the wharf, then the resistance is only one fourth; for the double wire may then be considered as a wire of double mass and only half length. Supposing the induction to be entirely accumulated in the 100 plates of Gutta percha referred [to] in my last letter, & that they were at one end of 50 miles of *air wire*, at the other end of which the electricity was to be discharged by successive taps, then I believe that the resistance would be the same as that with the 100 miles of water wire charged & discharged at *one* end only; & the effects the same. On the assumption that the conducting power of metal wires is directly as the sectional area & inversely as their length, a mile of copper wire of the $\frac{1}{112}$ of an inch in diameter should offer the same resistance; and a few feet of wet thread should produce the same result: – which from numerous familiar experiments with ordinarily charged Leyden batteries I have no doubt it would do.

But though such an effect in relation to time is due to length of wire, that cause is almost insensible here, for the experiments which you saw with Bain's printing telegraph (p. 9 of the notice) shewed that with 750 miles of *air wire* or even 1500 miles the retardation was scarcely sensible; while with the *induction or underground wire* it was 1 and 2 seconds.

This long *time* I believe to be due to that conduction which every insulator shews more or less and which therefore follows upon every act of induction; as I have shewn in my old researches, see paragraphs 1323. 1324 & the other paragraphs these referred to. As soon as the 100 miles of water wire are charged inductively, the two electric states begin to travel through the gutta percha between the two surfaces; and hence the leaking of electricity which always occurs. There is as *true* a conduction through the Gutta percha of $\frac{1}{10}$ of an inch thick as through the copper wire 100 miles long; but the amount is so different that the conduction of Gutta percha is almost infinitely small when compared with that of copper. Nevertheless this act of conduction causes that the electricity leaves in part the surfaces of the wire & opposed water, & penetrates the gutta percha; so that the particles of Gutta percha next the wire become positively charged & those next the water negatively charged (the wire being first charged Positive). This charge occupies *time* and at the wharf Mr Statham[2] was continually occupying time for contact with the battery, to charge, as he said, the wire fully. Then when the wire is discharged it requires the time again for the return of the Electricity from the Gutta percha and it is this time which enabled me to divide the charge into as many as 40 distinct portions.

My thoughts are so familiar with these considerations, which flow as natural consequences from principles long since published, that I am apt to consider them as of little importance and not worth pointing out. Your notes make me think that perhaps I have been too brief and ought to have enlarged more upon the principles of insulation and conduction and the many beautiful conditions & effects that flow from them.

I am My dear Sir
Very Truly Yours
M. FARADAY

[1] See Letter 534.
[2] Undoubtedly an employee of the Telegraph Company.

542 M. FARADAY to W. WHEWELL, 27 February 1854
[Trinity College Library, Trinity College, Cambridge, previously unpublished]

Royal Institution
27 Feby 1854

MY DEAR DR. WHEWELL

I send you a copy of a report of a F. E. here:[1] – it is an account of some remarkable results obtained by experiments with long insulated telegraph wires subject to induction & I think the phenomena & their causes will interest you.

I am told there is some hope that you will favour us with a lecture on Education. Permit me to say how much it would gladden me to have your thoughts upon the higher points of this great subject brought before the audience in our lecture room. The social phenomena presented by the reception of table turning etc.[2] fully shew that for those who esteem themselves amongst the fully educated there is still an education of the mind required.

There is no one whom I should so much like to hear upon mental education as yourself.

Ever My dear Sir,
Your faithful Servt
M. FARADAY

Our Managers meet this day week is it likely we may then hear of your assent?

1 See Letter 534, fn. 3.
2 See Letter 519.

543   M. FARADAY to E. W. BRAYLEY, 28 February 1854
[*R.I., previously unpublished*]

Royal Institution
28 Feb.ʸ 1854

MY DEAR SIR

In signing certificates it is not my inclination but my rules which govern. I am sorry your case does not come in my rules but perhaps I am wrong & have forgotten and you may have a paper in the P. Trans. *then I sign at once.* In the absence of that qualification the other is some striking and philosophical work or operation like the construction of the Crystal Palace – or the first Submarine telegraph cable or some other object of equal interest & importance that I may be a judge of. I am very sorry that I cannot do myself the pleasure of signing on the present occasion but I am obliged to deny myself almost weekly at this time of the year

Ever Truly Yours
M. FARADAY

544   M. FARADAY to A. DE LA RIVE, 1 March 1854
[*Bibliothèque publique et universitaire de Genève, ms. 2316, f. 80–1, B.J. 2, 327*]

Royal Institution
1 March 1854

MY DEAR FRIEND

Your kindness and invitation moves our hearts to great thankfulness youwards: but they cannot roll back the years and give us the strength & ability of former times. We are both changed; my wife even more than I; for she is indeed very infirm in her limbs, nor have I much expectation that in that respect she will importantly improve: – but we are both very thankful for each others company and for the abundant blessing God has granted to us. I do not think it probable that either of us shall cross the sea this year or move a hundred miles from home; but we shall often during the Summer recall to mind your very pleasant invitation.

Your volume & the new matter I shall look forward to with eagerness. My little report I have no doubt you have received ere this. you will there perceive how much the induction you referred to in your letter has to do with the phenomena described

Now in reference to your questions;[1] and first whether I have ever obtained induction currents through liquids not being metals? – I have not worked on the subject since 1832 – At that time I obtained *no current* with a tube of Sulphuric acid (Exp Res. 200) but the current obtained in metals passed through liquids (Exp Res. 20). I should not at all despair of obtaining the current by the use of Electromagnets and thick wire Galvanometers (3178) but I never have obtained them

With regard to the second question I have never seen any reason to withdraw from the opinion I formed in the year 1834 that water & such liquids could conduct a very feeble portion of electricity without suffering decomposition. I venture to refer you to the paragraphs in the Exp. Researches namely 968 to 973, also 1017 and 1032. I have never contested the point because having once advanced it I have not since found any reason to add or alter; – and I left it to make its way. You will find at the end of Par 984 reference to a point which has always had great weight with me. When electrolytes are solid as in the case of nitre or chloride of sodium at common temperatures or water at or below o°F.; and when they according to all appearances *cannot* conduct as electrolytes, they still can conduct electricity of high tension; as is shown at par: 419 to 430. If they have this power to such a considerable degree with electricity able to open the gold leaves, it is almost certain they have it to a certain degree with electricity of lower tension; and if the solid electrolytes have such power I cannot see any reason why their liquefaction should take it away. It would seem to me rather unphilosophical to admit it for the solid and then, without proof, to assume that it is absent in the liquid: for my part, I think the proof is all the contrary way. The power seems to be present in a very low degree but I think it is there. So much for that matter.

If I were in your company I should have a long chat with you about Palagi's experiments.[2] I cannot understand them as to any new principle that is involved in them; and if there be not a new principle I fear they are only mistakes; i.e imperfect forms of old results where the two developed forces are before hand present. I cannot conceive it possible that if a sphere (metallic) of 3 inches diameter be inside a metallic sphere of 12 feet (or any other) diameter & touching its side, its mere removal into the centre of the large sphere or any other position in it will cause any electricity to appear.

Adieu My dear friend for the present

Ever Affectionately Yours
M. FARADAY.

718

[1] See Letter 532.
[2] Alessandro Palagi, 'Sulle variazioni elettriche a cui vanno soggetti i corpi allorche si allontano, o si avviginano fra di loro', *NASN*, 8 (1853), 365. There is a French translation (to which Faraday probably is referring) in *ASPN*, 25 (1854), 372.

545 M. FARADAY to A. DE LA RIVE, 7 March 1854
[*Bibliothèque publique et universitaire de Genève, ms. 2316, f. 82–3, B.J. 2, 330, PM, 4 s., 7 (1854), 265*]

Royal Institution
7 March 1854

MY DEAR FRIEND

Your question whether I have ever succeeded in producing induction currents in other liquids than mercury or melted metals, as for instance in acid or saline solutions?[1] has led me to make a few experiments on the subject, for though I believed in the possibility of such currents, I had never obtained affirmative results: I have now procured them, and send you a description of the method pursued. A powerful Electromagnet of the horseshoe form, was associated with a Grove's battery of 20 pairs of plates. The poles of the battery were upwards, their flat end faces being in the same horizontal plane; they are 3.5 inches square and about 6 inches apart. A cylindrical bar of soft iron 8 inches long and 1.7 in diameter was employed as a keeper or submagnet: the cylindrical form was adopted, first, because it best allowed of the formation of a fluid helix around it; and next, because when placed on the poles of the magnet and the battery connexions made and broken, the magnet and also the keeper rises and falls through much larger variations of power and far more rapidly than when a square or flat faced keeper is employed; for the latter if massive has, as you know, the power of sustaining the magnetic conditions of the magnet in a very great degree when the battery connexion is broken. A fluid helix was formed round this keeper having 12 convolutions, and a total length of 7 feet; the fluid was only 0.25 of an inch in diameter, the object being to obtain a certain amount of intensity in the current, by making the inductive excitement extend: to all parts of that great length, rather than to produce a quantity current by largeness of diameter, i.e by a shorter mass of fluid.

This helix was easily constructed by the use of 8.5 feet of vulcanized caout-chouc tube, having an internal diameter of 0.25 & an external diameter of 0.5 of an inch: such a tube is sufficiently strong not to collapse when placed round the iron cylinder. The 12 convolutions occupied the interval of six inches, & two lengths of 9 inches each constituted the ends. This helix was easily and perfectly filled, by holding it with its axis perpendicular, dipping the lower end into the fluid to be used & withdrawing the air at the upper; then two long clean copper wires 0.25 of an inch in diameter, were introduced at the ends, and being thrust forward until they reached the helix, were made secure by ligaments, and thus formed conductors between the fluid helix and the Galvanometer. The whole was attached to a wooden frame so as to protect the helix from pressure or derangement when moved to & fro. The quantity of fluid contained in the helix was about 3 cubic inches in the length of 7 feet. The Galvanometer was of wire 0.033 of an inch in diameter and 164 feet in length, occupying 310 convolutions: it was 18 feet from the magnet & connected with the helix by thick wires, dipping into cups of mercury. It was in the same horizontal plane with the magnetic poles & very little affected by direct action from the latter.

A solution formed by mixing 1 vol. of strong sulphuric acid & 3. of water was introduced into the helix tube, the iron keeper placed in the helix, & the whole adjusted on the magnetic poles in such a position, that the ends of the copper connectors in the tube were above the iron cylinder or keeper, and were advanced so far over it as to reach the perpendicular plane, passing through its axis: in this position the lines of magnetic force had no tendency to excite an induced current, through the metallic parts of the communication. The outer ends of the copper terminals were well connected together & the whole left for a time, so that any voltaic tendency due to the contact of the acid & copper might be diminished or exhausted: after that the copper ends were separated & the connexions with the Galvanometer so adjusted, that they could be in an instant either interrupted, or completed, or crossed, at the mercury cups. Being interrupted, the magnet was excited by the full force of the battery & thus the direct magnetic effect on the Galvanometer was observed; the helix had been so arranged, that any current induced in it should give a deflection in the contrary direction to that thus caused directly by the magnet; that the two effects might be the better separated. The battery was then disconnected & when the reverse action was over, the Galvanometer connexions were completed with the helix; this caused a deflection of only 2° due to a voltaic current generated by the action of the acid in the helix on the copper ends: it shewed that the connexion throughout was good, and being constant in power, caused a steady deflection, and was thus easily distinguished from the final result. Lastly the battery was thrown into action upon the magnet, and immediately the galvanometer was deflected in one direction, & upon breaking battery contact, it was deflected in the other direction, so that by a few alternations, considerable swing could be imparted to the needles. They moved also in that particular manner, often observed with induced currents, as if urged by an impact or push at the moments when the magnet was excited or lowered in force; and the motion was in the *reverse* direction, to that produced by the mere direct action of the magnet. The effects were constant. When the communicating wires were crossed, they again occurred, giving reverse actions at the galvanometer. Further proof that they were due to currents induced in the fluid helix, was obtained, by arranging one turn of a copper wire round the iron core or keeper in the same direction as that of the fluid helix, and using one pair of plates to excite the magnet; the induced current caused in the copper wire was much stronger than that obtained with the fluid, but it was always in the same direction.

After these experiments with the highly conducting solution, the helix was removed, the dilute acid poured out, – a stream of water sent through the helix for some time, distilled water then introduced and allowed to remain in it awhile, which being replaced by fresh distilled water, all things were restored to their places as before & thus a helix of pure water submitted to experiment. The direct action of the magnet was the same as in the first instance but there was no appearance of a voltaic current, when the galvanometer communications were completed; nor were there any signs of an induced current upon throwing the magnet into and out of action. Pure water is too bad a conductor to give any sensible effects with a Galvanometer & magnet of this sensibility & power.

I then dismissed the helix, but, placing the keeper on the magnetic poles, arranged a glass dish under it & filled the dish with the same acid solution as before; so that the liquid formed a horizontal fluid disc 6 inches in diameter nearly, an inch deep & within 0.25 of an inch of the keeper; two long clean platinum plates dipped into this acid on each side of the keeper and parallel to it, and were at least five inches apart from each other; these were first connected together for a time, that any voltaic tendency might subside, and then arranged so as to be united with the galvanometer when requisite as before. Here the induced currents were obtained as in the first instance, but not with the same degree of strength. Their direction was compared with that of the current induced in a single copper wire passed between the fluid and the keeper, the magnet being then excited by one cell, & was found to be the same. However, here the possibility exists of the current being in part or altogether excited upon the portions of the wire conductors connected with the platinum plates; for as their ends tend to go beneath the keeper & so into the circuit of magnetic power formed by it and the magnet, they are subject to the lines of force in such a position, as to have the induced current formed in them; and the induced current can obtain power enough to go through liquid, as I shewed in 1831. But as the helix experiment is free from this objection, I do not doubt that a weak induced current occurred in the fluid in the dish also.

So I consider the excitement of induction currents in liquids not metallic as proved; and as far as I can judge, they are proportionate in strength to the conducting powers of the body in which they are generated. In the dilute sulphuric acid, they were of course stronger than they appeared by the deflection to be; because they had first to overcome the contrary deflection which the direct action of the magnet was able to produce: the sum of the two deflections in fact expressed the force of the induced current. Whether the conduction by virtue of which they occur is electrolytic in character or conduction proper I cannot say. The present phenomena do not aid to settle that question, because the induced current may exist by either the one or the other process. I believe that conduction proper exists and that a very weak induction current may pass altogether by it, exciting for the time only a tendency to electrolysis, whilst a stronger current may pass partly by it & partly by full electrolytic action.

I am My dear friend

Ever most truly yours,
M. FARADAY.

1 See Letter 532.

546   M. FARADAY to A. DE LA RIVE, 8 March 1854

[Bibliothèque publique et universitaire de Genève, ms. 2316, f. 84, B.J. 2, 335]

Royal Institution
8 Mar 1854

MY DEAR DELA RIVE

I send you enclosed a letter[1] in such shape that you may publish it if you think it worth while. It has been copied so as to be a little better in writing than if you had had the original. I wish I could have written it in French – As the experiments arose out of your question I send the matter to you first if you publish it in the Bibliotheque[2] then I shall afterwards give my rough copy to the Philosophical Magazine as the translation from your Journal. If you should not find it expedient to print it, then I would alter the heading a little and send it to the Phil Mag as original – Do exactly as you like with it

Ever My dear friend
Yours Affectionately
M. FARADAY

1 See Letter 545.
2 The Letter was published in French in *ASPN*, 25 (1854), 267.

547   LORD WROTTESLEY to M. FARADAY, 8 March 1854

[I.E.E., previously unpublished]

Wrottesley
8 Mar 1854

DEAR SIR

The Parliamentary Committee of the British Association appointed to watch over the interests of Science have considered that it would greatly assist them in the due performance of that duty if they were occasionally favored with opinions from distinguished cultivators of Science in whose judgment and discretion confidence may be securely reposed, of a kind calculated from the subject matter to which they relate to afford valuable information as to the objects, to which the labours of the Committee might be most beneficially directed –

I have therefore to request that you will be so kind as to send me at your earliest convenience a reply to the following query,

Whether any and what measures could be adopted by the Government or the Legislature to improve the position of Science, or of the Cultivators of Science in this country?[1] –

> I remain
> Yours truly
> WROTTESLEY
> /Chairman/

[1] See Letter 549.

548   M. FARADAY to W. WHEWELL, 10 March 1854
[*Trinity College Library, Trinity College, Cambridge, previously unpublished*]

> Royal Institution,
> 10 Mar 1854

MY DEAR DR. WHEWELL

I am tempted once more before you answer our application to write for having got hold of the enclosed bit of lectures and *men* I wished you to see how desirable it would be that we should have a discourse either at *the beginning* or *the end*, general in its nature and shewing the idea of education as needed for all classes of men & minds – mental education which in a man of thought goes on within him from first to last. No man could do this in my opinion as you would do it.

Are circumstances such as to enable you to do it with convenience & satisfaction to yourself.

> Ever
> Yours Faithfully
> M. FARADAY

Dr. Daubeny
   1. On the importance of the study of chemistry as a means of education for all classes of the community.

Dr. Tyndall
   2. On the importance of the study of physics as a means of education for all classes.

Mr. Paget[1]
   3. On the importance of the study of Physiology as a means of education.

Dr. Booth[2]

4. On the importance of mathematical studies as a means of education.

Dr. Hodgson[3]

5. On the importance of the study of Social economy as a means of education.

Dr. R. Latham[4]

6. On the importance of the study of language, classics, *etc.* as a means of education.

(on fourth sheet, in Whewell's hand – The Liniment does not seem to afford me any relief –)

[1] James Paget, later Sir James Paget, Bart. (1814–99), Fellow of the Royal College of Surgeons and, after 1858, surgeon-extraordinary to the Queen.
[2] James Booth (1810–98), mathematician.
[3] William Ballantyne Hodgson (1815–80), economist.
[4] Robert Gordon Latham (1812–88), Professor of English language and literature in University College, London.

549 M. FARADAY to LORD WROTTESLEY, 10 March 1854
[*J. H. Gladstone, 'Michael Faraday', London, 1872, 144; B.J. 2, 336*]

Royal Institution,
March 10th, 1854.

MY LORD, –

I feel unfit to give a deliberate opinion on the course it might be advisable for the government to pursue if it were anxious to improve the position of science and its cultivators in our country. My course of life, and the circumstances which make it a happy one for me, are not those of persons who conform to the usages and habits of society. Through the kindness of all, from my sovereign downward, I have that which supplies all my need; and in respect of honors, I have, as a scientific man, received from foreign countries and sovereigns those which, belonging to very limited and select classes, surpass in my opinion any thing that it is in the power of my own to bestow.

I can not say that I have not valued such distinctions; on the contrary, I esteem them very highly, but I do not think I have ever worked for or sought after them. Even were such to be now created here, the time is past when these would possess any attraction for me; and you will see, therefore, how unfit I am, upon the strength of any personal motive or feeling, to judge of what might be influential upon the minds of others. Nevertheless, I will make one or two remarks which have often occurred to my mind.

Without thinking of the effect it might have upon distinguished men of science, or upon the minds of those who, stimulated to exertion, might become distinguished, I do think that a government should *for its own sake* honor the men who do honor and service to the country. I refer now to honors only, not to beneficial rewards; of such honors I think there are none. Knighthoods and baronetcies are sometimes conferred with such intentions, but I think them utterly unfit for that purpose. Instead of conferring distinction, they confound the man who is one of twenty, or perhaps fifty, with hundreds of others. They depress rather than exalt him, for they tend to lower the especial distinction of mind to the commonplaces of society. An intelligent country ought to recognize the scientific men among its people as a class. If honors are conferred upon eminence in any class, as that of the law or the army, they should be in this also. The aristocracy of the class should have other distinctions than those of lowly and highborn, rich and poor, yet they should be such as to be worthy of those whom the sovereign and the country should delight to honor, and, being rendered very desirable and even enviable in the eyes of the aristocracy by birth, should be unattainable except to that of science. Thus much I think the government and the country ought to do, for their own sake and the good of science, more than for the sake of men who might be thought worthy of such distinction. The latter have attained to their fit place, whether the community at large recognize it or not.

But besides that, and as a matter of reward and encouragement to those who have not yet risen to great distinction, I think the government should, in the very many cases which come before it having a relation to scientific knowledge, employ men who pursue science, provided they are also men of business. This is perhaps now done to some extent, but to nothing like the degree which is practicable with advantage to all parties. The right means can not have occurred to a government which has not yet learned to approach and distinguish the class as a whole.

At the same time, I am free to confess that I am unable to advise how that which I think should be may come to pass. I believe I have written the expression of feelings rather than the conclusions of judgment, and I would wish your lordship to consider this letter as private rather than as one addressed to the chairman of a committee.

I have the honor to be, my lord, your very faithful servant,

M. FARADAY

[1] See Letter 547.

550 W. WHEWELL to M. FARADAY, 12 March 1854
[Trinity College Library, Trinity College, Cambridge, previously unpublished]

Trin. Lodge,
Cambridge,
March 12, 1854

MY DEAR DR. FARADAY,

I do not know anything which could weigh so much with me, in making me wish to give a lecture at the R.I., as your thinking it would be likely to be interesting and informative. I think I have a few thoughts " On the influence of the History of Science upon Intellectual Education" which perhaps may not have occurred exactly in the same form to other persons, and which may serve to answer the speculations which may be delivered, on the influence of special branches of Science. If you think this likely to answer the purpose of the R.I. I should suppose such a lecture could come best at the beginning of the series; and in that case, I would propose myself for such a lecture to be delivered, I suppose, soon after Easter. You will let me know whether this proposal appears to you worth following out – and believe me,

Always truly yours,
W. WHEWELL

551 M. FARADAY to W. WHEWELL, 14 March 1854
[Trinity College Library, Trinity College, Cambridge, previously unpublished]

Royal Institution,
14 Mar 1854

MY DEAR DR. WHEWELL

Your letter has been a very great gratification to our Committee and to myself: – they have asked me to convey our very sincere thanks to you for your great kindness. Saturday the 28th of April is the first lecture of the series for which day I conclude we may now make the arrangement with the title you have given me " On the influence of the history of science upon intellectual education"

As I sent you a list of names, I may as well tell you that I did not intend to join in the series, just because I do not feel competent; but our Managers wish it very much & I may not be able to resist the wish, in which case, in order that I may be safe, I think I must confine myself to something like personal experience or observation on mental education,[1] and shall probably come the Saturday after you.

Ever Your faithful Svt,
M. FARADAY

[1] See M. Faraday, 'Observations on mental education', *ERCP*.

726

[*I.E.E., previously unpublished*]

Naples
ce 21 mars 1854

MON ILLUSTRE AMI!

Merci, mille fois merci, des paroles si bienveillantes que vous avez eu la bonté de m'écrire – elles ont soulagé mon coeur et rendu mon esprit susceptible d'apprécier toute l'importance de vos nouvelles et magnifiques découvertes Ainsi les physiciens ont voulu à toute force perseverer dans leur idée de mesurer la vitesse absolue de l'electricité pour chaque éspèce de conducteur métallique, lorsque vous leur aviez annoncé depuis longtems, que cette vitesse dependait de la tension du fluide transmis . . . . . Or le fait est venu confirmer les prévisions du génie, et la science professionelle se trouve justement punie de la sotte préference accordée à ses propres routines.

Tout le monde doit bien convenir aujourd'hui que l'electricité se propage plus ou moins lentement de l'une à l'autre extremité d'un même fil télegraphique, selon qu'elle subit une induction laterale plus ou moins intense. Maintenant, si j'ai bien compris votre pensée, l'induction abaisserait le dégré de tension; et de cet abaissement resulterait l'alteration observée de la vitesse du courant eléctrique.

Permettez, mon illustre ami, que je vous soumette une objection qui pourrait s'elever contre cette manière de voir. La cause du retard qu'eprouve le courant eléctrique, ne serait-elle pas analogue à ce qui se passe dans un conduit destiné à alimenter une série de citernes placées le long de sa course? Parce que le tems que l'eau emploie à parcourir toute la longueur du conduit est plus long lorsque les citernes sont vides que lorsqu'elles sont pleines ou fermées, il n'en resulte pas pour cela que le liquide marche plus vite dans le second cas que dans le premier.

En me voyant avancer une espèce d'attaque contre votre theorie sur l'origine commune des forces d'induction et de transmission n'allez pas croire, je vous en prie, que je rejette absolument cette théorie si simple et si elegante, ni que je soutienne l'egalité de vitesse pour toute espèce d'eléctricité dynamique: car, je me sens, au contraire, très-incliné à admettre, et l'identité des causes qui produisent les phénomènes de la transmission et de l'induction, et l'inegale vitesse des courants eléctriques par suite de leurs divers dégrés de tension. Je crois même que cette dernière proposition pourrait se démontrer directement par l'expérience.

Supposons, par exemple, deux longs fils métalliques egaux, isolés, et communiquant, par leurs extremités les plus éloignées, avec deux galvanomètres de même sensibilité, dont les bouts libres soient plongés dans le sol. Imaginons, en outre, deux piles ou eléctro-moteurs voltaiques à tensions très-differentes, mais produisant des déviations à peu près égales sur les deux galvanomètres susdits

727

lorsqu'on les fait communiquer respectivement, par un de leurs poles, avec l'extremité la plus rapprochée des fils; tandis que l'autre pole est en communication avec la terre. Supposons enfin que, par un moyen quelconque, on puisse établir ou interrompre simultanément les communications des piles avec les fils.

Le mouvement successif des deux galvanomètres pendant l'expérience ne conduirait-il pas à la démonstration cherchée? Et ne verrait-on pas l'index magnétique correspondant au circuit de la pile composée d'un grand nombre de couples à petites surfaces sortir plus vite de sa position d'equilibre que celui qui appartient appartient [*sic*] au circuit de la pile formée d'un petit nombre de couples à grandes surfaces?

Je voudrais bien savoir votre opinion là dessus; et, dans le cas affirmatif, je serais vraiment enchanté de vous voir prendre les dispositions nécessaires pour mettre en oeuvre ce projet d'expériences. Je le serais d'autant plus, qu'en faisant quelques essais pour construire un eléctroscope très-sensible j'ai acquis la conviction qu'un fait parfaitement analogue existe à l'égard de l'electricité statique.

On transmet à un metal isolé une forte charge eléctrique moyennant un mince et long conduit de ces matières à moitié conductrices que Volta appellait *semi-* [illeg.] On fait ensuite communiquer l'extrémité libre du conduit avec le sol; et, malgré cela, le corps métallique entouré d'air sec et tranquille se conserve electrisé pendant des journées entières. Ainsi le principe eléctrique, qui avait d'abord parcouru le conduit, ne peut plus retroceder par la meme voie lorsque sa tension a atteint une certaine limite d'abaissement.

Au moyen de cette propriété j'espère me procurer un eléctroscope analogue à celui de Bohnenberger,[1] mais debarassé des imperfections qu'on lui a souvent reprochées. Cet instrument indiquera immediatement et nettement la nature de l'eléctricité explorée; et il aura en outre l'avantage de montrer, si je ne me trompe, que le principe eléctrique ne rayonne pas comme la lumière, et la chaleur, qu'il ne se déplace pas par influence de l'extremité antérieure à l'extrémité postérieure, des métaux isolés, et qu'il se propage réellement dans toute sorte de corps par une suite de polarisations moléculaires comme vous l'admettez depuis longtems contre l'avis opposé de la presque totalité des physiciens.

La construction de cet eléctroscope est assez avancée et j'espère vous en envoyer bientôt une description complete. Mais, de grace, repondez d'abord aux observations précédentes et veuillez bien me pardonner si, par des motifs déduits de ma position actuelle, je vous prie d'adresser votre reponse, ainsi que tout autre envoi de papiers, livres ou brochures, a Mr Flauti Secrétaire perpétuel de l'Académie Rle des Sciences de Naples – je vous serais même fort obligé si vous vouliez avoir la grande bonté de transmettre cet avis au Secrétariat de la Société Royale d'Edimbourg, lorsqu'il s'offrira une occasion de lui écrire – La maniere la plus sure, la plus prompte, et la plus économique de nous faire parvenir les envois c'est de les expédier *par Marseilles et les paquebots de la Mediterranée.* Excusez ces details, recevez encore une fois mes plus vifs remerciements et croyez moi pour [illeg.] votre tout dévoué admirateur et ami

MACÉDOINE MELLONI

P.S. Nous ne recevons plus ici, en fait de journaux scientifiques, que les Archives des Sciences naturelles de Genève et les Annales de Chimie, de Physique et d'histoire naturelle de Paris. Si, en lisant le Philosophical Magazine, les Annales de Poggendorf [*sic*], ou autres feuilles periodiques, vous y trouviez des articles interessants en physique, ou s'il vous arrive de publier la moindre chose dans ces journaux ou ailleurs, vous accompliriez une oeuvre vraiment charitable en nous les envoyant, manuscrits ou imprimés par la voie indiquée tantôt –

[At bottom, in Faraday's hand:]
I expect the smaller intense pile would tell quickest but there are many points to include in the consideration. See Clarke.

[1] Gottlieb Christian Bohnenberger (1732–1802), writer on electricity.

553 G. B. AIRY to M. FARADAY, 22 April 1854 [copy]
[*Royal Observatory, Herstmonceux, Astrology-Optics, 1853–4, Sect. 4*]

Royal Observatory
Greenwich
1854 April 22

MY DEAR SIR

Simultaneously with the Ozone observations made here, we have had observations made at the Hospital Schools and on the declivity of Lewisham Hill (Dartmouth Terrace). You know the locality generally, the three are nearly but not quite in a straight line: the distance of the Hospital Schools about 1300 feet, that of the Lewisham station 1 mile. I enclose you the results. Also those at Bexley Heath.

The reason for my troubling you with these is that I am struck with their discordance. They seem to have no particular connexion, except that on the whole the morning numbers are larger than the evening numbers. In other respects they are so unlike that they seem to suggest, – either that our modus operandi is wrong, or that the phaenomenon registered is something so very local as to be of no particular use.

Pray instruct me on all this.

I am, my dear Sir,
Yours very truly
G. B. AIRY

[*Royal Observatory, Herstmonceux, Astrology-Optics, 1853–4, Sect. 4*]

Royal Institution
26 April 1854

MY DEAR SIR

The impression produced on my mind by your reports is first that observers have not yet learned what is requisite for a safe or a constant observation on their own part and next what circumstances about any given locality may affect the result. I do not know how far your observers have compared themselves with themselves or with others but without some proof of certainty in the results at one place it would be hardly worth while comparing them in different places. The following questions will illustrate my meaning.

Does an observer making three or four simultaneous observations in the same place obtain a like result by all? – if there is a difference what is the extent?

Does another observer obtain the like accordance or discordance with himself in the same place? – What is the state of accordance between him & the former observer?

Do observations made on two or four sides of the observatory by the same person agree together? – if not is the difference constant?

Do those made by *two observers or more* simultaneously in these different places agree for the same place & time?

If the results are satisfactory & the power of observing seems to be obtained then observations at places further apart would be required. I imagine a great difference is to be expected between a clear open space and the neighbourhood of a building and I conceive that no general results can be expected to agree well before the influence of all minor circumstances has been ascertained – the corrections in fact worked out.

Ever My dear Sir
Truly Yours
M. FARADAY

555 M. FARADAY to the Editors of the Philosophical Magazine and Journal, 20 April 1854

[*P.M., 4 s., 7 (1854), 396*]

Royal Institution,
April 28, 1854.

GENTLEMEN,

A communication has been just brought to my notice on some remarkable phænomena presented by subterraneous electro-telegraph wires observed and described by M. Werner Siemens of Berlin, in a communication bearing date April 15, 1850. They are the same phænomena as those shown to me by Mr.

Latimer Clarke, and used in my communication (inserted in your Magazine for March 1854, p. 197) as illustrations of the truth of my ancient views of the nature of insulation, induction and conduction. It is only justice that I should refer to them; and I think they are so interesting, that you will be willing to reprint the account, very slightly abbreviated, which I send you; the effects are produced with wires covered with gutta percha and laid in the earth.

"A very remarkable phænomenon is constantly observed on long, well-insulated telegraphic lines. Suppose one extremity, B, of the wire be insulated, and the other, A, be connected with one pole of a battery of which the other touches the earth; at the instant of communication a brief current is observed in the near parts of the wire in the same direction as the instantaneous current which would exist if the extremity B were connected with the earth; on lines of perfect insulation no trace of this current remains. Suddenly replacing, through the action of a commutator, the battery by an earth conductor, a second instantaneous current is obtained of an intensity nearly equal to the first, but in the inverse direction. Finally, breaking the communication of A with the battery and also the earth, so as to insulate this extremity, and uniting the end B at the same instant with the ground, an instantaneous current is observed nearly equal in intensity to the former, and this time in the same direction as the first, $i.\,e.$ as the continuous current of the battery. This last experiment can only be made on a double subterranean line having the two extremities A and B at the same station. One might at first sight suppose these phænomena to be due to secondary polarities developed on the wire, but many facts oppose such a conclusion. 1. The phænomena are more striking as the wire is better insulated. 2. The currents are much more brief than those due to secondary polarities. 3. Their intensity is proportional to the force of the battery, and independent of the intensity of any derived current that may occur in consequence of imperfect insulation; it follows that the intensity of the instantaneous currents can greatly surpass the maximum intensity which secondary currents in the same circuit could acquire. 4. Finally, the intensity of the instantaneous currents is proportional to the length of the wire, whilst an inverse relation ought to occur if the currents were due to secondary polarities.

"The phænomena are easily comprehended if we recall the beautiful experiment by which Volta furnished the most striking proof of the identity of galvanism and electricity. He showed that on communicating one of the ends of his pile with the earth, and the other with the interior of a non-insulated Leyden battery, the battery was charged in an instant of time to a degree proportional to the force of the pile. At the same time an instantaneous current was observed in the conductor between the pile and the battery, which, according to Ritter, had all the properties of an ordinary current. Now it is evident that the subterranean wire with its insulating covering may be assimilated exactly to an immense Leyden battery: the glass of the jars represents the gutta percha; the internal coating is the surface of the copper wire; the external surface is the moistened earth. To form an idea of the capacity of this new kind of battery, we have only to remember that the surface of the wire is equal to 7 square metres per kilometre. Making such a wire communicate by one of its ends with a pile, of which the other extremity is in contact with the earth, whilst the other extremity of the wire is insulated, must cause the wire to take a charge, of the same character and tension as that of the pole of the pile touched by it: – that is what came to pass in the first of the instantaneous currents described. In Volta's experiment, on breaking the communication between the pole and the battery and connecting the two coatings of the latter by a conductor, an ordinary discharge was obtained: – to this discharge correspond the two instantaneous currents which are observed in opposite directions at the two extremities of the charged wire, on communicating their extremities with the earth, to the exclusion of the pile. It will be understood, also, that the first instantaneous current, namely, that which is connected with the charge of the wire, ought to be equally produced, though of a lower intensity, even when the other extremity of the wire is in communication with the earth. The instantaneous current then precedes the continuous current, or, if the statement be preferred, is added to it at the first moment. This instantaneous current has an intensity much greater than that of the continuous current; doubtless because in the act of charging the wire, the electricity in going to the different points of the wire passes through paths so much the shorter as the points to be charged are nearer to the pile."

The above is from the *Annales de Chimie*, 1850, vol. xxix. p. 398, &c.

> I am, Gentlemen,
> Your very faithful Servant,
> M. FARADAY.

556 G. B. AIRY to M. FARADAY, 12 May 1854 [copy]
[Royal Observatory, Herstmonceux, Astrology-Optics, 1853–4, Sect. 4]

> Royal Observatory,
> Greenwich
> 1854 May 12

DEAR SIR

Since receiving your letter about Ozone, I have carefully examined into the circumstances of observation. The observers are so closely connected, and their habits are so completely formed one upon another, that I do not conceive that there is any risk of discordance from personal peculiarity. But another fact has come out which may have something to do with it, and concerning which I wish to learn whether it is recognized (it is new to me).

The fact is, that the tint of the paper sometimes *goes off*. In early morning it is sometimes deeply coloured, and by 9 o'clock the colour has nearly vanished. If at such a time a strip of the paper is torn off early and dipped into water, it gives a full purple: while that which remains, if treated in the same way at a later hour, shews no colour or very little.

I cannot say with certainty that this diminution of tint is different at different places, but I am inclined to think that it is.

I am, my dear Sir,
Yours very truly
G. B. AIRY

557 A. DE LA RIVE to M. FARADAY, 13 May 1854
[*I.E.E., previously unpublished*]

Genève
le 13 mai 1854

MON CHER & DIGNE AMI,

J'ai reçu successivement vos excellentes lettres du 1er & du 8 mars,[1] & je viens vous en adresser tous mes remerciements. – L'intéressant mémoire que vous m'avez envoyé m'est arrivé juste à temps pour figurer dans le numéro de la *Bibl. Univ.* qui paraitra le 15. Pour aller plus vite en besogne, nous nous en sommes partagé la traduction Marcet & moi, mais j'ai revu le tout. Je suis bien reconnaissant que vous ayez pensé à me donner la primeur de cet article & de la découverte importante qui y est renfermée. Je ne crois pas possible que le courant d'induction déterminé directement dans un liquide, comme il l'est dans votre expérience, puisse être d'une nature électrolytique; ne pourrait-on pas s'assurer de ce qu'il en est, en voyant si en ne laissant passer plusieurs fois de suite qu'un des deux courants d'induction, les électrodes sont ou non polarisées; ils ne doivent l'être que peu ou point si le courant n'est pas électrolytique.

Je vous enverrai immédiatement le n° de la *Bibl. Univ.* où votre article va paraitre; permettez-moi de vous envoyer les précédents qui ont paru en *janvier* & *fevrier* ainsi que ceux qui paraitront à l'avenir. Je serais bien heureux de les voir figurer dans votre bibliothèque. – Vous trouverez dans le même numero de *mars* la traduction complète de vos belles recherches sur les fils télégraphiques qui m'ont enfin donné la solution de cette question relative à la soi-disante vitesse de l'Electricité, qui m'avait toujours embarassé.

Je regrette bien d'être obligé de renoncer au plaisir de vous voir cet été Madame Faraday & vous; j'espère, si Dieu le permet, aller dans un an ou 15 mois vous faire une visite en Angleterre; je remets toujours le moment de faire ce voyage qui me sera bien pénible à cause des souvenirs que j'ai dans ce pays. Mais la douceur que j'aurai de voir quelques amis que j'y ai encore sera une compensation à mes impressions pénibles.

J'espère que vous avez reçu mon premier volume Français que je vous ai fait envoyer de Paris; je travaille avec vigueur au second qui est bien difficile à faire dans l'état actuel de la science.

Veuillez avoir la bonté de me rapeller au bon souvenir de Madame Faraday & agréez, vous aussi, Monsieur & excellent ami, l'assurance des sentiments respectueux & affectueux

de votre tout dévoué
A. DE LA RIVE

¹ See Letters 544 and 546.

558 M. MELLONI to M. FARADAY, 18 May 1854
[*I.E.E., previously unpublished*]

Moretta di Portini pres Naples
ce 18 Mai 1854.

CHER ET ILLUSTRE AMI!

J'ai suspendu jusqu'à present ma reponse à votre lettre du 19 Avril dans l'espoir de pouvoir vous envoyer, d'un jour à l'autre, la description complète de mon nouvel eléctroscope [*sic*].¹ Mais la crainte que ce retard ne soit sinistrement interpreté m'oblige à vous ecrire ces lignes, afin de vous dire d'abord, que vos souffrances m'ont profondément affligé, et que je ne doi[ ]sse [reading doubtful] de faire les voeux les plus ardents pour un prompte retablissement dans l'état de parfaite santé – Je vous remercie ensuite bien vivement, mon excellent ami, de la peine que vous vous êtes donnée pour rectifier mes idées à l'égard de votre ingénieuse théorie sur les relations que vous établissez entre l'induction la conductibilité l'isolement et la capacité eléctrique des corps . . . . . Ayez la bonté d'attendre quelques semaines, et peut être pourrais-je decider la question de savoir si dans les phénomènes de l'induction et de la conductibilité il y a simple polarité moléculaire ou transport réel de fluide eléctrique de l'une à l'autre extremité des conducteurs isolés comme on l'admet encore dans la plupart des traités de physiques . . . Vous comprenez bien que mes esperances de reussite sont essentiellement fondées sur l'appareil thermoscopique dont je vous parlais tantôt . . . . Sa construction avance et, malgré les nombreuses difficultés artistiques, et economiques qui semblaient s'accumuler exprès pour m'empêcher d'atteindre le but, je puis déjà vous annoncer *avec certitude* que cet instrument a complètement réussi – J'ai supprimé le conducteur imparfait dont je vous parlais dans ma lettre précedente; mais son emploi primitif m'a conduit à une heureuse application d'un principe nouveau, ou plutôt à l'application d'une consequence jusqu'à present negligée des principes connus au moyen de laquelle mon appareil a acquit une sensibilité et une netteté d'indications vraiment étonnantes. Pour vous en donner une idée je dirai que, *dans son état actuel d'imperfection*, il donne des deviations de 20 a 25° sur un cercle d'un decimètre

734

de diametre par le contact de la lame zinc et cuivre soudée de Volta; et que ces déviations se maintiennent assez longtems pour permettre d'explorer tout à son aise, *jusque dans les tems les plus humides*, l'espèce d'electricité dont elles dérivent. –

Je crois qu'avec cet instrument, porté à son dernier dégré de perfection, on parviendra à faire rejeter définitivement, même par ses propres partisans, le principe de M. Palogi[2] d'une prétendue eléctrisation des corps par le simple changement de distance; principe qui n'est, selon moi, qu'une consequence des phénomènes d'induction dûs à l'eléctricité developpée par le frottement des corps mobile sur les tubes ou les tringles qui servent à le rapprocher du corps fixe. – Il me semble enfin que nous pourrons employer cet instrument avec succès pour voir s'il y a réellement de l'eléctricité dégagée pendant l'évaporation des liquides, dans l'acte de la végetation, et dans une foule d'autres questions analogues qui ont été, si je ne me trompe, fort mal étudiées dans ces derniers tems à cause de l'emploi impropre du galvanomètre . . . Et, pour en citer un seul exemple, quel rapport y a-t-il entre les courants electriques *que l'on développe artificiellement* par le contact, direct ou indirect, des extremités du galvanometre, avec les feuilles et les racines d'une plante arrachée du sol, et le degagement supposé de l'electricité statique dans l'etat naturel de cet être organique? . . . .

Je finis en renouvellent mes voeux les plus ardents pour le retablissement de votre précieuse santé et en me déclarant avec toute l'effusion de mon ame

votre très-affectionné et très reconn.[t]
Serviteur et ami
MACÉDOINE MELLONI

[1] See Letter 552.
[2] See Letter 544, fn. 2.

559 M. FARADAY to C. R. LESLIE,[1] 25 May 1854

[*R.I., previously unpublished*]

Royal Institution
25 May 1854

MY DEAR SIR

It gives me great pleasure to think that I may in any way be useful to you as it very [*sic*] agreeable to my thoughts to suppose I have any knowledge which can bear upon your high & intellectual pursuit: – leaving you to judge of the applicability of what I may say, I shall plunge at once into the middle of your letter. We only know of two states of existence for the water in the atmosphere, one as clear transparent vapour the other as the vesicles which form clouds, or what is commonly known as visible steam. We have no philosophical reason for supposing that in the first state it can produce the blue colour of the sky; for all experiment goes to shew, that, in that state, it is as transparent & colourless as the air itself. Neither, if we were to assume that the local colour of water is blue, and that in the state of transparent vapour this colour is retained, would that account for a blue sky; for supposing the whole of the atmosphere to its very summit, were retained at the high temperature of 80°F, and that it were saturated with aqueous vapour, still the quantity of water present if condensed into the liquid state would not make a layer of more than $13\frac{1}{2}$ inches in depth. But considering the rapid diminution of temperature upwards, and other circumstances affecting the quantity of water present as transparent vapour at any one time in the atmosphere, we cannot suppose there is ever more than one fourth of this amount, and I leave you to judge how utterly insufficient this Would [*sic*] be to produce the blue skies seen in this country, much less those of Italy and other parts of the world. Three inches in depth of the Rhine water at Geneva, which is as blue as any water I know of, if held in a glass vessel between the eye & the sky would give scarcely an appreciable effect of colour.

But the other state of "vesicles" appears to be sufficient to account for the blue colour, *not because of any colour they have in themselves*, but because of their optical effect on the rays of light passing through the atmosphere My own knowledge does not render me competent to give an opinion on this matter; but I place confidence in the investigations of a high mathematician, M. Clausius, whose paper you will find (& I think read with interest) in Taylor's memoires:[2] and to facilitate your access to it I send you my copy, which if you can return it in a week or two I shall be obliged. This paper begins at p 326 and you will see that by the time he arrives at the end p. 331, he considers that the *blue colour* of the sky, as well as the *morning & evening red* are fully accounted for

In reference to another part of your letter, which speaks of air without water being invisible, and therefore of the sun as intensely luminous and without halo or rays, and the space around appearing black; there is reason to believe that such effects (except the rays) would occur. As to the rays, the irradiation of a very brilliant center of light does not depend upon the atmosphere, but upon effects produced in & by the parts of the eye; and would occur if the atmosphere could be entirely removed. On the other hand there is no reason to believe that the presence of water in the atmosphere, in its perfectly dissolved state, would produce any of the effects you refer to or change the appearances from those presented by perfectly dry air. It is more probable that the vesicles Clausius & others speak of, are the cause of the general diffusion of the light coming from the Sun to the earth, which takes place even in the clearest atmospheres

Believe me to be
My dear Sir
Very faithfully Yours
M FARADAY.

[1] Charles Robert Leslie (1794–1859), artist and art historian.
[2] *TSM*, 1853, 326.

Royal Institution
29 May 1854

MY DEAR FRIEND

Though feeling weary & tired I cannot resist any longer conveying to you my sincere thanks (however feebly) for the gift of your work in French. I have delayed doing so for some time hoping to be in better spirits but will delay no longer. for delighted as I have been in the reading of it. my treacherous memory begins to let loose that which I gained from it; – for when I read some of the summaries a second time, I am surprised to find them there & then slowly find that I had read them before The power with which you hold the numerous parts of our great department of science in your mind is to me most astonishing & delightful and the accounts you give of the researches of the workers & especially those of Germany exceedingly valuable & interesting to me – May you long enjoy & use this great power for the good of us all. – We shall long for the second volume but we must have patience for it is a great work that you are engaged in

You sent me also the Numbers of the Bibliotheque for January February & March & there again your kindness to me is deeply manifested & with me is deeply felt: but do not trouble yourself to send me the succeeding numbers for I have the work here & see it with great interest for it is to me a channel for much matter that otherwise would escape me altogether. I wish I could send you matter oftener. but my wishes far outmeasure my ability. My portfolio contains many plans for work but I get tired with ordinary occupation & then my hands lie idle.

Your theoretical views from p. 557 and onwards have interested me very deeply and I am glad to place them in my mind by the side of those ideas which serve to aid discovery & development by suggesting analogies and crucial experiments and other forms of test for the views which arise in the mind as vague shadows however they may develope into brightness. I have always a great difficulty about hypotheses from the necessity one is under of holding them loosely & suspending the mental decision. I do not know whether I am right in concluding that your hypothesis supposes that there can only be a few atoms in each molecule and that these are arranged as a disc or at all events disc fashion i.e in the same plane it seems to me that if we consider a molecule in its three dimensions it will be necessary to consider the atoms as all having their axis in planes parallel to one only of these directions however numerous these atoms may be – I speak of course of those bodies which you consider as naturally magnetic p 571. Perhaps when I get my head a little clearer I may be

737

able to see more clearly the probable arrangements of many atoms in one molecule. But for the present I must refrain from thinking about it

Our united kindest remembrance

Ever My dear friend
Your faithful
M. FARADAY

561 M. FARADAY to G. B. AIRY, 8 June 1854
[*Royal Observatory, Herstmonceux, Astrology-Optics, 1853 and 1854, Sect. 15, previously unpublished*]

Royal Institution
8 June 1854

MY DEAR SIR

Many thanks for your note. Curiously enough I wrote in March to Mr. L. Clarke about experiments as to any change in velocity of conduction dependant on the character of the current as to quantity & intensity; for Melloni wished for some results.[1] Mr. Clarke said he would make the experiments – and a week ago sent me all the results which I sent off at once to Melloni at Naples They are the same as those you refer to.

Did Mr. Clarke tell you the curious fact that some of the instruments connected with the *underground wires* have had their needles *reversed* & in some cases the *wires melted* – I suspect they have been struck thrgh [*sic*] the earth (where near the surface) by lightning

Ever My dear Sir
Yours Truly
M. FARADAY

[1] See Letter 552.

562 M. FARADAY to H. BENCE JONES,[1] 30 June 1854
[*R.I., previously unpublished*]

South Cliff Cottage
Shanklin
Isle of Wight
30 June 1854

MY DEAR FRIEND

I do not know why I write to you but that you are a friend and are called specially to my mind by any indisposition coming over me or my wife. She has I suppose caught cold very easily and in order in part to avoid the consequences we have removed from Ventnor where we were to this place. But at Ventnor her ear plagued her & since we have been here (the second day now) a serious gathering occurred in it causing her much pain & trouble – Now I think it is

738

going off after breaking – & she is easier but very deaf & very weak – She has brought no medicine or prescription with her hoping all from the air & place that was needful. I have an impression (and she has also) that the frequent syringing with warm water has made the ear susceptible to cold – perhaps the blistering has helped. I dare say all will come right again but the fact is I am somewhat of a coward on my wife's account and so I trouble you. If there is nothing to say do not think of writing. The place is very beautiful and the birds singing sweetly; and we are now on the top of the cliff. I am quite well and idling to perfection – it is the only thing that suits me. I forget where Lady Millicent[2] & the family are at present but I hope in such health as to cheer you. What a blessing health is? I hope you are enjoying it – and with it a cheerful active mind

Ever My dear friend
Yours faithfully,
M. FARADAY

[1] Henry Bence Jones (1813–73), physician and Hon. Secretary of the Royal Institution, 1860–73. The author of *The Life and Letters of Faraday*, 2 vols., London, 1870.
[2] Dr. Jones' wife.

563 M. MELLONI to M. FARADAY, 1 July 1854
[*I.E.E., previously unpublished*]

Moretta de Portini
ce 1er Juillet 1854

CHER ET ILLUSTRE AMI

J'ai recu, il y a quelques jours, les documents relatifs aux expériences que vous avez eû la bonté de faire faire à ma requisition par l'ingenieur en chef de la compagnie anglaise des télégraphes eléctriques:[1] elles m'ont beaucoup intéressé et je ne manquerai pas d'en rendre compte à mes collegues dans la premiere séance de notre académie des sciences . . . il se pourrait que l'exemple d'une société particulière si favorable aux recherches scientifiques induisit enfin le Ministre de l'instruction publique de Naples à fournir les petites ressources que l'Académie lui a demandées depuis longtems pour mettre en oeuvre mon projet d'expériences magnetiques autour du Vesuve . . . . . Quoiqu'il arrive, recevez mes plus vifs remerciments pour cette nouvelle preuve de votre précieuse amitié et soyez bien convaincu qu'elle restera profondément gravée dans mon coeur!

Le nouveau modele de mon eléctroscope sera bientôt fini et je ne manquerai pas de vous en envoyer de suite la description.[2] En attendant je vais vous communiquer quelques resultats obtenus avec l'ancien modele, fort incomplet sans aucun doute, mais bien superieur, comme je vous le disait à tout les autres eléctroscopes, soit pour la sensibilité, soit pour la netteté des indications. Ces resultats me paraissent en général favorables à votre ingenieuse theorie de l'induction et de la conductibilité eléctrique; il y en a cependant quelques uns dont je ne puis encore me rendre compte et je vous serai bien obligé si vous vouliez m'éclairer là dessus. Voici les faits que je vais résumer le plus brièvement possible.

Il faut premettre [*sic*][3] d'abord qu'un corps est complètement garanti des actions d'attraction et de repulsion provenant d'une source eléctrique extérieure lorsqu'on l'abrite convenablement par un écran de métal mis en communication avec le sol. Cela posé, vous concevrez qu'avec mon appareil, un écran percé, et un petit bâton de cire d'espagne eléctrisé je puis facilement étudier *la transmission* des milieux de differente nature pour *la force eléctrique rayonnante*. Or je trouve que cette force ne se propage jamais immédiatement dans les substances solides et liquides, comme quelques physiciens semblent l'admettre à l'égard du verre; mais toujours par la voie imédiate [*sic*], c'est-à-dire de couche en couche; ce qui rentre parfaitement dans vos idées. Cependant je ne comprends pas d'une maniere bien nette comment *la radiation eléctrique* parvenue à la surface du milieu se propage egalement dans tous les sens de sa masse, et surtout, comment *elle se renverse* [reading doubtful] *complètement dans certaines circonstances*

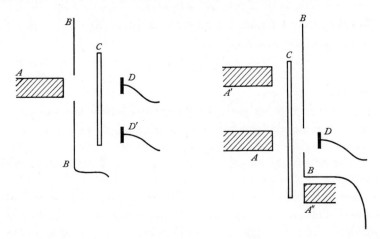

Soit *A* le corps eléctrisé, *B* l'ecran percé, *C* le milieu soumis au rayonnement electrique, *D* l'electroscope. L'action a lieu tout aussi bien lorsque l'eléctroscope est en face de l'ouverture que lorsqu'il se trouve placé en *D'*. De plus – Si l'on transporte la lame interposée *C* du côté de la source eléctrique, on observe encore le même effet en plaçant cette source en *A*, *A'* ou *A''* –

Dans ces differents cas ce n'est pas le seul mouvement de l'index eléctroscopique à l'état naturel que l'on obtient, mais aussi la qualité de l'electricité transmise, qui est toujours la même que celle de la source: en sorte que le petit baton de cire d'espagne porté en A, A' ou A'' augmente toujours la divergence initiale de l'index eléctroscopique lorsque l'instrument a été d'abord eléctrisé dans le même sens que celui du corps inducteur et diminue toujours cette divergence dans le cas contraire.

Les resultats sont les mêmes, quelle que soit la propriété isolante ou conductrice du milieu interposé et paraissent seulement un peu plus intenses pour les corps conducteurs, qui doivent être comme vous le pensez bien maintenus à l'état d'isolement. Ceux ci peuvent même recevoir une disposition au moyen de laquelle on démontre que dans le phenomène de l'induction des substances conductrices il n'y a point ainsi qu'on le dit, de transport du fluide eléctrique de l'une à l'autre extremité du corps. Je prends deux disques egaux, C', C'' de fer blanc ou de laiton bien mince, je les reunis ensemble par un fil metallique; et, après avoir fixé l'un de ces disques, C' par exemple, contre l'ouverture centrale de mon ecran communiquant avec le sol, j'eléctrise positivement l'eléctroscope, j'approche le baton frotté de cire d'espagne d'abord en C', puis en C'', et, j'observe à chaque fois le mouvement de l'index eléctroscopique. S'il est vrai, comme on l'admet, dans tous les traités de physique, que dans un corps conducteur isole soumis à l'induction, *le fluide homologue est repoussé jusqu'à l'extremité la plus eloignée*, on devrait evidemment avoir une diminution de la divergence eléctroscopique beaucoup plus grande dans le premier cas que dans le second; ce qui n'est point; car on obtient un effet à peu près egal dans les deux positions du corps eléctrisé. Le transport supposé de l'une à l'autre extremité du corps métallique isolé n'existe donc pas.

On dirait même au premier abord, d'après l'ensemble des faits qui précèdent, que le phénomène de l'induction développe dans le corps induit une seule espèce d'electricité; ce qui serait en opposition avec tout ce que nous savons sur cette branche de la science. Mais il est facile d'expliquer cette anomalie apparente en reflechissant que *le fluide de nom contraire à celui du corps inducteur ne peut être que dissimulé*, et que, par consequent, il ne saurait exercer son action à travers l'epaisseur de la lame des disques ou des lames interposées, telles minces qu'elles soient; tandis que le fluide homologue est doué de tension et repandu en proportion plus ou moins grandes sur toutes les faces du conducteur, moins celle qui est en regard du corps eléctrisé.

Je me trompe beaucoup ou le theorème fondamental de l'induction eléctrique, tel qu'on le trouve ordinairement énoncé, devrait être modifié de maniere à ne pas confondre deux effets complètement distincts: l'état eléctrique pendant l'induction et après le contact et l'eloignement du corps inducteur. On connait parfaitement ce qui arrive dans ce dernier cas, et pas assez ce qui se passe dans le premier. En effet les moyens de l'analyse expérimentale sont alors soumis à une grave objection. Vous dites qu'un eléctroscope eléctrisé donne deux actions continues lorsqu'on l'approche des deux extremités de votre cylindre métallique isolé soumis à l'induction. Mais l'instrument porté successivement à ces deux extremités est en des conditions toutes differentes: car il éprouve lui même une action inductive qui depend de sa proximité au corps inducteur – Abritez vos instruments derrière une lame métallique convenablement placée et mise en communication avec le sol; et vous arriverez comme moi, à la conclusion, *qu'une seule electricité est sensible pendant l'induc[tion]*, [ms. torn and missing] parcequ'elle se trouve à l'état libre, tandis que l'autre est dissimulée, et par consequent insensible. Ne serait-il pas plus convenable de presenter le theoreme de l'induction electrique sous la forme suivante?

Quand on approche un conducteur isolé d'un corps electrisé, le fluide naturel de ce conducteur est en partie décomposé: une certaine quantité du principe homologue est repoussée à l'état de tension sensible; la portion correspondante du principe contraire est attirée et dissimulée.

Dites-moi, de grace, votre opinion sur tout ce que je viens d'ecrire, et croyez moi pour toujours – – – – – votre très fervent admirateur et ami

MACÉDOINE MELLONI

P.S. Prenez garde de ne pas mettre une autre fois mon nom avant celui de Mr Flauti[4] dans l'adresse de vos lettres . . . . . autrement l'artifice ne servira à rien autre chose qu'à entraver davantage notre correspondance – – –

[Notes added by Faraday]   *Reply to Melloni July 31, 1854*

Results – contained in Exp Researches of 1837 & 1838. Series 11–14
    Do not know if one or two fluids 1298 note – is of no consequence 864 [?]
    In induction only the surface of the inducteous body excited and that only where the induction lines fall on it 1220. 1 1295. 301
    The induction is limited by the inducting surfaces 1231. 97. 361. 72. 483.
    The lines of inductive force 1231. 306. 441. 50.
    Induction not through thinnest metal except by conduction final – so not through uninsulated Gold leaf even
    Induction lines curved 1215. &c 1219. 21. 4. 30. 376. 449, 614.

Figs 7.8.9.10.11.12.

    Induction lines – their lateral relation 1224. 97. 1449
    Induction case   to Walls 1436 – mixed results. 1337. 1566. 1679
    Induction lines transferred to approached conductors 1225. 1449
    No destruction of force & dissimulated electricities 1684
    Charge always inductive 1177. 8.   and Viceversa
    Summary 1667–78–84
    Exp Research Vol II. pp. 263   also 279. good. concentric vessels
    Net covers screen – repels. &c. Wire Gauge. &c. – impermeability to induction

¹ For French translations of the Letters between Faraday and Latimer Clark see, M. Melloni, 'Sur l'égalité de vitesse que prennent les courants électriques de tensions différentes dans le même conducteur', *ASPN*, 27 (1854), 30.

² M. Melloni, 'Descrizione dell'elletroscopio di sua invenzione', *MASN*, 1 (1852–4), 335.

³ There is no such word in French. See 'premettere' in Italian – to say first of all, to state in advance.

⁴ Vincenzo Flauti (1782–1863), mathematician and Secretary of the Neapolitan Academy of Science. By addressing letters to Flauti, Faraday could save Melloni the postage.

564   M. FARADAY to H. BENCE JONES, 4 July 1854
[*R.I., previously unpublished*]

South Cliff Cottage
Shanklin,
Isle of Wight
4 July 1854.

MY DEAR FRIEND

Your letter was very kind and your words & advice of great value to us. The gathering in my wife's ear must have been very serious; occurring chiefly, or at first, in the left ear, – it extended or was joined in by the right ear; and though things are improving, & we believe steadily, yet much fluid or discharge comes from both. She has not been out of this house since we came into it and not much out of her room: but today appearances improve. She has taken one of the pills (on Monday), has great faith in them, & takes another tonight: – Your thought even, however distant the possibility was, of coming here was very kind, but to think of such a thing would have grieved us very much. We hope you found Lady Millicent well, & all hearty & happy. We have a surgeon here & a good doctor & surgeon at Ventnor – but a word of yours on paper seems of far more value than a long examination & consideration by a stranger – and so I wrote – for the moral as well as the *physical* help; – and both came. The pain in the head was at first, & especially at nights, very sharp & great: – it still continues but is changed in character being more of a heavy dull throb but is very distressing at times. We have not poulticed the ears but syringed them with warm water & used the cotton as you said. I suppose we must expect these series of changes as the parts slowly recover their tone. My wife takes the quinine as you directed

Ever My dear friend
Your grateful
M. FARADAY

[*I.E.E., previously unpublished*]

Moretta de Portini près Naples
12 Juillet 1854

CHER ET ILLUSTRE AMI

Dans ma dernière lettre j'élevais quelques doutes à l'égard des consequences que l'on a cru pouvoir deduire jusqu'à present des experiences qui servent de base au theoreme fondamental de l'induction électrostatique. Ces doutes ont passé dans mon esprit à l'état de certitude depuis qu'il m'a été permis de les soumettre à l'épreuve de l'analyse experimentale: et me voilà aujourd'hui bien convaincu que l'énoncé du théoreme susdit doit être essentiellement modifié.

Veuillez, de grace verifier les faits que je vais decrire, et si vous les trouvez exacts, comme je n'en doute point, ayez la bonté de les communiquer à la *Société Royale* et d'enfaire inserer la traduction dans les *Transactions philosophiques*.

Lorsqu'on approche d'un corps électrisé *A* un conducteur isolé *BC*, le principe électrique contraire à celui de *A* se developpe en *B*, l'homologue a [reading doubtful] *C*. En effet si on place; d'après la méthode d'Aepinus un corps métallique, isolé en contact avec l'une ou l'autre extremité du conducteur et si on l'approche ensuite d'un électroscope chargé d'une électricité connue, on obtient une action négative pour le contact *B* et positive pour le contact *C* lorsqu'*A* est électrisé positivement; et on a, au contraire, une action positive pour *B* et negative pour *C* dans le cas opposé où *A* est électrisé negativement.

Pour abréger l'expérience et la rendre peut être encore plus significative, il suffit d'avoir recours à la methode Wilke, qui consiste à composer le conducteur *BC* de deux pièces détachées que l'on separe, sans les toucher, sous l'influence électrique pour les eloigner ensuite de *A* et les presenter successivement à l'électroscope: car alors on trouve constamment les deux pieces électrisées en sens opposé, l'anterieure possedant toujours l'état électrique contraire à celui de *A*. Enfin, si on ne separe les deux pieces qu'apres l'éloignement de *A* on n'y observe plus aucune trace d'électricité, chacune d'elles se montrant alors à l'etat naturel: preuve evidente qu'il n'y a eû pendant l'expérience aucune transfusion électrique de *A* en *BC* et que les phénomènes presentés par ce dernier corps proviennent uniquement de l'électricité naturelle de *BC* troublée dans son etat d'equilibre par la presence de *A*.

Le developpement des deux principes électriques dans un conducteur isolé par la simple action d'un corps électrisé placé à une certaine distance est donc un fait incontesté et incontestable.

Cependant les preuves experimentales que je viens de citer ne demontrent cette verité *qu'après l'action de A, et non pas pendant que cette action est en train de s'exercer, comme on l'admet dans tous les traités de physique*

Vous pouvez vous convaincre, dit-on, de l'existence réelle des deux électricités en presence du corps inducteur, soit en approchant successivement de *B* et de *C* le même électroscope électrisé, soit en suspendant le long de *BC* une série de pendules a fil de lin: car les signes électroscopiques sont contraires aux deux extremités du cylindre, et la pendule correspondante se mouvent en sens opposé lorsque vous en approchez un corps chargé d'une électricité connue.

Je reponds que ces expériences ne sont guère concluantes, puisque les appareils employés pour explorer l'etat électrique des deux bouts du cylindre sont soumis, eux mêmes, à l'influence de *A* et subissent en *B* une une [*sic*] perturbation électrique bien autrement intense que celle qu'ils eprouvent en *C*. Ne serait-il pas possible que le changement des actions attractives en repulsives, ou viceversa, derivât tout simplement de cette perturbation électrique *de l'analyseur* et non pas de la qualité differente des électricités qui dominent en *B* et en *C*?

Pour resoudre la question il faudrait donc trouver le moyen de soustraire les instruments à l'action perturbatrice des corps inducteur. Or ceci ne presente aucune difficulté. Prenez une lame métallique et fixez-la verticalement dans le voisinage du conducteur de la machine électrique, après l'avoir mise en communication avec le sol: Approchez du côté opposé une petite balle de moëlle de sureau suspendue à un long fil de lin: et vous pourrez tourner tant qu'il vous plaira le plateau de la machine, tant que le petit pendule dévie le moins du monde de la direction verticale. Les choses ne se passent pas tout-à-fait de même lorsque le pendule est isolé et électrisé; car alors celui ci eprouve une certaine tendance à se rapprocher de la lame; mais cette tendance dérive uniquement d'une *réaction* developpée par l'électricité du pendule, et n'a rien à faire avec la force électrique provénant de l'autre côté de la lame; comme on peut s'en convaincre, soit en supprimant l'électricité du conducteur, soit en lui communiquant successivement les deux principes électriques: car dans l'un et l'autre cas l'inclinaison du pendule ne subit pas la moindre variation. Au reste l'attraction *de réaction* que la lame métallique en communication avec le sol exerce sur le pendule électrisé diminue rapidement, comme toutes les forces de ce genre, lorsque la distance augmente; en sorte que elle devient sensiblement nulle à un fort petit éloignement de la lame.

Maintenant, si on tient d'une main un électroscope chargé d'une électricité connue et de l'autre une lame métallique et que l'on approche l'instrument tantôt de *B* et tantôt de *C* en le preservant soigneusement de l'influence de *A* au moyen de la lame maintenue à une certaine distance, on voit ces extremités du cylindre *BC exercer toutes les deux la même éspece d'action électrique sur l'instrument*, *C* étant toutefois doué d'une action plus puissante que *B*.

Autrement: si on attache le long du cylindre *BC* la serie connue des pendules accouplés, et qu'on la soustrait à l'induction directe de *A* par des lames métalliques, convenablement placées, une baguette électrisée de verre, transportée successivement au dessus de chaque couple normalement à l'axe *BC* de et soigneusement abritée de l'action de *A* par une lame métallique qui communique avec le sol, *augmente ou diminue toutes les divergences des couples*, selon que *A* est électrisé positivement ou negativement. On peut même faire cette expérience d'une maniére beaucoup plus frappante en disposant la baguette parallelement à l'axe du cylindre; car alors *toutes les divergences subissent en même temps la même phase d'augmentation ou de diminution*; ce qui dissipe D'UN SEUL COUP DE BAGUETTE, les illusions que nous nous étions formées à l'egard des tensions électriques contraires développées sur les parties anterieure et posterieure du corps soumis à l'induction.

En variant la forme de ce dernier corps on peut enfin rendre l'experience independante des ecrans qui servent à preserver les instruments d'analyse de l'action directe de *A*. Imaginons, en effet, que l'on ôte la partie cylindrique de *BC* moins une bande superieure assez forte pour soutenir les surfaces hémisphériques placées à ses extremités: supposons ces surfaces terminées interieurement par un plan muni d'un leger pendule à fil de lin. L'appareil étant isolé et fixé à une certaine distance de la machine électrique en activité, on voit les deux pendules s'ecarter simultanément des surfaces planes correspondantes; l'antérieur moins que le posterieur; mais *tous les deux en vertu de l électricité positive*, comme cela resulte evidemment de leur repulsion commune sous l'action électrique de la baguette de verre, portee successivement en *B* et en *C*. La même repulsion s'obtient lorsqu'on remplace l'hemisphere anterieur *B* par un disque très mince; ce qui prouve l'existence de l'électricité positive jusque tout près de la surface tournée vers *A*. Il va sans dire que si *A* est electrisé negativement, le sens électrique des apparences observées s'en [reading doubtful] renverse, et que l'electricité negative est la seule sensible dans les diverses parties de l'appareil –

Ainsi *le cylindre BC soumis à l induction de A ne développe, a l'etat de tension apparente, que la seule electricité homologue à celle du corps inducteur. L'électricité contraire est completement dissimulée et ne devient sensible qu'après la separation et l'isolement des parties anterieures de BC et la suppression de la force inductrice*

On pourrait croire, au premier abord, que l'existence de l'électricité homologue à celle du corps inducteur jusque dans la partie antérieure du corps induit est en contradiction formelle avec les expériences de Coulomb et des autres physiciens qui ont trouvé cette partie électrisée en sens contraire. Mais la contradiction n'est qu'apparente et s'explique naturellement par les deux phases [reading doubtful] opposées de tension insensible ou sensible que prend successivement *sur le plan d'épreuve* une des deux espèces d'électricité. En effet supposons, pour fixer les idées, que *A* soit positif et que le point anterieur du cylindre *BC* touché avec le plan d'epreuve possede une seule unité d'électricité sensible et quatre [*sic*] [reading doubtful] d'électricité dissimulée, qui dans ce cas sera negative. Au moment du contact, le plan d'épreuve sera électrisé positivement, puisque le seule unité electropositive possede l'etat de tension apparente. Mais lorsque ce plan chargé de $+1$ d'électricité sensible et de -4 d'électricité dissimulée, s'éloigne de A pour subir l'essai de la balance de torsion, la dernière éspèce d'électricité acquiert, elle aussi, l'état de tension, neutralise la positive et reste en excès de trois unités. Si le point touché possedait trois unités d'électricité dissimulée et deux de sensible, le plan d'épreuve, positif pendant le contact de BC et la presence du corps A, accuserait sur la balance de torsion une electricité négative egale à une seule unité. Enfin, le plan d'épreuve serait [reading doubtful] encore positif au moment du contact avec BC, mais ne donnerait plus à la balance de torsion aucun signe d'électricité apparente si le point touché possedait des proportions egales du principe électrique sensible et du principe électrique dissimulé. – Il est inutile de s'occuper des points placés au delà de cette limite, parceque on ne trouve plus alors dans les deux cas que la seule tension électropositive.

Tout se reduit, comme on le voit, à une lutte plus ou moins inégale des deux électricités qui donnent, tantôt un resultat et tantôt une autre, selon qu'elles se trouvent dans un état de developpement semblable ou dissemblable.

Ainsi la dénomination de *point neutre*, adoptée par Coulomb pour signifier la partie du corps induit où les deux principes électriques possèdent la même intensité, n'est pas, au fond, inexacte. Je crois cependant qu'elle doit être rejetée parcequ'elle tend à donner une idée fausse de la distribution de l'électricité sensible pendant le phénomène de l'induction: car alors le point en question ne se trouve pas à l'etat naturel, et manifeste, au contraire, comme nous venons de le voir, une certaine tension électrique de même éspèce que celle du corps inducteur.

Il n'y a pas de doute que la principale cause de l'erreur où nous étions tous tombés jusqu'à ce jour n'ait été l'apparence trompeuse presentée par les pendules accouplés le long du cylindre métallique soumis à l'induction. En voyant les divergences de ces pendules plus fortes vers les deux bouts que dans la partie centrale du cylindre; et trouvant, d'autre côté, que les extremités de ce même cylindre donnaient des électricités differentes lorsqu'on les separait, à l'état d'isolement, dont l'action de la force inductive, on était naturellement porté à en deduire que les divergences extrémes n'étaient pas produites par le même principe.

Maintenant si vous me demandez la cause de cette singuliere disposition de l'electricité sensible dans le cylindre soumis à l'induction, je repondrais franche-ment que je ne saurais encore la formuler d'une maniere bien nette. Cependant l'explication qui me parait la plus plausible c'est que l'électricité homologue à celle du corps inducteur une fois developpée dans le corps induit, tend à s'y repandre d'apres les lois connues de la distribution électrique: et nous savons que dans un cylindre la tension est toujours moindre à la partie centrale qu'aux étremités [*sic*]. C'est vrai que l'électricité rencontre à l'extremité voisine du corps inducteur une force de repulsion plus puissante qu'à l'autre bout: aussi y a-t-il de ce côté un phénomène perturbateur que l'on supprime, je ne sais trop pourquoi, dans tous les traités de physique. Les doubles pendules s'inclinent vers *A* malgré l'électricité homologue dont ils sont pourvus: comme cela arrive toujours lorsqu'on met un corps mobile faiblement électrisé en presence d'un corps fixe doué d'une forte dose de la même éspèce d'électricité, et l'inclinaison des fils qui soutiennent les deux balles de sureau attachées à chaque couple dérivent de la même force attractive, produit naturellement entre les deux pendules une augmentation de divergence.

Mais en revenant à la nouvelle forme sous laquelle, je crois indispensable d'énoncer le théoreme fondamental de l'induction électrostatique, il est facile de voir qu'elle ne complique pas inutilement l'explication des faits qui en dependent: bien au contraire, elle tend à les présenter sous un point de vue unique et invariable, le seul qui soit réelement rationnel et conforme à l'observation.

Ainsi, par exemple, si les deux électricités induites se trouvaient contemporainement existantes à l'état de tension dans notre cylindre horizontal muni de pendules, comme on l'a supposé jusqu'à ce jour, elles devraient aussi exister dans le même état sur la partie métallique verticale et isolée d'un électroscope mis en presence d'un corps électrisé. Or, pourquoi en touchant la garniture superieure de l'appareil et en soustrayant ensuite l'instrument à l'action de la force inductrice, le trouvons nous électrisé en sens contraire? Evidemment parceque la seule électricité homologue était, sous l'action du corps inducteur, douée de tension et mobile; tandis que l'autre était privée de tension et de mobilité. Dans le premier cas on faisait donc une supposition totalement differente de celle qu'il fallait adopter pour avoir l'explication du second. Cette contradiction manifeste n'existe plus dans le nouvel énoncé des phénomènes électriques développés par influence, où l'etat different des deux électricités, que l'on imaginait pour se rendre compte de la charge inductive des électroscopes, est admis comme un fait démontré directement par l'expérience.

On pourrait citer aisément d'autres exemples analogues. On pourrait montrer surtout, comment l'énonciation exacte des états où se trouvent les deux principes électriques d'un corps isolé sous l'action de la force inductive permet de concevoir leur developpement sans avoir recours au transport de ces deux principes de l'une à l'autre extremité du corps induit. . . . Mais ce serait là une véritable temerité d'ecolier envers son maître. . . . Voila pourquoi je m'arrête tout court en me declarant comme toujours, bien sincerement

votre tout-devoué admirateur et ami
MACÉDOINE MELLONI

566 LYON PLAYFAIR to M. FARADAY, 19 July 1854[1]

[*Portfolio of portraits of Honorary Members of the Ipswich Museum, Sir Harold Hartley, previously unpublished*]

32 Ludbroke Square,
Notting Hill
19th July/54

MY DEAR PROFESSOR

The Scotchmen, myself being an atom of that nation-loving race, are very desirous to make the Meeting of the Association at Glasgow a successful one. The Meeting takes place on the 12th Septr. in a Town situated on a *moderately clean river*, the seat of badly smelling Chemical Manufactures, but within 2 hours of Loch Lomond where Rob Roy became a hero, by remaining unhung as a thief, & within 3 hours of Loch Katrine where the fair lady of the Lake, her father & array of followers mysteriously inhabited an island on which two little Bushmen would scarcely be able to squat with our present vast ideas of space –

I hope all these attractions will lead you to Glasgow where as the Clyde claims no relationship with the Thames, I can promise you a warm reception.

Yours Sincly
LYON PLAYFAIR

[1] This letter seems to refer to the meeting of the British Association at Glasgow in 1855, and is probably wrongly dated 1854.

567 M. FARADAY to SIR T. BYAM MARTIN,[1] 7 August 1854

[*British Museum, Add. mss. 41, 370, f. 333, previously unpublished*]

Royal Institution
7 Aug 1854

MY DEAR SIR BYAM

I send you herewith the best answer I can make to your enquiries. [Ref: Proposal by Lord Dundonald,[2] f. 328]

Ever Your faithful Obt Servt
M. FARADAY.

f. 334 – Observations &c. Royal Institution 7 August 1854.

Very few of the questions are so put that I, in reference to their chemical or physical character, can give any consistent or distinct answer to them. The proposition is correct in theory, *i.e.* dense smoke will hide objects, and burning sulphur will yield fumes that are intolerable, and able to render men involved in them incapable of action, or even to kill them: but whether the proposition is *practicable* on the scale proposed and required, is a point so little illustrated by any experience, or by any facts that can be made to bear upon it, that for my own part I am unable to form a judgment. I have been on the crater of Vesuvius and to leeward of the mouth; and have seen the vapours (which are very deleterious) pass up over my head and go off down the wind in a long and not rapidly expanding stream. I have, by changes in the wind, been involved in the vapours, and have managed with a handkerchief to the mouth and by running, to get out of their way. I should hesitate in concluding that ten or twenty vessels could give a body of smoke, the columns of which, at a mile to leeward, would coincide and form an impervious band to vision a mile broad; but I have no means of judging, for I know of no sufficient facts that can be of use as illustrations of the proposed applications.

In reference to the burning of sulphur and formation of sulphurous acid, I may remark, that, as 400 tons of sulphur have been spoken of, perhaps the following considerations may help to give some general ideas, in the present state of the proposition, as to the probable effect of its fumes. If a ship charged with sulphur were burning in a current of air, a continuous stream of sulphurous acid fumes, mingled with air, would pass off from it. This stream, being heavier than air, would descend and move along over the surface of the water; and, I expect, would sink perpendicularly and expand laterally, so as to form a low broad stream. Its noxious height would probably soon be less than 15, or perhaps even 10, feet, (but I cannot pretend to more than a guess) and its width by degrees more and more. The water over which it would have to move, would tend continually to take part of the noxious vapour out of it. Now 400 tons of sulphur would require 400 tons of oxygen; and that it would find in about 1740 tons of air. Supposing that this product were mixed with ten times its bulk of unaltered air, it would make near upon 20000 tons of a very bad mixture; and one, which if a man were immersed in it for a short time, would cause death. Supposing that the 20000 tons of mixed deleterious air were converted into a regular stream, 30 feet high and 300 feet wide, then it would be about 6500 feet or a mile & a quarter long. Such is a representative result for 400 tons of sulphur, and hence an idea may be formed of the time during which with a given velocity of wind, the places involved in the stream may remain subject to its effects.

In respect of the seven questions, there is scarcely a point in them to which I am able to give an answer of any value.

As to 1.; I suspect much larger quantities of matter will be required than is supposed. – I do not imagine that if burnt in heaps coals would burn fast enough to give the smoke required.

2. The data are wanting.

3. I suspect the upper part of high buildings would frequently be free from the sulphurous vapours; and that sets or eddies of fresh air from above would occur behind.

4

5

6 The lateral extent at the distance of a mile very doubtful – would need proof.

7.

The proposition is, as I have said, correct in theory, but in its results must depend entirely on practical points. These are so untried and unknown, and there are so few general facts bearing on the subject, that I have the utmost difficulty in speaking at all to the matter. These circumstances must plead my excuse for the very meagre character of the only observations which I am at present able to offer. All I need add is, that if the project were known or anticipated, it would not be difficult for the attacked party to provide respirators, which would enable the men, in a very great degree or even altogether, to resist a temporary invasion of an atmosphere such as that described.

M. FARADAY

1 Sir Thomas Byam Martin (1773–1854), Admiral of the Fleet.
2 Thomas Cochrane, Tenth Earl of Dundonald (1775–1860), famous naval commander in French Revolutionary and Napoleonic wars. His proposal was to take Cronstadt by filling old ships with sulphur, igniting it when the wind was favorable and let the ships drift to shore. The sulphur dioxide thus wafted over Cronstadt would force the garrison to surrender. See *LPW*, 482.

568   J. BARLOW to M. FARADAY, 10 August 1854
[*I.E.E., previously unpublished*]

Lake of Geneva,
Aug. 10th (1854)

MY DEAR FARADAY,

How are you all? I trust that nothing of a harassing or distressing nature shortened your visit at [illeg.]. I saw your name in the newspaper among those of the Lord Mayor's guests on the 14 of July but I think that the list (as in the cast of Queen's Belles) was made from those who were invited not from those who were seen at the entertainment. . . . Our journey has been very prosperous hitherto and I earnestly hope that the weather has been as fine in England as that with which we have been favoured.

– At Paris we were joined by Charles Hewes[1] (the nephew & brother of your friend) and with him we have since been traveling – our route has been Bale (see new railroad) Geneva – by the Münster Thal, Neufchatel, and Rolle – then to that lovely village of St. Gervais (near Sallanches) & Chamouni, where we spent a fortnight – I mean dividing the time between St. Gervais and Chamouni. At Chamouni I met a man whose name I could not find out, though I ought to know it familiarly. He is a Fellow of Trinity College Dublin. He had Brougham's paper on light referred to him. He was one of the first in making magnetic observations after Gauss's fashion. He knows you personally, and he asked me whether certain observations of Kreil[2] at Prague on the moon's influence on the magnet had not made you revise your views? (meaning of course your paper of 1850–51) – He is a light-haired man, about 40, & has a wife, a luxury allowed to Irish Fellows.[3] . . . . .

. . . When I was last at Geneva, De la Rive was at Vichy. He is due at home now – Mr. Drummond ought also to be at Geneva by this time. I hope to send you news of both. I dined at [illeg.] with M. Marcet – a distinguished-looking young Spanish lady was on a visit to his daughter. This girl is a Pigano,[4] and there is a curious story connected with her. . . . Her uncle fell desperately in love with a beautiful Spanish lady. *Her* friends objected, because they felt assured that her excessive beauty would ensure for her a still more eligible match – *His* friends were equally adverse, because they had heard the girl's mother ill spoken of. He yielded to their representations. He promised to give up the marriage, & only stipulated for their assent to his visiting his love for the last time to bid her farewell – She was then at a country house high in the mountains. She received him with bitter reproaches, and avowed her disbelief in his attachment. He challenged her to put him to the test. She said "If you really love me you will not refuse to take off your coat & swim across the ice-cold "pond yonder".

Excited as he was, he plunged in caught a pleurisy from which he never recovered but died within a twelvemonth. The Heroine of this curious romance *is the present Empress of the French.*

. . . Geneva Aug. 11th, 4.00 P.M.

a thousand thanks in Mrs. Barlow's name and my own for your letter, which was cordially welcomed by both of us.. My wife had one of those obscure attacks (which sometimes harrass her,) while we were in the Münster Thal. It gave way to a mustard poultice but so did the cuticle also. There must be something particularly malignant in the [illeg.] of that district. .

We have indeed enjoyed the glorious scenery which has daily been presented to our view in such rich abundance. From Montigny we went to Villeneuve by Monthey [reading doubtful] (instead of Bix) and the prospect including a bridge over the Rhine was one of the most striking I ever witnessed. . Snow mountains – an amphitheatre of near rocks, not too near, a foaming river, and most luxuriant foliage – – This richness of verdure is of course the result of previous rains: but it is very brilliant. – I earnestly hope that the sunshine is on its way to England. . . . . .

You are sure to succeed in what you do for the Institution: – I quite agree with you that Percy is a great prize. – – If your health and inclination enable you to give the Christmas Lectures, I shall be very sanguine for next year. – I hear that a Mr. Hawkins,[5] who is restoring those apocryphal animals the

Megatherium &c for the Crystal Palace is thinking of writing to propose to give us an Evening next year. Do you know anything about him? If you meet any of the Paleontologists & happen to think of it, inquire – But we have many sterling men who will help us. To say nothing of yourself & Tyndal. Owen has promised. so has Grove after his fashion. If you write to Airy you will poke him I am sure – In short we are sure to get on..

Mrs. Barlow keeps urging me so constantly to remember her most earnestly to you and Mrs. Faraday and Miss Jenny[6] if she is with you that I fear I am going over a thrice uttered effusion (instead of a thrice told tale) but it is genuine.

Ever your attached [reading doubtful] JOHN BARLOW

I will write again & tell you where to direct to us – I hope that we shall be at Munich in the beginning of next month.

[1] I am unable to identify Mr Hewes further.
[2] Karl Kreil (1798–1862), Director of the Central Institution for Meteorology and Terrestrial Magnetism of Vienna.
[3] The description appears to fit Humphrey Lloyd (1800–81) except for his age. Light-haired men often do not look their age.
[4] I am unable to discover what a Pigano is. A Spanish family, perhaps?
[5] Benjamin Waterhouse Hawkins (1807–89), sculptor, who applied his art to illustrating geology and palaeontology. See his 'On Visual Education as applied to geology, Read before the Society of Arts, May 17, 1854', London, 1857.
[6] Probably Jane Barnard.

569 F. C. O. VON FEILITZSCH to M. FARADAY, 11 August 1854
[*I.E.E., previously unpublished*]

Greifswald in Prussia,
Aug. 11, 1854.

MOST HONOURABLE SIR!

Three years ago I had the honour to send you my researches about the physical distinction of magnetic and diamagnetic bodies.[1] By your kindness and under your protection they were admited [*sic*] in the Philosophical Magazine and consequently they were bespoken from several sides, thereby it was caused, that in the Archives des sciences physiques et naturelles de Geneve well founded doubts could by [*sic*] raised against my opinions,[2] I were obliged to assert their rightness, but on the other side I was convinced from the principle defended by me, that the magnetism and the diamagnetism were only identical excitations of the matter, and it grew my task to maintain it by new researches. You have treated my first notices with so much indulgence, that I dare to hope you, the creator of this new disciplin [*sic*] will take it as a prove of my respects, that I put at your benevolence the results of my new treatise. On the other hand it is my duty vis-a-vis of you, as well as of all who got knowledge of my first paper, to

753

confess my error and to put some better thing in its place. If I had succeded to gain your approbation, my highest wishes were accomplished. You will kindly allow me to send you the german treatise,[3] as well as a short extract, that I have written in your language, trusting that you will excuse its incorrectness.

I am, Sir, your
most devoted servent [sic]
DR. VON FEILITZSCH
Professor at the university of Greifswald

[1] See Letter 442.
[2] See J. Tyndall, 'De la polarité diamagnétique', *ASPN*, 27 (1854), 215.
[3] F. C. O. von Feilitzsch, 'Ueber Herrn de le Rive's Theorie der von der Magnetkraft abhängigen Erscheinungen', *AP*, 169 (1854), 248.

570   J. BARLOW to M. FARADAY, 13 August 1854
[I.E.E., previously unpublished]

Hotel de York
Spa,
Aug 13 /54

MY DEAR FARADAY

You could have had no misgiving when you were writing your letter, as to the amount of pleasure it would afford us. We are glad to think of you & Mrs. Faraday enjoying pure air and quiet, & hearing, as I trust you do, good news from Miss Barnard. You will be glad that my wife is well. I am rather feeble, my right eye is not yet restored. My right hand is very slow in writing, and I am soon tired in a walk.. Luckily these infirmities do not diminish the pleasure I experience from intercourse with valued friends..

– – Of course we shall gladly acquiesce in your outlay for Tyndall's Lectures. I only hope that his optics may not be "higher" next year than the intellects of his hearers. I think it very important that our Lectures should be original, & such as can only be given by the original research of the Lecturer; that they should be illustrated by striking experiments, so as to present a beautiful outline-map of the subject, such as any one, who would give continuous intelligent attention to the Lecture, would both apprehend and retain. Such were your own Saturday Lectures in old time. Now I dread the tendency of Tyndall's Lectures to become abstract – Illness and the meetings of the R. Soc. Council, deprived me of many of them last Spring but I thought some of them I did hear, difficult, especially as there was no text book for the student to refer to. This remark I would apply, with greater force, to the chemical lectures except the last. Many of these have been quite out of the comprehension of any but chemists. – Within the last few years Jermyn Street has supplied the wants of those who require detailed & deep instruction.

But I have prosed too long on this subject. I was very glad to get a cheerful note from Tyndall on the eve of his departure. He said nothing about Lectures, but he talked hopefully of the issue of his researches into the gases' interference with the waves of heat.

I do not know that there has been any enterprise of yours in which I have more cordially bidden you "God speed" than in your efforts for the scientific degree. It will be the motive for high powers, now too much neglected, as judgment and accuracy, being cultivated; and it will constitute an order of men, much needed now, to fulfil very important purposes in society. Then it will enormously add to the usefulness of mathematical proficients, also may be induced to compete for it. Mr. Hudson,[1] one of the Assistant Tutors of Trinity, is here: he tells me that, as yet, little has been done in the scientific Tripos at Cambridge – you would have few sympathizers at Spa. There are pretty walks & drives; & the geological structure of the hills is interesting – But nothing is thought of except gambling. Though, for many reasons, I abstain from playing, I often go to the Tables to watch the curious succession of events which occur, and to listen to the still stranger inferences which are drawn from them. As, during the plagues infallible preventives and cures were sold, so here people profess to have devised schemes which *must* win. Some of these are extremely plausible, and it has been an occupation to me to detect their fallacy, and to try to demonstrate the mathematical certainty that those, who play long enough, must lose. There have been wonderful games – an Englishman won £1200 two days ago. This is as good for "the bank" as a fire is for an insurance office. It is already said to have made £60,000 and the season is little more than half over. . . .

I hear that the same cause which you assign has diminished the [word illeg.] all over central Europe.

Mr. [illeg.] sends his cordial remembrances. Mrs. Barlow her love to Mrs. Faraday with my thanks for her few lines.

> Ever, dear Faraday,
> your attached friend
> JOHN BARLOW

[1] E. T. Hudson (1825–75) received his B.A. in 1849.

571   G. B. AIRY to M. FARADAY, 19 August 1854

[*I.E.E., previously unpublished*]

> Royal Observatory
> Greenwich
> 1854 August 19

MY DEAR SIR

I have some thought of trying pendulum experiment [*sic*] in a mine, as I did (unsuccessfully) a good many years ago. At that time I saw R. W. Fox, and he was possessed with the idea that the vibrations of a pendulum might be influenced by magnetic currents in the rocks about it. I should be very much obliged if you will tell me *in the first place* whether you think that there can be any such attraction: and if so, of what kind. I may point out what would be the effects of different kinds of force (A) If the force were a steady vertical force, it would be injurious (B) If the force were always opposed to the motion it would not be injurious (C) If the force aided the motion in the approach to perpendicular position and opposed it in the recess from perpendicular position, it would be injurious. – *In the second place,* would such force be annihilated by destroying the insulation of the pendulum.//I regret to trouble you with what may be foolish questions: – but if there is any reality in the thing it may be important – and to whom else can I go for information?

I am, my dear Sir,
Yours very truly
G. B. AIRY

572   SIR T. BYAM MARTIN to M. FARADAY, ca. 20 August 1854[1]

[*British Museum, Add. mss. 41370, f. 371, previously unpublished*]

MY DEAR MR. FARADAY

I am ashamed to think how long I have neglected to thank you for the interesting paper you sent to my Committee at the Admiralty; the fact is I was taken seriously ill at the moment when we brought our business to a close and have been made to keep my papers out of sight since that time.

I not only beg to thank you for your observations in reply to our questions but permit me to ask if there is not some fee usual, and due, for your obliging services – I am ignorant in such matters, and beg you will tell me candidly what is customary

[1] See Letter 567. Also Letter 574.

573   J. PLÜCKER to M. FARADAY, 21 August 1854

[*I.E.E., previously unpublished*]

Bonn
21st of August 1854

DEAR SIR!

I take liberty to present to you two new papers. One of them is from Poggendorff's Annalen; the other one I was obliged to write being this year Dean of the faculty.[1] I thought it proper to explain at this occasion, what I think the present state of our knowledge of the magnetism of gazes and crystals. Belonging to this subject several assertations were attributed to me, I never made. I passed myself through different errors. Therefore I wished to precise my present meaning.

I join to this parcel other copies of the latin paper for the Reverend Secretary of Royal Institution, to Mr Grove and Prof Tyndall.[2] Your porter may, without giving you any trouble, deliver them by occasion.

I set off instantly for visiting my friends at Vienna.

Yours
most truly
PLÜCKER

[1] Plücker published two papers in *AP* in 1854. It is impossible to determine to which he is referring. See *RSCSP*. I am unable to identify the second paper.
[2] See Letter 410, fn. 2.

574   M. FARADAY to SIR T. BYAM MARTIN, 26 August 1854
[*British Museum, Add. mss. 41370, f. 372, previously unpublished*]

Royal Institution [stamped letterhead]
26 aug 1854

MY DEAR SIR BYAM

I have received your kind note and am very sorry to hear of your illness. There is no charge for I am not Professional. Do not get me into more consultations than can be helped. – I have just come away from another at Somerset House. I shall always attend to any thing *you* desire of me but wish the Admiralty – to procure other aid when they can

Ever My dear Sir Byam
Your faithful Servt
M. FARADAY.

575   J. BARLOW to M. FARADAY, 27 August 1854
[*I.E.E., previously unpublished*]

Dresden
Aug 27, 1854

MY DEAR FARADAY

You must write to me once more, as soon as you can do so without suffering. I am sure that that letter to me must have been a painful effort – The fingers cannot do their work satisfactorily when the nerves from the neck are irritated by disease & violence. . . We are very anxious also to have another report of Mrs. Faraday. She could not have made progress during your painful illness. Then I should desire to know which of the Porters has been in trouble. One naturally thinks of Lacy, who, I fear, is transmitting a dreadful constitution to his children. . . Of all the mysterious dispensations of Providence the fertility of mad, consumptive, & scrophulous families is, to me, the most inexplicable. It is, to my mind, the most (apparently) exceptional arrangement in the system of this world. . . I hope that I need not tell you that if the immediate administration of a sovereign or two will remove any part of the trial, I beg that you will advance it for me. . . . Our journey thus far has been very prosperous. I forget whether I wrote to you from Salzburg or from Ischl. We enjoyed the last named place extremely. The scenery is lovely, and the residence there of the Emperor & Empress does not spoil it. I saw them, one day, walking home from the village church (where they go every day) – She is prettier than the pictures of her: the expression of her countenance is very pleasing. I am told that she is very amiable & benevolent. From Ischl to Vienne over the lake of [illeg.] & by the fall of the Traun to Linz – from Linz by Danube-Steamer to Vienna – at Vienna six days, & then here by Prague, where we remained three, & where your prompt letter just caught me. – You perhaps heard that the cholera broke out in Munich soon after we left it. I was told that six people were lying dead in one day at the large hotel (the Bavaria) – May Liebig & Hofmann & all our friends have escaped! . . . My accounts from England represent this disease to be more under control now than on any of its former visitations. – Lord Jocelyn's[1] death seems to have been, in great measure, the result of his own imprudence: Lord Beaumont's[2] appears hardly to have been a case of cholera, and the reports which I hear from the Westminster hospital certainly indicate a very small proportion of deaths. . . . I quite fancy Schlagentweit's face. He is just the man to be panic-struck: if I at all understand these brothers,[3] neither of them would distinguish himself much if made to confront a danger of this kind. . . .

. . . As far as I can understand the patois of the people, there seems every prospect of an abundant harvest, except in fruit, which is neither good nor plentiful. . . .

The more I see of other countries, the less am I disposed to encourage that swaggering language which our countrymen indulge in when speaking about England. . . . Educated classes are, I imagine, much of the same calibre of morals every where: but I should guess that the educated bear a larger proportion to the uneducated all over central Europe than is the case in England. . . . Then, if one comes into details – of the English farmers, I have a very bad opinion – of the English (especially London) tradesmen I think very little better – The foreign shopkeeper perhaps takes advantage of you in his prices, but he does not send false bills, or parcels in which the goods you have paid for are not forthcoming. This has happened to me repeatedly from the most eminent of the (so called) most respectable London Tradesmen. – In England nothing could induce me to associate with what is called an "Evangelical clergyman" or with any one else who made a parade of religion, because I never knew any such who was not at heart an infidel, a debauchee, or a rogue or, at best, a tool of these characters. Now this does not seem to be the case in Roman Catholic Countries. The discipline of the confessional must restrain breaches of the moral law – Your Connection does the same thing by different machinery. Therefore I am always disposed to think well of and to confide in a member of it. . . .

. . . I beg your pardon for this outbreak. . . . Mrs. Faraday is however partly to blame for it. . She said that I should think your form of worship ridiculous – Now I cannot imagine any thing less possible to deride than the simplicity and earnestness of your ritual and I am sure that it must pervade the daily life of those who are exercised by it. . .

And yet there is the same earnestness in those who are well disciplined by the Roman system. I attended High Mass at St. Stephen's Cathedral in Vienna on the Birth-day of the Emperor. The Arch Bishop, assisted by a conclave of Bishops, officiated. There was the full Roman Pageant. – Robes, incense, lights, music – Diplomatists, & statesmen, and officers in splendid uniforms, assembled in the most picturesque groupes [sic] to give effect to the spectacle – This was at the high altar – at a side altar, very near this dazzling ceremony, a low mass was going on – perhaps fifty people were kneeling there. Not one of these raised his eyes or seemed at all conscious of what was going on so near him – In short, Priest & people did just what they would have done had they been alone in the Church. – No Protestant engaged in any of his services, would, as I am persuaded, be capable of such concentration – and yet these were people the majority of whom were in the humblest ranks.

Don't imagine that I am exalting R. Catholics further than the letter of my words expresses. – It is a religion which, it I know very well, I never could become attached to. Still I appreciate their accomplishment of their steadiness which it is so difficult to attain.

I will now release you. . . Do not think about all this effervescence but tell me how you, Mrs. Faraday and Miss "Jenny" are. . . If I can say or do any thing for you in Berlin, tell me.

Ever yours
JOHN BARLOW

[1] Robert Jocelyn (1816–54), eldest son of the third Earl of Roden.
[2] Miles Thomas Stapleton Beaumont (1805–54), Colonel commandant of 4 West York Militia at the time of his death.
[3] See Letter 452.

[*R.I., previously unpublished*]

Royal Institution
30 Aug 1854

MY DEAR BARLOW

You do not say where I am to address you or when so I write instantly that I may catch you at Dresden – though perhaps I shall decide to send it to Berlin as you ask whether you can do any thing for me there. Remember me in kindness to all friends there – there are three or four I think of writing to, but now that I am better the hot weather is so enervating that I am *lazier* than ever. We are getting on pretty well here. Lacy is better & his family & I shall not mention your kindness you can do what you like when you come back – Anderson had to lay up but is better indeed pretty well again. He had a boil or something in the neck that had to be opened – Miss Savage[1] has just gone for her holiday. Mr. Vincent will be here very soon & is very well. Tyndall is at work hard in the Laboratory & appears to be quite well We are now at Surbiton near Kingston but I am in town three or four days in the week at work. I am now very well. My wife, I hope improving; pretty well but very deaf & feeble in the limbs & head.

As to the world I know nothing of it here nor do I care much for it – if it will let me alone – but only think of the nuisance of being found out at Surbiton, & teased with visits; and invited by the *Mayor of Kingston* to *dine* at the *Venison feast* (annual) – &c &c It is all meant very kindly but such kindnesses are not in my way, and I feel it unkind in me to refuse them

I received a letter from Naples last Saturday which will grieve you Melloni died suddenly that is after a short illness on the 11th I think of this month (August) We had been corresponding vigorously on some scientific matter & instead of a letter from him I received the notice of death from his friend, M. Flauti of the Academy of Sciences there –

I must pass by your observations on religion &c & indeed must conclude in the briefest manner with our kindest wishes to you & Mrs. Barlow

Ever Yours
M. FARADAY

---

[1] Sarah Savage, housekeeper at the Royal Institution, 1835–65.

577   J. G. S. Van Breda and W. M. Logeman to
M. Faraday, September 1854[1]
[*P.M.*, *4 s.*, *8 (1854)*, *465*]

Haarlem,
September 1854

Sir,

The experiments on electro-dynamic induction in liquids which you have published in a letter to M. de la Rive,[2] have excited our lively interest, not only because the phænomenon appeared to us to be of importance in itself, but especially because it seemed likely to throw some light upon the manner in which electricity is propagated in liquids.

Do liquids conduct exclusively by electrolysis, or do they also possess a proper conductibility, similar to that of metals? An experiment that we have made may perhaps assist in the solution of this question. It is well known that the conductibility of liquids increases with their temperature, whilst the opposite effect takes place with the metals, a fact which is easily explained if we suppose that liquids, in general oppose less resistance to decomposition in proportion as their temperature is raised. If this explanation be the true one, the next thing to be ascertained is, whether a liquid will also exhibit this increase of conductibility for a current so weak as to traverse it without producing any apparent chemical decomposition. If this were the case, it would appear probable that the decomposition nevertheless took place, and that it was by its intervention that the current passed through the liquid. We have endeavoured to solve this question by the following experiment. We passed the current of a small Daniell's element through a column of distilled water 24 centimetres in length, contained in a glass tube of about 15 millimetres in diameter; the electrodes were of platinum wire. One of these electrodes was connected with the zinc pole of the battery, the other with one end of the helix of a galvanometer of which the wire made 1800 coils, the other end of which communicated with the copper pole. The tube was immersed in a water-bath, the temperature of which could be raised by means of a spirit-lamp. When the water was at 59° F., the needle of the galvanometer deviated 4°. When the lamp was lighted, this deviation was seen to increase regularly. At a temperature of 152°.6 F., the deviation was 7°, and at 190°.4 F. it was 11°. The increase of the conductibility of the liquid by heat was therefore proved, even when traversed by an excessively feeble current. Had any chemical decomposition of the water taken place during this experiment? Its direct result led to the belief that such was the case, but we were also fortified in this opinion by the following circumstances. When the liquid was cooled, the communications remaining untouched, the needle of the galvanometer no longer showed any appreciable deviation. When the direction of the current in the column of water was reversed, the needle immediately deviated 8° and returned insensibly, but in a short time to 4°, at which point it remained stationary. It was consequently an effect of the polarization of the electrodes that we observed in this case, a polarization which opposed the current at the first moment of its passing, without, however, being able to annul it, but which annulled it completely when it had become stronger by the passage of the stronger current through the heated liquid.

But is this polarization the peculiar effect, and consequently the irrefragable proof, of chemical action? There are many experiments which render this opinion, if not absolutely certain, at least exceedingly probable. We may mention in particular those of Schönbein, who found that the effect continues when the electrodes which have served to introduce a current into a liquid are immersed in another liquid through which no current has been passed, and also that effects exactly similar to those of the plates polarized by the current may be obtained by putting one of them only in contact with a gas (such as hydrogen or chlorine) for a very short time, and afterwards immersing them in acidulated water*. Some physicists, however, still maintain the opposite opinion. They explain polarization by an accumulation of electricity of different natures, either in the electrodes themselves, or in the adjacent portions of the liquid; these two electricities in recombining by a conductor uniting the two electrodes, after the connexion between these and the electromotor has been broken, would give rise to the current in the opposite direction to that of the latter, which is always observed in such cases.

It appeared to us that your *beautiful experiment on electrodynamic induction in liquids* might furnish a means of submitting this opinion to an experimental test, by trying whether the electrodes, employed in that experiment to conduct the instantaneous current of the fluid helix to the galvanometer, are or are not polarized by this current. To obtain a decisive effect it was necessary to reproduce the phænomenon with more intensity than when, as in your experiments, the question was merely to prove the phænomenon itself. For this purpose we made use of a tube of vulcanized Indian rubber, of about 1 centimetre in internal diameter and 13 metres in length. We twisted it round the two branches of the large electro-magnet intended for experiments in diamagnetism, which, if we are not mistaken, has the same form and the same dimensions as your own; it is covered by a coil of copper wire 3 millimetres in diameter and 180 metres long. The tube was entirely filled with a mixture of 6 parts by volume of water and 1 part of sulphuric acid. It was terminated at both ends by glass tubes of about 4 centimetres in length; into each of these passed a platinum wire of 1 millimetre in diameter, the portion of which immersed in the liquid was about 2.5 centimetres in length. All being thus arranged, the ends of the two platinum wires were connected with the galvanometer of 1800 coils which was placed at a distance of 10 metres. We had ascertained previously that at this distance the magnet did not exercise any sensible action upon the needles. The moment the two ends of the copper-wire coil of the electro-magnet were put in connexion with the poles of a Grove's battery of 60 large elements, arranged in a double series of 30, the needle of the galvanometer deviated suddenly about 40°, and returned, after oscillations which occupied between 1 and 2 minutes, to 0°. When the circuit of the pile was interrupted, the galvanometer deviated again about the same number of degrees, but in the opposite direction, returning again to 0° in the same manner. The needle returning in both cases to 0°, one would be tempted, at first sight, to think that there was no polarization of the electrodes. But the strong impulsion communicated to the very astatic system of the galvanometer by the induced current, causing the needles to oscillate during a considerable period as we have just stated, the circuit remaining always complete, it appeared possible that the polarization, if it existed, had already exhausted itself before the needles had arrived at a state of repose. To get rid of this difficulty we put the two electrodes in direct communication with each other by means of a copper wire of only 10 centimetres in length, although they still remained in connexion with the galvanometer. The induced current produced when the circuit of the pile was established, then passed by this wire rather than by the infinitely longer wire of the galvanometer, and the needles remained at rest. But when this wire was removed after the establishment of the communication with the pile, *we saw the galvanometer deviate instantly in an opposite direction to the deviation produced by the induced current of the preceding experiment, and rest, after a few oscillations, at 10°. By replacing the wire, then interrupting the circuit and again removing the wire, we saw the galvanometer deviate in the contrary direction, and rest, in the same manner, at about 10° on the other side of the divided arc.* In both cases the deviation diminished regularly by little and little until it became 0°; we did not exactly measure the time which this occupied, but it appeared to us to be about 30 or 40 seconds.

These experiments were frequently repeated, and always with the same result. We need not say that we always took the precautions pointed out by you, to prevent the effect of an induction in one of the metallic conductors.

Polarization therefore takes place in the electrodes which serve, not only to convey a current into a liquid, but to carry out the current induced in the liquid itself. It appears to us that this fact directly contradicts the theory which attributes polarization to an accumulation of the two electricities upon or around the electrodes; for in the present case not only would such an accumulation be infinitely less probable than in ordinary cases of polarization, but if it existed, it would necessarily give rise to a current not in a direction opposed to that of the principal current, but in the same direction.

May we therefore regard all polarization as an effect of electrolytic decomposition, and consequently as an irrefragable proof of the existence of this decomposition? If this be true, we shall be led to regard the opinion of those who admit the possibility of the transmission of a current, or of a portion of a current through a decomposable fluid without the occurrence of any decomposition, as resting upon very slight grounds. Whenever we have passed a current, however weak, through such a liquid, we have always observed an undoubted polarization of the electrodes.

We shall take the liberty to describe one other experiment, which is still more convincing in this respect than that described at the commencement of this communication. We immersed two plates of platinum, 6 centimetres in length and 5 centimetres in breadth, at a distance of about 1 centimetre from each other, in distilled water. One of these plates communicated with the ground by a metal wire; they had previously been carefully cleaned by heating to redness, and consequently, when put in communication with the galvanometer, did not produce any sensible deviation. But as soon as *a single spark* from a common electrical machine had been thrown upon the plate which did not communicate directly with the ground, and the communication with the galvanometer had been established, the needle deviated from 3° to 4° in one direction, and the same distance in the opposite direction when the current of the spark was passed through the water the other way. This deviation could be brought to 15° or more by throwing several sparks instead of one upon one of the plates, or by connecting the plate for a very short time with the conductor of the machine during the movement of its plate.

We fear that the importance of this letter will not be proportional to its length; if, however, its contents should seem to you to be worthy of attention, we shall be happy to see it published in any manner you think proper.

We remain, Sir, &c.,
J. G. S. VAN BREDA.
W. M. LOGEMAN.

* Poggendorff's *Annalen*, vol. xlvi. p. 109, and vol. xlvii. p. 101.[3]
[1] See Letter 583.
[2] See Letter 545.
[3] C. Schönbein, 'Beobachtungen über die elektrische Polarisation fester und flüssiger Leiter', *AP*, 122 (1839), 109, and 'Neue Beobachtungen über die Volta'sche Polarisation fester und flüssiger Leiter', *ibid.*, 123 (1839), 101.

578   J. BARLOW to M. FARADAY, 13 September 1854

[*I.E.E., previously unpublished*]

Paris
7 Rue 29 Juillet
Septr. 13th. (1854)

MY DEAR FARADAY

Since I wrote to you we have gone over much space, & have had many things to think about, recalling associations with yourself... From Berne we went to Interlaken, where I found your letter at the Poste Restante. We remained at Interlaken 3 weeks, and had 2¾ days of available [reading doubtful] weather. These small morsels of time we devoted to the Wengen Alp Reichenbach & Rosenhorn [reading doubtful]. From Interlaken we went to Vevay [*sic*] (& thence to Geneva) (by the Simmenthal). The weather was just beginning to close up: luckily one is not so dependent on the clearness of the atmosphere for valley and for mountain scenery.

. . . At Geneva we were very kindly received by De la Rive, Marcet &c and enjoyed ourselves for 11 days getting many glimpses of Mont Blanc, and witnessing De la Rive's phenomenon of the second pink which comes over the mountain on a fine evening – – After eleven agreeable days we quitted Geneva, & traveled post hither, coming over the Jura to Dijon. . . We have taken lodgings for a month, and I hope that we may meet at the beginning of October. . . . . . While at Berne I was invited to attend the meeting of a philosophical Society. – I was not able to do so – I regretted this afterwards as Wolf read two papers on interesting subjects. 1. Proving from a series of observations a connection between magnetic variations and the spots on the sun's disc. 2. Describing a method for making platinum malleable at a very little cost. . If there really is anything in these communications, they are very important. You will of course hear more about them if you have not done so already.

. . . . The political state of Switzerland is anything but satisfactory. – The 'Black' & 'White' parties (i.e. Conservatives & Radicals) abuse each other vehemently, but we cannot easily see what is the point of real principle at issue. The Black Conservative denounces the White Radical as a source of all sort of moral corruption – imputes to him the increase of drunkenness, & the growing depravity des moeurs. The White rejoins by impeaching the Black as a conspirator against [word illeg.] the rights of the poor. One effect of the triumphs of the White party at Geneva is sufficiently deplorable. They have, as you well know, ostracized the De la Rives Marcets &c. I see that all the old families regard Geneva as no longer the place of their interests. – And yet not withstanding that the intellectual Glory of the University has departed, the material prosperity of that town never could have been greater than it is now. . One cannot help thinking what a bribe it offers every day to France or to its starving neigbour [*sic*] Jevry. . . . . Marcet told me that, in the month of August, 6 inches of rain ($\frac{1}{5}$th of the average of the year) had fallen at Geneva.

. . . Delarive is going to write to you on one point in your recent researches on which he is not sure that he has got your exact thoughts. I told him that I had heard from you, and that you were working satisfactorily. – by the bye, in reference to another sentence in your letter, Bence Jones & Dubois Reymond are to meet at the Hotel des Bergers [reading doubtful] at Geneva on the 15Th.

I met Dr. Webster[1] in the street on Friday. He is full of the sea-serpent, which he declares that he & half a dozen other persons saw, going at the rate of 10 miles in 2 minutes, between Dieppe and Newhaven. He is ready to make any amount of declarations that it was no porpoise, grampus or anything of the kind. . . He has written to the Times, & will write to the Royal Society[2] – so let Owen beware.

... I found luckily two very good examples of your *"filings"* in my blotting book. I gave one to De la Rive, & the other to Dumas, with whom I dined yesterday.. He supports his station very elegantly. His son is Directeur de la Monnaie at Rouen –

... And now goodbye. If you can find 5 minutes to tell me of your welfare & that of Mrs. Faraday I shall be thankful – so will my wife – Miss Grant[3] offers her best remembrances.

Ever yours

JOHN BARLOW

[1] Possibly George Webster, M.D. (1797–1875), one of the founders of the British Medical Association in 1832.

[2] I find no mention of a sea-serpent in *PRS* or in *The Times*.

[3] I am unable to identify Miss Grant.

579 M. FARADAY to J. PLÜCKER, 19 September 1854

[*Nat. Res. Counc. Canada, previously unpublished*]

Royal Institution

19 September 1854

MY DEAR SIR

At the very time that I had sat down to write to you in sincere acknowledgement of your last kind letter I received the one of the 21st August and the papers.[1] The latter I immediately distributed giving the one copy to Dr Tyndall and sending the others to the houses of Mr Barlow and Mr Grove. You go on working earnestly and well a great pleasure to yourself an [*sic*] an honor to your friends and country and it is quite cheering to an old man like me to see it in your letters and your labours. Though cut off from the German language yet by dint of perseverance amongst some of my friends I get hold of the thoughts in your papers as well as of those in the papers of other worthies of your country but then my memory is weak and soon holds them but indistinctly and then I mourn a little for the labour of recovering all I want to know and of doing that again & again is more than health can bear I well know that if the time is come for me to cease running in the race I should be most ungrateful to murmer much. I ought rather to rejoice that I can enjoy the pleasure of looking on at the fine exertions of others

I have not been at the British Associations for some years so tomorrow I go off to Liverpool to be present for 2 or 3 days at the one now approaching. I hope you will be successful & happy at Vienna – You must need a holiday for when you talk of your labours three lectures a day & successful research you quite frighten me

I am Your Very true friend

M. FARADAY

[1] See Letter 573.

580   M. FARADAY to J. LATIMER CLARK,[1]
26 September 1854
[*Engineering Societies Library, N.Y.C., previously unpublished*]

26 Septr. 1854

MY DEAR SIR

I called yesterday to congratulate you I trust every day makes you more & more happy in your change Though I have no proper right still give my sincerest hopes & wishes to Mrs. Clarke as an offering of respect twds [*sic*] you & to her through you

Poor Melloni is dead. He left this life in the middle of the correspondence I had with him about your experiments. I sent him all the data you sent to me & he published some of them in a brief form. I was waiting for his further results but now I fear there is no reason [reading doubtful] to expect any more. Those he had in hand were imperfect & I fear he cannot have lived to finish them

Now the results which shewed that the force of a weak battery passed with equal rapidity along the line as that of a strong battery are very interesting to me. I could not keep copies of those sent to Melloni for want of time but if you could let me have them I think I should like to consider them in relation to my views and send a note or brief paper to the Phil Mag upon that point Can you favour me so far?

Ever My dear Sir
Yours faithfully
M. FARADAY

[1] Josiah Latimer Clark (1822–98) had recently taken the position as Engineer for the Telegraph Company of England.

581   M. FARADAY to SIR T. BYAM MARTIN, 14 October 1854[1]
[*British Museum, Add. mss. 41370, f. 374, LPW, 483*]

Royal Institution
14 Octr 1854

MY DEAR SIR BYAM

I have no doubt you have thought of the matter but I cannot resist referring to the combustion of I think above 2000 tons of Sulphur in the middle of a crowded town like Newcastle & *as regards a certain application*, the little comparative evil it has done

I am
My dear Sir Byam
Your faithful Servt
M. FARADAY.

[1] See Letter 567.

[*I.E.E., previously unpublished*]

Genève

le 27 8bre 1854

J'ai eu la visite de mon jeune ami M. *Vardet* qui a quitté huit jours chez moi à la campagne; il était bien *reconnaisant* d'une lettre qu'il avait recu de vous; c'est un jeune physicien bien distingué & qui [illeg.] loin. – [next sentence largely illeg.]. de faire [illeg.] un lettre à [illeg.] d'Tyndall dont j'ignore l'adresse[1]

MONSIEUR & TRÈS CHER AMI,

Je n'ai pas encore répondu à votre si bonne & excellente lettre du 29 mai[2] dont j'ai été bien touché comme je le suis toujours de tous les témoignages d'amitié que vous me donnez. A mesure que l'on avance en âge & qu'on voit les rangs de ses amis s'éclaircir autour de soi, on a d'autant plus besoin des marques d'affection de ceux qui vous restent, & quand surtout on a été frappé comme je l'ai été de manière à n'avoir plus qu'une moitié de vie, on est encore plus sensible aux consolations d'une amitié aussi sympathique & aussi sérieuse que la votre. Personne ne comprend mieux que vous que ce n'est plus dans ce monde que je dois chercher le bonheur & que mes pensées doivent s'élever plus haut.

J'ai su que vous aviez été pas bien cet été; j'espère que le repos vous aura fait du bien & que vous êtes maintenant tout-à-fait remis. Donnez moi de vos nouvelles dès que cela vous sera possible.

Vous me parlez dans votre lettre de l'hypothèse par laquelle je cherche à expliquer le magnétisme des corps & vous me faites l'objection que mes molécules devraient dans cette hypothèse, avoir la forme de disques. Cela semble en effet résulter de la conception que j'ai mise en avant. Cependant je ne crois pas que cette conséquence soit rigoureusement nécessaire.

Je distingue l'*atome chimique* de la *molécule intégrante*, celle-ci étant formée par un groupe plus ou moins considérable d'atomes chimiques. J'admets que dans les corps qui sous le même volume renferment le plus grand nombre d'atomes chimiques, les atomes sont beaucoup plus rapprochés les uns des autres dans la molécule intégrante d'où nait un courant électrique pour chaque groupe, par l'effet de leur polarité. Or que la molécule intégrante soit sphérique, cubique, octaëdrique ou rhomboëdrique, rien n'empêche les atomes de s'arranger de manière à former autour de la molécule des ceintures de courants tous parallèles les uns aux autres & dirigés dans le même sens. Le disque serait dans ce cas la section équatoriale d'une molecule sphérique. – Quand le fer n'est pas aimanté, les molécules intégrantes se disposent naturellement de façon que l'action naturelle de tous leurs courants soit neutralisée, ce qui constitue le cas d'équilibre. Mais dès qu'une source extérieure telle qu'un aimant ou un courant vient à agir, alors tous les courants moléculaires s'orientent, & le corps est aimanté.

Quant au diamagnétisme, je crois qu'il est dû à une action inductrice moléculaire du même genre que l'induction que vous avez découverte, mais avec cette
différence qu'elle persiste tant que la source qui la produit est présente. – Dès
lors [reading doubtful] les contacts moléculaires doivent être dans le corps
induit dirigés en sens contraire des courants inducteurs, ce qui explique la
répulsion exercée sur les corps diamagnétiques. Les dernières recherches de
Matteucci & celles de Tyndall sur la polarité des corps diamagnétiques sont
favorables à cette hypothèse. Je n'ai pas la place dans une lettre de développer
suffisamment mon explication; mais si vous me le permettez, je pourrai le faire
une autre fois. Je suis convaincu qu'on peut ramener à la même cause les
phénomènes du diamagnétisme et ceux de l'induction.

J'ai été très occupé pendant cet été de mon $2^{\underline{d}}$ volume qui est presque
entièrement achevé; j'espère que vous en serez content, c'est toute mon ambition, car il n'y a aucune opinion à laquelle je tienne autant qu'à la votre

Votre tout dévoué & affectionné
A. DE LA RIVE

¹ Note added at the beginning of the letter.
² See Letter 560.

583 M. FARADAY to J. TYNDALL, 31 October 1854
[*P.M.*, *4 s., 8 (1854), 465*]

Royal Institution,
Oct. 31, 1854

MY DEAR TYNDALL,

I send the enclosed letter from MM. Van Breda and Logeman¹ to you as an
Editor of the Philosophical Magazine. If you should judge it proper for insertion in that Journal, I shall be very happy to see it there, but will beg you to
accompany it on my part with the observation that it is not so conclusive in
proving the negative (a thing very difficult to do) as to move me at present
from the reserved condition of mind which I have recently expressed in respect
of this matter.

Ever yours truly,
M. FARADAY.

¹ See Letter 577.

584 M. FARADAY to G. B. AIRY, 8 December 1854

[*Royal Observatory, Herstmonceux, Sci. Soc., 1853 and 1854, Sect. 10, previously unpublished*]

R Institution
8 Decr. 1854

MY DEAR SIR

Mr Barlow has put me down for the Fr. Evg of Jany. 19th. i.e the first Evg You I think consent to favour us on [reading doubtful] the third ie Feby 2nd – Having undertaken the Juvenile lectures at Christmas extending to the 9th. Januy I feel I should be glad to be later in my Friday. Do not think I wish to draw on your good nature & so cause any inconvenience but if it should happen to be nearly the same to you, there are so many that would feel a delight in hearing you open our season that I thought I would put the case before you

Ever Yours faithfully
M. FARADAY

585 G. B. AIRY to M. FARADAY, 11 December 1854 [copy]

[*Royal Observatory, Herstmonceux, Sci. Soc., 1853 and 1854, Sect. 10, previously unpublished*]

Royal Observatory,
Greenwich
1854 December 11

MY DEAR SIR

The circumstances which determined my selection of the beginning of February (at least my preference of a time not earlier than that to an earlier time) is this – that the last four days of December and a portion of January are the only time when I can have a slight remission of labour and a little country life. Great things are guided by little ones, all the world over: and these moments of mine are ultimately determined by my children's school holidays.

It would upset my family arrangements very much, to engage to be in London on a definite day in January: although without doubt I shall have to come up on some days yet undefined.

I would do much to accommodate my movements to your wishes, but I am confident that the price which, in this instance, must be paid for it, is greater than you yourself would desire.

I am, my dear Sir,
Yours most truly
G. B. AIRY

Royal Institution,
February, 1855

My dear Mr. Faraday,

Few, I imagine, who read your Memoir in the last Number of the Philosophical Magazine,[2] will escape the necessity of reconsidering their views of magnetic action. We are so accustomed to regard the phænomena of this portion of science through the imagery with which hypothesis has invested them, that it is extremely difficult to detach symbols from facts, and to view the latter in their purity. This duty, however, is now forced upon us; for the more we reflect upon the results of recent scientific research, the more deeply must we be convinced of the impossibility of reconciling these results with our present theories*. In the downfall of hypotheses thus pending, the great question of a universal magnetic medium has presented itself to your mind. Your researches incline you to believe in the existence of such a medium, and lead you, at the same time, to infer the perfect identity of magnetism and diamagnetism.

In support and illustration of your views, you appeal to the following beautiful experiments: – Three solutions of protosulphate of iron are taken; the first, *l*, contains 4 grains; the second, *m*, 8 grains; and the third, *n*, 16 grains of the salt to a cubic inch of water. Enclosed in hollow globules of glass, all these solutions, when suspended in the air before the pole of a magnet, are attracted by the pole. You then place a quantity of the medium solution, *m*, in a proper vessel, immerse in it the globule containing the strong solution *n*, and find that the latter is still attracted; but that when the globule containing the solution *l* is immersed, the latter is *repelled* by the magnetic pole. Substituting elongated tubes for spheres, you find that when a tube containing a solution of a certain strength is suspended in a weaker solution, between the two poles of a magnet, the tube sets from pole to pole; but that when the solution *without* the tube is stronger than that *within* it, the tube recedes from the pole and sets equatorially.

Here then, you state, are the phænomena of diamagnetism. It is maintained by some, that, to account for these phænomena, it is necessary to assume, in the case of diamagnetic bodies, the existence of a polarity the reverse of that of iron. But nobody will affirm that the mere fact of its being suspended in a stronger solution reverses the polarity of a magnetic liquid: – to account for the repulsion of the weak solution, when submersed in a stronger one, no such hypothesis is needed; why then should it be thought necessary in the case of so-called diamagnetic bodies? It is only by denying that space presents a medium which bears the same relation to diamagnetic bodies that the stronger magnetic solution bears to the weaker one, that the hypothesis of a distinct diamagnetic polarity is at all rendered necessary.

The effects upon which the foregoing striking argument is based are differential ones, and are embraced, as already observed by M. E. Becquerel,[3] by the so-called principle of Archimedes. This principle, in reference to the case before us, affirms that the body immersed in the liquid is attracted by a force equal to the difference of the attractions exerted upon the liquid and the body immersed in it. Hence, if the attraction of the liquid be less than that of the immersed body, the latter will approach the pole; if the former attraction be the greater, the immersed body recedes from the pole, and is apparently repelled. The action is the same as that of gravity upon a body immersed in water: if the body be more forcibly attracted, bulk for bulk, than the water, it sinks; if less forcibly attracted, it rises; the mechanical effect being the same as if it were repelled by the earth.

The question then is, are all magnetic phænomena the result of a differential action of this kind? Does space present a medium less strongly attracted than soft iron, and more strongly attracted than bismuth, thus permitting of the approach of the former, but causing the latter to recede from the pole of a magnet? If such a medium exists, then diamagnetism, as you incline to believe, merges into ordinary magnetism, and "the polarity of the magnetic force", in iron and in bismuth, is one and the same.

Pondering upon this subject a few evenings ago, and almost despairing of seeing it ever brought to an experimental test, a thought occurred to me, which, when it first presented itself, seemed to illuminate the matter. Such illuminations vanish in nine cases out of ten before the test of subsequent criticism; but the thought referred to, having thus far withstood the criticism brought to bear upon it, I am emboldened to submit it to you for consideration.

I shall best explain myself by assuming that a medium of the nature described exists in space, and pursuing this assumption to its necessary consequences.

Let a cube, formed from the impalpable dust of carbonate of iron[†], which has been compressed forcibly in one direction, be placed upon the end of a torsion beam, and first let the line in which the pressure has been exerted be in the direction of the beam. Let a magnet, with its axis at right angles to the beam, and hence also at right angles to the line of pressure, be brought to bear upon the cube. The cube will be attracted, and the amount of this attraction, at any assigned distance, may be accurately measured by the torsion of the wire from which the beam depends. Let this attraction, expressed in degrees of torsion, be called a. Let the cube now be turned round $90°$, so that the line of pressure shall coincide with the direction of the axis of the magnet, and let the attraction a' in this new position be determined as in the former instance. On comparison it will be found that a' exceeds a; or, in other words, that the attraction of the cube is strongest when the force acts parallel to the line of compression[‡].

Instead of carbonate of iron we might choose other substances of a much feebler magnetic capacity, with precisely the same result. Let us now conceive the magnetic capacity of the compressed cube to diminish gradually, and thus to approach the capacity of the medium in which, according to our assumption, the carbonate of iron is supposed to be immersed. If it were a perfectly homogeneous cube, and attracted with the same force in all directions, we should at length arrive at a point, when the *magnetic weight* of the cube, if I may use the term, would be equal to that of the medium, and we should then have a substance which, as regards magnetism, would be in a condition similar to that of a body withdrawn from the action of gravity in Plateau's experiments. Such a body would be neither attracted nor repelled by the magnet. In the compressed cube, however, the magnetic weight varies with the direction of the force; supposing the magnetic weight, when the force acts along the line of compression, to be equal to that of the medium, then if the force acted across the line of compression, the magnetic weight of the cube would be less than that of the medium. Acted upon in the former direction, the cube would be a neutral body; acted upon in the latter direction, it would be a diamagnetic body. If the magnetic capacity of the cube diminish still further, it will, according to your hypothesis, become wholly diamagnetic. Now it is evident, supposing the true magnetic excitement to continue, that the cube, when acted on by the magnet in the direction of compression, *will approach nearer to the magnetic weight of the medium* in which we suppose it immersed, than when the action is across the said line; and, hence, the repulsion of the cube, when the force acts along the line of compression, must be *less* than when the force acts across it.

Reasoning thus from the assumption of a magnetic medium in space, we arrive at a conclusion which can be brought to the test of experiment. So far as I can see at present, the assumption is negatived by this test; for in diamagnetic bodies the repulsion along the line in which the pressure is exerted is proved by experiment to be a *maximum*‖. An ordinary magnetic excitement could not, it appears to me, be accompanied by this effect.

The subject finds further, and perhaps clearer, elucidation in the case of isomorphous crystals. It is not, I think, questioned at present, that the deportment of crystals in the magnetic field depends upon their molecular structure; nor will it, I imagine, be doubted, that the molecular structure of a complete crystal of carbonate of iron is the same as that of an isomorphous crystal of carbonate of lime. In the architecture of the latter crystal, calcium simply takes the place which iron occupies in the former. Now a crystal of carbonate of iron is attracted most forcibly when the attracting force acts parallel to the crystallographic axis§. Let such a crystal be supposed to diminish gradually in magnetic capacity, until finally it attains a magnetic weight, *in a direction parallel to its axis*, equal to that of the medium in which we assume it to be immersed. Such a crystal would be indifferent, if the force acted parallel to its axis, but would be repelled, if the force acted in any other direction. If the magnetic weight of the crystal diminish a little further, it will be repelled in all directions, or, in other words, will become diamagnetic; but it will then follow, that the repulsion in the direction of the axis, if the nature of the excitement remain unchanged, will be less than in any other direction. In other words, a diamagnetic crystal of the form of carbonate of iron will, supposing magnetism and diamagnetism to be the same, be repelled with a *minimum* force when the repulsion acts parallel to the axis. Here, as before, we arrive at a conclusion which is controverted by experiment; for the repulsion of a crystal of carbonate of lime is a *maximum* when the repelling force acts along the axis of the crystal. Hence I would infer that the excitement of carbonate of iron cannot be the same as that of carbonate of lime.

Such are the reflections which presented themselves to my mind on the evening to which I have referred. I now submit them to you as a fraction of that thought which your last memoir upon this great question will assuredly awaken.

Believe me,
Dear Mr. Faraday,
Yours very faithfully,
JOHN TYNDALL.

* Some of the reasons which induce the writer to hold this opinion are given in the Bakerian Lecture of the Royal Society for the present year.
† For an ample supply of this most useful mineral, I am indebted to the kindness of J. Kenyon Blackwell, Esq., F.G.S.
‡ Phil. Mag. Sept. 1851; Pogg. *Ann.* 1851.
‖ Phil. Mag. Sept. 1851.[4] Pogg. *Ann.* 1851.
§ Phil. Mag. Sept. 1851.[5] Pogg. *Ann.* 1851.

[1] The footnotes marked by symbols, not numbers, are Tyndall's.
[2] See Letter 588, fn. 2.
[3] E. Becquerel, 'De l'action du magnétisme sur tous les corps', *AC*, 3 s., 28 (1850), 283.
[4] John Tyndall, 'On Diamagnetism and Magnecrystallic Action', *PM*, 4 s., 2 (1851), 165.
[5] *Ibid.*

587   J. PLATEAU to M. FARADAY, 6 February 1855
[*I.E.E., previously unpublished*]

Gand,
6 février 1855

MON CHER MONSIEUR FARADAY.

Il y a bien long-temps que je n'ai eu l'honneur de causer un moment avec vous; Je saisis donc avec joie l'occasion que m'offre l'envoi de la troisième livraison de ma petite *Physique*,[1] livraison que vous recevrez sous bandes par la poste. Cette livraison termine la physique des corps pondérables; la première moitié seulement est de moi; la seconde, qui se compose de l'Acoustique, est de M. Quételet. J'ai joint à l'exemplaire qui vous est destiné, un second exemplaire que je vous prie de vouloir bien remettre de ma part à M. Wheatstone. Dites lui, je vous prie, que la froideur qui semble exister entre lui et moi me fait grande peine. Je l'ai, à la vérité, importuné un peu à propos de la reproduction non realisée de ma *deuxième série* dans les *Scientific Memoirs*, et aussi à propos d'une analyse de ce travail, que je désirais faire insérer dans un Journal anglais;[2] mais je vous ai également importuné, et pourtant vous n'avez pas cessé de me témoigner de l'amitié; tâchez, je vous prie, de la ramener à de meilleurs sentiments envers moi.

J'ai lu avec admiration le compte rendu de vos belles expériences sur les effets de l'induction latérale dans un long fil métallique recouvert d'une substance isolante et plongé dans l'eau. Que nous preparez-vous encore? Il y a quelque temps que vous n'avez rien publié à ma connaissance, et je m'attends à l'apparition de quelque nouveau prodige.

Quant à moi, débarassé maintenant de l'encyclopédie populaire, j'ai repris la suite de mon travail sur les masses liquides sans pesanteur, et deux nouvelles séries sont fort avancées. Je regrette bien vivement que ce sujet soit si éloigné de ceux qui vous occupent: Car il en résulte que vous ne pouvez y prendre un grand intérèt; cependant vous serez convaincu, je l'espère, que c'est une mine féconde en résultats.

Agréez, mon Cher Monsieur Faraday, l'assurance de tous mes sentiments de respectueuse affection.

Jh PLATEAU
Place du Casino, 22.

¹ See Letter 480.
² See Letter 480.

588   M. FARADAY to G. B. AIRY, 9 February 1855
[*Royal Observatory, Herstmonceux, Astrology-Optics, Tides, 1855 and 1856, Sect. 8, previously unpublished*]

Royal Institution
9 Feby. 1855

MY DEAR SIR

I should not like to draw a conclusion from the phenomenon you describe except upon more numerous and personal observations. Mr Latimer Clarke has told me that he has evidence of currents produced in underground wires referable (he thinks) to atmospheric inductions upon the surface & substance of the earth at different localities & unless yours be a *constant* phenomenon it may be of that kind.

As to the sea water battery – you must not rely upon it before you have tried it for some time – A change of fluids (which for a time includes the condition of fresh fluids & fresh surfaces) may answer for a short time & yet the new fluid may not be satisfactory in the long run.

I have not seen your letter to Mr Barlow yet but I have been ill & confined to my room[1] I dare say he will shew it to me in due time. In the meantime I send you a paper from the Phil. Mag. The speculative part I have no more opinion of than I have of the many speculations that float about (and must float) in mens minds but the experimental part contains many nuts which at present are hard to crack.[2]

Ever My dear Sir
Yours Truly
M. FARADAY

[1] See *B.J.* 2, 352. The letter concerned Airy's views on Faraday's ideas of the conservation of force and action at a distance. *LPW*, 507.
[2] M. Faraday, 'On some points of magnetic philosophy', *PM*, 4 s., 9 (1855), 81.

589 W. WHEWELL to M. FARADAY, 12 February 1855
[*Trinity College Library, Trinity College, Cambridge, previously unpublished*]

Trinity Lodge,
Cambridge,
Feb. 12, 1855

MY DEAR DR. FARADAY

I have received papers containing your speculations on magnetism and especially the paper in the Phil. Mag. on Magnetic Philosophy.[1] I have read them with great interest, as I always read your speculations; but they require more time and leisure before I can fully possess myself of your views. At this imperfect stage of thought, and at the risk of proposing difficulties which your former papers have solved, will you allow me to make a remark on your notions as there given.

Your lines of magnetic force whether or not they contain the true theory, are an admirable way of exhibiting the facts; and I have always ascribed the success with which you have unravelled so many very complex phenomena to your starting from these lines. I do not say that they do not contain the true theory, or come nearest to it; for I think we are arriving at a point when the other two theories which you mention not only cannot explain but cannot express the facts. And if the lines of physical force come to be the only way of expressing the laws of phenomena they *must* be accepted at least till they are resolved into something else. Now what I have to say is this: I do not think that the facts of magnetism alone, even those in your new paper, are the strongest examples or any examples of *this* peculiar advantage of the physical lines of force. So long as we confine ourselves to magnetism alone (paramagnetism) all the facts can be explained by the existence of two fluids. All your facts of chambers in which the magnetic force vanishes flow easily from that theory: for a self-repelling fluid is necessarily concentrated at edges and points: and the theory of two mutually

776

attracting self-repelling fluids includes, so far as I see, all the facts by which you reduce the universal duality of the forces. – But when instead of confining ourselves to one kind of polarity magnetism, we take in the related polarities, electric or voltaic currents, then your lines of force become the only way, so far as I see, of exhibiting the facts. I can make nothing of the other theories in that case, and I have not seen any attempts to apply them coherently. And the same is the case with diamagnetism. I do not see that either of the other theories enables us to explain the most obvious facts. Now what I have to say is this; the advantage of the physical lines of force theory thus residing in its application to diamagnetism and voltaic currents in their relation to magnetism, it would be a great boon to the ordinary thinker if you could explain it more fully in these relations. Your application of it to voltaic currents always makes me wonder at the clearness and readiness with which you conceive the relations of space, but I fear is not intelligible to ordinary readers. It might be made so by figures, diagrams, of the physical lines copiously used, and exhibiting many kinds of examples of the application of your views. And the same is the case with the application of the lines of force in diamagnetic phenomena. We – [reading doubtful] ordinary readers – would like to see the lines of force drawn in such cases as you have given in page 10 of this last paper, and in many other cases. It is probable that you have explained this matter in some of your previous papers; but it has I conceive a special bearing upon your present attempts to show the advantages of the lines of physical force. Your theorem (p. 33) "pointing in one direction or another is a differential action due to the convergence or divergence of lines of force" etc. is a very curious proposition; and seems to me, or rather is, so far as I see, the only way of exhibiting the facts; but it wants much development to make it intelligible to us: and I want you to give it this development, by diagrams, copious and various, as well as by experiment. Excuse my liberty; I want to have all possible light thrown upon us from your abundant internal light.

Yours always truly,
W. WHEWELL

1 See Letter 588, fn. 2.

590   M. FARADAY to W. WHEWELL, 23 February 1855

[*Trinity College Library, Trinity College, Cambridge, previously unpublished*]

Royal Institution
23 Feb.ʸ 1855

MY DEAR DR. WHEWELL

Your letter was very acceptable to me for it gives me courage, and I am heartily thankful to you for it. I have given many figures of lines of force at different times, and briefly refer you to them. Thus in the Paper on Magnetic conduction (2797) there are figures at 2807. 2821. 2831. 2874. 2877. 2972. 2993. The paper on lines of Magnetic force (3099) has a plate full of figures in reference to their delineation (3234) drawn from nature; and the paper on Physical lines (3243) also has a plate. Still I think that, as you suggest, figures more numerous still would be very useful. I have, however, been in some degree deterred from pressing these matters too hard, because I wanted to see how far that which has been advanced might be accepted or justified; and also because I wanted to trace more clearly to myself the origination & developments of the lines of force round a wire carrying a current; through & about a helix – without or with an iron core; and amongst wires & helices in juxtaposition. Above all I want to obtain some *clear* idea of the coercitive force, & how it is that an electrohelix, having but weak powers itself as a magnet, can raise up (or arrange) such a powerful system of lines when an iron core is introduced. I have other matters too in hand, regarding magnecrystallic action, which I hope to develop soon & think may turn out well. Your recommendation, however, shall not be forgotten & I shall probably soon begin to collect cases for illustration.

I conclude I am right in believing that if diamagnets & diamagnetism had been known to us before we knew any thing at all of Paramagnets & paramagnetism, the theory of two magnetic fluids would have applied to it, but could not then have included paramagnetism. It is this idea which makes me earnest in speaking of chambers of little or no action & places of weak magnetic action; for though the old theory of two fluids can account for them, they are not the less important to me who do not believe in that theory. I see in them proofs that the dualities must be related externally to the magnet; & so they come in as necessary consequences of the principles both of paramagnetic & diamagnetic action; but I hope to make all this clearer by degrees; & my hopes are greatly strengthened by the growing admission that the lines of magnetic force represent at present fairly the facts of magnetism. Into what they may ultimately resolve themselves, or to what they may lead I am sure I cannot say; but if I can only convert the theory of magnetic fluids, & that of electric currents, into two stools; the fall to the ground between them may be more useful than either of them as a seat in a wrong place.   I am

My dear Dr. Whewell,

Yours faithfully

M. FARADAY

591 M. FARADAY to J. BARLOW, 28 February 1855

[B.J. 2, 355]

Royal Institution,
February 28, 1855.

MY DEAR BARLOW,

I return you Airy's second note.[1] I think he must be involved in some mystery about my views and papers; at all events, his notes mystify me. In the first, he splits the question into (*a*) action inversely as the square of the distance, and (*b*) metaphysics. What the first has to do with my consideration, I cannot make out. I do not deny the law of action referred to in all like cases; nor is there any difference as to the mathematical results (at least, if I understand Thomson and Van Rees),[2] whether he takes the results according to my view or that of the French mathematicians. Why, then, talk about the inverse square of the distance? I had to warn my audience against the sound of this law and its supposed opposition on my Friday evening, and Airy's note shows that the warning was needful. I suppose all magneticians who admit differences in what is called magnetic saturation in different bodies, will also admit that there may be and are cases in which the law of the inverse square of the distance may not apply to magnetic action; but such cases are entirely out of the present consideration.

As to the metaphysical question, as it is called. If the admitted theory of gravitation will not permit us to suppose a new body brought into space, so that we may contemplate its effects, I think it must be but a poor theory; but I do not want a new body for my speculations, for, as I have said in the Friday evening paper,[3] the motions of either planet or comet in an ellipse is sufficient base for the strict philosophical reasoning; and if the theory will not permit us to ask a question about the conservation of force, then I think it must be very weak in its legs. The matter in the second note is quite in accordance with my views *as far as it goes*, only there is at the end of it a question which arises, and remains unanswered: When the attractive forces of the earth and moon in respect of each other diminish, what becomes of them, i.e. of the portions which disappear?

Ever, my dear Barlow, yours truly,

M. FARADAY.

[1] See *B.J.* 2, 352.
[2] See W. Thomson, 'A mathematical theory of Magnetism', *PT* (1851), 243, and R. van Rees, 'Over die theorie der magnetische krachtlijnen van Faraday', *VEKNIW*, 1 (1854).
[3] *PRI*, 2 (1854–8), 6.

[*P.M.*, *4 s.*, *9 (1855), 253*]

Royal Institution,
March 14, 1855.

MY DEAR TYNDALL,

In relation to your letter of last month*, I write, not for the purpose of giving what might be taken as an answer, but to say that it seems to me expedient and proper to wait and allow the thoughts that my papers may raise, to be considered and judged of at their leisure by those who are inclined to review and advance the subject. Perhaps, after a respectful interval, I may be induced to put forth such explanations, acknowledgements, or conclusions, as the state of the subject may then seem to render necessary or useful.

In the mean time, the more we can enlarge the number of anomalous facts and consequences the better it will be for the subject; for they can only remain anomalous to us whilst we continue in error. I may say, however, that the idea you suggest presents no difficulty to me; for having on former occasions (Exp. Res. 2501.) had to consider the magnecrystallic phænomena presented by the same body in different media, and having found the magnecrystallic difference unchanged in the media, I have no difficulty in conceiving that a body (as bismuth), which in the amorphous state is of the same magnetic character as the medium around it, shall, when employed as a crystal, be paramagnetic in one direction and diamagnetic in another (3157.). What happens in a medium may, according to my knowledge of the facts, happen in space; and is in full accordance with Thomson's clear paper[2] on the theory of magnetic induction in crystalline bodies†.

In respect of the effects of pressure, to which you refer in your letter, we cannot easily draw conclusions on either side until we know better what pressure does. I am not aware whether you consider that pressure on bismuth, whilst it makes the metal more diamagnetic in one direction than another, also makes it more diamagnetic as a whole than before; or whether you suppose it *less* diamagnetic in the transverse direction of the pressure than at first. Gmelin says, on the authority of Marchand and Scheerer (vol. iv. p. 428), that the density of bismuth is diminished as pressure upon it is increased, and extraordinary as the fact seems, gives densities of the following degree for increasing pressures, 9.783, 9.779, 9.655, 9.556; a change in texture at the same time occurring. If the statement be true, then the line of pressure in your beautiful experiments may be the line of *least density* or of *least approximation*, though I hardly know how to think so; still it becomes difficult for us to draw reasons from the constitution of a compressed body, until we know what happens during the compression, although no difficulty arises in considering it, after compression in one direction, like to a magnecrystallic substance.

You are aware (and I hope others will remember) that I give the lines of force‡ only as *representations* of the magnetic power, and do not profess to say to what physical idea they may hereafter point, or into what they will resolve themselves. Advancing no principle, I say, that the hypothetical fundamental ideas already advanced, when taken in relation to the body of facts now known, are self-contradictory and inapplicable. The following points, namely, – that the *direction* and *polarity* of lines of magnetic force are always shown truly by the electric current induced in metal moving within their influence; – that the dualities of electricity and magnetism are always respectively and essentially related; – that the dualities of an isolated magnet are not related back in straight lines through the magnet; – are to my mind not hypothetical in character, but easily proveable by experiment: – and they, with the considerations arising from the principle of the conservation of force, seem to me to be left unexplained by, and in opposition to, the usual hypotheses. No difference arises about the laws of magnetic action and their mathematical development; and that, simply because they are as yet applied only partially, and thus far are in accordance with *all* the views taken, including mine. When the attempt is made to apply them so as to include at once *paramagnetic*, *diamagnetic*, and *electromagnetic* phænomena, and at the same time to deduce them from *one* hypothetical cause, then they may become so large and yet precise as to enable us to distinguish between true and false assumptions. On my part I endeavour not to assume anything, but only to draw such conclusions from the assumptions already made, and the phænomena now discovered, as seem subject to experiment and tangible by facts.

Some persons may feel surprised that I dwell upon points which are perfectly and mathematically explained by the hypothesis of two magnetic fluids, as, for instance, places of little or no action (3341. &c.). My reason is, that being satisfied by the phænomena of diamagnetism, &c. that that hypothesis cannot be true, all these and such like phænomena acquire a new character and a high importance which they had not before, and amongst other philosophical uses, point most emphatically to the essential relation of the dualities and their equivalency in power. They do not contradict the old hypothesis when that is partially applied, but they are not the less strong and striking as evidence in favour of the view of lines of force.

I am, my dear Tyndall,

Yours very faithfully,

M. FARADAY.

---

* Phil. Mag. 1855, vol. ix. p. 205.

† Phil. Mag. 1851, vol. i. p. 177.[2]

‡ It is nearly twenty-four years since I first called attention to these lines; Exp. Res. 114, note.

[1] The footnotes marked by symbols, not numbers, are Faraday's.

[2] W. Thomson, 'On the theory of magnetic induction in crystalline and non-crystalline substances', *PM*, 4 s., 1 (1851), 177.

593 G. B. AIRY to M. FARADAY, 15 March 1855 [copy]

[Royal Observatory, Herstmonceux, Astrology-Optics, Tides, 1855 and 1856, Sect. 8, previously unpublished]

Royal Observatory
Greenwich
1855 March 15

MY DEAR SIR

You may perhaps remember that I troubled you a little while ago about some galvanic currents that disturbed us. Upon mapping the wires and studying the connexions, we found that there was a connexion with a Battery not duly considered: and upon examining the Battery we suspected imperfect insulation. So I have mounted the Battery upon potted-meat-pots surrounded by inverted saucers, and all the strange currents have ceased. And so ends that Great Mystery.

That imperfect insulation is an odd thing. I wonder why the power of the battery did not go off in full force.

I am, my dear Sir,
Yours very truly
G. B. AIRY

594 M. FARADAY to G. B. AIRY, 16 March 1855

[Royal Observatory, Herstmonceux, Astrology-Optics, Tides, 1855 and 1856, Sect. 8, previously unpublished]

Royal Institution
16 Mar 1855

MY DEAR SIR

Many thanks for your note I am glad you have found out the mystery and that Mrs Airy [*sic*] kitchen apparatus has turned to account. It always interests me when some deep difficulty is aided by the application of common things for then principle shines forth – Are your troughs made of Gutta Percha? I suppose not

Mr Walker has been telling me of your clock at the London Bridge station, and I intend to go some day very soon & look at it. I suppose your activity has made Le Verrier[1] active also at the Paris observatory. The announcements of changes there seem at least to look like it.

Ever My dear Sir
Yours Very Truly
M. FARADAY

[1] Urbain Jean Joseph Le Verrier (1811–77), astronomer and discoverer of Neptune.

Giessen
am 16ten März 1855.

Hoch verehrter Herr!

Vor zwei Jahren habe ich einige Versuche über die Electrolyse der Silber:
und Kupfer: Lösungen, des reinen Wassers und der verdünnten Schwefelsäure
bekannt gemacht, durch welche die Proportionalität der Stromstärke mit der
Zersetzung, immerhalb sehr weiter Gränzen Bestätigung erhielt.[1] Dieselbe
Frage ist seitdem wieder von verschiedenen Physikern und in verschiedenem
Sinne discutirt worden. Eine allgemeine Geltung des electrolytischen Gesetzes
wurde insbesondere hinsichtlich der Wasserzersetzung bestritten. Hierdurch
veranlasst, habe ich mich ebenfalls wieder mit diesem Gegenstande beschäftigt.
Es ist mir gelungen, mit Hülfe Wollaston'scher Spitzen die Zersetzung des
Wassers und der wässrigen Lösungen durch electrische Ströme sichtbar zu
machen, welche, wenn sie ganz zur Electrolyse verwendet werden, doch nicht
merhr als 2,14 C.C. Wasserstoff im Laufe eines ganzen Jahres, d.h. stündlich
den vierten Theil eines Cubick-Millimeters zu liefern vermögen.[2] Diese
Angaben sind durch die denselben zu Grunde liegenden Messungen, welche ich
der Öffentlichkeit übergeben habe, wie ich glaube genügend gerechtfertigt. Sie
dürften daher wohl geeignet sein die Annahme zu widerlegen, dass das Wasser
einen in Betracht kommenden Theil des galvanischen Stroms, nach Art der
Metalle zu leiten, im Stande sei.

Wenn man freilich das Verhalten der gemeinen Electricität in Betracht
nimmt, wenn man bedenkt, wie geringe Mengen dieser Electricität erfordert
werden um sehr bedeutende Spannungs-Effecte hervorzubringen, so bleibt
immer noch die Möglichkeit, dass ein, allerdings sehr kleiner und vielleicht
durch die Magnetnadel gar nicht messbarer, aber immerhin ein Theil des
electrischen Fluidums durch das Wasser in ähnlicher Weise wie durch
Metalldrähte geleitet werde.

Hinsichtlich dieses Punktes ist es mir nun kürzlich geglückt einige zum
Theil neue Erfahrungen zu sammeln, welche ich mir erlaube Ihrer Beachtung
vorzulegen; in der Hoffnung dass sie auch in Ihren Augen dazu beitragen
werden, den Umfang der Geltung jenes wichtigen Gesetzes, durch dessen
Entdeckung Sie zur Verständniss der chemischen Wirkungen des electrischen
Stroms die einzige ganz allgemeine und zugleich die festeste Grundlage
gegeben haben, um ein Bedeutendes zu erweitern.

Wenn die beiden Conductoren der Electrisirmaschine durch einen Multipli-
catordraht in ununterbrochne Metallverbindung gesetzt werden, so wird
bekanntlich der Übergang beider Electricitäten zu einander so vollständig
vermittelt, dass durch Annäherung der Hand an den einen oder andern der
Conductoren, ja selbst durch Berührung, Electricität in wahrnehmbarer Menge

nicht abgeleitet werden kam. D.h. die Stellung der Galvanometernadel wird dadurch nicht merklich verändert. Der durch den Draht laufende Strom hat also ganz die Beschaffenheit eines galvanischen Stroms angenommen.

Mittelst einer Scheibenmaschine von 32 Pariser Zoll Durchmesser der Glasscheibe konnte ich bei dieser Art Schliessung Ströme erzeugen, welche die Nadel des von mir benutzten Galvanometers (einer Tangentenbussole) um 20 bis 24° ablenkten. Galvanische Ströme von dieser Stärke wirken auf das Wasser ganz dem electrolytischen Gesetze entsprechend und zwar erhält man auf 20° Ablenkung stündlich fast genau 0,01 C.C. Wasserstoffgas. Erfahrung und Rechnung zeigen sich so weit in befriedigender Übereinstimmung. Eine gleich kräftige Wasserzersetzung glaubte ich daher von der Einwirkung der gemeinen Electricität erwarten zu dürfen. Auch schien diese Annahme gerechtfertigt zu werden, als destillirtes Wasser in den Schliessungsbogen der Conductoren eingeschlossen wurde und man zu den Electroden Platinspitzen nahm. Vor dem Wasserstoffpole erhob sich, genau so wie unter der Einwirkung einer galvanischen Kette, bei gleicher Stromkraft eine ununterbrochne Säule äussertst feiner Gasbläschen, während die von dem Sauerstoffpole aufsteigende Gaslinie unverkennbar weniger massenhaft war, auch die Folge der einzelnen Bläschen viel deutlicher erkennen liess. Erscheinungen vor demselben Charakter konnten übrigens auch durch schwächere Reibungsströme hervorgerufen werden und blieben selbst dann noch wahrnehmbar als nach allmäliger Abnutzung und Bestäubung der Reibzeuge die Nadel kaum noch einen Strom anzeigte.

In denselben Schliessungsbogen wurden nach Wiederherstellung der Maschine zugleich mit dem Wasser, verdünnte Schwefelsäure und Lösungen von Glaubersalz und Kupfervitriol eingeschaltet; und zwar so, dass der Übergang von der einen Flüssigkeit zur andern durch Wollaston'sche Spitzen stattfand. In welcher Ordnung nun diese Flüssigkeiten aufeinander folgen mochten; die drei erst genannten verhielten sich stets in ganz gleicher Weise, und so wie vorher für das Wasser beschrieben wurde. In der Kupferlösung entwickelte sich Gas nur an der Sauerstoff-Electrode. Nachdem die Einwirkung zwei Stunden gedauert hatte konnte man aber auch den Kupferabsatz an der negativen Electrode sehr deutlich erkennen. Dieses Verhalten der Kupferlösung haben Sie in den Experimental-Untersuchungen namentlich hervorgehoben und als chemisch electrische Zersetzung erkannt. Somit ist wohl kaum zu bezweiflen, dass die gleichzeitigen Vorgänge in den andern Flüssigkeiten ebenfalls electrolytisch waren.

Gleichwohl habe ich nicht unterlassen die Gase selbst auf ihre Natur zu prüfen. Zu diesem Zwecke diente ein enges, nur 1 Linie weites Glasrohr, an dessen oberem Ende ein Platindraht in der Art eingeschmolzen war dass er etwa drei Linien weit frei in das Innere eindrang. Dieses Rohr mit reinem luftfreiem Wasser gefüllt, wurde mit dem unteren offnen Ende in ein Glas mit Wasser eingetaucht. Dann liess man reines Wasserstoffgas in den oberen Raum treten, bis die Flüssigkeit 4 oder 5 Linien unter das Ende des Platindrahts herabgesunken war. So entstand ein kleiner eudiometrischer Apparat in welchem, wie ich mich durch Vorversuche überzeugte, die geringste messbare Menge Sauerstoff angezeigt wurde, indem sie eine verhältnissmässige Menge des Wasserstoffs unter dem Einflusse eines durch den Platindraht geleiteten Funkenstroms verschwinden machte.

In diesem Eudiometer-Rohr wurde nun abwechselnd das von der negativen und das von der positiven Platinspitze aufsteigende Gas gesammelt, und jedes besonders auf seine Beschaffenheit geprüft. So überzeugte ich mich durch wiederholte Versuche, dass an der einen Spitze nur Wasserstoff, an der andern nur Sauerstoff entbunden wurde. Die einzelnen Versuche erforderten ein lange Zeit fortgesetztes Drehen der Scheibe, zum Theil aus dem Grunde, weil die Wirksamkeit meiner Electrisirmaschine nicht lange ungeschwächt aushielt. Um z.B. 2 Linien Wasserstoffgas zu sammeln bedurfte es 4 Stunden Arbeit.

Das Resultat blieb in der Qualität und, soweit man aus der für die Gewinnung des Gases erforderlichen Zeit ein Urtheil ziehen durfte, auch in der Quantität ganz gleich, wenn man die vorher gut leitende Verbindung der beiden Conductoren der Maschine durch eine kurze Luftschicht unterbrach. Erst als nach allmäliger Vergrösserung der Unterbrechungsstelle die Platinspitzen zu leuchten anfingen, tratt auch im Verhältniss der Gasentwicklung eine auffallendere Veränderung ein. Die Gasmenge vermehrte sich, um so bedeutender, je tiefer, bei verstärkten Schlägen die von der Spitze ausströmende züngelnde Flamme in das Wasser eindrang; dabei wurden die Gasblasen mit Gewalt nach allen Richtungen umhergeschleudert. Allerdings erhielt man jetzt an beiden Drahtspitzen ein Gemenge von Sauerstoff und Wasserstoff; allein die eudiometrische Probe zeigte, sobald nur der Versuch lange genug fortgesetzt worden war, entschieden auf der positiven Seite einen Überschuss von Sauerstoff, auf der negativen einen Überschuss von Wasserstoff. Es ist hieraus wohl kaum eine andere Folgerung zu ziehen, als dass der Wollaston'sche Versuch ein zusammengesetztes Phänomen darstellt, wobei die stets vorhandene Electrolyse von einer bald mehr, bald weniger starken durch Erhitzung bewirkten Zersetzung begleitet ist.

Jene chemisch electrische Zersetzung bleibt selbst dann nicht aus, wenn auch nur eine einzige Wollaston'sche Spitze, und ausser dieser keine andere Electrode in das Wasser taucht. Ich habe diesen sonderbaren Versuch, dessen Sie in der dritten Reihe Ihrer Experimental-Untersuchungen Erwähnung thun, in folgender Weise wiederholt. Ein zugespitzter Platindraht wurde aus einiger Entfernung gegen die Oberfläche des Wasserbeckens gerichtet, in welchem die Wollastonsche Spitze unter dem Eudiometer-Rohr so aufgestellt war, dass das sich entbindende Gas gesammelt und dann geprüft werden konnte. War nun der zugespitzte Draht mit dem positiven Conductor, die Platinspitze mit dem negativen in leitender Verbindung, so entwickelte sich an der letzteren reines

Wasserstoffgas; im umgekehrten Falle erhielt man Sauerstoffgas. Der andere Bestandtheil des Wassers musste sich folglich an der die Wasseroberfläche berührenden, durch den zugespitzten Draht electrisirten Luftschicht ausgeschieden haben. Die Richtigkeit dieses Schlusses wird durch den folgenden Versuch noch direkter bewiesen. – Der zugespitzte Draht wurde in ein zweites Eudiometer-Rohr eingeschmolzen, welches von gleicher Weite mit dem früheren war, und wie dieses theilweise mit Wasser und darüber soweit mit Wasserstoff gefüllt wurde, dass das Ende des Drahts 5–6 Linien von der Wasserfläche entfernt stand. Als nun das aus dem Glasrohr hervortretende Drahtende mit dem negativen Conductor verbunden wurde, die Wollastonsche Spitze aber mit dem positiven, so vermehrte sich die Gasmenge im zweiten Eudiometer-Rohr. Sie nahm dagegen ab, sobald man umgekehrt verfuhr, und das Drahtende zu dem positiven Conductor leitete. Bei dem letzten dieser Versuche war gleichzeitig das von der Wollaston'schen Spitze (die diesmal mit dem negativen Conductor verbunden war) aufsteigende Gas aufgefangen worden. Dabei zeigte sich nun, dass die Gasmenge in diesem Rohr ungefähr in demselben Verhältnisse zunahm, als sie sich in dem andern vermindert hatte. Gase wenn sie, wie in diesen Versuchen durch eine verstärkte electrische Spannung die Fahigkeit angenommen haben, das electrische Fluidum überzuführen, können also ähnlich den metallischen Oberflächen die Rolle einer Electrode übernehmen.

Genehmigen Sir schliesslich verehrter Herr die Versicherung der ausgezeigneten Hochachtung womit ich die Ehre habe zu zeichnen.

H. BUFF

---

[1] H. Buff, 'Über die electrolytische Gesetz', *AP*, 161 (1853), and 164 (1853).
[2] Buff's calculation here is in error. 2 cc. of gas would be produced in about a month's time.

595a H. BUFF to M. FARADAY, 16 March 1855[1]
[I.E.E., previously unpublished]

Giessen,
16 March, 1855

DEAR SIR,

Two years ago I published some researches upon the electrolysis of silver and Copper solutions, of pure water and dilute sulphuric acid, from which the dependence of the amount of decomposition upon the strength of the current received Confirmation within very wide limits. This same question has since been discussed by different physicists and from different points of view. The general application of the electrical law has however been disputed particularly with respect to the decomposition of water. Induced by this circumstance I have been again occupied in the examination of this subject. I have succeeded by the aid of Wollaston's points in rendering evident the decomposition of water and of aqueous solutions by the electric current, which if entirely used for electrolysis does not liberate more than 2.14 Cubic centimetres of hydrogen in the course of a whole year, i.e. the fourth part of a cubic millimetre per hour. These statements are I think sufficiently justified by those which I have published, upon which they are founded.

They seem therefore well calculated to refute the assumption that water is capable of conducting an appreciable portion of the galvanic current like metal.

On considering the deportment of common electricity and reflecting how small a quantity of this electricity is required in order to produce very considerable effects of tension, the mind is impressed with the possibility that a certain portion of the electric fluid small indeed and perhaps no longer measurable by a magnetic needle, is conducted by water, in the same way as by metallic wires.

With regard to this point I have recently succeeded in collecting some new facts, which I may be permitted to bring under your notice: in the hope that they may in your eyes also, contribute to the further confirmation of that important law, by the discovery of which you have laid at once the most general and the firmest foundation for the comprehension of the chemical action of the electric current.

If the two conductors of an electrical machine be placed in unbroken metallic union by a galvanometer wire, it is well known, that the passage of the two Electricities from one to the other is so completely effected, that even by touching either of the conductors with the hand, electricity is not carried off to any appreciable extent, i.e. the position of the needle of the galvanometer does not become perceptibly changed. The current passing through the wire has therefore essentially acquired the nature of a galvanic current.

By the use of a plate machine of 32 parisian inches in diameter, and by closing the circuit in this way I was enabled to produce a current which deflected the needle of the galvanometer which I employed (a tangential needle) 20° to 24°. Galvanic currents of this strength act upon water in a manner quite in accordance with the law of electrolysis, and in fact by a current deflecting the needle 20°, very nearly 0.01 of a cubic centimetre of hydrogen is collected per hour. Experiment and theory thus agree perfectly in this respect. I thought therefore that I might reasonably expect an equally powerful decomposition of water by common electricity. And this opinion appeared to be justified, for on interposing distilled water as a part of the circuit of the conductors, and using platinum points as the Electrodes, there arose from the negative pole (just as by the action of a galvanic current of equal strength) an unbroken series of bubbles of gas, whilst the stream of gas rising from the positive pole was unmistakably less coherent and the succession of the individual bubbles much more distinctly recognisable. Effects of the same character could be produced also by weaker frictional currents and remained perceptible even when the needle scarcely

787

indicated the passage of a current after the gradual wearing of the rubber and its becoming covered with dust. Into the same closed circuit after the restoration of the machine dilute sulphuric acid, acid solutions of glauber's salts and of sulphate of Copper, were introduced with the coating in such a manner that the passage from the one fluid to the other took place through the Wollaston's points.

Now in whatever order these solutions followed each other, the three above mentioned always comported themselves in a perfectly similar way, and as has been described in the case of water. In the copper solution gas was only disengaged at the positive electrode, but after the action had been continued for two hours the deposition of copper on the negative Electrode could be very distinctly perceived. This deportment of copper solutions you have specially brought forward in your "experimental researches" and recognised as an electro-chemical decomposition. Hence it can scarcely be doubted that the simultaneous actions in the other fluids were likewise electrolytic.

I have however, not omitted to examine the nature of the gases themselves. For this purpose I employed a narrow glass tube (only $\frac{1}{10}$th of an inch in diameter) into the upper end of which a platinum wire was sealed in such a way that it projected within the tube to the extent of about a quarter of an inch. This tube was filled with pure water free from air, and inverted in a glass of water. Then pure hydrogen gas was allowed to rise to the upper end, until the fluid had sunk about half an inch below the end of the platinum wire. Thus was obtained a small eudiometrical apparatus in which, as I had convinced myself by previous trials, the smallest measurable quantity of oxygen could be indicated since it would produce an appreciable diminution of the hydrogen under the influence of an electric spark passed between the platinum wires.

In the eudiometric tube the gases disengaged from the positive and negative platinum poles were now collected. In this way I convinced myself by repeated experiments that from the one pole only hydrogen, and from the other only oxygen was disengaged. Each individual experiment required the turning of the plate to be continued for a very long time, partly because my electrical machine did not retain its state of activity for a long time undiminished. In order e.g. to collect $\frac{1}{5}$Th of an inch of hydrogen gas four hours work was necessary.

The result remained the same as to quality, and as far as an opinion could be formed from the small quantity of gas disengaged in the necessary time also as respects quantity, whether the conductors of the machine be joined as in the preceding experiments by a good conducting union, or interrupted by a short stratum of air: only on gradually increasing the interrupting space the platinum points began to become incandescent and a remarkable change took place in the disengagement of gas. The quantity of gas increased in the same measure as the lambent flame emanating from the points, during the augmented changes penetrated deeper into the water; and the bubbles of gas were tumultuously disengaged in all directions. A mixture of oxygen and hydrogen was now collected from the points of both wires, but the eudiometrical examination indicated, as soon as the experiment had been continued long enough, that at the positive pole an excess of oxygen, and on the negative an excess of hydrogen of liberated. There is scarcely any other inference that can be drawn from this observation than that Wollaston's experiment is a mixed phenomenon, that the regular electrolysis which is always going on is accompanied by a more or less powerful decomposition produced by the heating of the electrodes.

This electro-chemical decomposition does not cease even when only a single Wollaston's point and no other electrode is immersed into the water. I have repeated this curious experiment, which you have mentioned in the third volume of your 'experimental researches', in the following way. A pointed platinum wire was arranged at a short distance from the surface of a vessel of water in which the Wollaston's point was so placed under the eudiometer tube that the gas disengaged from it could be collected and subsequently examined. The pointed wire was now placed in contact with the positive conductor, and the platinum point with the negative, when pure hydrogen was liberated upon the latter, whilst under the reversed circumstances oxygen gas was then liberated.

The other constituent of the water must have been drawn off by the pointed wire into the electrified atmosphere, between it and the surface of the water. The correctness of this conclusion is proved by the following experiment. The pointed wire was fused into a second eudiometer tube of the same width as the former, and like it, partly filled with water, and above it with just so much hydrogen that the end of the wire stood at about half an inch distant from the surface of the water. Now when the end of the wire projecting from the glass tube was connected with the negative conductor, and the Wollaston's point with the positive, the volume of gas increased in the second eudiometer tube. On the other hand a diminution was observed when the circumstances were reversed, and the end of the wire united with the positive conductor. In the latter of these experiments the gas rising simultaneously from the Wollaston's point (which in this instance was connected with the negative Conductor) was simultaneously collected. It was then observed that the quantity of gas in this tube had increased, in the same proportion, as it had diminished in the other. Gases, when by an increased electrical tension (as in these experiments) they have acquired the power of conducting the electric fluid, thus become capable of playing the part of electrodes like metallic surfaces.

Believe me
dear Sir
Yours very sincerely
H. Buff

[1] Translation made for Faraday.

Royal Institution,
7 April 1855.

MY DEAR FRIEND

I must just write you a letter though I have nothing to say; i.e. nothing philosophical; but I hope to feel with you that when philosophy has faded away, the friend remains. Do not think that I cannot & do not rejoice in reading and understanding all that your vigorous mind produces, but for myself, I feel I have little or nothing to return; and though when my sluggish mind is moved, I can think determinately & write decidedly, yet being once written I fall back into quietude, and leave what has been said almost uncared for or unthought of; & so it is that I do not (illeg. – teaze) you in letters with much of my philosophic opinions.

I am afraid too of the Post, for though I send you now & then a report of a Friday Evening meeting, being assured that they will go without charge to you, yet as to papers from the Philosophical Magazine I am in the greatest uncertainty. I receive daily papers from abroad which are charged two, three or four shillings, and am absolutely obliged to refuse many; and when they tell me at the post office here that such a paper can go to the continent at so much, I am in fear of some mistake, &, that inadvertently I run the risk of taxing my friends beyond their patience. However, I have sent you, by a friend, a paper from the Philosophical Magazine, which perhaps you have seen already; & so I will say no more about it: – except that Mr. Twining[1] (the friend) is an excellent Gentleman as you will find if he personally comes in your way.

But of other matters: – I hope & desire that you should enjoy good health & spirits and that your work will be a cheerer to you; – and further, that as you turn from it to graver thoughts & back again, *both* should minister peace & contentment to your mind. What a world this is! How the whole surface of the earth seems about to be covered with the results of evil passions. – Ambition – contest – inhumanity – selfishness. – Thou shall love thy neighbour as thyself, – how the extreme reverse of this shapes its self into the forces of Honor, Patriotism, Glory, Loyalty, Romance &c. &c. Happy for us that there is a power who overrules all this to his own good ends, and who will one day make manifest the truth & cause the light to shine out of the darkness.

I shall hope soon to hear of the volume of the work, – & again to know that you are yourself in good strength; & whilst in the flesh, still working on your way. – I am very well, much as before, continually failing in memory; but since I have given up lecturing & the occupations which require memory, I have been very well & cheerful & free from giddiness. – My dear wife also, though infirm, is in good mind & we go on our way rejoicing in each others company.

Ever My dear friend Yours faithfully,
M. FARADAY

[1] Possibly Thomas Twining (1806–95), advocate of technical education and popularizer of science.

597 M. FARADAY to P. T. RIESS, 7 April 1855
[*Darmstaedter Collection, Westdeutsche Bibliothek, Marburg, previously unpublished*]

Royal Institution
London
7 April 1855

MY DEAR SIR

It was a very great pleasure to me to receive your kind letter;[1] – and written in such English as made me ashamed of my ignorance of the German language. I never cease to regret the latter circumstance; for I am aware of the great stores of knowledge in that language which would then be open to me in relation to my especial pursuits, and which some how or other the system of publication in our country almost entirely shuts out from me. I have several times within the last 15 years set about acquiring it, but a result over which I have no power, namely, a gradually failing memory, has on these occasions made the labour of head so great, that I have been obliged to refrain from such an endeavour, as also from many others. You gave me your book some time back. I looked at it eagerly; but both by its language & its mathematical developments (for the use of symbols requires memory) it was shut out from me; and so I placed it in our library, where I am very glad to find it is of great use to others

Your observations upon M.ʳ Clarkes experiments[2] (for M. Melloni) are very interesting to me & I cannot doubt that you are right. I can see no difference of an essential kind, between the current produced by a Leyden Jar & that of a Voltaic battery, and your experiments & conclusions appear to me to be fully applicable to the case and perfectly justified. I think Melloni could have been but little acquainted with the great body of facts belonging to Electricity, Static & dynamic; – perhaps he had only begun to enter upon the subject, and was caught, as all men are, by first appearances. I had several letters from him; & in relation to his conclusions on induction, I had written him a very long letter (in reply to a like long one from him) against his views & statements. I heard from M. Flauti, the Secretary of the Academy at Naples, that it was received after his death, & had been read at the Academy (which was not however my intention). It was my hope that it would have led him to revise his conclusions before he published them. From what you tell me I conclude that he had already published them; & I am sorry for it.

Your letter to me for which I thank you very much indeed, makes me think that you approve of the correction which I put into the Philosophical Magazine, of Mellonis erroneous representation of Mr L. Clarkes last results.[3] As they were represented in the Italian journal, the diagram could only confuse the mind & give conflicting ideas.

I am My dear Sir
With Very Great Respect
Your Obliged & faithful Servt
M. FARADAY

[1] See Letter 614.
[2] See Letter 563.
[3] M. Faraday, 'Further Observations on associated cases, in Electric Induction, of Current and Static Effects', *PM*, 4 s., 9 (1855), 161.

---

598   A. DE LA RIVE to M. FARADAY, 15 April 1855
[*I.E.E.*, *previously unpublished*]

Genève
le 15 avril 1855.

MONSIEUR & TRÈS CHER AMI,

Je suis profondément touché de la bonne pensée qui vous a mis la plume à la main pour m'écrire quelques mots d'amitié qui m'ont été encore plus doux & plus agréables que ne m'aurait été l'annonce d'une grande découverte. A mesure que l'on devient vieux (& j'ai 53 ans) on sent toujours plus le prix des sentiments élevés & Chrétiens & la valeur d'amis comme vous avec lesquels on est en si pleine sympathie sur des points aussi essentiels. – J'ai passé de mauvais moments ce printemps. – Voilà cinq ans bientôt que j'ai perdu une amie comme on n'en a qu'une & je sens chaque année un vide & un isolement plus grands quoique je sois entouré de nombreux & charmants enfants & même de quatre petits enfants. Ce sont d'immenses objets d'interet, mais ce ne sont pas des seconds vous-mêmes. Refléchissez que je n'ai ni soeur, ni belle soeur, en un mot aucune femme de ma génération avec qui je puisse parler de mes enfants, à qui je puisse communiquer mes impressions; je voudrais souvent être plus vieux.

Ma santé physique s'est beaucoup améliorée; je suis très bien portant maintenant. Aussi, vais-je en profiter pour aller passer un mois à Londres afin d'achever de corriger les épreuves de mon second volume qui ne me parviennent ici que très irrégulièrement. Je serai à Londres du 10 ou 15 Mai & j'irai reprendre ma chambre de *Suffolk Place* (Haymarket) dans la maison où était mon bon ami J. L. Prevost & qui est occupé maintenant par son neveu Alexandre qui m'a offert l'hospitalité de la manière la plus aimable. Vous n'avez pas d'idée combien je serai heureux de vous voir, de retrouver ce regard bienveillant, cette amitié si douce dont vous m'avez toujours gratifié.

J'ai eu beaucoup de peine à finir mon second volume en [reading doubtful] le chemin qu'avaient fait plusieures questions depuis que je l'avais rédigé; il m'a fallu changer complètement certaines parties telles par exemple que la thermo-électricité; & bien des points de l'Electro-chimie ont du subir des modifications. Néanmoins je suis assez satisfait des résultats auxquels je suis parvenu, & j'espère que vous le serez aussi. J'ai cherché à éclaircir bien des points par la voie expérimentale, & j'ai eu sous ce rapport un auxiliaire précieux dans l'un de mes élèves Mr Soret[1] qui, après avoir passé quatre ans dans le laboratoire de M' Regnault, est établi maintenant à Genève où il travaille très bien & beaucoup.

J'ai bien reçu & lu avec beaucoup d'intérêt tout ce que vous m'avez envoyé & que vous avez publié sur le magnétisme & le diamagnétisme. Je persiste à croire à la polarité diamagnétique & je vous transmettrai mes raisons en même temps que je vous demanderai de vouloir bien faire quelques expériences avec des appareils que j'apporterai, & qui me paraissent pouvoir être de nature à éclaircir la question. Je n'ai point voulu parler de vos dernières recherches dans la *Bibl. Univ.* avant de m'en être entretenu avec vous. – Au fond la grande différence entre vous & moi, c'est que je suis tout *moléculaire* & que vous êtes tout *force*. – Je crois à un principe *passif* aussi bien qu'à un principe *actif*. – Mais cette discussion nous mènerait trop loin.

Au reste il y a deux points sur lesquels nous nous entendrons toujours; le premier c'est que les faits, & les faits bien observés doivent dominer toutes les théories; le Second c'est qu'au-dessus des pauvres lois de la nature dont nous ne saisissons que des lambeaux, il existe un Etre qui dirige tout le monde matériel aussi bien que le monde moral, par sa providence d'une manière continue & générale. – Quand on est d'accord là dessus ainsi que sur tout ce qui touche aux sentiments du coeur, on peut bien différer sur quelques points de détail, sans danger pour l'amitié. –

Mes souvenirs respectueux & affectueux à Madame Faraday; j'espère que sa santé est bonne ainsi que la vôtre. A bientôt & croyez, Monsieur & cher ami, aux sentiments de profonde & ancienne affection

de votre dévoué ami

A. DE LA RIVE

[1] Jacques Louis Soret (1827–90), later Professor of Medical Physics at the University of Geneva and, after 1856, Editor of *ASPN*.

599 A. S. TAYLOR[1] to M. FARADAY, 24 April 1855
[*I.E.E., previously unpublished*]

15 St James' Terrace
Regents Park
April 24. 1855

MY DEAR FARADAY

I have great pleasure in replying to your question from authentic documents in my possession[2]

There was no nitrate of potash on any part of the premises.

There were 128 tons of Nitrate of Soda, and there were 2800 tons of sulphur Of these quantities there were in the seat or focus of explosion 47 tons of sulphur and 45 tons of nitrate of soda. These quantities were in a strong vault in the basement, – the sulphur being exposed and occupying the lower part of the vault: – and on a tarpaulin, placed on the sulphur, were piled the bags containing the nitrate of soda. The capacity of the vault was such that these articles (which alone were in this vault) – reached to within a foot of the ceiling.

There was a large quantity of sulphur amounting to some hundreds of tons stored between the entrance to this vault and the Woollen factory in which the fire commenced. This probably ignited, as it was in contact with the Woollen-factory-wall, and thus communicated like a train (reading doubtful) to the sulphur on the lower floor of the vault

The quantity of sulphur consumed was enormous. It flowed out in rivers of blue fire from the two ends of the building, and made its way into the Tyne, realizing the description of Phlegethon given by the poets.

Any documents in my possession with a plan of the building and an official table of the whole contents at the time of the conflagration are at your service.

I send for your perusal my Report to Lord Palmerston which you can return to me on Friday evening next Believe me

Dear Faraday
Yours most truly
ALFRED S. TAYLOR

[1] Alfred Swaine Taylor (1806–80), Professor of medical jurisprudence and lecturer in chemistry at Guy's Hospital.
[2] See Letter 581. Also, *LPW*, 482.

600   W. T. BRANDE to M. FARADAY, 19 May 1855
[*Ms. Collection of Dr E. T. Conybeare, OBE, No. 12, Catalogue of Historical Manuscripts Commission, previously unpublished*]

Tunbridge Wells
19 May 1855

DEAR FARADAY

Many thanks for your prompt attention to my request. It has enabled me to gratify the curiosity of an intelligent friend here, and who, being a great Microscopist, said nothing about the smallness of the sample – When Sodium can be had for half a crown a pound, I presume Aluminum [*sic*] may be produced for five shillings so that perhaps at no very distant period, it may be better known – and the next generation may see roofs covered with it –

If your wife has not forgotten the existence of such a person, remember me kindly to her and believe me

My dear Faraday
always very truly yours
WM THOS BRANDE

If you will be good enough to leave *the 8ᵛᵒ Volume* in the Hall, I will call or send for it in the course of next week – in the mean time accept my best thanks for your kind remembrance of your old Colleague.

601   W. SNOW HARRIS to M. FARADAY, 20 May 1855
[*I.E.E., previously unpublished*]

Plymouth,
20 May 1855

MY DEAR FARADAY

You have been always so generous & kind to me upon Philosophical Subjects, that I feel ashamed at offering any large apology for this further intrusion on your valuable moments. – I am however desirous to satisfy my mind upon one or two points in which I am now deeply interested, will you then permit me to submit the following points to you.

First – let me ask whether you consider the following expᵗ. as a fair illustration of the evolution of Electricity during Chemical action

– Expᵗ: – put some coarse grains of the impure Zinc of commerce into a glass bottle *A* pour on them dilute sulphuric acid the water will decompose and hydrogen will escape at *h* – If during the effervescence a gold Leaf Electrometer be applied to the glass vessel *A* its leaves will diverge freely –

Well then here is clearly a development of common Electricity during chemical action

– Now if I clearly understand you in your views of current force – in the pile – Pure zinc or amalgamated zinc is not acted on in this way The Water will not be decomposed although there may arise a large Electrical Tension between the Metal and the fluid – directly a metal such as copper is put into the liquid & made to touch the zinc then Chemical action ensues and we have a current –

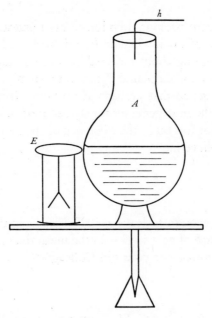

Now I want to satisfy my mind as to what takes place when we use Iron or impure zinc – here we have at once the same result as is brought about by the introduction of the copper plate – in the impure zinc I suppose it is the presence of other metals which brings about the result – but how of Iron – say *pure* Iron will not filings of pure Iron cause chemical action in dilute acid without the presence of another metal?

With respect to what is called the "Contact Theory" I have carefully read through the subject and I am obliged to conclude – that it is perfectly *untenable* – the Phenomena of the Pile in all their generality upon Volta's simple view of the source of power are quite impossible –

Finally I would ask – whether it may not appear to you upon further reflection that some confusion & misapprehension arises in the application of the terms positive & negative to the metals exhibiting Electrical disturbance after *contact* – say I bring a plate of *Zinc* to touch a plate of *Copper* and I find that Electricity has passed or is supposed to have passed from the *Copper* upon the Zinc – Surely in this case the Copper should be called the *positive* metal & the Zinc the negative – whereas Zinc is called *positive* now it is a cardinal point in your philosophy that the surface *from* which Electricity flows is to be considered positive – your *anode* for example is opposite the *positive* Electrode – positive because the current flows from it – reciprocally for the Cathode

In ordinary Electricity we consider the prime Conductor positive in the Glass Machine because it gives off Electricity & the conductor of the rubber negative because it takes up Electricity from the Prime Conductor. Now this is precisely what by the Contact Theory the Copper does in relation to the Zinc it appears to me, that the views of pos & neg as originally expressed in the contact experiments should be reversed – I remain My dear Faraday

most truly & sincerely yours
W. SNOW HARRIS

I suppose in the Paper in the Trans for 1801 by Wollaston[1] page 427 – In which he says "If a piece of zinc and a piece of Silver have each an extremity immersed in dilute acid &c &c &c – the zinc is dissolved &c he does not mean *pure* zinc but the Zinc of commerce

[1] William Hyde Wollaston, 'Experiments on the chemical production and agency of electricity', *PT* (1801), 427.

602   J. GASSIOT to M. FARADAY, 28 May 1855
[*I.E.E., previously unpublished*]

Clapham Common
28 May 1855

MY DEAR FARADAY

During the progress of your lecture last Friday Evening[1] it occurred to me that the question you had raised as to conduction proper might be explained by some experiments I made a few years since & which are described in a paper published in the RS. transactions (*PT* 1844)[2] – it appears to my mind to explain that peculiar action which arises in a Voltaic Battery when it is thrown into a state of tension *before* actual Electrolysis takes place, and that this is similar to the induced state of an Electrified Body previous to its receiving the actual discharge from the Electrical Machine

I will briefly describe the Experiment – Charge in the usual manner (taking care to keep the outer portion of each cell dry) a number of cells or series of a Voltaic Battery sufficient to diverge the leaves of Gold leaf Electroscopes – One of which is attached to the + and the other to the − terminal, introduce into the circuit a delicate Galvanometer and two platinum wires the ends of which rest on a piece of bibulous paper saturated with a solution of Iodide of Potassium (as in original Experiment) – the Battery and entire apparatus being insulated – in this state the leaves of the Electroscopes will diverge one with + and the other with − Electricity. When all is thus arranged touch with a wire or with the finger either terminal, the leaves of the electroscope will collapse, while those of the instrument attached to the other terminal will diverge with increased intensity – repeat this by touching first one and then the other terminal, the alternating and progressive effect shews some action must be passing through the entire Battery, but the needle of the Galvanometer (let the instrument be ever so delicate) is not deflected nor is there the slightest trace of Chemical action in the solution of Iodide of Potassium.

If as in my water Battery the terminals are brought sufficiently near to allow a spark to pass, or let the circuit be completed for a moment of time the deflection of the needle takes place & Iodine is evolved –

Have we not in this conduction proper through the battery without Chemical action

Believe me
My Dear Faraday Yours truly
JOHN GASSIOT

[1] M. Faraday, 'On magnetic hypotheses', *PRI*, 1 (1851–4), 457.
[2] John Gassiot, 'A description of an extensive series of the Water Battery; with an account of some experiments made in order to test the relation of the electrical and the chemical actions which take place before and after the completion of the Voltaic Circuit', *PT* (1844), 39.

603   T. PHILLIPPS to M. FARADAY, 2 June 1855

[*I.E.E.*, *previously unpublished*]

2 June 55

MY DEAR DR FARADAY

Many thanks for yr translation, wch enables me to see that the actual production of the metal is not so costly & intricate as I supposed; for it appears by the Comptes Rendus that one of the experimenters produced it by a Blow-pipe, in *globules*. To produce it in *Ingots* like Mr Deville, wd be both costly & intricate, & it *must* be produced in that form to make it *pay*. But perhaps a more simple method may be discovered by *yourself* before long.

Mr Wohler told me the process which he used, but it seems he does not obtain it in Ingots, altho' the specimen which he sent to me might be called a *thin* Ingot.

I am translating all the Passages in the Comptes Rendus relating to aluminium. Repeating my thanks for your kindness believe me

Very truly yours
THOS. PHILLIPPS

PS. I find a family of Faraday in Worcestershire; are you from my county?

[*I.E.E., previously unpublished*]

Vichy
le 17 juin 1855

MON CHER MONSIEUR & AMI,

J'ai reçu votre bonne petite lettre qui m'a bien touché comme tout ce qui me vient de vous. Vous avez été surpris de ma détermination; mais vous le serez moins quand vous connaitrez l'amie qui a bien voulu consentir à se réunir à moi pour que nous terminions ensemble les jours que la Providence daignera encore nous accorder sur cette terre.

Amie & contemporaine de ma chère première femme ainsi que de ma belle soeur Louisa Marcet, veuve de l'un de mes collègues & amis qu'elle a perdu il y a 16 ans, Madame Maurice Fatio[1] était pour moi une de ces amies précieuses, si rares à trouver, soit à cause de la communauté des souvenirs qui nous unissaient, soit à cause de la tendre affection qu'elle avait pour mes enfants, soit surtout à cause de l'élévation de son caractère & de ses sentiments si profondément chrétiens. Il a fallu pour la décider à s'unir à moi qu'elle cherchât & vît dans ce parti qu'elle a fini par prendre après deux mois d'hésitation & de scrupules, une direction providentielle, qu'elle y reconnût la volonté de Dieu. Or les circonstances qui ont accompagné cette époque d'incertitude ont été telles qu'il a semblé véritablement que notre union était voulue par Celui qui gouverne l'Univers. Ainsi c'est sous son regard & sous Sa divine protection que nous nous sommes unis en implorant sur nous sa bénédiction au nom de notre Seigneur Jésus-Christ.

Voilà, Monsieur & cher ami, les circonstances qui ont accompagné l'événement si sérieux & en même temps si doux qui vient de s'accomplir pour moi. Je suis convaincu que vous me pardonnerez ces détails que justifie l'amitié si précieuse que vous m'avez constamment témoignée & dont vous m'avez toujours donné tant de preuves. J'espère que cette amitié ne me fera jamais défaut & j'ose y compter. —

Je compte être à Londres vers le 8 ou le 10 juillet pour y terminer l'impression de mon second volume qui a été retardée, j'ignore pourquoi. J'espère que vous me permettrez d'aller pendant ce temps passer quelques moments avec vous de temps à autres. Il y aurait même une ou deux expériences que j'aimerais bien faire avec vous, si cela vous est possible.

Je suis encore à Vichy jusqu'à la fin de Juin & je dois passer huit à dix jours à Paris avant d'aller à Londres pour terminer quelques affaires relatives à mon fils cadet qui vient de sortir de la Ecole [*sic*] Polytechnique où il a achevé ses deux années d'une manière honorable, car il est sorti le $25^{\text{ème}}$ sur une liste de 110. Mais j'ai préféré qu'il ne prît en France aucun service ni militaire, ni civil; & il va maintenant poursuivre ses etudes Scientifiques. —

Agréez, Monsieur & trés cher ami, l'assurance des sentiments les plus affectueux de votre tout dévoué

A. DE LA RIVE

[1] The Fatio family was of the Genevan aristocracy.

605 M. FARADAY to C. R. WELD, 6 July 1855
[*R.S., previously unpublished*]

6 July 1855

MY DEAR SIR

I cannot doubt that any paper by Mr Joule[1] must be proper for the Transactions but I am unable to judge of the peculiar merits of the one you send me. The object is (I conclude) to obtain data the best fitted to form the foundations of mathematical investigations into the nature of the electro-magnetic forces. Having no mathematical knowledge I am not competent to say whether the data here supplied are so direct in their consequences as to be thus fitted for that purpose. With my rough geometrical mode of looking at things I should have liked to know the number of spirals (which vary) in the different helices; – and the influence of the difference of helix diameter for the different bars: – also having a helix *constant* in diameter & length of wire, the difference caused by having the iron (of the same weight & length) in the form of a rod or a cylinder so as to be in one part or another of the space within the helix; – and other variations. But for ought that I know the mathematicians may not require these particularities but may be able with a given & constant length of wire to proceed at once from the data Mr. Joule gives. I have no doubt that the experiments are well & carefully made. I conclude that the iron was of like quality in all the cases & well annealed

Dr. Tyndall is abroad at present: when he returns he will have the paper & your notes.[2]

I am

Yours Very Truly

M. FARADAY

[1] The paper was not printed in the *PT*. It may be the basis of Joule's short notice 'An account of some experiments with a large electro-magnet', *BAASR* (1855), Pt. 2, 12.
[2] See Letter 619.

['*The Times*', *9 July 1855, 8*]

Royal Institution,
July 7, 1855

SIR,

I traversed this day by steamboat the space between London and Hungerford
Bridges, between half-past one and two o'clock. It was low water, and I think
the tide must have been near the turn. The appearance and smell of the water
forced themselves at once on my attention. The whole of the river was an
opaque pale brown fluid. In order to test the degree of opacity, I tore up some
white cards into pieces, and then moistened them, so as to make them sink
easily below the surface, and then dropped some of these pieces into the water
at every pier the boat came to. Before they had sunk an inch below the surface
they were undistinguishable, though the sun shone brightly at the time, and
when the pieces fell edgeways the lower part was hidden from sight before the
upper part was under water.

This happened at St. Paul's Wharf, Blackfriars Bridge, Temple Wharf,
Southwark Bridge, and Hungerford, and I have no doubt would have occurred
further up and down the river. Near the bridges the feculence rolled up in
clouds so dense that they were visible at the surface even in water of this kind.

The smell was very bad, and common to the whole of the water. It was the
same as that which now comes up from the gully holes in the streets. The whole
river was for the time a real sewer. Having just returned from the country air, I
was perhaps more affected by it than others; but I do not think that I could have
gone on to Lambeth or Chelsea, and I was glad to enter the streets for an
atmosphere which, except near the sink-holes, I found much sweeter than on
the river.

I have thought it a duty to record these facts, that they may be brought to the
attention of those who exercise power, or have responsibility in relation to the
condition of our river. There is nothing figurative in the words I have employed,
or any approach to exaggeration. They are the simple truth.

If there be sufficient authority to remove a putrescent pond from the neighbourhood of a few simple dwellings, surely the river which flows for so many
miles through London ought not to be allowed to become a fermenting sewer.
The condition in which I saw the Thames may perhaps be considered as exceptional, but it ought to be an impossible state; instead of which, I fear it is rapidly
becoming the general condition. If we neglect this subject, we cannot expect
to do so with impunity; nor ought we to be surprised if, ere many years are
over, a season give us sad proof of the folly of our carelessness.

I am, Sir, your obedient servant,
M. FARADAY.

607 M. FARADAY to J. LIEBIG, 17 July 1855
[Bayerische Staatsbibliothek, Munich, previously unpublished]

Royal Institution
London
17 July 1855

MY DEAR LIEBIG

Now that I think of writing to you, it seems very long since I wrote last, and I seem as if I had left a pleasure unenjoyed: – but I have often thought of you, & had thoughts even of seeing you; though ever as the proposed time drew near, things before unthought of grew into realities, & the dreams which seemed sometimes as lively as realities, passed away; – & so it is with our life and so I suppose it ought to be. But the thoughts of you are pleasant; and my wife & I often think of the days at York, and then set too, to imagine what the years between then & now have done with you. I do not mean as to *progress*, *discovery*, and *fame* for that we know; but as to the personality of the *Man Liebig*, whose company and converse we enjoyed so much there, that it has left an enduring impression on my failing memory. We both desire to recall ourselves *by that time* to your kindliest remembrance of us.

And now I want to ask you to do me a favour if it lies within your power. – My nephew Mr Frank Barnard, who desires to improve himself in Art as applied in Art manufacture, has been in Paris for some years & now purposes to visit Munich, that he may profit by its schools & Art treasures. I should be glad if you could give him the opportunity of a few minutes conversation, and if you know what he ought to do to gain admission to the places of study, to tell him. He is earnest to advance himself, but of course needs the information, which he can gain only by enquiry: If you can in this respect put him in the way it will be a great kindness to him & to me. I am quite sure he will not trouble you more than you will desire.

I hardly know who of my friends is in Munich with you: – for my memory fails me & I forget persons in relation to places. I know that I have many friends every where, & not as I am aware of one enemy or one who dislikes me. I ought to be grateful.

Ever My dear Liebig
Yours Most truly
M. FARADAY

608 A. DE LA RIVE to M. FARADAY, 26 July 1855
[*I.E.E., previously unpublished*]

Paris
jeudi 26 juillet 1855

MONSIEUR & TRÈS CHER AMI,

J'apprends par mon ami Prevost que vous êtes encore à Londres & que vous ne quittez cette ville que lundi prochain. Monsieur Tyndall m'avait induit en erreur en me disant, il y a déjà 15 jours, que vous aviez déjà quitté Londres. Ce motif joint à d'autres avait fait que j'avais prolongé sans regret mon Séjour à Paris. Maintenant l'arrivée de mon frère & de deux de mes enfants m'oblige de retarder mon départ jusqu'à lundi prochain 30 juillet. J'arriverai donc à Londres seulement ce jour là ou le lendemain matin mardi 31, désirant passer le dimanche tranquille & ne pas être en voyage ce jour là.

Maintenant je viens vous demander si je ne pourrai pas aller un matin vous faire une visite à la campagne & si vous ne revenez point quelquefois à Londres de la campagne où vous serez. – Vous comprenez combien je tiens à vous serrer la main & à m'entretenir quelques instants avec vous. – Veuillez donc avoir la bonté de m'écrire deux mots chez MM. Morris Prevost & ce pour me donner vos instructions.

Je compte rester à Londres 10 à 15 jours pour corriger les épreuves qui m'attendent, puis j'irai faire un tour en Ecosse avec ma femme & l'une de mes filles que j'emmène avec moi. Je repasserai donc de nouveau à Londres vers la fin d'Août. J'espère donc bien avoir le plaisir de vous voir, d'autant plus que, comme vous le savez, je n'ai pas à Londres un plus excellent ami que vous.

Agréez, Monsieur & cher ami, l'assurance de mes sentiments dévouées & les plus affectueux

AUG[e] DE LA RIVE

609 M. FARADAY to J. TYNDALL, 6 October 1855
[*R.I., Tyndall's Journal, previously unpublished*]

Sydenham,
6th Oct. 1855

MY DEAR TYNDALL,

I was put into a very mixed mood by your last letter; glad to hear from you that you were out of the turmoil, had enjoyed the beauties of the lakes and were happily at home again: but sorry for some annoyances which I saw you had met with at Glasgow.[1] These great meetings, of which I think very well altogether, advance science chiefly by bringing scientific men together and making them to know and be friends with each other; and I am sorry where that is not the effect in every part of their course, I know nothing except from what you tell me, for I have not yet looked at the report of the proceedings: but let me as an old man who ought by this time to have profited by experience, say, that when I was younger I often misinterpreted the intentions of people, and found that they did not mean what at the time I supposed they meant, and further that as a general rule it was better to be a little dull of apprehension when phrases seemed to imply pique, and quick on the contrary when they seem to convey friendly feeling. The real truth never fails ultimately to appear, and the opposing parties are, if wrong, sooner convinced when replied to forbearingly than when overwhelmed. All I want to say is that it is better to be blind to the results of partisanship, and quick to see good will. One has more happiness in oneself in endeavouring to follow the things which make for peace. You can hardly imagine how often I have been heated in private when opposed, as I have thought unjustly and superciliously, and yet, have striven and succeeded I hope in keeping down replies of the like kind, and I know I have never lost by it. I would not say all this to you if I did not esteem you as a true philosopher and friend.

I have not been altogether idle but I am of necessity very slow now. I have not read the journals, because when able I have been at work and writing a paper. The latter goes on slowly but I think will be a useful contribution of facts and may help to advance the logic of magnetism a little, though not much. The secret of magnetic action is like a Sebastepol at least in this point that we have to attack it in every possible direction and make our approaches closer and closer on all the sides by which we can force access. My working is mainly with magnecrystals and the effects of heat upon them.

You say "I am still here" but do not say where the 'here' is; and my memory is so treacherous that now I have written the letter I shall not be able to send it until I go to London: but whenever you receive it believe me to be as ever

Yours very truly
M. FARADAY

My wife's best remembrances.

1 The *BAAS* met at Glasgow in 1855. The Proceedings give no hint as to the nature of the controversy which Tyndall was involved in. In his Journal, however, he alludes to an argument with William Thomson and William Whewell which would seem to be the cause of his pique. See the manuscript of Tyndall's Journal at the Royal Institution. Journal VIa, 1855, 197.

610 M. FARADAY to C. MATTEUCCI, 2 November 1855
[*B.J. 2, 365*]

November 2, 1855.

MY DEAR MATTEUCCI,

When I received your last, of October 23, I knew that Tyndall would return from the country in a day or two, and so waited until he came. I had before that told him of your desire to have a copy of his paper, and I think he said he would send it to you; I have always concluded he did so, and therefore thought it best to continue the same open practice and show him your last letter, note and all. As I expected, he expressed himself greatly obliged by your consideration, and I have no doubt will think on, and repeat, your form of experiment; but he wished you to have no difficulty on his account. I conclude he is quite assured in his own mind, but does not for a moment object to counter views, or to their publication: and I think feels a little annoyed that you should *imagine for a moment* that he would object to or be embarrassed by your publication. I think in that respect he is of my mind, that we are all liable to error, but that we love the truth, and speak only what at the time we think to be truth; and ought not to take offence when proved to be in error, since the error is not intentional; but be a little humbled, and so turn the correction of the error to good account. I cannot help thinking that there are many apparent differences amongst us, which are not differences in reality. I differ from Tyndall a good deal in phrases, but when I talk with him I do not find that we differ in facts. That phrase *polarity* in its present undefined state is a great mystifier (3307, 3308). Well! I am content, and I suppose he is, to place our respective views before the world, and there leave them. Although often contradicted, I do not think it worth while reiterating the expressions once set forth; or altering them, until I either see myself in the wrong or misrepresented; and even in the latter case, I let many a misrepresentation pass. Time will do justice in all these cases.

One of your letters asks me, "What do you conceive the nature of the lines of magnetic force to be?" I think it wise not to answer that question by an assumption, and therefore have no further account to give of such physical lines than that is already given in my various papers. See that referred to already in the "Philosophical Magazine" (3301–3305); and I would ask you to read also 3299, the last paragraph in a paper in the "Philosophical Magazine," June 1852, which expresses truly my present state of mind.

But a physical line of force may be dealt with experimentally, without our *knowing its intimate physical nature*. A ray of light is a physical line of force; it can be proved to be such by experiments made whilst it was thought to be an *emission*, and also by other experiments made since it has been thought to be an *undulation*. Its physical character is not *proved* either by the one view or the other (one of which must be, and both may be wrong), but it is proved by the *time* it takes in propagation, and by its curvatures, inflexions, and physical affections. So with other physical lines of force, as the electric current; we know no more of the physical nature of the electric lines of force than we do of the magnetic lines of force; we fancy, and we form hypotheses, but unless these hypotheses are considered equally likely to be false as true, we had better not form them; and therefore I go with Newton when he speaks of the *physical lines of gravitating force* (3305 note), and leave that part of the subject for the consideration of my readers.

The use of *lines of magnetic force* (without the *physical*) as true representations of nature, is to me delightful, and as yet never failing; and so long as I can read your facts and those of Tyndall, Weber, and others by them, and find they all come into one harmonious whole, without any contradiction, I am content to let the erroneous expressions, by which they *seem* to differ, pass unnoticed. It is only when a fact appears that *they cannot* represent that I feel urged to examination, though that has *not yet* happened. All Tyndall's results are to me simple consequences of the tendency of paramagnetic bodies to go from weaker to stronger places of action, and of diamagnetic bodies to go from stronger to weaker places of action, combined with the true polarity or direction of the lines of force in the places of action. And this reminds me of a case you put in one of your letters, which to me presents no difficulty: — "*a piece of bismuth on which the pole p acts suffers an action on the part of the pole p′, which is the same as if the pole p′ did not act or was a pole of the contrary name.*" *p*, being an *S* pole, repels *b*, and sends it from a stronger into a weaker part of the field, i.e. from

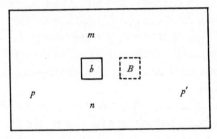

b to *B* ; then *p′* being brought up, and being also an *S* pole, *B* is no longer the weaker place of action but *b*; and hence the bismuth goes back. And that it is the weaker place of action can be shown by a minute magnetic needle or a crystal of bismuth, and in many other ways (3341, &c., especially 3350). But suppose *p′* is selected, an *N* pole, then the lines of force between *p′* and *p* are greatly strengthened in power, and the small needle or crystal bismuth, shows it to be so; but still *B* is no longer a weaker place of power than *b*, and if the bismuth can only move along the line *p p′* it must move from *B* to *b*, for *b* is the weakest place of action in that line; but this is a place of unstable equilibrium, and, as you know very well, if it can move in the line *mn*, it will move either towards *m* or towards *n*, as it happens to be on one or the other side of the axial line of the magnetic field.

These principles, or rather laws, explain to me all those movements obtained by Tyndall against which your note is directed, and therefore I do not see in his experiments any proofs of a defined or inverse polarity in bismuth, beyond what we had before. He has worked out *well* the antithetical relations of paramagnetic and diamagnetic bodies; and distinguished mixed actions, which by some have been much confused; but the true nature of polarity, and whether it is the same, or reversed in the two classes, is to my mind not touched. What a quantity I have written to you, all of which has no doubt been in your own mind, and tried by your judgment. Forgive me for intruding it. Ever truly yours,

M. FARADAY.

611 G. G. STOKES to M. FARADAY, 5 November 1855
[*I.E.E., previously unpublished*]

69 Albert St-
Regents' Park
London
Nov 5th 1855

MY DEAR SIR,

I have arranged to read your paper on the day of the first meeting (Thursday the 15th).[1] I intend only to take the first two sections that day and to take the 3d section the next.

Would you have the goodness to favour Dr. Murphy[2] with an abstract of the paper, such as you would wish to appear in the Proceedings?

I have been thinking over the setting of phosphorus, and it certainly seems to me that a non-crystalline and unstrained elongated diamagnetic body in a *perfectly* uniform field ought to set along the lines of force. I recollect that Thomson, in the paper in the Cambridge mathematical journal in which he first obtained mathematically the law which you had previously enunciated about going from places of stronger to places of weaker force,[3] stated without demonstration that a sufficiently small elongated body whether paramagnetic or diamagnetic would set along the lines of force. Such I imagine ought to be the way in which an elongated piece of phosphorus would set in an *absolutely* uniform field. That such a set is not observed in experiment is I think no valid argument against the theoretical conclusion. For even if we could obtain a mathematically uniform field the setting force would be so excessively small that it seems doubtful whether it could be experimentally observed, and the field between flat poles is demonstrably not mathematically uniform. The setting force arising from any deviations from uniformity in the field would depend on the first power of the inductive capacity of the substance, whereas the setting force in a *perfectly* uniform field would depend upon its square, and would be as nothing in comparison with the former, the inductive capacity of all diamagnetics being very small. Could a diamagnetic be discovered at all approaching in inductive capacity to soft iron I suppose the setting along the lines of force could be easily observed.

Believe me
Yours very truly
G. G. STOKES

[1] 30th Series, *ERE*.
[2] Possibly Edward William Murphy (1802–77), Professor of midwifery, University College.
[3] W. Thomson, 'On the forces experienced by small spheres under magnetic influence; and on some of the phenomena presented by diamagnetic substances', *CDMS*, 2 (1847), 230.

612 M. FARADAY to J. B. DUMAS, 15 November 1855
[*Arch. de l'Acad. des Sciences, Paris, Dossier Faraday, previously unpublished*]

Brighton
15 November 1855

MY DEAR & MOST ESTEEMED FRIEND,

You can hardly conceive the pleasure your letter gave me; the sight of the hand writing, the old kind remembrances, – and the present affection – all contributed to move me greatly. The honour had little or nothing to do with the matter;[1] – it was the feeling that you had not forgotten me, but that I was on your mind as I had been; – and for this I must truly thank you: – and before I leave this ground of true pleasure must ask you to join it with my most respectful remembrance to Madame Dumas; to whom also my dear wife sends her kindest remembrances as well as to yourself.

I have not been well; and having been ordered out of town, did not receive your letter until yesterday and as it has no date, was not aware that I ought to have written on the instant. This morning I have received a letter from Mr. Cole,[2] which leads me to suppose the great day of the Exposition is today. In any case I could not have been present.

You must not think that I do not esteem *very highly* the great honor, which you, and the Council have done me; and could I have been present on the great occasion, and so had the opportunity of beholding the Emperor, a flood of remembrances would have come back upon me (as they do now) of his extreme kindness on former occasions. I do not suppose that he can ever think of me; there is, now, no occasion: but if the circumstances now existant should cause any sound of my name before him in your presence, I hope you will (if proper) express to him the deep feelings of my heart; both in former things and in the present happy & I trust enduring union of France & England under his reign.

I am My dear friend
Most Truly Yours
M. FARADAY

[1] Faraday had been named Commander of the Legion d'Honneur. See Letter 621.
[2] Henry Cole (1808–82), who was at this time Secretary to the Royal Commission at the Paris Exhibition of 1855.

613 M. FARADAY to J. B. DUMAS, 17 November 1855

[*Arch. de l'Acad. des Sciences, Paris, Dossier Faraday, previously unpublished*]

Royal Institution
Saturday Evening, 17 Nov.ʳ 1855

MY VERY DEAR FRIEND

Coming home for an hour or two only I find your last letter & hasten to reply by the post. I trust you have my former one from Brighton by this time. Do not think for a moment that any expression meant kindly can be to me any thing but a pleasure – I do not know to what you refer. I should be grieved at any word touching my honor or affecting my moral character but any thing else is to me perfectly indifferent. What I chiefly & above all rejoice in is your good opinion & great kindness in the first place & then the added approbation & aid(?) of them upon your acts. To the Emperor I owe a deep debt of gratitude for I do not think that in this case he acts merely upon the conclusions of others but accompanies his most gracious act with a thought of good will on his own part. It is considerations of this nature which makes the honor so acceptable to me – for its own sake it is precious for the sake of these associated feelings it is very dear

Ever My dear friend
Yours most truly
M. FARADAY

614 M. FARADAY to P. T. RIESS, 19 November 1855

[*P.M., 4 s., 11 (1856), 1*]

London,
Nov. 19, 1855

MY DEAR M. RIESS,

I have only just arrived at the knowledge of a paper written by you on the action of non-conducting bodies in electric induction; for though I had seen it in Poggendorff's *Annalen*,[1] I could not read it. A translation has, however, appeared in the Philosophical Magazine for June of this year, vol. ix. p. 401,[2] and by it I find that I have failed to convey to your mind (and therefore, perhaps, to the minds of others) my true meaning; so that what you think to be my view, is in some very important points absolutely the reverse. You will not wonder that I am anxious to set myself right in such a matter with one who holds your high position in science. For that purpose I must refer to the pages of the Philosophical Magazine; for though I am not a judge of the strictness of the translation, I have no other means of access and reference to your paper.

At the bottom of page 402, the paper says that Faraday has endeavoured to establish the notion that "induction is not produced by the action of electricity across space, but that an electric body acts *only* on the contiguous particles of an insulating medium," &c. If you refer again to my papers, you will find that in the very beginning of that on induction (1165). I have especially limited the cases to those of *ordinary induction*, *i. e.* cases where matter is present; at (1215.) this expression is repeated; and again in vol. ii. Exp. Res. p. 267. Instead of saying that induction cannot occur across space, I have especially spoken of the case of a vacuum (1613–1616.), which case is enlarged upon in a letter to Dr. Hare, vol. ii. Exp. Res. p. 262. 266.

At p. 403, Phil. Mag., your paper says, "It follows from other experiments made by Faraday (1218.), that the induction would have been diminished had a conducting plate been introduced between the two; for, *according to Faraday's opinion*, the introduction of the conducting plate would have caused the induction to take place in curved lines around the edges of the plate, instead of in right lines through the intervening stratum of air." If this translation conveys your meaning, then I cannot find out what expression of mine has led you to suppose the above is my opinion. I have nowhere said or implied that the interposition of such a plate would have diminished the induction, or made it take place in lines only round its edges, or more curved than before. On the contrary, I know that because of such a plate more lines of force would have passed to the space occupied by it than before; that as far as regarded that portion of space, induction would be replaced by the better function of conduction; that instead of interfering with induction, it would have favoured the final result, although that result would be complicated by the form and size of the plate, the distances of it and the acting bodies, and by other circumstances, as your paper well shows.

The case of mine to which your paper refers as above (1218.), is one of those which I sought for as establishing the *possibility* of induction in curved lines, and is not given as a proof that it must *always* be in curved lines, which is very far from my thoughts. In it the metallic piece (ball, hemisphere or plate) referred to is *uninsulated*, not insulated (1218–1230.). It is also the conductor upon which the induction terminates, and not a conductor interposed in the course of the induction; cases so different, that much of the reasoning which belongs to one has no relation to the other. The latter case is not specifically referred to in the Experimental Researches, because I thought it thoroughly well known, but it is given in my letter to Dr. Hare, vol. ii. of collected papers, p. 263.

Perhaps the following mode of putting the matter will make my views on this point clear to you. Let *P* be an insulated charged body, inducing upon *N* an uninsulated metallic body, *np* being at first away. Then let *np* be introduced, 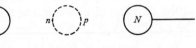 being a non-conductor equal to shell-lac or sulphur, but of the same specific inductive capacity as air; no change of the disposition of the forces will take place, for the particles of *np* will be polarized just as the particles of the air displaced by it were. Then consider *np* to be endued with conducting power, as if it were converted into a metal; its particles will now discharge to each other; the parts at *n* and *p* will be more negative and positive than they were before, because the sum of induction distance between *P* and *N* is shortened by the diameter of *np*, and so the induction is stronger; and instead of the lines of force from *P* to *N* passing round *np* (as your paper makes me to say), *more* will fall upon and pass through the space *np* now that it is a conductor than before when it was an insulator (1326. 1337. 1338.). I am sure I need make no further reference to these points, for I am satisfied that when you look at the paragraphs 1218. to 1230, and perhaps to vol. ii. Exp. Res. p. 279–284, you will at once see what my meaning was, and what my views are. The results according to them are precisely such as you describe at pp. 406, 407, Phil. Mag.

In your paper (Phil. Mag. p. 410), you describe an experiment which I know well, and consider as one of the strong proofs of the truth of my views. A plate of shell-lac is placed with its anterior face 12 inches from the positive knob of an electrical machine, and its posterior face 1 inch from the flame of a spirit-lamp, and then moved about before it; when taken away and examined, the anterior face is found by you charged negative, and hence you conclude, that, prior to the discharge of the posterior face by the flame, the induction had rendered the anterior face of the shell-lac negative, and the posterior face positive, just as would have happened with a metallic plate, and as far as I understand your paper, by a like act of conduction through its mass. Now my view of the induction agrees with yours as respects the anterior and posterior faces of the shell-lac plate; but it differs in two important points: it assumes that if the plate be supposed to consist of an infinite number of parallel plates, each composed of a single layer of particles, each plate has its anterior negative, and its posterior positive surfaces; and that the outer posterior positive surface is not the consequence of the transmission of electricity by the intervening *conducting* particles between it and the anterior negative surface, but of a transmission of the force by the polarity of the *insulating* particles. Upon so stating the case, one or two considerations arise fitted to test the relative value of the two views, and as yet they confirm me in mine.

If the shell-lac plate had had its anterior surface charged negatively, as the like surface of a metallic or conducting plate would have been, then that surface should not have remained exclusively charged on the removal of the plate from the induction; the shell-lac plate, like a conducting plate, should have been found charged over both faces and all its surface; for the same conduction which would permit the flow of electricity under induction, would permit the return to all parts when the induction was removed. As induction cannot be assumed for one part of the experiment and refused for the other, so I find this consideration alone fatal to your view, as I understand it from the translation.

The second consideration is of this kind. If the shell-lac plate whilst in the inductive position be considered, according to my view, as a mass of non-conducting particles polarized, then the action of the spirit-lamp will have been to convey, by convection, negative electricity to the posterior surface of the plate, to neutralize for the time its temporary constrained induced positive state; and it is *that* surface which (after the removal of the plate from the induction, and the return of the constrained state now no longer sustained by *P*) is to be considered as negatively charged, and not the anterior surface, the latter now being only held in a relatively negative state by the still remaining polarity of the particles between it and the really charged posterior surface. So, apart and beyond the argument derived from conduction, other determining considerations may thus be raised. If your view be the correct one, it is the anterior surface only which is charged negatively, and that by an inductive action half discharged; in my view, it is the posterior surface which has that state conferred on it by *convection* from the flame: – in your view the inner parts of the plate are in their natural condition; in my view they are still polarized, being retained in that condition by the posterior negative charge. Happily the question whether it is the anterior or posterior surface which is negatively charged, may be solved, though not by the indifferent approach of either side of the plate to a gold-leaf electrometer; for with either side, indications of negative electricity will be obtained; and if the excited surface be in both cases at equal distances from the electrometer plate, the action will be greater (because of specific inductive capacity) when the body of the shell-lac plate intervenes between the cap and the excited surface than when air only is interposed.

To make these points clear, once for all I will describe the plates I have used; and for easy reference to position, will give a diagram of the forms of experiment. One plate was of shell-lac, $4\frac{1}{2}$ inches square and 0.9 of an inch thick; the other was of sulphur, 5 inches square and 0.8 of an inch thick. A strong white silk thread was made   fast round the edges of each plate, and then a long loop of the like silk being fastened at the two corners of one side-edge, and a like loop at the two corners of the opposite side-edge, the two loops served as handles by which the plates could be insulated, and yet carried about or applied in any position to the electrometer. In the figure, *S* is one of these plates supposed to be seen edgeways; *P* represents the inductric or originally charged body, and *N* (whether flame, point, hand, or ball) the inducteous body; between these two, *P* and *N*, that induction takes place to which the plate *S* is, as far as regards the results of the experiment, subjected, and the effects of which are to be examined. The results were precisely alike with both sulphur and shell-lac plates. If P was made negative, they were also the same, but with inverted signs. I will describe those obtained with the shell-lac, and will always call that face towards P the anterior, and the face towards N the posterior faces of the plates.

Making P the end of the positive conductor of an electrical machine, and N an uninsulated metal ball or plate, then the shell-lac plate was put into its position, retained there for thirty seconds or more, was removed, examined by a gold-leaf electrometer, and found perfectly free from charge on either face or any part. The shell-lac plate was then restored to its position in the induction, and N made a spirit-lamp flame applied in the manner you describe. The shell-lac being taken away, was examined by laying the plate without friction on the cap plate of the electrometer. The shell-lac was found to give strong negative charge to the leaves, whichever face was on the cap; but the signs were much the strongest when the posterior face was in contact with the cap, showing, so far as that went, that the charge was really on that face.

According to my view of induction, that face of the plate had been charged negatively by the flame; for the portion of the induction between P and the flame could be destroyed by the convection dependent on the latter where air only intervened between it and towards P; but as the air in the direction of the conduction terminated at the posterior surface of the shell-lac, so the flame could convey its state of charge to that surface only, the insulating power and solidity of the shell-lac preventing further changes in that direction; hence the result already described. As the flame had power to charge the posterior surface, so it can discharge it, and accordingly by moving the flame for a moment parallel to that surface, and about an inch from it, the plate will be entirely discharged. The previous state of negative charge on the posterior surface of the plate will, if wished, remain for a minute, or two minutes, or even five or ten; and yet the momentary use of the flame discharges it entirely. The result accords perfectly with my view, but, as it appears to me, is entirely opposed to yours. Nor can I see how the assumption of any degree of conduction in the shell-lac, compatible with the acknowledged facts dependent on its insulating powers, can explain the result.

But it may be said, that the second application of the flame, instead of discharging the negative posterior surface, has really charged it positively to an amount equal to the supposed negative charge on the anterior surface, and so covers the effect of the latter more or less according to the thickness of the plate; and then the question is, is the plate entirely discharged, or is it now doubly charged, *i. e.* with one surface positive and the other negative? I find it to be *entirely* discharged; for if I place either surface on the cap plate of the gold-leaf electrometer, and then carefully bring an uninsulated metallic plate to the other surface, I find no effect on the electrometer; whereas there would be such an effect if the plate had been charged as a Leyden jar.

Or it may be supposed that the second application of the flame, though applied on the posterior side of the shell-lac, has somehow or other discharged the negative anterior surface. This is easily shown not to be the case, by the application of the flame on the anterior side, and then still stronger proofs than those already obtained appear against your view and for mine; for according to my view, such an application of the flame ought to cause the anterior face to acquire a positive charge, inasmuch as a second case of induction is set up, in which the posterior negatively charged face of the shell-lac is the inductric body, to which the flame plays the inducteous part as before, and by its well-known powers of convection transfers its state of charge to that surface of the shell-lac (formerly the anterior) now opposed to it; whereas on your view it ought to be simply discharged. The shell-lac plate was therefore placed before the charged body P, and the flame moved about before its posterior surface; then the plate was taken out of the inductive position and the flame moved before its anterior surface; after that it was examined by the electrometer. When the anterior face was on the cap plate of the instrument, the latter indicated a positive charge; when the posterior face was in contact with the cap, the instrument indicated a negative charge, being the same kind of electric charge for that face as before, but much weaker. The apparent weakness ought to occur, for now the negative charge of the posterior face is exercised inductively through the shell-lac towards the positive charge of the anterior face, and *vice versâ*; and this was proved to be the case by bringing the hand or an uninsulated metallic plate towards the upper anterior surface, whilst the posterior surface was in contact with the electrometer cap; for the negative divergence of the gold leaves then increased very greatly, the negative electricity being set free to a large extent from the induction of the positive anterior surface. And when the positive anterior surface was in contact with the cap of the electrometer, its highly charged condition could be exhibited in like manner. So the flame, carefully approached, can only discharge the side which has received a charge, and that only if approached on that side; if brought opposite the other side, it conveys to it the opposite electricity and leaves the plate doubly charged.

These experiments are by no means difficult or delicate, and are easily made in the most convincing and varied manner (a few simple precautions being taken), but always with the same results. P or the inductric body is best if of large surface. An excited glass rod, or, better still, an excited plate of gutta-percha (a shoe sole), are very good for the purpose; either may be brought to within an inch of the shell-lac or sulphur S, and still communicate no charge to it if discharging conductors be not near. A fine metal point may be used at N instead of the flame; or even conductors and contact be employed, as in the following manner. A sheet of gold-leaf was laid on the cap plate of the electrometer; P was put into place, and also the shell-lac or sulphur plate S, and the flame applied for a moment at N; then the plate S was removed and placed with its negatively charged posterior surface in contact with the gold-leaf on the electrometer; immediately the latter showed a strong divergence (often more than the instrument, though very large, could bear); but besides that, if an uninsulated wire was brought towards the cap or gold-leaf, the charged posterior surface was discharged with a spark, and the electrometer and shell-lac were left perfectly uncharged. It is but a very small step to coat the posterior surface with tinfoil beforehand, and then all the experiments can be repeated, using contact with an uninsulated body instead of the flame. Another step led to the coating of the anterior surface; the induction within the shell-lac between these surfaces and perpendicular to them being precisely of the same kind as if these coatings were away. If S, or the inducteous body, be made one that cannot at a distance communicate a charge to the posterior coating, being, for instance, an uninsulated metal ball or plate, then each of these coatings has for the time a polar condition like that represented by np in the first diagram of this letter, *i. e.* their anterior surfaces have negative charge, and their posterior surfaces positive charge, when a positive inductric body P is employed, and so long as the induction continues.

I think you doubt the existence of specific inductive capacity. You obtain the effects which I refer to it, but seem to explain them by some act of conduction in the shell-lac, like that in interposed metallic plates; indeed, by the same act as that which you suppose confers the assumed negative state on the *anterior* surface of the shell-lac plate. Now if any of the induction effects be due to such a conduction, this latter quality ought to appear in very numerous and various forms of experiment, especially if *time* be taken into account. I have taken the plate of sulphur, set it before P, applied the flame before the posterior surface, removed the plate, applied the flame before the anterior surface, and thus charged the sulphur negative and positive on the two sides, as before described, in less than four seconds, and to a considerable degree. That charge, thus quickly gained, the sulphur has retained apparently unimpaired for several minutes, and at the expiration of several hours it was still strongly charged. Now how could any conduction within the mass of the sulphur (of the nature of that which occurs in metals) have caused the appearance at its surfaces of the two electricities in a moment or two, and to twice the amount of what would have been evolved if air had been there, which conduction was yet not competent to effect their return in a period many hundred times as long? We have reason to believe that induction is sensibly instantaneous; for if we take the sulphur plate coated over the middle part of each face, and place a large metallic ball or plate for P opposite to it, three successive contacts, one to touch P and charge it, the second to touch for an instant the coating on the posterior surface of the sulphur, and the third to touch P and discharge it, are sufficient to put on the full inductive state through the sulphur and secure the resulting charge. By the use of a finger key these contacts can be made in the fiftieth part of a second, and by a little mechanical arrangement even much quicker; yet as far as I can find, the coated sulphur surface is as fully charged in this brief period as if the induction had been sustained for a minute or an hour. How are we to conceive that any degree of conduction of the sulphur consistent with the prolonged insulation which can follow, can have concurred to this brief and complete act?

The foregoing results appear to me to be crucial in their character, and to leave no question open as to the possibility of the action of interposed insulating matter being of the same nature as the action of interposed conducting matter in cases of induction. I would go further into them in explanation and illustration of my own views, and of the truthfulness of specific inductive capacity, if I thought it necessary; but I should have little more to do than repeat what is already said (and that many years ago) in the Eleventh Series of the Experimental Researches, and so I refrain.

The effect you mention at the bottom of page 404 and top of 405, Phil. Mag., is to me a very natural result of the high specific inductive capacity of shell-lac. In one place you say, in relation to it, that "no reason can be assigned why a *small piece* of shell-lac," &c.; but I cannot consent to accept that as a small piece which is in reality a small portion, not separated, of a large piece; as I could not say, that that was a small piece of metal which is only a small part of a large plate. A greater inductive capacity disturbs the lines and distribution of force in a manner equivalent to a certain amount of conductive power; and yet the two effects may be perfectly distinguished by such experiments and reasoning as that I have just applied to the examination of the condition of the shell-lac plate.

You will see, my dear Sir, that I am anxious to stand rightly before you; at the same time I would not have presumed thus far if I had not believed that there was some great misapprehension in your mind as to my opinions. You will perceive, also, that I find no reason to change any of my views of static induction as set forth in Series XI. I must confess, that as your paper has appeared in Poggendorff's *Annalen* and in the Philosophical Magazine, I should not like the case to remain before the scientific world just as it is, as it might be thought I acquiesced in the statements there made; and if I might suppose it would not be disagreeable to you I would put this letter into the Magazine, unless, indeed, you preferred some other mode of communication with the public. In the mean time I shall send it to you; and as many months have now elapsed since the publication here, I hope you will give me an early note saying whether you object or not.

I am, yours very truly,
M. FARADAY.

[1] P. Riess, 'Ueber die Wirkung nicht-leitender Körper bei der electrischen Influenz', *AP*, 168 (1854).
[2] P. Riess, 'On the Action of Non-conducting Bodies in Electric Induction', *PM*, 4 s., 9 (1855), 401.

615 T. STEVENSON to M. FARADAY, 19 November 1855

[*I.E.E., previously unpublished*]

Edinburgh,
Nov. 19. 1855

Private

MY DEAR SIR

Allow me to thank you for your kindness in sending me the notice regarding the polyzonal lens. In the Pamphlet[1] which my brother and I were forced although most reluctantly to publish we do not state that *Buffon* proposed the built lens although there is some doubt even as to this. But one thing *is certain* that Condorcet most distinctly described it as well as the means which it afforded of correcting spherical aberration. We know therefore that the polyzonal lens as now used in Lighthouses was first invented (for burning purposes only) by Condorcet in 1780 while Fresnel was the first to publish and the first to apply it to Lighthouses

With many thanks for your kind attention in which my brother joins

Believe me
ever faithfully yours
THOMAS STEVENSON

[1] David and Thomas Stevenson, *On Lighthouses*. I can find no citation of the actual publication. See Sir David Brewster, 'Reply to Messrs. D. and T. Stevenson's pamphlet on lighthouses', n.p., 1860.

616 J. N. CRICHTON[1] to M. FARADAY, 6 December 1855[2]

[*R.I., previously unpublished*]

Dundee
6 December 1855[2]

VERY DEAR BROTHER

Some of our Friends here say they have observed your name as one of the members of the British Association for the promotion of Science who are to hold a meeting at Glasgow on the 12th of this month and as Glasgow is only about three hours distant by Rail from this are anticipating that you may be induced to prolong your Journey to Dundee and so enjoy the happiness of being once more filled with your Company

If so ordered I need not not say how happy I shall be by your making my House your Home whilst here and again in my old age enjoying the Liveliness of your Company along with as many of the Brethren as the Room will contain

With kindest Regard to you Mrs F and all enquiring friends I am

Very Dear Brother
Affectionately Yours
J N. CRICHTON

[1] John Crichton (1772–1860), Surgeon and reader in the Glasite Church at Dundee.
[2] This letter must bear the incorrect month because the British Association meeting referred to took place in September.

617   F. Wöhler to M. Faraday, 10 December 1855
[*I.E.E., previously unpublished*]

Göttingen
le 10 Dec. 1855

Monsieur.

Permettez-moi d'abuser pour quelques moments de vôtre temps si précieux pour la science. Mr. Stein, dont j'ai fait la connaissance il y a quelques années et qui posséde des mines et des usines d'argent en Mexique, est rétourné de là à Darmstadt et a rapporté une masse de fer metéorique pésante 109 Kilogrammes (218 livres) et trouvée dans la vallée de Toluca. Il m'en a fait couper un échantillon et me l'a envoyé. C'est du veritable fer méteorique, [*sic*] characterisé par les belles figures, dites de Widmanstätten, qui se sont montrées en traitant une surface polie avec de l'acide nitrique étendue, et par une grande quantité de Nickel, qu'il contient. En outre on remarque sur sa surface un peu oxidée du sulfure de fer et du phosphure double de fer et de Nickel (le Schreibersit).

Mr. Stein désire vendre cette masse en entier et il croit pouvoir démander 350 livres Sterling. Il l'a déjà offert aux cabinets de Mineralogie à Vienne et à Berlin, mais on a répondu, que dans ce moment on n'ait pas disponible une telle somme d'argent pour un seul objet. Il a donc cru que peut-être le British Museum voudra acheter ce fer, et je lui ai promis de m'adresser à cet égard à Vous, Monsieur, n'ayant pas l'honneur de connaître le directeur de la section de minéralogie du British Museum.

J'ose donc vous prier, de vouloir bien me dire en deux mots, si peut-être à Londres on veut acheter cette masse rémarquable. Si vôtre réponse est Non, Mr. Stein se décidéra probablement de faire couper la masse et de la vendre divisée en des petits morceaux de 1 ou de 2 Kilogr. de pésanteur. Dans ce cas Vous voulez bien me dire, si le british Museum ou quelque autre personne désirera acheter des tels échantillons. Je pense qu'un morceau de 1 Kilogr. coutera à peuprès [*sic*] 4 livres Sterling.

Agréez, Monsieur, l'expression de la plus profonde considération, avec laquelle j'ai l'honneur de me nommer

Vôtre
très devoué
Wöhler.

618   P. T. Riess to M. Faraday, 10 December 1855[1]
[*R.I., P.M., 4 s., 11 (1856)*]

Berlin
10 December 1855.

My dearest Sir

In replying upon the letter with which you have honoured me,[2] I must at first claim your greatest indulgence for my english. I mean not the errors which are easily corrected, but the improper choice of words which in theoretical controversies is of consequence and which I have no hope to avoid. – Before I enter in the discussion of your remarks concerning my paper on induction, it may not be improper to say a word upon the old theory of static electricity. It appears to me, that a theory of a branch of the experimental sciences should be deemed good and not be abandoned, so long as it is sufficient to account for all facts known by applying a simple principle, be it paradoxical or not, and so long as it comes not in contradiction with itself or the theory of a congenial branch. The old theory of light has been abandoned, not because its principle of the emission of myriads of particles of light, endued with the greatest velocity and many perplexing properties, was highly paradoxical, but because it was found incompetent in accounting for the great class of phenomena of diffraction and polarisation. I see not the like in the old theory of electricity. Indeed it presumes the action at a distance and I agree entirely with you, that such an action is extremely difficult to conceive; but admit we not the like in the great theory of gravitation, and admit you not also this action in an extra-ordinary case of induction in electricity? The action at a distance consists here in the attraction of electricity of one kind and the repulsion of the other in every particle of matter and is illimited, that is to say: if an electrified particle E acts upon a particle of matter A, and a particle of matter B is placed wherever the action of E upon it is not hindered nor weakened and exists in the same amount as before. These premises granted, the theory accounts for the phenomena of Static electricity in the simplest manner. All these phenomena are instances of the arrangement of electricity upon the surfaces of bodies, and their arrange-ment is made dependent of the equilibrium of a number of forces which the electric particles exercise mutually on each other. Thus the electrostatic problems are changed into problems of pure mechanics and the principles of this science find their application. The advantage of this method is very great, it gives the result of each experiment as the sum of single actions which the mind conceives without difficulty, and leaves to the mathematier [sic] the pains to sum up the single effects and to give the amount of the sum. If this summation is often too complicated to be exactly effectuated, I think that not a fault of the theory, the more as it is in most cases not difficult to imagine by means of general considerations the final result. Therefore I have long ago, defended this theory against its – indeed not very dangerous – antagonists and I could not abstain from continuating the defence, as arose an adversary in the man whom I venerate as the greatest natural philosopher of the age.

Upon your first remark I reply that, writing on a case of induction in air, I gave your opinion on that induction and avoided intentionally to mention your opinion of a case, which not occurred. For, had I mentioned it, I would have been forced to add, that you admit solely a *limited* action at a distance,[1] and to explain, that this presumption in respect to the case beforehand is of the same consequence as if you denied that action at all. In respect to the reproof, made in the second remark, that I have misrepresented your meaning on the action of the conducting intermediate plates in induction, I must be the more anxious to disculpate me as, if I am not mistaken, this disculpation hits the very root of all differences between your theory of induction and the old one. I have said: it follows from your experiments that the introduction of a conducting plate between an inductric and an inducteous body would have diminished the action of the former upon the latter, because this action, according to your opinion, would pass in curved lines instead of in right lines through the air. In these experiments referred to, a rubbed shell-lac cylinder and, in contact with it, an uninsulated metallic disc have been employed and a *fact of proof* is given (exper. research. 1221) "that the induction of the shell-lac acts not through or across the metal,,. This fact of proof consists in the observation that a carrierball receives inducteously no charge or a weak one, if it is applied to the centre of the upper face of the disc, where the carrier is nearest to the inductric and no straight line can be drawn between both but through the metal; and the observation that the carrier receives a strong charge in the air in some height above the centre of the disc. Hence you conclude[2] "that the induction is not through the metal, but through the surrounding air in curved lines.,, I thought me entitled to presume that you would make the same conclusion from the same fact of proof in experiments of a varied form, and I thought it the more, as I saw no other way to account for this fact according to your theory. When the rubbed shell-lac cylinder is replaced by an electrified metallic globe, and a sufficiently large metallic plate is placed at some distance above the globe, the carrier receives only a weak charge from the centre of the upper surface of the plate (which is not in sight of the globe) and an increasing charge, if it is raised. If the plate is insulated, the carrier dares not be applied to the plate, but the charge increasing with the elevation of the carrier above the centre and the maximum of it in a certain hight [*sic*] is still remarked. Hence I conjectured, that you would consider the action of a metallic intermediate plate between an inductric and an inducteous body as *screening* the latter from the induction in straight lines of the former,[3] and I was confirmed in my conjecture by §. 1681[4] where you say "that the electric power is limited and exclusive,, Surely you will find this conjecture not to be a precarious one, if you see, that the philosophers who have adopted your views on induction, have made the same. Melloni has believed to screen his electroscopes from the induction of a conductor by the interposition of a metallic plate between both, and de la Rive relates with the same meaning the experiments with your differential-inductometer in his Traité d'électricité vol 1. p. 131 (it exists an english edition which I have not seen). He says: "si on interpose une lame métallique soit isolée, soit "mieux encore, communiquant avec le sol, entre *A* (the positively electrified "inductric plate), et *B* (the inducteous, which has been touched before) aussitôt "*B* donne des signes d'électricité negative tres forte, qui proviennent de ce que

"l'*induction cessant d'agir* sur elle etc Ainsi, mettre un disque métallique entre
"*A* et *B*, cela revient a [*sic*] remplacer *B* par un autre disque plus rapproché de
"*A* qu'il ne l'était, et par consequent le *soustraire à l'induction* de *A*.„

The metallic intermediate plate, insulated or not, is here said to have withdrawn a body to the induction, it is regarded as a screen which intercepts the
electric induction, how an opake body intercepts the light. I am extremely
satisfied that you partake not of this view, but I must confess that I cannot see,
how to account by the manner exposed in your letter, for the results which I
have obtained with intermediate conducting plates. Let *P* be the originally
electrified globe, *N* the uninsulated globe induced, *np* the metallic insulated

disc (edgeways seen) so interposed, that the line joining the centres of
the globes passes perpendicularly through the centre of the disc. According
to your view the faces *n* and *p* of the disc are more negative and positive, than
when the disc was of atmospheric air (the metallic disc away) and the induction
on *N* must be stronger than before. But really this is not always the case, the
induction on *N* appears strengthened or diminished, according as the intermediate metallic disc is small or large, is thick or thin. I am not able to supply
on your reasoning, what a difference occurs, when the disc *np* with the same
diameter has a thickness of 0.25 or of 0.04 of an inch. It seems to me, that in
both cases the electric state of the faces *n* and *p* should be greater than with the
air disc. And however with the thick metallic disc the induction on *N* appears
greater with the thin disc less, as in the case where no disc is present (p. 408 of
my paper).[5] When the thick disc is employed and therefore the induction on
N appears strengthened, if we touch the disc for a moment and insulate it
again, the induction on *N* is diminished. *Will* we say that the exalted state of *p*
is taken away by momentary touch, it is to be expected, that this state be fully
restored in the moment, where the disc is again insulated.[6] be it as it may, I
am not aware, that your theory admits the action of an inductric and an
inducteous body upon a third body to be independent of each other, and that
is, I believe, the essential point in which the two theories differ thoroughly.[7]
The old theory accounts in the simplest imaginable manner for all here concerned cases. It presumes that the three electric strata: upon the surface of the
globe *P* upon the face *n* and the face *p*, act independently of each other inducing
upon the globe *N*. If we denote with $f(P)$ the inductive effect of the globe *P*
on the globe *N*, with $-f(n)$ that of *n* (the sign $-$ says that the effect is contrary
to that of *P*) and with $f(p)$ the inductive effect of the face *p*, the theory asserts,
that in all cases the final effect on *N* is dependent of the amount of the sum

$f(P) - f(n) + f(p)$ and leaves it to the calculation to say, if the sum is greater or less than $f(P)$. In the sole case, where $f(p)$ vanishes, that is to say, when the intermediate metallic plate has been touched or is uninsulated, it can be said without computation, that the sum of inductive effects of globe and plate is less than the effect of the globe alone.

After having experimentally shown, that with conducting intermediate plates the induction can be strengthened as well as weakened, and with non-conducting plates weakened as well as strengthened I ventured to advance the opinion, that the action of plates of whatever nature have the same cause, viz. the arrangement of the electricities of opposite kind upon the surfaces of the plates. I examined roughly (if necessary it could be made very accurately) the arrangement of the electricities upon a metallic disc, and I concluded, that the electricities are arranged in a similar manner (not the same) upon a non-conducting disc. I concede that this conclusion is not inobjectionable, but I maintain, that it must be made necessarily at first and cannot be abandoned, unless it is proved false. The simple fact, that a non-conducting body is attracted by an electrified body, shows clearly, that the non-conducting matter as well as the conducting is instantaneously provided by induction with both electricities.

As a more direct proof of this induction upon insulators, without an essential connexion with the subject I treated of, I have described an experiment which occurred to me and which I had nowhere found. To this supplementary experiment belongs your third remark to which I proceed. A shell-lac disc is quickly moved once from above to below between a flame and the globe of the conductor of an electric machine (not "to and fro,,; I have indicated this error of translation to Prof. Tyndall in a letter dated 19 June)* The anterior face of the disc is found to be strongly negative. You agree with me, that without the flame both faces of the disc have been instantaneously provided by induction with negative and positive electricity, but you differ from me in respect to the explication of the experiment, in respect, as you say, to the manner by which the disc has been electrified and the part which the flame has acted in the final result. As to the first point, a mistake must have happened, inasmuch as I have nowhere mentioned my view on the manner by which the conducting and non-ducting bodies are excited by induction. I fear, that the word "distribution,, whereby the german word "Anordnung,, (which signifies "arrangement,,) has been translated, has caused the mistake. If it is said (p. 412) "there is no essential difference between the actions of conducting and non-conducting bodies, but inasmuch as the distribution of electricity upon them,, etc and further: "in conducting bodies the distribution of electricity,, etc (ibidem) my meaning is this: It is admitted that each intermediate plate, be it of conducting or of non-conducting matter, is by induction instantaneously provided with both electricities, which are arranged in a certain manner upon both faces of the plate. Upon a conducting plate I can specify by examination in every case the arrangement of the electricities and thereby account for the action of this plate upon a body in its vicinity and induced by an electrified body. Upon a non-conducting plate I cannot examine the arrangement of the electricities, but with a presumed arrangement I can also account for the action of this plate and therefore I must deny an essential difference to be between the action of conducting and non-conducting bodies in electric induction.[8] That the manner, whereby the induction is produced upon a conducting and a non-conducting plate, be alike in every respect, I have neither said nor meant.

As far as regards the result, indicated in my paper, of the experiment with the flame, it is neither uncertain nor equivocal. The shell-lac disc was moved only once from above to below between the positively electrified conductor of a machine and a spirit flame; the anterior face of it was laid with sliding contact[9] on the Knob of a gold-leaf electroscope; the disc was withdrawn and the electricity in the electroscope examined. Always negative electricity was found, weaker or stronger, the strongest, when the centre of the large disc had touched the knob and it was carefully breathed upon, whereof the reason is obvious. – I have imputed to the flame the essential part, of destroying the positive electricity of the posterior face. You have observed the fact that the posterior face is negatively excited, and you have hence drawn some consequences concerning the mode of induction on the plate which I cannot admit. The fact of the posterior face being negatively electrified appears to me a very complicated one and resulting from one of the two following causes, perhaps from both. Firstly: the flame is inducteously excited by the originally electrified body and imparts its negative electricity to the posterior surface. Secondly: the negatively electrified anterior face of the disc acts by induction upon the posterior face. Concerning the first assumption, I have concluded from experiments made on the electric properties of burning bodies (Poggendorff annals 61. 545) "that a flame, electrified by induction, acts upon a body in its vicinity by means of its electricity unlike – named to that of the inductric body. As to the second assumption a decisive experiment, as it appears to me, has been made and described by me vol 1. § 300 of my book on electricity. A shell-lac disc was held, by means of a handle, freely in the air and rubbed upon one surface (we will say, the superior) strongly with fur. Although it cannot be doubted, that the superior face was negatively excited, the inferior face was found also negative. On the contrary had the shell-lac disc lain upon an uninsulated metallic disc during the rubbing, and was after that the negative electricity of the superior face destroyed by the application of a flame (or the touching with a metallic plate, as instantly will be seen) the inferior face was found to be positive. After destroying this positive electricity, the superior face was again negative and thus continuating, alternately one face could be made positive the other negative. This experiment gave me the means to obtain easily an electrophorus with a positively excited cake. For that purpose the cake was laid in her uninsulated metallic mould, strongly rubbed with fur and inverted in the mould, so that the not-rubbed face was uppermost. Was this cake covered with its covercle (a metallic disc) I had an electrophorus which gave negative electricity instead of the common electrophorus giving positive electricity.

With respect to your fourth and last remark, I concede entirely, that it is not correct, to equalise a small portion of a large piece of shell-lac to a small piece of the same, what I have done p. 405 of my paper. But I believe to have rendered this incorrectness innoxious by referring to the end of my paper, where I have explained why a partial introduction of the non-conducting plate between the inductric and the inducteous body apparently diminishes the induction and strengthens it by complete interposition. I consider still this opposite effect of one and the same plate, together with the fact that the placing of the plate at the side of the inductric body increases the induction (p 411 at the bottom) very difficult to be explained by your theory of induction.

I have little hope to persuade you, my dear Sir, to modify your views on the action of insulators in electric induction, and, I confess, if I could, I would scarcely wish it. The great philosopher works best with the help of his own conceptions, his self-made tools whose imperfections he avoids by dexterous application. But these tools, so efficacious in his hand, are not only useless but very dangerous in the hand of others, and you know, what mischief, for instance, the conceit of electric screening has lately done in the hand of the since deceased italian philosopher. You will therefore not blame me, if I shall let follow to the publication of your remarks that of my reply. I cannot have any objection against the mode and place, which you choose for their publication, and I know, that immediately after the appearance of your letter Prof. Poggendorff will give a translation of it in his annals. I am, my dearest Sir,

Yours
most faithfully
P. Riess

* This I can certify: I would add, however, that I am not responsible for the translation which, on the whole, appears to be excellent. John Tyndall. [This note is in the same hand as that of the entire letter.]

[Notes by M. Faraday]

1. My view puts no limit to the action which is not paralleled in the case of light; where matter is, it is included in the action, where it is not, the action is considered as going on without it. M.F.

2. On the further side, the metal being always uninsulated. M.F.

3. If uninsulated, yes; if insulated no; – as regards the final result of all the actions (inductive & conductive) on the inducteous body. M.F.

4. (" 1681) a striking character of the electric power is that it is limited and exclusive, and that the two forces being always present are exactly equal in amount. The forces are related in

one of two ways, either as in the natural normal condition of an uncharged insulated conductor; or as in the charged state, the latter being a case of induction." M.F.

5. The induction of P is in my view not exclusively upon N but upon all surrounding bodies even to the walls of the room. When the metallic insulated disc np is changed in size the distribution of the induction is changed with it a small plate because of its thickness of conducting matter lessens the electric resistance between P & N and the induction on the latter is increased. a larger plate of the same thickness or even thicker may diminish the induction on N by a redistribution of the forces more induction upon surrounding bodies now taking place because of the extension of its periphery towards them. M.F.

6. I do not expect any restoration of the previous state of the disc and believe I know that it will *not* occur. A momentary uninsulating touch instantly brings on a new state of the induction & of the plate which is final & remains after the uninsulating contact is removed. The only disturbance of this state is the presence of the uninsulating wire which whilst it is there takes part of the induction on to itself; and the gradual discharge due to moisture & dust of the air & to imperfect insulation. M.F.

7. The question to my mind is the effect on the plate np dependant on or independant of internal conduction amongst its particles? if independant of internal conduction what is it dependant on apart from the polarity of the particles which I assume as the cause? Or again how can induction & insulation considered as contingent causes give as their result the same distribution of force? M.F.

8. Suppose a fluid insulating medium to exist between P and N and the solid interposed plate np to have like insulating power & inductive capacity as the medium as for instance shell lac in camphene or solid sulphur in melted sulphur are we to expect the two electricities to appear at the surfaces of the solid plate and not as I suppose in every section of both the fluid & the solid by planes supposed to pass through them parallel to the surfaces of the plate? Would not this be to attribute to insulating solids a power denied to insulating fluids and would it not also be equivalent to an admission that the solid could acquire a polar state under induction which yet would be denied to its particles? M.F.

9. I gave the one motion between the inductric body & the flame & obtained precisely the same results as those described in my letter. It is quite easy to ascertain which surface of the plate np is charged & whether Positive or Negative without ever making contact with the ball or cup plate of the electrometer but only by a near approach. I think it must be essentially necessary to avoid a sliding contact between the shell lac plate & the metal ball of the electrometer for I find that employing a perfectly uncharged plate & instrument and making such a contact, electricity is excited. The shell lac becomes positve & the metal negative, so that the moment the shell lac is withdrawn the electrometer diverges with negative electricity. M.F.

---

[1] Footnotes in parentheses are Faraday's. The letter as published here is transcribed from the original interleaved in Faraday's copy of his *ERE* at The Royal Institution. The notes by Faraday are taken from the published version.

[2] See Letter 614.

619   M. FARADAY to G. G. STOKES, 7 January 1856
[*R.S., previously unpublished*]

Royal Institution,
7 January 1856.

MY DEAR SIR

I do not see that I can change a single word of my former letter (6 July 1855).[1] Mr. Joules paper is intended for the use of the mathematicians and is one that I cannot pretend to judge on its merits The merits of the philosopher I know very well but you know them as well as I do

Ever Truly Yours
M. FARADAY

I return herewith the paper & my former note. MF.

[1] See Letter 605.

620   M. FARADAY to J. B. DUMAS, 14 January 1856
[*Arch. de l'Acad. des Sciences, Paris, Dossier Faraday, previously unpublished*]

Royal Institution
14 January 1856.

MY DEAR FRIEND

Wheatstone in telling me that he had seen you gave me the impressions very different to those that I had received from your letters: – he seemed to think that it was a duty for me to appear at Paris and went so far as to imply that you had said the Emperor expected it. I should be very grieved to think I could have appeared unthankful or less grateful than I ought to feel either in the Emperors eyes or in yours whose kind affection & approbation I most highly esteem; and having finished a course of lectures honored by the daily presence of our Royal Princes I now feel able to leave town for a few days so I propose running over to Paris & back in the middle of next week. but as I have no other object than to see you and do as I ought to do, so if you were not there I should have no desire to be there Tell me therefore whether I shall see you (and Madame Dumas) if I come and tell me whether on the whole I ought to come. Mr Hunt[1] of Canada has just given me your correct address & so I hope my letter will find you at once. Our joint & most sincere respects & remembrances to Madame Dumas.

Ever My dear friend
Your devoted & indebted
M. FARADAY

[1] Thomas Sterry Hunt (1826–92), Chemist and Mineralogist for the Geological Survey of Canada.

621 M. FARADAY to J.-G.-V. FIALIN,[1] 19 January 1856
[*B.J. 2, 358*]

Royal Institution,
January 19, 1856.

M. LE COUNT,

I am led to believe that I ought to thank the Emperor personally for the high honour he has done me in creating me a Commander of the Legion of Honour, especially when I call to remembrance circumstances of personal communication in former times.

May I beg the favour of the conveyance of the enclosed to its high destination.

I have the honour to remain, your Excellency's most humble, obedient servant,

M. FARADAY

[1] Jean-Gilbert-Victor Fialin, Comte de Persigny (1808–72), one of Napoleon III's earliest adherents, and, in 1856, French Ambassador to London.

622 M. FARADAY to his Imperial Majesty the Emperor,
19 January 1856
[*B.J. 2, 358*]

Royal Institution,
January 19, 1856.

SIRE,

I fear to intrude, yet I also fear to seem ungrateful; and before your Majesty I would rather risk the former than the latter. I know not how to return fit thanks for the high and most unexpected honour which your Imperial Majesty has conferred upon me in the gift of the Degree of Commandant of the Legion of Honour. I cannot promise to deserve it by the future, for the effects of time tell me there are no hopes that I should hereafter work for science as in past years. I can only offer a most grateful and unfailing remembrance of that which to me is more than honour – of the kindness of your Imperial Majesty to one such as I am; and I feel deeply affected by the thought that even I, by your Majesty's favour, form one link, though a very small one, in the bands which I hope will ever unite France and England.

Hoping and believing that your Majesty will accept my earnest thanks and deep-seated wishes for your Majesty in all things, I venture to sign myself as

Your Imperial Majesty's most humble and most grateful servant,

M. FARADAY.

623 M. FARADAY to J. B. DUMAS, 19 January 1856
[*Arch. de l'Acad. des Sciences, Paris, Dossier Faraday, previously unpublished*]

Royal Institution
19 January 1856

MY DEAR KIND FRIEND

Yours of Yesterday has decided me. I will come but I will come when the year is more advanced. But your letter has made me very bold and I have done a thing which I should not have had courage to do without it. I have written to the Emperor. and sent it through your Ambassador here. I had had a notice from the Chancellerie of the Legion of Honor and wrote a reply to it with sincerest thanks, but durst not do more. Now I have been very bold I hope not too bold. and I *am* sure that *you* will do me the justice to believe I would not intrude. Thinking to see you before very long, I am ever more & more Yours affectionately.

M. FARADAY

624 W. DE LA RUE to M. FARADAY, 9 February 1856
[*I.E.E., previously unpublished*]

London,
110 Bunhill Row,
Feby 9th 1856

MY DEAR MR. FARADAY,

Subsequent experiments have shewn me that we were a little too impatient the other day: – the solution of gold I now have, and of which you have a portion gives films, but they are much thicker than those first obtained by me – and I fail even now in getting thin ones.[1] A little free *hydrochloric* acid very much modifies the colour of a neutral solution of the chloride, and is apt to cause the gold to become crystalline, but I have not yet succeeded in so tempering the solution so as to get the first degree of tenuity.

One important result of our failure is this that I obtain films so thick that they may be as well lifted up on the copper with the long hole as gold leaf – and on Monday I will endeavour to thicken some by Voltaic means and let you know the result.

———

———

Glass, Clock-glasses; Chas. Wm. Price. 20 Clerkenwell Green Gold Leaf (our man) Law No 1–2 Northside Bethnal [reading doubtful] Green Glass Plates
Edward & Wm. H. Jackson, 315 Oxford Street

———

———

I find that bad as my memory is that I was right and that we have another broken spindle similar to one we have turned down to make a cone for you – if you will kindly let me know its diameter and length I will make this one the same: it is now being softened (annealed). We have more-over a broken square spindle 27 inches long which will plane up to $4\frac{1}{8}$ square and this might be cut off to the length you desire bent to make a good horse shoe by combining with the two cones, and we might perhaps get enough for two ends besides.

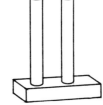

I had the bottle of liquor with suspended gold in it – the copper plates I retain for a day or two in the hope of giving you some films on them.

I am Very truly Yours
WARREN DE LA RUE

[1] See M. Faraday, 'Experimental relations of gold, and other metals, to light', *PT* (1857), 145.

---

625 K. W. KNOCHENHAUER to M. FARADAY, 20 March 1856
[*I.E.E., previously unpublished*]

Meiningen (Duché de Saxe)
le 20 mars 1856.

MONSIEUR,

Je Vous prie d'excuser, que j'ose Vous incommoder encore une fois, mais Votre lettre adressée à Mr. Riess, que j'ai trouvée dans les Annales de Poggen-dorff[1] et que j'ai lue avec un très grand intérêt, contient un passage, dont je désirerais une courte explication. Vous dites dans la note (8), ajoutée à la lettre de Mr. Riess, „que les phénomènes de la capacité inductive spécifique sont acceptés aujourd'hui". Ne croyant pas, que de ces expériences de Mr. Riess, qui effacent presque toute différence entre les corps isolateurs et les corps conduc-teurs, Vous dériviez une approbation de Vos phénomènes, je Vous prie de me dire, où se trouvent de nouvelles expériences publiées sur cet objet. Elles auraient pour moi un intérêt particulier, parceque [*sic*] moi aussi j'ai publié après ce Mémoire de Mr. Riess, que Vous avez examiné si complètement, quelques expériences sur la capacité inductive des isolateurs, qui sont insérées dans les Annales de Pogg. (1854) XCII p 407. Les anciennes disputes qui ont eu lieu entre Mr. Riess et moi ne me permettaient pas de discuter toutes ses expériences; c'est pour cela que je me suis borné à répéter et à prouver Vos expériences données dans la Série XI, croyant que ces expériences ne peuvent être expliquées selon „la théorie ancienne", nom fort bien choisi. –

Si Vous ne le trouvez pas arrogant de ma part, j'ajouterai qu'il y a peutêtre [*sic*] une explication plus facile au lieu de celle, que Vous avez donnée dans la note (5). D'après mes expériences citées dans „Beiträge zur Electricitätslehre"[2] p. 79 la quantité (m) de l'électricité induite par une plaque sur une autre est donnée par la formule $m = a/b+x$, où a et b sont des constantes, qui dépendent de la grandeur des plaques et x en mesure la distance.

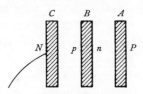

Pour mes grandes plaques je trouvai [sic] $a = 37$ et $b = 37,5$, supposé que x soit donné en lignes. Maintenant soit la plaque A chargée d'électricité positive et B représente une plaque de métal isolée, interposée entre A et la plaque C non-isolée, sur laquelle on cherche l'électricité induite; supposons que la distance x entre A et C soit de 12 lignes et que B se trouve à 6 lignes de A, supposons outre cela, que dans notre cas, où les plaques sont plus petites, les constantes a et b soient = 30,0 et 30,5 et que les quantités d'électricité positive et négative sur les deux faces de B soient égales, nous aurons dans les cas divers 1) que la plaque B est éloignée 2) que cette plaque a une épaisseur de 0,04 pouces = 0,5 lignes 3) que la même plaque a une épaisseur de 0,25 pouces ou de trois lignes, la quantité (m) d'électricité négative sur la plaque C:

$$1) \quad m = \frac{30}{42,5} = 0,706$$

$$2) \quad m = \frac{30}{36,5} \times \frac{30}{36,0} = 0,685$$

$$3) \quad m = \frac{30}{36,5} \times \frac{30}{33,5} = 0,736.$$

Ce sont les mêmes résultats que ceux qu'ont fournis les expériences de Mr. Riess, mais qui sont tout-à-fait d'accord avec Vos idées.

Je saisis cette occasion de Vous renouveler l'assurance de la haute estime avec laquelle j'ai l'honneur d'être

Monsieur
Votre très dévoué et très
obéissant serviteur
K. W. KNOCHENHAUER.

[1] See Letters 614 and 618. Also, 'Ueber die Wirkung nichtleitender Körper bei der elektrischen Induction; von M. Faraday und P. Riess', *AP*, 173 (1856), 415.

[2] K. W. Knochenhauer, *Beiträge zur Elektricitätslehre*, Berlin, 1854.

626   M. FARADAY to A. DE LA RIVE, 21 March 1856
[*B.J. 2, 375*]

Royal Institution
Mar 21, 1856

MY DEAR DE LA RIVE

Though unable to write much I cannot longer refrain from acknowledging your kindness in sending me such a remembrance of you as the *Vol ii* and in giving utterance to the great delight with which I have read it. I rejoice to think that such a work should be reprinted in the English language for now when asked for a good book on Electricity, I know what to say. I will not say that I envy you for your wonderful stores of knowledge regarding all that concerns our beloved science but I cannot help contrasting your power with mine and wishing for a little of the ability by which a mind such as yours calls up to present remembrance what it had found worthy to lay up in its treasury.

But we both have reasons of a higher nature than any that science can afford to be thankful for that we have received & not to forget the many benefits bestowed upon us and I hope that I am not envious of you or of any man but would rather rejoice in your exaltation. With the kindest remembrance of Madame De la Rive & of yourself

I am My dear friend
Most truly Yours,
M. FARADAY

627   J. PLÜCKER to M. FARADAY, 24 March 1856
[*I.E.E., previously unpublished*]

Bonn
24/3 56.

DEAR SIR!

Looking at the date of your last kind letter,[1] I am very much surprised that my silence had been so long a one. Being another time by election at the head of the University, I am for a year rather intirely [*sic*] distracted from scientific working. Therefore, that I may not fall into my former indolence, I write to you the very first day of „vacances". [*sic*]

My best thanks for your last interesting paper.[2] There is one conclusion in it, I fully adopt. The paramagnetic induction is augmented by the reciprocal action of the particles of the induced body. The diamagnetic induction must be *weakened* by the same reason. When the contrary would be proved by experiment, I shall be forced to give up diamagnetic polarity. But ancient experiments dont encourage myself, to take up again this „experimentum crucis". –

Since several years doubts rose in my mind against the theory I had imagined to connect together the complicated magnetic phenomena, exhibited by crystals. In crystals with only one optic axis, acted upon by a magnetic pole, this axis may be theoretically regarded as a line of polarity, or as the direction of resulting magnetic action. In biaxial crystals I (badly) imagined two such lines of resulting magnetic action, of which depends the position of the crystal between the poles. No experiment contradicted this theory, till July last I undertook a new series of experiments. With the same flexibility of mind, I modified before the theory, when forced by new discoveries, I now altogether give it up, substituting to it a new one, which gives to the various observed facts a new interpretation. I comunicated, on Mr. Moigno's demand, a first account of it in the Cosmos, September last, when I was in Paris.[3] Cutting of the introductory phrase and the Epilogue you will find my own words. Unhappily I got no copy to send it to you. – To the former two axes I substitute two new ones, depending upon the crystalline structure of the crystal. When the crystal suspended between the two poles, in such a way that one of these two axes be perpendicular, *there is no extraordinary magnetic action.* These two axes for instance, in the case of „cyanure rouge de fer et potasse" are placed in the plane of the two optic axes, both systems of axes have the same midle [*sic*] line, only the angle included by the magnetic axes is about 42°, while the angle included by the optic axes is only 20°. &c &c.

When you say any part, that my theory does not hold, you mean surely that theory „octroyée" to me by Mr. Tyndall.[4] The phrase I at first employed may be translated allso [*sic*] into Englisch: [*sic*] „the force which produces this repulsion is independent of the magnetic or diamagnetic condition of the mass" (Phil. Trans. 1855 p 2) but its real meaning was „the force exists in both cases, „the mass may be either magnetic or diamagnetic." Thus it was understood by *all* germain [*sic*] philosophers I know.

Mr Tyndalls laws printed with italic letters in his paper p. 12 & 13 signifie [*sic*],[5] I think, nothing at all. Indeed how may you observe the magneto-crystallic action if not by the displacement of a diamagnetic body from the equatorial to the axial position, of a paramagnetic body from the axial to the equatorial? Mr Tyndall fights against my theory of two conflicting forces, which never did exist (p. 13). The fact is that I gave 1849 before he published any paper, an mathematical expression of the force (couple) emanating from the pole of a Magnet and acting upon an uniaxial crystal. This expression contains two terms with opposite signs ($\pm$), indicating that the whole force may be mechanically divided into two forces, acting upon the crystall [*sic*] in opposite sense. You may call them conflicting forces; whether of both predominates depends on the distance from the poles. I *never* theoretically admitted a magnetic action on an ideal line, in conflict with the comon magnetic or diamagnetic action. After fighting against a theory, which never was mine, Mr T. gives in the Appendix (p. 44 seq.) the very same explication I gave 1849 to explain by a popular fact the principle of my calculus, relating to uniaxial crystals.

After having given to you, I hope in an intelligible Englisch, these incomplete explications, a stone, as we say in German, is fallen from my breast. Instead of fruitless discussions I think it more proper to present to the Roy. Society an elaborate paper,[6] containing the general theory of magnetocrystallic action founded on a new series of experiments. I have all reason to hope that the new theory will be generally adopted; it is no more contradicted by Poisson's, Green's & Thomson's calculus based on molecular action.

Dear Sir! The extreme kindness, with which you received my very first experimental researches is that moment in my scientific life, at which I look bak with the greatest satisfaction. When recently I had the honour to be elected a Foreign membre [*sic*] of the Royal Society, the origin of it is to be found only in that kindness.

With all my heart and for ever
Yours

PLÜCKER.

[1] This letter is missing.
[2] 30th Series, *ERE*.
[3] J. Plücker, 'Action du magnétisme sur les axes des cristaux', *Cosmos*, 7 (1855), 391.
[4] John Tyndall, 'On the nature of the Force by which Bodies are repelled from the Poles of a Magnet; to which is prefixed an Account of some Experiments on Molecular Influences', *PT* (1855), 1. See the footnote on p. 2 marked by an asterisk for Plücker's phrase.
[5] *Ibid.*, 12 and 13.
[6] J. Plücker, 'On the magnetic induction of crystals', *PT* (1858), 543.

628 M. FARADAY to J. PLÜCKER, 8 April 1856
[*Nat. Res. Counc. Canada, previously unpublished*]

Royal Institution
8 April 1856

Private

MY DEAR PLÜCKER

I have been and am suffering from much weariness and giddiness in the head and have, in consequence, delayed writing several days in hopes I should feel better; but as that is not the case, I will not delay any longer replying to your last, since I think you will be wishing for my answer. I am very sorry for the sort of feeling which seems to have arisen between You and Tyndall, and would do all I could to remove it; but I know the great difficulty having had several of these cases before, and never found that much good could be done. I laboured hard in that between Du bois-Reymond & Matteucci, but I do not think with any good result. It is a pity; – for I cannot but believe that Science may be pursued, and the most opposite notions be entertained, by two parties, who yet can be on most open & friendly terms with each other. My memory is so imperfect now, that I am in a very bad condition when I want to recall the points about which differences arise, and I cannot recollect to what you may refer at that part of your letter "when you say any part that my theory does not hold you mean surely that theory "octroyée" to me by Mʳ Tyndall." I think I have seen the gradual development of your thoughts since the first forthcoming of your most beautiful results in Magnecrystallic action. You like all of us, have *developed* and as the facts came forth, your views & reasoning enlarged with them, but I do not recollect that Tyndall ever offered or that I ever drew from him my understanding of your views. Tyndall and I differ in toto on some points – but we do not differ in our friendly views because of that. He considers that his last paper in the Philosophical Transactions establishes a reverse polarity in bismuth; I believe it simply shews in an extensive & perfect manner the complete antithesis of Iron & bismuth which however was known before.

Of course all the points regarding discovery or the precedence of one philosophers views before another, in respect of date, can be settled perfectly by reference to dates of published communications; and when I have occasion to make historical statements, which I have had to do in regard to both Davy & Wollaston,[1] I thought it best to make them as direct & brief as possible, – to publish them in the journals, & then to leave them. I never thought it wise or effectual to mix philosophical development and controversial matter together; and therefore I agree heartily with your words when you write "instead of fruitless discussions I think it more proper to present to the Royal Society an elaborate paper containing the general theory of magneto-crystallic action founded on a *new series* of experiments." I have not been able for several years to occupy myself with the Royal Society or its management, & therefore do not know what its guiding principles are now; but the rules were (formerly) to admit no matter that had already been published elsewhere, nor any controversial matter, – nor any merely hypothetical matter; and on the whole I think they are very good rules, & have always tried to conform to them

And now my dear friend I hope this cloud will soon pass away. I always try to forget such points as these; and when I meet with a controversial passage in a paper, endeavour to prevent it from exerting the least influence on my mind; and the fact is, that I cannot, & do not want to, remember the passages in Tyndalls paper which seem to have annoyed you. If I saw them now I do not believe they would cause me to come to any conclusion that I should not arrive at without them; for I naturally doubt such passages in all cases.

Long may you labour as you have done for the good of science; & one thing I think I learn from your letter, – that you are in good health & excellent working condition. For my own part, I look with great thankfulness to my own personal share in the work, as to a thing that *has been* and is passing away; but it has left me cheerful, and happy in watching the pursuits of others – that

band of brothers which has done so much in these last years of time for the
advancement of science

Ever My dear Plucker
Yours Most Truly
M. FARADAY

[1] M. Faraday, 'Reply to Dr. John Davy's "Remarks on certain statements of Mr. Faraday contained in his 'Researches in Electricity'"', *ENPJ*, 20 (1835–6), 37, and 'Historical Statement respecting Electro-Magnetic Rotation', *QJS*, 15 (1823), 288.

629   K. W. KNOCHENHAUER to M. FARADAY, 17 April 1856

[I.E.E., previously unpublished]

Meiningen,
le 17 avril 1856.

MONSIEUR,

En Vous remerciant sincèrement de la lettre, dont Vous avez eu la bonté de m'honorer, j'ose Vous présenter une traduction du mémoire publié en 1854 dans les annales de Poggendorff.[1] Ce n'est pas que j'espère Vous communiquer rien de nouveau, car mes expériences ne sont qu'une répétition des Vôtres, le seul point, auquel je Vous prie de prêter quelque attention, c'est l'observation, qu'une plaque d'un corps isolateur n'a qu'une faible influence sur l'induction, quand elle est séparée des deux plateaux condensateurs, tant de l'un que de l'autre, tandis que son influence s'augmente, quand elle touche le plateau, qui contient l'électricité induite, et encore plus, quand elle est en contact avec le plateau, qui reçoit l'électricité libre. (Voyez Votre Série XI–1271). Quelle que soit la cause de ce résultat, soit que la formation des lignes de force, douées de polarisation, en pénétrant par divers milieux s'affaiblisse par une espece de réflexion, comme nous le trouvons dans la lumière, soit que l'affaiblissement provienne de ce que les molécules de deux corps, qui se touchent, ne sont pas en contact parfait, peutêtre [*sic*] cette observation Vous donnera l'occasion de demander à Mr. Riess[2] selon l'ancienne théorie une explication complète des observations, où les plaques isolatrices remplissent tout l'espace entre les plateaux condensateurs. Il me serait très important, que par Votre autorité Vous pussiez amener une telle explication, car comme elle ne me parait pas possible sans supposer que l'électricité pénètre par le corps isolateur même et outre cela par les corps de diverse épaisseur jusqu'à une profondeur dépendante de l'épaisseur, on pourrait examiner très facilement cette hypothèse, en employant des *plateaux* condensateurs, d'où les corps isolateurs se laissent retirer commodement, aussi ceux, qui doivent s'être remplis d'électricité selon l'ancienne théorie. Une telle explication complète me serait outre cela très importante pour les expériences, que j'ai publiées depuis quelques années sur le courant de la batterie secondaire et surtout pour celles de cette espèce qui sont comuniquées dans les rapports des séances de l'Académie de Vienne en novembre 1855. Bien sûr que ces expériences ne peuvent être expliquées sans supposer un certain arrangement des molécules ou, comme je le nomme, une chaîne formée des molécules du fil, que parcourt le courant de la batterie primaire, d'ailleurs sans supposer que des lignes de force transfèrent cet arrangement sur le fil conducteur de la batterie secondaire, et que cette nouvelle chaîne cause la charge de cette batterie et par cela le courant qu'elle excite, il m'est impossible à présent de trouver en Allemagne des physiciens, qui veuillent se donner la peine de répéter ces expériences, parce qu'ils sont convaincus que des expériences sont faites mal-adroitement, qui amènent les idées de lignes de force et surtout les idées que l'électricité n'est qu'un arrangement et qu'un mouvement particulier des molécules. Pour surcroît de malheur Mr. Riess a publié en 1854[3] aussi quelques expériences de ce même genre, mais d'une manière à déranger parfaitement les résultats; en conséquence il a assuré que ces observations sont tellement compliqués [sic] qu'elles ne méritent pas d'être continuées.

Excusez-moi, Monsieur, je Vous prie, d'avoir abusé si long-temps de Votre patience, et agréez l'assurance de la haute estime, avec laquelle j'ai l'honneur d'être

Monsieur
Votre très dévoué et très
obéissant serviteur
K. W. KNOCHENHAUER.

[1] K. W. Knochenhauer, 'Ueber den Einfluss der Nichtleiter, auf die Stärke der electrischen Induction', *AP*, 169 (1854), 407.
[2] See Letters 614 and 618.
[3] P. Riess, 'Ueber die Wirkung nicht-leitender Körper bei der electrischen Influenz', *AP*, 168 (1854), 401.

630   C. MATTEUCCI to M. FARADAY, 1 May 1856
[*P.M., 4 s., 11 (1856), 461*]

May 1, 1856

MY DEAR FRIEND,

I think I have already told you that for some time past I have been making experiments in electro-physiology. Allow me now to communicate to you the results of my work.

I have lately succeeded in demonstrating and measuring the phænomenon which I have called *muscular respiration*. This respiration, which consists in the absorption of oxygen and the exhalation of carbonic acid and azote by living muscles, and of which I have determined the principal conditions and intensity compared with that of the general respiration of an animal, has been studied particularly on muscles in contraction. I have proved that this respiration *increases considerably* in the act of contraction, and have measured this increase.

A muscle which contracts, absorbs, while in contraction, a much greater quantity of oxygen, and exhales a much greater quantity of carbonic acid and azote, than does the same muscle in a state of repose. A part of the carbonic acid exhales in the air, the muscle imbibes the other part, which puts a stop to successive respiration and produces *asphyxy of the muscle*. Thus a muscle soon ceases to contract under the influence of an electro-magnetic machine when it is enclosed in a small space of air: this cessation takes place after a longer interval of time if the muscle is in the open air, and much more slowly still if there be a solution of potash at the bottom of the recipient in which the muscle is suspended. Muscles which have been kept long in vacuum or in hydrogen are nevertheless capable, though in a less degree, of exhaling carbonic acid while in contraction; this proves clearly that the oxygen which furnishes the carbonic acid exists in the muscle in a state of combination. According to the theories of Joule, Thomson, &c., the chemical action which is transformed, or which gives rise to heat, is also represented by a certain quantity of *vis viva*, or by an equivalent of mechanical work. I have therefore been able to measure the *theoretical work* due to the oxygen consumed, taking the numbers which I had found for muscular respiration during contraction, and in consequence the quantity of heat developed by this chemical action, and finally this *theoretical work* according to the dynamical equivalent of heat. I have compared this number with that which expresses the *real work* which is obtained by measuring the weight which a muscle in contraction can raise to a certain height, and the number of contractions which a muscle can perform in a given time. It results from this comparison, that the first number is somewhat greater than the second, and the heat developed by contraction ought to be admitted among the causes of this slight difference: these two numbers are therefore sufficiently in accordance with each other.

I completed these researches by some new studies on *induced contraction*, that is to say, on the phænomenon of the irritation of a nerve in contact with a muscle in contraction. A great number of experiments lately made on the discharge of the torpedo, and on the analogy between this discharge and muscular contraction, have led me to establish the existence of an electrical discharge in the act of muscular contraction. The general conclusion to be drawn from these researches is, therefore, that the chemical action which accompanies muscular contraction developes in living bodies, as in the pile or in a steam-engine, heat, electricity, and *vis viva*, according to the same mechanical laws.

Allow me to describe to you briefly the only one of these experiments which can be repeated in a lecture, and which proves the principal fact of these researches, although it is limited to prove that muscles in contraction develope a greater quantity of carbonic acid than those in repose. Take two wide-mouthed glass phials of equal size, 100 or 120 cub. centims.; pour 10 cub. centims. of lime-water (eau de chaux) into each of these phials. Prepare ten frogs in the manner *of Galvani*, that is, reducing them to a piece of spinal marrow, thighs and legs without the claws, which are cut in order to avoid contact with the liquid in the phials. The cork of one of these phials is provided with five hooks, either of copper or iron, on which five of the prepared frogs are fixed. Through the cork of the other phial are passed two iron wires, bent horizontally in the interior of the phial; the other five frogs are fixed by the spinal marrow to these wires. This preparation must be accomplished as rapidly as possible, and both the phials be ready at the same instant, and great care taken to avoid the contact of the frogs with the sides of the phials or the liquid. When all is in readiness, with a pile of two or three elements of Grove, and with an electro-magnetic machine such as is employed for medical purposes, the five frogs suspended on the two iron wires are made to contract. After the lapse of five or six minutes, during which time the passage of the current has been interrupted at intervals in order to keep up the force of the contractions, agitate gently the liquid, withdraw the frogs, close rapidly the phials, and agitate the liquid again. You will then see that the lime-water contained in the phial in which the frogs were contracted is much whiter and more turbid than the same liquid contained in the other phial in which the frogs were left in repose. It is almost superfluous to add, that I made the complete analysis of the air in contact with the frogs according to the methods generally employed.

Yours faithfully,
A. MATTEUCCI.

631   M. FARADAY to J. LIEBIG, 1 May 1856
   [*Universitetsbiblioteket Uppsala, previously unpublished*]

R. I.,
1 May 1856.

MY DEAR LIEBIG

I have long been desirous of writing to you, but laziness or weariness (and I think more of the latter than the former) have until now hindered me. I want to thank you for your great kindness shown to my nephew Mr. Frank Barnard. I assure you he is very sensible of it, and expresses himself in strong terms to us, upon this matter. He seems to find himself far more in a home atmosphere than he did at Paris. His sister Jane, whom you may remember meeting here and who is of a warm affectionate temperature [*sic*], feels very strongly your kindness to her brother. I have to thank you, too, for your kindness in sending me a photograph of Mr. Barlow. Your Munich photographs delight me very much; for I am not fond of those which I see about in London, coloured up so highly that all simplicity is taken away from them. I suppose the owners think them fine & elaborate, I think them common place & often vulgar.

As to science, I have little to say in my own name. I would say much in Yours; – but *that* perhaps you would wish me to be silent about. Nevertheless, my deep admiration of your character & your services to the good cause will steal out, so personal these few words – When I sit too, to think, I become headachy & giddy & think to no purpose; so am content to wait for what may be suggested or occur. I shall have a commonplace paper or two to send you at some opportunity, but they are only evidences of the will to work & think, not of the power.

> Ever my dear Liebig,
> Yours Most truly
> M. FARADAY

632 A. DE LA RIVE to M. FARADAY, 14 May 1856
[*I.E.E., previously unpublished*]

> Genève
> le 14 Mai 1856

MONSIEUR & TRÈS CHER & EXCELLENT AMI,

Je n'étais pas à Genève quand votre lettre y est arrivée;[1] elle m'a été expédiée à Paris où je me trouvais alors en séjour avec ma famille ayant été passer quelque temps dans cette ville auprès de mon fils second qu'y [reading doubtful] achève ses études. Je viens vous remercier de votre bon & aimable souvenir. Si vous saviez combien je tiens à tout ce qui vient de vous & combien je suis touché de votre excellente amitié pour moi. C'est de toutes les distinctions ou plutôt de tous les services que m'a rendus la Science celui de beaucoup que j'apprécie le plus. Car qu'est-ce que le reste à côté de ce qui concerne le coeur? *Vanité des vanités*, le plus souvent.

J'ai appris avec chagrin que vous aviez été un peu souffrant & que vous aviez été au bord de la mer vous faire un peu de bien. J'espère que ce remède vous aura réussi; mais il vous faut du repos; il faut que cette tête qui travaille toujours, sache s'habituer à rester quelquefois un peu oisive. Il n'y a que le coeur auquel il soit permis de ne jamais se reposer; mais chez vous tout est actif la tête & le coeur. Je sais bien que ce n'est pas sur cette terre que nous pouvons & que nous devons espérer trouver le repos; le vrai repos, [illeg.] & salutaire, nous ne pourrons le trouver que dans le Sein de Dieu; mais il ne nous est pas interdit cependant d'en chercher un peu l'avant goût dès ici bas.

J'ai profité de mon séjour à Paris pour voir bien des choses intéréssantes & en particulier les nouvelles expériences de Foucault,[2] & celles de Mr. Bernard[3] le physiologiste, qui sont très curieuses. – J'ai moi-même entrepris quelques nouvelles recherches sur les phénomènes d'induction qui ont lieu avec de très grandes vitesses, & j'ai trouvé pour les faire, de grandes facilités dans le Conservatoire des Arts & Métiers où l'on a mis avec beaucoup d'obligeance à ma disposition les instruments & les aides dont j'avais besoin. Je ne tarderai pas à publier le résultat de ces recherches que mon fils qui m'a aidé à les faire, continue sans moi depuis que j'ai quitté Paris.

Vous avez peut-être vu dans le dernier n° de la *Bibl. Univ.* que Mde [reading doubtful] Soret & moi nous avons réussi à montrer que l'eau est décomposée même dans la propagation de l'électricité qui résulte de l'induction statique.[4] C'est en nous servant d'eau [illeg.] isolée d'une bouteille de Leyde que nous avons obtenu ce résultat.

Mon frère qui est à Londres dans ce moment serait bien heureux s'il pouvait avoir le plaisir de vous voir avant son départ; j'espère qu'il me rapportera de bonnes nouvelles de vous. – Ma femme me charge expréssement de la rapeller à votre bon souvenir & à celui de Madame Faraday. Veuillez aussi présenter mes respects à Madame Faraday.

Votre tout dévoué & affectionné ami
A. DE LA RIVE

[1] See Letter 626.
[2] Jean Bernhard Léon Foucault (1819–68), inventor of the Foucault pendulum for illustrating the rotation of the earth on its axis. It is of these experiments with the pendulum that de la Rive speaks.
[3] Claude Bernard (1813–78), the discoverer of the glycogenic function of the liver. It is impossible to decide what experiments de la Rive refers to here for Bernard was working on a number of things. See *RSCSP* for the papers he published in 1856.
[4] J. L. Soret (1827–90), 'Sur la décomposition électro-chimique de l'eau servant de conducteur dans les phénomènes d'induction électro-statique', *ASPN*, 31 (1856), 204.

633 K. W. KNOCHENHAUER to M. FARADAY, 15 May 1856
[*I.E.E., previously unpublished*]

Meiningen,
le 15 mai 1856

MONSIEUR,

Vous trouverez sûrement très importun que je Vous incommode encore une fois, surtout où Vous êtes hors d'état d'examiner Vous-même les faits, ce que je regrette beaucoup. Cependant Votre lettre m'ayant convaincu, que l'induction doit être étudiée encore plus profondément pour dérober tout appui à l'ancienne théorie, je me suis aussitôt résolu à entreprendre quelques nouvelles recherches. Et voilà, comme je le crois, que Vos lignes de polarisation se laissent démontrer tout clairement par les expériences, j'espère donc pouvoir me prometre Votre indulgence, si j'ose Vous communiquer mes observations. – Du condensateur, dont les plateaux ont environ deux pouces de diamètre, je joignis le plateau inférieur au sol, et je communiquai au plateau supérieur de l'électricité positive, en le touchant avec la boule d'une bouteille de Leyden chargée plus ou moins fortement. L'intervalle des plateaux était rempli tantôt d'une ou de plusieurs plaques de verre (c'étaient les plaques *B C D* d'auparavant), tantôt les plaques étaient séparées l'une de l'autre par une couche d'air (quelques petits morceaux de verre interposés aux bords servaient à ce but), tantôt la plaque ne touchait que l'un des plateaux du condensateur, tantôt elle était éloignée de l'un et de l'autre. Toutes les fois après avoir retiré le plateau supérieur je trouvais la face supérieure de chaque plaque (c'est à dire celle qui avait été dirigée vers le plateau supérieur) chargée d'électricité positive et la face inférieure chargée d'électricité négative. Pour examiner cette charge j'avais muni l'électromètre à feuilles d'or d'un plateau, et après y avoir mis l'une des faces je couvris l'autre d'un autre plateau, afin d'en affaiblir l'influence, tout à fait de la manière, que Vous avez indiquée. – En voulant étendre un peu plus ces expériences, je me procurai encore 8 tables carrées de verre de vitre munies d'une mince couche de laque, de même 4 tables de soufre et une faible plaque de laque. Le tout exécuté comme auparavant, je fus étonné de trouver presque toujours sur les deux faces la même électricité, tantôt positive, tantôt négative, je répétai les observations avec les anciennes plaques et toujours les deux électricités sur les deux faces. Pour ôter l'électricité aux plaques, je plaçai les tables de vitre dans un forneau [*sic*], où elles s'échauffèrent un peu; mais ce moyen n'étant pas applicable à la plaque de laque, je fis usage d'une flamme d'alcohol, cependant sans atteindre mon but; même deux flammes ensemble des deux côtés de la plaque ne détruisirent point l'électricité. Aussi les tables de vitre ne voulaient pas perdre leur électricité, quand elles étaient exposées pendant quelques temps aux deux flammes. En examinant souvent les tables je trouvai qu'après l'usage de la flamme les deux faces étaient chargées d'électricité contraire, l'une d'électricité positive l'autre d'électricité négative. Dès ce moment tout était éclairci. Les plaques, qui se sont trouvées entre les plateaux du condensateur, sont chargées de deux espèces d'électricité, l'une recouvre legèrement les surfaces et peut être détruite tout à fait promptement quand on approche la plaque d'une flamme, l'autre a sa source dans la polarisation, n'est détruite qu'avec beaucoup de peine, et met la face supérieure en état positif, l'inférieure en état négatif. Les anciennes plaques, dont les surfaces étaient déjà un peu altérées par l'usage, perdirent l'électricité fugitive de la surface pendant le temps, qu'on les retirait du condensateur; aussi l'état de polarisation disparut après un quart d'heure environ, tandis que les nouvelles tables le conservèrent très long-temps, surtout les tables de soufre et de laque, où il resta même pendant quelques jours. – Maintenant la manière d'expériemenrer fut la suivante. Après avoir mis les tables sur le plateau inférieur du condensateur et les avoir couvertes du plateau supérieur, celuici était chargé plus ou moins fortement selon le nombre des plaques et aussitôt enlevé; alors j'examinais chaque plaque l'une après l'autre sur l'électricité libre en l'approchant de l'électromètre et sans faire usage du plateau affaiblissant, ensuite je promenais quelques moments chaque plaque devant la flamme, et enfin j'en examinais l'état électrique des deux faces, qui avait sa source

Les tables de vitre

	:avant l'usage :de la flamme	:après l'usage :de la flamme
1	pos.	régul.
2	nég.	,,
3	pos.	,,
4	nég.	,,

Les tables de vitre (charge forte)

	:avant l'us. :d.l.fl.	:après l'us. :d.l.fl.
5	pos.	régul.
6	nég.	,,
7	nég.	,,
8	pos.	,,

::Les tables ::de vitre

	:avant l'us. :d.l.fl.	:après l'us. :d.l.fl.
1	pos.	régul.
2	nég.	,,
3	pos.(faible)	,,
4	pos.	,,
5	nég.(fort)	,,
6	nég.	,,
7	pos.	,,
8	pos.	,,

Les tables d. vitre

	avant l'us. :d.l.fl.	après l'us. :d.l.fl.
D	—	régul.
1	pos.	,,
2	nég.	,,
3	pos.	,,
4	nég.	,,
B	—	,,

::Les tables ::de soufre

	:avant l'us. :d.l.fl.	:après l'us. :d.la flâme
1	pos (fort)	régul.
2	pos.(faible)	,,
3	nég.(faible)	,,
4	nég.(fort)	,,

::Les tables de vitres sont séparées l'une de l'autre par des couches d'air.

		:avant l'us. d.l.fl.	:après l'us. d.l.fl.	:avant l'us. :d.la fl.	:après l'us.:: :d.la fl.	:avant l'us.:: :d.l. fl.	:après l'us. :d. l.fl.
Les tables de soufre	D: 1:	pos.	régul.	régul.	régul.	5 : pos.	régul.
	2:	nég.(faible)	,,	6 : ,,		6 : nég.	,,
	3:	o	,,	7 : ,,		7 : nég.	,,
	4:	nég.(faible)	,,	8 : ,,		8 : pos.	,,
Les tables de vitre	1:	pos.	o	D: 1 : pos.			
	2:	nég.	o	2 : nég.			
	3:	pos.	o	3 : nég.(faible)			
	4:	nég.	o	4 : pos.(fort)			

Les tables de vitre avaient déja perdu l'état faible ::Avec 8 tables l'état de polarisation ne se conser [ms. torn] pas bien.

Les tables de vitre avaient déja perdu l'état de polarisation.

dans la polarisation. Voilà quelques séries. Les nombres donnent les plaques de haut en bas et le mot: régulièrement signifie que la face supérieure était en état positif, l'inférieure en état négatif.

Quelle que soit la cause de l'électricité libre, qui recouvre les tables, soit qu'elle vienne de l'air, qui se trouve entre les surfaces et qui reçoit aussi la polarisation, soit qu'elle ait une autre source, sûrement elle n'exerce aucune influence appréciable sur la charge du condensateur, et la distribution, qui paraît être modifiée par le degré de la charge, et de telle manière, que l'ancienne théorie n'en tirera aucun secours; aussi est-elle si faible que la flamme l'enlève aussitôt. La polarisation des tables, qui est retenue avec une si grande force, s'étend sans doute par toute la masse des tables, d'ailleurs elle serait aussi détruite par la flamme, et chacune des tables ne pourrait la montrer. Pour moi, je ne peux douter, que ces observations ne prouvent ce que Vous avez nommé les lignes de polarisation, et si Vous n'avez pas encore perdu la patience de répondre j'écouterais avec grand plaisir ce que Vous en jugez.

Agréez, Monsieur, l'assurance de la haute estime, avec laquelle j'ai l'honneur d'être

Votre très dévoué et très obéissant serviteur
KNOCHENHAUER

634   G. G. STOKES to M. FARADAY, 16 June 1856
[*I.E.E., previously unpublished*]

Pembroke College
Cambridge
June 16, 1856

MY DEAR SIR,

I have looked again for my piece of ruby glass, but without success. But I do not think it of much consequence. I distinctly recollect examining it for fluorescence, and finding that it had none, or at least no more than a colourless glass, none which could be in any way connected with the colouring substance. I distinctly recollect noticing that there was more "false dispersion" or scattered light than in colourless glasses, but it did not occur to me that this was connected with the colour by transmitted light. According to the best of an imperfect recollection the dispersing particles were somewhat sparse, not giving an apparently continuous beam like what is seen in the gold mixture from phosphorus. But I am by no means sure of this. It was fluorescence I was seeking after, and finding that this was only a case of "false dispersion" I paid little attention to it. I think it much more probable that the ruby glass I examined was like what you have examined than that my vague supposed recollection of the discontinuity of the dispersed beam was correct.

You have clearly shown that the colouring matter in the phosphorus-gold-mixture is in suspension, but I cannot believe that it is metallic gold.[1] Such a supposition is utterly at variance with my optical experience. I know of *no* instance in which the same substance exhibits two totally different characters as to absorption, such as do the $FeO.SO^3$-gold and phosphorus-gold mixtures. Many cases occur in which the tint is quite different according to the thickness looked through; but the prism shows that these are among the instances in which the identity of the character of the absorption is most markedly exhibited. Moreover the transmitted colour of the $FeO.SO^3$-gold mixture agrees, but that of the phosphorus gold mixture does not agree, with what might have been predicted from the reflected colour of gold. I can not help believing in the existence of a purple oxide.

Yours very truly
G. G. STOKES

[1] Throughout 1856, Faraday was working on the effect of finely dispersed gold particles in colloidal suspensions on light.

635   M. FARADAY to G. G. STOKES, 17 June 1856
[*Joseph Larmor, 'Memoir and Scientific Correspondence of the late Sir George Gabriel Stokes, Bart.', 150*]

Royal Institution
17 June 1856

MY DEAR SIR,

I am much obliged for your letter. Though I have a strong impression on the side of the question which admits that finely divided particles of gold may transmit ruby light, yet as I said I am by no means certain. I mean to work out the point. Electric explosions of gold wire seem to present an easy way of settling the question, as they may be made to occur in hydrogen, carbonic acid, and other gases; but I want to idle for a time, so I shall put your letter with my experimental notes and resume both together.

Ever truly yours,
M. FARADAY

636   J. LIEBIG to M. FARADAY, 27 July 1856
[*I.E.E., previously unpublished*]

München
27 July, 56

MY DEAR FARADAY,

I beg you to excuse myself for having so longtime delayed to answer your letter of the 1 May for which I beg to accept my best thanks.

Since last year I find myself engaged in a very stupid controversy with Mr

844

Lawes[1] of Rothamsted about Scientific principles in Agriculture. Having never read or understood my book he pretended to demonstrate by experiments that the Science of Chemistry could do nothing for practical Agriculture and that the knowledge of Laws of nature could not be of any use in practical farming! Mr Lawes is, I believe, a manufacturer of manure and by my disputing his scientific position and showing that his conclusions are erroneous he thinks to loose his customers; This is, I fear, the reason that he went so far as to attack my good faith in an Article (No 36) of the Journal of the Roy. agric. Soc. of England.[2] I was obliged to write an article for the Same journal, which will appear in the N° of July and in which I hope to have succeeded in uprooting his errors.[3]

You have always the good fortune, to find for all your works and investigations a well disciplined public which acknowledged gratefuly [sic] and accepted with thanks the immense services you rendered to Science and to mankind; but in Chemistry and its applications to Agriculture and Physiology I have to deal with a set of people without any Scientific education and who know, or believe to know, all these things better than the natural philosopher himself. I despair sometimes to be able to convince them of the most simple truth. It is that sort of people who believe on walking tables and all kind of nonsensical theory's [sic]. Being occupied during ten years with other researches I did not care about the opposition of the so called practical men, but last year I became aware that they fighted with a Shadow and that they failed to discern the truth which my theory contained. I should never have thought to answer any articles, if the questions which are involved in that controversy were not of such great importance to mankind. We are advanced far enough to decide the question about the right way to produce more corn and more meat from the same surface of land. The fortune and income of most people depend on them.

I should think that you could do a great deal of good by a lecture „on the methods to apply Scientific principles to practical purposes„ next winter in the royal institution! Perhaps you have the goodness to read my article in the Journal of the Roy. Agr. Soc. and it is possible you find matter in it for such a lecture. If my conclusions and inferences have your assent, I am sure all this opposition will cease and a truly scientific agriculture will commence.

Mr Fr. Barnard[4] is an excellent young man we like him very much and are always glad to see him in our house; he is not coming so often as we wish it and it requires mostly an formal invitation to see him; he is to [sic] strict an Englishman. The german custom is to go to take thea [sic] with his friends without these ceremonies. Mr. Barnard is very assiduous and I hear that his professors are much satisfied by his progress. We talk very often of you, his aunt and his aimable Sister. Pray express my kindest regards to them!

Dear Faraday I am with all my heart

Yours very Sincerely
JUSTUS LIEBIG

(Excuse my horrible english!)

845

20-2

1 John Bennet Lawes (1814–1900), founder of the Rothamsted experimental farm. Lawes, in 1842, by treating phosphates with sulphuric acid created the artificial manure industry.
2 John Bennet Lawes and J. H. Gilbert (1817–1901), 'On some points connected with Agricultural Chemistry; being a reply to Liebig's "Principles of Agricultural Chemistry",' *JRAS*, 16 (1855), 411. J. H. Gilbert was a chemist and partner of Lawes.
3 J. Liebig, 'On some points in Agricultural Chemistry', *JRAS*, 17 (1856), 284.
4 See Letter 631.

637 M. FARADAY to T. ANDREWS, 27 July 1856
[*Science Museum, S. Kensington, previously unpublished*]

Royal Institution
27 July 1856

MY DEAR ANDREWS

It gave me great pleasure to receive your kind letter and I shall make myself present to you as soon as I can – We start either tomorrow or Tuesday Morning for Paris & Paris only for I long to see my kind friend Dumas. Very sincere thanks to you for your offer of help & I dare say I shall use some of it: – but the fact is that my memory fails so fast that I dare not trust myself alone so I avail myself of the kind aid & care of my brother in law Mr. George Barnard who accompanies me expressly that he may relieve me in all matter that he can – in fact I am in his hands. He settles when we start and has arranged where we shall go: – he takes all the care of money passports hours. routes – Hotels – calls &c and I trust you will let me present him to you – he is an artist – and knowing Paris pretty well I commit all things into his hands

My kindest remembrances if they may be called so to Mrs. Andrews – I want here to have some of the feeling towards me that her husband has i.e I want her to think of me kindly & favourable – it is very pleasant

Ever My dear Andrews
Most truly Yours
M. FARADAY

638 J. PLATEAU to M. FARADAY, 5 August 1856
[*I.E.E., previously unpublished*]

Gand,
5 Août, 1856.

MON CHER MONSIEUR FARADAY.

Vous recevez sans doute en même temps que cette lettre, trois exemplaires de la *troisième série* de mes recherches sur les figures d'équilibre des liquides;[1] veuillez accepter l'un d'eux et offrir le second, de ma part, à la Société Royale et le troisième à l'Institution Royale. Cette troisième série, jointe à la dernière partie de la *deuxième* forme un ensemble contenant une théorie complète de la constitution des veines liquides lancées par des orifices circulaires et soumises ou non à l'influence de mouvements vibratoires. Ne lisez pas cette troisième serie, car elle ne peut être comprise si l'on ne s'est bien pénétré de celle qui la précède, et le genre de vos propres recherches vous éloigne trop de ce qui concerne les théories capillaires pour que je désire que vous preniez cette peine.

D'ailleurs, j'ai à vous prier de vouloir bien perdre pour moi, d'une autre manière, une petite portion de votre temps, et j'espère que vous ne me refuserez pas; voici ce dont il s'agit; je m'occupe en ce moment à mettre en ordre, pour la publication, un ouvrage que j'avais commencé il y a un grand nombre d'années, et qui est sur le point d'être terminé: c'est une bibliographie en partie analytique des phénomènes subjectifs de la vision tels que la *persistance des impressions*, les *couleurs accidentelles*, &c.[2] Or, je trouve dans mes notes, que l'invention du *Thaumatrope* est due au docteur Paris, et qu'il l'a décrite dans un ouvrage intitulé: *Philosophy in sport made science in earnest*; mais j'ignore le lieu et la date de la publication de cet ouvrage, qui parait n'exister dans aucune bibliothèque de Belgique, et cependant je dois nécessairement l'insérer dans ma bibliographie.[3] Maintenant l'ouvrage étant anglais, ou plutôt, je pense, américain, je me suis dit qu'il devait exister dans les bibliothèques de Londres. Vous me rendriez donc un grand service, si vous vouliez bien prendre la peine de chercher ce même ouvrage, et, si vous le trouvez, de me faire connaître le lieu et la date de la publication, le volume dans lequel se trouve la description du Thaumatrope, et enfin la page où commence cette description.

Si l'ouvrage du Dr Paris est postérieur à l'année 1800, ces renseignements me suffisent, mais s'il a paru dans le siècle précédent, j'aurais besoin de quelque chose de plus, et je ne vous le demande qu'en tremblant, car je sens que je deviens indiscret; si le passage où il est question du Thaumatrope n'est pas long, vous compléteriez le service que j'attends de votre obligeance en le faisant copier pour le joindre aux renseignements précédents; Seulement veuillez ne pas oublier que cela est inutile si l'ouvrage est de notre siècle, et que, si le passage est étendu, je ne veux dans aucun cas que vous vous donniez cet embarras.

Vous me pardonnerez, j'en suis certain d'abuser ainsi de vos bontés pour moi, quand vous réflechirez qu'il m'est absolument impossible d'aller par moi-même consulter les bibliothèques etrangères.

J'ai reçu les différents exemplaires de vos travaux, que vous m'avez fait l'honneur de m'envoyer; les trois derniers serviront à étendre et à compléter vos magnifiques recherches sur le dia-magnétisme; mais permettez-moi de vous exprimer ici toute mon admiration pour l'une de vos découvertes antérieures: Je veux parler de l'induction statique latérale exercée par un courant électrique dans un fil métallique recouvert de gutta percha et plongé dans l'eau.[4] Qui aurait pu s'attendre à pareille chose? Qui aurait pu s'imaginer que la vitesse de transmission de l'électricité eprouverait dans ce cas, un retard considérable? Du reste on est habitué à vous voir enfanter des merveilles.

Encore une fois, mon Cher Monsieur Faraday, Veuillez me pardonner mon importunité, et avoir d'avance mes remerciements.

Agréez l'assurance de tous mes sentiments de respectueuse affection

J[H] PLATEAU

[1] J. Plateau, 'Recherches expérimentales et théoriques sur les figures d'équilibre d'une masse liquide sans pesanteur', 3ème série, *MASB*, 29 (1857).
[2] Joseph Plateau, *Bibliographie analytique des principaux phénomènes subjectifs de la vision, depuis les temps les plus reculés jusqu'à la fin du XVIIIᵉ siècle, suivie d'une bibliographie simple pour la partie écoulée du siècle actuel*, Brussels, 1878–84.
[3] John Ayrton Paris, *Philosophy in Sport made Science in Earnest! being an attempt to illustrate the first principles of Natural Philosophy*, n.p., 1827.
[4] See Letter 543, fn. 3.

639 M. FARADAY to T. ANDREWS, 12 August 1856
[*Science Museum, S. Kensington, previously unpublished*]

Royal Institution
12 Aug 1856

MY DEAR ANDREWS

Your note shocked me very much and my thoughts continually turn to poor Regnault.[1] Mr. Barnard and I were with him at Sevres for several hours together on the previous Friday and saw all his apparatus there and how he mounted himself up in his chair to read his manometer which I think 30 or 40 feet high. I cannot help supposing it was in some of these places he was engaged when he fell & yet cannot call to mind any chimney like that you speak of. When I read the account to Dr. Bence Jones he seemed to hope that the case was not so bad as your note supposed: he thought that though the concussion must have been very great yet that the symptoms were not desperate. I hope it is so and that by this time there is some degree of recovery I shall be very anxious until I know. Mr Barnard will be passing through Paris in a day or two perhaps he may bring me good accounts

I reached home in safety the same day that I left Paris & with a strong remembrance of all your kindness – It was time that I should return for I found when I reached home that I wanted 2 or 3 days rest before I could get out of the exhaustion into which I fell. Now I am quite well again

With kindest regards to Mrs Andrews & remembrances to all friends

I am My dear Andrews
Ever Truly Yours
M. FARADAY

[1] Victor Regnault suffered a severe concussion from a fall in 1856.

Gand,
14 août 1856.

Mon Cher Monsieur Faraday.

Je viens vous témoigner toute ma reconnaissance pour l'obligeance extrême avec laquelle vous avez bien voulu m'envoyer les renseignements relatifs au thaumatrope; ils sont précis, et me suffisent complètement; il ne me reste qu'à vous prier de nouveau de me pardonner l'embarras que je vous ai causé.

J'ai cependant à me plaindre de vous: je vois, par votre lettre, que vous avez été récemment à Paris; comment la bonne pensée ne vous est-elle pas venue de retourner en Angleterre par la Belgique, et de me faire une visite à Gand? J'aurais eu tant de plaisir à vous recevoir. Mais Hélas, quand les savants se décident à pénétrer en Belgique, c'est à Bruxelles qu'ils vont, et il est bien rare qu'ils passent par ici.

Veuillez accepter encore l'hommage d'une note que je viens de publier sur les théories récentes de la constitution des veines liquides,[1] et dont j'ai l'honneur de vous adresser par la poste, trois exemplaires ayant les mêmes destinations que ceux de mon mémoire: Je vous ai engagé à ne pas lire ce dernier; mais je désirerois beaucoup que vous voulussiez bien lire ma note; elle n'est pas longue et cela vous prendra peu de temps. Vous vous rappelez sans doute que, par vos bons offices, la première série de mes recherches sur les figures d'équilibre a été reproduite dans les *Scientific Memoirs* de M. Taylor, mais qu'il n'en a pas été de même de la deuxième série, quoique vous ayez également bien voulu engager M.r Taylor à la faire traduire. Il résulte de là que mes premières expériences sont aujourd'hui bien connues dans votre pays, tandis que celles de ma deuxième série y sont probablement à peu-près ignorées, et qu'ainsi, par exemple, les physiciens anglais en sont toujours aux anciennes idées sur la théorie de la constitution des veines liquides; j'en ai acquis la preuve en lisant, dans le philosophical magazine de 1854, le compte-rendu d'une leçon de M.r Tyndall, ayant en partie les veines liquides pour objet et dans laquelle il n'a pas mentionné mes théories:[2] or, si vous voulez bien prendre connaissance de ma note actuelle, si, après l'avoir lue, vous êtes convaincu, comme je l'espère, et si dans vos conversations avec les savants l'occasion se présente de parler de ce sujet, vous pourrez me rendre un grand service en contribuant efficacement à répandre mes idées et à dissiper ainsi des erreurs accrédités.

Ne répondez pas à cette lettre, je vous ai déjà fait perdre assez de temps, et je ne veux pas que vous en perdiez davantage à cause de moi.

Agréez, Mon Cher Monsieur Faraday, l'assurance de tous mes sentiments de respectueuse affection.

J.H Plateau

P.S. j'apprends qu'il y a du mieux dans la situation de Mr Regnault, et tous les savants s'en félicitent comme moi; vous êtes du reste, sans doute, au courant de son état.

[1] J. Plateau, 'Sur les théories récentes de la constitution des veines liquides lancées par des orifices circulaires', *BASB*, 23 (1856), 737.
[2] J. Tyndall, 'On some Phaenomena connected with the motion of Liquids', a lecture delivered at the Royal Institution on May 19, 1854 and reported in *PM*, 4 s., 8 (1854), 74.

641 M. FARADAY to J. BARLOW, 20 August 1856

[*R.I., previously unpublished*]

Royal Institution,
20 August 1856

MY DEAR BARLOW

I have just received your kind remembrance and intend if I can to catch you whilst you remain at Heidelberg by this letter. I hardly knew whereabout you were & so was delighted with your letter as all was fresh to me We both hope that Mrs. Barlow and yourself for you wanted it have enjoyed & benefited by your journey thus far By the bye are you on your way to Vienna to the Congress of Scientific Men there? Tyndall set off some days ago for the Glaciers & Vienna & Dr. Bence Jones started this morning intending also to reach the Austrian Capital. As you are at Heidelberg give my kindest remembrances to Professor Bunsen I have sent him a paper now & then though I had not the pleasure of his acquaintance but the Chevallier Bunsen & I used often to talk of him and if you come across the former I hope you will convey the expression of my respect & remembrance to him. He has that of all men here

There is a philosopher in Bunsen's Laboratory Matthiessen[1] who sent us some specimens of Lithium Calcium etc I dare say you remember them – will you make kindest remembrances to him from me – I hope he goes on working – I cannot doubt it under such a master having himself such a mind. It is very pleasant to hear of Plucker & the rest you speak of – I was in Paris for 7 days going out of it to Fontainbleau from Saturday to Monday I saw so many kind friends there that I cannot remember them Dr. Andrews was there & we had the rare luck of seeing the Catacombs with a Prince Gortschakoff – there was not much in them except associations & a fine large stock of phosphate of lime in the form of 3000000 skulls skeletons *etc* A more interesting thing was the sight of an Aluminium operation in a reverberatory furnace – the Sodium & the Chloride of Aluminium *etc* which was used in the one operation being enough to fill more than a couple of Buckets – when the slag & the Aluminium was drawn off the latter appeared in portions among the former like round flattened globules 2 inches in diameter. They were also preparing Sodium. – *three* retorts were sending forth their streams at once.

Dumas was very well and very kind so was also Biot, Regnault, Despretz, Le Verrier & all Poor Regnault have you heard of his accident – I was with him for 3 or 4 hours at Sevres & also at the Academy. Two days after he fell a height of not more than 9 feet – alighted on his feet, but with such a concussion on the brain that when found he knew nobody & could see nothing he remained insensible for a long while & was despaired of. However time has gone on & he is a little better & though far from being out of danger there is more hope of him than there was at first.

My wife is pretty well. Jane is at Newcastle. We go to a little house at Hornsey next Wednesday. All the repairs & other matters go on well & steadily. The weather which had been very hot whilst I was in Paris is now rainy and we have even had heavy floods in the midland counties Good bye to you both for the present may you come back to us strong & rejoicing.

Ever Affectly Yours
M. FARADAY

[1] Augustus Matthiessen (1831–70), chemist and later (1862) Professor of Chemistry at St Mary's Hospital, London.

642   J. LIEBIG to M. FARADAY, 17 September 1856

[*I.E.E., previously unpublished*]

Munich
17 Sept 56.

MY DEAR FARADAY,

It is so long ago that I received your kind letter of the 1 Mai that I am quite ashamed to answer it. I always thought that I could communicate to you some news of interest, but I was unfortunate enough to have nothing worthy of faraday! I occupied myself in the last 5 months with agriculture and what is worse with a controversy in agriculture of the most absurd kind.[1] The truth of certain natural laws which some have done me the unwanted honour to call my theory, has been attacked by so called practical men and the questions involved in this controversy seemed to me of such importance for the material progress of nations and for the welfare and prosperity of millions that I determined to enter the lists in defense of them. If you take the trouble to read my paper in the Journal of the Roy. agric. Society No xxxvii Vol xvii Pt. 1,[2] you will understand all what I have to say. My dear friend, my disappointment is very great of being obliged to defend things so simple! By that controversy I have lost all my confidence of the possibility of improving agriculture by teaching scientific principles. What I taught during 15 years has had no effect whatever, it has taken no root. What a singular being is the mind of man. The walking tables, mesmerism and similar nonsense attracts the attention of thousands and the most simple and important truths find their enemy's [*sic*] and opponents and always successfull in opposing them! There was not in England and not in Germany a single man who did take the trouble to signalise the open errors, mistakes and misrepresentations of Mr Lawes and Gilbert about my views! the unknown force acting in the moving tables found hundreds of zealous defensors! I can not find the key for that! You are in this respect in a much better situation; no person believes in your department to understand the questions better than yourself but there is no ignorant medical man or no farmer who does not believe to understand medical or agricultural questions better than the natural philosopher who has thoroughly investigated them! I am dominated by the desire to establish a school of practical farming for the education of teachers of practical Agriculture. It seems to me that there is no other way of showing the application of Scientific principles. It must be done in a large Scale and I am confident to Succeed. I think I could do for Agriculture what I have done 30 years ago for the practical education of experimental chemists. All my friends tell me that it is a folly to give up the most brilliant position which a man of Science has ever held, but I am tired of lecturing; there are so many others which would do it quite as well; I am sick of my Schoolmastership and all my happiness depends to get rid of it. I have to regret that my friends in England hastened 3 years ago to [sic] much to give me in that testimonial a signe [sic] of acknowledgment. If this matter would have been brought before Parliament by the Duke of Argyle – perhaps the english nation would have voted for me a pension which might have given me full liberty to resign my professorship. By this supply I should be in position to spend 3–4 months in Scotland or England and to devote all my powers to agricultural questions. The royal agric. Society has to dispose of large sums annually and a great deal of good could be done by it. But all that is to [sic] late!

Mr. Barnard tells me that he is returning next month to England and to remain there; I am sorry that he is leaving us. We like him all very much; he is such a good natured, honest young man, openhearted and true! he devoted every minute of the day to his studies and I am glad to hear him say that the Stay at Munich was really useful to him. I wish very much that he might direct his attention to introduce in England the Painting with soluble Glas, [sic] of which Mr Barlow has given an interesting lecture. Mr Barnard has all the facility of learning the little secrets of our celebrated Kaulbach[3] to which I introduced him and I think it would give him a start in London. It is something new and most analogous to his painting in water colours or aquarell.

My wife begs to unite with me in kind regards to Mrs. faraday and your nieces. It is my warmest wish to see you and your Lady in Munich and to show you our beautiful mountains. You could repose yourself and enjoy the most solitary life.

Believe me dear faraday
yours very truly
JUSTUS LIEBIG

[1] See Letter 636.
[2] See Letter 636, fn. 3.
[3] Wilhelm von Kaulbach (1805–74), Bavarian painter and illustrator.

643 M. FARADAY to J. LIEBIG, 3 October 1856
[*Bayerische Staatsbibliothek, Munich, previously unpublished*]

Royal Institution
London
3. October 1856

MY DEAR LIEBIG

Your letter, received a few days ago; grieves me, since it shews that you feel very much, the opposition set up by some to your views, and the principles you so effectually advocate.[1] – I say effectually, for though present obstruction arises the truth must ultimately prevail. But we know, as a matter of universal experience, that it never makes way at once; but has to fight through a long course of resistance, arising from invested interest, pride of knowledge falsely so called, retention of old habits, prejudice, &c. and all these your great truths must meet with, just as every other advancing part of science has and is still meeting with, as I think I, for one, perceive in my own department. Moreover I think you are hardly aware of the strong hold your name, and principles, have upon our general population; and of those here who speak for them. Daubeny[2] I believe is one of the latter; – and Playfair, on one of the last Friday Evenings (May 30th). in our Institution in referring to the chemistry of Agriculture (which was his subject) to Mr Lawes and to you, spoke up most earnestly for your views, as he had a right to do; and was, as I can testify, well responded to by the feeling of our audience:[3] – as far as I could judge true Agricultural chemistry is making its way as well as could be expected, considering the enormous mass of persons in the country requiring instruction and the very unprepared state for it in which they were not many years ago. But as I said before how can a man expect, in his own life time, to be truly, recognised; it requires more than one generation to give currency to his highest truths.

Your expressions with regard to my Nephew[4] are most kind and acceptable; and give great comfort to his parents and family. He speaks of you in a manner shewing his deep sense of gratitude for all your kindness, and his respect and veneration for you as a commanding intellect amongst those by which you are surrounded. We hope to see him soon, & to perceive the influence of the minds amongst which he has been sojourning. – His sister thanks you gratefully for him and desires to be remembered. Tell the Baroness, that my wife and I are deeply indebted to her for thinking of us, and, scarcely hoping for any personal opportunity of expressing our feelings, desire *now* to thank her most heartily, with you, for your wishes in our favour – I am becoming old dear

Liebig, and I am losing my memory, & with it the means of enjoying many pleasures; but no loss of memory can make me altogether forget the abundance of mercies I have received & am in possession of, amongst which I hope & ask for the continuance of a contented & cheerful spirit for the short remainder of days.

Ever My dear friend
Yours Most truly
M. FARADAY

[1] See Letter 642.
[2] Charles Daubeny, the Oxford Chemist.
[3] Lyon Playfair, 'On the Chemical Principles involved in Agricultural Experiments', *PRI*, 2 (1854–8), 289.
[4] See Letter 642.

644   M. HESS to M. FARADAY, 5 October 1856
[*I.E.E., previously unpublished*]

Paris,
33, Rue de l'Est,
le 5 octobre 1856

MON VÉNERABLE MAITRE!

J'ai l'insigne honneur de vous remettre ci-jointe une feuille qui peut-être vous interessera, Monsieur, à cause de la matière qu'elle traite, plutôt qu'à cause de la manière tout à fait insuffissante avec laquelle j'ai essayé de la traiter dans une ébauche plus que superficielle.

La feuille que j'ai l'honneur de vous remettre, est un extrait d'une introduction que j'ai publié dans une revue francaise. Elle a déjà paru l'année passée 1855, dans le même mois où Mr. *Foucault* a fait l'expérience que je cite à la fin de la brochure. Il est assez heureux pour moi qu'un an plus tard, c'est à dire dans l'année courante 1856, Mr. *De la Rive*, qui n'avait certainement pas connaissance de mes petits travaux, pas plus que je ne pouvais avoir connaissance de son deuxième volume qui a paru il y a seulement quelque mois, aît terminé ce second volume par la même citation de l'expérience de M. *Foucault* à l'appui de sa théorie qui a une grande analogie avec celle émise dans ma petite brochure. Bien que ma théorie ne coincite pas complètement avec celle de M. De la Rive, cette dernière arrive pourtant à supposer aussi une *rotation d'atomes*, supposition qui est le point principale sur lequel j'appuis une nouvelle théorie de la *gravitation*.

Ce n'est que depuis les dernieres commotions politiques qui m'ont conduit forcement de l'Allemagne, ma patrie, en France, où je demeure comme exilé, que j'ai commencé à m'occuper sérieusement de physique et de chimie, attiré principalement par les ingénieuses recherches et expérimentations, par lesquelles vous avez demontré la liaison qui existe entre l'électricité et l'action chimique.

Conduit par votre opinion sur l'insuffissance de la théorie des atomes pour expliquer les phénomènes électro-chimiques, et desiré de trouver les rapports presentés par vous entre la gravitation et ces phénomènes, j'ai essayé de me rendre compte de ces rapports par une théorie qui n'est, en effet, qu'une hypothése, [sic] tant qu'elle ne sera constatée par l'expérimentation. Mais, quoique je ne désespére pas à parvenir un jour de constater ma théorie par des expériences scientifiques, il est pourtant de mon devoir à vous communiquer, mon vénerable maître, mes tentatives théoriques.

Comme vous verrez, Monsieur, je ne suis pas adversaire absolu de la théorie des atomes. Mais si je crois qu'elle rend bien compte des phénomènes de la chaleur et de la lumière, de même que des actions chimiques, je ne suis pourtant pas de l'avis de M. *De la Rive* quant à sa théorie génerale [sic] des phénomènes électriques. Pour que l'électricité puisse se propager, M. De la Rive suppose toujours un milieu contenant des atomes chimiques, et il explique p. ex. l'arc voltaïque dans le vide par une décharge d'atomes chimiques qui s'en vont d'un bout du conducteur à l'autre. Il y a une objection capitale qui s'oppose à cette theorie. L'électricité s'echappe de la surface des corps conducteurs isolés par l'air, et cela d'autant plus que l'air est rarifié davantage; ce qui a conduit *Mateucci* à supposer qu'elle s'en échapperait entièrement, dans le vide parfait. Il faut en conclure que l'électricité peut exister indépendante d'atomes chimiques – ce qui n'exclut pas que l'éther soit précisément de l'electricité combinée, accumulee, et plus ou moins condensée. Mais cette condensation qui peut produire aussi des atomes, ou de centres, formant le milieu par lequel se propage la chaleur et la lumière, doit produire originairement des atomes beaucoup plus dilatés que les atomes chimiques ou le milieu par lequel se propage p. ex. le son qui impressionne l'oreille, parce que le son se propage infiniment moins vite que la chaleur et la lumière. Je suis donc porté à croire que l'arc voltaïque est produit par l'accumulation de l'électricité et la formation d'atomes étheriens qui réagissent en se condensant et produisent la lumière et la chaleur – et je crois que si l'on pouvait déterminer une condensation, ou une accumulation plus forte de l'electricité dans le vide, il pourrait en resulter la formation d'atomes chimiques, si toutefois les difficultés expérimentales ne seraient insurmontables. Mais beaucoup de difficultés qui paraissent insurmontables, ne le sont pas pour vous, Monsieur; et si vous ne trouvez pas mon hypothése trop folle, peut-être vous vous occuperez de cette expérimentation difficile. – On arriverait par une telle expérimentation à expliquer la formation des nébuleuses dans l'espace, où je suppose de l'électricité accumulée de plus en plus par les déperditions que les corps celestes, et notamment les soleils, éprouvent pendant toute leur existence.

Je vous demande mille fois pardon, Monsieur, de vous entretenir de théorie qui ne sont que des hypothéses dans l'état actuel des sciences. Mais je crois que c'est précisément à un savant si éminent, comme vous, Monsieur, de constater par des expériences ingénieuses les liens déjà pressentis par vous, Monsieur, qui existent entre la gravitation et tous les autres mouvements dynamiques de la matière.

Si vous le permettrez, Monsieur, je vous enverrai mes travaux à mesure qu'ils seront publiés, en commençant par une nouvelle théorie du soleil que je publie maintenant dans une revue naturaliste allemande.

Vous me feriez infiniment heureux, Monsieur, si vous vouliez me daigner de votre avis sur mes tendances [reading doubtful] théoriques. – Agréez, en attendant, vénérable Maître, l'hommage qu'un de vos plus grands admirateurs se permet de vous offrir en comptant sur votre indulgence.

MAURICE HESS
33, Rue de l' Est

645 W. DE LA RUE to M. FARADAY, 11 October 1856
[*I.E.E., previously unpublished*]

London,
110 Bunhill Row,
October 11 1856

MY DEAR MR FARADAY,

I returned only yesterday from Paris through which I passed on my way homeward from Caen in Normandy. I met Graham there and we called together on Pelouze[1] who informed us that Mitscherlich was staying at the Hotel des Princes. – we called but he was unfortunately out. The Paris Mint is overwhelmed with gold which it fails to manufacture fast enough to supply the place of the place [*sic*] of the absent silver five-franc pieces, and much uneasiness exists in Paris as to the result of this monetary disturbance. The processes of manufacture in the Paris mint appear to me to very rough more especially in the founding and rolling of the metals as more than 20 $p\%$ of "blanks" are rejected for errors of weight or defects, and upwards of 10 $p\%$ of the coined pieces & I believe in the London Mint the total rejections do not exceed 5 $p\%$ in both stages.

GOLD LEAF

The deploraizing [*sic*] effects which I noticed in gold leaf were obtained by putting the gold leaf on a copper frame with a long slit in it and holding a

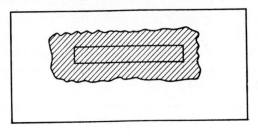

series of these inclined before a lighted taper at an angle of 45° & viewing the transmitted light through a Nichol's prism which was revolved in the hand. I have not repeated the experiment but I will do so.

Yours very truly
WARREN DE LA RUE

¹ Theophile Jules Pelouze (1807–67), chemist.

646 W. DE LA RUE to M. FARADAY, 13 October 1856
[*I.E.E., previously unpublished*]

London,
110 Bunhill Row,
October 13 1856

MY DEAR MR FARADAY

I have repeated the experiment with the gold leaf: –

I find that light passing through a gold leaf held at an angle say of 45° – is polarized, and hence that an obscuration and lightening are produced alternately if the light is viewed through a Nicholl's prism made to rotate.

If the light is first polarized and the analyzer arranged to produce obscuration then the interposition of the gold leaf renders the flaw visible, as you state in your note.

I believe that your explanation is the true one for both cases, and hence that there is no true polarization produced by the gold leaf *in consequence* of the compression by [reading doubtful] hammering.

Yours Very truly
WARREN DE LA RUE

647 M. FARADAY to [no addressee], 1 December 1856
[*R.I., previously unpublished*]

51A Kings Road
Brighton,
1 Decʳ 1856

MY DEAR FRIEND

I purpose writing out an account of the little philosophic incident which interested you so much the other evening, though it is very possible that the interest may sink when the facts are plainly described. A Lady, in walking about her bedroom, ran a needle into the great toe; on searching the floor a part of a needle was found, and there was every reason to believe, from the sensation & other circumstances, that the pointed end, being broken off, was left in the toe: yet neither a friend nor a surgeon could find it there About two months after, and when doubts were entertained by some whether any needle was there or not, I proposed to settle *that* question, & if there, to say in what part of the toe it then had its place, & what was its direction. The following were the means employed. A fine sewing needle was well magnetized & a piece about 1/8th of an inch long was broken off. Then a filament of cocoon silk, about an inch long, had one end attached to the middle of the little magnet by a touch of soft cement, & the other end to the handle of a camel hair brush. In this way a minute test magnetic needle was obtained, which pointed well under the earths power, & could easily be brought near any part of the toe. The toe being examined by this needle, shewed occasional deflexions of the latter, which, being imperfect as indications, still seemed to imply that a piece of the broken needle was there, but rather deeply situated Now, the means of increasing these indications and making them tell their story more perfectly was applied, and upon the following principles. – A piece of unmagnetized needle will affect a little magnet at a distance very feebly, compared to the same piece magnetized: – the unmagnetized piece will affect either end of the test needle alike, whereas the magnetized piece will affect the opposite ends in different ways, attracting one & repelling the other; – A piece of unmagnetized needle can be magnetized at a distance by a magnet of sufficient power, & as well, whilst in the toe as out of it: – also its magnetic state can be reversed if the inducing magnet be reversed, and further it can be, by management, unmagnetized, and being without magnetism is not rendered magnetic whilst the lines of force of the inducing magnet are perpendicular to it. Upon these principles I started, employing a single bar horse shoe magnet made by Logeman, with the poles so far apart that I could introduce my thumb between them. This magnet was brought up to the toe, then taken away & the part examined by the indicating needle, the indication was not stronger than before; hence one of two conclusions was probable; either there was no piece of needle there, or its position was at right angles nearly to the line joining the poles of the inducing magnet when it had been applied – So the latter magnet was employed again in a different position, & now the indicating needle told its story beautifully: shewing the little magnet which had been formed within the toe and which by its power, attracted one end of the needle & repelled the other. A few more trials with the inducing magnet shewed in what position it was able to act most strongly on the hidden needle, and then the position of the magnetic axis of the former indicated the position of the latter. Reversing the position of the inducing magnet instantly changed the magnetism of the buried needle, and now that point of the skin which before attracted the marked end of the indicating needle, repelled it strongly & attracted the other end. It was beautiful to see, when the indicating needle was carried round a given spot on the surface of the toe, how one end always pointed towards that spot; & even moved as if striving to dip down to it. Another indication, which will interest you, was afforded: The direction of the piece of needle and the locality of *one* end was clearly shewn; then came the question where may the other end of the piece be and what is the probable length of the whole? By carrying the indicating needle about the toe, it was found that the opposite end of the piece, though it exhibited an influence over the indicator, did not come near the opposite surface of the toe, but was buried deep in the flesh; and the piece, though manifestly piercing deep, & almost perpendicularly into the flesh, did not come near the other side. I guess it therefore to be about the third of an inch long. Presently we may tell if the needle travels and which way it is going: – all of which will be of great interest to us, who look on philosophically, and likewise to the unlucky possessor of this illustration: who I trust however will soon be able to make the experiments in her hand instead of her foot.

And now my friend here we are very comfortably situated in dry & largish rooms at 51-A Kings Road – and though all tender (I am best) yet we all think it will do us good. I think if you could pop in to a cup of tea – you would approve of our locale & arrangements. Winter is very strong on the outside though perhaps he is going but we do not let him come into the house. Hoping that all with you are pretty well in which hopes as well as for those for yourself my wife & Jeannie joins me

I am
Ever Truly Yours
M. FARADAY

We have no occasion for a Dr. but cannot remember the name of the one you spoke of.

648 M. FARADAY to J. G. MACVICAR,[1] 29 December 1856
[*R. Coll. of Physicians, previously unpublished*]

Royal Institution
London W
29 Decr 1856

MY DEAR SIR

I hasten to thank you for your paper & letter. You work vigorously; & it is well you do so; for your work is before you. I am free to say you are far in advance of me, for I am only an experimentalist, & cannot enter into the very numerous views of natural bodies & forces which have been put forth; otherwise than as they arise in my own mind from my own results. As it is I am esteemed by many to be very heterodox, but I just work on, forgetting as age comes on, many of my own choices of thought which I would have been very glad to retain, & afraid to embarras [*sic*] myself with the reasonings of others. Let us hope we are all advancing more or less towards truth though it may be by different roads

Yours Very Truly
M. FARADAY

649 J. PLÜCKER to M. FARADAY, 2 January 1857
[I.E.E., previously unpublished]

Bonn
January 2, 1857.

DEAR SIR!

I thank you heartily, Sir, for your last very kind letter, I got several months ago, after having exposed to you openly my feelings with regard to Prof. Tyndalls paper.¹ I did so convinced as I was, that you were above all such personal disputes and I fully adopt all conclusions of your letter. My intention never was to bring before the Royal Society any personal question, nor even any question of priority. I felt myself so much indebted to English men of Science that I would think it „mal placé" to provoke personal discussions, if not forced to do so. When ever I shall be so happy to see you again, I would be much interested to speak to you without any „arière [*sic*] pensée". But for the moment it will be sufficient to declare to you, that I have no animosity against M T. as I think he has none against myself I will not examine the motives he had, when he suggested to me ideas, which never were mines [*sic*], and which I think absurd. I ask only to be the interprete [*sic*] of my own words, if these words, especially when translated, admit a double meaning, or rather I ask only to restitute their true meaning, laid down in many papers, in the most explicit [*sic*] manner in a paper, whose date is anterior to Mr Tyndalls first publication about the subject. The way how that may be done is indifferent to me.

I fully succeeded this last time to sustain the theory of magnecrystallic action by analytical calculous [*sic*] as well as by experiment. I am enabled know [*sic*] to determine by calculous the position of equilibrium of a crystal, when suspended between the two poles along any direction whatever, as well as the relative number of its oscillations in any two suspensions. And, vice versa, having determined by observation any position of the crystal, however suspended, or the relative number of its oscillations, I can calculate the position of its magnetic axes.

I wanted an [*sic*] biaxial crystal to verify the theory. By far the best would have been ferrocyanite of potassium. But I did not succeed to get a perfectly clear crystal of this salt large enough to furnish a sphere (10 mm or 15 m [*sic*] diameter); till now all my labours to get such a crystal were lost. Therefore I recurred to formicate of copper, which I made crystallise myself. Under Prof. Beer [*sic*]² valuable cooperation I had a complete success. I got very curious facts deduced by calculous and verified by experiment.

Encouraged by yourself, Sir, I think the results I obtained not unworthy to be laid before the Royal Society as a „temoignage de ma réconnaissance". (Then I may in a note rectify Prof. Tyndals [*sic*] assertions (Phil. Trans. 145 I p. 2).) Only my bad English gives me some trouble, but I prefer to send an original paper incorrectly written, like this specimen then [*sic*] to have a german paper translated into a good English but not exactly rendering my meaning.

My best whishes [*sic*] for your health. With all my heart

Yours
Plücker

1 See Letter 628.
2 August Beer (1825–63), Extraordinary Professor at the University of Bonn.

650 M. Faraday to W. Whewell, 3 February 1857

[*Trinity College Library, Trinity College, Cambridge, previously unpublished*]

Royal Institution,
London W,
3 Feby 1857

My dear Dr. Whewell

The following are references.

Thomson – On Poisson's *Magnecrystallic* views[1] – Phil. Mag. March 1851, page 177.[2] Perhaps Thomson has something more about the matter in 1854, Comptes Rendus xxxviii pp. 632. 637.[3]

As to lines of Magnetic force you will find the *test experiments* described at p 28 of the accompanying paper Par 3351 &c. of Exp Res.

Van Rees has a mathematical paper in Poggendorfs Annalen 1853, vol xc p 415,[4] – he is opposed to my views but says they give the same mathematical results as the views of Ampere or Coulomb or Weber

Thomson says that the lines represent truly the Magnetic forces & even more simply than the representative idea of Coulomb Phil Mag 1854, viii. p 53[5]

Another paper besides that on *some points* has turned up[6] – I send it because pp. 4.5.6.7 has reference to what we said about Gravity

Ever faithfully yours,
M. Faraday

1 D. Poisson, 'Mémoire sur l'équilibre et le mouvement des corps cristallisés', *MAS*, 19 (1842), 3.
2 W. Thomson, 'On the theory of magnetic induction in crystalline and non-crystalline substances', *PM*, 4 s., 1 (1851), 177.
3 W. Thomson, 'Remarques sur les oscillations d'aiguilles non cristallisées de faible pouvoir inductif paramagnétique ou diamagnétique, et sur d'autres phénomènes magnétiques produits par des corps cristallisés ou non cristallisés', *CR*, 38 (1854), 632.

[4] R. van Rees, 'Ueber die Faraday'sche Theorie der magnetischen Kraftlinien', *AP*, 166 (1863), 415.

[5] W. Thomson, 'On the mathematical Theory of Electricity in Equilibrium', *PM*, 4 s., 8 (1854), 42.

[6] I am unable to identify this paper.

651   J. PLÜCKER to M. FARADAY, 14 March 1857
[*I.E.E., previously unpublished*]

Bonn,
March. 14,. 1857.

MY DEAR SIR!

I take liberty to send to you the announced paper on the magnetic induction of crystals[1] – not without some hesitation. Is it not rather strange that a Professor of Bonn presents so large a paper to the Royal Society! [punctuation doubtful]

Not being acquainted with the „coutumes" of this Society, I have written a few word [*sic*] to the foreign Secretary. I pray you, Sir, to send to him the paper with the letter, if this be the way. In addressing it to you, I principally wished to offer to you the occasion to look previously at the paper and especially to the note (p. 6) concerning Prof Tyndall. I think there is no offense given to him.

Tis now exactly ten years ago, I made the first observation on the new way opened by yourselves [*sic*]. After many disappointments I finally succeeded – I think so at least – to give a theory of all the various phenomena and to support this theory, in verifying experimentally the numerical values derived from it. Let me refer here only to the experiments with a sphere of formicate of copper. You may directly find after some trials, what I have called the magnetic axis of this salt, a crystal when suspended along one of these axes (including an angle of 50,°) not being acted upon in an extraordinary way. You may obtain them by counting the oscillations of the crystalline sphere, when successively suspended along any two determined directions. You may get them by observing its position, when suspended along any known direction and hence deduce its position, when suspended along *any other* direction (p. 53–57). You may lastly determine them by a curious method, wich [*sic*] I applied to crystallised bismuth – to get exact number [*sic*] my sphere of formicate of copper wanted a different torsion – wire (note p. 65).

Excuse me, Sir, in giving to you so much trouble. I hope you are well. With all my heart

Yours
PLÜCKER

PS. If there be *any* inconvenient [*sic*] to lay my paper before the Royal Society, I beg you to put it aside and to burn the letter to the foreign secretary.

¹ See Letter 627, fn. 6.

652 M. FARADAY to G. B. AIRY, 21 March 1857
[*Royal Observatory, Herstmonceux, Astrology-Optics, 1857 and 1858, Sect. 8*]

Albemarle S^t. W.
21. March 1857

MY DEAR SIR

I thank you heartily for your two notes – It was very difficult to see what an interval of nearly an hour meant – but the identical time of the phenomena brings all together

Nevertheless as an experimentalist I am thinking about the possibility of proving the existence of the Element of *time* in Magnetic phenomena: – and though we cannot look for hours or minutes or seconds, still even should it be so small as with light itself – there seems a possibility of ascertaining it. – All will depend upon the power we may have in diminishing the *time* of *obstruction*. – I acknowledge that I have not much hope; but a proof in the affirmative would be of such extreme value to the consideration of a force acting at a distance, that I think much labour & thought would not be thrown away in trying for it, even if the results should at last be negative

Ever Truly Yours
M. FARADAY

653 M. FARADAY to J. PLÜCKER, 23 March 1857
[*Nat. Res. Counc. Canada, previously unpublished*]

Royal Institution,
23 March 1857

MY DEAR SIR

Let me acknowledge, first your letter of the 2nd January, and now the letter & paper which I received only a few days ago. The paper I have read & sent on to Professor Miller¹ of Cambridge who is now the Foreign Secretary of the Royal Society: & I have sent with it the letter to Admiral Smyth who has left the Secretaryship since his elevation in rank. Your paper appears to me to be a very carefully elaborated work. but I am quite unable to enter into the mathematical part of it. The Formate of copper appears to have been of great service in your investigation

With regard to the note at p 6. I hardly know what to say² – I understood that you & Tyndall met each other at Vienna & I was in hopes that you would have come to a thorough understanding with each other – I do not mean that you would have agreed in conclusion because every scientific man has a right to his own – but that both sides would have found reason to believe that the other did not charge him with wilful misstatement – Dr Tyndall thinks that you have implied such a charge and says that whether you meant it or not your words conveyed the meaning in which he understood them to many others in the same sense as to himself – I suppose that as long as you say they did not convey that meaning & *could* not convey it. he will think he can only clear himself from the charge of *wilfully* misrepresenting you by proving that they did convey it. and so the disturbed feeling is kept up. – In the present case I should have thought that such explanations as we frequently have in our House of Commons would have been satisfactory – There when one party says they did not mean to convey a certain impression the other party is immediately satisfied that there was no intention to convey that impression – But such things as these are far more easily settled by word of mouth than by letter & that was the reason why I hoped much from your meeting at Vienna – I am very sorry for this affair I do not remember the expressions referred to and would[3]

[1] William Hallowes Miller (1801–80), Professor of Mineralogy in Cambridge University.
[2] This note appears on page 545 in *PT* for 1858.
[3] The rest of the letter has been lost.

654 M. FARADAY to J. CLERK MAXWELL, 25 March 1857
[*Lewis Campbell and William Garnett, 'The Life of James Clerk Maxwell', London, 1882, 519*]

Albemarle St. W.,
25$\underline{^{th}}$ March 1857.

My Dear Sir – I received your paper, and thank you very much for it.[1] I do not say I venture to thank you for what you have said about "Lines of Force," because I know you have done it for the interests of philosophical truth; but you must suppose it is work grateful to me, and gives me much encouragement to think on. I was at first almost frightened when I saw such mathematical force made to bear upon the subject, and then wondered to see that the subject stood it so well. I send by this post another paper to you;[2] I wonder what you will say to it. I hope however, that bold as the thoughts may be, you may perhaps find reason to bear with them. I hope this summer to make some experiments on the *time* of magnetic action, or rather on the time required for the assumption of the electrotonic state, round a wire carrying a current, that may help the subject on. The time must probably be short as the time of light; but the greatness of the result, if affirmative, makes me not despair. Perhaps I had better have said nothing about it, for I am often long in realising my intentions, and a failing memory is against me. – Ever yours most truly,   M. FARADAY.

¹ Probably a copy of his 'On Faraday's Lines of Force' which was read before the Cambridge Philosophical Society on 10 December 1855 and 11 February 1856. The printed paper appeared in *TCPS*, 10 (1864), 27.
² M. Faraday, 'On the Conservation of Force', *PRI*, 2 (1854–8), 352. See Letter 670.

655 L'Abbé F. Moigno to M. Faraday, 27 March 1857
[*I.E.E.*, *previously unpublished*]

2 rue Servandoni
27 mars 1857

Mon cher Monsieur Faraday

Je vous remercie de m'avoir envoyé de bonne heure le résumé de votre belle leçon Sur la conservation des forces. Je me Suis empressé de l'analyser et vous trouverez la première partie de mon travail dans la livraison du cosmos que vous recevrez en même temps que cette lettre.

A propos de votre lecture permettez moi d'appeler votre attention Sur une exposition que j'ai faite¹ il y a déjà longtemps des doctrines de Mʳ Seguin² Sur la cohésion. vous y trouverez exprimées des idées très conformes aux Votres Sur la pesanteur et la Nature des dernières molécules de la matière. Permettez moi malgré vos nombreuses graves et Savantes occupations de vous prier instamment de lire ces quelques pages trop peu connues il me Semble. J'ose aussi vous conjurer, dussé-je paraitre importun de lire dans ma traduction de la corrélation des Forces physiques de Mʳ Grove,³ l'ensemble des idées de Mʳ Seguin. C'est un homme excellent, un véritable philosophe, qui a fait dans l'industrie une grande fortune, dont il a fait le plus excellent usage, c'est lui qui a fait toutes les dépenses de mon Cosmos jusqu'au jour où ce journal s'est suffi à lui-même. Il se désole de ne pas pouvoir appeler l'attention, et faire entrer dans le domaine de la philosophie naturelle, des doctrines qui lui semblent aussi vraies que nécessaires. Si à l'exemple de Mʳ de Humboldt vous voudriez être assez bon, après avoir lu les notes additionelles à l'ouvrage de Mʳ Grove, pour lui écrire une petite lettre de sympathie et d'encouragement, vous le rendriez bien heureux, et je vous l'en serais reconnaissant comme d'un grand bienfait. Ne me refusez pas cette grace. Personne n'est plus à moins [reading doubtful] que vous de comprendre et de juger cette Synthèse philosophe; l'explication de la *cohésion* et la théorie de la *distension* Sont [3 words illeg.] de bonnes choses qui méritent d'être étudiées.

Si vous rencontrez Mʳ Tyndall, j'oserai vous prier de lui dire que j'ai éprouvé un grand plaisir à developper sa théorie si simple et si vraie des phénomènes des glaciers.⁴ J'ai été heureux aussi de rendre justice à votre si bon ami Mʳ Andrews⁵ en analysant sa note sur la décomposition bipolaire de l'eau par l'électricité de tension. Mon temps est consacré tout entier à l'exposition des travaux, des découvertes et des progrès accomplis, c'est une besogne bien aride, bien fatigante, qui rapporte peu de gloire et de profits; mais il faut souvent se dévouer et s'effacer pour le bien de la Science; et je me conforme de bon coeur à cette sublime maxime de St. Jean: *Il faut qu'il croisse et que moi je diminue*. Les Savans anglais vous le Savez Sont chers à mon esprit et à mon coeur, j'ai traduit Grove avec bonheur, je traduirais avec plus de bonheur encore Vos recherches experimentales sur l'electricité, et peut être deciderai-je M.ᵣ Seguin a faire les frais d'une traduction française quand votre travail sera terminé. Je n'ai pas malheureusement vos deux premiers volumes complets, et le plus grand plaisir que vous pussiez me faire serait de me les envoyer avec votre Signature.

Je vous verrai certainement cette année en allant à Dublin prendre part aux réunions de l'association britannique.

Je Suis dans les Sentimens de la considération la plus respectueuse et [illeg.] affectueuse et la plus distinguée.

Votre très humble Serviteur
L'ABBÉ F. MOIGNO

¹ See F. Moigno, 'Recherches de la cause qui maintient les molécules des corps à distance; théorie de la distension comprenant la répulsion, la dilatation, la vaporisation, etc. etc., essence de la matière', *Cosmos*, 2 (1853), 371, 625.
² Marc Seguin (1786–1875), engineer and one of the enunciators of the principle of the Conservation of Energy.
³ W. R. Grove, *Corrélation des forces physiques, ouvrage traduit en français par M. l'abbé Moigno sur la 3ᵉ édition anglaise, avec des notes de M. Seguin aîné*, Paris, 1856.
⁴ J. Tyndall, 'On the Theory of Glaciers', *LG*, 7 February 1857. This article was translated and published in *ASPN*, 34 (1857), 177.
⁵ T. Andrews, 'On the polar Decomposition of Water by common and atmospheric electricity', *BAASR* (1855), Pt. 2, 46.

656 M. FARADAY to L'ABBÉ F. MOIGNO, 22 April 1857
[*National Maritime Museum, Greenwich, previously unpublished*]

Royal Institution
London
22 April 1857.

———
Private
———

MY DEAR ABBÉ MOIGNO

To day I send off by the Railway Company three volumes of the Experimental Researches about which you enquired and which I trust you will do me the favour to accept – I send them by the Railway Company addressed to your name at 2 Rue Servandoni and I hope they will arrive safe. I have read your translation of Groves volume and the matter added by M. Seguin. The latter has interested me exceedingly and will keep my thoughts going for some time but it requires a great deal of thought to compare such a view with ones accustomed notions & ideas of matter especially if one tries to carry it out in relation to the different varieties of matter and their chemical and electrical relations one to another – and my thoughts are now very slow and soon weary by exertion. It is wonderful to the mind when one endeavours to form a conception of matter & of force – it would be still more wonderful if those who have dealt with these things did not strive to form a conception and though we cannot hope in this life to know the beginning or ending of these things still we may hope to develope an extra link in that part of the chain of reasoning which comes within our comprehension. At the same time I must confess my feeling of great insufficiency in these matters and am constrained to hold my views under continued subjection & cross questioning and not having the honor of knowing in the slightest manner M. Seguin I dare not intrude upon him my very hesitating views – or give any expression to the feeling of great pleasure which I have had in reading his vigorous & as it seems to me philosophic view. It is very encouraging to see how men's minds are moving These things cannot be developed quickly & M Seguin must not be disheartened – It requires a generation to pass away that prejudices may die out with it & though that has happened since the time of Montgolfier still the change required is of such extent that the dissolution of another may be needed before the mind is freed from her trammels

Believe me to be
Your faithful Servt
M. FARADAY

657 M. FARADAY to H. H. MILMAN,[1] 30 April 1857
[*Parl. Pap.*, *1857*, *Session 2*, *Vol. 24*, *149ff*]

R. I.,
April 30, 1857

MY DEAR DR. MILMAN

I wish I could write anything satisfactory, in reply to your note about the marbles in the British Museum. I examined them, in respect of their condition as to dirt, on the 24ᵗʰ instant; and more particularly a Caryatide, No. 128; the Shaft of a Column, No. 118; and some of the Metopes in the Elgin Gallery. The marbles generally were very dirty; some of them appearing as if dirty from a deposit of dust and soot formed upon them, and some of them, as if stained, dingy and brown. The surface of the marbles is in general rough, as if corroded; only a very few specimens present the polish of finished marble: many have a dead surface; many are honey combed, in a fine degree, more or less; or have shivered broken surfaces, calculated to hold dirt mechanically.

I found the body of the marble beneath the surface white. I found very few places where the discolouration seemed to be produced by a stain penetrating the real body of the unchanged or unbroken marble. Almost everywhere it appeared to be due to dirt (arising from dust, smoke, soot, etc.) held mechanically by the rough and fissured surface of the stone.

The application of water, applied by a sponge or soft cloth, removed the coarsest dirt, but did not much enlighten the general dark tint. The addition of rubbing, either by the finger, or a cork, or soft brushes, improved the colour, but still left it far below that of a fresh fracture. The use of a fine, gritty powder, with the water and rubbing, though it more quickly removed the upper dirt, left much imbedded in the cellular surface of the marble.

I then applied alkalies, both carbonated and caustic; these quickened the loosening of the surface dirt, and changed the tint of the brown stains a little; but they fell far short of restoring the marble surface to its proper hue and state of cleanliness. I finally used dilute nitric acid, and even this failed; for, though I could have gone on until I had dissolved away the upper marble, and left a pure surface, even these successive applications, made, of course, with care, but each time producing a sensible and even abundant effervescence, and each time dissolving enough marble to neutralize the applied acid, were not sufficient to reach the bottom of the cells and fissures in which dirt had been deposited, so as to dislodge the whole of that dirt from its place.

The examination has made me despair of the possibility of presenting the marbles in the British Museum in that state of purity and whiteness which they originally possessed, or in which, as I am informed, like marbles can be seen in Greece and Italy at the present day. The multitude of people who frequent the galleries, the dust which they raise, the necessary presence of stoves, or other means of warming, which, by producing currents in the air, carry the dust and dirt in it to places of rest, namely, the surfaces of the marbles; and the London atmosphere in which dust, smoke, fumes, are always present, and often water in such proportions as to deposit a dew upon the cold marble, or in the dirt upon the marble, are never-ceasing sources of injury to the state and appearance of these beautiful remains. Still, I think that much improvement would result from a more frequent and very careful washing; and I think that the application of a little carbonated alkali (as soda) with the water would be better than soap, inasmuch as the last portions of it are easily removed. It requires much care in washing to secure this result; but whether soap or soda be employed, none should be allowed to remain behind.

Dry brushing or wiping is probably employed in some cases; if so, it should be applied with care, and never, whilst the objects are damp, or from the conditions of the weather likely to be so. In several cases there is the appearance as if such a process had resulted in causing the adhesion of a darker coat of dirt than would have been produced without it; for convex, front, underlying

868

portions of a figure are in a darker state than back parts of the same figure, though the latter are more favourably disposed for the reception of falling dirt.

I am, my dear Dr. Milman,
Humbly and truly yours,
M. FARADAY.

[1] Henry Hart Milman, D.D. (1791–1868), Dean of St Paul's Cathedral and author.

658 M. FARADAY to G. B. AIRY, 18 May 1857

[*Royal Observatory, Herstmonceux, Astrology, Electricity-Optics, 1857 and 1858, Sect. 12, previously unpublished*]

1857 May 18 Monday Morg

MY DEAR MR AIRY

I have this moment learnt that there will be the Magneto electric light *this evening* at 8 o clk & after – at the Trinity house wharf Blackwall[1] – I cannot be there but if *you can – and wish –* and will ask for Professor Holmes[2] you will be admitted to the Wharf & lighthouse. I should think the best plan would be to go across in a boat to the Trinity Wharf landing place. Captn Poulter is the chief at the Wharf & if you mention my name or your own to him you will have every attention

In haste
Yours truly
M. FARADAY

[1] Faraday was engaged at this time in testing the efficacy of a light for lighthouses which was run by electricity from a dynamo. See *LPW*, 488.
[2] Professor Holmes was the inventor of the 'magneto-electric light'. I am unable to identify him further.

659 M. FARADAY to G. B. AIRY, 20 May 1857

[*Royal Observatory, Herstmonceux, Astrology, Electricity-Optics, 1857 and 1858, Sect. 12, previously unpublished*]

Albemarle St. W.
20 May 1857

MY DEAR SIR

I am very glad you have seen the Magneto electric light – Is it not a remarkable & wonderful source. If Professor Holmes agrees to what you propose I hope you will let me know I should like to see the light from the Observatory though I have already seen it from Woolwich. I do not know what arrangements are possible for Professor Holmes I think the means of variation at the

Wharf are but few but I cannot doubt that he will do all he can & that you require. – I should like him (if they can arrange it) to shew you an Argand lamp in a Parabolic reflector both with the naked electric light & with the same light in a reflector; & I should hope also that they could make both the lights traverse that you might see the coming on & passing away of the beam.

Ever Very Truly Yours
M. FARADAY

660 M. FARADAY to E. JONES,[1] 9 June 1857
[*B.J.* 2, *386*]

Royal Institution,
June 9, 1857.

MY DEAR SIR,

I have received your very kind letter and paper, and am delighted at such a result of my evening.[2] If nothing else had come of it but that, it would have been a sufficient reward; but much else has come, and I expect much more.

I do not think you can find in my papers any word or thought that contradicts the law of gravitating action. My observations are all directed to the *definition or description of the force* of gravitation with the view of clearing up the received idea of the force, so that if inaccurate or insufficient it may not be left as an obstacle in the present progressive state of science.

If I am wrong in believing that according to the present view the mutual gravitating force of two particles, *A* and *B*, remains unchanged, whatever other particles come to bear upon *A* and *B*, then the sooner I am corrected publicly the better.

If your view (whether old or new), that the power of *A* remains unchanged in amount, but is subdivided upon every particle which acts upon it, is the true or the accepted one, then I shall long to see it published and acknowledged, for I do not find it received at present. I have proved to my own satisfaction that such is the case with the dual powers electricity and magnetism, and it is the denial of it as regards gravity which makes up my chief difficulty in accepting the established view of that power. Your statement that *A* may attract or act on *B C* with a force of one, whilst *B C* act on *A* with a force of two, seems to me inconsistent with the law that action and reaction are equal; but I suppose I am under some misconception of your meaning.

The cases of action at a distance are becoming, in a physical point of view, daily more and more important. Sound, light, electricity, magnetism, gravitation, present them as a series.

The nature of sound and its dependence on a medium we think we understand pretty well. The nature of light as dependent on a medium is now very largely accepted. The presence of a medium in the phenomena of electricity and

870

magnetism becomes more and more probable daily. We employ ourselves, and I think rightly, in endeavouring to elucidate the physical exercise of these forces, or their sets of antecedents and consequents, and surely no one can find fault with the labours which eminent men have entered upon in respect of light, or into which they may enter as regards electricity and magnetism. Then what is there about gravitation that should exclude it from consideration also? Newton did not shut out the physical view, but had evidently thought deeply of it; and if he thought of it, why should not we, in these advanced days, do so too? Yet how can we do so if the present definition of the force, as I understand it, is allowed to remain undisturbed; or how are its inconsistencies or deficiencies as a description of the force to be made manifest, except by such questions and observations as those made by me, and referred to in the last pages of your paper? I believe we ought to search out any deficiency or inconsistency in the sense conveyed by the received form of words, that we may increase our real knowledge, striking out or limiting what is vague. I believe that men of science will be glad to do so, and will even, as regards gravity, amend its description, if they see it is wrong. You have, I think, done so to a large extent in your manuscript, and I trust (and know) that others have done so also. That I may be largely wrong I am free to admit – who can be right altogether in physical science, which is essentially progressive and corrective. Still if in our advance we find that a view hitherto accepted is not sufficient for the coming development, we ought I think (even though we risk something on our own part), to run before and rise up difficulties, that we may learn how to solve them truly. To leave them untouched, hanging as dead weights upon our thoughts, or to respect or preserve their existence whilst they interfere with the truth of physical action, is to rest content with darkness and to worship an idol.

I take the liberty of sending by this post copies of two papers. The one on conservation of force is, I suppose, that which you have read. I have made remarks in the margin which I think will satisfy you that I do not want to raise objections, except where the definition of gravity originates them of itself. The other is on the same subject two years anterior. If you would cause your view of gravity as a force *unchanging* in amount in *A*, but disposable in part towards one or many other particles, to be acknowledged by scientific men; you would do a great service to science. If you would even get them to say yes or no to your conclusions, it would help to clear the future progress. I believe some hesitate because they do not like to have their thoughts disturbed. When Davy discovered potassium it annoyed persons who had just made their view of chemical science perfect; and when I discovered the magneto-electric spark, distaste of a like kind was felt towards it, even in high places. Still science must proceed; and with respect to my part in the matter of gravitation, I am content to leave it to the future. I cannot help feeling that there is ground for my observations, for if there had been an evident answer it must have appeared before now. That the answer, when it comes, may be different to what I expect, I think is very probable, but I think also it will be as different from the present received view. Then a good end will be obtained, and indeed your observations and views appear to me to be much of that kind.

If it should be said that the physical nature of gravitation has not yet been considered, but only the law of its action, and, therefore, that no definition of gravity as a power has hitherto been necessary; that may be so with some, but then it must be high time to proceed a little further if we can, and that is just one reason for bringing the principle of the conservation of force to bear upon the subject. It cannot, I think, for a moment be supposed that we are to go no further in the investigation. Where would our knowledge of light, or magnetism, or the voltaic current have been under such a restraint of the mind?

Again thanking you most truly for the attention you have given to me and the subject, I beg you to believe that

I am, very gratefully, your faithful servant,

M. FARADAY.

1 Edward Jones was a minister in West Peckham, Maidstone.
2 Probably refers to Faraday's lecture 'On the conservation of force' given 27 February 1857.

661   J. PLÜCKER to M. FARADAY, 1 July 1857
[*I.E.E., previously unpublished*]

Bonn
1/7 57.

DEAR SIR!

Let me first thank you for the kind letter of the 23rd March and the interesting paper, I received nearly at the same time.[1] I learnd [*sic*] by the letter that you have sent my Memoir to Prof. Miller of Cambridge, the foreign Secretary. Since I got not the least notice about it, I fear therefore that I was ill informed with regard to the rules of the Royal Society, when I supposed, that papers, presented to the Society, (if approved) were published, in all cases announced in the proceedings. If the Memoir should get the honour to be printed, I would have found a friend, to eliminate the incorrectness of the language. My former views abandoned by myself since two years, being always reproduced in Journals (for instance by Mr Verdet[2] in the „Annales de Chimie") I am interested to have my Memoir published, but, under the actual circumstances, I think myself not entitled to publish its contents.

I fear, Sir, to annoy you, when speaking again about the difference with Prof. Tyndall. Being desirous to have this difference settled, I think it best, not to enter into any detail. Allow me only a few words in answering your letter. I dont know what reason Prof. Tyndall has to believe that I charged him with *wilful* misstatement. I published no word against him, except the note p. 6 of my paper, and whatever should be my personnel [*sic*] feelings, I would not publish such a charge. – With regard to Mr de la Rive's relation quoted by Prof. Tyndall, the fact is this.[3] After having showed to him all my experiments, he put to me, by letter, a great number of questions. These questions, difficult to be answered by yes and no, admitted partly a double meaning, you might

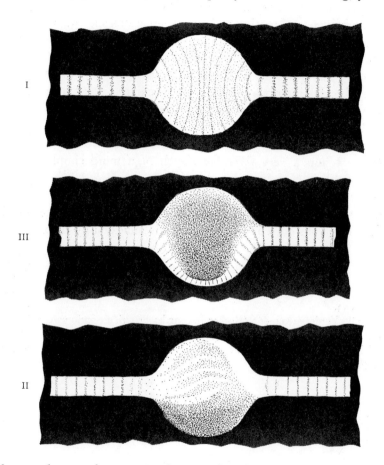

refer them to the pure fact or to its theoretical explication: I fear to have induced him myself to some expressions contrary to my own real meaning. – The reason of the misstatement is to be sought in some strange circumstances, by which I got my paper of 1849 (of which I gave you an abstract January 1850) published only 1852 and therein that it was not translated neither into English nor French.

I worked not much this last time. I got only confirmed my theory of the magnetic induction of crystals in some new cases. Lately too I made a series of experiments in order to get an explication of the stratification of light, exhibited first by Ruhmkorff's apparatus within certain rarified [*sic*] vapours, but equally obtained in every rarefied gaz and also by the electric spark or a series of them taken from a conductor, by retarding the decharge [*sic*] by means of less well conducting bodies. I have the opportunity here to obtain tubes of glass, of different forms, filled with any gaz or vapour whatever at a measured tension, through which you may send the electric charge by means of platina wires. The various experiments are beautiful. You may easily observe the influence of tension and heat, the various spectra, sounds etc. But MOST BEAUTIFUL is the effect, when the tubes are placed in the Electromagnet, in different ways, as well axially as equatorially. A tube 16–18 inches long showed many hundred blak [*sic*] intervals equally distant from each other; in other cases the blak intervals are larger and distant ¼ to ⅙ of an inch. The blak spaces are differently directed when put axially on the iron pieces of the Electromagnet. The current is under certain circumstances interrupted by the Electromagnetism It is impossible to give by a sketch an idea of the most splendid phenomena. I join a *very imperfect* sketch of a more simple case. (I the tube and the sphere contains rarefied hydrogen gaz, II & III the sphere is put in the equatorial direction on the iron pieces and the polarity comutated) Whatever may be the variety of appearances the *general* phenomena of inflection of the luminous current by the Magnet is indicated by theory.

With all my heart
Yours,
PLÜCKER

¹ See Letter 653.
² Marcel Emile Verdet (1824–66), 'Recherches sur les propriétés optiques développées dans les corps transparents par l'action du magnétisme', *AC*, 3 s., 41 (1854), 370.
³ J. Tyndall, 'On the nature of the Force by which Bodies are repelled from the Poles of a Magnet', *PT* (1855), 1.

662 M. FARADAY to J. LATIMER CLARK, 7 July 1857
[Engineering Societies Library, N.Y.C., previously unpublished]

7 July 1857

MY DEAR SIR

I am on the point of leaving town but hasten to acknowledge your letter. As I said before when you can do any of these things I shall be willing to look a little closer at them.¹ But how is it that the believers in these things make such a shouting out for the scientific men? Why do they not become scientific themselves and prove their own so called facts as scientific men prove their facts. If they are so much wiser than scientific men as to form a sure judgment when the latter are wrong why do they want to fall back upon them? To me this desire to include the men of science is a proof that they do *secretly doubt* what they wish to believe If they be the locomotives of knowledge why should they wait for that which to them is only a slow donkey cart jogging along the common road?

Ever Truly Yours
M. FARADAY

[In Latimer Clark's hand, at the end.] This has reference to some Spiritual Seances I asked Prof. Faraday to attend. LC

¹ See the note by Clark at the end of the letter.

663   M. FARADAY to J. PLÜCKER, 11 July 1857
[*Nat. Res. Counc. Canada, previously unpublished*]

Norfolk,
11 July 1857

MY DEAR PROFESSOR

I left town very shortly after receiving your last letter but not before I had inquired at the apartments of the Royal Society about your paper.¹ My memory is so bad, that I cannot recollect the circumstances under which I presented it, or the time; but I believe I wrote you word on that occasion. When I called lately I saw Mr Weld the assistant secretary, and found, from him, that the paper had been received and entered in a book: – he told me that Mr. Stokes the Secretary, was to communicate with you; but as there was no further note made, he concluded that he had not yet done so – Mr. Stokes is just married. I did *all I could* to expedite proceedings but as I do not belong to the Council or take any office I am quite without power in the matter. – I have myself presented a paper to the Royal Society – I believe it is to be printed though I have never been informed officially that that is to be the case. – I think it must be near a twelvemonth since I sent it in, but I have seen no printers proof as yet – The proceedings are indeed very slow.

With respect to You & Tyndall I cannot pretend to explain the misunderstandings which exist: – and having tried a little I do not think that any third person between you can be of any use. To be clear it requires that the parties should communicate directly, and plainly, with each other; and then I think it would be impossible not to discover where the mistake lies. He is at present abroad.

I am very glad that you are working on the stratified electric light. – I hope that you will very shortly give us the fundamental explanation of the phenomenon. I cannot help thinking that it will aid us in developing some very important points about the nature of the electric discharge. We would rejoice to understand, truly, the first principles of that very striking electric action.

The variation of the intervals to a certain degree at pleasure is exceedingly interesting – but what is the state of an interval?

I must conclude saying that I am as ever Very Truly Yours

M. FARADAY

[1] See Letter 651.

664 M. FARADAY to J. PLÜCKER, 27 July 1857
[*Nat. Res. Counc. Canada, previously unpublished*]

Royal Institution
27. July 1857

MY DEAR SIR

I seemed to have two or three of your letters unanswered & wondered at it but then I remembered that you had been *here* since some of them & we had talked them over. Your last I shewed as you desired to Mr. Gassiot & also to Dr. Tyndall The latter is now in Switzerland amongst the Glaciers I do not know whether you will see him at some of your German meetings. I have been obliged to give up thinking about the luminous current but whilst such as you Gassiot and others work at the subject I know it is progressing. The Arch which you shewed me corresponding to the Magnetic line of force and that other one of which you speak in one of your letters of like nature interest me very much inasmuch as their course seems to be directly at right angles to the course of the Electric current – The alternate light & dark parts of the stratified column are also exceedingly exciting. What is the essential difference of these parts? It is very easy to imagine a difference or even two or three kinds of it but what is the real difference?

Then again the question of transmission of the discharge across a perfect vacuum or whether a vacuum exists or not? *is* to me a continual thought and seems to be connected with the hypothesis of the ether. What a pity one cannot get hold of these points by some *experiments* – more close & searching than any we have yet devised

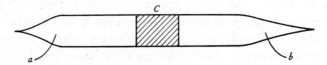

You seem surprized to have had the double current when one end of the Ruhmkorf was connected with the coating of the tube & the other with the wire. With Gassiot & myself this was an instant conclusion from the experiment with two coatings & is described in his paper as such.[1] A very pretty variation of it is made by connecting the two wires *a. b.* with one end of the

Ruhmkorf & the coating c with the other: double currents are obtained in both halves of the tube but in opposite directions as is shewn by their examination with a magnet

Ever

My dear Sir

Very Truly Yours

M. FARADAY

1 See J. P. Gassiot, 'On some experiments made with Ruhmkorff's induction coil', *PM*, 4.2., 7 (1854), 97.

665   J. PLÜCKER to M. FARADAY, 17 August 1857
   [*I.E.E., previously unpublished*]

Bonn

17.th Aug. 1857.

DEAR SIR!

During your glorious career of scientific researches it certainly may often happened, that you entered a question having very little hope to get a satisfactory result. Such is my case on the present occasion. There is held at Bonn from 18.th to the 24.th of September the 33.th [*sic*] [reading doubtful] meeting of the Germain Association. All is done to render it a splendid one, a great number of eminent men from all countries are expected. Every body would regard your presence as a most precious one. You dont like festivals, I know, – but you may move here quite free. You dont like traveling abroad, but changing the air of London and its environs with the air of the Rhine, will certainly do good to your health – when my own head is tired, I run away in any direction, and, when returned, I feel myself restored. Let me be the advocate of our Association, if I should succeed – a case more whished [*sic*] for by myself then expected – I shall be happy to take care of *all* regarding your stay here at Bonn. Having no office on this occasion you may fully dispose on me. – I dont expect any answer but in the extraordinary case of a favourable decision.

I thank you for your last kind letter, which announces me that the presented paper (addressed to the foreign Secretary) is not lost. With patience I'll expect its future destiny.

From all my heart

Yours

PLÜCKER

666 M. FARADAY to J. BARLOW, 19 August 1857

[*B.J. 2, 380*]

Highgate,
August 19, 1857.

I am in town, and at work more or less every day. My memory wearies me greatly in working; for I cannot remember from day to day the conclusions I come to, and all has to be thought out many times over. To write it down gives no assistance, for what is written down is itself forgotten. It is only by very slow degrees that this state of mental muddiness can be wrought either through or under; nevertheless, I know that to work somewhat is far better than to stand still, even if nothing comes of it. It is better for the mind itself – not being quite sure whether I shall ever end the research, and yet being sure, that if in my former state of memory, I could work it out in a week or two to a successful and affirmative result.

Do not be amazed by what I am telling you: it is simply the thing I remember to tell you. If other things occurred to my mind, I would tell you of them. But one thing which often withholds me, is, that if I begin a thing, I find I do not report it correctly, and so naturally withdraw from attempting it. One result of short memory is coming curiously into play with me. I forget how to spell. I dare say if I were to read this letter again, I should find four or five words of which I am doubtful, "withholds, wearies, successful," &c.; but I cannot stop for them, or look to a dictionary (for I had better cease to write altogether), but I just send them, with all their imperfections, knowing that you will receive them kindly.

Ever, dear Barlow, truly yours,
M. FARADAY.

667 M. FARADAY to J. PLÜCKER, 27 August 1857

[*Nat. Res. Counc. Canada, previously unpublished*]

Royal Institution
27 August 1857

MY DEAR SIR

Your letter is so kind that I cannot let it pass in silence, though it gives me pain to say no to you: – but, though I cannot come, I thank you and all my friends about you for the kindness. I should have rejoiced to have been amongst you all but the time is past; Years & their consequences limit our powers, & though I trust yours will long run on successfully, mine are drawing nigh to their end. The British Association is now I believe holding its meeting at Dublin and I was very kindly & considerately pressed to be there. But I am obliged to have *one* answer & only one to these friendly applications. Remember me to my friends. – May all be happy & successful with you.

Ever Very Truly Yours
M. FARADAY

668 W. DE LA RUE to M. FARADAY, 28 September 1857
[*I.E.E., previously unpublished*]

110 Bunhill Row,
London, EC
September 28 1857

MY DEAR MR FARADAY

I am greatly obliged to you for the copy of your paper on the relation of light to metals which I have nearly read through[1] – you have made a most interesting investigation of the phenomena, and will probably hereafter do much more in this same path. It was very scrupulous on your part to name me in your paper for the slight assistance I was able & glad to render.

The full moon was on the 4th of September, as you say, – but very early in the morning (5^h. 7m A M.) and as the photograph was taken on the 7th at the 14–15 hour (the 8th at 3° clock A M) nearly four days had elapsed, so that fully one fourth of the moon was in shadow: – added to which those parts most in shadow do not produce a sensible impression on the plate by the time the lighter portions are overdone; So that all the lunar surface visible to the eye is not depicted: – the original photograph, however, shows a little more than the copies taken from it, but not quite all that could be seen with the eyepiece.

Do not hesitate to do what you require with the fragments of speculum metal, they are quite at your disposal. If you would like to cast them into other forms it is easily done and they are very readily polished quite true: – will you allow me to put you in the way of doing this? It is quite easy and you would have no difficulty in doing it yourself much better than you will get it done by another, several specula are also very easy to make.

It is quite astonishing how much of the actinic rays is stopped by the atmosphere when the moon is situated, as it has been lately, at only a few degrees from the horizon – I could not obtain on the 25th the slightest impression of the moon in 25 seconds whereas in 5 seconds when well situated the plate is almost overdone. A slight haze which barely diminished Jupiter's light stopped so much of the actinic effect that I could not last night obtain the slightest trace of an image in 25 seconds under such circumstances, whereas in 12 seconds just previously I obtained a capital impression. I believe that there is room for a curious investigation in this direction. Did you try gold in its green & purple states in regard of its transmitting or excluding the actinic ray?

Yours Very truly

WARREN DE LA RUE

[1] M. Faraday, 'Experimental relations of gold, and other metals, to light', *PT* (1857), 145.

669 M. FARADAY to J. B. DUMAS, 6 November 1857

[*Arch. de l'Acad. des Sciences, Paris, Dossier Faraday, previously unpublished*]

Royal Institution,

6 November, 1857

MY DEAR & KIND FRIEND

I hope you will not be startled at my presumption but I had formed the rather ambitious thought of endeavouring (if you should sanction etc.) to convey to our Members at one of the Friday Evening meetings an idea of the remarkable and important views which you developed to us in some degree at Ipswich.[1] and first I have to ask you whether such a proceeding would be agreeable to you or whether for any reason or feeling you would rather I should not do it.

But in the next place if you see no reason against it but on the contrary are willing to let me touch so fine a subject before our members – then I am obliged to confess to you that I feel greatly startled in finding how much of that which you communicated to us & to myself personally my decaying memory has allowed to escape and though I have the sheet of paper on which you wrote me down a few pencil figures & a few rough lines and also the journal accounts of your discourse at Ipswich yet they do not sufficiently clear up my recollections to enable me to do that which I want to do, well.

And so my boldness extends to this. If in the first place it is agreeable to you that I should do it then have you any papers M S. or other that you could lend to me giving me an account of the results whether deduced from change of valence – or of solubility or progression of character or equivalent numbers, etc., etc. and the probabilities around it as the conclusion. As our audiences though they contain I am happy to say many high philosophers consist chiefly of persons who though gentlemen of high & liberal education are still not exclusively scientific (500 or 600 persons being present perhaps) so I generally introduce an experiment or strive to make them quickly comprehend any *point* which is under consideration: – as for instance in speaking of the progression of Chlorine, Bromine & iodine in reference to your views I should shew them these bodies. but such helps I could arrange and do not wish to trouble you about experiments unless indeed you have some which have occurred to yourself as fit illustrations. As to diagrams or curves I am at a loss for the few lines

I have do not now recall my memory except very vaguely to that which they represent.

Now I think I have said enough to frighten you. If I could obtain possession of the matter and give the subject well I should be greatly honored in the doing of it. but I should not like to put you to too much trouble. Any papers you may trust me with I will most carefully return and use them with every reservation that you may desire. If there is any thing yet published about them and you favour my proposition send me a reference to it. The evening would be in the middle or end of next January, but I should like to have possession of the matter (if I give it) by or before the beginning of the next year that I may study it at will.[2] Our kindest remembrances to Madame Dumas also to M. Dumas your son & to Madame Edwards.

Ever My dear friend. Yours faithfully
M. FARADAY

[1] See J. Dumas, 'Mémoire sur les équivalents des corps simples', *CR*, 45 (1857), 709, where Dumas discusses the relations between the chemical elements.

[2] There is no record of Faraday having delivered a lecture on this subject.

670 J. CLERK MAXWELL to M. FARADAY, 9 November 1857

[*I.E.E.*, *Lewis Campbell and William Garnett, 'The Life of James Clerk Maxwell',*
new abridged version, London, 1884, 202ff[1]]

129 Union Street
Aberdeen
9th Novr 1857

DEAR SIR

I have to acknowledge receipt of your papers on the Relations of Gold &c to Light and on the Conservation of Force.[2] Last spring you were so kind as to send me a copy of the latter paper and to ask what I thought of it. That question silenced me at that time, but I have since heard and read various opinions on the subject which render it both easy and right for me to say what I think. And first I pass over some who have never understood the known doctrine of conservation of force and who suppose it to have something to do with the equality of action & reaction Now first I am sorry that we do not keep our words for distinct things more distinct and speak of the "Conservation of Work or of Energy" as applied to the relations between the amount of "vis viva" and of "tension" in the world; and of the "Duality of Force" as referring to the equality of action and reaction.

Energy is the power a thing has of doing work arising either from its own motion or from the "tension" subsisting between it and other things.

Force is the tendency of a body to pass from one place to another and depends upon the amount of change of "tension" which that passage would produce.

Now as far as I know you are the first person in whom the idea of bodies acting at a distance by throwing the surrounding medium into a state of constraint has arisen, as a principle to be actually believed in. We have had streams of hooks and eyes flying around magnets, and even pictures of them so beset, but nothing is clearer than your descriptions of all sources of force keeping up a state of energy in all that surrounds them, which state by its increase or diminution measures the work done by any change in the system. You seem to see the lines of force curving round obstacles and driving plump at conductors and swerving towards certain directions in crystals, and carrying with them everywhere the same amount of attractive power spread wider or denser as the lines widen or contract.

You have also seen that the great mystery is, not how like bodies repel and unlike attract but how like bodies attract (by gravition [*sic*]).

But if you can get over that difficulty, either by making gravity the residual of the two electricities or by simply admitting it, then your lines of force can "weave a web across the sky" and lead the stars in their courses without any necessarily immediate connection with the objects of their attraction.

The lines of Force from the Sun spread out from him and when they come near a planet *curve out from it* so that every planet diverts a number depending on its mass from their course and substitutes a system of its own so as to become something like a comet, *if lines of force were visible*

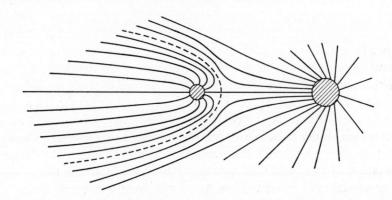

The lines of the planet are separated from those of the Sun by the dotted line. Now conceive every one of these lines (which never interfere but proceed from sun & planet to infinity) to have a *pushing* force, instead of a *pulling* one and then sun and planet will be pushed together with a force which comes out as it ought proportional to the product of the masses & the inverse square of the distance.

The difference between this case and that of the dipolar forces is, that instead of each body catching the lines of force from the rest all the lines keep as clear of other bodies as they can and go off to the infinite sphere against which I have supposed them to push.

Here then we have conservation of energy (actual & potential) as every student of dynamics learns, and besides this we have conservation of "lines of force" as to their *number* and total strength for *every* body always sends out a number proportional to its own mass, and the pushing effect of each is the same.

All that is altered when bodies approach is the *direction* in which these lines push When the bodies are distant the distribution of lines near each is little disturbed When they approach, the lines march round from between them, and come to push behind each so that their resultant action is to bring the bodies together with a *resultant* force increasing as they approach.

Now the mode of looking at Nature which belongs to those who can see the lines of force deals very little with "resultant forces" but with a network of lines of action of which these are the final results, so that I for my part cannot realise your dissatisfaction with the law of gravitation provided you conceive it according to your own principles. It may seem very different when stated by the believers in "forces at a distance", but there can be only differences in form and conception not in quantity or mechanical effect between them and those who trace force by its lines. But when we face the great questions about gravitation Does it require time? Is it polar to the "outside of the universe" or to anything? Has it any reference to electricity? or does it stand on the very foundation of matter – mass or inertia? then we feel the need of tests, whether they be comets or nebulae or laboratory experiments or bold questions as to the truth of received opinions.

I have now merely tried to show you why I do not think gravitation a dangerous subject to apply your methods to, and that it may be possible to throw light on it also by the *embodiment* of the same ideas which are expressed *mathematically* in the functions of Laplace and of Sir W. R. Hamilton in Planetary Theory.

But there are questions relating to the connexion between magneto-electricity and certain mechanical effects which seem to me opening up quite a new road to the establishment of principles in electricity and a possible confirmation of the physical nature of magnetic lines of force. Professor W. Thomson seems to have some new lights on this subject

Yours sincerely

JAMES CLERK MAXWELL

[1] Also in *LPW*, 511 (without diagram) where it is erroneously described as previously unpublished.
[2] See Letter 654.

[*B.J.* 2, *390*]

Royal Institution,
November 13, 1857.

MY DEAR SIR,

If on a former occasion I seemed to ask you what you thought of my paper, it was very wrong, for I do not think anyone should be called upon for the expression of their thoughts before they are prepared and wish to give them. I have often enough to decline giving an opinion, because my mind is not ready to come to a conclusion, or does not wish to be committed to a view that may by further consideration be changed. But having received your last letter, I am exceedingly grateful to you for it; and rejoice that my forgetfulness of having sent the former paper on conservation has brought about such a result. Your letter is to me the first intercommunication on the subject with one of your mode and habit of thinking. It will do me much good, and I shall read and meditate on it again and again.

I dare say I have myself greatly to blame for the vague use of expressive words. I perceive that I do not use the word "force" as you define it, "the tendency of a body to pass from one place to another." What I mean by the word is the source or sources of all possible actions of the particles or materials of the universe, these being often called the powers of nature when spoken of in respect of the different manners in which their effects are shown.

In a paper which I have received at this moment from the "Phil. Mag.," by Dr. Woods,[1] they are called the *forces*, "such as electricity, heat, &c." In this way I have used the word "force" in the description of gravity which I have given as that expressing the received idea of its nature and source, and such of my remarks as express an opinion, or are critical, apply only to that sense of it. You may remember I speak to labourers like myself; experimentalists on force generally who receive that description of gravity as a physical truth, and believe that it expresses all and no more than all that concerns the nature and locality of the power, – to these it limits the formation of their ideas and the direction of their exertions, and to them I have endeavoured to speak, showing how such a thought, if accepted, pledged them to a very limited and probably erroneous view of the cause of the force, and to ask them to consider whether they should not look (for a time, at least), to a source in part external to the particles. I send you two or three old printed papers with lines *marked* relating to this point.

To those who disown the definition or description as imperfect, I have nothing to urge, as there is then probably no real difference between us.

I hang on to your words, because they are to me weighty; and where you say, "I, for my part, cannot realise your dissatisfaction with the law of gravitation, provided you conceive it according to your own principles," they give me great comfort. I have nothing to say against the law of the action of gravity. It is against the law which measures its total strength as an inherent force that I venture to oppose my opinion; and I must have expressed myself badly (though I do not find the weak point), or I should not have conveyed any other impression. All I wanted to do was to move men (not No. 1, but No. 2), from the unreserved acceptance of a principle of physical action which might be opposed to natural truth. The idea that we may possibly have to connect *repulsion* with the lines of gravitation-force (which is going far beyond anything my mind would venture on at present, except in private cogitation), shows how far we *may* have to depart from the view I oppose.

There is one thing I would be glad to ask you. When a mathematician engaged in investigating physical actions and results has arrived at his own conclusions, may they not be expressed in common language as fully, clearly, and definitely as in mathematical formulae? If so, would it not be a great boon to such as we to express them so – translating them out of their hieroglyphics that we also might work upon them by experiment. I think it must be so, because I have always found that you could convey to me a perfectly clear idea of your conclusions, which, though they may give me no full understanding of the steps of your process, gave me the results neither above nor below the truth, and so clear in character that I can think and work from them.

If this be possible, would it not be a good thing if mathematicians, writing on these subjects, were to give us their results in this popular useful working state as well as in that which is their own and proper to them?

Ever, my dear Sir, most truly yours,
M. FARADAY.

¹ Thomas Woods (1815–?), physicist. The only paper published by Dr Woods in the *PM* in 1857 is 'On the time required by compounds for decomposition', *PM*, 4 s., 14 (1857), 346.

672 M. FARADAY to J. TYNDALL, 9 December 1857

[*P.M.*, 4 s., 16 (1858), 354]

Royal Institution,
Dec. 9, 1857.

MY DEAR TYNDALL,

Have the following remarks, made in reference to the irregular fusibility of ice, to which you drew my attention, any interest to you, or by an occasional bearing on such cases, any value in themselves? Deal with them as you like.

Imagine a portion of the water of a lake about to freeze, the surface S being in contact with an atmosphere considerably below 32°, the previous action of which has been to lower the temperature of the whole mass of water, so that the portion below the line M is at 40°, or the maximum density, and the part above at progressive temperatures from 40° upwards to 32°; each stratum keeping its place by its relative specific gravity to the rest, and having therefore, in that respect, no tendency to form currents either upwards or downwards. Now generally, if the surface became ice, the water below would go on freezing by the cold conducted downwards through the ice; but the successive series of temperatures from 32° to 40° would always exist in a layer of water contained between the ice and the dense water at 40° below M. If the water were *pure*, no action of the cold would tend to change the places of the particles of the water or cause currents, because, the lower the cold descended, the more firmly would any given particle tend to retain its place above those beneath it: a particle at *e*, for instance, at 36° F., would, when the cold had frozen what was above it, be cooled sooner and more than any of the particles beneath, and so always retain its upper place as respects them.

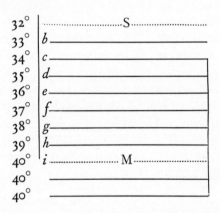

But now, suppose the water to contain a trace of saline matters in solution. As the water at 32° froze, either at the surface or against the bottom of the previously-formed ice, these salts would be expelled; for the ice first formed (and that *always* formed, if the proper care be taken to displace the excluded salts) is perfectly free from them, and PURE. The salts so excluded would pass into the layer of water beneath, and there produce two effects: they would make that layer of greater specific gravity than before, and so give it a tendency to sink into the warmer under layer; but they would also make it require a lower temperature than 32° for congelation; this it would acquire from the cold ice above, and by that it would become lighter and float, tending to remain uppermost; for it has already been shown that the diminution of temperature below 32° in sea water and solution of salts, is accompanied by the same enlargement of bulk as between 32° and 40° with pure water. The stratum of water, therefore, below the ice, would not of necessity sink because it contained a little more salt than the stratum immediately below it; and *certainly would not* if the increase of gravity conferred by the salts was less than the decrease by lowering of temperature. An approximation of the strata between the freezing place and the layer at 40° would occur, *i. e.* the distance between these temperatures would be less, but the water particles would keep their respective places.

When water freezes, it does not appear that this process is continuous; for many of the characters of the ice seem to show that it is intermittent: *i. e.* either a film of ice is formed, and then the process stops until the heat evolved by solidification has been conducted away upwards, and the next stratum of water has been sufficiently cooled to freeze in turn; or else the freezing being, so to speak, continuous, still is not continued at the same constant rate, but, as it were, by intermittent pulsations. Now it may well be, when a layer next the previously-formed ice, and containing an undue proportion of salts, has been cooled down to its required temperature for freezing (which would be below 32°), that, on freezing, the congelation will pervade at once a certain thickness of the water, excluding the salts from the larger portion of ice formed, but including them as a weak solution within its interstices. The next increment of cold conducted from the ice above would freeze up these salts in the ice containing them, at the same time that a layer of pure ice was formed beneath it. Thus a layer of ice fusible at a lower temperature than the ice either above or below it might be produced; and by a repetition of the process many such layers might be formed.

It does not follow necessarily that the layers would be perfectly exact in their disposition. Very slight circumstances tending to disturb the regularity of the water-molecules would be sufficient, probably, to disturb the layers more or less. Ice contains *no* air, and the exclusion of a minute bubble of air from the water in the act of freezing might disturb the direction and progress of the congelation, and cause accumulation of the extra saline liquid in one spot rather than another: so might the tendency to the formation of little currents, either arising from the separation of the saline water from the forming ice, or from the elevation of temperature in different degrees at those places where the congelation was going on at different rates.

The effect would not depend upon the quantity of salts contained in the freezing water, though its degree would. The proportion of salts necessary to be added to pure water to lower its freezing-point 1° F. may be very sensible to chemical tests; but the proportion required to make the difference $\frac{1}{100}$th or $\frac{1}{1000}$th of a degree would be far less: and if we suppose that only $\frac{1}{20}$th of a piece of ice is brought into the condition of melting before the rest of the mass, and that the salts in that proportion were originally in the *whole* of the water, then its quantity there may be so small as to escape detection except by very careful analysis. However, it would be desirable to examine the water chemically which is produced by ice distinguished by having in its interior much that liquefies before the rest.

It is easy to make ice perfectly free from air, and, as I believe, from salts, by a process I formerly described. It would be interesting to see if such ice had within it portions melting at a lower temperature than the general mass. I think it ought not.

Ever truly yours,
M. FARADAY.

673 M. FARADAY to C. HANSTEEN,[1] 16 December 1857
[*R.I., previously unpublished*[2]]

Royal Institution,
16 Decr. 1857

DEAR & HONORED SIR,

General Sabine has placed in my hands a letter from you, and I make it, I hope you will not think improperly, an occasion for writing to you, for the purpose of expressing my sincere admiration and respect; hoping that, as one who has been admitted into the circle of scientific men, I might be permitted to offer a word of testimony & praise to one who is a leader in that glorious band. Let me suppose that I have not been presumptuous in thus writing to you and in any case think as kindly of me as you can.

I thought also that I could better answer your enquiries in relation to Mr. Arndtsen[3] directly than through General Sabine. I am sorry that I cannot advance the wishes of that gentleman and yourself; but I must explain to you how it is. In the first place our Institution is not like your Universities. It is a private establishment: the Government does nothing for us, and we have no opportunities of receiving students. We have but one assistant and he is an ordinary workman. I formerly gave lectures to which the public were admitted by payment; but do not deliver any now, except six, once a year, at Christmas to the juvenile connexions of our members & subscribers. So you see we have no place for such an one as Mr. Arndtsen.

For the same reason I have never had any student or pupil under me to aid me with assistance; but have always prepared and made my experiments with my own hands, working & thinking at the same time. I do not think I could work in company, or think aloud, or explain my thoughts at the time. Sometimes I and my assistant have been in the Laboratory for hours & days together, he preparing some lecture apparatus or cleaning up, & scarcely a word has passed between us: – all this being the consequence of the *solitary & isolated* system of investigation; in contradistinction to that pursued by a Professor with his aids & pupils as in your Universities.

But besides all that, my dear Sir, I now work but little and at fitful moments; as my health will bear it. I am obliged to keep out of Society; – to avoid Societies; – and above all to forbear making new connexions and claims on my thoughts: for I find it quite difficult enough to perform my duty to the few that I do keep open, as you may suppose.

Nevertheless I esteem Mr. Arndtsen's desire as a very great compliment, and thank him & you for it. Will you say so much to him for me.

And now I must conclude, hoping you will believe me in truth & sincerely.

Your great & respectful admirer
M. FARADAY

[1] Christopher Hansteen (1784–1873), pioneer student of terrestrial magnetism.
[2] There is a copy of this letter in the Institut for Teoretisk Astrofysikk, Oslo, Norway.
[3] Adam Frederick Olaf Arndtsen (1829–?), Instructor in Physics at the Royal Military School at Christiana.

674   A. DE LA RIVE to M. FARADAY, 19 December 1857
[*I.E.E., previously unpublished*]

Genève
le 19 X^bre 1857.

MON TRÈS CHER & EXCELLENT AMI,

Je ne puis vous dire avec quel plaisir j'ai reçu votre bonne lettre du 30 Octobre. Parmi les jouissances que je dois à la culture de la Science; l'une des plus grandes, je vous assure, est de m'avoir procuré votre amitié, héritage précieux que j'ai reçu d'un père qui serait heureux de penser que je vous ai pour ami. Je jouis des bonnes nouvelles que vous me donnez de vous même; vos 66 ans m'ont étonné; vous êtes si jeune d'esprit, de corps & surtout de coeur, qu'on ne peut croire que vous avez passé la soixantaine. – Mais vous avez su arranger votre vie de manière à ne pas la dépenser dans ce qui use l'âme & le corps, & par dessus tout vous avez eu le bonheur de la conformer aux sentiments chrétiens qui seuls sont un guide infaillible.

Quant à moi, si j'ai eu une vie plus agitée sous bien des rapports, plus coupée & surtout non moins bien employée que la votre, je dois cependant bénir la Providence de tous les biens qu'elle m'a accordées. J'ai eu de grands malheurs, de grands désappointements, de grands soucis, mais j'entrevois une vieillesse calme & douce, sérieuse plutôt qu'heureuse, car à mon âge le bonheur complet n'est pas possible. Au reste un trop grand bonheur ne vous permettrait pas de vous detacher graduellement de cette vie pour tourner ses regards & ses espérances plus haut, & j'en suis venu à ce moment où il faut savoir mettre un intervalle entre la vie & la mort, en cherchant à se mettre à l'abri des agitations & des tracas du monde.

Enfin j'ai achevé mon ouvrage sur l'Electricité; vous allez recevoir ce 3ème & dernier volume, & si vous daignez y jeter les yeux, vous me comprendrez quand je vous dirai qu'à lui seul il m'a couté plus de travail & de peine que les deux autres réunis. L'électricité animale surtout m'a occasionné plus d'une année de travail persévérant. Je suis impatient de savoir ce que vous penserez de ma théorie sur l'origine de l'Electricité atmosphérique & sur celle du Magnétisme terrestre. J'ai éprouvé une grande jouissance à l'occasion de ce dernier volume dans le concours utile que m'a prêté mon fils cadet; vous verrez qu'il ne s'est pas trop mal tiré de ce qu'il a fait dans ce volume. Il vient de faire pour la *Bibl. Univ.* un extrait du mémoire que vous m'avez envoyé & dont je vous remercie infiniment; ce mémoire nous a vivement intéressés & mon fils a désiré en faire l'analyse. Il a commencé & poursuit un grand travail sur l'induction, sujet qui lui parait l'un des plus curieux de la physique; j'espère qu'il parviendra à obtenir quelques résultats importants. Il prend souvent dans ma bibliothèque les volumes que vous m'avez donnés & qui renferment la collection de vos mémoires.

Quant à moi, je jouis de revenir au laboratoire & je suis certain [reading doubtful] de suivre à ses recherches que m'a suggéré le travail que j'ai été obligé de faire pour composer mes trois gros volumes. Que de choses encore à faire dans ce champ inépuisable. Dès que j'aurai achevé une partie de ces recherches, j'aurai soin de vous faire part des résultats que j'aurai obtenus, si du moins ils le méritent.

Mon fils ainé est devenu depuis cette année le Rédacteur en chef de la *Bibliothèque Universelle*; il a trouvé là une occupation très intéressante & en même temps assez assujétissante, ce qui est assez précieux[1] dans le temps où nous vivons. C'est surtout la partie littéraire & des Sciences morales qui est son domaine.

Voilà bien des détails intimes; mais vous me les avez demandés & je les dois à votre amitié; permettez moi d'ajouter encore que toute ma famille est bien portante, grâce à Dieu, & que la Providence m'a accordé la faveur d'avoir une compagne qui est une amie dont tous les jours j'apprécie davantage la valeur. Elle me charge de la rappeler à votre bon souvenir ainsi qu'à celui de Madame Faraday à qui je vous prie de présenter mes compliments les plus affectueux.

Votre tout dévoué & affé
AUG. DE LA RIVE

Serait-ce indécent de vous prier de faire parvenir la lettre ci inclus à notre ami Wm Henry dont j'ignore l'adresse

Je ne vous ai rien dit de notre séjour de sept mois en Italie qui a trés bien réussi & où j'ai éprouvé des jouissances dont je ne me croyais plus susceptible. – J'ai eu un bien grand plaisir à voir un instant cet été Mr Tyndall à qui je compte écrire incessamment; faites lui en attendant mes meilleurs compliments –

[1] 'précieuse' pencilled over the word in the text in another hand.

675   J. PLÜCKER to M. FARADAY, 27 December 1857

[*I.E.E., previously unpublished*]

Bonn
27/12 57.

MY DEAR SIR!

My best thanks for your interesting paper on the Relations of gold to light, which I received some time ago. I tried myself to prepare one of your purple fluids, but – you will think me a bad experimentalist – I did not succeed. I was much interested to get such a fluid, being itself a bad conductor, but containing well conducting particles in suspension, in ordre [*sic*] to examine if no particular arrangement of these particles would appear, when electric currents of different kind were send through it. The discharge of Electricity through the tubes, exhibiting the stratified light, cannot be a transport of light, or luminous matter from one end of the tube to the other. There is, I think, within the tube a distribution of ponderable matter produced by the discharge, that matter becoming luminous by it, while the discharge is a dark one, as you call it, from one luminous place to another one.

I had the opportunity to examine a great number of tubes containing traces only of matter of a different kind. Since I showed the beautiful effect they present, at the Meeting of Bonn, several hundred of them have been sent to all countries, except till now to England. If any of my English friends had assisted to the meeting, I would have found the opportunity to send to you and to Mr Barlow some of them. – Since that time I observed a quite new series of phenomena, which exhibit a very fine appearance. I can, in a few words give no better account of them but by saying, that I am enabled by means of the electric light, to *render luminous your lines of magnetic force*.

There is round the positive electrode (where heat is produced) a luminous atmosphere, sometimes of some inches in diameter, separated by a dark space from the Stratified light. By means of the Magnet this light is concentrated, if the electrode be a single point, to a brightly coloured line of magnetic force, passing through that point. If the electrode be a platina wire every point of it produces such a luminous curve. The system of all these curves constitue [*sic*] luminous surfaces of different forms, depending only upon the position of the poles. By commutating the polarity these luminous curves and surfaces of magnetic forces do *not* change.

What will do the light surrounding under different circumstances the *negative* Electrode?

In a paper sent to Poggendorff. I gave a first account of these curious phenomena.[1] When printed I'll send to you a copy of it.

With all my heart
Yours
PLÜCKER

[1] J. Plücker, 'Ueber die Einwirkung des Magneten auf die elektrische Entladung in verdünnten Gasen', *AP*, 179 (1858), 88.

[*I.E.E., B.J.* 2, *395*]

Observatory,
Chritiania [*sic*],
30 Dec. 1857

DEAR AND HONORED SIR.

I thank you heartily for your letter of 16 Decbr. at first while you have written yourself, as you could better declare the circumstances – and secondly while I thereby have received an autographic letter from a man, which I in many years have honoured as one of the chief notabilities "in rebus magneticis". I preserve with delight and perhaps a little vanity letters from different English scientifical notabilities, as Sir Joseph Banks, Sir David Brewster, Professor Airy, Prof. Forbes, General Sabine, Prof. Barlow and others; and to this treasure I now can add yours.

Professor Oersted was a man of genius, but he was a very unhappy experimentator; he could not manipulate instruments. He must always have an assistant or one of his auditors, who had easy hands to arrange the experiment; I have often in this way assisted him as his auditor. Already in the former century there was a general thought, that there was a great conformity and perhaps identity between the electrical and magnetical force; it was only the question how to demonstrate it by experiments. Oersted had tried to place the wire of his galvanic battery perpendicular (at right angles) over the magnetical needle, but remarked no sensible motion. Once, after the end of his lecture as he had used a strong galvanic battery to other experiments, he said, "let us now once, as the battery is in activity, try to place the wire parallel with the needle". As this was made he was quite struck with perplexity by seeing the needle making a great oscillation (almost at right angles with the magnetic meridian). Then he said: "let us now invert the direction of the current", and the needle deviated in the contrary direction. Thus the great detection was made; and it has been said, not without reason, that "he tumbled over it by accident". He had not before any more idea than any other person, that the force should be *transversal*. But as Lagrange has said of Newton in a similar occasion: "Such accidents only meet persons, who deserve them." You completed the detection by inverting the experiment, by demonstrating, that an *electrical current* can be excited by a *magnet*; and this was no accident, but a consequence of a clear idea. I [word illeg.] your many later important detections, which will conserve your name with golden letters in the history of magnetism.

Gauss was the first, who applied your detection to give telegraphic signals from the observatory in Göttingen to the physical hall in a distance of almost an English mile from the observatory.

I very well understand your situation. I can also not work in company with other persons, and I read not much, for not to be distracted from my own way of thinking. I allow that thereby many things escape me, but I fear to be distracted upon sideways. "Non omnia possumus omnes". Every one must follow his own nature.

I have translated an extract of your letter, and sent it to Göttingen to Mr. Arndtsen.

In the summer 1819 I visited in long time almost every day the library in "Royal Institution" in order to extract magnetical observations (declination and inclination) from old works, which our University was not in possession of, for instance "Haculuyt"[1] [*sic*] [reading doubtful] and "Purchas his pillegrims"[2] [*sic*] etc; so I am acquainted with the place of your activity.

I have in this year received your portrait from Mr. Lenoir in Vienna, as also of Sir David Brewster. They shall decorate my study on the side of Oersted, Bessel, Gauss and Struve.

> Believe me Sir sincerely your
> very respectful
> CHR. HANSTEEN

[1] Probably Richard Hakluyt, *Divers voyages touching the discoverie of America*, London, 1582.
[2] Samuel Purchas, *Purchas his Pilgrim*, London, 1619.

---

677 A. THOMPSON D'ABBADIE[1] to M. FARADAY,
21 January 1858
[*I.E.E., previously unpublished*]

> Paris,
> rue Bellechasse 31,
> 1858 Jany. 21

MY DEAR SIR

Some time ago you were kind enough to inform me that your heavy glass is not to be had in England. As I am in great want of it I have tried to persuade several glass manufacturers to undertake the making of it, and at last Messrs Mars & Clémandot of Paris have consented if I can be fortunate enough to obtain from you answers to the following queries for they do not like to make several trials.

1. What are the ingredients? 2 their proportions. 3. Are they melted at a low or a high heat? 4. is there any particular process (in French, *tour de main*) necessary to prevent the formation of Striae and the Separation of ingredients according to their density? 5. What sort of crucible was employed by you? 6. How much of the glass did you find it convenient to make at once? 7. what was the Size of the largest *pure* bit of your heavy glass.

I do not wish to encroach on your valuable time by requesting an answer in your own hand, but I hope that you may be kind enough to direct one of your assistants to pen the answers to the foregoing questions and send them, *not* prepaid, to me at rue Bellechasse 31 Paris.

23-2

It is with much reluctance that I here venture to trespass on your time, but the only frenchman who ever made glass with an index of refraction equal to 2, & even then in small quantities & impure, is now dead, & if you do not come to my help I am afraid that I must give up my plan of improvement in Astronomical instruments. I hope at all events that I may some day be able to return your preceeding kindness towards me, & remain

ever most truly yours
ANTOINE D'ABBADIE
Correspt. de l' Institut

[1] Antoine Thompson d'Abbadie (1810–97), astronomer and explorer.

678 J. P. GASSIOT to M. FARADAY, 30 January 1858
[*Faraday's 'Diary', 7 (1855–1862), 423*]

30th Jany. 1858[1]
Saturday, 10 o'clock.

MY DEAR FARADAY,
    After you left I made the following experiment:

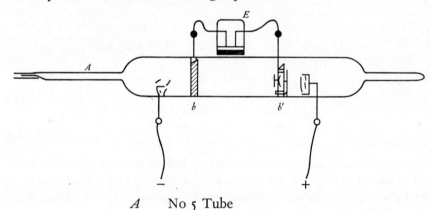

A   No 5 Tube
b, b'   2 Clips attached to
E   a Dble. leaf Electroscope

Whether the clips *were as in figure* or *separated to their fullest extent* or *nearly in contact*, the leaves of the Electroscope always *repelled*, shewing that at no time were there signs of opposite states of Electricity on the Tube.
    When Wheatstone saw the Experiment in this (or a similar tube), he considered the striae as mere cases of induction, alternating + and −; if the experiment is correct this cannot be the case – at all events I give you the fact as I observed it,

Believe me
truly yours
J. P. GASSIOT

[1] According to *B.J.* 2, this letter was dated by Faraday.

679 W. Snow Harris to M. Faraday, 27 March 1858

[*I.E.E., previously unpublished*]

4 Windsor Villas
Plymouth,
27 March 1858

My dear Faraday

You have always been so kind and considerate toward me that I have really very conscientious scruples, in venturing upon this communication which I fear must to some extent intrude on your valuable time and attention but the fact is I am now seriously engaged on what I hope may be at least a useful Work to be entitled "Statical and Dynamical Electricity"[1] and which will comprise I hope the existing state of Electrical Philosophy to the present time under an original form & containing something more than is constantly repeated over & over again in Works of this kind – I have now a very completely fitted apartment with Instruments for daily investigation – some good may be done in this way and future times will judge of the real merits of my Work. This also is much better than vanishing discussions of a controversial kind

– Now it is most important to me to be assured that I fully & clearly comprehend all your advances in your immortal Work "Experimental Researches" Which I am ever studying. It is really very difficult to say what questions bearing on Electrical force it does not treat. –

When you say 1177 "that it is impossible to charge a portion of matter with one Electrical force independently of the other" I suppose you mean to say that the opposite force always appears somewhere – or is always called up: now I want to avoid collision with this view & the common notion that an insulated conductor may be electrified either *positively* or *negatively* When I throw sparks from the positive Conductor of the Elec! Machine upon the Insulated metal Ball *A* may it not be said to remain in a certain sense charged with one of the Electrical forces? – can we say that the opposite force is at the same time also called up on this positively electrified Ball *A*?

As all charge is necessarily determined to the Surface – it seems a delusion to talk of charging the Ball *A* itself at all. I believe you agree in the Idea that the Ball is the mere terminating or beginning of that peculiar condition of the Intervening dielectric medium external to it. – I should imagine that the depth of the charge whatever it be upon the surface of the Ball is infinitely small yet it has certainly possession of the metallic particles – and there is a stratum of dielectric particles also outside it charged with the same Electricity – this we see by Franklins [*sic*] Experiment with the Leyden Jar and moveable coatings moreover you can not easily deprive the Metal of this charge for if an Electrified Ball be whirled round in the Air with any Velocity by means of a silk line – still the charge remains – so I think the Metal must hold some of the Charge as

895

Metal – and probably by attractive force for the Electrical agency Then again we have the outer stratum acting sensibly through the medium around it. Thus if we apply metallic discs *ab* to a dry Glass disc *abc* one on each side and charge *a* in the usual way *b* being for the time connected with the Earth – remove the charged discs *ab* by the insulators *mn* – each will be found Electrified – but one + the other minus – now the glass disc itself shows the Electricity of the charged side *a* every where the charge left under disc *a* upon the glass acts freely

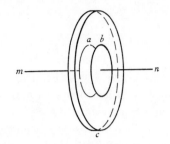

upon an Electrometer through the Glass and is radiated as it were from the opposite surface – what should we say – supposing an objector were to remark upon the Theory that metal disc *a* charged positively ought to induce *negative* Electricity upon the Glass beneath it – and so we should find negative not positive Elec.ʸ upon the glass – In any new work on this subject (which is greatly wanted) the whole form of expression as to language requires to be altered and we must study to adapt description by approximate terms to the real state of things taken in all their generality I should never for example talk of Electrical Fluids but rather of Electrical force – or of the charging of Metallic Balls or other Conductors with Electricity as if the whole mass were independently affected &c &c

In reply to Dr Hare[2] you put the case of 3 Bodys(?) *ABC*

A is directly + originally
B + on one surface and – on the other
C – you say.

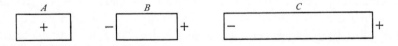

I think we must consider *C* as a polar charge also in a certain sense – If connected with the Ground the whole is but another Conductor and what may be called the positive force must exist in *C* at an infinite distance as If its extension were limited thus

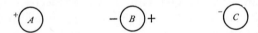

but the + of *C* is with unlimited extension a vanishing quantity

So again the charge upon *A* is disturbed by reaction of *B* placing its two extremitys [*sic*] on somewhat dissimilar plates – we might have an arrangement such as to bring the distance force of *n* into a plate of neutrality or even to pass that limit in which case *A* would be polarly charged.

As you have defined the case in your reply to Dr Hare it is all well enough. I had much correspondence with some French Philosophers relative to Conduction across a vacuum & your notion of considering forces only as mere force without taking into the account solid indivisible Atoms – you are aware that my little unpretending Work has been Translated into French by M. Gernault Professor of Physics à l'Ecole navale à Brest – under the Title of "Lecons Elementaire D'Electricite" – They have much difficulty in conceiving all this on the other side of the Water and I had hard work to explain to them what we were to really understand by your Theory It may appear silly to many persons – but I can not see what mere space or distance has to do with the question. If two Bodys [*sic*] are so circumstanced as to have *nothing* between them – they must be considered for all practical purposes as touching each other. Thus Body *A* and mere space *a* and Body *B* would Electrically con-

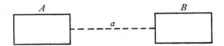

sidered be as one Body *AB* and the whole would suffer Inductive charge [reading doubtful] from a charged Body *C* in each case alike. – With respect to

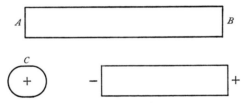

positive & negative Electricity – I believe the real difference to consist in the operation of the same force in different ways. Take a Spiral Spring *ab* at rest

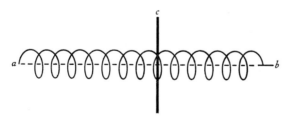

with a central fixed bar *c*; and let the ends *ab* be connected through the Spring by a cord *ba* – extend the cord at *b* in direction *ab* the result will be the extension of the Spring in direction *cb* and compression in *ac* thus If we allow the Spring

897

to react on Spirales [*sic*] by expansion *b* reacts by contraction – I call the extremity *b* negative force, extremity *a* positive force if you like. I think opposite Electricitys [*sic*] have some analogy to this –

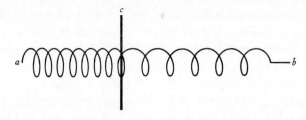

Do you know any case of friction in which Amber gives positive Electricity?

always yours
W. S. HARRIS

[1] I find no such treatise listed either in the catalogue of the British Museum or in that of the Library of Congress.
[2] See Letter 245.

680   M. FARADAY to C. V. WALKER,[1] 3 April 1858
[*Patent Office Library, London, previously unpublished*]

Brighton
3 April 1858.

MY DEAR SIR

I have an impression that the Specific inductive capacity of Gutta Percha is nearly 2. but I cannot remember the exact experiments: – as to Trinidad bitumen I cannot say any thing.

When an electric current is sent into a submerged insulated wire the effect may for the moment be considered as two fold. one part *dynamic* dependant on the current; – the other *static*, dependant on the momentary charge of the wire: Both may be resolved into one law of action. acting *along* & *across* the wire, but with infinite degrees of difference in the two directions; the difference being as great as that of *insulation & conduction*. Your question refers to the *static* part. i.e the induction of the wire through the gutta percha towards the iron coating or towards the water outside. Now the true principles of static induction (as I have understood them & endeavoured to promulgate them for many years past) offer no advantage from the expedient you propose. Suppose the diagram to represent a section of a telegraph cable *a* being the central wire, – *b* gutta percha, – *c* a continuous metallic tube – *d* gutta percha, – and *o* either the outer iron wire or the water. On sending a positive current through *a* it, for the moment, induces laterally across *b c* & *d*. the action terminating at *o* where

898

[reading doubtful, ms. blotted] it raises up the negative state. If you attempt to charge *c* positive at the same time with *a* the charge given to *c* will induce outwards towards *o* not inwards towards *a* – indeed pos *a* will induce a *negative* state on the inside of *c* & a positive state on its outside; which, with that given

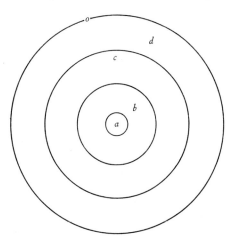

to it purposely, will act with increased force towards *o* rendering its inside equivalently negative. – As regards pure static action you will see these principles stated in the last paper I sent you; and I should expect as concerning *static* action, that *a* would be in a better state with *c* away i.e. replaced by gutta percha.

Then there come the dynamic inductions If a momentary current be sent through either *a* or *c* it tends to send a reverse currents [*sic*] through the other; and therefore if like short currents were sent through *a* & *c* at once, they would affect each other. – You may think it worth while making experiments of this kind. Only I may observe, that, as the two states must be kept up throughout the whole length of the cable there seems no reason, theoretically, why *a* & *c* should not coalesce that is be made into one central wire & all the electric current thrown into it.

I am My dear Sir
Very Truly Yours
M. FARADAY

[1] Charles Vincent Walker (1812–82), Secretary of the London Electrical Society and electrician to the South Eastern Railway Co.

681   M. FARADAY to C. F. WINSLOW,[1] 26 April 1858[2]

[*Boston Daily Advertiser, Tuesday 26 October 1858*]

Royal Institution,
London,
April 26, 1858.

Dear Sir: – I write at once to acknowledge your letter and your paper on the relations of the sun and the earth. I am very glad to see you occupied on the subject, and certainly have been very much surprised by your monthly table of earthquakes and volcanic eruptions. The relation of these mighty terrestrial phenomena to the distance at which our earth is placed from the sun at the time, seems as if it could only be referred to the amount of heat received at the time from the sun, or else to some function of gravity varying, as it does, in accordance, as to time, with the phenomena. I sincerely wish you may establish your view, i.e. may by further examination of the phenomena prove it to be the truth. We none of us want anything but the truth, but when the truth is in a new direction and aside from our preconceived notions, we are often very slow to receive it. I should be very glad to find some effect of gravity that might be considered complementary to the variation of that force by change of distance, but the thought is very coldly received here. I see no reason to change my own impressions; but I should rejoice to find them receiving either expansion or correction from such views as yours.....I do not imagine that I shall hear from either —— or ——, on the subject of your paper. I doubt whether either are as yet favorable to such views as ours. If the views be truth, it will require time for them to make their way. Still they are announced, and I am persuaded will progress, though probably not much in the present generation.

I am, sir, your very obliged servant,
M. FARADAY

[1] Charles Frederick Winslow, M.D., (1811–77), author of a number of works on cosmology. Perhaps his most important book was *Force and Nature; Attraction and repulsion, the radical principles of energy discussed in their relations to physical and morphological developments*, London, 1869.
[2] See Letter 692.

682   A. DE LA RIVE to M. FARADAY, 10 May 1858

[*I.E.E., previously unpublished*[1]]

Genève
le 10 mai 1858

MON CHER AMI,

Ayant appris par mon ami le profr Marcet que vous vous occuperez Monsieur Gassiot & vous, des effets lumineux si remarquables que produisent les décharges électriques de l'appareil inducteur de Ruhmkorff dans les tubes de

Geissler, & de l'influence que le magnétisme exerce sur ces décharges, je viens vous rappeler que j'avais le premier signalé cette influence sous une forme différente, il est vrai, mais plus remarquable, à mon avis, que celle qu'a fait connaitre Mr Plucker. La note qu'a publiée à ce sujet le savant physicien de Bonn[2] m'a engagé à répéter mon expérience & m'a fait sentir la nécessité d'ajouter à sa description quelques détails sur la manière de la reproduire avec un succès certain. Du reste je viens d'avoir l'occasion, dans un Séjour tout récent que j'ai fait à Berlin, de la faire dans le laboratoire de Mr Magnus[3] en présence de cet illustre physicien & de Messieurs Riess, Dove,[4] Dubois-Reymond & Wiedemann,[5] qui ont tous été témoins de la facilité avec laquelle elle réussit.

J'ai déjà décrit, soit dans une lettre adressée à Mr Regnault & insérée dans les Comptes rendus de l'Académie des Sciences de Paris de 1849 (T.29), 'soit dans mon Traité de Electricité [sic] (T.II p. 308) l'appareil destiné à montrer l'action dont il s'agit. Il consiste [reading doubtful] dans un ballon dans l'intérieur duquel est une tige de fer doux entourée, sauf à ses deux extrémités d'une couche isolante très épaisse; une des extrémités de la tige se trouve à peu près au centre du ballon, tandis que l'autre, sort du ballon par une tubulure de manière à pouvoir être placée sur le pole d'un électro-aimant. Les décharges électriques s'établissent, quand l'air est suffisamment raréfié dans le ballon, entre l'extrémité intérieure de la tige de fer & un anneau métallique qui entoure cette tige par dessus la couche isolante dans sa portion la plus rapprochée de la tubulure.

La première fois que j'avais fait l'expérience, je m'étais servi pour produire les décharges d'une machine hydro-électrique d'Armstrong; plus tard je fis usage d'une machine électrique ordinaire, seulement le phénomène était moins prononcé, ce qui tient à la moins grande puissance de la source électrique & surtout à la moindre continuité des décharges. Mais, comme la machine d'Armstrong n'est pas d'un maniement commode, j'ai vu qu'on pouvait la remplacer avec avantage par l'appareil d'induction de Ruhmkorff en faisant communiquer l'une des extrémités du fil induit avec la tige de fer doux, & l'autre avec l'anneau intérieur de cuivre au moyen d'un fil de métal soudé à cet anneau, & qui traverse la tubulure en restant isolé du fer doux. Je dois ajouter qu'il est nécessaire, pour le succès de l'expérience, que le ballon renferme une certaine quantité de vapeur dont la tension soit de 4 à 6 millimètres de mercure; la vapeur d'eau qui reste ordinairement dans le ballon quand on y fait le vide à 3 ou 5 millimètres près, est quelquefois suffisante pour la production du phénomène; mais il est préférable d'y introduire directement cette vapeur, & mieux encore une vapeur provenant d'un liquide plus volatil, tel que l'alcool, l'éther, ou le sulfure de carbone; la vapeur d'essence de térébenthine m'a donné également un bon résultat. Il suffit, pour introduire ces vapeurs, de faire une première fois le vide dans le ballon, d'y faire entrer l'air en l'ouvrant audessus d'un flacon renfermant le liquide dont on veut introduire la vapeur qu'on chauffe légèrement si, comme l'essence de térébentine il n'est pas suffisamment volatil; puis on fait de nouveau le vide dans le ballon à 4 ou 6 millimètres près.

Une fois l'appareil ainsi disposé, on fait communiquer l'électrode positive de l'appareil de Ruhmkorff avec la tige de fer doux & la négative avec l'anneau; on voit aussitôt un ou plusieurs jets lumineux distincts partir du sommet de la tige & former entre ce sommet & l'anneau des lignes courbes semblables à celles de l'oeuf électrique; en même temps la partie supérieure de la tige est couverte de points brillants agités comme les particules d'un liquide en ébullition. Aussitôt qu'on aimante la tige de fer doux en la plaçant par sa base sur le pole d'un fort électro-aimant, les jets lumineux prennent un mouvement rapide de rotation extrêmement prononcé & parfaitement visible, dans un sens ou dans un autre, suivant que le pole de l'électro-aimant est Nord ou Sud. En même temps les points brillants qui étaient sur le sommet de la tige de fer disparaissent & sont chassés sur les bords où ils forment un anneau lumineux qui tourne comme les jets & dans le même sens. Quand on change la direction des décharges induites, le sens de la rotation est renversé.

Sans m'arrêter aux différents détails du phénomène & qui varient avec la nature des vapeurs qu'on a introduites dans le ballon, sujet sur lequel je reviendrai incessamment, je me bornerai pour le moment à remarquer que lorsque la rotation dure un certain temps, les jets s'épanouissent & finissent par former autour du cylindre de fer doux une [illeg.] cylindrique lumineuse presque continue qui tourne avec une grande rapidité, mais dont la rotation est souvent difficile à saisir dans ce cas à cause de la continuité de la lumière. Pour obtenir de nouveau les jets dont la rotation est si sensible, il faut arrêter le passage des décharges & réintroduire de la vapeur.

Sans insister, de nouveau sur l'analogie que présentent les phénomènes électromagnétiques lumineux que je viens de décrire avec l'Aurore Boréale, analogie que j'ai exposée dans mon *Traité de Electricité* [sic] (T.III p. 292), je ne puis m'empêcher cependant de saisir cette occasion pour rappeler en faveur de cette analogie l'observation que vient de faire le Docteur Robinson (*Phil. Mag. April 1858*),[7] que la lumière de l'Aurore Boréale possède comme la lumière électrique, la propriété de rendre fluorescentes les substances qui en sont susceptibles, propriéte qui est due [reading doubtful] à la présence chez les deux lumières également des rayons les plus réfrangibles.

Agréez, &c. . . .

A. DE LA RIVE

Mon cher & excellent ami,[8]

Marcet qui arrive de Londres me dit que vous n'avez pas réussi à reproduire mon expérience de la rotation de la lumière électrique; or, comme à mes yeux cette expérience a une grande importance soit en elle même, soit pour la théorie de l'Aurore Boréale & que je viens de la faire à Berlin avec le plus grand succès, je vous envoie sous forme de lettre, quelques détails à ce sujet que vous me feriez un vrai plaisir, si cela est possible, de faire insérer dans le *Phil. Mag.* J'y tiens d'autant plus que Mr Plucker à l'air de s'attribuer le mérite d'avoir trouvé le premier l'influence du magnétisme sur les décharges, tandis que je l'avais déjà fait connaitre en 1849 dans ma lettre à M' Regnault. – Au reste ce n'est pas la première fois que Mr Plucker laisse quelque chose à désirer dans ses rapports avec les autres savants; on le sait bien à Berlin & demandez le à Tyndall & à vous même.

Je vous écrirai plus en long incessamment, j'ai fait un petit voyage des plus intéressants en Allemagne & à Berlin; j'espère que vous êtes bien ainsi que Madame Faraday; mes meilleures amitiés à M' Tyndall. – M'autorisez-vous à vous appeller dans ma lettre: *Mon cher ami?* Ce titre m'est bien doux, comme vous le savez.

Marcet m'a parlé des belles expériences qu'il a vues à Londres avec les tubes de Geissler; je les ai aussi vues & répétées à Berlin soit chez Riess, soit chez Dove avec qui j'ai analysé la lumiere de ces décharges [4 words illeg.] lumière qui présente une disposition particulière des raies du spectre. C'est un sujet bien curieux & intéressant dont le mérite revient plus à Mr. Geissler qui a eu l'idée de faire ces tubes & qui y a réussi, qu'à Mr Plucker.

Vous me trouverez bien mauvais, vous qui êtes toujours si bon, à l'endroit de Mr. Plucker, mais cela vient de ce que a entendu Marcet. Il semblait que le physicien de Bonn avait tout fait dans ce sujet. – Permettez-moi de vous prier de demander en grâce à Mr. Gassiott [*sic*] en lui présentant mes compliments les plus affecteux, de répéter mon expérience sur une grande échelle, en prenant un fort électro-aimant & une puissante machine de Ruhmkorff, montée avec 3 ou 4 couples de Grove ou de [illeg.]; je suis sûr qu'il sera récompensé de sa peine, car cette rotation est bien belle à voir.

Votre tout devoue & affe.

A. DE LA RIVE

Je ne vous ai pas remercié, je crois, de votre bonne lettre du 26 mars & de la notice qu'elle renfermait qui m'a fort intéressé. – Vous savez combien vos lettres me font toujours plaisir. –9

[End of letter torn.]

¹ For an English translation of this letter, see *PM*, 4 s., 15 (1858), 463.

² See Letter 675, fn. 1.

³ Heinrich Gustav Magnus (1802–70), Professor of Physics at the University of Berlin.

⁴ Heinrich Wilhelm Dove (1803–79), meteorologist and Professor at the University of Berlin.

⁵ Gustav Heinrich Wiedemann (1826–99), physicist and (in 1863) Professor of Physics at the Polytechnicum in Braunschweig.

[6] 'Extrait d'une lettre de M. Auguste de la Rive à M. Regnault', *CR*, 29 (1849), 412.

[7] T. R. Robinson, 'On fluorescence produced by the Aurora', *PM*, 4 s., 15 (1858), 326.

[8] This letter follows on directly with letter 682 so I have kept it a part of it. Clearly, the first part was for publication, the second was private.

[9] I have been unable to locate this letter.

683   A. DE LA RIVE to M. FARADAY, 19 May 1858

[*I.E.E., previously unpublished*]

Genève
le 19 mai 1858

MONSIEUR & TRÈS CHER AMI,

Si par hazard la lettre que je vous ai adressée, il y a quelques jours, n'a pas encore parue dans le *Phil. Mag.*, auriez-vous l'extrême bonté d'y faire ajouter le *post-scriptum* ci joint; vous m'obligeriez infiniment. (Voyez la 3ème page).

J'ai répété ces jours derniers l'expérience dont je vous ai parlé & j'espère ne pas tarder à publier les résultats assez curieux que j'ai observés, dans un mémoire spécial.

J'ai eu un peu de remords de vous avoir parlé, comme je l'ai fait, de M. Plucker; j'étais peut-être encore un peu trop sous l'impression de ce que j'en avais entendu dire; j'espère que vous m'avez pardonné. –

J'aimerais bien aller vous faire une visite cet été; mais cela m'est impossible; il faut remettre ce plaisir à une autre année, si Dieu me prête vie. Si vous saviez tout le plaisir que j'aurais à vous voir, à vous serrer la main, vous comprendriez mes regrets de ne pouvoir réaliser cette année mon désir. D'autant plus que nous devenons vieux & que nous n'avons pas de temps à perdre; nous n'avons probablement pas jusqu'aux 89 ans comme l'illustre Humboldt que j'ai trouvé encore avec toutes ses facultés & son entrain d'autrefois. – Mais il lui manque malheureusement toujours quelque chose que la grâce de Dieu pourrait seule lui donner & dont l'absence est même plus pénible à son âge –

Ma femme me charge de ses compliments les plus affectueux; elle ne vous oublie point pas plus que votre tout dévoué & affectueux   A. DE LA RIVE

–Post-scriptum à la lettre de M. A. de la Rive à M. Faraday du 10 Mai 1858[1]

P.S. Mon cher ami,

Dans ma lettre du 10 mai qui renfermait quelques détails relatifs à mon expérience de la rotation de la lumière électrique autour du pole d'un électro-aimant, j'ai omis un point assez important que je viens vous signaler. Parmi les vapeurs que j'ai introduites successivement dans le ballon vide d'air, celle qui m'a donné le résultat le plus brillant & en même temps le plus constant, est sans contredit la vapeur d'éther sulfurique à la tension de 10 à 12 millimètres de mercure. Non seulement la rotation est tres prononcée dans un sens ou dans l'autre, suivant la direction des décharges & la nature du pole magnétique, mais l'expérience peut se prolonger très long-temps sans que les jets en s'épanouissant, comme cela arrive avec les autres vapeurs, changent un peu l'apparence du phénomène ou la rendent au bout d'un certain temps plus difficile à saisir. Les stries sont aussi très apparantes & plus durables. – Cette différence tient probablement à ce que la vapeur d'éther est dans le ballon à un état de tension & de densité plus grand que les autres & qu'elle est moins vite décomposée par le passage des décharges électriques.

[1] See *PM*, 4 s., 15 (1858), 466.

684 M. FARADAY to A. DE LA RIVE, 24 May 1858
[*Bibliothèque publique et universitaire de Genève, ms. 2316, f. 87–8, previously unpublished*]

Royal Institution
24 May 1858

MY DEAR DE LA RIVE

I have received both yours; and sent them both to the Philosophical Magazine to have the parts which are *intended* for publication published. I have no doubt they will appear in the next Number. I began to translate them; but they were taken from me that they might be done at once. I gave Tyndall your message who returns his own remembrances. The tubes which Gassiot & I worked with were those of *his own construction* not those of Geissler. Plucker brought some of Geisslers to London & shewed us some effects. I have not, & cannot read, Plucker's note; but I did not understand from him that he claimed any merits in the observations of the ordinary effect of a magnet over the electric discharge through air, but for a special effect which occurs at the Negative metallic termination. When that (the discharge) takes place in a globe there is a diffused light in the globe or part of the globe, having its seat on the negative wire: – not the brighter; light – but another feebler one – When this is held between the strong poles of a very large & powerful magnet, they being about an inch apart, – all that kind of light collects itself into a plate, leaving the other parts of the globe *dark*. – Further, this plate has the Negative wire *as a base or section* & in fact is formed upon it; the breadth of the plate of light is formed by the length of the wire left exposed in the vacuum; – the thickness of the plate is coincident with the thickness of the wire; & the length of the plate is given by the globe, for its ends abut suddenly against the glass. This plate of light is always coincident with the *lines of magnetic force* and makes them visible as iron filings render them visible; – with this restriction, that no light is visible except for *those lines of force which pass through the negative wire* i.e through the discharging part of the negative wire for if half the wire be coated with an insulator no light lines of magnetic force pass through the coated part.

Plucker has shewn me this phenomenon not to its full extent but very decidedly & I understand that, that, was what he claimed.

I have not your letters at present; but I can understand your feelings about Plucker. Do not think that they surprize me. I profess to be a peacemaker & therefore say little about such matters, unless circumstances call for it: – but scientific morality is not altogether satisfactory.

Your kind expressions my dear friend delighted me. I speak to very few friends (and to no other philosopher) as I do to you: – and why? because I have a trust in you in respect of matters beyond science. My kindest thoughts & remembrances (as also my wife's) to Madame De la Rive. Others, still very kind, as they ought to be, to Your Son, Marcet, & other friends.

Ever My dear De la Rive
Yours
M. FARADAY

685 J. PLÜCKER to M. FARADAY, 28 May 1858
[*I.E.E., previously unpublished*]

Bonn
28Th May 1858.

MY DEAR SIR!

At first my most sincere thank [*sic*] for all your kindness to me during my last stay in London. I never will forget the heartty [*sic*] reception I received, without *any* exception.

I was very much vexed that I was not able to show you the magnetic action on the electric current in all its beauty and with all the singular facts in connexion. I had selected for this purpose the finest tube which Geissler ever made; I thought it changed, but really it was broken by Geissler when put into the box and exchanged by an ordinary one of a similar shape. Thus I was able only to give a general idea of the curious phenomenon.

Being returned home I was most anxious to examine the *induction* current within the tube, I am indebted for to Mr Gassiots kindness. There is indeed between the two tin covers a double current *of equal intensity* and opposite direction, as indicated already by Mr. Gassiots experiment. When put equatorially between the two iron pieces one of the two currents is thrown upwards, the other one downwards; over a single pole the two currents, separated by the Magnet, are deflected within the horizontal plane. When put axially upon the two iron pieces, the two currents, obliged by the Magnet to *cross* each other, present a beautifull phenomenon difficult to be reproduced by a drawing. When the tube is put in an oblique direction upon the iron pieces I got two *separated* bright spirals, the one dextrorsum, the other one sinistrorsum. In some distance from the Magnet (when the action on both spirals is less different) we get two similar spirals; the lower one is interrupted, when the tube touches the iron pieces.

It was quite unexpected to me, to get essentially the same double current, when I connected one of the wires of Ruhmkorff's coil with the platina wire of the tube, the other one with the tin cover.

The double induction current exhibits a variety of phenomena when provoked in tubes of a different shape and containing traces of different gazes. –

After closer examination of the Torricellian vacuum, made with the greatest care, I am persuaded now that our best vacuum does not at all transmit an electric current and therefore not offer a luminous phenomenon. The double induction current seems to be even than transmitted when, for want of *sufficient* ponderable matter within the tube, the ordinary current between the platina wires is stopped. (Perhaps the double induction current may be transmitted by traces of ponderable matter deposited in the interior surface of the tube). I used tubes of the shape of Mr. Gassiot's. In one instance the double induction current having passed through the tube for a short time with a constant intensity, I interrupted the current, and connected the two wires of Ruhmkorff's coil to the two platina wires in the extremities of the tube; I was struck to get a very bright ordinary electric discharge which did not exist before; but, after some time the discharge became an interrupted one and finally entirely stopped. This experiment may be repeated as often as you like.

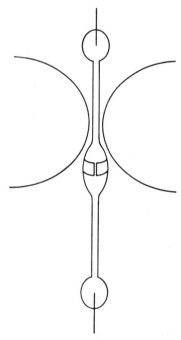

In order to verify the general law, according to which to the same colour corresponds the same refrangibility of rays, in the case of electric spectra produced in different most dilated gazes, I conducted the discharge of Ruhmkorff's coil through a double tube of this form.

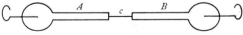

The two narrow tubes *A*, *B*, forming one straight line were connected to a platina wire *c*. One of the tubes contained traces of carbonic acid, the other one of hydrogene. Whatever might be the difference between the two spectra, the deflexion of the same colour in both spectra was the same. The strange appearances of the spectra are partly produced by contrast; I think also that some effect is to be attributed to fluorescent light.

There is, I think, no doubt that the blue colour in English tubes, corresponding to the green one in ours, is produced by imixed lead. I procured German glass, containing lead: tubes made of it gave a most intensive blue colour.

Lately I got a new case of magnetic light. Putting a tube of the shape *A*, in the equatorial position, with one of its narrow parts between the two poles, its larger middle part touching laterally the two iron pieces, I observed in the horizontal plane a fine magnetic luminous arch (*a*) completely seperated [*sic*] from the electric current. The two extremities of the arch touched the interior surface of the glass, as the magnetic arches do, which pass through the negative electrode. But in the new case the arch in the midst of the tube *is not at all directed by any conducting wire*.

You would oblige me very much, Sir, by communicating my observations, as you did in a former case, to Mr. Gassiot and also to Mr. Tyndall, who kindly intends to give an abstract of my papers, (the third did not yet appear) in the Philosophical Magazine.

I beg you, dear Sir, to present my respects to Mad. Faraday, and to Revd. John Barlow, the amiable Secretary of Royal Institution.

Ever yours
PLÜCKER

686   J. PLÜCKER to M. FARADAY, 28 June 1858
   [*I.E.E., previously unpublished*]

Bonn
28/6 58.

DEAR SIR!

I got the last number of the philosophical Magazine with de la Rive's letter, who characterizes my experiments as his own under a different form.[1] Allow me a few words. Davy's[2] and de la Rive's beautifull experiments are inscribed into the annals of science. In both cases the free luminous arch is substituted to the moveable copper wire, to which in your original experiments the current is bound. In that sense de la Rive's experiment of 1849 is that of „Faraday's pendulum". I published a series of experiments of the same kind which in like manner emanate imediately from yours and may be easily predicted.

But there is a second series of experiments, which I described in my first paper, of quite a different description. Such is the rupture of the current too. A copper-wire cant [*sic*] change its form under the influence of the Magnet, an electric beam, starting from a fixed point, can. The new class of phenomena show this change of form of the luminous current in a most splendid way. I am enabled now to explain the connection of these phenomena with the experiments you made about thirty years ago[3] and particularly with the mathematical law deduced from them by M. Biot and Laplace.[4]

The form which a flexible current assumes when in equilibrium under the influence of the Magnet is given by the following laws.

1.° When the current is free only to move on a given surface (that arrives, for instance, in the case of the double helix in Gassiot's induction tube) each moveable element of the current, acted upon by the magnet, is to be, by this action, compelled perpendicularly against the given surface: therefore the line perpendicular to the element and the line of force passing through it, must be a normal to the surface.

2.° When the flexible current, starting from a fixed point, is free to move in any direction whatever, each of its elements must be directed thus, that there is on it no action not at all emanating from the Magnet; id est it must be directed along a line of magnetic force. Whence you may imediately conclude that the whole current, when in equilibrium, is bent along the line of magnetic force passing through the fixed point.

I hope, my dear Sir, you will be satisfied by the simplicity of these new laws.

Most truly yours
PLÜCKER

PS. Since my last letter I observed a great variety of new facts. I am preparing a fourth paper. My third one is printed since a month but I could not yet obtain the copies. With regard to the two spirals, I mentioned in my last letter, by a „lapsus pennae" I said one dextrorsum the other one sinistrorsum. But both are either dextrorsum or sinistrorsum (independently of the direction of the primitive current of Ruhmkorff's coil and of the polarity of the Magnet) the tube in its oblique position being inclined either $+45°$ or $-45°$ to the equatorial plane.

[1] See Letter 682.
[2] See the footnote at the end of de la Rive's letter, *PM*, 4 s., 15 (1858), 466.
[3] M. Faraday, 'Electro-magnetic current', *QJS*, 19 (1825), 338.
[4] I am unable to identify these references.

687   G. B. AIRY to M. FARADAY, 12 August 1858 [copy]
[Royal Observatory, Herstmonceux, Misc. Corres., 1857–1859, A–K, Sect. 19, previously unpublished]

1858 August 12

MY DEAR SIR

Thank you for the Quartz threads, which arrived but a month ago, when I was going up the Tarantaise.

I returned from Switzerland ten days ago. I missed Tyndall at the Grimsel by one day, for which I am sorry. But I visited the Unter Aar Glacier in my own way, and am equally interested and puzzled. I did not see any of Tyndall's lenticular masses of ice there[1] but I saw plenty on the Eismear of the lower Grindelwald Glacier.

I should like much to live for a time in Agassiz's cottage[2] by the Aar glacier. Without some such near residence little can be done.

I am, my dear Sir,
Yours very truly
G. B. AIRY

[1] See J. Tyndall, 'On the Structure and Motion of Glaciers', *PM*, 4 s., 15 (1858), 365.
[2] Louis Agassiz (1807–73), the great naturalist and geologist.

688   J. D. FORBES to M. FARADAY, 14 August 1858
[I.E.E., previously unpublished]

Pitlochry
Perthshire
14 Augt 1858

MY DEAR SIR

I was very much obliged to you for your letter of the 23^d July, & especially for the expressions of regard which it contains & which I can assure you that I heartily reciprocate.

I am also much obliged by your remarks on my little paper;[1] on which I shall not trouble you with more than a few additional words.

I hope however that you will resume consideration of a subject which you are so well able to illustrate & which is still to a certain extent obscure.

I cannot doubt that regelation takes place between Ice & Metals. The pile of Shillings, though perhaps the simplest is not the only Experiment I have tried; but is so easy that I hope you will repeat it. I have frozen in like manner a Bronze letter presser of several pounds weight firmly to Ice in a warm room: but this requires a long time.

I do not see anything contradictory to the views which I have advanced, in the other experiments you mention. The finely triturated Ice – or Mr. Harrisons crystalline laminae when in contact with an indefinite mass of water clearly

910

belong to the portion of the curve in my figure between *N* and *O*, or to the physical boundary between water & Ice having a temp. intermediate between 31.7 and 32.0 & possessing the plastic quality proper to that intermediate state,

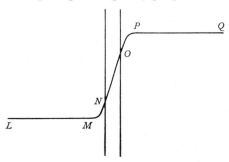

just as in the case of wax, tallow, or fusible metal, when portions brought into contact by a gentle pressure become moulded into one another's substance by molecular cohesion. Further in the case you mention where a quantity of finely triturated particles of ice are taken in the hand and squeezed together, I seem to understand perfectly why "regelation" takes place: – you have drained or squeezed away all the *perfect water* from the mass, & the molecules of plastic ice ceasing to receive heat from the perfect water [which is operating a minute fusion at the surface of each particle *without communicating the smallest quantity of heat to its interior*] the condition of the Ice becomes that of more or less hard Ice not being in contact with perfect water, & this is what is called regelation.

I had last the pleasure of seeing you at Greenwich in Oct 1851. Since the end of November in that year I have been more or less of an Invalid – at times severely ill – which will account for my comparative inactivity in matters of Science. I trust that your health is good & will long continue so.

Yours sincerely
J. D. FORBES

[1] J. D. Forbes, 'Sur quelques propriétés que présente la glace près de son point de fusion', *CR*, 47 (1858), 367.

689 M. FARADAY to J. TYNDALL, 2 September 1858
[*B.J.* 2, 407]

Royal Institution,
September 2, 1858

MY DEAR TYNDALL,

I might not have written to you again, but for the receipt of your letter by my wife, detailing the ascent of Monte Rosa, and the enormous indiscretion I have committed thereupon. What shall I say? I have sent it to the "Times."[1]

There, the whole is out. I do not know whether to wish it may appear to-morrow, or next day, or not. If you should dislike it, I shall ever regret the liberty I have taken. But it was so interesting in every point of view, showing the life and spirit of a philosopher engaged in his cause; showing not merely the results of the man's exertions but his motives and his nature – the philosophy of his calling and vocation as well as the philosophy of his subject, that I could not resist; and I was the more encouraged to do so because, from the whole character and appearance of the letter, it showed that it was an unpremeditated relation, and that you had nothing to do with its appearance, i.e. it will show that, if it should appear. How I hope you forgive me. Nobody will find fault with me, but you. It came too late for the "Philosophical Magazine," but if the "Times" does not put it in, I shall send it to the "Philosophical Magazine," However, as this is only the 3rd of the month, there is time enough for that.

I won't give you any scolding. I dare say my wife will when you see her. "Êtes vous marié?" indeed. I cannot help but feel glad you have done it now it is done; but I would not have taken the least portion of responsibility in advising you to such a thing.

I have no philosophy, and no news for you. I feel just out of the world – forgetful, and dull-headed in respect of science, and of many other things, but well and content, as I have great reason to be.

Good-bye, my dear friend, ever truly yours,

M. FARADAY.

Friday morning, 3rd. The letter is There.

[1] See *The Times*, 3 September 1858, 10. I have not reproduced the letter here for it appears to have been addressed to Mrs Faraday.

690 A. DE LA RIVE to M. FARADAY, 25 September 1858
[*I.E.E., previously unpublished*]

Genève
le 25 7ᵇʳᵉ 1858

MON CHER & EXCELLENT AMI,

Il me tarde de répondre à votre bonne lettre de ce printemps, & de vous en remercier. Quoique je n'aie eu aucune communication directe avec vous depuis cette époque, je n'ai pas moins été au courant de vos nouvelles par plusieurs amis communs, & en particulier par M – Hoffman que j'ai eu le plaisir de voir il y a quelques jours. Je sais que vous allez bien, grâce à Dieu, & que vous êtes toujours aussi jeune d'esprit & de corps. J'espère que votre tête ne vous fait pas souffrir; il me semble que depuis quelques années elle va aussi bien physiquement qu'intellectuellement. Dieu vous maintienne le plus long-temps possible dans cet état satisfaisant qui est une bien grande douceur pour vos amis.

Les enfants de notre bonne amie Madame Marcet m'ont demandé de faire une petite biographie de leur mère. Je m'occupe de ce travail qui est toujours un travail délicat & difficile. Il y a un point sur lequel vous pouvez me donner une information, & je viens vous prier d'avoir la bonté de me la donner. Est-il vrai que c'est la lecture des *Conversations sur la Chimie* qui vous a inspiré le premier gout pour la Chimie & la Physique & a déterminé la direction de vos travaux? Si cela est vrai, m'autorisez-vous d'en faire mention dans ma notice sur Madame Marcet?[1] Voilà les deux questions auxquelles je vous demande de vouloir bien me répondre; vous me rendrez un vrai service.

Un autre service que je vous demande encore, ce serait, si cela vous est possible, de donner à mon jeune ami Monsieur Alexandre Prevost, l'indication des Constructeurs d'instruments d'optique qui pourraient lui fournir des informations sur la quantité de verre optique de Dagart [reading doubtful] qu'on consomme en Angleterre. Monsieur Dagart va probablement transporter son établissement à Genève, & les personnes qui s'intéressent à cet établissement qui sera important pour notre pays, tiendraient à avoir ce renseignement. J'avais engagé Monsieur Prevost à recourir à votre complaisance pour cet objet; peut-être l'a-t-il déjà fait. – En tout cas je vous remercie d'avance des facilités que vous pourrez lui fournir pour cet objet. Il ne s'agissait que de lui donner peut-être une introduction auprès des personnes compétentes à cet égard, & personne ne peut mieux le faire que vous.

Pardonnez moi mon indiscrétion, Monsieur & cher ami; vous y êtes accoutumé, voilà tout ce que je puis vous dire pour mon excuse; ma femme me charge de ses meilleurs compliments pour Madame Faraday & pour vous & je vous prie de recevoir l'expression de mes sentiments les plus affectueux

AUG^E DE LA RIVE

Veuillez, quand vous verrez M' Tyndall, lui exprimer tous mes regrets de ce que je ne l'ai pas vu à son passage à Genève; je lui écrirai incessamment. –

[1] I am unable to discover a published notice by de la Rive on Mrs Marcet.

691 M. FARADAY to A. DE LA RIVE, 2 October 1858
[*Bibliothèque publique et universitaire de Genève, ms. 2316, f. 87, B.J. 2, 401*]

Hampton Court
2 October 1858

MY DEAR FRIEND

Your subject interests me deeply every way; for Mrs Marcet was a good friend to me, as she must have been to many of the human race. I enterd the shop of a bookseller and bookbinder at the age of 13, in the year 1804, remained there 8 years, and during the chief part of the time bound books. Now it was in these books, in the hours after work, that I found the beginnings of my philosophy. There were two that especially helped me; the Encyclopaedia Britannica, from which I gained my first notions of Electricity; and Mrs Marcets conversations on chemistry, which gave me my foundation in that science. I believe I had read about phlogiston etc in the Encyclopaedia, but her book came as the full light in my mind. Do not suppose that I was a very deep thinker or was marked as a precocious person; – I was a very lively, imaginative person, and could believe in the Arabian nights as easily as in the Encyclopaedia. But facts were important to me & saved me. I could trust a fact, – but always cross examined an assertion. So when I questioned Mrs Marcets book by such little experiments as I could find means to perform, & found it true to the facts as I could understand them, I felt that I had got hold of an anchor in chemical knowledge & clung *fast* to it. Hence my deep veneration for Mrs Marcet; first as one who had conferred great personal good & pleasure on me; – and then as one able to convey the truths and principles of those boundless fields of knowledge which concern natural things to the young, untaught, and enquiring mind.

You may imagine my delight when I came to know Mrs Marcet personally; – how often I cast my thoughts backward delighting to connect the past and the present; – how often when sending a paper to her as a thank offering I thought of my first instructress; – and such like thoughts will remain with me

I have some such thoughts even as regards *your own father*: – for when, later in life, I was first at the Royal Institution and then abroad with Sir H. Davy, your father was one of the very earliest, I think I may say *the first*, who personally, at Geneva, and afterwards by correspondance, encouraged and by that sustained me.

Though I have not seen M. A. Prevost I have had a letter from him & written a reply. I am afraid I shall be very useless for I have no knowledge of the opticians & am without the information he wants. An alien as regards Society, & of very bad memory, I cannot either pick up, or lay up, information of that kind; but thought the Dollonds might inform him.

My wife desires her kindest remembrances to you & Madame De la Rive. She keeps pretty well but cannot walk many yards. We are now at Hampton Court, in the house which the Queen has given me. We shall use it in the summer months, & go into town in the cold weather & the Season. I believe it will be a comfortable pleasure for the few years that remain of life; – but hope for a better house shortly; – and we may do that without presumption, seeing through whom it is that we obtain right to such a hope

Ever My dear friend
Yours Affectionately
M. FARADAY

[*I.E.E., previously unpublished*]

West Newton.
Mass
Nov. 5, 1858

MY DEAR SIR

Your valuable note dated at London April 26th[1] was received & I felt highly flattered by it. Notwithstanding your conclusions are not understood nor appreciated by astronomers & mathematicians – & because my doctrine of cosmic repulsion has been treated more contemptuously than by mere coldness by several opinionated mathematicians here, who could not see how cosmic repulsion could exist without destroying the force of gravitation, I value your encouraging words very highly.

The subjects of researches such as yours & mine, are very abstruse for common thinkers, & especially to astronomers educated strictly in the Newtonian faith do they seem like unnecessary innovations. These latter as teachers, think but little, & communicate to others what they were severaly [*sic*] taught: To think anything else would be heresy. They never think how rejoiced Newton would have been to be surrounded by such light & accumulated physical knowledge as we possess in these days. Nor what progress he would himself make on his own discoveries. Little by little however the world will wake up, & even astronomers like Arago in his last days will question the universe for *the other great secret* which has been so long hidden beneath the glare of the sublime Newtonian discovery.

The recent comet will greatly enlarge our knowledge of the forces at work within cosmic masses. Seen through the great equatorial telescope at Cambridge, as related to me by the Elder & younger Bond,[2] the translucent sphere was in a violent state of agitation, throwing up constant disruptions from its central parts toward the sun & these luminous outbreaks were then swept off behind the nucleus, that is in lines away from the sun as if some repulsive force proceeded from the sun which seized upon them & swept them off in rapid currents into space to produce luminous appendages. The elder Bond even assured me that it seemed as if some other force besides that of gravitation did exist in space & that it seemed to proceed from the sun. But he was greatly perplexed for an explanation of the phenomena, & said astronomers were very tender about admitting any other force than gravitation. I am truly glad, my dear Mr Faraday, that that comet, so beautiful, so wonderful, so full of tidings from infinite space & the hand of God, so full & overflowing with the secret forces which abide in the atoms of all cosmical spheres, should appear in *our* days & gladden *our* eyes & strengthen *our hearts* with the prospect of the increasing physical knowledge which must the sooner, open upon the world.

About the time I received you [*sic*] letter I received one also from M. Alexis

Perry [*sic*]³ of Dijon whose investigations on lunar agency in producing earth-quakes became known to me some time after I published my views in 1853, on *Solar* causation of the same phenomena. – The letters from both of you were read with great interest by a number of my friends who urged me by all means to have them published as an honor to their authors, as a means of advancing science, & as due to myself inasmuch as my views had been publicly ridiculed by two prominent & leading mathematicians in this country. I hesitated a long time, but an eminent scientific friend & prominent gentleman in Boston urged me so strongly upon the point that I consented to place copies of both the letters at his disposal – that is the philosophical portions of them. Now, my dear Sir, what do you think – This friend took them to the Boston Courier, a newspaper conducted with some ability, one of those editors is a Professor at Cambridge, & the organ of the Cambridge party or school or influence what-ever it may be called. – They were kept 3 weeks & then my friend had some difficulty to get them back & offered to pay for their insertion. But they would not publish them at any price, even as advertisements. I was surprized at this last, but not surprized that they were unwilling to publish at mere request; for in my controversy with Prof. Pierce⁴ last year on "The Sun & Continents", The Courier espoused his cause as he was the pride of Cambridge. It was however the only journal in Boston, or the United States who did take his part, & I saw the Courier was still in his interest or under his advisement or control. – The editor of the Boston Advertizer however very gladly availed himself of the opportunity to publish them as he esteemed them too valuable & of too much public & scientific importance to be longer suppressed.⁵ – I can only hope, the publication of your note will not meet your disapproval. – The next day after their publication, the *Courier* appeared with a short notice of "a new step in Cometology", announcing that "Prof. Pierce of Cambridge had at length" discovered or "accomplished" the theory of the Curvature of the comets tail "& had not "abstracted" the idea of it "in form nor substance from any Winslow, Warner, Peter's,⁶ or Bond." I smiled & wondered what the discovery was. Yesterday morning the Courier announced the Discovery itself – & it is no less a novelty than that the tail is the result of *repulsion whose force is about three & one third times as great as that of gravitation*! –

In your note you said you "should be very glad to find some effect of gravity that might be considered complimentary to the variation of that force by the change of distance" – As I view this department of nature it seems to me all magnetic force & its congeners or convertabilities, are secondary powers arising from disturbance of equilibrium in the two primal forces of attraction & repulsion at work among atoms. – It is a question with me now, the solution of which I am earnestly seeking, whether force does not exist & may not, independent of matter – whether it did not originally: – & did not also have existence prior to matter. In my contemplations I can divide forces into strata

916

(so to speak & illustrate thought by physical conditions) – & allowing matter to have affinities for gravitation which after certain accumulation, engenders a capacity for the manifestation of repulsion. I obtain the first class of phenomena – The play between these fundamental forces on atoms brings into existence – or manifestation to our senses – the second class including heat, light, magnetism, electricity. – which also I strongly suspect lie in latent or unappreciated conditions to our senses, outside of matter – the excitation of atoms by the dynamic play of condensation ie gravitation & [illeg.] only creating a capacity to receive forces whose fountains are boundless or rather would be boundless in space if matter was set at liberty from attachment to all force. As nature exists matter, & force, both primal & secondary with all their combinations & complications, are united, their relations only changing to produce all the phenomena of the physical world palpable or conceivable by our profoundest researches. – My idea might be illustrated by conceiving all forces united into a homogeny, like a ray of common light which dissolved by a prism presents a multitude of parts all possessing different functions or powers. Our mental prism may be clear enough one of these days, to dissolve the great secret of nature now hidden in the action & reaction of matter & force. At any rate it is by the *study of atoms* alone that progress can ever be *surely* made. However these atoms may accumulate never fear to follow the fundamental force as an increasing magnitude however mighty the mass may become. Gravitation is a unit in an atom – it is only a magnified unit in a world according to the number of atoms it embraces. So with repulsion: and in the mighty play of these accumulated forces we get heat light & magnetism, in proportion to the *amount* of matter & the *activity* of the primal forces which produce motion among the atoms. – In planets & comets these are more active the nearer the mass is to the sun & they must vary according to its distance from the sun. –

The earth is full of phenomena the opposite of gravitation. Did it ever occur to you that the growth of any tree is an act the contrary of gravitation & that the repulsion between atoms, which carries it upward, may be a mere conversion of the mundane force of gravitation into another living power – a compound of *magnetism* & *life?* – All these things are marvellous & I beg you to consider them. I am very truly Yours

C. F. WINSLOW

[1] See Letter 681.
[2] William Cranch Bond (1789–1859), director of the Harvard College observatory.
  George Phillips Bond (1825–65), successor to his father (in 1859) as director of the Harvard College Observatory.
[3] Alexis Perrey (1808–82), Professor at the University of Dijon. For his many papers on earthquakes, see *RSCSP*.
[4] Benjamin Peirce (1809–80), mathematician and astronomer.
[5] See Letter 681.
[6] Christian Henry Frederick Peters (1813–90), in 1858, was Director of the Litchfield Observatory in Clinton, N.Y.

Bonn
9th of Jan. 1859

MY DEAR SIR!

I thank you, sir, for your last kind letter of the 27[Th] of July, and would not answer it without comunicating to you some new results regarding the electric discharge through gaz vacua. I had observed already the double current – mentioned in your letter – which is produced in Gassiots tube, if only one tin-cover is touched by one wire of Ruhmkorff's coil. I had made use of it in order to confirm the theoretical views, contained in my paper of the 15[Th] of July. I closer examined double currents in a recent paper in order to get analogies with the negative light, constituting the magnetic curves and surfaces. I think it probable that this light, starting from its electrode returns to it in the same way. – If the current find resistance of any description in a longer evacuated tube it partly returns on its own way (will it not be the same in *very* long isolated copper wires?).

But by far the principal object of my last longer paper[1] (sent before Christmas, to Poggendorff) are the curious appearances of *positive* light which are as characteristic as those of negative light, already described. Let me try to give in a few words a general idea of them. From each of two electrodes entering an evacuated sphere of glass starts a peculiar kind of light. Even if the distance of the electrodes be a few millimeters only, there is produced no current; the double light, filling all the sphere is separated by the magnet. Suppose, for instance, an airvacuated [*sic*] sphere, through which are conducted two platina

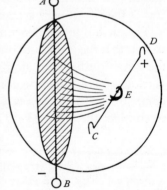

wires, equally distant from the centre and directed perpendicularly to each other. Put the sphere upon the two ironpieces of the Electromagnet, let the negative wire *AB* be vertical, the positive one axial ⸱,⸱ let the south polarity (the polarity of the North of the Earth) be behind. Then all the surface of the axial and vertical circle passing through *AB* will be illuminated with beautiful violet light, while the reddish yellow positive light is concentrated in *E* the midst of *CD* and from *E* it moves in a fine spiral toward *AB*. Between the comencement of the spiral and the positive wire *CD*, there is a small dark interval 𝈸 . The spiral does *not reach AB*.

After having changed the polarity of the magnet, the appearance of the illuminated circle will not change, but instead of the single spiral, you will get two spirals, starting from the two ends *C* and *D*, both turned in the same way,

918

but in opposite way as before ☽ ☾. After a comutation of Ruhmkorff's coil the phenomena totally change.

In my paper I described a great number of similar phenomena, especially with regard to the propagation of *positive* light. In admitting an electric particle – *sit venia verbi* – starting from the different points of the positive wire towards the negative one and applying to its movement the well known law of the action of the Magnet on a moved electric particle – I became enabled to predict all phenomena observed, regarding the concentration of the positive light in certain points of its wire, as well as the curves, which it follows towards the negative wire. With other words, the same laws, which determine the action on a formed current are applicable to its formation.

In our case the positive light goes all the way towards the negative wire; here the combination of both electricities takes place, accompanied with chemical action and production of heat. The magnetic light, which has nothing to do with the current itself, may probably take its origine [*sic*] from these same sources.

If the air be less rarefied *all* changes. Accidentally my above mentioned sphere got a fissure through which air entered M O S T slowly. The electric light opposed by an [*sic*] by a greater resistance to the magnetic action. The magnetic light of the circle *AB* disappeared, the positive light of the spirals became better defined and, at a certain period, the spiral above indicated by a few lines had a most striking resemblance with Donati's comet.

The indications of the nature of the electric discharge given to me by the magnet seems now, for the greater part, to be exhausted. Its analysis by the prism remains rather unexplored [*sic*]. I would be happy if I could myself show to you the spectra of pure gazes, presented by the positive light on its way to the negative wire. The number of those spectra, observed by myself, is always increasing. The spectrum of mercurial vapour (at the ordinary temperature) is the most brilliant and the most instructive too (The light in my tube of Gassiot is produced by this vapour).

The discontinuity of the index of refraction in the gaz-spectra is very extraordinary. If you observe through a telescope a narrow aperture illuminated by electric hydrogene-light, you will see a red band, we may suppose under an angle of 3′–15′. (For my researches I wanted exact measures of angles) In interposing a prism of flint, you will observe *under the same angle* on a dark ground three fine bands, the first one is red, the second bluish green, the third violet. The second band is distant from the first about 3°, the third about 5°. Hence you deduce three different absolute indices for the electric hydrogene-light.

The pure gaz-spectra are only obtained by the current of *positive* light through most rarefied vacua. The light of the negative wire gives the spectrum of the gaz, mixed with bands depending upon the metal of the wire. &c &c &c –

919

Poggendorff was not so kind to send me copies of my paper, I am not able therefore to send some to England. I am anxious to know Gassiots new results, perhaps your own, if the seducing power of the object be great enough. Excuse me if I am too long. Pray give my respects and compliments [reading doubtful] to Mad. Faraday and believe myself with all my heart

Yours

PLÜCKER

1 See J. Plücker, 'Ueber die Constitution der electrischen Spectra der verschiedenen Gase und Dämpfe', *AP*, 183 (1859), 497.

694   B. C. BROOST to M. FARADAY, 14 January 1859
[*I.E.E., previously unpublished*]

14 Savile Row W,
January 14, 1859.

MY DEAR SIR

Pray do not think that in what I said last night I alluded in any way to the observations made in a lecture of yours formerly on the *force of gravity*; which indeed were not at the time at all present to my mind, & which, if my recollection be accurate, were based on an entirely different view of the subject.

All that I intended to say was that in physics not less than in metaphysics, there are boundaries beyond which, not only from the want of opportunities of experience, but also from the want of adequate powers of comprehension, the Human Intellect can not penetrate; & that we must be content to accept certain facts as well established, of which we can offer no explanation by referring them to any more general principle. For example: that there are good grounds for believing that there is something pervading the universe corresponding to Newtons [*sic*] notion of an Ether, I do not doubt; but if we venture further than this, & attribute the mutual attraction of masses of matter to the operation of such an ether, we do but substitute one simple fact for another simple fact, & endeavour to explain one thing by another thing which is equally inexplicable.

I dare say that you have forgotten, but I have not forgotton a conversation which I had with you long ago, in which I believe that you expressed yourself as agreeing with me in the opinion that of the ultimate structure of material bodies we neither have, nor can have any actual knowledge, & that neither the ordinary hypothesis of solid impenetrable molecules, nor Boscovich's hypothesis of mathematical points, which are centres of attraction & repulsion, is anything more than a contrivance for bringing these things down to the level of all limited comprehension.

I owe you some apologies for occupying so much of your time, & I can only make up for it by asking you not to think it necessary to take the trouble of writing an answer to what I have written.

Yours most truly
B. C. BROOST

695 M. FARADAY to Mrs MARY SOMERVILLE,
17 January 1859

[*Martha Somerville, 'Personal Recollections, from early life to old age of Mary Somer-ville, with selections from her correspondence', London, 1874, 292*[1]]

Royal Institution,
17th January, 1859.

MY DEAR MRS. SOMERVILLE,

So you have remembered me again, and I have the delight of receiving from you a new copy of that work which has so often instructed me;[2] and I may well say, cheered me in my simple homely course through life in this house. It was most kind to think of me; but ah! how sweet it is to believe that I have your *approval* in matters where kindness would be nothing, where judgment alone must rule. I almost doubt myself when I think I have your approbation, to some degree at least, in what I may have thought or said about gravitation, the forces of nature, their conservation, &c. As it is, I *cannot* go back from these thoughts; on the contrary, I feel encouraged to go on by way of experiment, but am not so able as I was formerly; for when I try to hold the necessary group of thoughts in mind at one time, with the judgement suspended on almost all of them, then my head becomes giddy, and I am obliged to lay all aside for a while. I am trying for *time* in magnetic action, and do not despair of reaching it, even though it may be only that of light. *Nous verrons.*

I have been putting into one volume various papers of mine on experimental branches in chemistry and physics.[3] The index and title-page has gone to the printer, and I expect soon to receive copies from him. I shall ask Mr. Murray to help me in sending one to you which I hope you will honour by acceptance. There is nothing new in it, except a few additional pages about "*regelation*" and also "gravity." It is useful to get one's scattered papers together with an index, and society seems to like the collection sufficiently to pay the expenses. . . . Pray remember me most kindly to all with whom I may take that privilege, and believe me to be most truly,

Your admirer and
faithful servant,
M. FARADAY

[1] I have used the Boston edition of 1874.
[2] The ninth edition of Mrs Somerville's *On the Connexion of the Physical Sciences* appeared in 1858.
[3] M. Faraday, *Experimental Researches in Chemistry and Physics*, London, 1859.

696 Mrs MARY SOMERVILLE to M. FARADAY,
1 February 1859
[*R.I., B.J. 2, 424*]

Florence
February 1, 1859

MY DEAR DR. FARADAY

I cannot tell you how much I have been delighted and gratified by your letter, and by your kind acceptance of my book. I should not have dared to send it to you from any merit it may have in itself, but I have no other way of offering the tribute of my most sincere and heartfelt admiration of your transcendent discoveries of the laws and deep mysteries of nature.

I fear from what you say that I may have expressed myself ambiguously with regard to your views of gravitation. I certainly did not mean to do so, for on the contrary, they convey to my mind the most perfect conviction, and I only hope you may live to complete what Newton began, by the discovery of that one comprehensive power of which gravity and all the correlative and convertible forces are but parts – Meanwhile I wish you success in your research for time in magnetism, which there can be no doubt you will accomplish, having already so beautifully connected magnetism with light, whose velocity is known.

I fear you tax your health too severely; subjects so abstruse as you are accustomed to consider must fatigue even your mind, which makes occasional repose necessary; so I wish you would come here & amuse yourself for a little; we should be indeed delighted to see you, and there are many things that would interest you.

Many thanks for the volume of your papers and researches, which you intend to send to me; it will be a very precious gift – Mr Somerville and my daughters desire to be kindly remembered to you, and be assured that I am ever,

with sincere friendship, yours,
MARY SOMERVILLE

697 M. FARADAY to J. H. GLADSTONE, 2 July 1859
[*J. H. Gladstone, 'Michael Faraday', London, 1872, 178*]

Royal Institution of Great Britain,
2d July, 1859.

MY DEAR GLADSTONE, –

Although I have frequently observed lights from the sea, the only thing I have learned in relation to their *relative brilliancy* is that the average of a very great number of observations would be required for the attainment of a moderate approximation to truth. One has to be some miles off at sea, or else the observation is not made in the chief ray, and then one does not know the state of the atmosphere about a given light-house. Strong lights like that of Cape Grisnez have been invisible when they should have been strong; feeble lights by comparison have risen up in force when one might have expected them to be relatively weak; and after inquiry has not shown a state of the air at the light-house explaining such differences. It is probable that the cause of difference often exists at sea.

Besides these difficulties there is that other great one of not seeing the two lights to be compared in the field of view at the same time and same distance. If the eye has to turn 90° from one to the other, I have no confidence in the comparison; and if both be in the field of sight at once, still unexpected and unexplained causes of difference occur. The two lights at the South Foreland are beautifully situated for comparison, and yet sometimes the upper did not equal the lower when it ought to have surpassed it. This I referred at the time to an upper stratum of haze; but on shore they knew nothing of the kind, nor had any such or other reason to expect particular effects.

Ever truly yours,
M. FARADAY

698   J. PLÜCKER to M. FARADAY, 3 July 1859
[*I.E.E., previously unpublished*]

Bonn
3/7 59.

MY DEAR SIR!

I thank you very much for your last kind letter. allow me to answer it in giving a short notice on a new paper, printed just now in Poggendorffs Annalen.[1] I get a series of beautifull electric spectra by conducting the discharge of Ruhmkorff's Apparatus through a capillar [*sic*] tube. Two larger spheres or cylinders, into which the electrodes enter, cõmunicate by means of such a tube. The apparatus contains traces only of any gas or vapour. The general fact is that such a spectrum consists of a certain number of distinct coloured bands, having each the same largeness as the aperture has, when directly observed, without the interposition of the prism: i.e. the light in the spectrum is expanded in a certain number of discontinuous rays, each of which has a certain refrangibility, a certain length of wawe. [*sic*]

In hydrogen-gaz there are only three such rays, which I called H_α, H_β and H_γ. H_β exactly coincides with Fraunhofer's dark line F. H_α and H_γ are very near to C and G. The new bright lines may be most easily observed and their position measured with the greatest accuracy.*) They replace with great advantage Fraunhofers dark lines in determining the indices of refraction &c.

The bright bands of Oxigen are quite different ones, but not so easily obtained. Most brilliant are these bands in Chlore, Brome, Iod, Mercury, and especially in Chloride of tin (which partially is decomposed). In the larger parts of the apparatus the discharge through the Chloride is of a deep blue colour, in the capillar tube it shows the finest colour of pure gold. (When a larger tube is placed upon the Electromagnet golden lightnings, directed by the magnetic force continually move through the blue coloured space – a most beautifull and striking experiment.) Metallic Sodium, within an atmosphere of rarified hydrogen-gaz presents, when heated only one brilliant yellow ray. The spectrum of Nitrogen is the richest in colours. The space of the Red Orange and Yellow is divided by 17 dark lines in 18 bands of the same largeness. The violet bands are very brillant [sic]. Accordingly this gaz produces fluorescens [sic] in a high degre [sic] (Hydrogen-gas does not). Phosphorous, when heated in an atmosphere of rarified hydrogen, extinguished the spectrum of this gaz, without producing new bands. &c &c &c.

The spaces between the bright bands is either absolutely blak [sic] or of a greyish colour, or they are faintly coloured according to their place in the spectrum.

The aperture of the Goniometer, illuminated by the gaz, appears in my observations under an angle of 3 minutes, so does every single bright band in the spectrum. Smaler [sic] bands are never observed, larger bands are frequently. In the midst of bands, smaler then [sic] 6′ a bright line is often seen. Bands larger than 6′ are commonly divided by dark lines in two or more single ones, according to their largeness. Nearly all the violet part of the Nitrogen-spectrum offers striking instances of this case.

By diminishing the aperture of the Goniometer separated bright lines are finally obtained, some of them constituting groups. The refraction of these lines exactly equals to the refraction of the middle line of the former bands.

There is no doubt that the questioned spectra belong to the *gaz* only, the metal of the electrodes has nothing to do with them. I think, properly speaking, there exists no „electric light." The gazes become luminous by the current, Indeed what ought to be the enormous heat of the traces of the gaz within the capillar tube of the apparatus by which the temperature of the thik [sic] glas [sic] of this tube is increased 20° C and more. The difference of colour in smaler and larger parts of the same apparatus depends on the difference of heat.

I dont mention here any of the curious chemical actions produced within the spectra tubes and indicated by the spectra themselves. –

With regard to the stratification of light I observed many new phenomena, but my theoretical views are rather not promoted by them. The most curious fact is this. The *luminous discharge* which passes through certain tubes (one of them was about 6″ long and 1″ thik) is in all its length, by the Magnet, transformed into *a dark discharge of the same intensity*. This is easily shown, if such a tube, placed upon the iron pieces of an Electromagnet, comunicates with another tube in some distance from it. Then both tubes become luminous by the same electric discharge as long as the Electromagnet does not act, under its magnetic action the light in the first tube disappears, in the second tube it remains quite unaltered.

But all such phenomena are very difficult to describe: I whished [*sic*] I could *show* them to you. Unhappily our most uncertain political situation is till now not at all favourable to visit England this year.

Pray, dear Sir, present my respect, to Mad. Faraday. With the sincerest feelings of veneration

Yours
PLÜCKER

* I allways used a larger Goniometer comonly called of Babinet.
¹ See Letter 693, fn. 1.

699 M. FARADAY to Mrs DEACON,¹ 12 August 1859
[*B.J. 2, 428*]

The Green,
Hampton Court, s.w:
August 12, 1859

MY DEAR C[AROLINE],

I am a little tired, dull, and unable to work, or even to read; so I write to you. I have your letter before me, and so that is a moving cause; and it is rather grave, and that renders the cause more effectual. I never heard of the saying that separation is the brother of death; I think that it does death an injustice, at least in the mind of the Christian; separation simply implies no reunion; death has to the Christian everything hoped for, contained in the idea of reunion. I cannot think that death has to the Christian anything in it that should make it a rare, or other than a constant, thought; out of the view of death comes the view of the life beyond the grave, as out of the view of sin (that true and real view which the Holy Spirit alone can give to a man) comes the glorious hope; without the conviction of sin there is no ground of hope to the Christian. As far as he is permitted for the trial of his faith to forget the conviction of sin, he forgets his hope, he forgets the need of Him who became sin, or a sin-offering, for His people, and overcame death by dying. And though death be repugnant to the flesh, yet where the Spirit is given, to die is gain. What a wonderful transition it is! for, as the apostle says, even whilst having the first-fruits of the Spirit, the people of God groan within themselves, "waiting for the adoption, to wit, the redemption of the body." Elsewhere he says, that whilst in "the earthly house of this tabernacle we groan earnestly, desiring to be clothed upon with our house which is from heaven."

It is permitted to the Christian to think of death; he is even represented as praying that God would teach him to number his days. Words are given to him, "O grave, where is thy sting? O death, where is thy victory?" and the answer is given him, "Thanks be to God, who giveth us the victory through our Lord Jesus Christ." And though the thought of death brings the thought of judgment, which is far above all the trouble that arises from the breaking of mere earthly ties, it also brings to the Christian the thought of Him who died, was judged, and who rose again for the justification of those who believe in Him. Though the fear of death be a great thought, the hope of eternal life is a far greater. Much more is the phrase the apostle uses in such comparisons. Though sin hath reigned unto death, much more is the hope of eternal life through Jesus Christ. Though we may well fear for ourselves and our faith, much more may we trust in Him who is faithful; and though we have the treasure in earthen vessels, and so are surrounded by the infirmities of the flesh with all the accompanying hesitation – temptations and the attacks of the adversary – yet it is that the excellency of the power of God may be with us.

What a long, grave wording I have given you; but I do not think you will be angry with me. It cannot make you sad, the troubles are but for a moment; there is a far more exceeding and eternal weight of glory for them who, through God's power, look not at the things which are seen, but at the things which are not seen. For we are utterly insufficient for these things, but the sufficiency is of God, and that makes it fit for His people – His strength perfect in their weakness.

You see I chat now and then with you as if my thoughts were running openly before us on the paper, and so it is. My worldly faculties are slipping away day by day. Happy is it for all of us that the true good lies not in them. As they ebb, may they leave us as little children trusting in the Father of mercies and accepting His unspeakable gift.

I must conclude, for I cannot otherwise get out of this strain; but not without love to Constance, and kindest remembrances to Mr. Deacon . .

Ever, your affectionate uncle,
M. FARADAY.

¹ His niece.

700 G. B. AIRY to M. FARADAY, 16 August 1859
  [*I.E.E., previously unpublished*]

Royal Observatory,
Greenwich,
London, S.E.,
1859 August 16.

MY DEAR SIR

I want your assistance in a practical galvanic matter.

I am about to introduce a method of altering the rate of a clock by what is in fact a diminution or an increase of the gravity of the pendulum: thus effected.

To the pendulum is to be lashed a bar-magnet pointing up-and-down. To the clock case is to be fastened an ordinary galvano-magnet bobbin without its iron core, so that one pole of the magnet will, in the vibrations of the pendulum, sweep close over the pole of the bobbin. And when we send one current through the bobbin, it attracts the magnet and accelerates the clock: with the opposite current, the clock is retarded. All this works well. Now I want your information as to the best form of the bobbin or other convolution of wires. Ought it to be a bobbin? Ought there to be any particular relation of inside diameter to outside diameter? Ought the bobbin to be long or short? &c &c &c.

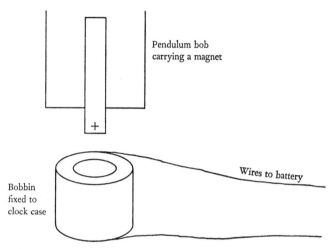

Pendulum bob
carrying a magnet

Bobbin
fixed to
clock case

Wires to battery

I am, my dear Sir,

Yours very truly
G. B. AIRY

701 G. B. AIRY to M. FARADAY, 19 August 1859
[*I.E.E., previously unpublished*]

Royal Observatory,
Greenwich,
London, S.E.,
1859 August 19

MY DEAR SIR

Your note shews clearly how difficult it is for a person who is possessed of all circumstances to think of detailing them sufficiently to any body else. I will supply my deficiencies as well as I can: and if you see the matter clearly, please to give me your advice: and if you do not see the matter clearly, *do not trouble yourself to write*, but wait till we can meet.

1. The pendulum carrying the magnet is to vibrate through an arc of $2\frac{3}{4}$ inches, or thereabouts.

2. Through the whole of this arc, the magnet pole is to be (*a*) attracted to, or (*b*) repelled from, the coil which is below. In the case (*a*), the pendulum's vibrations will be made quicker; in the case (*b*) they will be made slower.

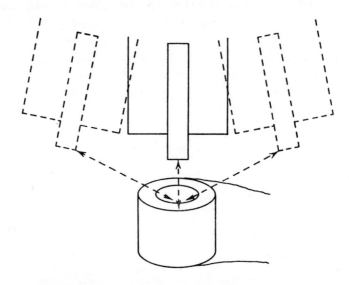

3. The dotted lines in the figure shew the extreme positions of the pendulum. The barbed lines shew the direction of force required in different parts of the vibration.

4. The case (*a*) is to be produced by turning on the battery in one direction, and the case (*b*) by turning on the battery in the opposite direction.

5. I expressly exclude iron core, because there would, when no battery is in action, be an attraction between the magnet and the iron core independent of battery, at times when I demand to have no attraction at all.

6. So the questions now are, Is the coil the most advantageous form of employment of current?

7. And if so, what shape and dimensions may be best?

I am, my dear Sir,
Yours very truly
G. B. AIRY

['*Papers on subjects connected with the Duties of the Corps of Royal Engineers contributed by Officers of the Royal Engineers, and East Indian Engineers*', *new series, 9 (1860), 47*[2]]

Note by the Inspector General of Fortifications.[3]

Having observed in the "Times" a letter from Professor Faraday, explaining a very simple mode of treating water that was contaminated by receptacles of lead in the neighbourhood of the sea (a matter of great interest at many military posts), I requested him to favour me with a note on the subject, with the addition of any simple practical remedies, if such there were, for the presence of lead in water arising from other combinations; and the folowing answer from that eminent chemist cannot be too generally promulgated and attended to among those who have charge of establishments on the sea coast.

Royal Institution,
7th Oct., 1859

MY DEAR SIR JOHN,

I consider your request relating to the leaded water an honour, and in replying may add an observation or two to the original matter. The case at first was simply that of certain waters, which, having been collected from rain by roofs, gutters, pipes, or cisterns of lead, were contaminated more or less with the metal. All water so obtained has not been found thus affected, and there is much difference and uncertainty about the mutual action of lead and water in different cases. When rain water falls upon surfaces of lead it is apt to act on them, and the water thus contaminated, by standing exposed to air, generally clears itself from the dissolved lead, the metal separating as a carbonated precipitate, and falling to the bottom. But when the sea-spray has access to the leaded surfaces, the action of the rain water is such that the dissolved lead does not separate in this way, or if it does, only after a much longer time. It is such water as this that I recommend to be treated with carbonate of lime. Enough whitening or levigated chalk is to be mixed with the fluid to make it of the consistency of good milk (though more will do no harm), and the whole is either to be filtered or to stand until clear. I have never yet found any sample of water poisoned as above that was not freed from the lead by this process; and from the actions that occur in the laboratory I have no doubt that if two or three pounds of such powdered chalk were put into a cistern, and stirred up occasionally after rain, it would keep the water free from lead.

Now my consideration was entirely confined to cases of the above kind, and to the service of the Trinity House. I might say much more to you about the modes of testing for lead in water, so as to discover its presence, and, within certain limits, its proportion, and also about the clearance of lead from all domestic waters by filtration or otherwise, but I have always found that chemical practice was required to make such knowledge available, and that for that reason it was nearly useless in the hands of the public. When, too, a particular case becomes mixed up with the numerous cases that may be associated with it, I think it often disappears from view, and the whole are after a time forgotten. Hence I prefer adhering to the case of adulteration arising from the joint action of salt water, or sea spray, and lead; and I have the full confidence that if it arise at any of your military posts at home or abroad, no difficulty will be found in the effective application of the remedy.

I am, My dear Sir John,
Your very faithful servant,
M. FARADAY

[1] Sir John Fox Burgoyne, Bart. (1782–1871), Inspector General of Fortifications.
[2] 'Account of a mode of purifying water contaminated by lead, contained in a letter to the Inspector General of Fortifications from Professor Faraday, F.R.S.'
[3] In text of letter.

703 C. W. PASLEY to M. FARADAY, 17 October 1859
[*I.E.E., previously unpublished*]

High Elms,
Hampton Court, S.W.
Monday Morning the 17th October 1859

MY DEAR SIR,

I should like to have a few minutes conversation with you on a subject very interesting to me, and of some importance to the Service of the Country.

It relates to Pontoons, which have always been my hobby horse, as you may perhaps recollect. I proposed decked copper canoes shaped like Boats and the late General Blanshard[1] also of the Engineers proposed tin cylinders with paraboloidal ends. The midsections of the two are as below

When a heavy weight such as a Gun presses them down to within 4 inches of the surface of the water, Pasley's pontoon requires more than a Ton of additional weight to press it down to the water's edge, whilst Blanshard's from having so little capacity in the upper part would be in great danger of sinking, and after each heavy gun whether drawn by men or horses passes over any *one cylinder*, the moment that this is relieved of the weight there is a violent rebound of the superstructure in rear of the gun that flies up as if it were forced by a powerful spring. Thus a very dangerous oscillation or rather undulation of the roadway is occasioned, that has a tendency to frighten horses, and was the cause of an accident in the Pontoon Bridge formed over the Thames at Runnymede, when a 9 Pounder Gun of a field battery went over into the river with Drivers and Sappers employed as Pontoneers on the same side, because they

PASLEY   BLANSHARD

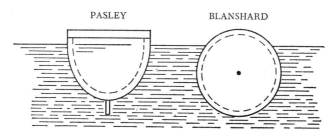

cannot stand in safety on a cylindrical surface, so that they were obliged to jump in to save themselves. On this occasion 2 out of 6 horses (then in the shafts) were drowned the others saved by cutting the traces. The Men some of whom could not swim escaped. I should have mentioned before, that both sorts were sent out to Bombay for trial, by order of the Court of Directors of the East India Company in 1826 and were tried in a creek subject to the action of the Tides for a short time, in two or three years after which, Blanshards tin cylinders having become a mass of rust and dust were thrown away and mine were adopted as the standard Pontoon for India and are still established as such.

I now wish to bring them forward again to supersed [sic] the tin cylinders, and my object is to consult you about the properties of copper, iron and tin. – The latter has been proved to be destructible even in the brackish water of the Medway to guard against which, the men are obliged to carry the cylinders down to the river and gently deposit them on the surface of the water, instead of launching them like boats, and in landing them, on leaving off work, they lift them out with equal care, and in the meantime my Exercise has been adopted by Blanshard whilst his are afloat. Part of the men having mud boots for wading into the river manage this business of the launching and landing. The others carry up or down the bank which may be steep. In fact whenever the paint is rubbed off the thin iron follows it and holes are eaten through it by the action of the water. Even on grass or on the smoothest fine sand, the same effect takes place, so that they must never touch the ground.

If you take a walk this morning will you do me the favor to call, or I will call on you at one o clock P.M. which is our luncheon time, for which as you know I do not care, or only employ a quarter of an hour at most

I remain, My dear Sir
Yours very faithfully
C. W. PASLEY

---

[1] Thomas Blanshard (1807–59).

704　M. FARADAY to H. BENCE JONES, 26 October
[probably 1859][1]
[R.I., previously unpublished]

Royal Institution [stamped letterhead]
Wednesday 26th Oct

MY DEAR BENCE JONES

I did think of calling on you; but went to Sir B. Brodies instead and as I am told to keep in I write *least you should hear of my matters otherwise* & not that they are serious. This morning I awoke without pain & found I was lying in blood which had issued from one or two small punctures or apertures in the scrotum. the scrotum itself being also black & charged with blood. Mr. Cutler refers it to the breaking of a small blood vessel during my violent recent sea-sickness – All is going on well now & there is no more effusion – I have only to take care. We have come home for good so all is right with us & I hope with you. I shall see Sir B. Brodie on Friday morning but expect there is nothing to do.

Ever Yours
M. FARADAY

[1] See Letter 708.

705　M. FARADAY to W. THOMSON, 28 October 1859
[British Museum, Add. mss. 48983, previously unpublished]

Royal Institution [stamped letterhead]
Albemarle St. W
28 Oct[r] 1859.

MY DEAR THOMSON

I have received by post a number of diagrams – apparently lines of magnetic force with transverse lines – perhaps lines of direction of motion – but there is no explanation of their particular object – nor any note with or about them – Are they from you? I have a vague notion that you spoke to me about some such thing but have forgotten all about it

Is your delicate static electrometer manufactured yet? and if so what is the *price* of a most delicate one? – It ought to be sensible at a distance. If we require one can you order its making?

I think I heard you speak of some other electrometer employed by Dollman[1] & another employed in the investigation of Ohm's law – or am I mistaken

Ever Truly Yours
M. FARADAY

[1] Possibly Francis Thomas Dollman (1812–99), architect, though I find no reference in Dollman's works to electrical experiments.

[*King's College Library, Newcastle upon Tyne, previously unpublished*]

2 College,
Glasgow,
Oct 31, 1859

My dear Sir

The diagrams which came to you by post were from Professor Clerk Maxwell. He wished to speak of them to you at Aberdeen but I suppose did not find an opportunity in the closely packed time.

The curves represent lines of force, or lines of motion of a fluid, in various cases in which their directions are all parallel to one plane. In every such case the set of curves which cut a set of lines of force perpendicularly are themselves a set of lines of force for another case; and therefore each of the diagrams bears a double interpretation. The best electrical application is to lines of atmospheric-electric force in the neighbourhood of a long straight mound, or mountain ridge, or trench [reading doubtful], with a section of any form – In such a case you will see that, except near the ends of the line of elevation or depression, the lines of force will all be parallel to one plane, namely to any plane perpendicular to that line. Among Maxwell's diagrams you will find one, for instance, which shows the lines of electric force in the neighbourhood of a long semicylindrical mound. The surfaces which we mathematicians call surfaces of equal potential (after George Green's definition) will be shown in the diagram by the lines

perpendicular to the lines of force. In the case of the semicylindrical mound, the surfaces of equal potential commence, at the earth, with the plane & curved surface of the earth, & approximate to parallel planes, at greater & greater heights. The curves showing these surface [*sic*], are lines of motion of water round a long cylindrical bar carried in a direction perpendicular to its length –

I am now having a reflection electrometer made for Kew, to act as a self recording instrument for atmospheric observation. The same kind of instrument will I believe be the best for general experimental purposes in which an electrometer of the highest sensibility is required. It will also answer for lecture illustrations, but for elementary instruction perhaps one such as you saw at Aberdeen showing [reading doubtful] its whole action and construction, and distracting the mind less from the electrical topic, may be preferred. I could have an instrument of either kind constructed for you if you please, and it would be a great pleasure to me to take charge of it should you wish to have one made. The last which I had made (much improved on the one you saw) cost £11. I do not think the appliances for reflection will add much to the cost, but I shall soon be able to have an exact estimate sent should you desire it.

Believe me
Yours very truly
WILLIAM THOMSON

707   M. FARADAY to W. THOMSON, 2 November 1859
[*British Museum, Add. mss. 48983, previously unpublished*]

London. W.
Royal Institution
2 Nov.ʳ 1859

MY DEAR SIR

I am very much obliged for your last. and have been looking over the curves with its assistance. I do not find the particular case of a long mound in the earth which you refer to but I think I have understood all except perhaps one. By the writing of the address I think they came to me from *you* so I return them to you by post with many thanks to you and Profʳ Maxwell.

I am very glad too to hear of the Electrometer My reason for writing to you was as follows. Our Managers have a fund founded by Sir Henry Holland for the purchase of certain pieces of apparatus it is limited in extent but if in consideration I find that one of your electrometers is a suitable object I mean to propose it. I think we should need the reflexion appliances inasmuch as we ought to make all our apparatus serve to demonstrate to the Members the facts & discoveries in science. When your instrument comes to View and you have as you say a more exact estimate I should be very glad to know.

Both your instrument and your application of it to atmospheric electricity interest me most deeply. Are you inclined (supposing it would suit with your convenience) to tell the story to our Members on one of the Friday Evenings of the next season.? It would be a very great pleasure to me to hear you here

I often think of Mrs. Thomson & her sisters & the friends at Aberdeen. Pray remember me correctly as well as kindly to your wife

Ever Very Truly Yours
M. FARADAY

2 College,
Glasgow
Nov 7, 1859

My dear Sir

The diagrams were drawn for you by Clerk Maxwell but they chanced to be addressed by Mr. Macfarlane, my assistant, whose hand is often mistaken for mine. They were left for him to look at for a day at Aberdeen, as he had been engaged in drawing some similar sets of curves to illustrate atmospheric electricity.

I now send you two of them which show the lines of atmospheric force in the neighbourhood of elevations and depressions of various forms

If you cover the lower part of No (1) placed with "Air" up, with the piece of white paper marked "Earth", you will see what I said regarding the semicircular mound. If you take the same diagram with one of the sides up, and cover the lower part with the piece of paper with the curved indentation, place it in the position indicated by the marks ⌗ and ∗ , you will see the aëril field of electric force over a ravine. If you cover the central circle of the same diagram with the circle of paper, placing the two points which are marked on one side of it in the positions in which curves meet making angles outside the circle, you will see the lines of force about a conducting cylinder insulated in a uniform field of electric force. The curves cutting those lines of force at right angles, are the lines of flow of water meeting and bending round a cylinder held perpendicular to the stream: or the lines of magnetic force about a cylinder of infinitely diamagnetic substance placed in a uniform field of magnetic force.

I showed the corresponding set of diagrams for a sphere, instead of a cylinder, at the meeting of the British Ass^n at Belfast in 1852.[1]

If you cover part of No 2 with the paper marked "Tableland" in the manner indicated, you will see the lines of force over a piece of stratified sea coast, with land rising vertically and sloping up to a level according to a regular curve. The same diagram turned the other way shows lines of force over a straight mountain ridge, or elevated mound, of the form shown in section by the marked curve.

All these illustrations are applicable only when there are no electrified clouds or masses of air in the neighbourhood.

I must ask you to pardon me for troubling you with all this, which I do only because, from your letter, I thought you might be interested in illustrations of atmospheric electricity

If you desire it I shall send you all the other diagrams immediately, or I shall bring them with me to give you the first time I have an opportunity of seeing you.

To myself it would be a great pleasure, although accompanied with not a small degree of anxiety, to have the prospect of giving a lecture on Atmospheric Electricity to the Royal Institution. My time during the session of the College here is engaged with scarcely any interval long enough to allow me to undertake anything at a distance, before May. If however it should be desired that I should lecture on Atmospheric Electricity on one of the evenings after the 1st of May, I shall be willing to do so.

I shall not omit to let you know as soon as possible how I succeed in the way of reflecting electrometers. I hope soon to have one ready to try.

I heard of you yesterday from Mr Crawford, and was sorry to learn that you had suffered from the rough work in the Channel.[2] I hope now you are feeling quite well again.

With kind regards in which Mrs Thomson joins, I remain, Yours very truly

WILLIAM THOMSON

[1] W. Thomson, 'On certain Magnetic Curves; with applications to Problems in the Theories of Heat, Electricity and Fluid Motion', *BAASR*, 22 (1852), 18.
[2] See Letter 704.

709   W. THOMSON to M. FARADAY, 17 November 1859
[*I.E.E., previously unpublished*]

2 College,
Glasgow
Nov 17, 1859

MY DEAR SIR

I have made an experiment today which illustrates remarkably the electro-polar state which you have always urged must exist in the particles of an electrolyte between two metals having different degrees of affinity for one of its elements; and I cannot deny myself the pleasure of immediately telling you of it.

An uninsulated can of water was placed so as to discharge its contents through a vertical copper pipe and fine nozzle of copper in a stream breaking into drops after about an inch, and falling into an *insulated* jar connected with an electrometer. A tube of metal, either zinc, composition (chiefly copper), or common sheet copper, was sometimes held round the stream of water and sometimes it was left simply with air and the walls of the room round it. In the last mentioned case the electrometer quickly showed strong negative, because the air of the room and a plate glass electrical machine not far off which had been in use, electrified the *uninsulated* metal tube & issuing stream *negatively* by influence. When a *copper* tube was held round the stream the electrometer showed little or no effect. When a piece of bent sheet zinc was held in the hand round the stream, & the vertical copper pipe was touched by the same hand, the electrometer shewed nothing or slight positive. When a metal wire connected the sheet zinc round the stream with the copper pipe from which the stream issued, the electrometer very quickly gathered a strong negative charge. In 30 sec: it showed 65° negative. When a composition metal (nearly copper) tube

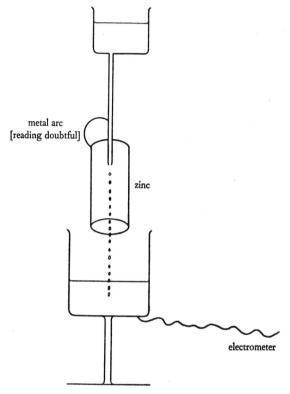

metal arc
[reading doubtful]

zinc

electrometer

was used, the electrometer gathered 7° neg. in the 30 sec: When a wide zinc tube, about 6 inches diameter & 12 inches long was held vertically so that the stream broke into drops about its centre the electrometer gathered negative quickly, provided the zinc was connected by metal with the copper from which the water issued. By using a well *insulated* support a spark may readily be obtained by allowing the charge to gather. I shall write to you when I have got one.

That the result must be as I found it seemed obvious before I made the experiment, from the following considerations. If the two water arcs (moist cotton wicks for instance) shown on the sketch are brought together a current flows in the direction shown by the arrowhead. Hence before the ends of the water arcs are united it must tend to flow and these opposed ends must be

937

oppositely electrified; – that connected with the zinc positively and that connected with the copper negatively. If drops from the former are allowed to fall through a hole in the zinc they must each carry away, negative electricity, (by the dynamical power of the gravitation of the water, and communicate it to any conductor into which they may be allowed to fall.

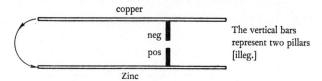

copper

neg

pos

The vertical bars
represent two pillars
[illeg.]

Zinc

This explains completely Volta's contact & separation experiment, by electro-chemical action, if there be any moisture present between the plate. For at the instant when the last point of metallic contact still exists the moist film on the copper surface must be negative to the moist film on the zinc surface; and the thinness of the separating air must make the quantity large even for a small difference of potentials between the opposed water surfaces. Immediately & even after contact (the insulation by glass handles being perfect) each metal has and keeps the electricity its (assumed moist) surface had when opposed to the

copper

zinc

other, and thus the copper shows negative and the zinc positive after separation. It would be important to try volta's experiment in artificially dried atmospheres of various gases.

The experiment which I made today was done by the aid of my divided ring electrometer – Perhaps one cell Daniell would, as the electrometer stood in the experiment, have given about 2° – The effects I observed are capable of indefinite accumulation, [illeg.] the extent I had them would I believe have shown on a gold leaf electrometer.

Believe me Yours most truly,
WILLIAM THOMSON (T.O)

P.S. I think I must ask that, if wanted to lecture on atmospheric electricity, I should have some time later than the 7th of May, as I fear I should have no time for preparation sufficient before the 1$^{\underline{st}}$ of the month.

710   M. Faraday to W. Thomson, 19 November 1859

[British Museum, Add. mss. 48983, previously unpublished]

Royal Institution
19 November 1859

My dear Sir

Your experiment[1] is most beautiful & striking and a wonderful proof of the extent to which experiment may be carried by those who engraft it on principle. I think I understand the whole of it and I conclude you can make the dropping water bring away either P or N electricity according as the nozzle from which the jet issues & the cylinder round the jet are of this or that metal.

I conclude I am right in assuming that static induction is set up all the time across the air between the breaking stream & the surrounding cylinder but what a curious variety of cases may be devised in that case since water issuing from the same vessel with different jets & these surrounded by cylinders of different metals would give so many changes from one water source

Suppose Voltas experiment of contact and separation were made in perfectly dry naphtha or out of schist it ought to give no result if contact were made at dry places of the metals. Whereas if a portions [*sic*] of the surface were wetted & then contact made a result should be obtained. I shall be anxious to hear of your educated results

There are five fridays after the 7th of May – but do not delay your evening longer than is necessary

Respectful remembrances to Mrs. Thomson from Yours ever truly

M. Faraday

[1] See previous letter.

711   J. Clerk Maxwell to M. Faraday, 30 November 1859

[I.E.E., previously unpublished]

Marischal College
Aberdeen
1859 Nov 30

Dear Sir

I am a candidate for the Chair of Natural Philosophy in the University of Edinburgh, which will soon be vacant by the appointment of Professor J. D. Forbes to St Andrews If you should be able from your knowledge of the attention which I have paid to science, to recommend me to the notice of the Curators, it would be greatly in my favour and I should be much indebted to you for such a certificate.

I was sorry that I had so little time in September that I could not write out an explanation of the figures of lines of force which I sent you, but Professor W Thomson to whom I lent them, seems to have indicated all that was necessary, and most of them can be recognised from their resemblance to the curves made with Iron filings.

The only thing to be observed is, that these curves are due to the action either of long wires perpendicular to the paper or of elongated magnetic poles such as the edge of a long ribbon of steel magnetized transversely. By considering infinitely long currents or magnetic poles perpendicular to the paper, we obtain systems of curves far more easily traced than in any other case, while their general appearance is similar to those produced in the ordinary experiments.

All the diagrams have two sets of lines at right angles to each other and the width between the two sets of lines is the same so that the reticulation is nearly square. If one system belongs to poles, the other belongs to currents, so that if the meaning of one be known, that of the other may be deduced from it.

I remain
Yours truly
JAMES CLERK MAXWELL

712 M. FARADAY to W. THOMSON, 8 December 1859

[*British Museum, Add. mss. 48983, previously unpublished*]

Royal Institution [stamped letterhead]
Brighton
8 Decr 1859.

MY DEAR THOMSON

I have been away from home, so am able *only now* to read & answer your letter. I did not write in reply to Mr MacFarlane, for his account voiced so many ideas & doubts, that I thought I would wait for more matter. You puzzle me greatly; & I am in great doubt, because I never can *judge* an experiment or make up my mind about it *without seeing it*. No description suffices to answer all the mental inquiries that arise about the conditions. As you say, you have just got hold of Voltas experiment; only you refer to the air place, where the zinc & copper oppose each other for that cause of the final effect, which he finds in the place of metallic contact.

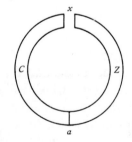

You seem to have made out that the place of excitement is really at x and not at a. I suppose if Voltas contact were effectual your charged index which placed at x goes either towards the z or c according it is neg or positive, ought to do the same thing if placed over a; for I do not see why the metallic contact there should undo or hide the electric state which it is supposed to bring on. How is this in experiment? Is your charged index indifferent at a & other places except at x, where there is separation?

940

You seem to refer the electric state at x to the mutual chemical relations of the zinc & copper; – as if the chemical relations of the air there went [reading doubtful] for nothing. How would it be, however, if the zinc & copper ring were in such different atmospheres as oxygen carbonic acid – hydrogen. &c the oxygen being ozonified if you like? Would they be indifferent. as you seem to expect naphtha will be. You might perhaps select atmospheres which would act more on copper than on zinc, as Sul Hydrogen; or at all events as much or more on silver than on zinc.

If the action be in & through the air place x., and that varies with distance, as I think you shew by an experiment, then, should not two half rings of zinc approximated in different degrees at x and a shew a difference of action at the two places, & therefore a difference of state? Or if metallic contact at a is required in the first instance, suppose that made by a metallic arc & the arc then removed, what state will the two opposed surfaces at a have? and also those at x?

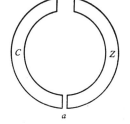

Suppose the contact at a made also by *water* & by *air* what are the results in comparison with those of contact by metal.

Does a piece of *Zinc alone* become positive in air i.e without any metallic contact with copper or other metal – I think I remember an experiment by De la Rive in support of the chemical origin of the electricity of the voltaic pile, in which, passing chlorine through a tube of platinum, he found either the issuing chlorine or the tube electric.

Supposing your charged aluminium index was over x, in figure page 2., it will go either towards the zinc or the copper, according as it has been rendered Pos or Neg – If the place x was closed the metals being there brought into contact, would the signs of electricity in the ring cease? and then on opening the place would they appear there again?

Is there *no* transfer of Electricity from copper to zinc at the place of metallic contact?

Is it possible that the metal of the index may act a part in the play at the place x.? It is evidently within the reach of the sources of action if they exist there; – or else it would not be affected: Would indexes of zinc, Gold, Copper, &c, behave differently one to another?

I dare say you have by this time answers to many of these questions & many others, that would, with me, arise in turn. But I shall wait to hear your news.

I understand your self acting condenser; but all the influencing circumstances can only be bound, as you are finding, by trial & experiment.

Kindest remembrances to Mrs. Thomson and heartiest wishes for your quick success. Remember that the more embarrassing the effects may be with you just now the more novel & important may be the principles involved in them.

Any thing regarding the first motions of Electricity among metals & surrounding exciting bodies must be of the utmost consequence to the progress of the science.

Ever Yours
M. FARADAY.

713   A. DE LA RIVE to M. FARADAY, 9 December 1859
[*I.E.E., previously unpublished*]

Genève
le 9 X^{bre} 1859

MONSIEUR & TRÈS CHER AMI,

Qu'il y a long-temps que je n'ai eu de vos nouvelles. J'ai su par Tyndall qui nous a fait une visite cet été, que vous étiez bien & toujours aussi actif. Quant à moi j'ai passé aussi un bon été & je me prépare à donner cet hiver quelques *lectures* (pour employer le mot anglais) sur les phénomènes naturels. Je suis fatigué, je vous l'avoue, de l'envahissement de la Science industrielle & je trouve que les oeuvres de Dieu dans la nature méritent bien aussi, & peut-être plus encore que celles de l'homme dans les arts, d'attirer l'attention & d'exciter l'admiration. Je me propose donc dans ces lectures d'examiner successivement les phénomènes naturels qui sont dus à l'attraction, à la chaleur, à la lumière & à l'électricité. Si je vous dis tout cela, c'est que j'ai un service à vous demander. Edmond Becquerel m'a écrit que vous aviez donné une leçon dans laquelle vous aviez réussi à montrer les phénomènes de phosphorescence à un auditoire nombreux en la projetant sur un écran.[1] – Avez-vous publié cette lecon? & dans ce cas auriez-vous la bonté de m'en envoyer un exemplaire? en tout cas serait-il indiscret de vous demander quelques détails sur la manière dont vous avez opéré.? Si vous m'envoyez un article imprimé, vous n'avez qu'à le mettre sous bande, mais [en] plus il faut l'affranchir; je crois que c'est une affaire de quelques pences. L'autre jour on m'a demandé pour un numéro du Quarterly qu'on n'avait pas affranchi frs. 43.50^{c.} de poste, tandis qu'avec 10 pence on l'aurait affranchi. – Quant aux lettres il est inutile de. les affranchir.

J'ai lu avec beaucoup d'intérêt le dernier mémoire de Mr. Gassiott [*sic*];[2] je suis très occupé dans ce moment du même sujet & j'espère ne pas tarder à faire connaître les résultats assez intéressants que j'ai obtenus. J'ai aussi quelques autres travaux d'un autre genre sur le métier que j'espère mener à bien avant le printemps. Si Dieu me prête vie, j'ai toujours le projet d'aller faire avec ma femme & mes deux filles cadettes, une visite à nos amis de Londres le printemps prochain. Ce sera probablement la dernière, car je me fais vieux & passé un certain age il convient aussi bien pour le *moral* que pour le *physique* de rester chez soi, d'adopter une vie calme & serieuse & de savoir mettre un intervalle entre la vie & la mort afin de pouvoir se receuillir avant de paraitre devant Celui qui doit nous juger.

Ne trouvez-vous pas que plus on avance dans la vie, plus on sent le besoin de penser au ciel plus qu'à la terre; mais au milieu de tant d'intérets & de préoccupations, cela m'est bien difficile & j'ai des moments de découragement qui ne doivent pas vous étonner vous qui mieux que personne comprenez ce que je dois éprouver. Il m'est doux de pouvoir vous parler ainsi; vous êtes le seul de mes amis Scientifiques auquel je puisse me confier & m'entretenir de ces sujets. C'est que vous êtes mieux qu'un ami Scientifique, vous etes pour moi un ami Chrétien & ce titre que vous me permettez de vous donner est, vous le savez, bien doux pour moi.

Ma femme me charge de ses compliments les plus affectueux pour vous & pour Madame Faraday; je vous prie de me rappeler aussi à son bon souvenir

Yours faithfull [*sic*]

A. DE LA RIVE

[1] See *PRI*, 3 (1858–62), 159.
[2] There are a series of papers by Gassiot on electrical discharge in rarefied gases and vacua which appeared in 1858–9. See *RSCSP*, 2, 780, items 15–19.

714 M. FARADAY to A. DE LA RIVE, 16 December 1859

[*Bibliothèque publique et universitaire de Genève, ms. 2316, f. 91–2, previously unpublished*]

Royal Institution
16 Decr 1859

MY DEAR DE LA RIVE,

Your letter was a very agreeable surprize I cannot tell when I wrote to you last but know I often think of you and that with very great pleasure since it is in the belief that you can understand more of the power of God than what can be gained by the study only of his material works Yet how wonderful they are I think yours is just the mind to revel amongst them as the evidences in natural things of his eternal power & Godhead and though I do not like when speaking of them in a common lecture to deal irreverently with religion by drawing it in at second hand I think it is impossible to forget who hath ordered them.

I have no doubt you have Becquerels papers from the Annales de Chimie[1] whether he will be able (or Ruhmkorf for him) to send you some of his phosphori I do not know. I had some from him very beautiful. They are preparations of the Sulphurets of Strontia, lime and baryta – He pulverizes them & then having gummed a paper surface (a circle 8 or 9 inches in diameter) he sifts the powder over it & when all is dry knock off the loose powder & a pure phosphorescent surface is left Having an Electric lamp with a lens & a divergent beam – placing the expanded hand on the surface & then throwing the beam on to it for a moment the result is beautiful for on showing it to the audience after the hand is removed there is its black form impressed on a sheet of light.

943

These phosphori on paper or exposed to air will not keep. Those I had are all insensible now as I found the other day: or I would have sent some by post – but kept in tubes hermetically sealed up they remain good for years

When Becquerel speaks in his letter to you of my experiments on a screen[2] I suppose he refers to fluorescence as well as phosphorescence The fluorescence is most powerfully produced by the rays at the violet end of the spectrum So by throwing the spectrum obtained by passing a divergent beam from the Electric lamp through a prism placed near the lens of the lamp; cutting off the red orange yellow rays etc by a screen placed near the prism – a beam of feeble light is obtained on the large white screen well fitted to bring out the fluorescent results of Uranium glass – [illeg.] etc

I have sent you a printed report of my evening.[3] by the regulations here it seems to require only a penny stamp but I have been so often disappointed by the uncertainty of the Post office proceeding that I have not usually sent these unimportant papers to you. I only hope you will not have more to pay The report is not worth more However in it you will see described a phosphoroscope which I had made for the evening & which answered exceedingly well especially with the nitrate of uranium I think you will have no difficulty in comprehending it The cylinder described was in a vertical position and no part of it more than 10 or 12 inches distant from the Electric focus It was closely made & blackened so that no light escaped outwardly but such as was brought out by the phosphorescent or fluorescent substance

I am glad to hear that you think of paying England a visit I look upon you as a young man – and then again as a strong young man. I know you can go on working in a manner which astonishes me I look on & admire – I rejoice with you & Madame de la Rive and though I wish for the power of imitating I do not envy you It is surely my time to rest. A new year is coming and a new period & life may they be happy to us and ours is the earnest & I desire it to be the only wish of your old friend

My wife desires to join me in the sincerest thoughts of good to you and Madame de la Rive.

Ever My dear friend
Affectionately Yours
M. FARADAY

[1] E. Becquerel, 'Recherches sur divers effets lumineux qui resultent de l'action de la lumière sur les corps', *AC*, 3 s., 55 (1859), 5; 56 (1859), 99; 57 (1859), 40.
[2] See Letter 713.
[3] *Ibid.*

715   M. FARADAY to Mrs POLLOCK,[1] 4 January 1860

[*Burndy Library, Norwalk, Conn., Michael Faraday Collection 73, previously un-published*]

4 Jan.ʸ 1860

MY DEAR MRS. POLLOCK

You will think me sadly remiss in thanking you for your kind letter & thoughts but coarse [?] things & the concerns of the lectures have so taken up my time that I have been really unable fitly to express myself I write a line or two of a note & then forget what is written & how the construction of the sentence runs & get all wrong & give it up – and this I have done more than once

But I value your favours greatly – and your boys visit & their kindness in thinking of me & now I remember that they have only just returned home and might like to hear an odd lecture or two If they do pray let them run in as they pass using my name at the door

I am sorry you were dull at Christmas but hope better things of you We are getting on pretty well here My wife & niece having much cold in the body but warm remembrances for you Jeannie has lost her voice so that I am really too quiet

Again & Again Ever Yours
Most Truly

M. FARADAY

Love to all whom I dare send it to I would not be in debt for such a precious thing as that & yet I do not want it to be by measure

M F

1 Wife of Sir William Frederick Pollock (1815–88), jurist. The Pollock family was close to Faraday. See Letter 67.

716   J. J. WATERSTON[1] to M. FARADAY, 20 January 1860

[*I.E.E., previously unpublished*]

26 Royal Crescent
Edinburgh
January 20 1860

SIR

In a paper that I am drawing up for the Philosophical Magazine (entitled – "*On the Gradient of Density in saturated vapours and its development as a physical relation between bodies of definite chemical constitution*)[2] – I have made use of your observations on the condensible gases that appeared many years ago in the Phil: Trans:[3] To do so with effect I have to reduce the temperatures to the standard scale of the air thermometer

945

The following is the extract from your memoir describing the means employed to measure the low temperatures obtained

"*In order to obtain some idea of this temperature (i.e. the temperature of the liquid carbonic acid and ether bath)[4] I had an alcohol thermometer made, of which the graduation was carried below 32° F[5] by degrees equal in capacity to those between 32° &[6] 212°*"

I have assumed that the length on the scale of this thermometer corresponding to 10° was uniform and that it was found by comparing the reading with a thermometer of mercury between 0° & 32° On this assumption we can reduce the temperatures very precisely to the air thermometer by means of M. Pierre's[7] observations on the expansion of absolute alcohol – The results exhibit your observations at these extremely low temperatures to be in conformity with the general law of density of saturated vapours

I shall be highly obliged if you can inform me if I am right in assuming that the scale of your thermometer was thus determined or was it formed as usual with mercurial Thermometers viz: by plunging into melting ice and boiling water & dividing the interval into 180 equal parts for degrees

It is perhaps too much to expect you to remember such particulars so far back, but it is of so much importance in establishing a general principle in science that I have ventured to intrude

I am

Sir

Your obedt humble servt

J. J. WATERSTON

[1] John James Waterston (1811–83) one of the pioneers in the creation of the Kinetic theory of heat.

[2] I can discover no such paper. There is a paper by Waterston entitled 'On a law of Liquid Expansion that connects the volume of a Liquid with its Temperature and with the Density of its saturated Vapour', *PM*, 4 s., 21 (1861) that may be the one referred to here.

[3] M. Faraday, 'On the Liquefaction and Solidification of Bodies generally existing as Gases', *PT* (1855), 155.

[4] The material in parentheses is Waterston's, not Faraday's.

[5] Fahr., in original.

[6] 'and' in original.

[7] Joachim Isidore Pierre (1812–81), later (1867) Dean of the Faculty of Sciences at Caen. For his many papers on the expansion of various liquids, see *RSCSP*.

[*Sir Hugh Chance, Stourbridge (on loan to the R.I.), previously unpublished*]

Royal Institution
8 Feby 1860.

SIR

In reply to your letter of the 1st instant, I have drawn up a set of enquiries which, in my opinion, it would be necessary to make, and have answered, *before* any proposal to introduce the lime light into a lighthouse could be considered. These I beg to submit to the consideration of the Deputy Master and Elder brethren. As far as I am concerned, such preliminary enquiries and answers would be required in every like case.

I am Sir
Your faithful humble Servnt
M. FARADAY

Enquiries, etc

1 The Trinity House cannot undertake to consider a mere proposition, or an imperfect arrangement; but only such subjects as are presented to them in a practical state.

2 The T. H. cannot undertake to work out, or perfect, the application of a proposition, though it may feel justified in undertaking to test a perfected arrangement, upon good reasons and data being submitted to it.

3 In order to enable the T. H. to judge whether a proposition made to them by parties, not practically experienced in the service of lighthouses, is well founded and has been thoroughly considered, it is desirable that certain questions should be answered; not from expectation only, but upon principle and from experience. These, in the present case, may be founded upon the requisites for a *first order fixed light*; and may be as follows.

4 What is the quantity of light proposed to be supplied; expressed either in relation to a central Fresnel lamp of four wicks, or to an ordinary Argand burner such as is used in a reflector?

5. The number of jets of gas required to ignite the lime?

6. The quantity of oxygen required for 12 hours?

7. The current price of the oxygen? i. e the cost of materials, wages, repairs, and any other current expence

8. The manner of storing the oxygen?

9. The nature of the gas fuel? – the quantity required in 12 hours?

10. How is the gas fuel to be obtained? How is it to be stored?

11. What is its current price for 12 hours; including material, wages, repairs, and other current expences?

12. What is the shape and size of the lime or focal light? How often will it require renewal? – How, or where, is it to be obtained? – and what will be its current cost?

13. What degree of steadiness will the light possess? Is it *now* as steady as a well burning lamp, or is it unsteady like a lamp in draughts? – or does it sink and rise at intervals?

14. Will the attention of the keeper be, of necessity, perpetual? – If not, for what intervals has the light been left, as yet, without falling off in character?

15. What is the vertical height, and horizontal width of the *most* intense part of the luminous objects? – and what the height of the part which may be called, generally, intensely luminous?

16. What number of persons would it be necessary to employ *upon the spot*, in relation to the lighthouse? – and what would be their occupations?

17. What buildings or outhouses for retorts, gazometers, etc, and what habitations, besides those now belonging to a first-order lighthouse, would be required?

18. Are the means of obtaining the light considered as applicable, only in favourable situations, or in all ordinary situations? In the latter case, let the reply have relation to such a lighthouse as that at Dungeness or Flamboro' head.

19. Are there any exceptional cases where the light could not be applied with advantage; – as the Needles – Eddystone – Bishops – Longships – Plymouth breakwater – Casquets – Longstone – Bell Rock – Skerryvore [reading doubtful] – Stack – Smalls – Tuskar – and others? If so, are they supposed to be few or numerous?

20. Will the service of the lime light make it dependant upon the neighbourhood of a town? – or if not so dependant, – what kind of annual supplies, – or supplies at considerable intervals, will probably be required?

21. What will be the probable *outfit* of the apparatus; with the buildings necessary for it and for the accomodation [sic] of the extra staff required?

22. What will be the nature of the necessary repairs?

23. What will be the *whole current expence* of the application of the lime light? (Including Royalty, etc)

The Trinity House cannot authorize any chance of interference with the *certainty of lighthouse action* by the introduction of any uncertain or *un*proved arrangements – tending to disturb the actual service of the light. It therefore requires full proof of the fitness of any proposed arrangement, *before* considering its introduction into a lighthouse

Any failure in such preliminary proof, or any serious departure in the results, from the answers given to the questions 4. 5. 6. 7. 9. 10. 11. 12. 13. 14. 16. 17. 18. 20. 23., which can be as well obtained out of a lighthouse as in it, will be considered as shewing that the proposed application has not been sufficiently matured; – and, if not removed by further investigation and proof, will lead to the conclusion, that the method is not applicable to the service of lighthouses.

M FARADAY

¹ Deputy Master of Trinity House.

718 G. B. AIRY to M. FARADAY, 9 March 1860

[*I.E.E., previously unpublished*]

Royal Observatory,
Greenwich,
London, S.E.,
1860 March 9

MY DEAR SIR

I wish to consult you about the location of magnetism in a steel bar – [illeg.] a dipping needle.

We have one needle of our dipping-needle-apparatus which without any visible reason gives us a great deal of trouble. Its results are very discordant, but the means of results (in masses) come out very fairly: *but*, they differ very steadily from the mean results of other needles by about ½ a degree.

The use of a dipping needle rests entirely on the assumption that, when the magnetism is reversed by the ordinary double-touch process, the new poles lie in the same line in which the old poles lay.

Now do you think it likely that there may be such perverse heterogeneity in the steel of the magnet that, when it is infected with one kind of magnetism, the magnetic axis may tend (steadily on the whole, though with some irregularities) to lie in one line: and that, when it is filled with the opposite magnetism, the magnetic axis may (steadily on the whole) be disposed to lie in a different line, inclined to the former at an angle of 1°?

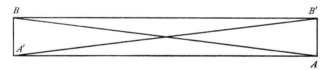

As thus: – *B* and *A* the boreal and austral poles at first, *B'* and *A'* the boreal and austral poles after reversion?

I am, my dear Sir
Yours very truly
G. B. AIRY

719 M. FARADAY to J. PLÜCKER, 29 March 1860

[*Nat. Res. Counc. Canada, previously unpublished*]

Royal Institution
29. March 1860

MY DEAR PROFESSOR

It is a long while since I have written to you – too long but the fact is that the writing a letter or any action that calls upon memory is a burden to me – and not merely that but often makes my head ache and obliges me to cease – I am fit for nothing now but small gentle acts of thinking – I have just read over your last letter and the description therein given of the light of the discharge in narrow tubes & the spectra which you obtain. They seem to me very wonderful but I cannot as I read retain the case of each vapour sufficiently to compare one with the other in my mind – or the phenomena altogether with – the luminous phenomena before known. In fact the luminous phenomena of the Electric discharge across very rare media are so numerous so varied *so indicative* and yet as it appears to me so little understood in respect of their *law* or fundamental principle that I *can not* retain them in my mind – for I have no memory & memory only can keep hold of them

But though I cannot discuss these beautiful phe- [*sic*] phenomena with you I can enjoy them & your success in the development of them & I doubt not that some day the whole beautiful encircling cloud of luminous results will open out into perfect order & intelligence & you will either produce that result or be a chief leader in obtaining it

In the mean time I commend myself to you as an old worker in science one that loves to look on the present bands of worker [*sic*] & as far as he can to keep up a relation with them if it be only by reminiscences & the memory of past times. And so it is that I write you now though I have no science to send you and am ashamed that I have not written before to thank you for yours & to say how heartily I am

My dear Professor
Your Obliged
M. FARADAY

720 M. FARADAY to P. N. BERTHON, 19 April 1860
[*Sir Hugh Chance, Stourbridge (on loan to the R.I.), previously unpublished*]

Royal Institution,
19 April 1860

SIR

Several of the answers from the lime light company, are not direct to, or sufficient for the questions; I will briefly point them out.

Q.6. "The nature of the gas fuel?" "The quantity required in 12 hours?" The answer has no reference to it but is about *coke* and *oxygen*

Q.7. "How is the *gas* fuel to be obtained? – How is it to be stored?" – The answer has no reference to the questions.

Q.8. "What is its (the gas fuel) current price for 12 hours including materials, wages, repairs and other current expences?" The word *its* in my query is written *the* in the company's paper and may perhaps explain why the answer has no reference to the question.

Q.12. "What is the vertical height and horizontal width of the most intense part of the luminous object? and what the height of the part which may be called generally intensely luminous?" By luminous object I mean the whole cylinder of lime at the ignited part: – and being three inches in diameter or about 9 1/2 inches in circumference I conclude, by the answer, that there are in that circumference, six spots, half an inch wide, of most intense ignition; – that these being surrounded by less ignited parts, may be considered as extending to an inch in width; – and that there are six intervening dark portions, each between 0.6 and 0.7 of an inch wide.

Q.16. asks whether there are any exceptional cases such as the Needles, Eddystone, Bishops etc etc. These (by the answer) do not seem to be known. Reference is made to the convenience of storing, building, etc and the exceptions are said, if any, to be where these conveniences do not exist.

Q.18. Relates to outfit. The answer seems to imply that the Fresnel apparatus would be dispensed with and gives no estimate on that point.

Supposing these answers had been to the purpose, or that direct answers may *now* be supplied, then comes the point, how far will they be justified and sustained in practise. At the close of the company's letter, it is not doubted, that, the directors will obtain permission to exhibit their light *in a lighthouse*, subject to the rules and regulations of the Trinity Corporation. My letter, containing the enquiries (8. Feby 1860.) did not go so far as that, as you will see at the end: – for it requires *full proof* of the fitness of any proposed arrangement, *before* considering its introduction into a lighthouse: and says that any failure in such preliminary proof, or any serious departure in the results from the answers given to the questions, will be considered as shewing that the proposed application has not been sufficiently matured etc. I see no reason at present to alter that course as far as I am concerned in watching the matter

> I have the honor to be
> Sir
> Your Very Obedt. Humble Servant
> M FARADAY

---

721 M. FARADAY to J. T. CHANCE[1], 23 April 1860
[*Sir Hugh Chance, Stourbridge (on loan to the R.I.), previously unpublished*]

> Royal Institution [stamped letterhead]
> London W.
> Albemarle St
> 23 April 1860

MY DEAR SIR

Mr Airy tells me he found one of your finished apparatus much out of adjustment and that he required to raise the lamp stand 5/16 of an inch to correct it. I have perhaps no right to ask you if this is so – or is so for any reason. I have no doubt if it be so you have a reason for it – but think it may be some mistake of his

Ever Truly Yours
M FARADAY

[1] Sir James Timmins Chance (1814–1902) was a member of the glass manufacturing firm of Chance Bros. and Co. in Birmingham. For his work on Lighthouses, see James Frederick Chance, *The Lighthouse Work of Sir James Chance*, London, 1902.

722   J. T. CHANCE to M. FARADAY, 24 April 1860
[*Sir Hugh Chance, Stourbridge (on loan to the R.I.), previously unpublished*]

Framstead,
Birmingham,
24 April./60

MY DEAR SIR,

I am obliged by your letter of yesterday – . When Profsr. Airy first inspected the apparatus the lamp was placed with the top of its burner 28 mm below the focal plane.

With the height of flame then attained, 20 mm was found to be about the best distance of the top of the burner from the focal plane. – This is the chief point to which I imagine Profsr. Airy to refer – viz. the best distance of the burner below the focus. –

I believe that 20 mm is not unusually adopted by the Trinity House – or about that distance.

At all events the position of the focal plane in the flame is still an undecided one – and a very important one –

On a subsequent examination of the apparatus which Profsr. Airy saw, I determined still to adhere to 28 mm: – but I made a slight alteration in the position of the lower prisms in their panels. I have never seen a better light than the one attended to: – I should like you greatly to have inspected it –

I am glad to hear of your success with the electric light – for fixed lights.

In a sixth order Light (150 mm indy. a height of flame equal to 1 mm (say) = 1/25th. of an inch, ought (even supposing parallel emergence) to spread over 20 miles from the horizon inwards (say) at an elevation of 400 ft. –

The remaining distance to the shore can be provided for by the bottom prisms.

There will be an end I suppose of large apparatus.

Yours truly
J. T. CHANCE

723 H. E. ROSCOE[1] to M. FARADAY, 26 April 1860

[*I.E.E., previously unpublished*]

Owens College,
Manchester,
April 26th 1860

MY DEAR MR. FARADAY

You will I know be interested to hear that Bunsen has discovered a new alkaline metal – discovered it by a method which, it seems to me, is for our Science of Chemistry what Adams's & Leverrier's discovery of the planet Neptune is in Astronomy.

I believe I mentioned to you, when I saw you last, that Bunsen and Kirchoff are engaged at present upon what they term "Spectral Analysis"[2] i e, the identification of the constituents of a body by means of the various colours which these constituents impart to the flame. You will probably have read a short notice given by Stokes in the Phil: Mag: a month or two ago of Kirchoff's most interesting and important discovery of the cause of the Fraunhofers [*sic*] lines in the Solar Spectrum.[3]

Making use of this important discovery, Bunsen finds that every (or almost every) elementary body or its compounds imparts to a colourless flame light of a definite degree of refrangibility – Soda for example giving a spectrum consisting of two narrow bright bands corresponding exactly in refrangibility to the dark line D in the sun's spectrum. In this way, if a mixture of the Salts of Ba. Sr. Ca. Mg. Li. K. Na be made – & if $\frac{1}{10}$ of a milligramme in weight of such a mixture be placed in a colorless flame (of Hydrogen – or Coal gas & air) and if the resulting coloured rays be allowed to pass through a prism, the spectrum thus formed will show bands of light in different positions, *each one* of which corresponds to, & is produced by *one* of the constituents of the mixture. Thus at one glance the presence of each of these substances – in a mere trace of such a mixture – may in one moment with certainty be detected.

Bunsen has found Lithium in all the potashes which he has examined, also in 20 grammes of Sea-water!

Now examining in this way the alkalies he has found a substance which in its spectral relations is different from any of the 3 known fixed alkalies (K.Na. Li)[4] – but up to the present time he has not found it in quantities sufficient to enable him to isolate it or to obtain the Chemical analogies of its salts –

I need not insist on the immense importance of these investigations & the new & vast areas they open out –

I intend going to Heidelberg in the summer, & on my return I should be glad, if you think it adviseable, to give an account of these experiments on one of your Friday Evenings in the spring.

Ever my dear Mr. Faraday truly yours

HENRY E. ROSCOE.

[1] Henry Enfield Roscoe (1833–1915), chemist and (later) spectroscopist, Professor of Chemistry in Owens College, Manchester.
[2] See R. W. Bunsen and G. Kirchhoff, 'Chemische Analyse durch Spectralbeobachtungen', *AP*, 186 (1860), 160.
[3] See [G. G. Stokes], 'On the Simultaneous Emission and Absorption of Rays of the same definite Refrangibility; being a translation of a portion of a paper by M. Léon Foucault, and of a paper by Professor Kirchhoff', *PM*, 4 s., 19 (1860), 193.
[4] R. Bunsen, 'Ueber ein neues, dem Kalium nahe stehendes Metall', *MAWB* (1860), 221.

724 M. FARADAY to J. T. CHANCE, 4 May 1860
[*Sir Hugh Chance, Stourbridge (on loan to the R.I.), previously unpublished*]

Royal Institution
4 May 1860

MY DEAR SIR

Can you & will you help me. I want a short right angled prism of glass of about this size the thickness *a* being from 3/4 to 1 inch It is for total reflexion so that the three right angled faces would require polishing but the two triangular faces not. The point however is that it should be moderately good

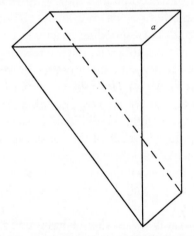

glass and if I set our workers here about it I shall be delayed by the plea that perfect glass is not to be had. Does it so happen that you occasionally may have a spare piece not perfect but moderate in quality which you could let me have out of which I could get a prism cut approaching the size I have drawn. If I am imprudent in my enquiry tell me so at once.

Many thanks for your reply to my Airy note[1]

With kindest remembrances to Mrs Chance believe me Ever Truly Yours

M FARADAY

[1] See Letter 722.

[Sir Hugh Chance, Stourbridge (on loan to the R.I.), previously unpublished]

Royal Institution
11 May 1860

SIR

The additional answers obtained from the Universal lime light company are to the point, except, that to question 18.[1] The question is "What will be the probable *outfit* of the apparatus, with the buildings necessary for it and for the accomodation [*sic*] of the extra staff required?" You will see that the answer makes no reference to the buildings, gazometers, retorts, and extra staff required.

The answers generally are such, as, in my opinion, to justify the Trinity House in permitting a trial on a full scale, of the applicability of the lime light to lighthouse purposes: provided it can be done so as to give full practical information on all matters, and without injury or interruption to the service. Such a trial should be sustained night after night for a given time, that the following, amongst other, points may be tested, namely; – the character and power of the light (that being at the time under general observation) – its constancy – its liability to accidents – its capability of replacement by the ordinary central lamp – its call on the keepers attention – the requisite number of persons for the service – the manufacture and storing of the gases – the quantity of gases consumed – the cost in full of the gases – the cost of wages – the cost of outfit and whole expence.

It is not for me to judge where such a trial could be best made: but wherever made, I think it should depend upon its own appliances as much as a lighthouse removed from the neighbourhood of a town and placed on a distant coast. I think too, it should be subject to the continual observation of external night watchers; and if they be mariners, or such as are concerned in lighthouse action, so much the better. The South Foreland upper light is an admirable station for observation; but perhaps cannot be permitted to be used on this occasion. The Purfleet lighthouse might serve, but would not be under good observation, or observation in all directions. I think a *fixed light* is the proper condition in which the light should be observed. If Purfleet, however, or any such situation, were chosen, it would not be necessary to have six jets on the lime, nor could they all be watched, by persons external to the lighthouse: perhaps three would do; only, this would not make the full call on the nightly supply of gas, and so far would leave the trial imperfect

Will you allow me to say that not having the answers to my questions, nor copies of them, I find myself frequently at a loss, when I desire to refer to them

I have the honor to be
Sir
Your Very humble Servant
M FARADAY

[1] See Letter 716.

726 G. G. STOKES to M. FARADAY, 8 June 1860

[*I.E.E., Joseph Larmor, 'Memoir and Scientific Correspondence of the Late Sir Gabriel Stokes, Bart.', 1, 150*]

14 Bellvue Terrace,
Southern Portsmouth
8 June 1860

MY DEAR FARADAY,

I found your paper at the R. S. and took it here to read.[1]

I am nearly sure you asked me to read it and give you my opinion about it. I will answer on that supposition.

I own my own opinion is against sending it in for the *Transactions*. It might have done as coming in incidentally in the body of a paper containing positive results but it seems to me it would scarcely do for an independent communication to the Transactions, a communication I mean made at one time though forming part of a train of experimental enquiry. If such negative results had the effect of correcting a commonly entertained expectation, or if the author's previous labours had led those who had followed them to regard a positive result as probable, or even not unlikely, the case might be different. But to my mind the antecedent probability of a positive result was too slender to justify the publication, in such a solemn manner as in the Transactions, of a negative result.

I should not myself expect a change in the temperature or electric state of a body even if one could transfer it to a place where gravity was only half what it is at the surface of the Earth; but even if a change were to be effected under these circumstances one could hardly expect to render it sensible in merely passing from the bottom to the top of a tower. To my mind the antecedent probability of a positive result is the product of two (to my mind small) fractions expressing the separate probabilities.

I write on the supposition that the change to be expected was one due to a change in the gravitating relations of the experimental mass – to a change for example from a place of strong to a place of weaker gravity – and not merely to a motion with or in opposition to the force of gravity: Such I take to be your view.*

A sentence at the top of p. 2 will require modification. "The so called variation of gravitating force by change of distance, can only be taken into account in either astronomical or cosmical phenomena: neither of which can be made the subject of experiment." This statement is too absolute because the change *is* taken into account in Cavendish's experiment.

I don't think there would be any objection to the paper's appearing in the proceedings. I should be glad if you would take the opinion of some one else.

I remain here till Tuesday when I go to Town.

Yours very truly
G. G. STOKES

* or rather that you would think such a change, if it could be effected, more likely to yield a positive result.

[1] The paper, on the relation of gravity to other forces, was never published. See *LPW*, 466.

727 M. FARADAY to G. G. STOKES, 11 June 1860

[*J. Larmor, 'Memoir and Scientific Correspondence of the Late Sir Gabriel Stokes, Bart.', 1, 151*]

Royal Institution,
11 June 1860

MY DEAR STOKES,

I am very grateful for your kindness, though I had not ventured to presume on troubling you except by the general question whether the account was worth appearance in the Proceedings or anywhere else at the R.S. I quite go with you in all you say, and think that the paper had better be withdrawn altogether if it can be. I want no other opinion than yours and my own.

I hope my acknowledgments will catch you at Southsea or at least follow you to London safely.

Every your very obliged,
M. FARADAY

728 W. THOMSON to M. FARADAY, 12 June 1860

[*Silvanus P. Thompson, 'The Life of William Thomson Baron Kelvin of Largs, London', 1910, Vol. 1, 410*]

Thornliebank, Glasgow
June 12, 1860

MY DEAR FARADAY—

The insurance trial regarding the Atlantic Telegraph, for which I expected to be summoned to London before this time, has been put off until the end of the month, and I expect to be required to attend between the 25th and the 1st of July.[1] I shall call to see you if you are in London, and to ask if you are disposed to come out to Kew along with me, where I shall have to go to look after the recording atmospheric electrometer. I have made several attempts to discover, if possible, indications of electric force in the air over the surface of two liquids, such as sulphate of zinc and sulphate of copper, separated by a porous partition, but as yet with no result. I think there must be something to be found; and probably strong in such a case as caustic potash and nitric acid, since these two liquids when substituted for acidulated water next the zinc and platinum of a galvanic element increase its electro-motive force very largely. I yesterday had an opportunity of observing something with my portable electrometer during thunder. No lightning was visible, but I could perceive the instants of the discharges that gave rise to audible sound by sudden motions of the needle. The thunder came about 20 seconds later than an impulse of this kind, several times, from which I judged that it was about 5 miles distant. The motion of the needle was more sudden than that which takes place when the conductor with the match burning is suddenly insulated. When this is done the needle gradually deflects without vibration, and shows nearly the full effect in 5 or 6 seconds. The changes yesterday were so sudden as to leave the needle vibrating, and were therefore *inductive* beginnings of the electric change in the conductor which the burning match completes. Besides the larger impulses which I was able to connect with the thunder, there was a constant flickering of the needle, which seemed to show that between flash and flash sufficient to make audible thunder, there were countless smaller discharges. On a small scale the same thing is produced and is indicated by the needle in the same way when shreds or fibre assist disruption of the air in any "field of electric force" in connection with experimental apparatus.

The ordinary atmospheric changes, although sometimes very rapid, for instance doubling the force in a minute or less, are not instantaneous, and show their effect by a gradual motion of the needle without vibrations. It seems certain that such changes are produced by motions of electrified air, while those I observed yesterday must have been due to discharges. – Believe me, my dear Faraday, every truly yours,

WILLIAM THOMSON.

[1] William Thomson was the leading scientific figure in the laying of the Atlantic cable.

729 M. FARADAY to W. F. COWPER,[1] 3 August 1860
[*Burndy Library, Norwalk, Conn., previously unpublished*]

Hampton Court Green
3 Aug. 1860.

DEAR SIR

I found your letter on returning from certain lighthouses. I do not see how I can help you in the Szerelmy-Ransome matter. I do not know M Szerelmy, and I believe he wishes to keep his process secret. I answered your enquiries as well as I could with the knowledge I had; and have no objection to the matter as it appears in the printed returns to the House of Commons, though I would rather have had my letter (which you consider private) amongst the rest.

If you consider an analysis necessary for your object, I conclude that some of the Professional men attached to the Government, at the Jermyn Street Museum, – Woolwich; or elsewhere will be the proper persons to undertake it – For my own part I think *time* (as I said in that letter) is the *only* test of such a practical matters [*sic*]

I have lately had a visit and a threat of legal proceedings from Mr. Davis [reading doubtful][2] on account of my answers to your questions. I will candidly

958

confess that such results, cool, in some degree, my willingness to answer all enquiries made of me by the Governmental boards. If I thought that such a case were likely to occur again I would make *all* my letters *private* to prevent like results. Whenever you give me the pleasure of being any way useful to you again, I hope you will help me to keep clear of the parties: – whose object is of course profit

> I am Sir
> Very faithfully Yours
> M. FARADAY

1 William Francis Cowper (1811–88), Baron Mount-Temple, M.P. for Hertford, 1835–63.
2 Possibly James Edward Davis (1817–87), barrister.

730 M. FARADAY to W. F. COWPER, 4 August 1860
[*Burndy Library, Norwalk, Conn., previously unpublished*]

> 4 August 1860

Private

DEAR SIR

When I was first called in to form some kind of judgment respecting the preservation of the stone work, I was to be guided by the appearance and state of the prepared specimens, and these alone. When I met M. Szerelmy at the Houses of Parliament, the engagement with him was already made; as Sir Chas. Barry, who was then present, told me: – but he was permitted to retain his secret. I tasted the liquid in one of his buckets, and have no doubt it was an alkaline silicate: – but I did not take any of it, nor ask him for it, as he would have then kept me to secrecy, and I did not chose [*sic*] to be in that position. I should not have thought it honest to take any of his preparation without his knowledge. I think you ought to have some security that he is dealing honorably & fairly with you; – but the permission was given long ago that he might retain his secret, – and unless he freely yields up the knowledge I do not know what you can do; except to decline upon principle dealing with a person who has a secret, and over whom, consequently, you can have no hold.

I hope you understand that, in my opinion, a process, whether secret or open, whether guided by most promising principles or altogether by rule of thumb, can only be judged of by the proof of times action.

> I have the honor to be
> Dear Sir
> Your Very faithful Servnt
> M. FARADAY

[*I.E.E.*, *previously unpublished*]

Bonn
4Th of August 1860.

MY DEAR SIR!

I thank you for the kind letter of March 29Th and deeply regret, to learn from it, that your state of health is not a quite satisfactory one. The same told me Prof. Baumert[1] of Bonn, who met you at the Oxford Meeting.

Chevallier [*sic*] Bunsen – as he was called when Prussian ambassador in London – who resides now among us, speaks of you with great enthousiasm [*sic*], remembering with pleasure the happy hours, he passed with you. He charged myself to present to you his respects.

I sent an Abstract of my researches on the electric discharge through evacuated tubes to the Royal Society, October last, to be printed in the Proceedings.[2] Prof. Stokes informed me three months ago, that my paper was either already printed, or would be printed imediately. But since I heard nothing about it. I whished [*sic*] I could show you the beautifull coloured lines of the spectra of the different gazes, by which these gazes are fully characterised and chemically analysed. Since Prof. Bunsen examined in the same way the (generally less well defined) spectra of Kalium Sodium, Lithium, Calcium, Strontium and Barium, proving that these spectra solely depend upon the mere metal, like gases are determined by one of their brillant [*sic*] spectra-lines. In this way he detected a new metal,[3] varying [reading doubtful] among the above mentioned, on examining the spectra of the residue from mineral waters, which he introduced into the flame of a gaz-lamp. A Chemist would certainly obtain curious results by a closer examination of gaz spectra. Some rather bold conceptions of mine, concerning for instance the beautifull spectra of chlorine, brome and iodine had hitherto no success.

Since my last communication I got only a few results concerning the gaz spectra. The spectra remain the same, the gazes may be rarefied, as they are in Geissler's tubes, or in the state of ordinary density. In this last case too, the discharge of a stronger apparatus of Ruhmkorff's easily passed through them, when contained in a capillar tube. – In order to prevent the influence of the Electrodes I recently substituted to my former spectra tubes

other ones into which no wire enters: the gazes

included becoming luminous by *induced* currents   . The spectra thus produced are equally beautifull.

I'll take liberty to send you by occassion [*sic*] my last paper on the magnetic condition of the different kinds of mica, compared with their optical properties.[4] The plane of the two magnetic axes is always perpendicular to the plane of the two optic axes, whatever may be the angle of these axes. When the plane of the two magnetic axes passes through the shorter diagonal, the plane of the two optic axes passes through the larger one and vice versa. The middle lines of both systems of axes are the same. Mica if optically uniaxial is equally so magnetically. If the angle of the axes be small, there is no rule indicating what system of luminous vibrations (either parallel to the longer or to the shorter diagonal) is more absorbed. This last result seems favourable to the views of Mr de Sénarmont, who thinks that the different micas are composed of two normal species having their optic axes within two planes perpendicular to each other.[5]

I beg you, Sir, to present my respects to Mad. Faraday. With all my heart

Yours
PLÜCKER

[1] Friedrich Moritz Baumert (1818–65), organic chemist and Professor at the University of Bonn.
[2] J. Plücker, 'Abstract of a series of Papers and Notes concerning the Electric Discharge through Rarefied Gases and Vapours', *PRS*, 10 (1859–60), 256.
[3] See Letter 723.
[4] J. Plücker, 'Das magnetische Verhalten der verschiedenen Glimmer und seine Beziehung zum optischen Verhalten derselben', *AP*, 186 (1860), 397.
[5] Henri Hureau de Sénarmont (1808–62), 'Observations sur les propriétés optiques des micas et sur leur forme cristalline', *AC*, 3 s., 34 (1852), 171.

732   M. FARADAY to J. T. CHANCE, 4 August 1860
[*Sir Hugh Chance, Stourbridge (on loan to the R.I.), previously unpublished*]

Royal Institution
4 Aug 1860

MY DEAR SIR

Have you perchance a fragment or a bad piece of one of the upper reflectors which you could bring to Whitby next week and by which we could see practically what amount of change in position would suffice to make the image of the horizon travel over a certain small angle?

Ever Truly Yours
M FARADAY

733 M. FARADAY to J. T. CHANCE, 13 August 1860

[*Sir Hugh Chance, Stourbridge (on loan to the R.I.), previously unpublished*]

Royal Institution
13 Aug 1860

MY DEAR SIR

You offered at one time to give me a drawing of your curves &c but I had in the mean time sent it back. That makes me ask your help in this way Can you give me a drawing full size on a big sheet of cartridge paper of the position of your pieces of glass? I want to consider for myself in conjunction with experiment on a good lamp where I think the focal points should be taken. I do not want the angles of each piece with great accuracy but their position in relation to the lamp, so as to give their distance from it, & the angles which the rays proceeding from it to them make with the horizontal ray – also the distance between the burner & focal plane

Ever My dear Sir
Truly Yours
M FARADAY

734 M. FARADAY to J. T. CHANCE, 14 August 1860

[*Sir Hugh Chance, Stourbridge (on loan to the R.I.), previously unpublished*]

Royal Institution
14 Aug 1860

MY DEAR SIR

Had the lamp at the North lighthouse at Whitby been adjusted before our survey of matters on the 9th instant?, or was it as you left it originally and as it was when the Astronomer Royal saw it?[1] Were you with him there? and what was the judgment regarding the upper reflectors formed from observation within the lanthorn at that time?

Ever Truly Yours
M. FARADAY

The bundle of photographs and the drawing have been found. They came to me but I return them to Mr. Wilkins for conveyance to M. Soutler[2]

[Note by James Chance]

North Whitby

Lamp 27 *mm.* below focal plane of lenses. Same position as it has always been – not capable of adjustment – no change made.

Lamp not in center.

[1] See Letter 722.
[2] This perhaps refers to a M. Sautre. See Letter 743.

735 M. FARADAY to J. T. CHANCE, 17 August 1860

[*Sir Hugh Chance, Stourbridge (on loan to the R.I.), previously unpublished*]

The Green
Hampton Court
17 aug 1860

MY DEAR SIR

I have made my report to the Trinity House Yesterday –

I have received *no* written account or statement from the R Commissioners or the astronomer Royal nor do I believe that the Trinity house has. We had no other means of gaining our information than you had with us

I cannot send you my report though I should be very glad that you and all should see it: – it belongs to the Trinity house & therefore I have not the power. I expect they will write to you for I have advised that you should put a new & effectual lamp & readjust the South house if with such a lamp it may seem to you to require adjustment. Carefully leaving the North light alone in all things that it may serve for a standard of comparison. I have suggested that when the South light is rectified both for lamp and adjustment we ought to have some means of comparing it at Sea with the North light so as to shew the effect of the adjustment with the old lamp & then both of adjustment & new lamp – i.e to get if possible the effect of the right lamp and the effect of the right adjustment separably – Perhaps this may be a little difficult

If it was understood that you were to write to the Trinity Board do so – I should be wrong in any way to change or guide your intentions in respect of any understanding between you & the Deputy Master. I have said that you were quite willing to make any change that the Trinity house would require

Ever My dear Sir
Very Truly Yours
M. FARADAY

736 M. FARADAY to J. T. CHANCE, 23 August 1860

[*Sir Hugh Chance, Stourbridge (on loan to the R.I.), previously unpublished*]

Royal Institution[1]
23 aug. 1860

MY DEAR SIR

Let me ask you on one or two points – which I have omitted to note

1 { the distance in the fitting room to the first test place [14 yards][2] do. to the extreme test place [22 yards] (= 66 feet)

2 { the distance in the yard to the first observing place [62 yards] to the furthest observing place [105 yards]

3. height of the focal plane above the burner [28] mm

4 { the focal point of the *upper*[3] reflectors either in relation to the burner or the focal plane [10 mm above focal plane]

5 { Where do your foci cross in relation to the burner or cotton [*see other page* (over)]

6 Do the final diagram & in rela to dip, refraction, &c refer to Whitby or only an imaginary case?

   [They refer to W HI TB Y: viz.:[1] *apparent dip* = 17′ 40″
                                    real   = 15′ 14″]

                                                    Ever Truly Yours
                                                    M. FARADAY

Sorry to trouble you but my memory lets things slip.   M F

[Questn: I presume that this question relates to the *lower* reflectors. My construction of foci (so far as I have at present arrived) is thus

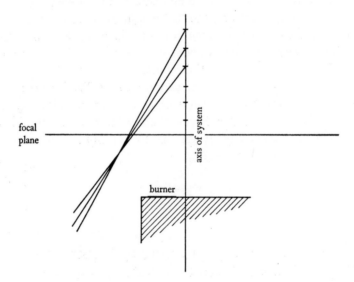

---

[1] Royal Institution stamped letterhead.
[2] These figures in square brackets are by Chance. They were written over Faraday's question marks.
[3] Underlined by Chance.

M. FARADAY to J. T. CHANCE, 25 August 1860
[*Sir Hugh Chance, Stourbridge (on loan to the R.I.), previously unpublished*]

Royal Institution [stamped letterhead]
25 aug. 1860

MY DEAR SIR

I have just time to acknowledge your letter & thank you. I give you much trouble.

When I came home and compared your real experimental foci with those I had obtained by a first rough tentative proof (on paper only) I was gratified to find that I was not far from you for I accept your determinations as real practical results – I had made a point 21 mm above the burner and 50 mm from the central vertical towards the side of the lower reflector a common focus for the illuminating rays going to the middle of the face of each reflector. In like manner I had adopted for a first approximation a point 26 mm above the burner and 31 mm from the vertical axis of the system on the side opposite to the upper reflectors as a common focus for them. This would give on the vertical axis foci varying from 45 to 125 mm – instead of the constant French focus of 38 mm

I had taken a point higher & nearer to the vertical axis but think that experiment with such a flame as one has a right to expect will give the former numbers or something near to them – I wonder what you will get by experiment How I should like to come & experiment with you

With sincere respects to Mrs. Chance – and what I forgot very many thanks for her kind intentions regard the Infant Orphan Asylum[1] & little Leighton.[2]

Believe me to be
Ever Truly Yours
M FARADAY

[1] This was one of the charitable institutions for which Faraday actively solicited support.
[2] I am unable to identify little Leighton.

738   M. FARADAY to J. T. CHANCE, 4 September 1860
[*Sir Hugh Chance, Stourbridge (on loan to the R.I.), previously unpublished*]

Royal Institution
4 Septr 1860

MY DEAR SIR

I do not know how much room I shall want, so I take something larger than a sheet of note paper. Let me acknowledge yours of the 1st, and then say, that I was yesterday at the Trinity House, and was authorized fully to write to you in its name; of which you will hear generally from the Secretary: – and let me say at once, that in your reference to expence, and even of your own willingness to defray it for the good of the cause, that cannot be thought of for a moment. The Trinity House desire, by me, certain things to be done, both at your works and at Whitby; and of course will pay the expences. I have told the Deputy Master that you were quite willing to help in every way that you could.

Focal points. I have reported to the Trinity House my theoretical conclusions regarding a change in these: – and the degree of change. I have also reported what you have done in respect of the *lower reflectors*; – have stated what I saw at your works, and my perfect satisfaction with the results as given by the Russian lights; – and have recommended a point 20 mm above the burner and 50 mm from the axis, towards the reflector, as the focus hereafter to be used for the adjustment of the *lower reflectors* for a chief horizontal beam. The dip to be taken into account whenever that is necessary.

For the *upper reflectors* I have made a first report (by theory) of a point, 27 mm above the burner and 32 mm from the axis, on the side *opposite* to the reflectors. From certain experiments I made here with a very excellent lamp, I deduced a point, 30 mm above the burner and 32 mm from the axis. Now can you help us (I should not like to go elsewhere), by putting up a lamp and an upper pannel [*sic*] of reflectors, and adjusting the latter to *this* focus: I would then come down and we would see what the result is. The lamp I used was a very excellent one; perhaps too excellent to be taken as a standard (though I see no reason why not). It burnt between 6 and 7 pints of oil in 4 hours; but it was very steady and without smoke all the time. Still, I should be glad if you could adjust a *second upper pannel* of reflectors, to a focus 30 mm above the burner and only 28 mm from the axis; that we may make our experiments more decisive & instructive.

As *to Whitby*: – leave the North light as it is and deal only with the South light. I mentioned to you to put a new lamp, such as you approve and will be responsible for. It is our opinion that the person who supplies the optical part, ought to supply and be responsible for the lamp in future. Then readjust the lamp for the dioptric part, having respect to the dip to the horizon; – readjust the lower reflectors from the focal point decided upon to the sea horizon; and readjust the upper reflectors *from the focal point we shall determine upon when you have the experimental pannels ready.*

When however the Whitby light is thus adjusted, we want to make the experiment as instructive as possible. Now the light includes 180° of the horizon; and there are four sets of pannels or frames, each of about 45°. I propose to leave the first upright set of pannels unchanged (except for the dioptric part which will alter with the lamp); to correct the upper and lower reflectors of the second upright set, to the foci we shall determine upon: – to correct the reflectors of the third set to the *other trial foci* we shall adopt; – and to leave the fourth set of reflectors unchanged. Then in sailing round the

966

lighthouse we shall have the successive observations and always the North light to refer to as a standard.

You have the Smalls light in hand. Though the time of the contract is drawing near, yet I am authorized to wish you to delay the adjustment of the parts, until we have determined the new foci. I need not say how glad I shall be to have the two experimental pannels ready for observation soon.

I fancy I shall have to come down to you soon to examine two Red sea lights for the Board of Trade. To give the power of examining them, (and lights generally) as I should like to do in the future; even a fixed light ought to stand on a *revolving* platform; – for I shall want to observe from the flame place to a distant point which may (upon a scale) represent the horizon. Can this be?

You will probably have heard that the Russian Engineer wrote to me,[1] and that I gave him my opinion on the lights.

I shall be very glad to hear & see your results as to the light thrown up into the air; – and all else (as you well know) that you obtain. The flame of a lamp is favourable as respects the sea light. We shall have more anxiety on that point with the electric light.

I may have to run up & down to & from Spon lane, but I must not be always a trouble to you. I must find some place near at hand, if we are always to examine the apparatus upon the works; and I certainly think that is best.

Ever my dear Sir
Most truly Yours
M FARADAY

[1] I cannot identify the Russian engineer.

---

739 M. FARADAY to J. T. CHANCE, 7 September 1860
[*Sir Hugh Chance, Stourbridge (on loan to the R.I.), previously unpublished*]

The Court,
Hampton Green [*sic*],
Friday 7th Sept^r (1860)

MY DEAR SIR

I have only just had yours here. I will come down on *Tuesday Morning* the 11th; same hour as before – to the same station, of which I cannot remember the name just now. (Edgbaston?)

I am very happy to think of being with you & very much obliged to you & Mrs. Chance for the kindness. But *think of this*. I do not want *any* body to interpret the circumstances as an indication of favouritism. I would much rather deny myself a pleasure than give rise to *that*: – and as I may want to spend two nights at Birmingham I thought it would be a good & an early opportunity to

cut up that thought either here or in France, if there were an Inn, – at or near
Spon Lane works, – I would not mind how small, if clean

Ever Truly Yours
M. FARADAY

740 E. BECKER[1] to M. FARADAY, 12 September 1860
[*I.E.E., previously unpublished*]

Heidelberg (im Waldhorn)
Sept. 12, 1860

MY DEAR MR FARADAY,

Before I left England, you have allowed me to write to you from time to
time, and to tell you what I am doing. Six months have passed since that time,
so rapidly indeed, that I can hardly believe it. My life has been rather mono-
tonous, & in such cases time seems to fly very fast, and if one stops then
occasionally & looks back upon that portion of one's life, old friends, not seen
since, recur first to the mind & one cannot conceive that it is really so long
since we last met them, or heard of them.

The month of March I spent in visits to relations and friends in different
parts of Germany & in the beginning of April I took my abode at Bonn for 3
months and began the work which I had set me for the next twelvemonth, viz:
to make myself acquainted with the present state of physical science in all its
branches which includes the recovery of what I knew, but had forgotten, – and
the reading up of what has been *added* during the last ten years. By changing my
place of residence during that year, I intended to become acquainted with the
different professors of physical science at several of our Universities. Accordingly, in the beginning of July I came to Heidelberg, where I am still, & I have
had the pleasure of seeing more or less of Plücker & Beer at Bonn, of Kirchhoff,
Bunsen and Helmholtz here, & last week I went to Carlsruhe to the Congress
of Chemists where I expected to find & did find many old acquaintances from
Germany & England. However, my principal work is done in my own room
& consists in nothing but reading – and rather hard and dry work it is. Not
that after two years' abstinence I did not feel the pleasure of being able to
devote all my time to science again; but in experimental science, to become
acquainted with new facts or to form a clear notion of phenomena, without
either making an experiment, or seeing it made, – is difficult & appears dry, if
compared with what it would be, if I had the assistance of experiment and
observation. I feel that without this, I shall require much longer time before I
find myself sufficiently prepared & yet, that my notions will not be so clear. To
procure all the apparatus and instruments necessary for an experimental study
of physical science, would be equivalent to the purchase of a whole & physical
laboratory, which exceeds the means of any private individual; on the other

hand the existing physical laboratories of our Universities are not accessible to me, before I have attached myself to one of them as a lecturer in physics (and then only by permission of the Professor) and yet this is the very position for which my present studies are to form the *preparation*. – When at Giessen, the other day, on a visit to my old friend and master Buff, I mentioned to him the difficulties I laboured under, & he expressed his opinion, that my present mode of study was not the right one, that I ought not to go on *reading* up the *whole* of the science, but begin at once a special experimental investigation of my own, purchase the necessary apparatus, which need not be very expensive, & that I would find that I profit a great deal more in that way, not only in that branch to which such investigation belongs, but also in other branches of physics. – This is the precise course which, according to my idea, I would have followed *after* the intended *general* preparation. Buff thinks, that the latter is useless, that the first will to a great extent fulfil the same purpose better, & that, if there are other branches in which I should feel the necessity of reading, that might be done bye and bye, while the principal work ought to consist in an experimental investigation, and not in reading

I have since considered the subject on all sides & I think, I shall follow Buff's advice; that the course he proposes is an infinitely more interesting & agreeable one, but this consideration *alone* would not have induced me to follow it.

I had intended to spend several months next winter at Berlin; but under the circumstances, I just mentioned, when I am obliged to purchase apparatus &c, I shall not select so expensive a place as Berlin for my residence, but rather choose one of our small Universities, perhaps Giessen itself, where I have old friends, and particularly the kind advise [sic] of Buff, while anywhere else my acquaintance with the professors is new & I cannot expect their taking any interest in me. – It remains yet for me to choose a subject for the special investigation I am about to begin. –

Now I have given you a short sketch of my life & of what has occupied my mind. I may add, that since I came to Heidelberg, I have taken my mother to me, & so given her a new home, while I have formed one for myself; should I go to Giessen in November, she would come with me again.

At Carlsruhe, I heard from Gladstone that you are well and vigorous and that you often meet on the Lighthouse Committee. I hope you have not entirely discontinued the subject of the connection of gravitation with the other forces. Dear Mrs Faraday, I am afraid, will not have much enjoyed the retreat at Hampton Court, bad as the weather has been; I trust, however, that she is well. With my kindest regards to her & Miss Barnard

> I remain
> Yours very truly
> E. BECKER

[1] E. Becker was a physician who had spent some time at Queen Victoria's court.

741 M. FARADAY to J. T. CHANCE, 14 September 1860
[Sir Hugh Chance, Stourbridge (on loan to the R.I.), previously unpublished]

Royal Institution
14 Septr 1860

MY DEAR SIR

I caught the Deputy Master to day and advanced matters

You will receive a letter at once authorizing you. etc etc

The Trinity House (by desire of the Board of Trade) ask me for a general estimate of expence of the experiments I am making; – and so I have to ask you: – as it must be charged separately from the service of the lighthouse. I think all I did with you & all we shall have to do at Whitby in the first instance may be considered as experiment: except perhaps the lamp; which if it remains permanently, will be charged to the lighthouse. – Can you send me an idea of a general sum; about – etc

In the mean time you can go on with the alterations at the Whitby South lighthouse: – but the Deputy Master will not be ready to visit it with the Commission before Wednesday the 3rd of October, – because of the Queens visit to the continent etc. I shall want *to see it a couple of days before hand*

The *North light* to remain untouched either as to lamp or adjustment.

The *South light*

To have a good lamp – raised so that a point in the axis 28 mm above the burner shall be in a line passing through the center of the lenticular band to the sea horizon – the chimney of the lamp to be six feet high from the bottom of the glass

To adjust the lower reflectors of all the octants alike to the sea horizon: – namely by a focus 20 mm above the burner & 50 mm from the axis towards the reflectors

To adjust the four octants of upper reflectors also to the sea horizon but from different foci – there being for the most Northern octant 20 mm above the burner

and – 30 – from the axis

for the next toward the South. 28 mm up

and 30 – aside from axis

for the third – 30^1 mm up in the axis

for the most southern octant 28 mm up

and 40 – aside from the axis

We *must* have the French Focus in so I have left the 20 mm up and 40 – aside – out

I think I have mentioned all the points –

Ever your truly Obliged
M. FARADAY

---

¹ '38' pencilled above '30', not in Faraday's hand.

742   M. FARADAY to J. T. CHANCE, 15 September 1860
[*Sir Hugh Chance, Stourbridge (on loan to the R.I.), previously unpublished*]

15 Septr 1860
RI.

MY DEAR SIR

I think I have written 28 mm instead of 38 mm for the height of the French focus for the *third* octant at Whitby If so I have no doubt you will correct it.

Ever Truly Yours
M. FARADAY

743   M. FARADAY to J. T. CHANCE, 17 September 1860
[*Sir Hugh Chance, Stourbridge (on loan to the R.I.), previously unpublished*]

RI.,
17. Septr 1860

MY DEAR SIR

Yet another change. I think we ought to have *one Octant* adjusted as regards the reflectors altogether by the French regulation i. e Octant No. 3. Notwith-standing the elevation of the lamp, the true comparative effect of the different adjustment will be seen when the lenticular zone is veiled. I send you a copy of a paper which I do not call a report because I have no right to send you reports – you will see the part marked in the Margin & the general interest of the whole. Please let me have it again

Ever Truly Yours
M. FARADAY

744   M. FARADAY to J. T. CHANCE, 21 September 1860
[*Sir Hugh Chance, Stourbridge (on loan to the R.I.), previously unpublished*]

Hampton Court Green
Royal Institution[1]
21 Sept. 1860

MY DEAR SIR

I have only just had your letter here – so write to the Royal Hotel. Whitby. You just touch the thing that completely puzzles me namely the French arrangement I am most anxious not to meddle with the North light at all but keep that as a record of the past state – Then I think we cannot spare two octants for the French adjustments. Yet as M. Sautre[2] & the French authorities say that such dip as the North Ireland – which is near 200 feet is unimportant, I should be sorry not to include *proof* of the effect: – though having [reading doubtful] that as the French have it we do not correctly compare the pure effect of different foci.

I cannot but think that the Trinity House *will expect to see one of the octants as M. Sautre would have it and have the power of comparing it with an octant as we should have* [reading doubtful] *it* – the lamp being the same & to this purpose I had directed Octants 2 & 3. of the other two octants 1 & 4 I should be sorry to lose the instruction we hope to derive from them. No. 1. I expect will throw the light more to the horizon. No. 4 more below it – and even more below it than No. 2. Yet you speak well of it as if you wished for it. If we throw either out in order to introduce the *French foci subordinate to the Sea horizon*: I should wish it to be Octant 4. (focus 28 above & 40 aside). What do you think of that.

I asked you for a round sum as estimate of expences Has it escaped your memory or have you sent it in to the Trinity House? I have to add a few pounds to it before it goes in

Ever Yours
M. FARADAY

Could you get the correct bearings by the compass of the division lines between the Octants. I suppose the agent will be kind enough to give them to you?

Yours
MF

1 The words 'Court Green' and 'Royal Institution' are crossed out in the ms.
2 I am unable to identify M. Sautre. Could be Soutre.

745 M. FARADAY to J. T. CHANCE, 25 September 1860
[*Sir Hugh Chance, Stourbridge (on loan to the R.I.), previously unpublished*]

Royal Institution,
25 Sept.ʳ 1860

MY DEAR SIR

Thanks for your letter of yesterday. I have no right to interfere with the Red Sea lights at present and leave them to you – I gave notice to MM. Parkes and Wilkins[1] [reading doubtful] that the lamps must be with them –

When at Whitby M Massilin said it would be easy to turn the illuminating apparatus but the nuts broke & there was not time Now can this be done and that safely so as to allow of the partial revolution of the illuminating apparatus so as to bring any of the Octants into a given direction and that without disturbance of the adjustment in relation to the lamp & the sea horizon for as Capt.ⁿ Ryder[2] suggest [*sic*] that would much facilitate our observation at Sea Thus if the vessel were at sea 5 miles off opposite Octant no. 2 and 2' were allowed for each observation then the signals & order might be as follows

Signal from the ship

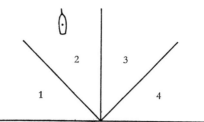

held	Octant	2	on for	2′
bring	———	1	———	2′
bring	———	2	on for	2′
bring	———	3	———	2′
bring	———	4	———	2′
bring	———	3	———	2′

bring ——— 2 in & then stop until the next signal from the ship This would include only 10′ for the actual moving time and the longest interval during which the mariner would be deprived of the South light would be only 6′ for No. 4. – Then the ship might sail of(f) to 10 miles and repeat signal & series – again at 15 or 20 miles and repeat Then we would if practicable shade off the lenticular part – & observe at three distances back again with the reflectors only

I have been to the Trinity House today & ascertained that this removal of the light for 6′ would not produce any harm & might be allowed. If you therefore can make the apparatus rotate (by hand of course) without introducing harm or error do so and let know when done

Ever My dear Sir
Truly Yours
M. FARADAY

[1] Possibly William Parkes (1812–89), civil engineer and designer of lighthouses. I am unable to identify Mr Wilkins.
[2] Alfred Phillips Ryder (1820–88), Captain, R.N.

746 M. FARADAY to J. T. CHANCE, 1 October 1860
  [*Sir Hugh Chance, Stourbridge (on loan to the R.I.), previously unpublished*]

Royal Institution [stamped letterhead]
Albemarle St.
1 Oct[r] 1860

MY DEAR SIR

Where you are I don't know or whether you had my letter about rotating the S. light apparatus: but I dare say you have received it. The piece of reflecting prism which you sent me was left at the Whitby light but can you let me have on the part of the Trinity house two such pieces corresponding to near the top & the bottom of the upper set of reflectors[1] that I may practically consider the best method of observing a distant object in them? Shall we be able to rotate the S. light?

Ever Yours Truly
M. FARADAY

[1] Underlining in wider pen, perhaps by Chance? The back of the letter is covered with notes and calculations, in pencil, perhaps also by Chance.

747   M. FARADAY to J. T. CHANCE, 2 October 1860

[*Sir Hugh Chance, Stourbridge (on loan to the R.I.), previously unpublished*]

The Green,
Hampton Court,
Tuesday, 2 Oct.ʳ 1860
11 0 clk. A.M.

MY DEAR SIR

Our posting has been sadly embarrassed. I have only just received yours of the 29th Sept.ʳ

The Deputy Master has I think appointed the 11th for the reunion at Whitby & has told Capt.ⁿ Ryder so as his letter tells me – The 4th would not do because of the moon – I will write to the Trinity house immediately to clear up the point & will say that I have that I have said the 11th to you [*sic*]

I intend to do as you say come to York on Monday the 8th & to Whitby the next morning.

I hope you will get this in time to free you for Birmingham

As the Trinity house will *as I suppose* not be at Whitby before the Thursday the 11th do not mind me at Whitby. If I find somebody who can turn the apparatus for me that will be all I shall need & that will do on the Thursday Morning

Ever My dear Sir
Yours
M FARADAY

748   M. FARADAY to B. VINCENT, 12 October 1860

[*Wellcome Medical Historical Library, previously unpublished*]

Royal Hotel
Whitby
Friday 12 Oct.ʳ 1860

MY DEAR FRIEND

I fear we are tied up here for some days longer & cannot stir. We are hard at work in the lighthouse and have to wait for the wind – Perhaps we may be able to go out tonight – perhaps tomorrow night – and perhaps not If I do not see you on Sabbath day you will know the cause. Both bodies i. e the Trinity house & the Royal Commission are here & I cannot leave them and though they respect the Sabbath we might have to work up *to* the Sabbath or within an hour of it so I must just wait & trust

Could you give the enclosed to Mr Anderson & could you also advance him 4 or 5 pounds until I come back? it will help me & him greatly

As to the great matter I say little of it here It is constantly in my thoughts but

I cannot write much about. Nor is that needed – it is in better hands than mine and in his working & guidance in whom I hope to trust for surely he made us and not we ourselves and he guides his own as a shepherd his sheep

> With deep love I am
> Very dear brother
> Yours
> M FARADAY

749 M. FARADAY to E. BECKER, 25 October 1860
[*R.I., B.J. 2, 439*]

> The Green
> Hampton Court
> 25th October 1860

MY DEAR DR. BECKER

It was a great delight to me to receive your very pleasant and affectionate letter last month.[1] It told us so much about your proceedings & concerns, as to shew that you knew we had a very strong interest in all you were doing, and were likely to do; and it has given great pleasure to Dr. Bence Jones and some other friends, besides. First I rejoice that you have your mother with you, and I cannot help imagining all the interest she will feel in hearing of your doing, and looking at you, & realizing the change and improvement that some years have made. A mother must make something of a home to you; and by home I imagine an arrangement very different to a Palace. You must have had a strong feeling for *home joys & happiness*: – for the *calm & peace* of such a place, to leave a Palace for the hopes of it; especially when that Palace was one where you were esteemed so highly I think the very feelings that induced you to make the change will help to create that home at last which will be the reward to you for it. Well, whatever change you may make in your life, we shall not alter in our thoughts about you.

I have been greatly interested in reading your account of your proceeding, at Bonn, Heidelberg, & Giessen. I am not competent to form an opinion of the best mode of pursuing science in Germany by a German mind; but the advice of Buff is that which would soonest fall in with my own thoughts and ways – I could not imagine much progress by reading only, without the experimental facts & trials which could be suggested by the reading. I was never able to make a fact my own without seeing it; – and the descriptions of the best works altogether failed to convey to my mind, such a knowledge of things as to allow myself to form a judgment upon them. It was so with *new* things. If Grove, or Wheatstone, or Gassiot, or any other told me a new fact & wanted my opinion, either of its value, or the cause, or the evidence it could give in any subject, I never could say any thing until I had seen the fact. For the same reason I never could work, as some Professors do most extensively, by students or pupils. All the work had to be my own. I know very well that my mind is particularly constituted; that it is deficient in appreciation: and, further, that the difficulty is made greater by a failing memory. Nevertheless you will understand how my thoughts fall in with Buffs opinion; and how terrified I should be to set about learning Science from Books only. However, what we call accident has, in my life had much to do with the matter; for I had to work & prepare for others before I had earned the privilege of working for myself, and I have no doubt that was my great instruction and introduction into physical science.

You have seen many of my friends. When you see them again, or any one think kindly of me, commend me to them. I long to know more of Scientific men than I do; but I dare not try to increase my privileges in that direction by writing, for such an occupation soon grows up, & then becomes too large for my head to carry. I am indeed even beginning to be sorrowful in *reading*, because I cannot store up what I read; – cannot keep it in remembrance.

Our friends here are I think pretty well. Dr. Bence Jones has only lately returned from the Continent – Tyndall is at home & well at work. – Wheatstone, Gassiot, &c. I see little of just now. I heard that Sir Benj. Brodie thought of giving up the Presidency of the Royal Society, but cannot say.

I feel as if I were leaving much unsaid in this letter, but it will not come to mind. I do not forget you & all your kindness. Nor does my Wife & Niece who send their kindest remembrances.

Believe me to be
My dear Dr. Becker
Ever faithfully Yours
M. FARADAY

1 See Letter 740.

750 M. FARADAY to J. G. MACVICAR,[1] 25 October 1860
[*Royal College of Physicians, previously unpublished*]

Royal Institution
25 Oct! 1860

MY DEAR SIR

I am very much obliged by your kindness. I shall have the opportunity of looking at your Tractate carefully after a week or two. but I am obliged to make a wonderful difference in respect of the manner in which I accept or hold at arms length a fact or body of facts and the superstructure which we of necessity raise upon them. Thanking you most heartily for your kindness

I am My dear Sir
Most Truly Yours
M. FARADAY

1 John G. Macvicar (1800–84), former Professor of Natural History at St Andrews University; in 1860, he was minister of Moffat, Dumfriesshire.

751 M. FARADAY to J. T. CHANCE, 26 October 1860

[*Sir Hugh Chance, Stourbridge (on loan to the R.I.), previously unpublished*]

Royal Institution
Friday, 26 Oct.ʳ 1860

MY DEAR SIR

I got your note today & accompanying it one from Mr Parkes – Yours says come on Thursday – & Mr Parkes says there is no hurry. Moreover he says I am to hear from the Board of Trade. I do not know what to do amongst three announcements all in different stages So I think I will decide on coming to you on Monday next the 29th. Leaving here by the 9.15. getting to Birmingham about 1 o' clk – getting a good lunch at the Railway hotel & securing a bedroom – reaching Spon Lane by 2.8 [?] – and then working on by day light and night time as it may be needful. Then if necessary I could [reading doubtful] be at the works also next morning. But you must not let me put you out by what I say and any change *you* make shall suit me.

I am just going to write Mr Parkes [a] word: I do not know whether he intends to be at Birmingham That I must leave to him

Ever Truly Yours
M. FARADAY

752 M. FARADAY to J. T. CHANCE, 1 November 1860

[*Sir Hugh Chance, Stourbridge (on loan to the R.I.), previously unpublished*]

Royal Institution
1, Nov.ʳ 1860

MY DEAR SIR

Yesterday afternoon I caught the Deputy Master. He sanctions the Experiment with the dioptric panel and also the delay of the Smalls apparatus, not unnecessarily but for the two or three weeks – That light will be 125 feet high – I have not yet sat down to the diagram. When the S Whitby light is finished you will let me know. The N Whitby light remains I think until next season

I found that the Trinity house had printed my last report[1] without telling me – so that there are errors of the press. – Being without the previous reports it reads to me imperfect. I send you a copy however & I also send the 1st and 2nd report that you may see how they hang together: – Return me the two latter.

Ever Truly Yours
M. FARADAY

[1] See 'Report . . . to the Deputy-Master and Brethren of the Trinity House', *Parl. Pap.* (1861), [2793] xxv.

753 M. FARADAY to J. T. CHANCE, 5 November 1860
[*Sir Hugh Chance, Stourbridge (on loan to the R.I.), previously unpublished*]

Royal Institution
5 Nov 1860

MY DEAR SIR

I thank you for your letter I return that of M. Hyeen.[1] I see no objection to his having a copy of the report and send you one: – but have written to ask that it should be revised & amended & would rather that were were [*sic*] done, before any more were given away I will attend to the "Farnes" and the "Hamstead"[2]

Ever Yours
M. FARADAY

[1] Lieutenant, R.N. See Letter 754.
[2] Lighthouses.

754 J. T. CHANCE to M. FARADAY, 6 November 1860
[*Sir Hugh Chance, Stourbridge (on loan to the R.I.), previously unpublished*]

Hamstead
Birmingham
6.Th November 1860.

MY DEAR SIR,

I am much obliged for your note. I have distinctly explained to Lieut Hyeen that he must not make any communication to others until he has the revised report.

In reference to the term 'focus', allow me to suggest the insertion of a *definition* simply, in a postscript or elsewhere, if you think it worth while to regard this point at all.

Considering a section of the reflectors made by a plane through the vertical axis of the whole apparatus, the 'focus' (as intended in your report) is the common point of intersection, within the apparatus, of the light transmitted from a distant object by the middle of each prism respectively.

Considering the *whole* apparatus of reflectors, the 'focus' becomes a circle (except where it is on the axis) the radius of that circle being the distance 'aside'.

I am just going to Whitby. On my return I will furnish you with a statement of what has been done, in regard to permanent adjustment

Most truly yours
J. T. CHANCE

755 M. FARADAY to J. T. CHANCE, 7 November 1860
[*Sir Hugh Chance, Stourbridge (on loan to the R.I.), previously unpublished*]

Royal Institution
7 Nov. 1860

MY DEAR SIR

Your notes are always very acceptable and your hints & suggestions too.

I suppose when you return from Whitby you will put up an experimental lens panel. I must, under the circumstances, meddle with the matter; else I feel I should willingly leave all to you; – but I suppose the pronoun *we* will best serve our purpose, unless you object.

I feel much uncertainty whilst endeavoring to decide by theory & diagrams (without experiment) upon the points (foci) for the lenticular band. On the other side I send my present impressions but expect that you have obtained some better results and with a more definite correction. When we come to an experimental trial for the purpose of deciding for the *Smalls*, I shall hope to have both the *experimental* panel, and another as *now adjusted*, up on the frame at once: so that we can turn first the light of one & then of the other on to the same white surface or screen; that we may be able to judge of the amount & position in both cases. The difference between a high & a low flame is also much on my mind; especially as we are so frequently liable to the latter unawares

When you set about the matter I should like if you could let me know several days before hand when you might want me down; that I might arrange things here

Ever Truly Yours
M. FARADAY

[this is vertical in original]

| 34 | 34 | 32 | 30 | 28 | 27 | 26 | 25 | | 25 | | 25 | 25 | 25 | 25 | 25 | 24 | 24 | 24 mm |

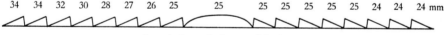

above the burner in the axis of the flame

756 W. CROOKES[1] to M. FARADAY, 15 November 1860
[*E. E. Fournier D'Albe, 'The Life of Sir William Crookes', London, 1923, 53*]

November 15, 1860

DEAR SIR,

Last Christmas I was kindly allowed the privilege of attending and reporting your course of Lectures in the *Chemical News*.[2] I venture to hope that the manner in which I then acquitted myself of the responsibility of transferring your language to print will not cause you to withhold a similar permission on the occasion of your forthcoming course "On the Chemical History of a Candle."

I remain, Sir,

Truly yours,

WILLIAM CROOKES

¹ William Crookes (1832–1919), chemist and pioneer investigator of cathode rays.
² Crookes was editor of the *Chemical News*.

757 M. FARADAY to W. CROOKES, 15 November 1860
[*R.I., E. E. Fournier D'Albe, 'The Life of Sir William Crookes', London, 1923, 54*]

R.I.

15 Nov., 1860

Private

DEAR SIR,

I take your request as a great compliment and as far as I can give it you have my full permission My only fear is that I may not do credit to your good opinion. I know that my memory fails and I know that the character of the lectures must fail with that. I had wished to cease lecturing altogether but circumstances induce me to consent for this season. The wish on any account to withdraw is a trouble to me in some sense for I really have had great pleasure in talking to the children. However I will do my best.

Ever Truly Yours,

M. FARADAY

758 J. T. CHANCE to M. FARADAY, 21 November 1860
[*Sir Hugh Chance, Stourbridge (on loan to the R.I.), previously unpublished*]

Hamstead

21 Nov. 1860

MY DEAR SIR

I have in repeated experiments tried what positions of the respective bands composing a lenticular panel will send the brightest light in a given direction compatible with a divergence downwards.

I have not yet had a panel constructed to show the total effects because it is important that you and I should first agree upon the approximate arrangement inasmuch as the lenticular zones can be fixed only once for all, not being individually independent like the reflecting prisms.

I have already mentioned that I find 21 to 23 mm a good position above the burner for the focus of the middle belt. As, however, 24 mm hits all the zones *above* the middle one, I propose that a point in the axis 24 mm above the burner shall be that through which shall pass the focal lines (i.e. through the middle of each lens), of all the zones from the middle one upwards.

This agrees very well with *your own* diagram, confirmed however by experiments as to the actual brightest light, the respective foci being observed *subsequently*. In regard to the lower zones, below the middle one, I recommend the common focal point to be 12 mm above the burner and 32 mm in front of the axis; giving the foci in the axis as follows: *first* below the middle belt

	18
2nd	20
3rd	22
4th	23 1/2
5th	24 1/2 to 25
6th	26
7	27
8	28

I shall be glad to know whether you so far approve of the foregoing arrangements, as to agree to the experimental lens being at *once* constructed accordingly.

This can be done in 2 or 3 days after receiving your reply.

Most truly yours
JAMES T. CHANCE

759 M. FARADAY to J. T. CHANCE, 21 November 1860
[*Sir Hugh Chance, Stourbridge (on loan to the R.I.), previously unpublished*]

Royal Institution
21 Nov.ʳ 1860

MY DEAR SIR

I have your notes & thank you heartily for them

I have sent your Whitby report with mine to the Trinity House – Send the bill of the alterations to the Trinity House (Not being experimental)

Your report of your results makes me fear that you find the same wave-ring in conclusions that I found in my mode of considering the matter here – for you make a sudden jump from belt No. 1 to belts Nos. 2.3.4.5. etc. and get results the opposite to Stevensons

I should like when I come to see the effect of *each rib* and the effect of the *whole* panel; – and if possible the latter compared with an ordinary panel – I suppose the effect of each rib & of all the ribs together could be had in the day time in your dark gallery – by the use of screening for the ribs of the panel and a whitened surface to the door end of the gallery – and then I suppose that the corrected panel & an ordinary panel could be compared across the yard at night time upon a whitened screen or wall in the distance – Is this so.

Now there is a good deal of observation in all this – and a good deal of preparatory work. Shall I come down next Monday at the usual time? & then if need be I could stop & work on the Tuesday or even longer – It is very desirable to have our minds settled

I should like to compare the same panel & ribs using a high & a low flame – This can be done easily if we have a *ready* means of shading the panel by two pieces of canvas so as to shew us any one rib by itself when wanted.

If you approve of Monday please let me know as soon as you can.

Ever Truly Yours
M. FARADAY

760   M. FARADAY to J. T. CHANCE, 22 November 1860 [copy]
[*Sir Hugh Chance, Stourbridge (on loan to the R.I.), previously unpublished*]

Royal Institution
22 Nov 1860

MY DEAR SIR

I trust you have mine of yesterday – as I now have yours

I think I must come and look at the *individual bands* – Will next Monday do?

You will evidently obtain more light for the Sea by the lower zones – but a very chief point is the *maximum light* for the horizon

In diagram the lines to the four lower belts *touch the cotton*. Of course the parts of the flame lateral to the great or axial plane may compensate for this but I cannot well judge of that on paper. I must come & see

Ever Yours
M FARADAY

761   M. FARADAY to J. T. CHANCE, 23 November 1860
[*Sir Hugh Chance, Stourbridge (now on loan to the R.I.), previously unpublished*]

Royal Institution
23 Nov.̲ 1860

MY DEAR SIR

Time gets on very fast and when December once comes in I shall find it difficult to leave London. So I will come to you on Monday as my last letter said to see the separate ribs at all events

I had yours just now and like your plan of determining the lamp place – I am anxious about the colours – & the way in which they will *experimentally* combine on the screen – but cannot say much in a note

Our notes cross continually – but I will come on Monday & we must try to use our time effectively.

Are the numbers determined by one set of bands sure to be right for the bands of other pannels? [*sic*] I shall have your answer to that & other questions on Monday.

Ever Yours
M FARADAY

762 J. T. CHANCE to M. FARADAY, 29 November 1860

[*Sir Hugh Chance, Stourbridge (on loan to the R.I.), previously unpublished*]

Hamstead
Birmingham
29th Nov: 1860

MY DEAR SIR,

I trust that you arrived comfortably at London last night: I was very sorry to hear of your detention at the Spon Lane Station.

I feel quite sure that no conclusions should be deduced from the images on the white paper, from the *whole set together* of the upper, or lower ribs, any more than from the image from the whole panel.

The only safe way is that which you & I have followed viz. – to decide the focus of *each rib separately.*

They cannot be taken together, except at such a distance as to see nearly the same part of the flame simultaneously from all the belts or ribs; that is, many miles away.

I will send you, in a day or two, coloured drawings of the respective images of the flame, received on the white paper from the different ribs, & the middle belt; so as to indicate the *relative positions* of those images, and to shew the way in which they would be one above another when the light comes from the whole panel.

I will take the 20 mm focus, & the 28 mm focus, as two separate cases; and for each case there shall be marked the level line for each rib, to assist the eye.

Possibly before you come to any conclusion for lights *generally*, you might like to view at a good distance the effect upon the eye through the whole panel of different positions of the flame, from 28 mm down to 18 mm above the burner.

This can be readily done, & would seem to be quite worth the extra trouble for so important a matter.

For the 'Smalls' Light however, I fancy that your present data, as derived from Tuesday's experiments will enable you to decide upon the positions of the bell & ribs in reference to the burner.

Most truly yours
JAMES T. CHANCE

763 M. FARADAY to J. T. CHANCE, 30 November 1860
[Sir Hugh Chance, Stourbridge (on loan to the R.I.), previously unpublished]

Royal Institution
30 Nov.ʳ 1860

MY DEAR SIR

I arrived at home all well and I hope you enjoyed your dinner
I think I remember up the results pretty well.

As concerns the Manufacturer I do not see how he can adjust his panel without taking each rib separately; which I think is what you mean. As to the party examining; he is to have the right of examining each rib separately *from foci given*: & (I think) that we agreed that in respect of the dead level the focus for the chief band & upper ribs was to be 20 mm (the chief band being the starting point) and for the lower ribs 11 up & 36 aside. Will not this be right for the Smalls? or shall 20 be made 21?

As the Smalls light is 125 feet above the water will there not be 12 1/2 minutes of dip to the Sea horizon? and will not this require a lamp elevation for the refractors of about 3.3 millimeters?

Ever Truly Yours
M. FARADAY

764 G. B. AIRY to M. FARADAY, 3 December 1860 [copy]
[Royal Observatory, Herstmonceux, Pure Math. and Misc. Sci., 1862 (Mar.)–1865 (Apr.), previously unpublished]

1860 December 3

MY DEAR SIR

Can you assist me in the following matter of lamp-lighting.

I want to use the optical image of a common gas-burner, not an Argand (which the mobility and various inclinations and other circumstances do not permit) but the common fish-tail, by whatever name known. Now a large portion of this flame is black, thus

which gives me a most inconveniently shaped image. Now can you contrive to make vivid combustion go on there? I suppose that the air is there combining with the gas, and not yet sufficiently combined. Can you supply the air before the gas emerges into expanse, [*sic*] so that it will be ready to blaze at once? Or can any thing else be done?

I am, my dear Sir,
Your most truly
G. B. AIRY

765 M. FARADAY to G. B. AIRY, 4 December 1860
[*Royal Observatory, Herstmonceux, Pure Math. and Misc. Sci., 1862 (Mar.)–1865 (Apr.), previously unpublished*]

Royal Institution,
4 Dec.ʳ 1860.

MY DEAR SIR

I do not know how to render the dark part of the fish tail flame luminous whilst the other parts are retained unchanged in form extent & brightness. By mixing some air with the gas before hand you will change the character of all the parts. I can judge only very imperfectly of the flame & its conditions not knowing exactly what you require – I suppose putting the flame edgeways so that the bright & obscure parts should mutually cover each other would not serve your purpose Practically you have as much light from the flame in one direction as in the other

Many thanks for your note about the light house lamp

Ever Most truly Yours
M. FARADAY

766 J. T. CHANCE to M. FARADAY, 6 December 1860 [copy]
[*Sir Hugh Chance, Stourbridge (on loan to the R.I.), previously unpublished*]

Hamstead,
Birmingham,
6th December 1860.

MY DEAR SIR,

Many thanks for the copy, now returned, of your report.[1]

page 2 – line 6 from top.
"much higher & varying points" –

perhaps it would be better to this effect: – "focal points in the axis varying from about 18 mm to 30 mm above the burner"; – because the words "*much higher*" apply to only a few of the lower ribs.

Page 3 – line 7 from top.

What do you think of adding that "even with a very high flame the focal points of the middle belt & upper ribs cannot be raised higher than 23 mm or 24 mm above the burner without sending the brightest light to the sky". Without some such limitation, it might be inferred from your description that for high flames the focus might be allowed to ascend to 28 mm or more.

I do not think that the foci of the *lower* ribs would have to be changed for any increased height of flame.

page. 1. line 11 from bottom the word "to" should be "as"

I feel no anxiety as to 20 mm for the "Smalls" Light: – for if at any time it is wished to lower the burner, either 1 mm or more, no harm whatever would be done to the upper or lower reflectors, by the small quantity involved.

I say nothing about the notions of the Royal Commrs. – Profr. Airy – etc etc in regard to the lens experiments, because you are sure to learn their opinion from themselves when you see them

Very truly yours

JAMES T. CHANCE

P.S. I enclose Chance Bros & Co.'s account for the 2nd set of Exps.

1 'Report of experiments at Birmingham on the focal points of the lenticular panel of a fixed first order lighthouse apparatus', *Parl. Pap.* (1861), [2793] xxv.

767 M. FARADAY to J. T. CHANCE, 11 December 1860
[*Sir Hugh Chance, Stourbridge (on loan to the R.I.), previously unpublished*]

Royal Institution
Tuesday, 11 Decr 1860

MY DEAR SIR

With respect to the Small's and my examination of it – my time is becoming very limited. Can you let me know when you will want me.

I could come next Thursday ⟨or Friday⟩[1] (13th or 14th) but would have to return the same day.

I could come next Friday leaving London after 1/2 p. 3 o clk but should have to return on the Saturday

I could come if necessary on Thursday the 20th (in Evg.) returning on the next day

After that I could not be with you before the 10th January 1861

Let me know which of these it must be.

I should like very much to see a lens up in your dark chamber & examine where its maximum light would fall as respects the dead horizon To repeat in fact Stevensons Experiment[2] there. But now that our experiments are finished

& that you have sent in your account as the T H desired I have no right to say
any thing about it

Ever Yours
M Faraday

¹ 'or Friday' crossed out in ms.
² See Letter 752, fn. 1.

768   W. Snow Harris to M. Faraday, 22 December 1860
[*I.E.E., previously unpublished*]

6 Windsor Villas
Plymouth
22 December 1860

My dear Faraday

Did it ever occur to you to consider, what difference there is, if any between
the state of a coated Plate of Glass charged in the usual way directly from the
Electrical Machine – and a Plate of Glass excited on one side with a coating on
the other side only – and then a second Coating applied after the manner of the
Electrophorus and an Experiment by Cigna. – To make myself very clear Let
Fig 1 represent the First case .. Fig 2 the excitation case by Friction over an

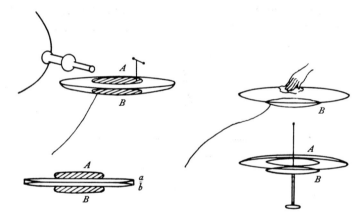

under coating B. Fig 3 the subsequent application of an upper Coating A – It
appears to me that the latter case Fig 3 is really not the same thing as Fig 1
[Faraday's note in margin – "Yes"] – or is it a charge at all of the system in the
way of Fig 1 The small Spark which is perceptible on joining A and B suppose
B insulated is so far as I see a mere affair [reading doubtful] of the two coatings
– If I unite A and B Fig 1 by a bent metal Wire – I neutralize or discharge that
system – and I can get nothing more out of the Cover A except so far as some
small residuary charges may be obtained in the way you have described Expt.
Researches 1246 – But in the Case of Fig 3 when I unite the coatings AB by a
metal wire I merely equalize the forces between the Coatings whatever may be

the consequent change in the intervening Dielectric – I do not *discharge* the system as in Case Fig 1 – This is seen by the continued bearing off Electricity by Induction through the Instrumentality of the Cover

In Fig 1 we charge & Polarize the system by *Foreign aid* as it were. In Fig 3 & 2 we merely develop the Electricity of the Glass itself – There is certainly some difference here which it might be well to elucidate Now with respect to your Exp.^t sec 1246 I have no doubt of the accuracy of your Researches but I think nevertheless there is more yet behind. – Beccaria[1] says that in a compound Gls Plate of 2 laminae Fig 4 – coated as before; each ½ plate will be + on one Side and − on the other.

I have been lately studying with very much attention this subject. I have repeated all the Experiments of *Cigna*,[2] *Symmer*[3] & others – I have certainly found with you that most commonly on separating the Plates one Plate is + without any negative Induction – the other − without any positive Induction –

But all these sort of Experiments are very precarious + I think in *situ* one surface must be + & the other − because the two plates *a* & *b* Fig 4 cohere & that forcibly – now as opposite Electricitys attract it follows that the near surfaces must be in opposite Electrical states – It is the act of separation which disturbs the condition

You can certainly have a glass Plate + on one side & − on the other – Now let me just remark, that it does not follow because we find on presenting each

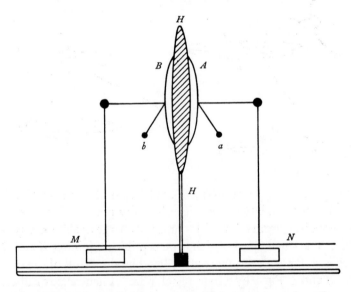

side of a Electrified Plate of Glass to an Electroscope – the Electroscope is similarly influenced by *both* sides, that therefore both sides of the Glass are Electrified – suppose I excite a disc of Glass on *one* Surface only – that excitation may as easily influence an Electroscope through the Glass on the one side as through the air on the other – (I do not consider here the question of Specific Inductive Capacity.) – nay more the side or surface opposite the excited surface may have a slight negative state but which you *can not detect* because the positive Electricity of the opposite Surface (suppose the excitation +) prevails & conversely Well as I said – you can obtain both + & − coincident surfaces if you will balance or equalize the force Let *H H* [word illeg.] Fig 5 be an insulated Glass disc about a foot in Diameter *AB* two moveable Coatings or covers about 7 Inches Diameter set upon vertical Insulators & moveable Bases *NN* so that the Coatings may be withdrawn on each side from the Glass, let *ab* be two Electroscopes of divergence connected with the coatings *AB*. Charge either side *A* in the usual way, giving side *B*, a temporary communication with the Ground. Then Electroscope *a* on the charged side diverges – but Electroscope *b* exhibits no Induction – connection with Ground being withdrawn – still we can not doubt but that the whole Dielectric is Polarized – In fact if we withdraw the Coatings Electroscope *b* diverges with neg Electricity whilst *a* is Positive – But you get no negative Indication from the Glass – both sides appear to give positive Electricity – but that is because the Positive Electricity of the excited side *A* predominates.

Replace the Covers & repeat the charge – Electroscope *a* being divergent and *b* tranquil – remove the connection of *b* with the Ground – and now by an Insulated metal Ball *G* of an Inch Diameter abstract Electricity from the predominant side *A* by degrees Electroscope *b* on the negative side

begins to rise – go on untill the divergence of *a* & *b* is alike or nearly so again withdraw the Covers: one is + the other − of course – but now the glass surfaces exhibit the same opposite states one is + the other − That is suppose you present one to Gold Leaves divergent with either Elect^y, (say Positive) the one side of the Glass increases the Divergence whilst the other causes the Leaves to close But I must not tax your patience further – Avogadro has written most capitally on this subject[4] – he draws a distinction between Electricity of the Coatings – Electricity of the Glass &c &c Nicholsons Journal – Octavo – Vol 21 page 288

believe me to be
My dear Faraday
always yours most sincerely
W. SNOW HARRIS

[1] Giacomo Battista Beccaria (1716–81), *A Treatise upon Artificial Electricity, in which are given solutions of a number of electric phoenomena, hitherto unexplained*, London, 1776.
[2] Giovanni Francesco Cigna (1734–90), student of electricity.
[3] Robert Symmer (?–1763), F.R.S. Author of a number of papers on electricity.
[4] A. Avogadro, 'Considerations on the State in which a Stratum of nonconducting Matter must be, when interposed between Two Surfaces ended with opposite Electricities', *NJ*, 21 (1808), 278.

[Sir Hugh Chance, Stourbridge (on loan to the R.I.), previously unpublished]

Hamstead,
Birmingham
2nd January 1861

MY DEAR SIR,

I wish you all the compliments of the New Year.

Concerning the Smalls Light: – I have only yesterday surmounted the various practical difficulties, of an unforeseen kind, which have developed themselves in the actually carrying into effect the new plan of adjusting the different members of a fixed light refractor.

I believe that the plan may now be said to be practically successful, so that *workmen* may be entrusted with the execution of it.

It has been impossible for me to say until now at what height in the apparatus the focal plane would most conveniently be placed, because that height depended partly on the altered breadths of the ribs below the middle belt. Before, therefore, I dare have one single reflector fixed, I was compelled to wait for the completion of a panel of refracting ribs.

Everything will now proceed uninterruptedly; and I am in great hopes that the whole apparatus will be ready for inspection by the 10th of January: – but as I do not feel perfectly certain of this, I should prefer your naming some day in the week *after* next week, if equally convenient to yourself; – *and I shall feel obliged by your letting me know by the return of post what that day will be* in order that I may keep myself disengaged.

I gave you some time ago an unfinished table of the dips for different heights of tower, prepared according to the suggestion of Captn. Ryder. In that table the angles were those *at the sea*: – and they had to be reduced by 1/7th to obtain the visible angles at the apparatus.

In the enclosed table the angles are the *actual visible angles* at the apparatus: and the correction for refraction adopted in the calculations is that which the astronomer Royal has been kind enough recently to communicate to me.

For the 'Smalls' Light the dip is 10′ 54″ (for 125 feet in height) and the corresponding quantity at the axis of the apparatus is nearly 3 mm, as you have given to the Trinity Board.

The angle of divergence which illuminates from the sea-horizon up to the one mile distance from the lower is only (about) *1* degree.

Apart from the new arrangement of the foci of the fixed refractor, the plan of *internal* observation in the adjustment is a most important step in the Art of Dioptric Apparatus and is well worth all the trouble which it has involved.

Most truly yours
JAMES T. CHANCE

770   M. FARADAY to J. T. CHANCE, 10 January 1861
[*Sir Hugh Chance, Stourbridge (on loan to the R.I.), previously unpublished*]

Royal Institution
10 Jany. 1860[1]

MY DEAR SIR

To my sorrow & regret I have been attacked by the cold & the sciatica and am forbidden by Dr. Bence Jones to leave town or my home until the cold diminishes and my state changes. I am very sorry but there is no hopes of my seeing you next Monday & what is worse I cannot now fix any other day. I just managed to reach the Trinity house today & told the Deputy Master these things

I thank you very much for the table of angles which you have sent me & which I omitted to acknowledge in my last because I hoped to see you

The Deputy Master wished me to tell you that until you have finally placed the lamps in the Whitby lighthouses he cannot make his final report to the Board of Trade but must keep the matter open in a certain manner until then

When we meet we can talk of these matters

Hoping that You and Mrs Chance have escaped any serious injury from the cold I am

My dear Sir
Ever Truly Yours
M FARADAY

[1] A mistake for 1861.

771   J. PLATEAU to M. FARADAY, 18 April 1861
[*I.E.E., previously unpublished*]

Gand,
18 Avril 1861.

MON CHER MONSIEUR FARADAY.

J'ai l'honneur de vous adresser, par la poste, trois exemplaires du mémoire que je viens de publier.[1] L'un d'eux vous est naturellement destiné, et je vous prie de vouloir bien offrir le second, de ma part, à la Société Royale et le troisième à l'Institution Royale.

Le procédé que j'ai employé jusqu'ici, savoir l'immersion d'une masse d'huile dans un mélange d'eau et d'alcool, présente certaines difficultés à cause de l'influence des changements de température et d'un reste d'action chimique entre les liquides; en outre il exige beaucoup de temps. Or, dans le mémoire actuel, je décris un procédé tout différent, qui n'exige d'autre embarras que la préparation d'un certain liquide, et qui, une fois ce liquide formé, permet de réaliser la plupart de mes expériences avec une extrême facilité, une grande promptitude, et d'une manière beaucoup plus belle que par le premier procédé.

Si vous me faites l'honneur de répéter quelques unes de ces expériences, surtout celles des paragraphes 18 et 19, je suis convaincu que vous y prendrez un vif intérêt, et si je pouvais espérer que vous ou M. Tyndall voulut bien les montrer publiquement dans une séance de l'Institution Royale, je serais tranquille sur l'avenir de mes Recherches en Angleterre; tandis que depuis l'apparition de ma deuxième série, elles paraissent n'avoir plus excité, dans votre pays aucune attention.

J'espère que votre santé est maintenant tout à fait rétablie, et je m'attends à voir apparaître, un jour ou l'autre, quelque nouvelle merveille venant de vous.

Agréez, Mon Cher Monsieur Faraday, l'assurance de tous mes sentiments d'affection.

Jʰ PLATEAU

P.S. J'écris à M. Tyndall pour lui faire aussi la prière que je vous ai adressée ci-dessus.

J'ai à peu près terminé ma 6ᵐᵉ série et j'espère qu'elle pourra paraître d'ici à quelques mois; j'y etudié la théorie des systemes laminaires du paragraphe 18 de la série actuelle, leur mode de génération, et la condition que doit remplir une charpente polyédrique pour donner un système parfait.

¹ J. Plateau, 'Recherches expérimentales et théoriques sur les figures d'équilibre d'une masse liquide sans pesanteur', *MASB*, 33 (1861).

772 J. T. CHANCE to M. FARADAY, 22 April 1861
[*Sir Hugh Chance, Stourbridge (on loan to the R.I.), previously unpublished*]

Hamstead,
Birmingham
22 April 1861

MY DEAR SIR

Last week a new kind of lamp intended by me for the South Lighthouse at Whitby, was inspected at the Trinity House.

Mr. Masselin who was present at the inspection has reported to me certain facts concerning the proportionate quantity of oil consumed in the lamp in comparison with others tried at the same time which seem to throw great doubt upon the propriety of measuring the performance of lamps by the consumption of oil apart from other considerations. As you have taken great interest in these matters you will excuse my writing to you upon the subject. – Now, according to Mr. Masselin's statement the flame of the new lamp was by no means inferior to that of the others; & yet its consumption of oil in a given time was by far the least. The new lamp admits of producing an immense overflow, 1st because any degree of regular pressure is practicable & 2dly Because each of the Concentric wicks is separately supplied with oil. – Now Mr. Masselin & myself consider that this excessive overflow prevents a great evaporation of non-luminous gas from the oil, whereas that waste by evaporation occurs in lamps where the overflow is not sufficient – . The waste of oil in this case would be similar to the waste of fuel in furnaces, from which smoke is emitted. Whatever, however, may be the theory; the facts, wh: I believe that Mr. Masselin cannot have erroneously observed, suggest further investigation, before the consumption of oil is allowed to be taken as a measure of the due performance of a lamp. –

Yrs. very truly
JAMES T. CHANCE

773   M. FARADAY to J. T. CHANCE, 23 April 1861
[*Sir Hugh Chance, Stourbridge (on loan to the R.I.), previously unpublished*]

Royal Institution
23 April 1861

MY DEAR SIR

I have had your letter but I can say little to it. All my experience has been that when the oil is fairly burnt the light produced is in proportion to the quantity of oil but I have had only small experience with light house lamps It is quite within the range of the possibility that the same quantity of oil may produce different quantities of light according as it is burnt

If I understand rightly you consider that your lamp with *excessive overflow* gives more light for the same quantity of oil than the French or Scotch lamp do. That is a point to be established by experiment and comparison & is a very important point if established

Ever My dear Sir
Yours Truly
M FARADAY

774   W. DE LA RUE to M. FARADAY, 25 April 1861
[*I.E.E., previously unpublished*]

the Observatory,
Cranford,
Middlesex, W
April 25 1861

MY DEAR FARADAY

The following particulars of the Eclipse you may like to have

the Sun's semidiameter	$15' - 44''.8$
The Moon's computed for my station at the epoch of totality	$16'\ 33''$

The *ratio* of the Moon's diameter
to the sun's diameter measured
on the photographs is as 1.05244 to 1   }   16′. 34″.3
which gives you the Moon's
semidiameter

Duration of totality at my station	Min sec 3 – 25
Motion of the Moon during the totality computed	93″
Measured on photographs	93″.4
Motion during one minute the time of exposure of the first plate	27″.22
The nearest approach of the centres of the Sun & Moon	14″

————————

Arrived at Bilbao 9th July partially overcast
           10   –   do   do

Arrived at Risabellosa 11 – cloudy

Instruments arrived in
the evening

Got the meridian
by Sun's observations 12   partial cloud
                     13   half cloud

first solar photograph 14   cloud in morning
                          clear afternoon
             15   cloudless
             16   cloudy
             17   cloudy

day of eclipse ——————— 18 cloudy up
to 11.ʰ 38 min

a photograph lost }
by clouds passing }
over the Sun   }   h   min
                 at 2.   12

——————————

——————————

In respect of the amount of light at the period of totality: – I am inclined on reflecting to think that the light in the sky must after all have been greater than that of the sky illuminated by the full moon because assuredly fewer stars were seen at the period of totality than are visible at the epoch of full moon. The colour of the light was unquestionably very different from moonlight and the appearance of objects illuminated by it so very different to that we ever see under ordinary circumstances that it is difficult to render an exact account of it even to oneself and almost if not quite impossible to impart to others any idea of the peculiarity of the phenomena we witnessed. Grand beyond description was the appearance to the naked eye of the dark bronze moon surrounded by the silvery corona in a sky of an intensely dark indigo blue in its immediate neighborhood but passing through a sepia tint into a very bright orange close to the horizon. The distant mountains appearing, perhaps by contrast, of an intense blue. The colours of all objects completely changed, they were all dulled and to my eye a sort of violet-bronze tinged all things at a little distance yet the paper on which I was drawing still looked white & I could distinguish very well the various tints I had prepared to compare with the luminous prominences. It required a very strong mental effort to recall me back to my real task when I had once lifted my eyes away from the telescope, & I heartily regretted at that time that I had ever undertaken to head the photographic expedition.

Yours Very sincerely
WARREN DE LA RUE

775   W. DE LA RUE to M. FARADAY, 26 April 1861

[*I.E.E., previously unpublished*]

110 Bunhill Row, E.C.
April 26 1861

MY DEAR FARADAY

You will think at last that I am boreing [*sic*] you with letters. I wrote you one last night or rather this morning at 1° clock after I had been chasing round Saturn's satellites which I suspect are greater in number by three than those known.

Some particulars I could not supply not having all my papers at home. They are as follows:

Totality	h	m	sec
Began at Risabellosa	3.	0.	39.1
Middle	3.	2.	21.6
Ended	3.	4.	4.1
Greenwich mean Time			
		min	sec
The duration being		3	.25

I think that when you asked me yesterday about the meaning of a certain shaded portion on each side of the central line on Vignolles' map[1] and certain other lines parallel to the shaded zone I did not quite understand your question and hence could not have given you the fitting answer on thinking over your question I am able to answer more to the purpose

The central zone, (shaded) includes all those parts of Spain where the duration of the total eclipse was three minutes and this being a long time and only 35 seconds less than the longest duration in any part of Spain it was made prominent so that intending observers might place themselves here & there in any position convenient to themselves; it being desirable however that they should spread themselves as much as possible.

The lines parallel to most favorable zone [*sic*] indicates still where the Eclipse *was total* from the position where there was simple contact only (and duration o) to other positions where the duration was that indicated on the particular parallel to the central line.

Yours Very sincerely
WARREN DE LA RUE

[1] Charles Blacker Vignoles (1793–1875) had campaigned in Spain against Napoleon. He was one of the founders and early Presidents of the Institution of Civil Engineers.

776   M. FARADAY to the Astronomer Royal, 27 April 1861

[*Royal Observatory, Herstmonceux, Sci. Soc., 1860 (Oct.)–1863 (Apr.), Sect. 24, previously unpublished*]

27 April 1861.

MY DEAR SIR

Next Friday I shall endeavour to convey De la Rues [*sic*] Eclipse matter to our Members He & I have very different notions in regard to you He thinks that we shall be neglecting you if we do not send you tickets, &c. I think you must be tired of Eclipse matter even when good & that it will be an impertinence in me to suppose that the evening can interest you We only want to do what will be most agreeable to you remembering always your kindness Let us neither intrude on nor neglect you and consider that your face company or hand writing will always admit you & yours here

Ever faithfully Yours
M. FARADAY

777   G. B. AIRY to M. FARADAY, 29 April 1861 [copy]

[*Royal Observatory, Herstmonceux, Sci. Soc., 1860 (Oct.)–1863 (Apr.), Sect. 24, previously unpublished*]

Royal Observatory
Greenwich S E,
1861 April 29

MY DEAR SIR

Thank you for your very considerate note just received. I think it is not only better but right and proper that I should not appear at the R. Institution Lecture. I am conceived officially (not truly)[1] to have a broad knowledge of the Anglo-Hispanic Eclipse expedition which penetrates into every observation and into the consequences of every observation. Possessing (officially)[1] this knowledge I should appear (also officially)[1] not as a learner but as a critic. A Dieu ne plaire! say I.

But my ladies are most anxious to hear you, and as Mrs. Airy has been talking about it earnestly for days past, I think it very likely that she has already posted a note to you. Let me state in their favour – as if they were strangers – that my wife and eldest daughter were observers of this eclipse, and that my wife was observer of the eclipse of 1842: at the same time they do not possess that consummate breadth of knowledge to which I have alluded as attaching, and peculiar, to myself. So if you can authorize my wife and three ladies to hear you, I shall be much gratified.

I am, my dear Sir,
Yours most truly
G. B. AIRY

[1] Square brackets in ms.

778   G. B. AIRY to M. FARADAY, 15 May 1861

[*I.E.E., previously unpublished*]

Royal Observatory,
Greenwich,
London, S.E.,
1861 May 15

MY DEAR SIR

A matter has come out in the examination of the Greenwich Magnetical Observations (which examination was one of the occupations that made me unfaithful to my lecture-engagement), on which I greatly want your opinion.

The diurnal changes of the forces acting on the magnet (including all forces that act in the plane of the Greenwich horizon) follow a very singular law, which I can explain only by supposing that the radiation of the Sun upon the sea, as distinguished from the land, produces an attraction of the north or marked end of a magnet at Greenwich: and that it is this excitement of the North Atlantic Ocean which mainly produces the diurnal inequalities of magnetic force. The radiation upon the land of Africa seems to produce little or no effect.

Now I want to ask you whether this harmonizes with other known laws of the mediate effect of solar radiation?

I do not doubt, from all that I have seen of atmospheric *electricity*, that any cause which promotes the absorption of aqueous vapour into the air will produce *electrical* effect [*sic*] the electricity being of the nature of frictional electricity. But this is so totally different from magnetism or *galvanism* in all its modes of development, and the exhibitions of accidental atmospheric electricity and accidental terrestrial galvanism are so totally unconnected, that I hardly expect any explanation to follow from that consideration.

———————

The examination of the luno-diurnal inequality shews a tidal throb of magnetism occurring in every lunar day twice towards and twice from the Hudson's Bay direction. Can you suggest any explanation of this?

———————

I am, my dear Sir,
Yours most truly
G. B. AIRY

779 G. B. AIRY to M. FARADAY, 7 July 1861
[*I.E.E., previously unpublished*]

The Grange,
Keswick,
1861 July 7

MY DEAR SIR

Your kind acquiescence in the proposal of the British Association sets me at liberty to a great extent.[1] If it is not contradicted by subsequent communication before my return, I will so far act on it as to pass through Manchester and see the capabilities for a lecture.

The subject of Comets, on which you invite my remarks, is a most puzzling one. I am a firm believer in Laplace's nebular hypothesis, and I do not doubt that he is correct in thinking comets to be stray bits of the cosmical nebulous matter: and this, in process of time, would undoubtedly assume the spherical or nearly spherical form in which we see comets when distant from the sun and in which we see their heads when they are near the sun. So, if comets would preserve their condensed form, I should be quite satisfied. But the difficulty is in the nature and motion of their tails and envelopes. The head of a comet is found to move under the mechanical laws of gravitation, *exactly* as if it had *no appendage whatever*. And the motion of the tail cannot be explained on mechanical laws, supposing it in empty space; and is still more opposed to them if in a resisting medium. It appears to me therefore that the tail of today cannot be the same as the tail of yesterday. I cannot imagine it to be any thing more real than the beam of light in a dusty atmosphere, which travels when the perforated board through which the sunlight passes is moved. But how to account for such a cometary beam (especially so crooked as it was in the case of Donati's comet), and how to explain three covers like three glass shades successively one within another (as appears to hold with this comet) I cannot at all conjecture. It appears to me that all that has been suggested by Bessel,[2] Faye,[3] and twenty other people, has added nothing to our knowledge or our plausible suppositions.

I want to discuss with you another subject, that of thunder-storms. I have lately gone through two sharp ones. In no. 1, there was one thunder clap which commenced by an instantaneous very heavy ringing sound which gave the idea that an Armstrong shot of enormous size had struck the cliff with very great force, the rest of the peal not remarkable. During the remainder of the storm we remarked that, with the utmost regularity, the peals were alternately strong and weak. (I have since thought that the weak ones might be only echoes, which in these mountains sometimes come after a long interval: but I think that here the intervals were too long). – In the storm no. 2, almost every peal began with a low noise, but very un-uniform, much resembling the sound of a military rocket, lasting perhaps three seconds, and then followed by very heavy rolls. Now as the light sound could not be an echo of the heavy one (because it preceded it), and as the heavy sound could not be an echo of the light one (because it was heavier), is it possible to conceive these as having any other relation than that of a train of gunpowder to a magazine? – In any case, my best thanks will be due to any body who will give me a plausible conjecture on the causes of the heavy introductory shot in No. 1 and of the light introductory fizz in No. 2.

I am, my dear Sir,
Yours very truly
G. B. AIRY

[1] I am unable to discover to what this refers.
[2] Friedrich Wilhelm Bessell (1784–1846), mathematician and astronomer. See his many papers on comets in *RSCSP*.
[3] Herve Auguste Etienne Albans Faye (1814–1902), Professor of Astronomy at the Ecole polytechnique. See *RSCSP* for his papers on comets.

780 M. FARADAY to Miss MOORE,[1] 14 August 1861
[*B.J. 2, 448*]

The Green,
Hampton Court,
August 14, 1861.

MY DEAR FRIEND,

I have been writing to you (in imagination) during a full week, and the things I had to talk about were so many that I considered I should at last want a sheet of foolscap for the purpose; but as the thoughts rose they sank again, and oblivion covers all. And so it is in most things with me; the past is gone, *not* to be remembered; the future is coming, *not* to be imagined or guessed at; the present only is shaped to my mind. But, remember, I speak only of temporal and material things. Of higher matters, I trust that the past, present, and future, are *one* with me, and that the temporal things may well wait for their future development.

As with you, so with us; the harvest is a continual joy: all seems so prosperous and happy. What a contrast such a state is to that of our friends the Americans, for notwithstanding all their blustering and arrogance, selfwilledness, and nonsense, I cannot help but feel drawn towards them by their affinity to us. The whole nation seems to me as a little impetuous, ignorant, headstrong child under punishment, and getting a little sobering experience, quite necessary for its future existence as a decent well-behaved nation amongst nations.

Ever your faithful friend,
M. FARADAY.

---

[1] Probably the Harriet Moore who made a number of water-colour paintings of Faraday's quarters and laboratory at the Royal Institution during the 1850s.

781 M. FARADAY to J. PLÜCKER, 17 September 1861
[*I.E.E., previously unpublished*]

Royal Institution
London
17 Sept.ʳ 1861

MY DEAR PROFR. PLUCKER

The progress of decay in memory takes from me all recollection of when I wrote to you. Of late years I have kept a record of letters from abroad which I receive and of those I write in answer – but of late I find I forget to record I have nothing to write about to you but I cannot let drop the kind feeling which is betwixt us and so I write without reason or excuse. I have indeed one thing to do – to acknowledge a very kind letter from you but the date is so long ago that (if I have not written in reply) I will not say how long it is

Your results on the gas spectra are exceedingly interesting. What a wonderful branch of research that of the luminous lines has become. and great honor belongs to Kirchoff [*sic*] & Bunsen for what they have done in the matter[1] I was tempted to think a little about it but when I tried to experiment a little my memory of the results failed & I was obliged for the time to give it up

I am now luxuriating in the Country & in idleness.

Ever My dear Professor
Yours
M. FARADAY

[1] See Letter 723.

782 M. FARADAY to A. DE LA RIVE, 19 September 1861
[*Bibliothèque publique et universitaire de Genève, ms. 2316, f. 93–4, previously unpublished*]

Royal Institution
19 Sept.ʳ 1861

MY VERY DEAR FRIEND

I cannot tell when I wrote you last. Of late years I have kept a note, but I suppose I have forgotten to note. Having no science to talk to you about, a motive, which was very strong in former times, is now wanting: – but your last letter reminds me of *another motive* which I hope is stronger than Science with both of us; and that is the future life which lies before us. I am, I hope, very thankful that in the withdrawal of the powers & things of this life, – the good hope is left with me, which makes the contemplation of death a comfort – not a fear. Such peace is alone in the gift of God; and as it is he who gives it, why should we be afraid? His unspeakable gift in his beloved son is the ground of no doubtful hope; – and *there* is the rest for those who like you & me are drawing near the latter end of our terms here below. – I do not know however why I should join you with me in years. I forget your age. But this I know (& feel as well) that next Sabbath day (the 22nd) I shall complete my 70th year. – I can hardly think myself so old as I write to you – so much of cheerful spirit; – ease – & general health is left to me; – & if my memory fails – why it causes that I forget *troubles* as well as pleasure; & the end is, I am happy & content

I know you to be so too. Long may it continue with you and Madame De la Rive your dear Partner, whom I know to be joined with you.

What can we wish for more, either for ourselves or our dearest friends and you are one of mine.

Ever Yours affectionately
M. FARADAY

[*I.E.E., previously unpublished*]

Présinge
le 23 7bre 1861

TRÈS CHER & EXCELLENT AMI,

Je ne puis assez vous dire combien j'ai été sensible à votre bonne lettre du 19 [7]^bre que j'ai reçue il y a deux jours. J'ai bien pensé à vous hier 22 7bre. Pensez aussi à moi le 9 Octobre, car, ce jour là j'achève ma 60ème année ou plutôt je commence la 61ème Quand on est arrivé à cette époque de la vie, dix ans de différence sont bien peu de chose, car la vieillesse existe aussi bien pour l'homme de 60 ans que pour celui de 70. Laissez-moi donc me considérer comme votre contemporain, comme je suis déjà votre ami. Ce sentiment m'est infiniment doux.

Vous avez bien raison. Cette paix si nécessaire surtout quand on approche du terme de la vie, ne peut se trouver que dans la confiance en Dieu, dans cett(e) foi simple & vive de l'enfant qui remet tout entre les mains de son père. Vous avez cette paix, c'est un immense bonheur pour vous. Je cherche à l'avoir & j'ai peine à y parvenir au milieu des mille préoccupations dont ma vie est remplie. Cinq enfants dont trois mariés sont l'origine de bien des jouissances, mais aussi de bien des soucis; & quoique je me dise souvent qu'il faut s'en remettre à Dieu qui pourvoira à tout, j'ai de la peine dans la pratique à le faire comme je le voudrais.

Dans ce moment en particulier la santé de mon fils second me préoccupe péniblement. Après avoir fait peut-être un excès de travail cet hiver, il a été constamment très souffrant depuis le commencement du printemps. On a essayé de tout: eaux minérales, changement d'air, fer administré à haute dose, sans obtenir jusqu'ici grande amélioration. Cependant il semblerait depuis quelques jours qu'un mieux réel se manifeste. Il n'y a pas chez lui, grâce à Dieu, de mal organique; mais la prolongation d'un état de malaise aussi prononcé est nécessairement inquiétante. Cette indisposition de mon fils m'avait un peu détourné de mes travaux Scientifiques, vu que j'étais péniblement affecté de ne pas le voir travailler à côté de moi. – Mais si, comme je l'espère, son état s'améliore réellement, j'y reviendrai avec d'autant plus d'entrain que je m'en suis plus long-temps abstenu.

Pardon de ces détails; votre bonne amitié m'excusera de vous les donner.

Je n'ai rien su de Tyndall; je ne crois pas qu'il soit venu cette année visiter la Suisse; j'espère cependant qu'il est bien. Rappelez moi, si vous y pensez, à son bon souvenir en le remerciant de l'envoi de son beau mémoire sur les gaz.

Ma femme me charge expressément de ses compliments les plus affectueux pour vous & pour Madame Faraday au souvenir de laquelle je vous prie de vouloir bien aussi me rappeler.

Recevez vous même, tres cher & excellent ami, l'expression de mes sentiments les plus affectueux

Votre tout dévoué

AUG^E DE LA RIVE

Seriez-vous assez bon pour continuer à me donner encore de temps en temps
de vos nouvelles?

784 M. FARADAY to J. T. CHANCE, 7 October 1861
[*Sir Hugh Chance, Stourbridge (on loan to the R.I.), previously unpublished*]

The Green

Hampton Court

7 Octr 1861

MY DEAR SIR

I received your report on Saturday & at once sent it off to the Trinity House
I hope Mrs. Chance is with you WELL & that you are enjoying Bournemouth which however is a place I have never seen

Ever Yours Truly

M FARADAY

The lime light is going in at the S Freeland. It is very good & easy *in the
lanthorn practice* but the gas department has to be well tested. If ever applied –
it will want a set of focal adjustments etc altogether different to those of either
the oil lamp or the Electric Spark.

Again Yours

M FARADAY

785 M. FARADAY to the Managers of the Royal Institution,
11 October 1861
[*R.I., B.J. 2, 443*]

Royal Institution,

11 October 1861.

To the Managers of the Royal Institution.

Gentlemen.

It is with the deepest feeling that I address you.

I entered the Royal Institution in March 1813, nearly fortynine years ago;
and, with the exception of a comparatively short period during which I was
absent on the continent with Sir Humphry Davy, have been with you ever
since.

During that time I have been most happy in your kindness, and in the fostering care which the Royal Institution has bestowed upon me. I am very thankful to you, and your predecessors, for the unswerving encouragement and support which you have given me during that period. My life has been a happy one and all I desired. During its progress I have tried to make a fitting return for it to the Royal Institution and through it to Science.

But the progress of years (now amounting in number to three score and ten) having brought forth, first, the period of development, and then that of maturity; have ultimately produced for me that of gentle decay. This has taken place in such a manner as to render the evening of life a blessing: – for whilst increasing physical weakness occurs, a full share of health free from pain is granted with it; and whilst memory and certain other faculties of the mind diminish, my good spirits and cheerfulness do not diminish with them.

Still I am not able to do as I have done. I am not competent to perform as I wish, the delightful duty of teaching in the Theatre of the Royal Institution; and I now ask you (in consideration for me) to accept my resignation of the *Juvenile lectures*. Being unwilling to give up, what has always been so kindly received and so pleasant to myself, I have tried the faculties essential for their delivery, and I know that I ought to retreat: – for the attempt to realize (in the trials) the necessary points brings with it weariness, giddiness, fear of failure and the full conviction that it is time to retire. I desire therefore to lay down this duty; and I may truly say, that such has been the pleasure of the occupation to me, that my regret must be greater than yours need or can be.

And this reminds me that I ought to place in your hands the *whole* of my occupation. It is, no doubt, true that the Juvenile lectures, not being included in my engagement as Professor, were, when delivered by me, undertaken as an extra duty, and remunerated by an extra payment. The duty of research, superintendence of the house, and other services still remains; – but I may well believe that the natural change which incapacitates me from lecturing, may also make me unfit for some of these. In such respects, however, I will leave you to judge, and to say whether it is your wish that I should still remain as part of the Royal Institution.

I am Gentlemen, with all my heart;
Your faithful and devoted Servant
M. FARADAY.

Bonn,
Oct 22 1861.

Most Dear Sir,

I was most happy to get after a long intervall of time your amiable letter of September 17th, which I found, when returning home from the Midi de la France. I intended to send you a paper in August im̃ediately before leaving Bonn, but at that time of hard work it was rather impossible to me to recollect my mind in order to give you at the same time a short account of the german, the barbarian paper.[1]

The principal part of it is intended to confirm what I think a capital point in the theory of electric currents. Such a current passing through a wire, through a conducting fluid or through a gazeous substance – this substance being sufficiently abondant [*sic*] as it is the case for instance in the experiment of Delarive's [*sic*] rotating arch – obeys to the known laws of Electromagnetism. But if there be no sufficient quantity of matter, to present to the current a continuous and regular passage, these laws do not hold; they are to be replaced by other ones, equally well defined. If the gaz be most highly dilated the current (la courant naissant, cherchant son chemin), when solely under the influence of magnetic forces, proceeds along a magnetic curve i.e. along such a curve where it is not acted upon by magnetism. If No matter at all: no current.

Let the discharge of Ruhmkorff's coil pass between two points within a sphere of glass containing *no measurable* quantity of air; introduce into the sphere, while de [*sic*] discharge is passing a new portion of air, producing within it a tension of about 5 mm. During the introduction of air the appearance of the discharge will be totally changed and, under the action of an Electromagnet, it will be deflected in a quite different manner. This experiment is most surprising.

Since I was so happy to show you first, about four years ago, at the Royal Institution the peculiar spectra of gazes, heated by the current, this chapter of experimental inquiry has been worked out very much. At that time I was struck, thinking that a quantity of gaz, too small as to be indicated by the most delicate balance, might be analysed by the prism. MM. Bunsen and Kirchhoff, who, with the greatest success made use of the same kind of analysis, thought this analysis proper only to discover or to prove the existence of metals, especially of those of alcaloids. From my part in the contrary, I always thought that *every vapour* (of Sodium or of gold), if sufficiently heated in any way whatever – That *every gaz*, composed or not, has its own spectrum. The gaz, if a composed one, gives a peculiar spectrum in the case only where it is non decomposed by the heat. If the decomposition take place by and by, appearances are obtained, similar to dissolving views, the spectrum of one gaz (sulfuric acid for inst.) is passing into the spectrum of another one (of sulfurous acid). –

An account of my further researches will be comūnicated afterward. I thought it proper to join in a note to my paper a few remarks only. – I hope, dear Sir, you will take up again your meditations and experimental researches regarding the same objects.

I most recently fully succeeded to get spectral tubes, the light of which is as *bright* and *constant* as the light of my former tubes, but without any electrode. I think the spectral analysis of gazes will be highly promoted by means of them. I'll go to work.

If possible in any way I hope to see you next year in England and I will be most happy to see you again. Be so kind to present my respects to Mad. Faraday. My best whishes for your health. With all my heart and for ever

Yours

PLÜCKER

¹ J. Plücker, 'Ueber die Einwirkung des Magnets auf die electrische Entladung', *AP*, 189 (1861), 249.

787   G. B. AIRY to M. FARADAY, 22 October 1861 [copy]

[*Royal Observatory, Herstmonceux, Sci. Soc., 1860 (Oct.)–1863 (Apr.), Sect. 24, previously unpublished*]

1861 October 22

MY DEAR SIR

Shame on me that I have left a note of yours so long unanswered!

I would willingly be excused from giving a lecture from this time to the end of my natural life. But I owe you one, and I will if possible discharge my debt on April 11.

But then comes the old difficulty – what shall be the subject?

I hope that something may present itself before April; at this moment I see nothing.

I am, my dear Sir,

Yours very truly

G. B. AIRY

788   M. FARADAY to G. B. AIRY, 23 October 1861

[*Royal Observatory, Herstmonceux, Sci. Soc., 1860 (Oct.)–1863 (Apr.), Sect. 24, previously unpublished*]

23 Octr. 1861

MY DEAR SIR

Very hearty thanks for your letter – Comets? Why not. You know what to ask about them if you cannot yet tell us the answers – & to give their state as a problem only is to do a great deal

Ever Yours

M. FARADAY

789 M. FARADAY to J. T. CHANCE, 28 October 1861

[*Sir Hugh Chance, Stourbridge (on loan to the R.I.), previously unpublished*]

Royal Institution
28 October 1861

MY DEAR SIR

I have sent on your report of the N. Whitby light to the Trinity House

You wrote to me from Bournemouth – how you run about? I hope Mrs. Chance & the little or rather young ones are quite well

Your kind & free offer about the investigation of foci for the lime light is very grateful to me – I do not know how we could do without you. We go (i.e. a committee) out to sea on Wednesday or Thursday night to look at the light – & there will be much to do in the retort & gas house – and in the matter of expence before the light can be established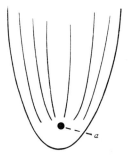

The individual lights are of about this shape and size the maximum light being at *a* & this spot is slightly *sunk* into the lime in consequence of a depression which is formed by the current of gases – there are eight of these lights placed at equal distances round an *opaque* cylinder about 3 1/2 inches in diameter. As all the light that goes to any part of the optical apparatus is from the *front* & side of the lime but none from the back you will easily judge what a change would be required for the focal points especially for the upper reflectors

Ever Truly Yours
M FARADAY

790 M. FARADAY to the Duke of Northumberland,
15 November 1861
[*B.J. 2, 445*]

Royal Institution,
November 15, 1861.

MY LORD DUKE,

Is it essential to *yourself* that we should lose you? You are kind, you bear with us, you do not disturb our management, you justify it when submitted to you, you do all that we desire. No one can be to us the President that you are.

Mr. Pole has shown me your Grace's note; it, and the remembrance of all your former kindness, makes me thus bold to write.

That your Grace may know of my sincerity, I quote a small thing personal to myself. I am above seventy years of age, and with a bad memory, feel the thought of the Juvenile Lectures a burden to me. I have retired from them; but as the managers believe that the remembrance of past times, and the association of my name, is good for the Royal Institution, I still continue engaged to do what I can for the cause of science there. May I hope that your Grace will in the same way continue our President.

I should be deeply grieved if I did not think that your Grace will forgive me the freedom of this letter.

I am, my Lord Duke, your truly humble servant,　　　　　M. FARADAY.

791　M. FARADAY to J. T. CHANCE, 23 January 1862
[Sir Hugh Chance, Stourbridge (on loan to the R.I.), previously unpublished]

Royal Institution
23 Jany/62.

Private

MY DEAR MR CHANCE

My communication is quite informal but you will see that it has a bearing

Suppose the T. H. had occasion to send out a specification to the manufacturers of lights; – it ought not to be loose or it would not secure the degree of perfection they would desire; – it ought not to be too precise for they could not treat every point with precision or if they could might really enforce faults & take away from the Manufacturer the power & right of exercising his own intelligence: – and so the question arises as to what would be a good specification? Now I know you so well that I think you could put self aside and sketch out or draw up, the fittest possible specification, to be sent, not to middlemen but to the real Manufacturers. I do not think such a paper should be very long or very minute: – it should of course stipulate for a thorough examination of the optical action as security for the T. H.

What do you think of this matter? If I should find occasion to suggest to the T. H. that you should be consulted on this subject, either privately or more openly, would it be aggreable or disagreeable to you. At present I have only talked with one person on the subject, & quite at a distance. I would not say much until I knew your thoughts; – but I suspect the matter would be done best in the way I hint at; & think it might be right with, & agreeable to, all parties.

Ever My dear Sir
Yours
M FARADAY

792 G. B. AIRY to M. FARADAY, 17 February 1862 [copy]

[*Royal Observatory, Herstmonceux, Sci. Soc., 1860 (Oct.)–1863 (Apr.), Sect. 24,* *previously unpublished*]

1862 February 17

MY DEAR SIR

I appear before you in the character of a suppliant debtor; not denying my debt – on the contrary, resolved to discharge it when I can –, but soliciting delay for the payment.

I begin to think it impossible that I can lecture in April, as was arranged.

I had partly hoped that I should be able to tell you something about star-spectra, observed by a peculiar apparatus attached to our great telescope. The weather has much baffled me. My apparatus wants clear days for adjustment, and naturally wants clear nights for use: and both have been very deficient. From these causes, and the usual interruptions of winter, I have made no progress for the last 3 months or more.

I am now trying by experiment the different retentive powers, for induced magnetism, of malleable iron of different qualities, but the result of these would be comprised in very few words, and would interest nobody.

So I thought of your suggestion about Comets, and have carried Bessel's paper[1] (first on the subject in modern times) from my Official Room to my Drawing Room and back about 30 times, hoping to be able to get through its stubborn German. But no opportunity of beginning it has yet come. There is a great deal to be read on this subject.

And now – De la Rue has at last sent me his account of the 1860 eclipse – and I must take some editorial charge of the whole matter.

Now I think, if you can let me off for a time, there is fair prospect of the first or the third of the subjects which I have mentioned becoming available.

I am, my dear Sir,
Yours very truly
G. B. AIRY

[1] Possibly F. W. Bessell, 'Beobachtungen über die physische Beschaffenheit des Halley'schen Kometen', *AP*, 114 (1836), 498, which deals with the problem of the physical make-up of comets which interested Airy.

793 M. FARADAY to J. T. CHANCE, 17 February 1862

[Sir Hugh Chance, Stourbridge (on loan to the R.I.), previously unpublished]

Royal Institution
17 Feby 1862

MY DEAR MR CHANCE

I have received your paper & note

I have introduced all your additions & changes

I have sent it to the Deputy Master to see if there is any wish to make further alterations or any objection to what has been changed or added – and I have asked for a couple of reviews that we may each have one. I tried to make a reference in No. 11 not merely to the middle ray of the bundle passing through a given prism and its passage to the destined focus: but to the whole of the bundle that its focus should not be too far before or behind that of the middle ray. Perhaps you think that great exactness in this respect should not be required at present

Ever Truly Yours
M FARADAY

I think you have said quite enough on the above point

M F

In the part proposed to be inserted in the 7th division it says "& in each alternate one of these panels an inclined stay is to be added." I understand you to mean, of these *upper* panels

Looking at the drawing: – what is an upper panel? Are there eight? Where is the inclined stay to go, in the alternate panels? – and how can they all coincide optically with the standards of the lanthorn

Can the drawing go with the amended specification?

Perhaps the tracing you promised me will inform me on these points

Ever Yours
M FARADAY

794 M. FARADAY to J. T. CHANCE, 1 April 1862

[Sir Hugh Chance, Stourbridge (on loan to the R.I.), previously unpublished]

Royal Institution
1 April 1862

MY DEAR MR. CHANCE

I saw the Deputy Master yesterday, and after much conversation, in which many practical manufacturing questions arose, left him under the arrangement, that I was to write these questions to you, but that (as I wished) you had better answer *directly* to him as if they came from him.

The questions concern a revolving *red* light of the *first order*, for the S. W end of the island of Guernsey; and the desire is to have the intervals of light and darkness as 1:3 or 1:4 and this by means of a series of holophotal panels. Now as the divergence of the lens beam is about 6° or 7°, twelve lenses in the circle would give nearly these proportions. Then come the questions

Are you prepared to construct a holophotal apparatus of the first order, divided into twelve parts?

Or to suggest, as manufacturers, any other refracting or glass arrangement to obtain the desired effect?

Do you manufacture red glass? – What kind of red glass do you, from experience, believe to be best? – the gold ruby or the copper ruby?

In applying the red glass, do you think, as regards construction and efficacy, the red glass should be used as *sheets* introduced in the course of the ray *after* it has left the optic apparatus; i. e. as it goes seaward, or around the flame *before* the rays have reached the refracting parts etc? – and if around the flame, would the colour & glass stand the heat, supposing the lamp-glasses themselves were red? – Or could the light be coloured by a globe of red glass placed outside the lamp glass? – or any other form of red glass, perhaps of parts framed together? – which globes or frames you would be able to manufacture

Perhaps you can answer these enquiries off hand from your present knowledge. We do not want to give you much trouble, but are uncertain about the power of manufacturing according to the division into twelve parts etc

The Deputy master wished me to say that he had forgotten to bring away his drawing.

> Ever My dear Sir
> Yours Truly
> M FARADAY

795 G. B. AIRY to M. FARADAY, 20 April 1862 [copy]
[*Royal Observatory, Herstmonceux, Astrology-Optics, 1860 (Nov.)–1863 (Apr.), Sect. 8, previously unpublished*]

1862 April 20

MY DEAR SIR

Can you throw any chemical or galvanic light upon the following matter of prevention?

I have lately had several Navy Chronometers returned, principally I believe from service in rather humid tropical climates, injured by rust. On close examination it is found, in all the instances which have lately occurred, (I know not whether antecedently), that the white or clean steel is perfectly untouched, but the blued steel is heavily rusted.

It is a serious evil, because among the "blued steel" is included the balance-spring, the replacement of which is very expensive.

The bluing, I believe, is produced only by heat. I conceive that there is no pigment as in the lacquering of brass.

Now can you give me any theory on this? And can you suggest any way of curing it?

We commonly imagine that, when brass or gunmetal and steel are in contact, it is the steel which suffers by oxidation. But with different acids it is not so. I had some instruments inclosed in a sound oak box, and after some time I found the whole of the brass and gunmetal covered with a yellow oxide or salt, while the steel pins shone [reading doubtful] out with an almost preternatural brilliancy.

> I am, my dear Sir,
> Yours very truly
> G. B. AIRY

796 M. FARADAY to G. B. AIRY, 23 April 1862

[Royal Observatory, Herstmonceux, Astrology-Optics, 1860 (Nov.)–1863 (Apr.), Sect. 8, previously unpublished]

> 23 april 1862

MY DEAR SIR

When the electrochemical relations of two bodies are very nearly equal and because of changes in the surface state of the bodies very likely to be disturbed it is often impossible to tell why one gives way in a certain direction before the other. I have often known cases in which in the same medium the two bodies have alternated sometimes one getting a head [*sic*] of the other & sometimes falling behind it Both well polished steel & blued steel (which is an oxidation) I have seen sometimes well preserved & sometimes easily decay

You ask about prevention I remember but only imperfectly that many years ago I was shewn the rusty state of a clock that had been fixed into an oakwood case I believe it was South that shewed it to me On trying the wood as to any power it might have of producing this action it was found that when holes were bored by a gimblet in the wood & little strips of delicate litmus paper were placed in the holes that paper was reddened in the course of a day or two by the acid vapour which rose from the wood. The corrosion of the iron parts of the clock was referred to this vapour. I think I tried & found that a like effect on the test paper was produced by some pieces of Mahogany & not by others

Has this fact any bearing on the case of your chronometers & will it suggest a means of testing the wood of their boxes

> I am My dear Sir
> Very Truly Yours
> M. FARADAY

797 Report by M. FARADAY, 19 May 1862 [copy]

[Sir Hugh Chance, Stourbridge (on loan to the R.I.), previously unpublished]

Royal Institution.
19th May 1862.

SIR

On the 21st of February last I sent to you a report on the state of the Magneto electric light at Dungeness, and referring to the requisite care and intelligence of the keepers expressed my gladness when the Deputy Master & committee concluded that this case of the "Electric light ought to be made exceptional for the present; that two intelligent young men should be appointed keepers; that they with the engineers should be fully instructed; that after a certain time when declared competent they should be examined; – and if found competent the light should then be reopened with the engineer as chief keeper – etc"

Two such keepers named Burney and Chaplin have been appointed, instructed, and exercised; and on the 12th & 13th instants I was at the lighthouse (the Deputy master & commitee [*sic*] and also Profs.ᵣ Holmes & Mr. Jas. Chance being present) and examined these Keepers, both by word of mouth & practice with the light. I am of opinion that they, with the Engineer, are competent to take charge of the light, and therefore according to the intention above expressed the Electric light may be reopened whenever the Deputy master and Brethren may think fit; and so the real evidence respecting manageability – power of light – constancy of action – fitness for duty – permanency – peculiar advantages – and expense – may be obtained by continued & public use under the observation of the maritime world.

The steam boilers have been jacketted. The machine room with its ceiling put into excellent order. – Certain alterations in the lantern respecting the course of the stove pipe & a shelter from the rain and dust entry by the cowl have not yet been made, but should be done by or before winter.

I noticed in the former report that the prisms of the optic apparatus do not intercept all the light that proceeds generally towards them; and said that in an apparatus so new and original as this I was prepared to accept them for the present case, but that in future apparatus this escape should be provided against. This is my opinion still* In reference to a new optic apparatus Mr. Chance and I think there should be many changes in size, arrangement, adjustments etc but we reserve all these points for longer & future consideration, aided by the instruction that will arise from the results of experience. We believe the present apparatus is abundantly sufficient to supply every proof that can be desired to establish the fitness or the contrary of Magneto electric light for lighthouse purposes.

* These apparatus which are of the 6th order according to the modes and practices derived from the use of the oil lamp; for no other practice had these been obtained.

798 M. FARADAY to J. LEIGHTON,[1] 1 December 1862
[*R.I., previously unpublished*]

Royal Institution.
1 Decr. 1862.

MY DEAR SIR

Dr. Bence Jones tells me that you & he have met & have agreed about a Friday Evening for the 15th or 22nd of May. Some one standing by gave us at the meeting the impression that you would read the lecture As we are sure that you would do it better the less you read, so I venture to express a hope that you will not read more than you may find quite necessary for your own convenience

Ever My dear Sir
Yours Very Truly
M. FARADAY.

[1] John Leighton (1822–1912), writer. His discourse at the Royal Institution was *On Japanese Art*, London, 1863.

799 M. FARADAY to J. T. CHANCE, 18 December 1862
[*Sir Hugh Chance, Stourbridge (on loan to the R.I.), previously unpublished*]

London
18 Dec.ʳ 1862

MY DEAR SIR

I thought that the imperfections in the workings & shaping of the large back mirrors had interfered with suggestions of the nature of those contained in your letter of the 13th. Were a reasonably good image of the flame sent back to the space above the burner, the rays forming it might surely be useful. But with those mirrors which I have seen, the experiment with a candle flame gave a very bad result. I think I tried the mirrors at Whitby, & found a like bad result there. Lamps with such mirrors are said to burn badly and that may well be the case, with a powerful source of heat acting irregularly on one side of the burner and cottons. My impression is that they have been discontinued in different places, in consequence of experience having shown that they produced no good effect: but I have no personal knowledge of the matter.

Ever My dear Sir
Very truly Yours
M FARADAY

800 M. FARADAY to C. C. BLAKE, 21 January 1863

[*Burndy Library, Norwalk, Conn., Faraday Collection 12, previously unpublished*]

R Institution
21 Jan.ʸ 1863

SIR

Though it is against my rule (which is also the rule of Society) to reply as of course to a circular – yet I am induced to say that I am doing all I can to retreat from societies & cannot therefore join a new one. The pressure of general distress makes this quite necessary in my case

Very Truly Yours
M. FARADAY

801 M. FARADAY to SIR JAMES CLARK, 7 February 1863

[*B.J. 2, 463*]

Royal Institution,
February 7, 1863.

MY DEAR SIR JAMES,

Her Majesty our Queen has done me great honour (and a favour most especially welcome) in thinking of me in relation to our most worthy and glorious Prince, his late Royal Highness the Prince Consort. I do not know how to thank Her Majesty enough or well – may I hope that you will help me? I would, if I might, express my reverence for the Queen, the wife and the mother whose image dwells in the hearts of all her people. I wish that I were, as a subject, more worthy of her; but the vessel wears out, and at seventy-one has but little promise for the future. The fifty years of use in the Royal Institution has given me wonderful advantages in learning, many friends, and many opportunities of making my gratitude known to them; but they have taken the matter of life, and above all, memory out of me, leaving the mere residue of the man that has been, and now I remain in the house useless as to further exertion, excused from all duty, very content and happy in my mind, clothed with kindness by all, and honoured by my Queen.

Ever, my dear Sir James, your most faithful servant,

M. FARADAY.

802 M. FARADAY to J. LIEBIG, 23 July 1863

[*Gesellschaft, Liebig Museum, Giessen, previously unpublished*]

Royal Institution
London
23. July 1863

MY DEAR LIEBIG

The arrival of the English translation of your work on the Natural laws of Husbandry,[1] sent to me as *from the author* stirs up all my affection for him and makes me write to him; though I write no more philosphy [*sic*] or have any ability as an active philosophic mind. It is the past that moves me, the remembrance of all the dear thoughts & associations that I have in former years been permitted to share in; – & though I may have through wear & years to give up the race & fall into the rear yet it rejoices me to think that those who still run carry forward a kind remembrance of me. So thanks & again thanks my dear Liebig for the volume you have sent me Though I write from London I am not there at present for I am sent out of town to rest – not my body so much as my bad memory & mind

I hear of you continually and always as one of the powerful ones

Ever My dear friend
Truly Yours
M. FARADAY

¹ J. Liebig, *The Natural Laws of Husbandry*, edited by J. Blyth, London, 1863.

803 M. FARADAY to B. VINCENT,¹ 7 August 1863
[*R.I., previously unpublished*]

5 Clairmont Gardens
Glasgow
7. August 1863.

MY DEAR FRIEND

Your letter from Old Buckenham was a most welcome pleasure to all here: – to know that you had gone through the journey & with great hope that it might do good we trust that the hopes & the wishes have since been realized & then how cheerily you will presently return home. I conclude that the party consisted of yourself – Mrs Vincent & Annie Our constant thoughts are with you all & our love. Your letter made us very happy. Our letters about Mrs. Buchanan made us dull. It is well for us that our hope & trust should be exercised that it may be placed on him who will never forsake his people – who worketh all things together for their good.

We have been received most affectionately here by all. Mr. Baxter has not made his appearance here & therefore it is concluded (& indeed known) that the case is compromised and that he has returned to Dundee. In an hour or two we start for Dundee – are to be received by the kind daughters of our old friend Dr. Crichton – in the Old house in Tay Street. We purpose returning here on the Wednesday (12 Aug) and I purpose returning to London on the Wednesday (or perhaps the previous Tuesday) according to our first plan.

Mr. More Mr. Cowan, Mr. Sandeman & the friends here seem pretty well. Up to Wednesday Evening we had here our friends Mr Myddleton & Mr. Dyack from Aberdeen with their friend Mr. Sinclair and very pleasant it was to meet them.

My recollection is failing me so I will not try to call up more of the agreeable events that have passed here. I am in a medium state of cheerfulness. I do not allow myself to be troubled by my own thoughts more than I can help.

Very dear brother,
Yours Affectionately
M. FARADAY.

Jeannie's love to Mrs. Vincent & Annie & to you all.

¹ The people mentioned below were all members of the Sandemanian Church. Faraday preached at Dundee during this visit.

804 M. FARADAY to B. VINCENT, 20 August 1863

[*R.I., previously unpublished*]

Thursday, 20 Aug/63
London.

MY DEAR FRIEND

I waited until last Evening that I might see our Elders; &, knowing that my wife wrote to you yesterday, hoped you would not think me neglectful, in not doing so. I had indeed enough to do in writing to our friends in the North. According to the proposed arrangements I came home on Monday night by the Mail; – arrived here on Tuesday Morning, – wrote to Mr. Leighton to announce myself, – found last night that Mr. Whitelaw was able to join you next Saturday for the Sabbath day, and hope you will be cheered by his company and will meet him with cheerful news.

Mr Sandeman was so kind as to shew me your letter & we were glad thinking that it was cheerful. They often talk of you & look forward to coming events. I think I may say they are pretty well; but the pronoun *they* is so comprehensive that I ought to doubt least I forget some. We have enjoyed their company very much and found most hearty welcomes there. Indeed all have been as kind as they could be; and it makes one think what is there in or attached to ourselves that draws it forth.

Our visit to Dundee was very pleasant, but I dare not try to give you any account of it. I should fail in the facts & their order; – but love & kindness was every where.

The library is getting on but the time will be short. The Porters say they cannot do it in the time. The arranging the books in order has taken so much time (they being greatly out of order) that the period is not long enough. The part in *the Gallery* is all finished but in the part under the Gallery, they will have to leave much as they find it. You will see how that is when you return; & probably Hughes can be useful there. Our love to Mrs. Vincent & Annie Mr Leighton & Mr Whitelaw looked very well last night. Love to all friends with you, from

[M. FARADAY]

[*R.I., previously unpublished*]

Tuesday, 25 Aug/63.
Hampton Court.

MY DEAR FRIEND,

I cannot be sure that I wrote to you since my return from Scotland but *I think I did*. Your letter of the 21st. I received with much delight; and there was so much that we thought would be acceptable to the Church, both about yourselves & the brethren with you, that the chief part was read at the love feast: – the interest in it was not lessened by our remembering that Mr White-law was with you at the very time. – We were very sorry to hear of Mr Love-days attack; – it would indeed be a great loss to the brethren to lose in any degree his company & help, both in the worship and that constant happy occupation to which all are called, of building each other up as one body.

Last Sabbath day we were very grave here. We had to resign the privilege of the Lords supper. Discipline was in hand & all were not at peace. The trouble lies between my wife, Mr Geo Leighton & Miss Cumacher. – I cannot say much about it, but look anxiously to hoped for results tomorrow. – We shall be very glad to have our brother Mr Whitelaw back again, and also yourself dear friend, when the time arrives. I hope before that, that the Father of Mercies will have given one heart & one way to us, as a people whom he hath chosen in his great mercy & long suffering to be with him in his beloved Son Jesus Christ. How great is the love he hath manifested in him – it ought indeed to move us to love one another.

Your account of Mrs. Vincent tells both ways, and we can well feel for you in your anxiety about the end of the Journey. Let us trust that it will be as favourable as the beginning. Though you have settled in your thoughts to be here (i.e. at the R.I.) on the 1st or 2nd of September, yet if you find reason to be somewhat late I am sure your reason will be good & sufficient. You will see by the different parts of this note, that we wish for you *soon*, & yet that wish you not to *hasten too much*.

My mind wanders: – if I continue to write it will be just vain repetitions. Miss Cloudsley is here with us, and Mary Chuter Barnard, & my wife – all unite in love to you & your dear wife & daughter & to our friends with you; one & all.

Always yours Very Affectionately,
M. FARADAY.

806 M. FARADAY to J. PLÜCKER, 17 September 1863

[*Nat. Res. Counc. Canada, previously unpublished*]

17. Septr 1863,
London

MY DEAR PLUCKER

As soon as I had your letter I wrote to you (being at the time out of town) and said I should call on you at a given hour 11 o'clk yesterday morning. I went to your house found you were gone having left for Paris the day before and now have only the solace of writing so that when you return to Bonn you may find this poor written word from me It would indeed have cheered me to have seen your face & heard your voice speaking of science & your exertions for it. For my own part things change as they may well do in the latter years of an old man's life and leave me listless and ineffectual – If I could only remember – but I will not tease you for I think I have said all I ought to say to you, on former occasions.

I hope you enjoyed your trip to Newcastle.[1] I durst not venture into the crowd of friends & exciting matters: – the very thought of doing so oppressed me. I hear all went on prosperously & I am quite sure you would bear your part in the matter. If I could have been there invisible. I am very glad you came across M.^r & Mrs Deacon[2] they would have great pleasure in your company. Believe me to be ever

My dear Plucker
Your Affectionate friend
M. FARADAY

---

[1] The *BAAS* met in Newcastle in 1863.
[2] Faraday's nephew and his wife.

---

807 M. FARADAY to L. AGASSIZ, 20 October 1863

[*Harvard University, previously unpublished*]

Royal Institution
20 October 1863

MY DEAR AGASSIZ

I wish I could send you a book or some evidence of scientific occupation but all I can do now is to take a pen & thank those who work & remember me in connexion with work. I am very grateful to you for your *method of Study*[1] and for your opinion given in it of the transmutation question. I have little or no right to judge of it philosophically but the evidence the advocates give is so weak & feeble that I feel as if they had no more right than I have.

I have not met Mr. Lesley[2] yet & fear I may not for when I called yesterday at the Hotel they gave me to understand he was going away

Ever My dear Sir
Yours Most truly
M. FARADAY

[1] L. Agassiz, *Methods of Study in Natural History*, Boston, 1863.
[2] Probably Peter Lesley (1819–1903), American geologist.

808 A. QUÉTELET to M. FARADAY, 18 January 1864
[*I.E.E., previously unpublished*]

Bruxelles,
le 18 Janvier 1864

MON CHER ET RESPECTABLE AMI,

J'aurois du vous remercier depuis longtemps de la lettre obligeante que vous avez bien voulu m'adresser, à la fin de l'année dernière, pour la communication des publications de notre Académie. Cette communication Vous étoit due sous tous les rapports: si je ne craignois de blesser votre modestie, je dirois que nous devons avant tout nos travaux aux princes de la Science: et sous ce rapport nul ne y mérite mieux que Vous. permettez moi d'ajouter qu'à l'âge ou je suis, il est d'autres qualités que j'estime plus encore que les grands talents, je ne dirai pas les quelles, [*sic*] [reading doubtful] parceque je craindrois de blesser Votre modestie: je dirai seulement que s'il est des manifestations qui peuvent me toucher Vivement, ce sont celles qui me sont adressées par des gens de bien, par des hommes d'honneur devant les quels [*sic*] tous les autres doivent s'abaisser.

je me rappeleroi toujours avec plaisir les jours que j'ai passés en angleterre pendant l'exposition des différentes nations et les bontés dont vous m'avez comblé. je ne dois plus retourner en Angleterre, je Verrois avec trop de chagrin ce palais où se trouvait le meilleur des princes. je sais que vous le receviez avec plaisir à vos cours de physique et je sais toute l'estime particulière qu'il avoit pour vos talents et votre personne; c'est par ce motif que je ne crains pas de Vous en dire quelques mots.

Je vous serois bien reconnaissant, mon cher et illustre ami, si en pensant à la Belgique et à mon excellent ami Plateau, car je sais l'amitié que Vous portez à cet ancien confrère, vous vouliez bien penser quelques fois à moi, car je puis le dire, sans dépasser les limites du vrai, il n'est personne pour qui je professe plus de respect et d'estime. Excusez moi d'exprimer des sentiments qui peut être Vous paraitront polis, mais qui sont vrais avant tout et que je tiens à vous exprimer. Je vous prie de vouloir bien me rappeler au souvenir de Madame qui contribuait si fort à faire de votre demeure une des plus heureuses et des plus honorables que j'ai connues.

Je ne vous parlerai pas des souffrances que j'ai éprouvées moi même, de la parte de ma femme, de ma fille, de mon petit fils. Tous ces malheurs m'ont frappe presqu'en même temps. Ma fille a succombé un an avant l'excellent prince Albert et le même jour!

Adieu, mon excellent, mon Vénérable ami; j'ose me servir de cette expression puisque Votre excellente lettre m'autorise en quelque sorte à le faire. Recevez l'expression de ma plus profonde Vénération

Tout à vous
QUÉTELET

809   C. MATTEUCCI to M. FARADAY, 20 April 1864

[*I.E.E., previously unpublished*]

Turin,
20 Aprile [*sic*] 1864

MON CHER FARADAY

Je suis dans l'impossibilité de vous faire une longue reponse etant au lit malade depuis plusieurs jours e [*sic*] par consequent dans l'impossibilité de chercher parmi mes papiers les lettres de Daniell et de vous que j'ai recu il y a vingt ans. Ce dont je me rappelle positivement c'est le sens, ou l'esprit de la proposition que j'ai exprimé *improprement* en employant le mot *promis* que ni vous ni Daniell n'ont employé et ne pouvaient employer. J'ai compris alors et j'ai toujours eu cette opinion après que Daniell et Faraday après avoir vu toutes mes experiences d'Electro Physiologie, après que le Conseil m'avait donné la medaille me jugeaient digne d'etre F.M. et s'interessaient auprès de leurs amis pour cela. Telle est je crois la verité, comme c'est la verité que depuis quelques années on fait croire au Conseil Royal que l'électro-ton des nerfs, les variations negatives du courant musculaire, les molécules bipolaires, l'identité de l'electricite et du fluide nerveux sont des découvertes, tandis qu'elles ne le sont pas et que les seules decouvertes sur cela sont jusqu'ici celles que la S.R. a couronné avec le Copley Medal en 1844.

Je demande mille fois pardon de tout ce tracas, que mon inexperience et ma confiance dans des vrais titres ont soulevé et surtout de la peine que cela vous a cause a Vous à qui je dois une eternelle reconnoissance et a qui j'ai été et je serai toujours très devoué.

tout a vous
C MATTEUCCI

1021

810 M. FARADAY to J. B. DUMAS, 4 October 1865

[*Arch. de l'Acad. des Sciences, Paris, Dossier Faraday, previously unpublished*]

Royal Institution
4 October, 1865

MY DEAR & MOST HONORABLE FRIEND

I have just returned from the seaside ill, and very unable to act much. I was *rejoiced* to see your hand writing. I have lost my memory, but not memory of you & your constant kindness. If I have ever had an intimation of your Lavoisierian thought as regards myself it has utterly left me & in the present state of matters, I hope not, for in that case I shall appear most ungrateful in your eyes, and that I am not, for such a work published under the care of such a man as yourself in such a manner under such auspices would be a great honor to me & deserve all my thanks.

I am employing my dear Niece[1] to write all my letters for me – my memory will not go on from the middle of one line to the middle of the next – but I could not give the one, for you, out of my own hands. you will I am sure accept my feeble and broken exertions backed as they are by my plentiful & warm thoughts But I must bring this to a close for my hand threatens me with loss of its powers, and I must save power enough to write to M. Gauthier Villarez[2] according to your instructions.

I remember a warning that Madame Dumas once gave me that she was troubled by my hand writing. I am ashamed to send such writing as this but it is the best in which I can convey my most earnest respects I hope that will cause it to pass.

Ever my dear Dumas Yours
M. FARADAY

I would like to have recalled a few names to my memory but fear to make myself troublesome & when they arise fear to trouble you, and again, so many have passed away. St. Claire de Ville [*sic*] Lavoisier etc.

[1] Jane Barnard.
[2] The publishers of the *CR*.

811 J. SOUTH to M. FARADAY, 12 January 1866

[*I.E.E., previously unpublished*]

Friday Jany 12th. 1866
Observatory Kensington

MY DEAR OLD FRIEND/

It was with great grief, that I read in a letter written me at your kind wish, by your good niece, Miss Barnard, that it had pleased God to call from this world, your honest – able – and intelligent Assistant, the late Charles Anderson.

To your sensitive Heart, the Blow, I am sure, must be a severe one; for his long service, (38 years) and STRONG attachment to you, had made him, in Royal Institution scientific matters, almost, "PART AND PARCEL," of yourself.

The old Soldier, has I think, left behind him a Daughter to bewail his loss; but I am unacquainted with her position in society; if however, the Managers of the Institution, or any portion of them, wishing to shew their high sense of his long and valuable service to Science, think it right to do so, by giving to his Mortal remains a Funeral and suitable Monument in the Highgate Cemetery, or elsewhere, I shall have *great pleasure* in contributing any sum, which may be required – and also if deemed desirable, would give any further amount towards raising an Annuity for the Daughter of the British Soldier of 22 years service, and of 38 years standing as Chemical Assistant to Mr. Faraday in the Laboratory of the Royal Institution.

With greatest difficulty have I, since I received [reading doubtful] your niece's Letter on Wednesday night written this much in reply to it; for *unlike you*, I am not *blessed* with a Niece, most kindly to act as amanuensis to me. this must be my excuse for sending you such a scrawl, and that too, after so long an interval; nor is this all, as you begged your Niece to make the removal of our Friend, Charles Anderson, known to me, bear with me if I say, how truly grateful I should feel to her, if she would write out and send me a copy of it, at her leisure, for I have no one here to do it for me.

I saw Dixon my *honest* Oculist on Saturday, and he begged me, "on no "account whatever, to let any one persuade me, to submit to an Operation for "my Cataracts, as there would be scarcely a *chance* of it's success."

I am suffering much in the ligaments of the scapula, from a fall in the street which I had in October last, when I was nearly run over, and which I shall never lose – and my Cough threatens me almost with suffocation.

Sincerely hoping that you have entirely shaken off your recent attack, let me beg you to present my kindest regards and best thanks to Miss Barnard – My love to Mrs. Faraday and yourself & believe me to be ever My Dear Old Friend

Yours most sincerely & affectionately
J SOUTH

PS. Excuse all this bad writing, my right shoulder is so painful, & my paralytic hand so inefficient, that I can scarcely hold my pen; and my Cataracts so dense and so darkening, that I can scarcely perceive the nibs [*sic*] of my pen; the vision so imperfect that to get the best, I am obliged to fish for it; indeed all taken together, I am a miserable old man, who has lived to see almost all his friends die before him.

[*I.E.E.*, *previously unpublished*]

Friday Night Jany 12, 1866
Observatory Kensington

MY DEAR OLD FRIEND/

My Butler is just returned, having thanks to one of your Hall attendants, brought me a copy of *tomorrow's* Athenaeum Newspaper.

Unfortunately your dear Niece, did not give me the date of the good old Soldier's[1] removal from amongst us; I therefore have no means of forming any good idea, when the ordinary sepulchral arrangements, would require the Removal, or burial, of the ashes of our departed Friend.

But if necessary, I would take upon myself, the charge of purchasing a site in the Cemetery at Highgate or elsewhere, rather than suffer the Mortal Remains of our humble Friend, after 22 years exemplary service as a Soldier, and 37 or 38 years service, as Chemical Assistant to Mr. Faraday, in his Immortal Experiments made during that period (perhaps if [line illeg.] in the Laboratory of the Royal Institution, to lie promiscuously with the ordinary dead.

As a Soldier and as a philosopher of 57 years standing he has claims of a higher order, and it shall not be my fault, if he do not get them –

Will you make interest with Dear Miss Barnard & get her to Copy me this Letter.

My correspondence powers, are very feeble. Lord Rosse – Dr. Robinson – and others, are I dare say, surprised, that they do not hear from me concerning the mounting of my *large* Object Glass, which on the persuasion of Dr. Robinson, I gave the Dublin University nearly 3 years ago, and which I *fear* the Fellows of Trinity College will not mount in the *English* manner as I, aye and as Robinson gave me reason to suppose) they would, and which if he had not done, *no consideration upon Earth*, should have induced me to let it see Dublin – indeed during the last month, I refer [to it] *very much* of my increased illness, and discomfort.

Dr. Robinson in one of his unanswered Letters which now lies before me, on the table, writes thus, "I am now very sorry I took any part in inducing you "to give the object Glass to them; but I dont think that they will be very likely "to mount it till they get some new, and better men, among them" ("the fellows." [*sic*]

Lord Rosse writes; "It is strange there should have been no one competent "for the professorship in Ireland but Stoney[2] – Now Lord Rosse is Chancellor of the University – The Fact is to keep the Object from the certainty of being broken by Hamilton,[3] in his DRUNKENNESS, the Fellows were obliged to lock it and all its apparatus which in my confidence I gave them also, up. But I will say no more about it, "tamquam animus memori horret, lustaque refugit."

I know not what I have written, & cannot read it over to refresh my recollection – but will send it to the post with all its *many* faults – In a few days I shall, I feel, follow Anderson – pray let your niece Copy & send me her copy of this Letter – God bless you & all belonging to you; Adieu my good old Friend, Adieu

Yours ever affectionately
J SOUTH

PS I have left all your valuable lectures &c to the Royal Instit pray let them be kept in neat in very neat cabinets by THEMSELVES & I think their bindings should remain as they are, but you, my dear Faraday, are the best judge of that.

Ever More God Bless You
J S

[1] Sergeant Anderson.
[2] Bindin Blood Stoney (1828–1909), engineer and astronomer.
[3] Sir William Rowan Hamilton (1805–65), the great mathematician.

813   H. WILDE[1] to M. FARADAY, 16 January 1866[2]

[I.E.E., previously unpublished]

20 St. Anne's Place,
Manchester,

To Michael Faraday Esq. D.C.L., F.R.S., &c.

SIR,

During the last two years I have been much engaged in some researches in electricity, and the results which I have at length obtained are of such an extraordinary character, and are so intimately connected with the department of natural knowledge in which you have so long and successfully laboured, but more especially with your famous discovery of magneto-electric induction, that I feel particularly anxious, for several reasons, (not the least of which is the great regard I have for you as the founder of the subject of my research), to give you a brief outline of the results of my investigations, in anticipation of the more extended publication of them through the medium of some of the scientific journals.

Referring to your communication in the Philosophical Magazine for June 1852. "On the Physical Character of the Lines of Magnetic Force." paragraph 3273. when speaking of the remarkable and anomalous difference observed between the quantity of magnetic force in an electro helix, and in an iron core placed in its interior, you express your strong conviction, that, "In every point of view the magnet deserves the utmost exertions of the philosopher for the development of its nature, both as a magnet and also as a source of electricity,". You will, I think, be gratified to learn, that I have had the good fortune to accomplish something towards the elucidation of these interesting phænomena when I tell you, firstly, that I have found out the cause of the difference observed between the magnetic force of an electro helix and its internal iron core. Secondly, that I have also discovered that an indefinitely small amount of magnetism is capable of producing an indefinitely large amount of dynamic electricity. And again, that an indefinitely small amount of dynamic electricity is capable of developing an indefinitely large amount of magnetism. Thirdly, that I have demonstrated, experimentally, that the magnet is the most powerful, as well as the most economical, source of electricity yet discovered. and I have, besides, by means of the knowledge thus acquired, succeeded in constructing the most powerful generator of dynamic electricity which has been yet invented.

In pointing out an experimental distinction, which exists between the quantity of magnetism in an electro helix and its iron core, in the same paragraph (3273.), you remark, "that an unchangeable magnet can never raise up a piece of soft iron to a state more than equal to its own, as measured by the moving wire. (3219.)," (3222.).

This observation, derived as it was from exact experiment, and having nearly all the rules of analogy to support it, is not absolutely true, but holds good only, under the conditions in which the experiment was made, for if one or more permanent magnets, of the horse shoe or other shape, form part of a magneto electric machine, and if the direct current from the machine be transmitted through the coils of a large electro magnet by means of a commutator, then will the electro magnet acquire a very much greater amount of magnetic force than that which is possessed by the permanent magnets of the magneto electric machine, notwithstanding the intermittent character of the magneto electric current. Again, when the electro magnet in its turn, forms part of an electro magnetic machine, the armature of which is driven at about the same speed as the one belonging [to] the magneto electric machine, a very much larger amount of dynamic electricity is obtained from the former, than what is obtained from the latter. Moreover, when the direct electric current evolved from the second machine, is transmitted simultaneously through the coils of a still larger electro magnet of a third machine, a still further, and very large increase of magnetism and electricity is obtained, and by extending the series of exciting machines, or increasing their dimensions, the quantity of magnetism and electricity evolved may be indefinitely increased.

Enclosed is a photograph, which has been taken from a perspective drawing of the machines as they are arranged for working, and by means of the letters marked thereon, I will endeavour to give you a general idea of their construction and mode of action, until a more particular description of them is completed. Should you then consider my researches of sufficient importance to merit your attention, I shall have great pleasure in forwarding to you, a fuller and better account of them before publication also.

The magneto electric and electro magnetic machines are constructed on precisely the same principle, with the exception of the magnetic arrangement for exciting the armatures, and as the latter machine is shewn on a much larger scale than the former, reference will be made to it more particularly.

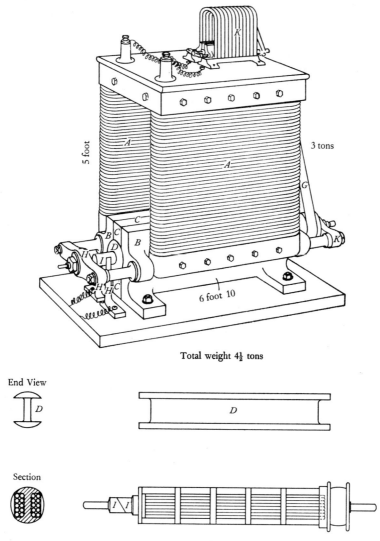

Total weight 4½ tons

A.A. Fig. 1. are the sides of an electro magnet formed of two plates of wrought iron enveloped with a large quantity of thick insulated copper wire. The upper ends of these plates are joined together by means of an iron bridge, which forms the top of the machine. The lower ends of the electro magnet are bolted to the cast iron sides B.B. of a compound cylinder of brass and iron B.C.B. the brass packings C.C. at the top and bottom of the cylinder, seperate

1027

the iron sides from one another. the latter, consequently, form the polar terminations of the electro magnet. The cylinder, as will be seen, is somewhat longer than the width of the electro magnet, and has a smooth and parallel hole bored through it from one end to the other. The length of the cylinder is five times the diameter of the bore, and as I have constructed many of them, for experimental purposes, with bores from one and a half to ten inches in diameter, I designate the different sizes of machines, from the bore or calibre of the magnet cylinder.

The armature D, represented in Fig. 2. without the coils, and in Fig. 3. complete, is made of cast iron, and is turned a small fraction of an inch less in diameter than the bore of the magnet cylinder. This armature is made to revolve concentrically, without touching the sides of the cylinder, in bearings provided for it in the brass crossheads $E.E.$, by means of a strong leather belt G. The alternating currents generated by the revolution of the armature can be taken from it all in one direction, by means of two steel springs $H.H.$ which are made to bear against the opposite sides of the commutator I. The currents of electricity can also be taken from the machine in alternate directions when required, by adjusting the springs so as to bear against the unbroken cylindrical part of each half of the commutator. The large electro-magnet is excited by the direct current from the small magneto-electric machine K, which stands on the wooden top of the electro-magnet, and is driven from the same driving shaft as that by which the electro-magnetic machine is driven.

In the following experiments, six small U shaped permanent magnets, eight inches long, and weighing about one pound each, were placed upon the cylinder of a one and a half inch magneto electric machine. Each magnet sustained a weight of about ten pounds, and the direct current from the machine was transmitted through the coils of the electro-magnet of a five inch electro magnetic machine, and the direct current from the latter, was, in like manner, transmitted simultaneously through the coils of the electro-magnet of a ten inch machine. This 10 inch machine is furnished with two armatures, one for producing quantity, and the other for producing intensity, effects.

The conductor on the quantity armature is 67 feet in length, and has a sectional area of 1.5 square inches.

The conductor coiled round the intensity armature is 376 feet in length, and has a sectional area of 0.25 of a square inch. These armatures are driven at a speed of 1500 revolutions per minute, and the armatures of the exciting machines at about 1800 revolutions per minute.

This combination of the machines, when in full action, is attended by the development of an amount of magnetism in the electro magnet of the ten inch machine, far exceeding anything which has hitherto been produced, together with the evolution of an amount of dynamic electricity from the quantity armature, so enormous, as to melt pieces of iron rod fifteen inches in length and a quarter of an inch in diameter. The electricity from the same armature will also melt fifteen inches of copper wire, one eighth of an inch in diameter.

When the intensity armature is placed in the machine, the electricity from it, will melt seven feet of No. 16 iron wire, which is about one sixteenth of an inch in diameter, and a length of 21 feet of the same wire, can be made bright red hot. Enclosed, are specimens of the different sized iron and copper wires so melted. All these, and the following results, are obtained from the alternating currents of the machine, without the intervention of the commutator.

The illuminating properties of this powerful arrangement, are, as might be expected, of the most splendid description, for when the polar terminations of the intensity armature are connected with rods of gas carbon half an inch square, the light which bursts from the points is of great volume and of the most dazzling brilliancy, each of the carbons being made red hot for a length of an inch and a half from the points. When the carbons are fixed in the beautiful apparatus for regulating the electric light recently invented by M. Foucault, behind which is placed a parabolic reflector twenty inches in diameter adjusted so as to cause the rays of light to diverge at a considerable angle, the light, when directed from the top of a lofty building, is sufficient to cast the shadows from the flames of all the street lamps upon the neighbouring walls for a distance of more than a quarter of a mile. When viewed from that distance, the light seems to fill the reflector completely, and is a very magnificient [sic] object to behold, the rays proceeding from it, having all the rich effulgence of sunshine.

A piece of the ordinary sensitized paper used for photographic printing, when exposed to the action of the light for five minutes, at a distance of five feet from the reflector, was blackened to the same degree as was a piece of the same sheet of paper after an exposure of ten minutes to the direct rays of the sun at noon on a very clear day in the middle of September last. Accept, Sir, the enclosed photograph of yourself, which has been printed by means of this light, from a negative taken at the Royal Institution by Mr Brothers of this city. (by the light of burning magnesium), and who was kind enough to lend me the plate.

The extraordinary calorific and illuminating powers of the machine are all the more remarkable, from the fact, that they have their origin in the six small permanent magnets before mentioned, which are only capable of sustaining collectively, a weight of 60 pounds. while the electricity generated from the small magneto electric machine, is, of itself, incapable of heating to redness, the shortest length of iron wire, of the smallest size manufactured.

The evolution of so large a quantity of dynamic electricity from the ten inch machine is only obtained, as you would anticipate, by a correspondingly large expenditure of mechanical force. In the practical working of the machine, I have found, that it is not necessary to employ the combination of magneto electric and electro magnetic machines, as described, for exciting the large electro magnet, since a two and a half inch magneto electric machine, as shewn in the perspective drawing, answers the purpose very well, as by means of it, fully two thirds of the maximum amount of power from the armatures of the 10 inch machine can be obtained. The following are the principal dimensions of the 10^{in} machine – Length of the magnet cylinder 50 inches. Total length of machine, 80 inches. Height, 60 inches. Width, 24 inches. – Weight of electro magnet without cylinder, about three tons. – cylinder one ton. – total weight of machine about 4 1/2 tons.

With respect to the cause of the enormous increase of magnetism developed in the large electro magnet, amounting to considerably more than 1000 times that of the permanent magnets of the magneto electric machine, I find, that a considerable number of currents or waves require to be transmitted through the electro helices of the electro magnet, before the iron acquires its highest degree of magnetism. Moreover, the number of currents or waves necessary for producing this high degree of magnetism, is diminished as the power of the exciting machine is increased. I have also found, that a spark can be obtained from the electro helices of the large electro magnet of the 10 inch machine, twenty five seconds after all connection with the exciting machine is broken.

This part of my investigations is closely connected with some of your own, but more particularly with the subject of your Ninth Series of Researches, and as I purpose making some observations thereon, as well as *on the nature of time*, and its influence in connection with the phenomena under notice, in any more extended communication, I will not trouble you at greater length with this part of the subject, nor with any further particulars of the construction of the machines. I am only sorry that they are not, at the present time, nearer London, or I might perhaps have had the pleasure of shewing them to you in operation, together with some other remarkable phenomena observed in connection with them, which I have reserved for a future communication.

I am, Sir,
Faithfully yours
H. WILDE.

¹ Henry Wilde (1833–1919), inventor of the dynamo called by his name.
² The letter was marked 'Received by post Tuesday 16 Jany 1866 MF'.

814 J. HENRY to M. FARADAY, 3 November 1866
[*I.E.E., previously unpublished*]

Smithsonian Institution,
Washington,
Nov. 3^{d}. 1866

MY DEAR SIR:

I write to request that you will inform me as to what is actually doing by the Light House authorities of England in the way of experiment with the electrical light and particularly with that derived from Wilde's apparatus.

Do not encounter the labor of giving this information with your own hand, but employ as I have done, an amanuensis.

I ask the information above-mentioned on account of the Light House Board of the United States, of which from its first organization I have had the honor to be a member. This Board consists of two officers of the Navy, two of the Army, all of high rank, and two civilians of scientific reputation, also a secretary from the Navy and another from the Engineer corps. Previous to the commencement of the war I gave but little attention to the subject, the business being principally conducted by the Secretaries, but during the war the officers of the army and navy being generally withdrawn from light house duty, I was obliged to devote much more time to it than previously, and in the absence of my colleague in the Board, Prof. Bache, who is still hopelessly excluded from active life, I am the principal scientific adviser.

A few years ago the subject of the materials of lighting was referred to me, and after examining all the different oils which had been proposed for the use of the light houses, I decided upon that manufactured from lard, and have succeeded in procuring its general introduction at all the light stations on the coast, except those of the entrance of harbors in which the smallest lamps are used. It has been proved conclusively that good lard oil is superior to sperm in lamps of all orders above the sixth. The change has been attended with a saving to the Government of at least 10,000 £. st. a year.

The Board has also referred to me the subject of fog signals, and in relation to this I have made a series of experiments from which it would appear that the trumpet of Daboll, in which the agitation of the air is produced by the vibration of a steel tongue, gives at least four times as much effective sound as that in air instruments in which the primary vibrations are produced by a film of air as in the ordinary whistle. The point to which we are now directing attention however, is to obtain the best kind of caloric engines or such as do not require water for the production of steam. There are three engines of this class, of which I think Ericson's is the least effective. In regard to fog signals, what is the experience of the English Light-house authorities?

The results obtained by Wilde if truly represented are remarkable, though perhaps not at variance with established dynamic principles, since it would appear that the effect is only commensurate with the amount of mechanical power expended. The fact stated that an electo-magnet [*sic*] retains a charge of electricity similar to that of the cable is not surprising, or that this at the moment of rupturing the circuit should increase the inductive effect; but I do not see that while in its statical condition it should increase the intensity of the magnetism of the iron. I have not however seen a full exposition of the principles of the apparatus, and therefore cannot speak definitely in regard to it.

[Letter continued in Henry's hand] I was gratified to learn from Mrs Bache who called upon you with her husband that you were looking quite well and that though you had given up scientific research you were enjoying apparently good health. I still retain a vivid impression of my visit to England and would be delighted to have an opportunity to repeat it; – but of this I have no prospect. I am still directing the affairs of the Smithsonian Inst[itut]ion and perseveringly endeavoring to carry out the plans which I originally proposed.

I am just called on to give the opening lectures at an Institution founded in Baltimore by Mr. Peabody[1] of London on an endowment of *one million of dollars* and I shall present to their Trustees the Royal Institution as a model of imitation.

Truly your friend
JOSEPH HENRY

[1] George Peabody (1795–1869), merchant and philanthropist.

INDEX OF CORRESPONDENTS

The figures in this index are letter numbers, not page numbers

INDEX OF HOLDERS OF LETTERS

The figures in this index are letter numbers, not page numbers

GENERAL INDEX

The figures in this index are page numbers; those in *italic* type indicate pages on which biographical details are given. The following abbreviations are used: MF for Michael Faraday, *RI* for Royal Institution, *RS* for Royal Society.

Airy, G.B. (*cont.*)

MF about telegraph wires, 713; MF replies, 714–15, 738; consults MF about unsatisfactory determinations of ozone, 729; MF thinks observers at fault, 730; observers said to be well-trained; test papers questioned, 732–3; consults MF about experiments with pendulum in a mine, 755–6; MF would like to exchange date of lecture with, 770; is unable to comply, 770; MF answers queries of, 775–6; MF to, on time in magnetic phenomena, 863; traces experimental difficulties to faulty insulation, 782; MF replies, 782; consults MF about magnetic regulation of clock, 926–7, 927–8; about a misbehaving dipping needle, 949; member of Lighthouse Commission, 951, 952, 986; consults MF about light of gas fish-tail burner, 984–5; MF replies, 985; MF invites him to a lecture on eclipse, 996; cannot attend himself, but wife and daughters wish to come, 997–8; reports daily inequalities in magnetism, and asks for explanation, 997–8; discusses comets and sound of thunder, 998–9; proposed lecture by (on comets?), 1006, 1009; consults MF about rusting of steel in chronometers, 1011–12; MF replies, 1012; mentioned by Moll, 206, by Barlow, 753, by Hansteen, 892

alcohol: flame of, 96–7; heated platinum wire in vapour of, 104; salts of lime in flame of, 164; fluorescence in electrified vapour of, 901

alkalies: in voltaic battery, 9, 11, 34; Mr Tatum lectures on, to City Philosophical Society, 24, 33; combination of carbon with, 35; vegetable, 146

Allen, W., *145n*; carries selenium mixture from Berzelius to MF, 144

alloys: of steel with other metals, 117–20; of iron and lead, 166

almond oil, does not thicken with cold, 327

aluminium: alloy of steel and, 118; in clays, 312; isolation of pure metal, 795, 798, 850

America, *see* United States of America

American Association for the Advancement of Science, meets at Cincinnati (1857), 632

Amici, G. B., *470n*; uses MF's heavy glass in microscopes, 469

ammonia: reactions of, with phosphorus chloride, 22, with chlorine, 28, with nitrogen chloride, 44; forms prussic acid with carbon, 35; solidified, 434, 438

ammonium chloride (muriate of ammonia): decomposed by battery, 10–11; reaction of chlorine with, 42–3; produced by reaction of nitrogen chloride with hydrogen chloride, 43–4; preparation of pure ammonium hydroxide from, 440

ammonium hydroxide: constituents of, 35, 36n; pure, required for polishing speculum of telescope, 440

ammonium nitrate, reaction of chlorine with, 42–3

ammonium phosphate, decomposition of, 22

Ampère, A.-M. (physicist, 1775–1836): MF on his theory and experiments on electromagnetism, 123, 124, 129, 130, 138, 210; MF to: on his discovery of rotation of current-carrying magnet, 130–2, discussing his work, 134–5, 153–4, thanking the Académie des Sciences through, 146–7, thanking him for constant kindness, 189–90, sending papers, 220; G. de la Rive refers to his work, 135, 136, 137; MF is indebted to, 372; mentioned by Hachette, 213, by Forbes, 224, by Melloni, 285, by Plücker, 567, by MF, 865

Anderson, Sergeant Charles, *171n*; MF's laboratory assistant, 171, 214, 328, 329n, 504; attendant at lectures by Brande, 348, and by Stokes, 685; begins his holiday (1853), 693; has been ill, 760; MF asks Vincent to advance money to, 974; death of, 1022–3

Andrews, T., *401n*; MF to: asking if he is willing to be recommended for a post at Toronto, 401, advising about 'rewards and Honors', 409–10, about British Association meeting at Belfast (1852), 663–4, 664–5, describing a trip to Paris, 846, on news of accident to Regnault, 848; with MF in Paris, 850; Moigno refers to his work on electrolytic decomposition of water, 865, 866n

angite, magnetic action on crystal of, 551

animal electricity: torpedoes, 61–2, 304; *Gymnotus*, 564, 565n; electric eel, 655; *see also* electrophysiology anion, term suggested by Whewell, 270, 272

Annales de Chimie et de Physique, MF writes for, 235–52

anode: term recommended by Whewell, 265–7 (instead of MF's suggested exode, 264–5); MF reports term apt to be misunderstood, 268; Whewell still prefers it, 269–70, 271

anorthoscope, 300–1

antimony: reaction of hydrogen chloride with, 20; affinities of, for chlorine and oxygen, 29; diamagnetic, 477, 482, 483–4; magnetic and optic axes in crystals of, 536, 541, 547, 566

Antinori, V.: with Nobili, uses letter by MF, published in Paris, as basis for paper on electromagnetism, 213n, 218, 224; MF details his experiments and publications, and corrects errors of, 235–52

apparatus in lectures, MF on, 53

Arago, F. (astronomer, 1786–1853): secretary of Académie des Sciences, 213; P. Barlow repeats experiments of, on magnetism of metals, 148–9; MF on experiments of, on electromagnetic rotation, 211; Antinori and Nobili misunderstand MF's references to work of, 237–9, 242, 244, 246, 247; Lardner sees observatory of, 288; introduces Le Play to MF; speaks in French Chamber on keeping Gay-Lussac as consulting chemist for artillery, 304, 305n; MF thinks of, in 1848 revolution, 524, 525; with A. de la Rive at Vichy, 631; old age of, 668, 915; obituary notice of, by A. de la Rive, 705; MF subscribes to statue of, 698; mentioned by G. de la Rive, 135, by MF, 220, 373, 431, 668, by Melloni, 285, 291, 699, by Harris, 405, by Napoleon Louis Bonaparte, 413, by A. de la Rive, 454, 455, 476

Arcet, J. P. J. d', *220n*; MF sends paper to, 220

Archimedes, principle of, 772

Archives de l'Electricité, A. de la Rive begs information from MF to be published in, 467

Argand lamp, 112, 677, 870; MF's ventilator for, 407

Arndtsen, A. F. O., *889n*; wishes to work at RI, 888–9, 893

arseniates, Dalton's paper on, 378, 379, 380

arsenic: reaction of hydrogen chloride with, 20; affinities of, for chlorine and oxygen, 29; magnetic and optic axes in crystals of, 536, 547, 566

arsenious acid: A. de la Rive wonders if odour attributed to ozone is not due to, 420–1

asphaltene, as fuel for steamships: MF answers query on, 274

Athenaeum club, 179; Moll asks MF to get friend introduced to, 273; lighting at, 278, 348; MF resigns from, 645, 646

Atlantic cable, 957, 958n

atmosphere: ozone in, 443, 636, 729, 730; lecture by MF on electricity of, 580; magnetism of, 589, 591, 595, 609, 613–14, 625, 629, 659; Quételet's observations on electrical state of, over the year, 615–18; proposed lecture by W. Thomson on electricity of, 934, 936, 938

atoms: MF on, 274, 414, 416n; arrangement of, in molecule, in relation to electrification and magnetization, 737, 768–9; Hess on, 854, 855; attraction and repulsion at work among, 916–17

Auckland, Lord, *508n*; MF to, as First Lord of the Admiralty, 508

Auldjo, M., carries letter from Fazzini to MF, 219

aurora borealis: calculations of height of, 380–1; theories about, 604–5; preparations for observing, magnetically, 605–6; and sun-spots, 670; and magnetic storms, 673; records of, for 10 years at Leith, 686–7; analogies between effects in electrified rarefied gases and, 902, 903

autograph: MF's in demand, 479, 892

Avogadro, A., *460n*; Thomson discusses paper by, on distribution of electricity on spheres in contact, 458, 459n; Harris quotes, 989

axiality: term proposed by MF, 530; Whewell comments on, 531–2, 564; of crystals, 536

azote, see nitrogen

Babbage, C., *168n, 207n*; collaborator with Herschel, 148, 149n, 167, and with Lardner, 262; Moll disagrees with his views

Becquerel, A.C. (*cont.*)
diamagnetism before MF, without realizing it was a new phenomenon, 471, 484; MF to, answering queries about his work, 608–9, 610–11; mentioned by MF, 220, 370, 373, 431, 482, by A. de la Rive, 455

Becquerel, A. Edmond, *554n*; to MF on 'painting with light', 702–3; attends lecture by MF, 942; 'phosphori' made by, 943–4; mentioned by A. de la Rive, 554, by MF, 608–9, 611, 613, by Plücker, 638, by Stokes, 677, by Tyndall, 772

Beek, A. van, *211n*; on poles of voltaic pile, 210

Beer, A., *861n*; with Plücker at Bonn, 860, 968

Bell, T., *612n*; MF to (as Secretary of *RS*), on papers submitted to *RS*, 611–12, 648–9, 654

Belli, G., *369n*; on charging of Leyden jars, 365

benzene, MF's discovery of, 84n

Berard, J. E., *286n*; on radiant heat, 285

Bergemann, C. W., *638n*; specimen of reputed new metal discovered by, is sent to MF, 637

Bermondsey, B. Abbott lives in Long Lane at, 15, 35–6

Bernard, Claude, *840n*; A. de la Rive sees experiments of, 839

Berthier, P., *220n*; mentioned by MF, 220

Berthollet, C. L. (chemist, 1748–1822): mentioned by MF, 129

Berthon, P. N., deputy master of Trinity House: MF to, about proposed use of lime-light for lighthouses, 847–8, 950–1, 955

Berwick-on-Tweed, steam pile-drivers for bridge at, 503

Berzelius, J. J. (chemist, 1779–1848): Davy on paper by, 114; MF on his theory of electromagnetism, 129, 130, 134; MF thanks him for selenium mixture, 144–5; sends MF ammonium vanadate, 199–200, 225; MF commends his accuracy, 202; MF proposes medal should be conferred on him, 208–9; Fox refers to his theory of relation of combustion and electricity, 275, 276; Kane refers to his theory on structure of ether, 282, 283; MF sends

thanks to Swedish Academy of Sciences through, 326–7; MF consults, about purity of Swedish copper, 398–9; suffers from bronchitis caused by hydrogen selenide, 635

Bessel, F. W., *999n*; on comets, 999, 1009; mentioned by Hansteen, 893

Bibliothèque Britannique, later *Bibliothèque Universelle*, 120, 121n, 184, 890

Biot, J.-B. (mathematician and natural philosopher, 1774–1862): work of, on polarized light, 288, 289, 476, 478n, 496; on Newton, 628, 629n; mentioned by Melloni, 285, 291, by Harris, 340, by MF, 373, 851, by Plücker, 684, 909

Birkenhead docks, steam pile-driver for, 503

Bischof, C. G. C., *543n*; Plücker obtains pure antimony from, 541

bismuth: diamagnetic, 470, 477, 482, 483–4, 488–9, 576, 589, 834; temperature and diamagnetism of, 520, 524; pressure and diamagnetism of, 780; magnetic and optic axes in crystals of, 528, 536, 537, 542, 547, 567, 569; magnetic influence on crystallization of, 545–6; MF on magnetic polarity in, 578, 806

Blackwell, J. K., F.G.S., supplies iron carbonate to Tyndall, 772, 774n

Blainville, H. M. D. de, *231n*; mentioned by Hachette, 230

Blake, C. C.: MF to, declining to join a society, 1015

Blanshard, Gen. T., *931n*; pontoons designed by, 930, 931

bleaching, alkali for, 179

blow-pipe, 100, 102; oxy-hydrogen, 204

Blumenbach, J. F., *262n*; Moll on lectures of, 260

Bohnenberger, G. C., *729n*; electroscope of, 728

Bonaparte, Napoleon Louis, *see* Napoleon III of France

Bond, G. P., *917n*; observes comet (1855), 915

Bond, W. C., *917n*; observes comet (1855), 915

books: MF's three boxes of, at *RI*, 65, 78; MF leaves letters and, in Geneva, 74; please MF more than anything else, 87

Boosey, T., bookseller, 200

Booth, J., *724n*; to lecture at *RI*, 724

Bordeaux, B. Abbott considers taking post at, 81

boron: affinities of, for chlorine and oxygen, 29

boron trifluoride, liquefied, 433, 438

Boscovich, R. G. (mathematician, 1711–87): point atoms suggested by, 416n, 920

Boston Advertizer, MF's letters to Winslow published in, 916

Botanical Gardens, Chelsea: MF visits, 14

Botto, G. D., *276n*; on thermo-electricity, 276

Boucherie, A., *550n*; inventor of process for preserving wood, 549

Boutigny, P. H., *452n*; carries letter from Peltier to MF, 451; his method of plunging hand into molten iron without harm, 549, 568

Bowyer, Mr, pharmacist, 32

Boyer, Mr, friend of MF in City Philosophical Society, 68, 73

Boyle's Statical Baroscope, 68

Braahsma, Mr, introduced to MF by Moll, 261, 273

Braconnot, H., *147n*; mentioned by MF, 146

Bramwell, George, 'a young lad', mentioned by MF, 92

Brande, W. T., *52n*, *559n*; lectures of, at *RI*, 49, 531; article in *Journal of Science* by, 126, 127n; MF relieved from attendance as assistant to, 155; *Manual of Chemistry* by, 226, 673, 674n; enquires about MF's health, and about a sample of aluminium, 795; mentioned by MF, 104, 109, 121, 158, 173, 394, 423

Brandis, D., *593n*; introduced to MF by Plücker, 592, 528

brass: smell of, 31; varnish for, 358; electrolytic gilding of, 376

Brayley, E. W., *216n*, 328–9; MF to: inviting to meetings, 216, on preferring to be called Mr rather than Dr, 260, thanking him for an extract, 689, about signing a certificate, 717

Breda, J. G. S. van, *619n*; MF to, about grant from *RS*, 619; Logeman and, to MF about their experiments on conduction of electricity through liquids, 761–4; MF sends letter to *Philosophical Magazine*, 769

Breguet, L. F. C., *397n*; electromagnetic machine of, 395–7

Brewster, Sir D. (natural philosopher, 1781–1868): and British Association, 201, 205; controversy between Moll and, 205, 207n, 261; work of, on radiant heat, 285, and on *muscae volitantes*, 418; and Philosophical Society, St Andrews, 688; to MF, 698; mentioned by Hansteen, 892, 893

Brighton, MF's visits to: 'to refresh', 209; 'to write my paper in peace and quietness', 315; to convalesce, 349; to get rid of a 4-month headache, 381; 'to *rest* the head and *work* it at the same time', 465; 'for the sake of rest and health', 536; *also*, 940

Bristol, Conybeare reports on foundation of Institution in, 143, 144n

British Association for the Advancement of Science: foundation of, 200–1, 203; meetings of: at Oxford (1832), 212; Cambridge (1833), 260; Dublin (1834), 282, 283n; York (1844), 423, 430; Southampton (1846), 497; Oxford (1847), 509; Swansea (1848), 527n, 536; Belfast (1852), 663–5, 935; Hull (1853), 706; Liverpool (1854), 766; Glasgow (1855), 749, 803, 817; Dublin (1857), 866, 878; Aberdeen (1859), 933; Oxford (1860), 960; Newcastle (1863), 1019

British Museum, MF consulted about condition of marbles in, 867–9

Brodie, Sir B. C., *501n*, *559n*; as MF's physician, 500, 932; attends Mrs Faraday, 664; thinks of retiring from *RS* Presidency, 976

Brodie, B. C., *559n*; MF to, on his proposed lectures, 558–9, 571

bromine: MF hopes to receive sample of, from Germany, 181; molecular weight of, 202; 'a disagreeable inmate', 609; spectrum of, 923, 960

bronze: corrosion of, by sea water, 215

Broost, B. C., on boundaries of physics and metaphysics, 920

Brougham, H., *147n*; mentioned by Pollock, 147, by J. Barlow, 757

Brown, Robert, *208n*, *490n*; MF describes Grove's work to, 490; mentioned by Moll, 206

Brugmans, A., *484n*: work of, on diamagnetism of bismuth, mentioned by Wheatstone, 483, by MF, 489

Brunel, I. K. (engineer, 1806–59): MF to, about P. Barlow's report on railways, 292

Brunel, M. I., *234n*; MF asked to advise on his attempts to use condensed gases as motive power, 233–4; consults MF about gases in the Thames Tunnel, 342–3

bubbles, in voltaic battery, 5, 6

Buchanan, G., *583n*; introduces G. Wilson to MF, 582

Buchanan, Mrs G., 641

Buchanan, Mr, of Edinburgh: mentioned by Forbes, 224

Buckland, Very Rev. W., *513n*; MF to, on soap bubbles, 513; unable to lecture because of illness, 541

Buff, H. (physicist, 1805–78): observes the aurora, 604; to MF about electrolytic experiments, (in German) 783–6, (translated) 786–9; advises Becker, 969; MF agrees with advice, 975–6

Buffon, G. L. L. de (naturalist, 1707–1788): mentioned by T. Stevenson, 817

building stone: MF consulted on durability of, 321–2, and on treatment for preservation of, 959

Bunsen, C. K. J., Freiherr von, *593n*; MF and, 850, 960; mentioned by Plücker, 592

Bunsen, R. W. von (chemist and inventor, 1811–99): spectroscopic work of Kirchhoff and, 953–4, 960, 1005; mentioned by MF, 850, 1001, by Becker, 968

Burgoyne, Sir J. F., *930n*; MF replies to enquiry from, about treating water to remove lead, 929–30

Bury, E., *449n*; to supply specimens of metal to MF, 446

Bussy, A. A., *434n*, on cyanogen, 434

cab drivers, strike of, 694

cadmium: MF hopes to receive sample of, from Germany, 181; tests for, 359; specific heat of, 377

caesium, discovered by spectroscopy, 953, 960

Cagniard de la Tour, C., *159n*; MF extends his work on application of heat and pressure to liquids, 427, 428, 432, 498; mentioned by MF, 158

calcium: affinities of, for chlorine and oxygen, 29; specimen of, sent to MF, 850; spectrum of, 960

calcium carbonate: oatmeal adulterated with, 253; magnetism of isomorphous crystals of iron carbonate and of, 773–4; removal of lead from water by, 929

calcium chloride: formed by reaction of lime with chlorine, 28; as dehydrating agent, 29

calcium phosphate: stock of, in skeletons in Paris catacombs, 850

calcium sulphide, phosphorescent, 943

calculating machine, Babbage's, 168n, 214, 262, 327n

Callcott, Sir A. W., *349n*; advises on lighting at Athenaeum, 348

calorimotor, Hare's, 130, 132n

Cambridge, scientific tripos at, 755

camphor: motions of, on water, 9–10, 13; Herschel mentions MF's experiment on, 160

candle, combustion and blowing out of, 97

caoutchouc, keeps MF and his wife warm and dry on outside of coach, 202

capillary phenomena, 543, 847, 849

carbon (charcoal): will not burn in chlorine, 19, 21, 22, 24, 26; compounds of chlorine and, 20n, 123, 124n, 139; compounds of alkalies and, 35; from alcohol, turpentine, wood, 63; from reaction of natural gas with chlorine, 77; in steel, 117, 399

carbon dioxide (carbonic acid gas): from combustion of diamonds, 62; liquefied, 140, 147; specific heat of, 377; solidified, 432, 433, 434; produced in respiration of muscle, and increased by contractions, 836–8; spectrum of, 908

carbon disulphide, fluorescence in electrified vapour of, 901

carbon monoxide, not liquefied, 434

carbonate: in water supply, 6; in stale voltaic battery, 34

Cardat, Monsieur, keeper of archives at Institut de France, 290, 291

Carnot, Lazare, *208n*; mentioned by Moll, 207

Carpmael, W., *408n*; *Law of Patents* by, 407

Cincinnati, rapid growth of, 633

City Philosophical Society: lectures at, 14, 26, 30n, 49; B. Abbott becomes a member of, 40

Clare, P., *381n*; travels with Dalton, 380

Clark, Sir J., *171n, 515n*; on examinations at London University, 169–71; MF to, about the Royal College of Chemistry, 514–15

Clark, J. Latimer, *697n, 767n*; to MF about electric telegraph, 697; MF refers to work of, 729, 731, 738, 775; MF congratulates, on new post, and would like account of his results, 767; MF agrees with Riess's comments on work of, 791, 792; MF to, about spiritualist seances, 874–5

Clausius, R. J. E. (physicist, 1822–88): MF refers to work of, on colour of sky, 736

clays: MF analyses, 312–13; laminations in, produced by voltaic action, 318

Clerk-Maxwell, J. (physicist, 1831–79): MF to, about his mathematical work on lines of force, 864–5; discusses idea of lines of force in gravity, 881–3; MF continues discussion, 884–5; sends MF diagrams of lines of force (through Thomson), 932–5; comments on diagrams, and asks for support in application for chair at St Andrews, 939–40

clocks: inclined-plane, 6; at London Bridge station, 782; electromagnetic control of rate of, 926–8; rusting of, 1012

clouds: new terminology for, 8; electrical state of, 400, 451–2; magnetic meridian and, 688

coal gas: lighting by, 83, 84n; heated platinum wire in, 103; compared with gas from pilchard oil, 112; not liquefied, 553

coal mines: Percy suggests electric spark to test for and explode gases in, 425–6; Airy asks about experiments with a pendulum in, 755–6

cobalt: in ancient glass, 88–9; specific heat of, 377; as impurity in manganese oxide, 404; magnetic, 454, 471, 488, 489

Cockary, Mr, member of City Philosophical Society, 98, 99n

Codrington, Sir E., *450n*; MF returns ship model to, 450

cohesion, forces of, 160, 161, 499

coke: difficult to burn, 204; cuts glass as diamond does, 505–7, 522; dust of, too sharp for use in polishing, 522

Colby, Lt-Col. T., *208n*; mentioned by Moll, 206

cold: absolute, 388; obtained by solid carbon dioxide and ether, 432; obtained by electricity, 380n, 452, 453n; *see also* frost

Colding, L. A., *573n*; introduced to MF by Ørsted, 571, 581

Cole, H., *808n*; MF receives letter from, about Paris Exhibition, 808

Colladon, J. D., *455n*; will carry diploma to MF, 455

colours: used by Greeks and Romans, 87–90, 92n; used in fresco painting, effect of hydrogenated lime on, 423–4; Dumas on use of zinc and iron oxides instead of lead compounds in, 549

Columbus, 468

combustion: in chlorine, 19, 28; in alcohol flame, 96–7; and electricity (Berzelius), 275

comets: proposed lectures on, 287–8, 1006, 1009; observations on, at Harvard, 915, 916; Donati's, 919, 999

compass, magnetic: Airy's correction of, 335–7

Condorcet, Marquis de (1743–94), inventor of polyzonal lens, 817

conservation of force, MF's work on, 864, 865; Clerk-Maxwell on, 881–3

Conybeare, D. H., to MF about electromagnetism, liquefaction of chlorine, and Institution at Bristol, 141–4

Conybeare, W. D. (geologist, 1787–1857), on relations of light and magnetism, 168–9

Conybeare, Mr, 'not aware of electromagnetic machines' (MF), 263

Copley Medal of RS: awarded to MF (1832, 1838), 324; to Matteucci (1844), 1021

copper: in voltaic battery, 4–5, 6, 10, 11, 12; decomposes hydrogen chloride, 20; in brass, 31; in ancient colours, 88, 89; magnetic, 149, 489; corrosion of, by sea water, 215; voltaic reproduction of engravings on, 343–4; purity of, for speculum metal, 398–9; pontoons of, 930

copper ammoniate, 11

copper chloride (muriate), in voltaic battery, 11, 16

copper formate, magnetic axes in crystals of, 860, 862, 863

copper oxides, MF on preparation of, 12; in clays, 318

copper sulphate, decomposed by voltaic battery, 5

copying machine, used for B. Abbott's letters, 70, 734

Cornwall Polytechnic Society, 318

Coulomb, C. A. de (experimental philosopher, 1736–1806): electrical measurements by, 458, 459; mentioned by MF, 534, 861, by Harris, 628

Cowper, W. F. (Lord Mount Temple), *959n*; MF to, about stonework at Houses of Parliament, 958–9

Cresson, J. C., *445n*; introduced to MF by J. Henry, 445

Crichton, J. N., *817n*; Dundee Sandemanian, 817, 1016

Crofts, Mr, introduced to Mitscherlich by MF, 309

Crookes, W., *980n*; has reported MF's Christmas lectures, and wishes to do so again, 978–80; MF gives permission, 980

Crotch, Dr, lecturer on music at Surrey Institution, 71, 72

crucibles, for making alloys, 120

Cruickshank, W., galvanic trough of, 14

Crystal Palace: 'the true architectural exponent of the feelings and wants of the present day' (J. Henry), 634; statues of prehistoric animals for, 752–3

crystallization: of sodium chloride, 33; vegetative, 36; forces of, 160, 161; polarity of, 300, 301–2, 468; influence of magnetism on, 545–6

crystals: effect of magnetic and electric forces on polarized light passing through, *see* polarized light; magnetic axes in, 528–9, 531, 535, 541–3, 546–8, 960–1; magnetic and optic axes in, 536–7, 546–8, 551, 561, 566–9; Thomson suggests experiments on magnetic action on, 559–61; Plücker on theory of magnetism in, 574–6, 831–3, 834, 860–1, 862; magnetism of isomorphous, 773–4

Cupid, B. Abbott's quotation on galvanism and, 9

Cuvier, G., *147n, 231n*; mentioned by MF, 146, by Hachette, 230

cyanite, magnetic and optic axes in, 547–8

cyanogen: solidified, 434; in solution of ammonia, 440

Daboll, C. L., fog-trumpet invented by, 1031

Dagart, Monsieur, manufacturer of optic glass, 913

Dalton, J. (chemist and physicist,1766–1844): works of, not collected, 378; asks for return of papers read at *RS*, 378–9; on height of aurora, etc., 380–1; his view of atoms, 416n

damasked surface, of Indian steel exposed to acid, 117

Daniell, E. R., barrister, brother of J. F. Daniell, 306, 423

Daniell, J. F., *191n*; 'constant battery' of, 328, 333, 334, 395; death of, 455; letters to MF from, sent to his daughter, 519; mentioned by MF, 190, 191, 301, 326, by Nicholl, 306, by Harris, 406, by Plateau, 419, by A. de la Rive, 421

Daubeny, C., *157n*; offers various speculations, 156–7; MF replies, 158–9; describes experiments, 203–4; to lecture at *RI*, 723; MF mentions, as supporter of Liebig, 853; mentioned by A. de la Rive, 453

Davidson, Mr, of Aberdeen: electromagnetic machine of, 404

Davy, Edmund, cousin of Sir Humphry, 195

Davy, Sir Humphry (natural philosopher, 1778–1829): *Elements of Chemical Philosophy* by, 15–16, 40, 41n; supports new theory about chlorine, 19, 22, 23, 29; on hydrogen chloride, 27–8; Bakerian lecture by (1811), 29, 30n; MF takes notes of his lectures, 31, 32n, 178; MF assists with experiments, 42–4, 93, 125, 126; MF travels with, 59–87, 90–2, 914; on ancient colours, 87–90; experiments by, on flames and combustion, 103–4; to MF from Rome, 114; and complaint against MF with regard to Wollaston, 125, 126, 127n; subpoenaed to give chemical evidence at a trial, 109; reports MF's work to *RS*,

Davy, Sir Humphry (*cont.*)
140; not quite satisfied with argument in MF's paper, 159; MF gives account of his first introduction to, 177–8; discovery of sodium and potassium by, 197n, 871; on molecular weight of iodine, 202; mentioned by Moll, 196, 205

Davy, Jane, wife of Sir Humphry: MF's difficulties with, 86–7; to MF about a copy of Sir Humphry's portrait for him, 510–11

Davy, John, brother of Sir Humphrey: experiments by, on chlorine, 27, 30n; MF comments on paper by, 834, 832n

Deacon, Caroline, niece of MF: MF chats with, about death, 925–6

Deacon, Mr and Mrs, Sandemanians, 641, 1019

death, MF on, 108, 925–6

De Candolle, A. P. (botanist, 1778–1841): A. de la Rive's memoir of, 455

definitions, MF enjoys, 17

De la Métherie, J. C., *197n*; editor, *Journal de Physique*, 196

De la Rive, A., *137n*; experiments by, on electromagnetic rotation, 135–6, 140, and on voltaic electricity, 210, 211n; to MF about exchange of periodicals, 184–5; MF replies, 186–7, and asks about journals for *RI* library, 317; MF to, on theory of voltaic battery, and on specific heats, 374–7; correspondence on ozone, etc., 420, 439, 453–4; on MF's work on relations of light and magnetism, 467; MF replies, with news of experiments on diamagnetism, 469–70; gives theory to explain MF's results on light, reports previous work on diamagnetism, and complains about *Philosophical Magazine*, 476–8; MF replies, 479–80; MF describes further experiments on diamagnetism, 486–90; made Foreign Member of *RS*, 494; in London, 550, 552; on returning home, suggests an experiment to MF, 554; MF has not been able to carry it out, 558; loses his wife (1851); MF condoles with him, and describes work on magnetism, especially of gases, 612–14; writes from Vichy, in bad health and sorrowful, 630–2; MF replies encouragingly, 634–5;

MF writes of failing health but contented spirit, 668–9; to MF in admiration and affection, 675–6; *Treatise on Electricity* by, (185), 689, 734, 737, 820, 831, 889–90; still sorrowing, 703–5; MF to, on their friendship, and telling of work on telegraph wires, 707–8; MF answers query from, on conduction of electricity by liquids, 718, and describes experiments on the subject, for publication if desired, 719–22 (publication arranged, 733–4); MF regrets his inability to visit, 717–18; on theory of magnetism, 768–9; MF to, 790; is coming to London (1855), 792–3; announces his re-marriage, 799–800; about his arrival in London, 803; on electrical effects in rarefied gases; claims priority over Plücker, 900–5; MF replies, 905–6; Plücker comments, 906; is writing memoir of Mme Marcet; asks MF about his early reading of her book, 912–13; MF replies, 913–14; is preparing lectures; asks about MF's experiments on phosphorescence, 942–3; MF replies, 943–4; MF to, 1001

expresses his religious faith, 675, 703, 768, 792, 793, 809, 889, 942–3, 1002; mentioned by Matteucci, 303, by W. Gregory, 403, by Quételet, 538, by MF, 694, by J. Barlow, 752, 765, 766, by Hess, 854, 855

De la Rive, G., *112n*; MF to: on preparation of illuminating gas, 111–12; on artificial plumbago, and on steel and alloys of steel, 117–20, on electromagnetism, 122–4, 138–9, on liquefaction of gases, 139–41, sending apparatus to illustrate electromagnetic rotation, 128–9; thanks MF for apparatus; describes electromagnetic experiments, 135–7; MF's grateful remembrance of, 914

De la Roche, F., *286n*; on radiant heat, 285

De la Rue, W., *557n*; sends on Nobert's request for heavy glass, 557; about Nobert's diffraction gratings, 557, 581–2; proposed for *RS*, 582; about an apparatus for observing effects of magnetism on polarized light, 646–7; about Saturn's rings, 700–1, and satellites, 995; about preparations of gold, 828–9, 879; about photography of moon and planets, 879–80; gives account of eclipse (1860), 993–5, 995–6, 1009

Deluge, MF discusses Universality of, 13

Descartes's system of vortices, 661

Desormes, C. B. (politician, 1777–1862): co-author with Hachette of paper on electricity from rotating copper plate, 223

Despretz, C. M., *220n*; sends papers on density of solutions and propagation of heat in liquids, 373–4; mentioned by MF, 220, 851

Deville, E. H. St C. (chemist, 1818–81): produces pure aluminium in ingots, 798

Devon, MF in, 60

diamagnetism: MF's discovery of, 466, 469–70, 471, 481–2, 488–9, 589, 608; use of term, 471–2, 518; Plücker's quantitative experiments on, 519–20, 526–7, 535; polarity in? 519, 562, 567–8, 576; Thomson on, 523–4, 534, 555–7; MF reports on paper by Ward on, 562–3; A. de la Rive on theory of, 769; Tyndall on theory of, 771–4

diamond: combustion of, 62, 204, 522; pure crystallized carbon, 63; identity of coke and, 505–6; MF speculates on conversion of coke or charcoal into, 509

diamond ring, sent to Nasmyth by Emperor of Russia, 522

Dickens, Charles (1812–70): asks for use of reports of MF's juvenile lectures in *Household Words*, 583, and for his sub-editor to attend a lecture, 583–4

dielectrics: Whewell suggests term, 307; induction through, 351, 361; Thomson asks about action of electrified bodies on, 459; MF replies, 460

diffraction gratings, 557, 581, 620

Dinsdale, Mr, proposes hydrogenation of lime for fresco painting, 423, 424

diopside, magnetic and optic axes in, 547

dispersive index of glass, effect of lead content on, 150

Dockray, Mr, MF receives papers from, 134

Dollman, Mr, electrometer used by, 932

Dollond, G., *189n*; on Glass Committee, 150n; mentioned by MF, 167, 171, 173

Dollond family, opticians, 188, 189n; enquiry from A. de la Rive referred to, 914

donarium, supposed new metal (later proved to be thorium), 637

Donny, F. M. L., *499n*; MF refers to work of, 499; Quételet conveys letter from MF to, 537

Dove, H. W., *903n*; mentioned by A. de la Rive, 901, 903

Downes, Lord (1788–1863): Clerk of the Ordnance, 177

Draper, J. W. (chemist, 1811–82): on radiations, 677, 678n

drawing, MF regrets ignorance of, 7

dress of different countries, MF comments on, 75–6

Drummond, T. (engineer, 1797–1840): lime-light of, 163–4, 345; *see also* lime-light

Drummond, Col. T., *177n*; corresponds with MF about lectures on chemistry to cadets at Woolwich, 175–7

Drummond's Bank, Edinburgh, 114

Du Bois-Reymond, P., *565n*; sends MF his books on electrophysiology, 564–5; MF thanks him, 579; MF as would-be peacemaker between Matteucci and, 833; mentioned by Acland, 597, by J. Barlow, 765, by A. de la Rive, 901

Du Fay, C. F. de C. (chemist, 1698–1739): Hare mentions his doctrine of two electric fluids, 388

Dulong, P. L., *231n*; secretary of Académie des Sciences, 230; Law of Petit and, 376, 377; mentioned by H. Davy, 114, by Melloni, 285

Dumas, J.-B., *231n*; Hachette sends MF papers by, 230; MF thanks, for his portrait and much kindness, 372–3; MF thanks Académie des Sciences through, 431; MF to, describing liquefaction of gases, 432–4; MF to, about *RS* policy on publication, and describing recent work, 480–2; publishes part of MF's letter, 487; MF introduces J. Barlow to, 497–8; his chemical types, 498, 499; converts diamonds to coke, 505, 509; MF to, about meeting of British Association, etc., 509–10; MF enquires about situation of, in 1848 revolution, 524; replies, 525–6; introduces Eichtal and Melsens; is elected deputy, 548–50; MF replies, 552, 555; MF regrets having failed to meet his son, 573–4; MF to, on occasion of admission to Légion d'Hon-

Dumas, J.-B. (*cont.*)

neur, 808, 809, 826, 828; MF longs to see, 846; MF wants to lecture on work of, on relations between the elements, and asks for details, 880–1; MF thanks, for a letter, 1022; mentioned by A. de la Rive, 494, by J. Barlow, 766, by MF, 851

Dundas, R. (Lord Melville), *216n*; MF to (as First Lord of the Admiralty), 215

Dundee: MF at, 509; MF with Sandemanians at, 817, 1016–17

Dundonald, Lord (10th Earl), *751n*; MF on poison gas proposal of, 749–50

Du Pasquier, A., *421n*; observations of, on arsenic, 420

Dupin, F. P. C., writer on British army, 202, 207n

Durkin, Mr (assistant at *RI?*), 485

dynamo, first effective, 263; Wilde's, 1025–30, 1031

Earth, electricity of, 400, 579–80

Earth, magnetism of, 124, 130, 136, 265; induction of magnetism in iron ball by, 149; Fox's instrument for determining, 277–8; observations of, by Sabine, 591–2, 599, 611–12, and at Royal Observatory, 656–7; MF on best way towards understanding, 658–9, 659–60; variations in, with number of sun-spots, 661–3, 670–3; annual and diurnal variations in, at different places, 678–9; variation of, twice in each lunar day, 997–8

earthquakes, 83; sun and, 670, 900; moon and, 916

Eastlake, Sir C. L., *425n*; MF reports to, about experiments on hydrogenation of lime, 423–5

eclipse (1860), 993–7, 1009

education: belief in table-turning reflects on state of (MF), 695, 716; Whewell and MF to lecture on, 726

Edward Albert, Prince of Wales: MF mentions having seen, 655

efflorescence, B. Abbott observes, 35

Egypt, steam pile-driver in, 502

Ehrenberg, C. G., *324n*; work of, on Infusoria, forwarded to *RS* by MF, 324

Eichtal, A. S. d', *550n*; introduced to MF by Dumas, 548–9, 552, 555

Ekman, Mr, engineer: introduced to MF by Berzelius, 199, 200

elastic surfaces, vibrating: MF's work on, 193–4, 204n

electric attraction and repulsion: Harris on, 340–1, 628; Airy on, 416–17

electric capacity, MF on use of term, 315

electric charge, 360, 384

electric column, de Luc's, 4

electric conduction and insulation, 367, 368, 388–9, 718

electric currents: induction of, by parallel currents, and by magnets on approach and removal, 210 (*and see* electromagnetic induction); directions of, in electromagnetic induction, 242–5; MF thinks present notions of, will soon pass away, 264–5, 267; laws of, and of mechanical collision, coincide (Whewell), 293; change of molecules in passage of, the same as in magnetization? (A. de la Rive), 454; speed of, 727, 733, 738

electric eel, 655

electric fluid or fluids, 33, 306, 367; kites to collect, 174; Du Fay's doctrine of two, 388; Harris has no belief in, 628

electric force, lines of, 459, 805, 836

electricity: B. Abbott's experiments on, 15 33; interconvertibility of magnetism and, 294; positive and negative, 267, 362, 796–7; from voltaic battery, contact and chemical theories of, 369–70, 374–7, 795–7; production of cold by, 380n, 452, 453n; mathematical theory of, 458–60; identity of galvanic and frictional, 697; *see also* animal electricity; atmosphere, electricity of; Earth, electricity of; electric currents; electricity, static

electricity, static: Brande's experiment on, 349; Harris's experiments and theories on, 337–42, 987–9; Hare criticizes MF's theory of, 382–92; MF replies, 360–9; Hare's further comments, 382–92; not produced on contact of metals, 376; on spheres in contact, 458; Whewell enquires about MF's theory of, 532; MF replies, 532–4; on concentric spheres, 718; Melloni's experiments on, 739–43, 744–8; MF corrects Riess on, 809–16; Riess replies, 818–21; MF comments, 824–5; Knochen-

electricity static (*cont.*)
hauer on non-conductors in, 835–6; Knochenhauer divides, into tenacious and superficial, 840–3; Thomson's experiment on induction of, 936–8; MF comments, 939

electrode, MF introduces term, 264

electrodynamic action: term introduced by Ampère, discussed by Whewell, 293–4; MF says the word implies a theory, 295

electrolysis: Whewell on measurement of forces in, 299; MF reports on a paper about, 412; Buff's experiments on, 783–9; *see also* batteries

electrolyte, MF introduces term, 264

electromagnetic induction, 204n, 212–13; Ampère finds copper made magnetic by adjacent current, 137n; magnetism of iron increased by current in coils of wire round (Moll), 197–8, (A. de la Rive) 454; magnets induce currents in wires on approach and withdrawal (MF), 210, 211, 219, 516–17, 892, (Fazzini) 219; MF details his experiments and publications on, 235–52 (in connection with paper by Antinori and Nobili, 213n, 218, 224); curves of, 532–4, in different substances, 709–10

electromagnetic machines: of Jacobi, 345, 346, 347; of Caxton, 263; of Breguet and Masson, 395–7; of Davidson, 404; of Wilde, 1025–30, 1031

electromagnetic rotation: (1) of current-carrying wire round magnetic pole and pole round wire (MF), 123–4; MF accused of stealing Wollaston's ideas on possibility of, 125–8; MF sends G. de la Rive apparatus to illustrate, 132–3; P. Barlow's experiment on, 132–3; Plücker on laws of, 684

(2) of current-carrying magnet about its own axis: MF to Ampère about his discovery of, 131–2

(3) magnetism induced in metals by rotation: P. Barlow continues Arago's experiments on, 148–9; caused by induction of currents in metal (MF), 211; Hachette on, 223

electromagnetism, MF's historical sketch of, 122, 126

electrometer, 370; Coulomb's, 325; Peltier's, 616, 618; Thomson's recording atmospheric, 932, 933–4, 957–8

electrophysiology: DuBois-Reymond's work on, 564–5, 579, 597; Matteucci's work on, 836–8, 1021; *see also* animal electricity

electroscopes, 376, 728, 734–5, 739–42

electrotonic state, 210–11, 296, 864

elements: MF gives number of, 313; Dumas on relations between, 880–1

Ellemeet, W. C. M. de Jonge van, *273n*; carries letter from Moll to MF, 273

Encyclopaedia Britannica, MF's early study of, 914

engravings on copper plates, voltaic copies of, 343–4, 347

Erman, P., *401n*; on electricity of the earth, 400

ether (etherial medium), hypothesis of, 628, 689, 876, 920

ether (sulphuric ether): heated platinum wire in vapour of, 103–4, 435; Kane's views on structure of, 282–3; under pressure, 427, 428, 432; in freezing mixture, 432, 434; fluorescence in electrified vapour of, 901, 904–5

ethylene (olefiant gas): specific heat of, 377; liquefied, 433, 438, 553

euchlorine, solidified, 438

evaporating basins, from Royal Porcelain Works, Berlin, 175

examinations in chemistry: for London University, 169–71; at Woolwich, 643–5

Exhibition of 1851 (London), 630, 634; Babbage's book on, 632; *see also* Crystal Palace

Exhibition of 1855 (Paris), 808

Experimental Researches in Chemistry and Physics, by MF, 921

Experimental Researches in Electricity, by MF, 209–11, 217, 225; collected and reprinted, 319, 324, 327, 347, 378, 422; translated, 397

experiments: in lectures, MF on, 58; 'need not quail before mathematics' (MF), 211; MF's dependence on, 975–6

explosions: of nitrogen trichloride, 42, 43, 44, 45, 46; of nitrogen iodide, 61; injuries from, 45, 83–4, 140, 141, 304; at Haswell Collieries, 425, 426n

Fabricius, observes sun-spots, 670

Faraday, James, nephew of MF, 278

Faraday, Margaret (born Hastwell), mother of MF: death of (1838), 316, 317; mentioned by MF, 63, 75, 90–1, by B. Abbott, 81

Faraday, Margaret (Peggy), younger sister of MF, 65, 69–70, 78, 82

Faraday, Michael (1791–1867) (personal references only):

end of apprenticeship, 38, 39n, 40; 'my turn is not architectural', 63; writes letter in French, 94; has a pupil twice a week, 115; describes his introduction to Davy and appointment at *RI*, 177–8 (*see also under RI*); his 'delicacy and dexterity of manipulation', 484; 'the beauties of nature are what I most enjoy', 640; 'only an experimentalist', 859; his 'solitary and isolated' work, 888; his regrets for ignorance, *see* German language, mathematics

his honours: elected Corresponding Member and Foreign Member of Académie des Sciences, 146, 431; given honorary degree at Oxford, 212; prefers to be called Mr rather than Dr, 260; remonstrates at mistaken announcement of his being knighted, 313; receives *RS* medals, 324, 500, 501n; elected to Swedish Academy of Sciences, 326–7; decorated by King of Prussia, 399–400; list of his honours, 422; elected to Swiss Society, 455; 'not a Sir in England' (but has Prussian knighthood), 513; made Chevalier of the Légion d'Honneur, 808, 809, 826, 827

his health: suffers from headaches, 49, 172, 558; injured by explosions, 140, 141, and by phosphorus, 420; his knee limits his motions, 278; has inflammation of the eyes (from volatilized metals?), 335; has breakdown in health, 348, 349n, (but walks 30 and 45 miles a day in Switzerland, 393); suffers from giddiness, 409, 507, 508, 509, 521; has lumbago, 414; has an attack of rheumatic influenza, 437; troubled by loss of memory, 450, 479, 508, 537, 878; teased with a misbehaving knee, 500; has teeth extracted, 585–6; has sore throat (quinsy) 640–1; can work slowly, but rapid changes make him confused and giddy, 664; complains of attack in the throat and deafness, 699; apart from failing memory is well and free from giddiness, 790–1; breaks small blood vessel after attack of sea-sickness, 932; suffers from cold and sciatica, 991; 'if my memory fails, why it causes that I forget troubles as well as pleasures', 1001

his life outside his work: engaged in paper-hanging, 35; his Sandemanian connection, 106–7, 640–1, 1016–17; a good singer, 107; has 'nearly useless conversation' with callers, 172–3; never dines out, 359 (except by royal command, 290); his autograph in demand, 479, 892; never meddles with politics and thinks very little of them as one of the games of life, 558; not a republican except as regards science, 597; keeps a volume of portraits and letters of scientific friends, 598, 608; resigns from Athenaeum because of 'diminution of income', 645, but has 'plenty of means left for all that is needful', 646; expresses his religious faith, to A. de la Rive, 634, 707–8, 790, 831, 943, 1001, to Vincent, 974–5

Faraday, Robert, elder brother of MF, 44, 70; and lighting of Athenaeum, 278, and of Devonshire House, 409; MF gives rights in a lighting invention to, 407; mentioned by MF, 64, 65, by B. Abbott, 70, 80, 81

Faraday, Sarah (born Barnard), wife of MF: writes letters for MF, 165; writes to Magrath from Switzerland, 393–4; suffers from inability to walk, 663–4, and from ear trouble, 738–9, 743; involved in dispute among Sandemanians, 1018; mentioned by J. Barlow, 759

Farley, John, chemist: mentioned by MF, 103, 105n

Farquharson, Rev. J., *381n*; calculates height of aurora, 380

Fatio, Mme Maurice, becomes A. de la Rive's second wife, 799

Favre, P. A., *709n*; congratulated by MF on his work on the relation of heat and chemical action in voltaic battery, 708–9

Faye, H. A. E. A., *999n*; on comets, 999

Fazzini, L., *219n*; to MF on electromagnetic induction, 219

Fechner, G. T., *377n*; defender of contact theory of voltaic electricity, 374

fees: to MF for lectures, 176, 177; to contributors to *Quarterly Journal of Science*, 182, 186, 191; to MF for advice to Admiralty, 229, 286–7 (no charge, 756, 757); for drawings of lecture-room at *RI*, 630

Feilitzsch, F. C. O. von (physicist, 1817–85): expounds a theory of magnetism, 599–603; sends paper with revised theory, 753–4

fermentations, should be included in study of chemistry, 170

ferrane, J. Davy's experiment on, 27

ferro- and ferri-cyanides, magnetism of, 520

Fialin, J. G. V., Comte de Persigny, *827n*; MF sends letter to Napoleon III through, 827, 828

filter paper: MF hopes to receive supply of, from Germany, 181

Fincher, J., Assistant Secretary, *RI*, 65, 69n, 70, 155

fire balls, 405

fireworks: at Ranelagh Gardens, 14; MF owns book on, 15; on sale in London (Fulminating Objects), 72–3

fishing and shooting, Davy and MF engage in (near Geneva), 68

flames: experiments on combustion and, 96–7, 98n, 103–4; sounds produced in tubes by, 112, 115, 116n; light produced by salts of lime in, 163, 164; Plücker's experiments on, 514; MF's experiments on magnetism and, 518, and on induction and discharge of electricity by, 813, 814; of fish-tail gas burner, 984–5

flannel: discs of, in voltaic battery, 5, 6, 10

Flauti, V., *743n*; letters to Melloni to go through, 728, 742; to MF about Melloni's death, and about MF's letter to Melloni, 791

floras of Tasmania, India, etc.: Hooker's work on, 711

Florence, MF at, 62

fluorescence: none in ruby glass, 843; in electrified rarefied gases, 902, 944

fluorine, 313; and chlorine, to be classed with oxygen or not? 61

fog signals, for lighthouses, 1031

Forbes, Dr, resigns chair of chemistry at Aberdeen to Gregory, 404

Forbes, J. D. (physicist, 1808–68): to MF about obtaining sparks from a natural magnet, 221–2, 224; carries letter from MF to Plateau, 231; on regelation, 910–11; moving from Edinburgh to St Andrews, 939; mentioned by Melloni, 285, by Hansteen, 892

Forbes and Co., Edinburgh bankers, 222, 224

force: Clerk-Maxwell defines, 881–2; MF's use of word, 884; Winslow on matter and, 916–17; lines of, *see* electric force, magnetic force, *and under* gravitation

Foster, J. L. (Irish judge and *FRS*, d. 1842), 145

Foucault, J. B. L., *840n*; experiments of, on pendulum, 839; apparatus of, for regulating lime-light, 1029; mentioned by Hess, 854

Fourcroy, A. F. de (chemist, 1755–1809): *Elements of Chemistry* by, 22, 25n

Fownes, G. (chemist, 1815–49): *Manual of Elementary Chemistry* by, 673, 674n

Fox, R. Were, *268n*; MF refers to letter by, on electricity, 267; to MF on analogies of heat, light, and electricity, 275–6; MF replies, 276–7; calculates height of aurora, 381; Airy refers to suggestion of, about magnetic influence on pendulum, 755–6

Francis, Mr, deals with English translation of Plücker's papers, 542–3

Franklin, Benjamin (1706–90): his doctrine of electricity, 390; Harris refers to experiments by, 626

Fraunhofer, J. von (physicist, 1787–1826): lines in spectrum observed by, 923, 953

freezing mixtures: ice and calcium chloride, 43; solid carbon dioxide and ether, 432, 434

Fresnel, A. J. (physicist, 1788–1827): on undulatory theory of light, 182, 567; applies polyzonal lens to lighthouses, 817

fritting, in glass-making, 152–3

frost: figures of, on glass, 16; and building stones, 322; and water in plants, 444; and fracture of iron, 447

furnaces at *RI*, for Glass Committee, 167, 169, 171, 173

Fuss, P. H. von, *347n*; mentioned by MF, 347

Galileo's instruments, at Florence, 62
Galvani, L., (discoverer of galvanism, 1737–98): mentioned by Du Bois-Reymond, 365, by Matteucci, 838
galvanic battery, *see under* batteries
galvanometer, vibration of needle of, 325, 713, 714
gambling, mathematics of, 755
gas: lighting by, in London, 83, 84n, 112; from pilchard oil, 111–12; for lime-light, 345, 950, 955; *see also* coal-gas
gas burner, fish-tail: flame of, 984–5
gas voltaic battery, Groves', 402, 490
gases: released in voltaic battery, 5, 6; MF works on liquefaction of, 140, 144, 147, 432–4, 438, 439; specific heats of, 377; magnetism without effect on polarized light passing through, 464, 466; velocity of, under pressure, 565; drying of, 582; as conductors and electrodes (Buff), 786, 789; Waterston enquires about thermometer used by MF in liquefaction of, 945–6; *work on magnetism of, see under* air, nitrogen, oxygen *etc.*;
    rarefied electrified: stratified light in, 873–4, 875–6, 900–2; effects of magnetism on, 891, 902–3, 905, 906–8, 918–19; effect of lead in glass on, 908
    spectra of, 919, 960, 1005–6
Gassiot, J. P., *329n*; on 'constant battery', 328–9; congratulates MF on his discoveries on relation of light and magnetism, and is sorry he did not follow up a suggestion of MF's on the subject, 478–9; MF to, about a coil of oiled silk and tinfoil, 705–6; to MF, on conduction through liquid without electrolytic action, 797–8; collaborates with MF in work on electrical effects in rarefied gases, 876–7, 894, 900, 905; mentioned by MF, 876, by Plücker, 906, 907, 908, by A. de la Rive, 942
Gauss, K. F., *262n*; Moll on, 260; magnetic telegraph of, 261, 892; magnetic observatory of, 299, 323; mentioned by Hansteen, 893
Gautier, A., *687n*; on sun-spots and terrestrial temperatures, 686

Gay-Lussac, J. L. (physicist and chemist, 1778–1850): on molecular weight of iodine, 202; MF writes to (for publication), on electromagnetism, 235–52; retained as consulting chemist for French artillery, 304, 305n; mentioned, 36n, by MF, 139, 220, by Moll, 196
Geissler, H., *684n*; makes apparatus for determining alcohol, 684
Geissler tubes, 900–1, 903, 906
Geneva, MF at, 60, 74
Genoa, MF at, 61
Gentleman's Magazine, contains 'some very foolish explanations' (MF), 17
geology: Liebig considers it over-represented at York meeting of British Association, and not scientific, 430; Museum of Economic, 693
German language, MF regrets his ignorance of, 175, 347, 491, 512, 521, 537, 577, 791
Gernault, Monsieur, translates work by Harris, 897
Gilbert, Davies (*PRS*, 1767–1839): MF to, about work of Glass Committee, 180–1; Hachette translates paper by, 182–3
Gilbert, J. H., *846n*; collaborator of Lawes, 852
Gilbert, W. (1540–1603), mentioned by Haldat, 639
gilding, electrochemical, 375–6, 377n
Girard, P. S. (engineer and physicist, 1765–1836): MF refers to work of, on solid particles in liquids, 228
glaciers: Tyndall and, 850, 865, 876, 910; Airy and, 910
Gladstone, J. H. (chemist, 1827–1902): MF to, about relative brilliancy of lights observed from the sea, 922–3; meets MF on Lighthouse Commission, 969
Glaisher, J. (astronomer, 1809–1903): Stevenson corresponds with, about aurora, 688, 689n
glass: transparent in one direction only, 10, 13; frost figures on, 16; optical, paper by MF on manufacture of, 181n, 182, 184, 190, 200 (*see also* Glass Committee)
    heavy (silica, boracic acid, and lead), made by MF, 469; found by MF to be diamagnetic, 469–70, 482, 488; MF sends specimen of, to Plücker, 512, 513–14;

glass (*cont.*)

Nobert begs for sample of, 557; d'Abbadie asks for directions for making, 893–4

passage of polarized light through, under tension, 473–4, 483, and when magnetized, 517; cut by coke, 505–7, 522; effect of lead in, on electric effects on contained rarefied gases, 908; enquiry about English purchases of optical, 913

Glass Committee, appointed by *RS* (1824) to seek means of improving optical glass, 150n; Herschel reports on specimens of glass for, 149–50; MF's work for, 151–3, 155–6, 169; furnace for, at *RI*, 167, 171, 173; expenses of, 180, 213; MF sends accounts of work of, to *RS*, 199

Gmelin, L. (chemist, 1788–1853): MF quotes, 780

gold: burns in chlorine, 19; affinities of, for chlorine and oxygen, 29; marble spangled with, 71; MF on effect of colloidal dispersions of, on light, 828, 829n, 844, 879, 880; Paris Mint overwhelmed with, 856; De la Rue on effect of (as gold leaf), on polarized light, 856–7

Good, I. M., lecturer at Surrey Institution, 71, 72

Gortschakoff, Prince, MF visits catacombs at Paris in company with, 850

Göttingen: Moll visits and describes, 260–1; magnetic observatory at, 299n

Gourjon, Monsieur: scientific-instrument maker, Paris, 281, 282n

Gourjon, Monsieur, of École Polytechnique, carries paper to MF, 400

Graham T., *310n*; asks MF to support application for chair at London University, 309–10; about velocity of gases under pressure, 565–6; *Elements of Chemistry* by, 673, 674n; mentioned by MF, 401, by Liebig, 429, by A. de la Rive, 856

Grant, Miss, friend of the Barlows, 694, 766

grass, effect of frost on, 444

gravitation: and vaporization, 160, 161; and electricity, 628–9; Whewell on ways of expressing, 661; idea of lines of force in, 683, 881–3; MF on, 779, 870–2, 884–5, 900, 916; Hess has new theory of, 854, 855; Winslow on, 916–17; Mrs Somerville

on, 922; Clerk-Maxwell's diagrams of lines of force in, 932, 933, 934, 935

Gray family, neighbours of Faraday, 70, 80, 109

Greeks, colours used by, 88–9

Green, G. (mathematician, 1793–1841): and mathematical theory of magnetism, 833, 933

Green, J. H., *457n*; delighted by MF's lecture on nature of matter, 457

Greenwell, Mrs, housekeeper at *RI*, 64, 65, 82

Gregory, Dr, to lecture at *RI* on London statistics, 360

Gregory, W. (chemist, 1803–58): answers query from MF about Turner's *Elements of Chemistry*, 403–4; thanks MF for copy of *Chemical Manipulation*; gives process for purifying silver, 411–12

Grove, Sir W. R. (scientist and judge, 1811–96): gas voltaic battery of, 402, 412, 490; sends MF a paper; previous paper not published by *RS*, 408; MF approves his paper on electrochemical polarity of gases, 654; to lecture at *RI*, 753; work of, translated by Moigno, 865, 866n; mentioned by A. de la Rive, 494, by Plateau, 545, by Plücker, 568, by MF, 569, 766

Guillemard, J., Secretary at *RI*: to MF, 154

Guinand, P. L., *156n*; glass made by, 155

Gulf Stream, 620, 621, 622

gunpowder: apparatus for firing of, under water, 331–5

gutta percha: as insulator, 708, 714, 716; specific inductive capacity of, 898

Gymnotus, MF's paper on electric force of, 564, 565n

Hachette, J. N. P., *132n*; sends MF Ampère's papers on electro-magnetism, 189; to MF, describing July Revolution (1830), 182–3; receives, reads to Académie des Sciences, and publishes, a letter from MF on electromagnetic experiments, 212–13, 224, 227, 229–31, 259 (*see also* Antinori); mentioned by MF, 130

Haldat, C. N., *640n*; claims priority for establishing universality of magnetism, 639

Halswell, Mr: friend of MF, going to Berlin, 174, 175

Hamilton, Sir W. R., *1025n*; mathematical work of, mentioned by Clerk-Maxwell, 883; his drunkenness referred to by South, 1024

Hampton Court, Queen gives MF house at, 914, 969

Hansteen, C., *889n*; MF to, about a student from Norway wishing to work at *RI*, 888–9; replies, 892–3

Harcourt, W. Vernon, 201n; on proposed foundation of British Association, 200–1; congratulates MF on his work on magnetism, 576–7

Harding, K. L., *262n*; Moll on observatory of, 260

Hare R. (American scientist, 1781–1858): calorimotor of, 130, 132n; *Chemical Compendium* by, 226; on MF's theory of electricity, 350–8, 359; MF replies, 360–9, 896, 897; answers MF, 382–92

Harris, W. Snow, *342n*; describes his experiments and theories on static electricity, 337–42; about lightning and lightning conductors, 405–6; about his experiments and theories on magnetism, 624–9; MF on paper by, 648–9; questions MF about electrolysis, and use of terms positive and negative electricity, 795–7; about static electricity, 895–8, 987–9; mentioned by Liebig, 429

Hastings, MF at, 202, 623, 624

Haswell Collieries, MF and Lyell investigate cause of explosion at, 425, 426n

Hatchett, C., 147n; elected Corresponding Member of Académie des Sciences, 146

Hauksbee, F., 629n; Harris refers to experiments by, 625, 628

Hawes, Sir B., *553n*; MF answers query from, on extraction of sugar, 553, 555

Hawkins, B. W., *753n*; perhaps to lecture at *RI*, 752–3

Hauy, R. J. (Abbé and mineralogist, 1743–1822): mentioned by Harris, 340

heat: generated in animal bodies by exercise, 8; radiant, 278–9, 280–2, 284–6, 288; theory of materiality of (caloric), 385–6, 392; Hare on conduction and radiation of, 386; mechanical equivalent of, 837; relation of chemical action and, in electrolysis, 709, *see also* specific heats, temperature

Hellyer, W. V.: MF answers query from, about asphaltene as fuel, 274

Helmholtz, H. L. F. von (physicist, 1821–94): mentioned by Becker, 968

Hennell, H., *166n*; MF on a paper by, 165

Henry, Dr: MF to, about publication of a letter, 694

Henry, J. (American physicist, 1797–1879): work of, on powerful electromagnets, 197, 198n, 208n; to MF, introducing H. James, 319–20, and J. C. Cresson, 445; MF sends drawings of lecture-room to, 629–30; replies, with account of travels in United States, 632–4, which is appreciated by MF, 640; enquires about electric light for lighthouses, 1030–2; mentioned by Hare, 391, by Peyron, 395, by MF, 499

Henry, W. (chemist, 1774–1836): *Elements of Experimental Chemistry* by, 225, 226n

Henslow, J. S., *607n*; enquires about display of elements in Ipswich Museum, 606–7, 609–10

Herapath, W., *122n*; new balance of, 122

Herapath, W. B., *698n*; supplies specimen of tourmaline, 698

Herbert, J., Secretary, Trinity House: advises MF of his appointment as scientific adviser in experiments on light, 302

Herschel, J. F. W., *207n*; collaborator with Babbage, 148, 149n; on Glass Committee, 150n; letters about glass, to MF, 149–50, and from MF, 151–2, 152–3, 155–6, 167; MF submits paper on vaporization to, 159; comments on, 159–60, 161–2; MF wishes comments to be added to paper, 162; dissents, 163, 164; MF asks about lime-light, 163; replies, 164; resigns from Secretaryship of *RS*, 167; his *Study of Natural Philosophy* praised by MF, 235; MF to: unable to supply copies of papers, 318–19, unable to analyse meteorite because of eye trouble, 335; MF answers queries from, about varnish for brass, and about cadmium, 358–9; writes about MF's work on light and magnetism, 461–3; MF replies, 463–5; proposes an experiment on passage of polarized light through glass under torsion, 473–4; MF prepares for, 475, and carries out experiment, 483; thanks MF, 486; MF to, about diffraction

Herschel, J. E. W. (*cont.*)
gratings, 620; MF forwards a letter from Wolf, 670; replies, 671–2; mentioned by Vernon Harcourt, 201, by Moll, 206, by MF, 211, 214, by Plateau, 545

Herschel, Sir W. *207n*; mentioned by Moll, 206

Hess, M., gives theory of electricity he would like MF to test by experiment, 854–6

Hewes, C., known to MF: mentioned by J. Barlow, 751

Higgins, W., *145n*; MF suggested as successor to, in chair at Dublin, 144–5

Hillhouse, Mr and Mrs, Sandemanians, 585

Hodgkin, Dr, mentioned by R. W. Fox, 276

Hodgson, W. B., *724n*; to lecture at *RI*, 724

Hofmann, A. W., *684n*; intends to show apparatus at *RI*, 684

Holland, antipathy to England in, 205

Holland, Sir H., *421n*; *707n*; carries letter from MF to A. de la Rive, 420; MF quotes his views on time required for mental operations, 664, 706; *RI* fund for apparatus founded by, 934

Holmes, Prof., with MF at inspection of Dungeness lighthouse, 1013

Home Office, MF consulted by, 508

honours for scientists, MF on, 409–10, 724–5

Hooker, J. D., *712n*; declines invitation to lecture at *RI*, 710–12

Hooker, Sir W. J., *713n*; library and herbarium of, 711

Hope, T. C., *222n*; magnet belonging to, 221

Howard and Gibson of Stratford, manufacturers of ammonia compounds, 440

Hudson, E. T., tutor at Trinity College, Cambridge: at Spa, 755

Hudson, J., *151n*, *222n*, *327n*; Assistant Secretary, *RS*, 222, 327, 347

Hudson, Mr, on specific gravity of glass, 151

Humboldt, A. von, *311n*; sends MF decoration from King of Prussia, 399–400; and association of sun-spots and magnetic variations, 672, 676; his *Cosmos* quoted by Stevenson, 688; mentioned by Quételet, 310, by A. de la Rive, 455, 904, by Melloni, 699, by Moigno, 865

Hume, J., *57n*; holds silica to be base of oxygen, 57

Hume, Mr, MF calls on, 109–10

Hunt, R., *483n*; MF intermediary between Herschel and, 483, 486; mentioned by Wilson, 635

Hunt, T. S., *826n*; gives MF Dumas's address, 826

hurricanes of West Indies, course of, 621

Hutton, J., *207n*; mentioned by Moll, 206

Huxtable, T., early friend of MF, 14; MF writes to, 40, 141

hydriodic acid, 202; solidified, 433, 438

hydriodic ether, 283

hydrobromic acid, solidified, 433, 438

hydrocarbons, MF interested in Mitscherlich's work on, 258

'hydro-carburet', gas issuing from earth considered to be, 77

hydrochloric acid (muriatic acid): formed in reaction of phosphorus chloride with water, 23, and of sulphur chloride with water, 24; metals in, 26, 31; water required for, 27

hydrogen: combines with chlorine to give hydrogen chloride, 19–20, 21, 24, 26; set free in reaction of potassium with hydrogen chloride, 20; forms water with oxygen, 21, 103; liberated (from water) by metal dissolved in hydrochloric acid, 26, 31; a volatile metal? 35; in charcoals, 63; compressed, MF's experiments on, 102; specific heat of, 377; 'bicarbonated', 202; treatment of lime by, 453–5; MF hopes to liquefy, 434; from electrolysed water, 787–9; rarefied electrified, 873, 874; spectrum of, 908, 923, 924

hydrogen arsenide, 283; liquefied, 433, 434

hydrogen chloride (muriatic acid gas): formed from hydrogen and chlorine, 19–20, 21, 24, 26; reactions of, with potassium, 20, 21, with ammonia, 25, with potassium permanganate, 29, with nitrogen trichloride, 43–4, 46; Davy's work on, 27–8; liquefied, 140, 433

hydrogen peroxide (bleaching principle produced in slow combustion of ether – Schoenbein), 435–7; differences between chlorine and, 442–3

hydrogen phosphide: compound of hydriodic acid and, 283; liquefied, 433, 438

hydrogen selenide, bronchitis caused by, 635

hydrogen sulphide: liquefied, 140; solidified, 433, 438

Hyeen, Lieut., R.N., and lighthouses, 978

ignition, spontaneous: of hemp containing oil, 316

ignorance, MF on public state of, 692, 716

inclined plane clock, seen by MF in shop window, 6

India, flora of, 711

india rubber, diamagnetic, 488

inductive capacity, 315; specific, 363, 815, 829–30; of gutta-percha, 898

inertia of electrodynamic current, Whewell on, 293

Infant Orphan Asylum, MF's support for, 965

influenza, theories about cause of, 635–6

infra-red rays, 68

iodine: Davy works on, 61, 68; crystals of, 160; molecular weight of, 202; spectrum of, 923, 960

ions, term suggested by Whewell, 270, 272

iridium, 208

iron: in water conveyed through pipes of, 5–6; reaction of hydrochloric acid and, 26; affinities of, for chlorine and oxygen, 29; alloys of, 117–20, 166, meteoric, 119, 120; in clays, 312, 318; production of, from ore, 399, 448; sound produced by bar of, at induction of current in, 426, 454; fractures and annealing of, 446–7; magnetic, 454, 481–2, 488; temperature and magnetism of, 489, 613; compounds of, are magnetic, 482, 489; molten, plunging hand into, 549, 568; specific magnetism of, 638, 710

iron carbonate: magnetic experiments on compressed cube of, 772–3; magnetism of isomorphous crystals of calcium carbonate and of, 773–4

'iron carburet', 118

iron sulphate, magnetic axes in crystals of, 528, 529, 535; optic and magnetic axes in crystals of, 561, 566

Jacobi, M. H., 346n; to MF, about voltaic copies of engravings, Drummond's light, and electromagnetic machines, 343–6; MF replies, 346–7

Jacques Hotel: MF hears music from, at RI, 47

James, H., 321n; introduced to MF by J. Henry, 319–20

Jocelyn, Lord, 759n; his death 'the result of his own imprudence' (J. Barlow), 758

Jones, E., 872n; MF sends papers to, 870–2

Jones, H. Bence, 728n; as MF's physician, 738–9, 743, 932, 991; mentioned by J. Barlow, 765, by MF, 850, 975, 976

Jordan, W., editor of Literary Gazette: MF to, correcting error, 313

Joule, J. P. (physicist, 1818–89): 'any paper by Mr Joule must be proper for the Transactions' (MF), 800, 826; and mechanical equivalent of heat, 837

journeyman, MF becomes, 36, 37

Joy, H., Irish Solicitor General, member of Dublin RS, 145

kaleidophone, 194, 257, 258n

Kane, Sir R. J., 283n; about priority for his views on structure of ether, etc., 282–3

Kater, H., 207n; mentioned by Moll, 206

Kaulbach, W. von, 853n; mentioned by Liebig, 852

Keil, Dr: in Utrecht, boasts of acquaintance with MF, 261; 'an impudent scoundrel' (Moll), 273

Kew, recording atmospheric electrometer made for, 933, 934

kilogramme, real value of, 192

King's College, London: subscriptions for, 172

Kirchhoff, G. R. (physicist, 1824–87): spectroscopic work of Bunsen and, 953, 1005; mentioned by Becker, 968, by MF, 1001

kites, MF on B. Smith's plan for, 174

knife: MF's is covered with copper, so that he cannot mend pen, 10

Knoblauch, K. H., 593n; mentioned by Plücker, 593

Knochenhauer, K. W. (physicist, 1805–75): to MF about inductive capacity, 829–30; about non-conductors in induction, 835–6; about experiments on static electricity, which he divides into tenacious and superficial, 840–3

Knox, Hon. G., member of Dublin RS, 145

Kreil, K., *753n*; mentioned by J. Barlow, 752

Kupffer, A. T., *311n*; mentioned by Quételet, 310

Kyan, J. H., *298n*; MF on tests of process for preserving wood invented by, 298

Lacépède, B. G., Comte de, *208n*; mentioned by Moll, 207

Lacy, porter at *RI*, 757–8, 760

La Fontaine, Davy's valet, refuses to go abroad, 85

Lagrange, J. L. (mathematician, 1736–1813): on Newton, 892

Lambert, J. H., *629n*; Harris refers to magnetic experiments of, 628

Lamont, J., *662n*; observes variations in mean declination of magnetic needle, 661, 670, 672

lamps: miners' safety, 98n; Argand, 112, 407, 677, 870; oil and gas, MF's ventilator for, 407; consumption of oil not measure of performance of, 992–3; *see also under* light-houses

Laplace, P. S., *401n*; on electricity of vapours, 400; mathematical work of, referred to by Clerk-Maxwell, 883, by Plücker, 909; nebular hypothesis of, 998

Lardner, D., *169n, 262n*; MF to, about chair of chemistry at London University, 168–9; proposes subjects for *RI* lectures, 262, 280; about his own proposed lecture(s) on comets, 287–8

Latham, Dr P. M., *349n*; as MF's physician, 348, 349, 350

Latham, R. G., *456n, 724n*; suggests terminology to MF, 456; to lecture at *RI*, 724

Laurent, P. A., *660n*; finds cycle of 10 years in magnetic records, 659

lava, cooled in sea water, 156, 158

Lavoisier, A. L., *401n*; and chlorine, 16, 27; *Elements of Chemistry* by, 22, 25n; opposed by De la Métherie, 197n; on electricity of vapours, 400

Lawes, J. B., *846n*; Liebig in controversy with, 844–5, 852, 853

lead: in water stored in cistern of, 6; affinities of, for chlorine and oxygen, 29; in ancient colours, 88; in glass, 149–50, 151–2, 155, 908; alloy of iron and, 166; Dalton poi-soned by (in porter and water), 380; removal of, from water, 929–30

lead acetate, decomposed by battery, 5

lead monoxide (litharge), decomposes chlorides, 33–4

lead oxide (red lead), among ancient colours, 88

lead silicate, refractive and dispersive indices of, 150

Leake, W. M., *298n*; mentioned by Moll, 206

Le Baillif, A. C. M., *478n*; observes diamagnetism of bismuth and antimony, 477, 482, 483–4

lecture-rooms, MF on best shape for, 50

lectures and lecturers, MF's views on, 49–50, 51, 102

legal cases: MF and others subpoenaed to give evidence in, but not called, 109; MF involved in (on new process for making malt), 110

Leighton, G., London Sandemanian, 1017, 1018

Leighton, J., *1014n*; to lecture at *RI*; MF hopes he will read as little of his lecture as possible, 1014

Lemon, Sir C. (founder of Statistical and Geological Societies, 1784–1868): MF to, on nature of electric agent, 267–8

Lenoir, Mr, Viennese photographer, 893

lenses: used for combustion of diamond, 62; polyzonal, for lighthouses, 817; manufacture of, for lighthouses, 1010–11

Lenz, H. F. E., *346n, 453n*; collaborator with Jacobi in work on electromagnets, 346, 347; produces cold by electricity, 452

Le Play, P. G. F., *305n*; carries letter from Arago to MF, 304

Lesage, G. L., *308n*; theory of gravitation proposed by, 308

Lesley, Mr, mentioned by MF, 1020

Leslie, C. R., *736n*; MF replies to query from, about blue colour of sky, 735–6

Leslie, Sir J. (mathematician and natural philosopher, 1766–1832): in *Encyclopaedia Britannica* on meteorology, 156, 157n; mentioned by Lardner, 288, by Whewell, 661

letters: MF to B. Abbott, on writing of, 3–4, 32, 45, 99, 101–2; MF yearns for, in Rome, 74–5

Le Verrier, U. J. J., *510n, 782n*; carries message from Dumas to MF, 509; mentioned by MF, 782, 851

Lewis, G. G., *654n*; accepts MF's resignation from post at Woolwich, 653–4

Leyden jar: electricity in, 349, 365; long wire with gutta-percha covering equivalent to, 704, 706, 708, 731

libraries: of Göttingen University, praised by Moll, 260; of *RI*, 1017

lichens, not found on London buildings, 322

Liebig, J. von (chemist, 1803–73): Kane refers to paper of, on structure of ether and alcohol, 282, 283n; sends greeting to MF after visit to England, 429–30; MF replies; describes work on liquefaction of gases, 437–8; writes about medical son seeking appointment in India, 663; thanks MF for help in obtaining appointment, 668; MF to, introducing nephew (Barnard), 802; MF thanks him for his kindness to Barnard, 838–9; on controversy with Lawes, 844–5, 851–2; commends Barnard, 845; is sorry he is leaving, 852; MF replies that time will enable truth to prevail, 853–4; thanks him for book on husbandry, 1015–16

light: MF's experiments connecting magnetism and, 461–3, 463–5, 466, 481; Whewell on different colours of, in polarization, 495–6; experiments can be made on, whether it is emission or undulation (MF), 805; velocity of, 922; produced by electricity in rarefied gases, *see under* gases; *see also* polarized light

Lighthouses: Bishop's Rock, 681; Cap Grisnez, 923; Dungeness, 1013; Eddystone, 680–1; Farnes, 978; Guernsey, 1011; Hamstead, 978; Nash Low, 665–7; North and South Whitby, 962–8, 970–4, 977–9, 981, 992, 1007; Purfleet, 955; Red Sea, 972; Smalls, 967, 977, 984, 986; South Foreland, 923, 955, 1003

lighthouses: lighting for, MF to advise Trinity House on, 302, 513; MF reports to Trinity House on effects of lightning at, and lightning conductors for, 665–7, 680–1; electric lighting for, 674, 869–70, 952, 1013; polyzonal lenses for, 817;

relative brilliancy of lights of, 922–3; lime-light for, 947–8, 950–1, 955, 1003, 1007; oil lamps for, 962–8, 970–4, 977–9, 992, 993; manufacture of lenses for, 1010–11; mirrors for lamps of, 1014

lighting: of lecture-rooms, 50; by gas, 83, 84n, 112, (Athenaeum) 278, 348, (Devonshire House) 409; by Drummond's lime-light, 345, 347; by arc light, 1029; for lighthouses, *see under* lighthouses; *see also* lamps

lightning: MF asks his nephew about a discharge of, 371; effects of, on ships, 341–2, on lighthouses, 665–7, 680–1, on telegraph wires, 738, on portable electrometer, 957; Harris on globular form of, 405

lightning conductors: on ships, 405–6; on lighthouses, 665–7, 680–1

lime: reaction of chlorine with, 28; experiments by MF on hydrogenation of, 423–5

lime-light, 163–4, 345, 347; for lighthouses, 947–8, 950–1, 955, 1003, 1007

linseed oil (unboiled), does not thicken with cold, 327

liquids: under pressure, 417, 419, 538; under pressure and heat, 427, 428, 498–9; spheres of, suspended in another liquid, 484; A. de la Rive asks about induction of electricity in, and transmission of electricity by, 705; MF replies, 718, and reports experiments on, 719–22; Van Breda and Logeman describe experiments showing conduction in to be due to electrolytic decomposition, 761–4; Gassiot reports conduction in, without electrolysis, 797–8

Literary Gazette, MF to editor of: correcting account of Nobili's paper, 218; correcting reference to himself as having been knighted, 313

lithium: specimen of, sent to MF, 850; spectrum of, 953, 960

litmus paper, shows that phosphorus trichloride is not an acid, 23

Lloyd, H., *649n*; MF on his theory of magnetism, 648–9; mentioned by J. Barlow, 751–2, 753n

Logeman, W. M.: Van Breda and, write to MF about their experiments on conduction of electricity through liquids, 761–4; MF

Logeman, W. M. (*cont.*)
  sends their letter to *Philosophical Magazine*, 769; magnet made by, 858
London: atmosphere of, and building stone,
  322; lecture on statistics of disease and
  mortality in, 360
London Bridge station, Airy's clock at, 782
London Institution, 165, 461; MF lectures
  at, 176; laboratory of, 402
London University: chair of chemistry at,
  declined by MF, 168–9; Clark on examinations in chemistry at, 169–71; opening
  of, 172; MF invited to join Central Board
  of Examiners of, 302–3
Lovelace, Lady, A. de la Rive on death of, 675
Lubbock, Sir J. (astronomer, 1803–65): and
  Halley's comet, 287, 288n
Lucca, MF at, 60
Lyell, Sir C. (geologist, 1797–1875), 426n;
  mentioned by A. de la Rive, 453

Macaire, I. F., *124n*; mentioned by MF, 123,
  by A. de la Rive, 453
machines: Babbage's calculating, 214, 262;
  pile-driving, 448–9, 502–3; *see also* electromagnetic machines
Mackenzie, R. S., *422n*; MF sends list of
  his honours and publications to, 421–2
Macvicar, Rev. J. G., *860n, 976n*; MF thanks,
  for papers, 859–60, 976
magnesium sulphate, decomposed by battery,
  5
magnetic fluid or fluids, hypothesis of, 776,
  778, 781
magnetic force, lines of: MF on, 612–13,
  682–3, 780–1, 805–6, 861; shown by iron
  filings, 648, 650–1, 652, 766; Whewell on,
  660–1, 776–7; Plücker on, 683–4; Stokes
  on setting of bodies along, 807; Clerk-
  Maxwell on mathematics of, 864; made
  visible in electrified gases (Plücker), 891,
  905
magnetic needle: variations in mean declination of, 661, 670, 672; affected by electric
  current (Ørsted), 892
magnetic storms, 656, 657, 658–9; and
  aurora, 673
magnetism: induction of, by electric current,
  137n, 197–8, 454; 'action of, is progressive
  and requires time' (MF), 217 (*see also*

under time); interconvertibility of electricity and, 294; permanent and induced,
  in correction of compass, 336; Plücker's
  quantitative work on, 519–20, 526–7, 535;
  von Feilitzsch's theory of, 599–603;
  measurement of, 593–4, 609, 613, 626;
  specific, 638; Haldat claims priority for
  establishing universality of, 639; Harris
  on laws of, 625–9; A. de la Rive's new
  theory of, 704; Tyndall on theory of,
  771–4; Whewell and MF discuss, 776–8;
  effect of, on polarized light, *see under*
  polarized light; *see also* atmosphere, magnetism of; Earth, magnetism of; *and* diamagnetism
magnetization, A. de la Rive on molecules
  during, 454
magneto-dynamic induction, 489
magneto-electric machines, *see* electromagnetic machines
magnets: lifting of weights by, 62, 197–8,
  203–4, 261; induction of electric currents
  by, 210, 211, 219, 516–17, 892; sparks
  from, 210, 218, 221–2, 229–30; large, for
  Royal Observatory, 298–9; checking
  vibration of, 323, 324–5; Whewell wants
  figures showing currents inside, 660
Magnus, H. G., *579n, 903n*; MF hears about
  Du Bois-Reymond's work from, 579;
  mentioned by A. de la Rive, 901
Magrath, E., *69n, 185n*; MF to, 165–6, 179–
  80, 202, 278, announcing his mother's
  death, 317, answering enquiries about his
  health, 349, 350, 381; Mrs Faraday writes
  to, from Switzerland, 393–4, and MF adds
  to letter, 394; MF to (as Secretary of the
  Athenaeum), sending his resignation, 645,
  646
Majocchi, G. A., *558n*; mentioned by MF,
  558
malt, MF reports on temperature in kiln-
  drying of, 109–10
man: 'a singular compound' (MF), 48;
  lessons taught by knowledge of manners
  and of (MF), 74–5
Manby, C., *378n*; MF advises, about purchase of books, 378
manganese, magnetic, 471, 482, 489
manganese oxide, cobalt and nickel as im-
  purities in, 406

manganese peroxide: as a lesser oxide with oxygen, 16; reaction of hydrogen chloride with, 29

Manning, G., Lieut. RN, adds postscript about charts to letter from Maury, 622

manufactory, transfer from laboratory to, 117

Marcet, A., *121n*; MF thanks, for book sent for review, 121; MF returns letter by Berzelius to, 129–30; death of, 139; mentioned by G. de la Rive, 137, by MF, 138, 326

Marcet, F., *185n*; with A. de la Rive in Geneva, 185, 186, 376; carries letters between MF and A. de la Rive, 705, 900, 902, 903; mentioned by MF, 694, by J. Barlow, 752, 765

Marcet, Jane, wife of A. Marcet, *121n*; her *Conversations sur la Chimie* introduces MF to chemistry, 121n, 913, 914; in London, 495, 675

Marcet, Louisa, sister-in-law of A. de la Rive, 799

Marchand, R. F. (chemist, 1813–50): mentioned by MF, 780

Marianini, S., *370n*; supporter of contact theory of voltaic battery, 369, 374

Marignac, J. C., *421n*; collaborates with A. de la Rive, 420, 442, 453, 477

Marsh, J., *149n*; collaborates with P. Barlow, 148

Martin, Sir T. B., *751n*; MF reports to, on Lord Dundonald's scheme, 749–51; thanks MF and enquires about fee, 756; MF replies, 757; MF to, on sulphur fire in Newcastle, 767

Marum, Martyn van, *193n*; mentioned by Moll, 191

Maskelyne, N., *207n*; mentioned by Moll, 206

masks, worn by Davy and MF when working with explosive compounds, 45, 46

Mason, T., jun., *329n*; makes Daniell battery, 328

Masselin, Mr, with Chance in inspection of new lighthouse lamp, 992, 993

Masson, A. P., *397n, 655n*; electromagnetic machine of Breguet and, 395–7; concludes electric current cannot exist in absolute vacuum, 655

mathematics: MF regrets his ignorance of, 7, 132, 134, 138, 154; MF on: 'experiment need not quail before', 211, 'sometimes glad I am not a mathematician', 292, 'all my mathematics consist in that rough natural portion of geometry which everybody has more or less', 295, 'may conclusions of, not be expressed in common language?' 885; Harris on determination of mathematicians to bend everything to principles of, 339, 628

matter: MF's speculations on, 457, 464–5, 491

Matteucci, C., *304n*; asks MF's support in obtaining a post in Corfu, 303–4; MF to, about lines of magnetic force, 804–7; to MF about his work on muscular respiration, 836–8, and electrophysiology, 1021; MF as would-be peacemaker between Du Bois-Reymond and, 833; mentioned by Hess, 855

Matthews, Mr, member of City Philosophical Society, 113

Matthiessen, A., *851n*; MF mentions, 850

Maury, M. F., *622n*; thanks MF for papers; asks him to work on electric and magnetic properties of sea water, 620–2

Mayo, T., *416n*; on MF's use of Atomic Doctrine, 414–16

mechanics: MF regrets ignorance of, 7; definition of, 17

Melloni, M., *279n*; sends papers on radiant heat, 278–9; recommends MF to have a 'thermo-multiplicator' made in Paris, 280–2; summarizes his work as possibly worthy of Rumford medal, 284–6; expresses thanks for Rumford medal, 289–90, for lectures on his work by MF at *RI*, 290–1, and for interest and support, 699; sends papers on magnetism of rocks, 698; about speed of electric current, 727–8; about a new electroscope, 728, 734–5; about his experiments and theories on induction, 739–43, 744–8; death of, 760; MF's answer to his letter on theories of induction is read to Academy at Naples, 791–2; Riess refers to his electroscope, 820; mentioned by W. Gregory, 403

Melsens, L. H. F., *550n*; Dumas to MF about process for extracting sugar invented by.

Melsons, L. H. F. (cont.)
549; MF writes to Colonial Secretary about, 555

mercuric chloride: preparation of chloride of phosphorus from phosphorus and, 22–3; from reaction of mercuric oxide with chlorine, 28, and of mercury with nitrogen trichloride, 45

mercuric iodide: crystals of, change colour when pricked, 698

mercuric oxide (red), reaction of chlorine with, 28

mercury: affinities of, for chlorine and oxygen, 29; reaction of nitrogen trichloride with, 45; spectrum of vapour of, 919, 923

Mercury (planet), transit of (1832), 224

metals: at very low temperature burn the skin, 16–17; give off smell when rubbed, 17, 31; several burn in chlorine, 19, 21; decompose hydrogen chloride, 20; dissolve in hydrochloric acid, with liberation of hydrogen, 26; affinities of, for chlorine and oxygen, 29; compounds of iodine with, 61; electric arrangement of, 119; magnetic arrangement of, 148–9; electrolytic preparation of, 412; magnetic, 488; compounds of magnetic, are also magnetic, 482, 489; supposed new, 637; Percy to lecture at RI on, 693; MF on relations of, to light, 828, 829n, 844, 879, 880; MF to Thomson about his experiments on motion of electricity among, 940–2; spectra of, 653; see also individual metals

meteorites: nickel in, 119, 120; elements in, 166–7; Herschel's (aerolite), 335; Mexican, offered to British Museum, 818

mica, magnetic and optic axes in, 960–1

Miller, J., 449n; 'my excellent friend' (Nasmyth), 446

Miller, W. A., 682n; Wheatstone arranges loan of apparatus to RI from, 681

Miller, W. H., 864n; Foreign Secretary, RS, 863, 872

Millington, J., 169n; mentioned by MF, 168

Milman, Very Rev. H. H., 869n; MF to, about condition of marbles in British Museum, 867–9

Milne-Edwards, H., 510n; carries packet from Dumas to MF, 509; mentioned by MF, 574

minerals: MF wants specimens of, from America, 174

Mint at Paris, A. de la Rive visits, 856

Mitscherlich, E., 175n; MF to: making introductions, 174, 309, asking for help in ordering apparatus, 175, mentioning Quarterly Journal of Science to be published by RI, 181–2, thanking Berlin Academy of Sciences through, 258; mentioned by Plücker, 511, by De la Rue, 856

Moigno, Abbé F. N. M., 538n; Quételet refers to work of, 538; to MF about translations he is making, and about Seguin, 865–6; MF sends his collected papers, and discusses Seguin's work, 866–7

molecules: change of, in passage of electric current, the same as in magnetization? (A. de la Rive), 454; arrangement of atoms in, 737, 768–9; electricity as a movement of, 836; hypothesis of solid impenetrable, 920

Moll, G., 189n; on the state of science in England, 187–9, 192–3, 195–6, 205–7, and in Germany, 260; publication of papers by, in England, 191–2, 197, 200, 204; electromagnetic experiments by, 191, 197–8, 203; to MF, about an imposter, 261, 273, and introducing a friend, 273

molybdenum, specific heat of, 377

Monferrand, J. B. de: MF receives Manuel d'Électricité by, from Ampère, 154

Monge, G., 208n; mentioned by Moll, 207

Monte Rosa, Tyndall's ascent of, 911–12

Montgaillard, Abbé G. H. R. de, 208n; mentioned by Moll, 207

moon: Nasmyth's observations of, 503, 523; and magnetism, 752; photography of, 879; and earthquakes, 916

Moore, Miss: MF to, mentioning American Civil War, 1000

morality, MF on, 37–8

Morrison, Mr, Percy mentions his observations on sounds produced by electric current, 426

Mossotti, O. F., 307n; MF reads paper by, on forces governing matter, and asks Whewell's opinion of it, 306–7; Hare refers to hypothesis of, 352

Munich: MF in, 76; MF's nephew in, 802, 838, 852
Murchison, Sir R. I., *510n*; mentioned by MF, 509
muriates, *see* chlorides, *also* ammonium chloride, sodium chloride, *etc.*
muriatic acid, *see* hydrochloric acid
muriatic acid gas, *see* hydrogen chloride
Murphy, Dr, mentioned by Stokes, 807
Murray, J., *105n*; on Davy's experiments, 103, 104
muscae volitantes, paper by Brewster on, 418
muscles: respiration of, increases with contractions (Matteucci), 836–8
Musschenbroek, P. van, *629n*; Harris refers to experiments by, 623, 628

Namier, Mr, working in laboratory of Berzelius, 144–5
naphthalene, paper by MF on, 157
Naples, MF at, 87
Napoleon, 59, 196, 207
Napoleon III of France: writes to MF from Fort of Ham (before coming to the throne), 413; appoints MF to the Légion d'Honneur, 808, 809, 826; MF's acknowledgement to, 827, 828
Nasmyth, J., *446n*; MF reminds, about promise to lend specimens of iron for lecture, 446; replies, describing specimens, 446–8; about his steam hammers and pile-drivers, 448–9, 502–3; about the surface of the moon; suggests experiment on hardening of steel, 503–4; MF replies, 504–5; on cutting of glass by coke, 505–7, 521–3; MF replies, 507
Natterer, J. A., *434n*; MF refers to work of, on liquefaction of gases, 433
needle, in flesh of toe, located by magnetizing it, 857–9
Neeff, C. E., *491n*; MF thanks for papers, 491
nerves: Peltier and Prévost on magnetization by current from, 379, 380; electrochemistry of (Du Bois-Reymond), 564
Newcastle-upon-Tyne: steam pile-drivers for bridge at, 502–3; conflagration of sulphur at, 767, 794
Newman, J., *64n*; friend of MF, 64, 65, 70, 78, 82, 111; money owed to, by Glass

Committee, 213; apparatus made by, 375 558, 691
Newton, Sir Isaac (1642–1727): definition of flame by, 96; MF compared with, 624–5; experiments by, on magnetism, 626, 628; Biot on, 628, 629n; his view of lines of force, 661, 683, 805; Lagrange on, 892; Winslow on, 915; his notion of an ether, 920; mentioned by MF, 10, by Mrs Somerville, 922
Niagara, Falls of, 72
Nicholl, Dr W., *180n*; as MF's physician, 179; MF consults, on terminology, 212n, 264, 268, 271; tells of a visit to Channel Islands, etc., 305–6
Nicholson, W. (scientist and inventor, 1753–1815): *Dictionary of Chemistry* by, 22, 25n; *Introduction to Natural Philosophy* by, 31, 32n
nickel: alloys of iron and, 119; in meteorites, 120, 818; as impurity in manganese oxide, 404; magnetic, 454, 471, 488; temperature and magnetism of, 489, 524, 613; salts of, magnetic, 489
Nicol, W., *290n*; double prism of, wanted by Melloni, 289–90
Nicol, W., printer, 165, 166n
Niepce de Saint-Victor, A., *550n*; process of photography invented by, 548–9, 552
nitric acid: reaction of nitrogen trichloride with, 44; liberates iodine from potassium iodide (as ozone does), 626
nitrogen (azote): a volatile metal? 35, 434; in nitrogen trichloride, 43, 46; from reaction of nitrogen trichloride with nitric acid, 44, and with mercury, 45; not liquefied, 434, 439; neither magnetic nor diamagnetic, 594, 599, 611; spectrum of, 924
nitrogen dioxide, not liquefied, 434
nitrogen iodide, detonating compound, 61
nitrogen oxides, magnetism of, 638
nitrogen trichloride: Davy and MF prepare and investigate, 42–4; further experiments with 'this terrible compound', 45–6
nitrous oxide, 9; liquefied, 146, 434; compound of chlorine with, 195; solidified, 438
Nobert, F. A., *557n*; begs piece of heavy glass from MF, 557; diffraction gratings made by, 557, 581–2, 620

Nobile, A., *231n*; carries letter from Hachette to MF, 231

Nobili, L.: Forbes refers to experiments of, on obtaining sparks from a magnet, 221, 222; *see also* Antinori

Northampton, Marquis of (1790–1851): as president of the *RS*, asks MF about new charter, 449–50; mentioned by Smyth, 473

Northumberland, Duke of (1792–1865): MF hopes he will not retire from chair of *RI*, 1007–8

Norwood, Faradays living at, 589

Nuremberg, 'two pennyworth of manufacture from' (MF), 228

oatmeal, MF analyses samples of, for the Admiralty (1832), 252–5, 286–7; MF asks for payment for the work on (1835), 286–7

ocean currents, 620–2

ochres, among ancient colours, 88, 89

Odling, W., *703n*; carries packet from E. Becquerel to MF, 702–3

Ørsted, H. C. (electromagnetist, 1777–1851): introduces friend to MF, and describes experiments on diamagnetism, 571–3; MF replies, 581; death of, 618; Hansteen describes, 892; mentioned by MF, 129, by Wheatstone, 194, by Plücker, 684, by Hansteen, 893

Ohm's law, 932

oil: pilchard, for production of illuminating gas, 112; MF engaged in work on combustion and flame of, 115, 116–17; decomposition of, by heat, 151, and by electricity, 185; spontaneous ignition of hemp containing, 316; effect of cold on different kinds of, 327

olefiant gas, *see* ethylene

optical illusions: Plateau describes his experiments on, and asks for a copy of MF's paper about, 231–3; Plateau acknowledges paper, and describes further experiments, 256–7

orangite (mineral), supposed new metal from, 637

Ordnance, Department of: MF consulted by, 508

O'Shaughnessy, Sir W. B., *689n*; MF mentions report by, 689

osmium, 208, 601

Owen, R., *541n*; MF to, about Buckland's inability to lecture, 541; to lecture at *RI*, 753

Oxford, MF given honorary degree at, 212

oxides, some decomposed by chlorine, 28

oxygen: supposed to be present in oxymuriatic acid (chlorine), 19, 20, 22; set free by chlorine from steam, 20, 21, and from some oxides, 28; forms water with hydrogen, 21, 103; affinities for chlorine and for, 29; chlorine and fluorine to be classed with? 61; and combustion, 96, 97; compressed, MF's experiments on, 102; not liquefied, 434, 438, 439; ozone produced from, 453–4, 477; magnetic, 576–7, 594–5, 598–9, 608, 611, 638; temperature and magnetism of, 595, 608, 613, 658, 659; from electrolysed water, 788, 789; used by contracting muscles, but muscles can contract without, 837; spectrum of, 923

oxy-hydrogen blow-pipe, 204

oxymuriates, *see* chlorates

oxymuriatic gas, *see* chlorine

ozone: Schoenbein's discovery of, 375, 377n, 420–1; MF on, 439; resemblances of Schoenbein's new bleaching principle (hydrogen peroxide) to, 435–6; Schoenbein describes further work on, 441–4; in the atmosphere, 443, 636, 729, 730; produced from oxygen, 453–4, 477; theory that influenza is caused by, 635–6

Paget, Sir J., *724n*; to lecture at *RI*, 723

Palagi, A.: MF refers to experiments of, on electricity in concentric spheres, 718, 719n, 735; mentioned by Melloni, 735

palladium: heated, in combustible vapours, 105; magnetic, 488, 601

Palmerston, Lord (1785–1865): Taylor's report to, on fire at Newcastle, 794

paper: in voltaic battery, 5; B. Abbott enquires about colour of, 32

Paradise, Mr, Sandemanian friend of MF, 641

paramagnetism: Whewell suggests term, 587; MF approves, 589

Paris: MF at, 61, 86; École Polytechnique at, in 1830 revolution, 183; Moll on Observatory at, 188; Lardner in, 288; MF to visit, about Légion d'Honneur, 826, 828 846, 850; Mint at, 856

Paris, J. A. (physician, 1785–1856): MF's introduction to Davy described to, 177–8; life of Davy by, 196; *Elements of Medical Chemistry* and *Pharmacologia* by, 226; Plateau asks for reference to invention of thaumatrope by, 847, 848n

Parker, J. W. (publisher, 1792–1870), 200

Parkes, Mr, and lighthouses, 972, 977

Parrot, G. F., *347n*; MF mentions, 347

Pasley, Gen. C. W., *311n*; MF analyses clays for, 311–13; on underwater apparatus for firing gunpowder, 329–31, 331–5; pontoons designed by, 930

Peabody, G., *1032n*; endows Institution at Baltimore, 1032

Pearsall, T. J., assistant to Faraday, 214

Peirce, B., *917n*; Winslow's controversy with, 916

Pelouze, T. J., *857n*; mentioned by De la Rue, 856

Peltier, J. C. A., *380n*; sends papers on meteorology, 379–80, 400–1, 451–2; MF cannot adopt his views on relation of Earth and space, 580

Peltier, young Mr; mentioned by MF, 580

Pentland, Mr, possible messenger between Melloni and MF, 290, 291

Pepys, W. H. (original manager and one-time Secretary of London Institution, 1775–1850): magnetic display by, 461

Percy, J., *426n*; sends specimens of metals, etc., 425–6; asks about freezing of water in capillary tubes, 444; to lecture on metals at *RI*, 693 ('a great prize' – J. Barlow, 752)

Perkins, J., on compressibility of water, 157, 158

perpetual motion, MF has contest 'with some Gents' on, 6

Perrey, A., *917n*; Winslow refers to his work on moon and earthquakes, 916

Perry, John, *207n*; mentioned by Moll, 206

Peters, C. H. F., *917n*; mentioned by Winslow, 916

Petit, A. T., (1791–1820), Law of Dulong and, 376, 377

Peyron, Monsieur, Professor of physics at Marseilles: carries letter and book from Peltier to MF, 379; on an electromagnetic machine; is translating MF's *Experimental Researches*, 395–7

Phillipps, Sir T. (antiquary, 1792–1872): thanks MF for information about aluminium, 798

Phillips, J., *605n*; observes the aurora, 604–5, 605–6

Phillips, R., *109n*; collaborates with MF, 123, 139; MF writes to, scientifically, 116–17, 178–9, 209–11, and socially, 172–3, 209; as editor of *Annals of Philosophy*, thanks MF for *Historical Sketch of Electromagnetism*, 122

Phillips, T., *414n*; MF has to cancel a sitting with, 414

Philosophical Magazine, 216; MF sends letters to, from Jacobi, 347, Plücker, 521, 551, Quételet, 624, von Feilitzsch, 753, and A. de la Rive, 905; MF to editors of: sending paper by himself, 359–60, account of Siemens' experiments on telegraph wires, 730–2, and letter from van Breda and Logeman on electricity in liquids, 769; A. de la Rive complains about, 477; MF replies, 480; *see also* Taylor, R.

phlogiston: MF expects old theory of, to be revived, 16

phosphates, paper by Dalton on, 378, 379, 380

phosphorescence: of phosphorus, 677; of sulphides, 943–4

phosphoric acid, does not sublime, 22

phosphoroscope, 944

phosphorus: burns in chlorine, 22; affinities of, for chlorine and oxygen, 29; detonation of nitrogen trichloride in contact with, 43; oxidation of, by ozone and by air, 443; diamagnetic, 470, 471, 482, 488, 589; excitation of, by irradiation, 677; effect of, on spectrum of hydrogen, 924

phosphorus chlorides, 22, 23, 24

photographs: from Munich, approved by MF, 838; of moon and planets, 879; of eclipse, 994

photography: Percy and Shaw investigate chemistry of, 426; new process for, 548–9, 552

physicist: MF dislikes the word, as translation of French *physicien*, 377

Pickersgill, W. H., *511n*; copies portrait of Davy for MF, 510

Pictet, M. A., *69n*; Davy visits, 68

Pierre, J. I., *946n*; on expansion of absolute alcohol, 946

Pietro Malo, Fuoco de: inflammable gas escaping from earth at, 77, 83

Plana, G. A. A., *308n*; mentioned by Babbage, 308

Plateau, J., *233n*; to MF about optical illusions, 231–3; sends his anorthoscope, 300–1; complains that letters and papers are not acknowledged, 417–18; thanks MF for letter, 418–19; becomes blind, 538; sends papers to MF, 543, 649, 774–5, 846, 849–50, 991–2; suggests a method for determining magnetism of gases, 543–5; enquires about publication of his papers in England, 570, 584–5, 649–50; asks for reference about thaumatrope for his bibliography on vision, 847; mentioned by Wheatstone, 484, by Moigno, 538

platina minerals, Berzelius's analysis of, 208, 209n

platinum: heated wire of, in combustible vapours, 103–4; alloy of steel and, 119; electrodes of, 374; negatively polarized by oxygen and chlorine, 436; magnetic, 488, 601

Playfair, J., *207n*; *Outlines of Natural Philosophy* by, 276, 277n; mentioned by Moll, 206

Playfair, Lyon (chemist, 1818–98): hopes MF will come to British Association meeting at Glasgow, 749; supports Liebig's views, 853, 854n

Plücker, J. (physicist and mathematician, 1801–68): to MF, sending papers on magnetism, 511; MF replies, and sends piece of heavy glass, 512; reports experiments on heavy glass, and on flames, 513–14, and further experiments on measurement of magnetism, 519–20; MF replies, 520; hopes to visit England, 524–5; after visit to England, reports further experiments, 526–7; MF refers to work of, 535; MF to, on magnetic axes in crystals, 536–7; to MF about magnetism and crystals, 541, 545–6, 546–8, 561–2; MF has his letters published in *Philosophical Magazine*, 550, 551, 552; thanks MF for election to *RI*; reports further work

on crystals, 561–2, 566–8; MF discusses his results, 569; continues to work on crystals, 574–6; MF discusses polarity, 577–8; to MF, introducing Brandis, 592–3; MF replies, 598; on magnetism of gases, etc., 637–8; on electromagnetic rotation, 683–4; MF to: 'want something to cheer me – so I have resolved to write to you', 706–7; replies, with account of experiments on induction, 709–10; sends papers, 756–7; MF replies, 766; on misapprehension of his work by Tyndall, 831–3, 860–1, 872–3; MF urges friendly feeling in controversy, 833–5, 863–4, 875; sends paper for *RS*, 862; hopes MF may come to meeting at Bonn, 877; MF replies, 878–9; on stratified light in electrified rarefied gases, 873–4; MF comments, 875–6; further work, 891; A. de la Rive claims priority over, 901, 903 (regrets his expressions, 904); MF comments to de la Rive on work of, 905–6; reports further work on electrified gases, 906–8, 908–9, 918–20; on spectra of electrified gases, 923–5, 960–1, 1005–6; MF admires his work, 950, 1000–1; MF misses seeing, in London, 1019; mentioned by Whewell, 331, by MF, 563, 850, by von Feilitzsch, 600, by Becker, 968

plumbago (graphite), 63; on surface of iron heated with charcoal, 115, 118

Poggendorff, J. C. (physicist and editor, 1796–1877): von Feilitzsch refers to work of, on diamagnetism, 600; mentioned by Matteucci, 304

Poisson, S. D., *292n*; to work on mathematics of induction, 291; work of, referred to by Mossotti, 306–7, by Thomson, 458, 861, by Harris, 628, by Plücker, 833; death of, 373

polarity: Hare discusses MF's conception of, 350–8 *passim*; MF replies, 361, 366, 368; Hare continues, with reference to induction, 382–3, 384; Plücker on, 519, 534, 562, 567–8, 576; MF uses word axiality in contra-distinction to, 530, 536; Whewell comments, on axiality, 531, and on Plücker's ideas of, 534; MF on Plücker's ideas of, 535, 577–8, 589; von Feilitzsch on, 599; A. de la Rive continues to believe

Quételet, A. (*cont.*)
death of Prince Consort, 1020–1; mentioned by Plateau, 301
quinine, MF on use of word, 225–6

railways: P. Barlow's report on, 292; effect of tremors from, on astronomical observations, 500; in U.S.A., 633
Ramsay, Mr, contractor for glass furnace at *RI*, 171, 173, 213
Ranelagh Gardens, MF and friends to meet at, 14, 20
razor strops, Nasmyth suggests coke for, 506, 522
razors, of rhodium-steel alloy, 118
Rees, R. van (mathematician, 1797–1875): work of, on mathematics of lines of force, mentioned by von Feilitzsch, 600, by MF, 779, 861
refractive index of glass, effect of lead content on, 150
regelation, 910–11
Regnault, H. V., *377n*; work of, on specific heat, 376; MF suggests his work on respiration is worthy of *RS* grant, 619; suffers from a fall, 848; is better, 850, 851; mentioned, 588n, by A. de la Rive, 494, 901
Reich, F. (physicist, 1799–1882): experiments of, on magnetism, mentioned by MF, 578, 581, by von Feilitzsch, 600
Reid, A., nephew of MF: MF answers a letter from, about a discharge of lightning, 371
Reid, Constance, niece of MF: MF to, 655–6
Reid, D., Sandemanian friend of MF, 641
Reid, D. B., *425n*; mentioned by MF, 423
Rennie, Sir J., *290n*; MF declines invitation from, 290
respiration: Regnault's work on, 619; of muscle (Matteucci), 636–8
rhodium, alloy of steel and, 118
Riebau, Mr, bookbinder: MF apprenticed to, 14; to visit *RI*, 95
Riess, P. T., *563n*; MF thanks, for letter; discusses Melloni's work, 791–2; MF corrects misapprehension in paper by, 809–16; replies to MF at length (for publication), 818–24; MF's notes on his reply, 824–5; mentioned by MF, 563, by

Knochenhauer, 836, by A. de la Rive, 901, 903
Rigaud, P., *204n*; mentioned by Daubeny, 203
Rippingham, Mr, lecturer at Surrey Institution, 71
Ritter, J., *211n*; 'secondary pile' of, 210
Robertson, W. (historian, 1721–93): Conybeare mentions *History of America* by, 468, 469n
Robinson, Dr: introduced to MF by Herschel, borrows money from MF and others, 235
Robinson, T. R., *145n*, *673n*; suggests MF should apply for chair at Dublin, 145; on fluorescence produced by aurora, 902, 904n; persuades South to give large object glass to Dublin University, 1024; mentioned by South, 440
Robison, John (scientific writer, 1739–1805): 627, 628
rock crystal, optic and magnetic axes of, 548, 551, 567
Rodney, HMS, struck by lightning, 342
Roget, P. M., *185n*; Secretary of *RS*, 185, 480; MF to, on *RS* business, 195, 199; MF refers to his determination of lines of magnetic force, 683
Roman Catholic services at Vienna, J. Barlow on, 759
Romans, colours used by, 88–9
Rome, MF at, 59, 63, 74–8, 84–92
Romily, Mrs: MF to, 495; mentioned by A. de la Rive, 467
Ronalds, H., apothecary, 110, 111n
Roscoe, H. E., *954n*; tells MF of spectroscopic discoveries, 953
Roscoe, T., *189n*; mentioned by Moll, 188
Rose, H., *638n*; confirms Bergemann's work on supposed new metal, 637
Ross, Sir J., *473n*; sends *RS* a claim on 'magnetized light', 473
Ross, Mr, instrument maker: mentioned by A. de la Rive, 646
Rosse, Earl of, *399n*; reflecting telescopes of, 398, 440, 441n; South on, 1024
Rousselle, Monsieur, carries letter from Hachette to MF, 227
Royal College of Chemistry, 514–15
Royal George, HMS: demolition of wreck of, at Spithead, 311n, 329, 334

Royal Institution (*RI*): MF appointed assistant at, 178; music from Jacques Hotel heard in, 47; MF's room at, 48n, 92, 93n; lecture theatre at, 50, 629–30, 632; doubts about continuance of, 65, 69n; debts of, paid off, 70; MF's interest in, 78, 168–9, 172; scientific meetings of members of, on Mondays, 113; Friday evening lectures at, 262, 359–60; MF on Brodie's dissatisfaction with, 558–9, 571; Plücker elected member of, 561; painters, etc., at work in, 693; porters of, 693, 757–8, 760; MF's Christmas lectures at, 699, 888, 979–80; MF resigns from Christmas lectures, 1003–4, 1007; library at, 1017

Royal Medal of Royal Society: awarded to MF (1835), 324, (1846), 500, 501n

Royal Military Academy, Woolwich: MF appointed to lecture on chemistry at (1829), 175–7, 179; MF's attendance at (two days a week), 645; MF resigns post at (1852), 653–4

Royal Navy: Airy on 'magnetic interests' of, 337; Harris on lightning conductors in, 341–2; *see also* Admiralty

Royal Porcelain Works, Berlin: MF hopes for evaporating basins from, 175, 181

Royal Society (*RS*): attacks on, and proposed reform of, 189n, 192; proposed exchange of journals of, 185, 187; MF (elected member 1824) going to Council of, 187; not able to attend Council of, 208, 209; MF asks for sealed paper to be placed in strong box of, 216–17; MF unwilling to stand for election to Council of, 234; MF asks permission to reprint his articles from journal of, 324; question of new charter for, 449–50; policy of, about publication of Fellows' work elsewhere than in the *Transactions*, 480–1, 487; A. de la Rive proposed for, 582; possible grant from, to assist research, 619; Plücker elected Foreign Member of, 833; MF has not been able for several years to occupy himself with, 834; delay in publishing by, 875; *see also* Bakerian lecture, *and* Copley, Royal, *and* Rumford Medals

Ruhmkorff inductive apparatus, 874, 900, 902, 903, 907, 923

Rumford Medal of Royal Society: awarded

to Melloni (1834), 289, 290, 291; to MF (1846), 500, 501n

Russell, Lord John, *713n*; MF offers to apply to, on behalf of Hooker, 717

Ryde, Isle of Wight: MF at, 278

Ryder, A. P., *973n*; and lighthouses, 972, 974, 990

Sabbath, Trinity House respects the, 974

Sabine, Sir E. (General and *FRS*, 1788–1883): reports observations on terrestrial magnetism, 591–2; MF commends paper by, 611–12; analyses larger variations in terrestrial magnetism, 659; on connection of magnetic variations and sun-spots, 671, 672, 686; to MF about Wolf's letter on sun-spots; claims priority for himself, 672–3; repeats his claim, 676–7; on annual and diurnal variations in magnetism at different places, 678–9; hands on to MF letter from Hansteen, 888; mentioned by Hansteen, 892

Saigey, J. F., *484n*; experiments on magnetism by, 484

St Petersburg: paddle-boat driven by electromagnetic machine at (1839), 345; steam pile-drivers for Cronstadt arsenal at, 503, 522

Salamè, Dr, 'an Italian Empiric': Quack Medicine of, 157

salary: of MF as scientific adviser to Trinity House, 302; of Professor of Chemistry at Toronto, 401

Sandeman, Mr: friend of MF in Glasgow, 1016, 1017

Sandemanians: MF (a member) and singing school of, 106–7; MF unfit for meeting of, because of dental trouble, 586–7; at Newcastle, 640–1; J. Barlow on, 759; at Glasgow, 1016; London congregation of, had to resign privilege of Lord's Supper, because all were not at peace, 1018

Sappings, Sir R., *208n*; mentioned by Moll, 206

Saturn: MF on rings of, 33; De la Rue on rings of, 700–1, and satellites of, 995

Saussure, H. B. de, *401n*; work of, on electricity in air above mountains, mentioned by Peltier, 400

Sautre, Monsieur (of French lighthouse service?), (962), 971, 972n

Savage, Sarah, *760n*; housekeeper at *RI*, 760

Savart, F., *194n*, *227n*; Wheatstone on MF's criticisms of work on sound by, 193, 194; Plateau refers to work of, on capillary phenomena, 543, 545n; mentioned by Hachette, 213, 227

Schaffhausen, MF visits Falls of the Rhine at, 76, 83

Scheele, K. W. (chemist, 1742–86): on reaction producing chlorine, 16

Scheerer, K. J. A. (chemist, 1813–75): mentioned by MF, 780

Scheiner, C. (astronomer, 1575–1650): observes sun-spots, 670

Schlagintweit, (H. R. A.), *618n*; carries MF's portrait to Quételet, 615; mentioned by J. Barlow, 758

Schoenbein, C. F., *377n*, *421n*; work of, on ozone, 375, 420, 421, 441–4; about his experiments on slow combustion of ether, yielding new bleaching principle (hydrogen peroxide), 435–7; suggests that ozone causes influenza, 635; ozonometer of, 696; on polarization of electrodes, 762, 764n; mentioned by Whewell, 588, by MF, 707

Schumacher, H. C., *618n*; Quételet mentions death of, 618

Schwabe, S. H., *662n*; observes and records sun-spots, 661, 662, 670, 673, 686

science: freemasonry of, 145; MF an anchorite in world of, 154; MF's desire to escape from trade and enter into service of, 178; detractors of English contributions to, 187, 188, 192–3, 195–6, 205; Napoleon and, 196; British Association for Advancement of, *see* British Association

scientist, word introduced by Whewell, 377, 378n

Scoresby, W., *615n*; asks advice about experiments on dimensions of electrified or magnetized iron, 614–15

sea-serpent, reported in English Channel, 765

sea water: specific gravity of, 108; corrosion of bronze and copper by, 215; Maury's questions on electric or magnetic properties of, 620–2; action of, on lead receptacles for water, 929

sebacic acid, in pilchard oil, 112

Seebeck, T. J. (physicist, 1770–1831): experiments on magnetism by, 484

Sefström, N. G., *200n*; sends ammonium vanadate to MF, 200, 225

Seguin, M., *866n*, *867n*; Moigno to MF about, 865–6; MF replies, 866–7

Selborne, Lord, *511n*; recommends an artist, 510

selenium: mixture containing, received by MF from Berzelius, 144; from Germany, mixed with much sulphur, 181; specific heat of, 377

Sérullas, G. S., *203n*; 'that clever and active chemist' (MF), 202–3; death of, 230

Shanklin, Isle of Wight: the Faradays at, 738

Shaw, Hope: MF to, saying he is unable to lecture anywhere other than *RI*, 699–700

Shaw, Mr: collaborates with Percy in work on chemistry of photography, 426

shell-lac: in alcohol, as varnish, 358; specific inductive capacity of, 816

Shepherd, Mr, member of City Philosophical Society, 33, 34n

shilling: MF analyses, for Babbage, 214

ships: struck by lightning, 341–2; possibility of electromotive power for, 345, 347; lightning conductors for, 405–6

Shuffleton's new dictionary (1813), 51

Shury, Mr, engraver, 122

Siemens, E. W. von (physicist and engineer, 1816–92): on subterranean telegraph wires, 730

silica (silex): base of oxygen gas? 57; in glass, 151–2, 155; in clays, 312

silicon fluoride, liquefied, 433, 438

silver: affinities of, for chlorine and oxygen, 29; ore of, from Potosi, 71; fulminating, 83; alloy of steel and, 119; volatilization of, 120; Herschel on mathematics of volatilization of, 159–62; electrolytic gilding of, 376; preparation of, from chloride, 411–12; magnetic properties of, 489

silver oxide: preparation of, from chloride, 411–12

Singer, S. W. (1783–1858): librarian of *RI*, 191, 193n

skin: Brewster asks what applications could hide red mark on, 698

sky, blue colour of, 735–6

Smart, Mr, lecturer at *RI*, 107

smells: of metals when rubbed, 17, 31; accompanying electric discharges (ozone), 375

Smith, A., member of *RI*, 202

Smith, B., brother of A. Smith: MF to, on his departure for America, 173–4; mentioned by MF, 202

Smithson, J., *634n*; J. Henry sends MF portrait of, 633

Smithsonian Institution, 1032; engraving of, 633, 640

smoke: collection of, on cracked ceilings, 32

Smyth, W. H., *473n*; tells MF of Ross's claim about magnetized light, 473; no longer Foreign Secretary of *RS*, 863

soap bubbles, 513

soap manufacture, alkali for, 179

soda, muriate of, *see* sodium chloride

sodium: affinities of, for chlorine and oxygen, 29; MF hopes to receive sample of, from Germany, 181; MF sees production of, 850; spectrum of, 924, 960

sodium chloride (muriate of soda): in voltaic battery, 5, 10, 11, 16; contains chlorine and sodium only, 16, 18; crystallization of, 33

sodium hydroxide (caustic soda): a hydrate of sodium, 35; Phillips sends MF a specimen of, 178–9; equivalence of potassium hydroxide and, in bleaching, etc., 179

sodium nitrate, in conflagration at Newcastle, 794

solenoid, use of term, 651, 653

Solly, E., *426n*; mentioned by Percy, 425

Somerset, Duke of (*FRS*, President of *RI*, 1775–1855): MF considers invitations of, as commands, 290

Somerville, Mary, *263n*; MF thanks, for copies of her works, 263, 921; carries paper from Paris to MF, 291; to MF, 922

Sorby, H. C., *426n*; mentioned by Percy, 426

Soret, J. L., *793n*, *840n*; assistant to A. de la Rive, 793, 840

sounds: produced by flames in tubes, 112, 115, 116n; by induced currents in iron bars, 426; by discontinuous currents in metals, 454

South, Sir J., *154n*, *189n*; Moll disagrees with, 153, 394; congratulates MF on election as Foreign Associate of Académie des Sciences, 431–2, and on *RS* Medals, 500; about Lord Rosse's telescope, 440–1; describes an accident to his finger, 500–1; about the large object glass given to Dublin University, 1024; on death of Sergeant Anderson; offers subscription for funeral or annuity to daughter, 1022–3; renews offer, 1024; mentioned by MF, 153, 394

South America, B. Abbott offered post in, 82

sparks: from magnets, 210, 218, 221–2, 229–30; from electric fish, 304

specific heats, 376–7

spectra: prismatic, 68; of lime-light, 163, 164; of potassium permanganate, 677; of electrified gases, 919; Bunsen and Kirchhoff's work on, 953, 960, 1005; of stars, 1009

Spencer, Mr, of *RI*? 72

sphondyloid, term suggested by Whewell, 651, 652–3, 657

spiritualist seances, MF on, 874–5

stannane, 28

stars: shooting, 311; variable, and sun-spots, 670, 673; spectra of, 1009

Statham, Mr, of Telegraph Company, 716

statical baroscope, Boyle's, 68

steam hammers, 502, 522

steam pile-drivers, 448–9, 502–3, 522

steel: experiments to improve, 112; Indian (wootz), 117; alloys of, 117–20; MF's papers on, 138; electrolytic gilding of, 376; hardening and tempering of, 448; Nasmyth suggests experiment on application of electric current during hardening of, 503–4, 505; as an alloy rather than a carburet of iron (Nasmyth), 506, 522; magnetism of, 710; rusting of white and blued, in chronometers, 1011–12

Stein, Mr, wishes to sell part of meteorite from Mexico, 818

Stenhouse, Dr, carries letter from G. Wilson to MF, 582, 583

Stevenson, J. (engineer, 1818–87): on polyzonal lens for lighthouses, 817; work of, mentioned by MF, 981, 986

Stevenson, Rev. W., *687n*; lists his observations on number of displays of aurora by

Stevenson, Rev. W. (*cont.*)
month over 10 years, 686–7; glad to let
MF inform *RS* of his work, 688–9
Stodart, J., collaborates with MF, 115, 116,
117, 139n; MF to, in distress about accusa-
tions of stealing ideas from Wollaston,
125–7
Stokes, G. G., *678n*; about apparatus for
proposed experiments at *RI*, 677–8, 685–6;
about reading MF's paper to *RS*, and about
setting of bodies along lines of force,
807–8; MF to, about paper by Joule, 826;
to MF about ruby glass, and suspensions
of gold particles, 843–4; MF replies, 844;
thinks MF's paper with negative results
should not be published, 956; MF concurs,
959; mentioned by Plücker, 960
Stoney, B. B., *1025n*; mentioned by South,
1024
Stromeyer, F., *262n*; Moll on laboratory of,
260
strontian, from Lake Erie, 174
strontium: affinities of, for chlorine and
oxygen, 29; spectrum of, 960
strontium sulphide, phosphorescent, 943
Struve, O. W., *701n*; on Saturn's rings, 701;
mentioned by Hansteen, 893
stucco, Roman, 89
Sturt, Mr, early friend of MF: death of, 165,
166n
sugar: method of extracting, from beet and
cane, 549, 552, 553
sulphur: reaction of chlorine with, 24; diamagnetic, 488; conflagration of, at Newcastle, 767, 794
sulphur chloride, reaction of water with, 24
sulphur dioxide: liquefied, 140; from volcanoes, 156; solidified, 433, 438; MF on
possible use of, as poison gas, 749–51, 767
sulphuric acid, experiment on induction of
current in, 719–21
sulphurous acid, *see* sulphur dioxide
sun: relations of earth and, 900; spectrum of,
953; eclipse of, 993–7, 1009
sun-spots, and terrestrial magnetism, 661–3,
669–73
Surbiton, the Faradays at, 760
surface: nature of, and emission and absorption of radiant heat, 285–6; increase of,
and intensity of magnetism, 626, 713, 714

Surrey Canal, MF and his brother wish to
see locks on, 17
Surrey Institution, 68, 73n; lectures at, 71–2,
83
Sussex, H.R.H. Duke of (1773–1843): elected
President of *RS*, 209, 211n, 234; MF considers invitations of, as commands, 290
Svanberg, A. F., *588n*; MF thanks, for
account of experiments, 588
Swanson, Mr, engraver, 195
Swedish Academy of Sciences, MF elected
member of, 326–7
Swiss Société de Physique et d'Histoire
Naturelle: A. de la Rive invites MF to
meeting of, 421, 453; MF elected Honorary Member of, 455
Switzerland: MF on, 75–6; MF on holiday in, 393–4; J. Barlow on politics in,
765
Sykes, Col. C. M.: MF to, about appointment in India for Liebig's son, a doctor,
663, 668
Symes, Dr, introduced to Ampère by MF,
146, 147
Szerelmy, Mr: secret process of, for preserving stonework, 958, 959
Symmer, R., *989n*; Harris repeats electrical
experiments of, 988

table-turning: MF's tests of, 690–2, 716;
Liebig mentions, 845, 851, 852
Talbot, W. H. Fox, *290n, 482n*; *RS* and
publication of papers of, 480–1, 487;
makes a photographic experiment at *RI*,
636–7; mentioned by Melloni, 289, by
Brewster, 698
tartaric and racemic acids, 208, 209n
Tasmania, flora of, 711
Tatum, J., lectures by, 14, 24, 33, 41; City
Philosophical Society meets at house of,
40; accident to, 83–4
Taylor, A. S., *794n*; on a conflagration of
sulphur, 794
Taylor, Brook, *629n*; Harris refers to experiments by, 625, 628
Taylor, Jeremy (Bishop, 1612–67): mentioned by Whewell as using term spondyl,
652–3
Taylor, Messrs J. and P., London: makers of
lighting apparatus, 112

1074

Taylor, Richard, *419–420n*; editor of *Philosophical Magazine*, 151, 359, 537, 550, 570, 584; publisher of MF's *Experimental Researches*, 378, 422; and papers by Plateau, 419, 647, 849

telegraph: magnetic, of Gauss, 261, 892; electric, 538, 633; printing, of Bain, 715; Atlantic, 957, 958n

telescopes: Moll's paper on invention of, 187, 192; specula for large reflecting, 398, 440; Nasmyth makes, as 'pet hobby', 522–3

temperature: in kiln-drying of malt, 109–10; and vaporization, 160, 161–2; between poles of a magnet, 514; dependence of intensity of magnetism on, 489, 520, 524, 594, 613, 658, 659; *see also* heat

Temps, Le: reports weekly meetings of Académie des Sciences, 259

Ten Eyck, P., *208n*; mentioned by Moll, 207

terminology: Nicholl on, 212, 264, 266, 271; MF replies to query from Babbage on, 225–6; MF on difficulties of, 360; Latham's suggestions for, 456; *see also under* Whewell

Thames, unhealthy condition of, 801

Thames Tunnel, noxious gases in, 342–3

thaumatrope, 847, 849

Thenard, L. J., *196n*, *444n*; reports properties of hydrogen peroxide, 442, 443; mentioned, 36n, by Moll, 169

thermal springs, and volcanoes, 204

thermometer, alcohol: used in experiments on liquefaction of gases, 946

Thilorier, C. St-A., *434n*; MF uses cooling mixture of, 432

Thomas, Monsieur, friend of Dumas: in London, 372

Thompson, L.: MF to, on liquefaction of gases, 553–4

Thomson, J. D., of Admiralty: MF to, 215, 229

Thomson, T. (chemist, 1773–1852): definition of chemistry by, 17

Thomson, W. (later Lord Kelvin, 1824–1907): to MF, commenting on a paper by Avogadro; is preparing a paper on mathematical theory of magnetism, 458–60; MF replies, 460; further on theory of magnetism, 523–4, 534, 555–7, 781n; suggests experiments on magnetic action on crystals,

559–61; argument between Tyndall and, 804n; and mechanical equivalent of heat, 837; MF gives reference to work of, 861; diagrams by Clerk-Maxwell sent to MF through, 932–3; electrometer of, 933–4, 957–8; proposed lecture at *RI* by, 934, 936, 938; on electrification of dropping water, 936–8; MF comments, 939; MF is puzzled by his report on electric state of metals in contact, 940–2; and Atlantic cable, 957, 958n; mentioned by MF, 779, 780, by Plücker, 833

thorina mineral, 208

thunderstorms: at sea, 320; portable electrometer during, 957–8; sounds of thunder in, 999; *see also* lightning

time, in electromagnetic phenomena: MF on, 217, 516–18, 715–16, 863, 864; Airy on, 515–16; Plücker on, 527

Times, The: reports paper by MF read at *RS*, 469, 479; letters of MF to: on table-turning, 690–2, on unhealthy condition of the Thames, 801, on treating water to remove lead, 929; Tyndall's letter on ascent of Monte Rosa sent by MF to, 911–12

tin: gives off smell when rubbed, 17; reactions of, with hydrogen chloride, 20, and with chlorine, 28; affinities of, for chlorine and oxygen, 29

tin chloride, spectrum of, 924

tin oxide: separates from water more easily if salt is added, 228; magnetic axes in crystals of, 561

titanium: oxide and carbonate of, not reduced in MF's furnace, 120; magnetic, 471, 488, 489

Tomlin, G., MF recommends him not to publish a paper on magnetic theory, 692

topaz: optic and magnetic axes in, 547

torpedoes (electric fish), 61–2, 304

tourmaline: magnetic polarity of, 567, 575; Brewster examines specimen of, 698

transmutation of elements, MF on, 1019

transparency, to light and to heat, 285

travelling, MF on, 60, 67–8

tree: growth of, contrary to gravitation (Winslow), 917

Trinity House: MF scientific adviser to, in experiments on light (1836–65), 302, 513;

vortices, Descartes' system of, 661

Vulliamy, L., *630n*; makes drawings of *RI* lecture-room, 629, 634

Wales, North: MF visits, 693

Walker, C. V., *329n*, *406n*, *899n*; paper of, on lightning conductors, 406; MF to, about currents in telegraph cables, 898–9

Walker, J., *667n*; report to Trinity House by MF and, 665

Walker, W., *52n*; MF mentions his lectures on astronomy, 50, 56

Wallace, W., *208n*; mentioned by Moll, 206

Waller, A., *684n*; buys Geissler's apparatus, 684

Ward, F. O.: MF to, about experiments to confirm or confute theories, 274

Ward, W. S., MF reports on paper on magnetism by, 562–3

Wartmann, E., *465n*; mentioned by MF, 463

water: decomposed by voltaic battery? 5; contaminants in, 6; motions of camphor on, 9–10; not formed in reaction of hydrogen with chlorine, 19; (as steam) decomposed by chlorine, 20, 21; formed by hydrogen and oxygen, 21, 103; reactions of, with phosphorus chloride, 23, and with sulphur chloride, 24; conducting power of, 31, 721; MF's analyses of, 107–8; purification of gases by washing with, 111, 112; under high temperature and pressure, 156–8; electrolysis of, 345, 787–9; freezing of, in capillary tubes, 444; diamagnetic, 482, 488, 489; distilled, no current induced in, 721; vapour of, and colour of sky, 735–6; decomposed by static electricity, 840; MF on freezing of, 885–8; boundary between ice and, 911

water battery, 798

water spouts, 61, 452, 453n

Waterston, J. J., *946n*; enquires about thermometer used in MF's work on liquefaction of gases, 945–6

Watkins, Mr, mentioned by MF as in possession of magnetic instrument, 277

Watson, T. T. W.: MF to, about test of electric light for lighthouses, 674

Watt, J., *207n*; mentioned by Moll, 206

Watts, Dr Isaac (hymn-writer, 1674–1748): recommends letter-writing, 3

Weber, W., *536n*: MF refers to work of, on magnetism, 535, 563, 569, 578, 806; mentioned, 299n, by Airy, 323, by Plücker, 576, by von Feilitzsch, 600, by MF, 861

Webster, Dr, sees sea-serpent, 765

Wedgwood: money owed to, by Glass Committee, 213

weights and measures, Moll's paper on, 192, 195

Weld, C. R. (Assistant Secretary and Librarian, *RS*, 1813–69): MF to, saying he is not a knight (in England), 513; MF to, reporting on papers by W. S. Ward, 562–3, and by Joule, 800

Wellington, Duke of (1790–1852): Moll on, 205–6

Wheatstone, C. (physicist and inventor, 1802–75): about MF's work on acoustical figures, 193–4; Plateau enquires about work of, on optical effects, 257; does not answer Plateau's letters, 417, 418; Plateau sends papers to, 419, 545, 775; undertakes translation of paper by Plateau, who enquires about progress, 584–5 (and again, 650); advises on explosion of gunpowder under water, 328; MF thanks, for information about 'prediscovery' of diamagnetism, 471; sends MF names of more 'prediscoverers'; suggests experiments, 483–4; paper by, on electric telegraph, 538; Stokes refers to apparatus of, 678; will lend apparatus, 681–2; tells MF he ought to go to Paris about Légion d'Honneur, 826; on Gassiot's experiments, 894; mentioned by De la Beche, 322, by Harris, 406, by A. de la Rive, 421, 453, by Plücker, 562, by MF, 683, by Gassiot, 894

Wheeler, Mr, involved in enquiry into malt, 110, 111n

Wheeler, T., *98n*; lectures at Surrey Institution, 71, 72; attends lectures at *RI*, 96

Whewell, W. (Master of Trinity College, Cambridge, 1794–1866): MF to, about notation in chemistry, 190–1; MF corresponds with, about terminology for electrolysis, 264–7, 268–72, 275, 284, 299; on MF's electromagnetic researches, 293–4; MF replies ('your letter was quite refreshing'), 294–6; would like to have discussion with MF, 297; makes suggestions

Whewell, W. (*cont.*)

on MF's work, and asks for copies of his papers, 299–300; MF can't supply papers; asks about term voltameter, 301–2; MF wants opinion on paper by Mossotti about forces governing matter, 306–7; further correspondence on terminology, 307, 314, 315–16, 377, 427–9, 471–2, 498–9; to MF asking about his work on light and magnetism, 465; MF replies, 466; suggests experiment on polarized light, 485; MF prepares to carry it out, 485; makes further suggestions, and asks for corrections for new edition of his book, 495–6; MF replies, 496–7; MF sends paper on diamagnetism; is glad he will lecture at *RI*, 512; other mentions of lectures at *RI* by, 528, 530, 531, 534, 563, 564, 723–4, 726; MF reports experiments on magnetism and crystals, 528–9; comments, 531; writes on MF's idea of induction in curved lines, 532; MF replies, 532–4; correspondence on terms terro- and para-magnetic, 586–8, 589–91; MF to, describing work on magnetic properties of gases, 593–5; another discussion on terminology, 651–3, 657; mentions Airy's wish for MF's advice on magnetic storms, 657; MF replies, 658–9; further on lines of magnetic force, 660–1; MF replies ('you frighten me'), 682–3; MF sends report on experiments on telegraph wires, 716–17; discusses MF's speculations on magnetism, 776–7; MF replies ('your letter gives me courage'), 777–8; MF to, sending references, 861; mentioned, 804n, by Vernon Harcourt, 201

Whiston, W., 629n; Harris refers to experiments by, 628

Whitelaw, Mr, London Sandemanian, 1017, 1018

Wiedemann, G. H., 903n; mentioned by A. de la Rive, 901

Wilde, H., 1030n; outlines his invention of dynamo, 1025–30; J. Henry on, 1030, 1031

Willis, Rev. R., 265n, 485n; suggests MF should have recourse to Whewell about terminology, 264; tells Whewell about lecture by MF, 485

Wilson, G., 583n; asks advice about drying gases, 582–3; on theory that ozone causes influenza, 635–6

Winslow, C. F., 900n; MF to, about his paper on relations of sun and earth, 900; replies in detail, 915–17

wires: for exploding gunpowder under water, 331, 334; telegraph (covered with gutta-percha), 697, 704, 706–7, 708, 898–9; effect of length of, 713, 714, 715–16; Siemens' experiments on, 730–2; Latimer Clark's experiments on, 730, 738, 775

Wöhler, F. (chemist, 1800–82): aluminium isolated by, 798; to MF about a meteorite the owner wishes to sell to the British Museum, 818

Wolf, R., 662n; on coincidence between number of sun-spots and degree of declination of magnetic needle, 661–2, 662–3; summarizes forthcoming paper for MF, 669–71; MF transmits paper of, to Herschel, 671–2; Sabine's claim to priority over, 672–3, 676; mentioned by Stevenson, 686, by J. Barlow, 765

Wollaston, W. H., 121n, 207n; supplies rhodium (which he discovered) to MF, 118; MF accused of stealing ideas of, 125–8, 834; approves paper by MF, 159; battery of, 333; mentioned by Moll, 206, by Harris, 797

'Wollaston's points' (Buff), 785, 786, 789

wood: proposed processes for preserving, 298, 549; acid vapours from some samples of, 1012

Woods, T., 885n; MF refers to paper on forces by, 884

Woods and Forests, Department of: MF consulted by, 508

Woolwich, *see* Royal Military Academy

wootz (Indian steel), 117–18

Wright, Mr: of Clarendon Hotel, next to *RI*, 693

Wrottesley, Lord (1798–1867): asks MF about possible government action to improve position of science or scientists, 722–3; MF replies, 724–5

Württemburg: MF in, 76

Young, J., 394n; mentioned by Mrs Faraday and MF, 393

Young, Dr T., *167n*; member of Glass Committee, 167; translates paper on light by Fresnel, 182; mentioned by Wheatstone, 193, by Moll, 206

Younghusband, C. W., *592n*; associated with Sabine in work on terrestrial magnetism, 592, 592

Zach, F. X., Freiherr von, *455n*; mentioned by A. de la Rive, 455

Zantedeschi, F., *568n*; mentioned by Plücker, 568

zinc: in voltaic battery, 4–5, 6, 10, 11, 12; malleable, 4, 9; solution of, in hydrochloric acid, 26; affinities of, for chlorine and oxygen, 29; in brass, 31

zinc carbonate, in clays, 318

zinc chloride, in battery, 34

zinc oxide, in battery, 6, 11, 34